# Jews in America

# Jews in America

*A Contemporary Reader*

Roberta Rosenberg Farber and
Chaim I. Waxman

**Brandeis University Press**
Published by University Press of New England
Hanover and London

Brandeis University Press
Published by University Press of New England, Hanover, NH 03755

Printed in the United States of America
5 4 3 2 1
CIP data appear at the end of the book

**Brandeis Series in American Jewish History, Culture, and Life**

Jonathan D. Sarna, Editor
Sylvia Barack Fishman, Associate Editor

Leon A. Jick, 1992
*The Americanization of the Synagogue, 1820–1870*

Sylvia Barack Fishman, editor, 1992
*Follow My Footprints: Changing Images of Women in American Jewish Fiction*

Gerald Tulchinsky, 1993
*Taking Root: The Origins of the Canadian Jewish Community*

Shalom Goldman, editor, 1993
*Hebrew and the Bible in America: The First Two Centuries*

Marshall Sklare, 1993
*Observing America's Jews*

Reena Sigman Friedman, 1994
*These Are Our Children: Jewish Orphanages in the United States, 1880–1925*

Alan Silverstein, 1994
*Alternatives to Assimilation: The Response of Reform Judaism to American Culture, 1840–1930*

Jack Wertheimer, editor, 1995
*The American Synagogue: A Sanctuary Transformed*

Sylvia Barack Fishman, 1995
*A Breath of Life: Feminism in the American Jewish Community*

Diane Matza, editor, 1996
*Sephardic-American Voices: Two Hundred Years of a Literary Legacy*

Joyce Antler, editor, 1997
*Talking Back: Images of Jewish Women in American Popular Culture*

Jack Wertheimer, 1997
*A People Divided: Judaism in Contemporary America*

Beth S. Wenger and Jeffrey Shandler, editors, 1998
*Encounters with the "Holy Land": Place, Past and Future in American Jewish Culture*

David Kaufman, 1998
*Shul with a Pool: The "Synagogue-Center" in American Jewish History*

Roberta Rosenberg Farber and Chaim I. Waxman, 1999
*Jews in America: A Contemporary Reader*

Murray Friedman and Albert D. Chernin, 1999
*A Second Exodus: The American Movement to Free Soviet Jews*

**In memory of**

**Horace H. and Bernice R. Rosenberg**

**Rabbi Nissan, and Sara R. Waxman**

## Contents

# Jews in America

# Introduction

The American Jewish population entering the twenty-first century is radically different from Jews who immigrated in the first two hundred years and from the large number of Eastern European Jews who embarked for America's shores at the beginning of the twentieth century. For many, the distinctive quality of being Jewish has all but disappeared. Inevitably, in the encounter between an immigrant and host culture, it is the immigrant culture that is most altered. Nevertheless, for a people who endured centuries of exile in foreign lands without losing their distinctiveness, the consequences of freedom in American life are difficult to understand and perhaps even more difficult to accept. In this volume we explore the ongoing transformation of the American Jewish population as it responds to the challenges of living in America. Specifically, we have chosen articles that focus on the challenge and response patterns that occur in the meeting between a traditionally rooted, religiously based culture and a modern, multicultural democracy.

Our approach to understanding Jewish life in America is largely interdisciplinary but with an overriding sociological perspective. We use this approach to capture the interaction between ideas and their expression within the many realms of social, personal, and political life. To do this we focus on the changing patterns of conflict and accommodation that result from the interaction between American and Jewish values.

As we come closer to the twenty-first century, conflict between traditional and modern values in American society has become more pronounced. According to Inglehart's extensive analysis (1990, 1997), this conflict is the result of radical changes occurring throughout advanced industrial societies. He notes that changes experienced in advanced industrial societies are so sweeping that they constitute a new societal paradigm and no longer move along the continuum of preindustrial to postindustrial traditionally used to characterize societies. Inglehart finds that the culture shift from a materialist to a postmaterialist value structure is better characterized by the term *postmodern*. We refer to these changes and discuss their consequences for the American Jewish population in our Conclusion.

The book is organized to enhance the learning experience. In Part I we present a sociological history of Jews in America (Waxman) to provide background for the remainder of the volume. Another perspective for examining the process of change experienced by American Jewish immigrants in their quest to Americanize is suggested by Chiswick. She adapts an economic model to explain the declining practice of Judaism and subsequent decline in Jewish identification.

Demographic changes, which underlie many of the issues examined in the reader, are discussed in greater depth in Part II. Rebhun, DellaPergola, and Tolts offer a population projection to the year 2020, identifying the various consequences of social and cultural changes, including but not limited to intermarriage, for the American Jewish population. Because family life constitutes the basis of social life, changes in the composition of the American Jewish family are also discussed in this section (Fishman) and regarded as basic foundation knowledge or information for the remainder of the volume.

The interaction between Jewish and American life is discussed throughout the reader, but in Part III we emphasize several key areas. Communal life often functions as a mediating structure for a minority culture. It must therefore respond in terms of its inner organization and function to the expectations of the larger host society. Elazar discusses Jewish communal life in these terms. Antisemitism, once a major force in understanding relations between Jewish life and thought and the more dominant non-Jewish society, is of a far less virulent type than it was in Europe. As a result, antisemitism no longer plays such a dominant role in shaping either non-Jewish American or American Jewish attitudes. Chanes discusses these changes, providing both a historical and a contemporary perspective on antisemitism in America. The success of pluralism in American society is nowhere better indicated than in the rising intermarriage figures for all racial, ethnic, and religious groups. Bayme examines the threat of intermarriage to the Jewish community from a Jewish organizational perspective. The role of women in American life and American Jewish life has dramatically changed. Fishman examines all sectors and denominations within Judaism, providing a cogent analysis of the interplay between American and Jewish values in the adaptation of feminist principles.

In Part IV, issues and expressions of American Jewish identity are discussed. We begin with an examination of the specific American values of political liberalism (Liebman and Cohen) and social justice (Legge), the behavioral implications of which have, by many Reform and Conservative Jews in particular, been regarded as a primary means through which to express one's Jewish identity. Waxman discusses the importance of Israel as a focus of one's Jewish identification across the spectrum of all denominations. This is then followed by an examination of the consequences of intermarriage for Jewish identification (Medding et al.). Cohen examines the impact of Jewish education on the formation of a Jewish identity. Farber concludes this section with an examination of the way in which the primacy of choice in American society determines the way in which a personal Jewish identity is constructed.

In Part V we examine the way in which the specifically religious and spiritual dimensions of being Jewish have been transformed as a consequence of the encounter with American values and society. Liebman's analysis pertains to all denominations within Judaism but particularly to the Reform and Conservative. Soloveitchik focuses specifically on the most insular of all the Jewish groups, the ultra-Orthodox. The point is that all Jews living within a larger society inevitably assume and express the values and lifestyles of that society. Within American life, where restrictions are few, if present at all, transformation nevertheless occurs across the religious denominational spectrum, even within groups that have chosen to live separately in a conscious, concerted effort not to change. Wertheimer looks at the cultural conflict expressed by the differing directions of denominational change.

In "Conclusion" the editors discuss the implications of trends and changes for Jewish life in postmodern America, focusing on the interrelated themes of identity, identification, and community as they are expressed in the interaction between and quest to express both American and Jewish values.

## References

Inglehart, Ronald. 1990. *Culture Shift in Advanced Industrial Society.* Princeton, N.J.: Princeton University Press.

———. 1997. *Modernization and Postmodernization: Cultural, Economic, and Political Change in 43 Societies.* Princeton, N.J.: Princeton University Press.

# Part I

## Establishing a Foundation for Contemporary American Jewish Life

1

Chaim I. Waxman

# The Sociohistorical Background and Development of America's Jews

The very first Jewish communities in the United States were settled by Sephardim, Jews of the Spanish-Portugese tradition who established their synagogues in that tradition. During the eighteenth and nineteenth centuries the majority of American Jews were of German and Central European background. During the second half of the nineteenth century and especially from 1880 to the mid-1920s, there was a massive wave of immigration from Eastern and Southern Europe. In this period of peak immigration, Italians were the largest immigrant group to enter America, and Jews from Eastern Europe were the second largest. Whereas in 1880 the American Jewish community numbered approximately a quarter of million (most of Central European background), during the years 1881 to 1923 about two and a half million Jews came from Eastern Europe. The floodtide of Eastern European immigration transformed the American Jewish community. Because the American Jewish community came to reflect the culture and concerns of this immigrant community, it is important to understand their cultural background.

The world of Eastern European Jewry was unique. In contrast to Jews in Central and Western Europe, Eastern European Jews lived in towns and villages—*shtetlach* in Yiddish—in which they were the majority. Their isolation from the larger society enabled them to develop and perpetuate a Jewish culture with a strong sense of in-group unity and with strong Jewish norms and values, many of which were religious in nature. They understood themselves as belonging to a Jewish "nation" or people, rather than simply a religion, a definition that derived from and was reinforced by both internal and external sources. As Daniel J. Elazar points out (see his essay in this volume), the Jewish community has traditionally been a unique blend of "kinship and consent," and it was almost natural that shtetl Jews perceived the Jewish community as extended family. This perception was not only theirs; the larger society also viewed them as a separate nation or people.

Their mode of life was less a matter of intentional individual choice and more a matter of familiarity and social and communal control.

Traditional Judaism was the religion of the shtetl and its culture as well. A Jew living in the traditional monoreligious culture of the shtetl would almost certainly have been confused by the Western distinction between religious group and ethnic group. To him or her there were only *Yidn* (Jews) and *Yiddishkei* (Jewishness, the Jewish way of life). To be a "good Jew" meant to behave in accordance with the norms of traditional Judaism as defined by the rabbis-scholars of the community.

Jews have traditionally had their own languages, and the language of the shtetl was Yiddish, which was a combination of a medieval German dialect and some Hebrew elements, as well as aspects of the local vernacular. Hebrew was the *loshen kodesh*, the "holy tongue," reserved primarily for religious rituals, including Scripture and prayer. For the masses, Yiddish was the *mama loshen*, the "mother tongue," which was used even to understand Scripture and for prayer. In this language of the shtetl, Jews expressed their deepest sentiments and most profound ideas. Those who knew the language of the country in which they lived used it only in their dealings with outsiders.

Occupationally, the Jews of the shtetl were middlemen engaged in commerce, trade, or skilled work. As a result of the abolition of serfdom in the early 1860s, the construction of railroads, and official attempts to promote industrialization, the economic situation of Eastern European Jewry increasingly worsened during the second half of the nineteenth century. These economic conditions, which reduced many to pauperism, along with the spread of the secular ideas of the Enlightenment, secular Yiddishism, secular Zionism, and secular socialism, overpowered the shtetl. As a closed society it could not withstand these forces. By the end of the century the shtetl was disappearing, and Jews who remained in Eastern Europe were moving to the larger cities.

Because their cultural and structural backgrounds in Europe were so different from those of German Jews and because the conditions in the United States had changed by the time of their arrival, the Eastern European Jewish immigrants developed very different patterns of organization from those of their predecessors. Ellis Island, in Upper New York Bay, was the major immigration station for those who arrived in the United States after 1892. And almost all Eastern European Jews who arrived after 1870 initially spent some time on New York City's Lower East Side.

The Eastern European Jewish immigrants arrived at a point during which the United States was rapidly becoming urbanized, and they settled in the ethnic neighborhoods in the country's largest cities. These settlement patterns led to American Jewry's becoming highly urbanized, a pattern that persists but has been steadily declining somewhat in recent years. Most Eastern European Jews arrived with no money and made their way to the Jewish neighborhoods, primarily on the Lower East Side in New York City, where they were assisted by relatives, friends, and/or representatives of the Hebrew Immigrant Aid Society.

For the millions who emigrated to the United States at the turn of the century, the change, though lifesaving for many, was nevertheless traumatic. Not only did they encounter alien social and cultural forces, they were frequently met with hostility, fear, and disdain from the earlier German Jewish immigrants, who were just beginning to feel comfortable with their own integration into American society.

To be sure, many of the German Jews perceived the Eastern European immigrants as uncouth, destitute, uncivilized, and therefore threatening to their own position in American society. In addition, when newly arrived Eastern European Jewish intellectuals began espousing socialism and when many Eastern European Jews became involved in and even assumed leadership roles in the newly emerging labor movement in the United States, many German Jews, who were essentially middle-class, were appalled. There was nothing novel in their fears; middle-class members of minority groups who are themselves of precarious status typically hold the lower-class members of their group in contempt. What was novel, however, was the manner in which the German Jews attempted to deal with their fears and hostilities. They did not, as other middle-class members of minority groups often have, totally reject and disassociate themselves from their lower-class brethren. Rather, they undertook to "Americanize" them as rapidly as possible.

One way they did this was to establish philanthropic organizations such as the Hebrew Emigrant Aid Society, which had local committees in more than two dozen cities throughout the United States and Toronto, Canada. Another was by establishing educational and training courses and schools for both children and adults.

The Eastern European Jewish immigrants strongly resented what they perceived as the snobbishness of the German Jews and especially the Germans' efforts to Americanize them, which the Eastern Europeans viewed as forced assimilation. Some Eastern European immigrants were so resentful of the German Jews that they embarked on massive efforts to establish their own network of religious, educational, and social service institutions, organizations, and agencies. For example, they founded their own Hebrew Emigrant Auxiliary Society, which subsequently merged with the Hebrew Sheltering House, also founded by Eastern European Jews, and became the Hebrew Immigrant Aid Society (HIAS), later a major international Jewish migration agency. Eastern European Jewish labor leaders in New York also organized a federation of Jewish labor unions, the United Hebrew Trades.

In 1887 the major Eastern European synagogues in New York City attempted to create a united Orthodox community and appoint a chief rabbi. After extensive deliberations and a search, they elected the popular and respected communal rabbi of Vilna (Vilnius), in Lithuania, Rabbi Jacob Joseph, who arrived in New York in 1888. The whole effort failed, however, because of the opposition of non-Orthodox rabbis; the vehement opposition of Jewish radicals, socialists, and anarchists; the resistance of ritual slaughterers to abide by the regulations that Rabbi

Joseph prescribed for the community; and the failure of the Orthodox synagogues to abide by their commitments to him. The effort, nevertheless, was a significant attempt by Eastern European Jewish immigrants to establish their own mode of Judaism in America.

One unique effort was the founding of extensive systems of organization, based on community of origin in Eastern Europe, known as *landsmanschaften*. These organizations catered to a host of economic, cultural, and personal needs, including mutual aid and interpersonal comfort for those undergoing a crisis. Some catered to the religious needs of their constituents as well. Founded in the late nineteenth century, many of these lasted well into the twentieth century, as suggested by a 1938 survey that found almost two thousand still in existence in New York City.

Between 1885 and 1923 twenty Yiddish daily newspapers were established in New York City. By 1924 seven of these were still in publication, and each represented a unique constituency. Despite the vehement objection of the Eastern European Jewish immigrants to the German Jewish attempts to Americanize them, the very creation of the Yiddish press, as well as the other institutions, organizations, and agencies that Eastern European Jews established, in fact helped to Americanize them. Such institutions helped the new immigrants overcome the severe cultural shock often experienced on arrival in the United States as well as teaching about American social and cultural systems and encouraging them to participate. In his study of the Yiddish press, Soltes ([1925] 1969) found it to be "an Americanizing agency" that nevertheless was cherished because it was determined by the Eastern Europeans themselves, rather than being foisted on them and controlled by others.

The Yiddish theater, which made its debut in New York on August 12, 1882, also played a role in acclimating the Eastern European Jew to American life. During its history it performed both indigenous Yiddish plays and translations into Yiddish of well-known non-Jewish plays.

Following the precedent established at the beginning of the nineteenth century by their Jewish predecessors, the Eastern European immigrants founded an array of new synagogues. According to Glazer, there were 270 synagogues in the country in 1880; "by 1890 there were 533; by 1906, 1,769; and in 1916, 1,901 . . . and there were perhaps scores or hundreds more that no census reached!" (Glazer 1972, 62).

The mushrooming of Orthodox synagogues during this period led in part to the prevalent but incorrect notion that all Eastern European Jewish immigrants were Orthodox when they arrived in this country and that only later did many of them and their children leave Orthodoxy for the Conservative and Reform synagogues or for no synagogue affiliation at all. This characterization is incorrect on several grounds. As mentioned before, throughout the nineteenth century, Eastern European Jewry, in the shtetl and elsewhere, was in major upheaval and change, including religious change. Many Jews in Eastern Europe had, in varying degrees, rejected the prevalent religious traditionalism. And many who maintained traditional Jewish religious patterns did so not so much out of an ideological commitment to Orthodox principles but simply because those were the cultural patterns they had internalized. When they emigrated to the United States, they founded synagogues because the synagogue was the central institution in their native communities. They founded Orthodox synagogues because those were the only kind they were familiar with. It would be more accurate to describe them as Orthoprax, conforming with Orthodox habit or custom, rather than as ideologically committed Orthodox Jews. Even among the Orthoprax, there were varying degrees of observance. In what might seem to be a paradox but is not, there were the "nonobservant Orthodox," whom Sklare (1972) defines as "heterodox in personal behavior but who, when occasionally joining in public worship, do so in accordance with traditional patterns" (46). Thus, while the Orthodox synagogue was the one chosen by the typical Eastern European immigrant who was so inclined, wide variations in intensity of religious commitment and a complete religious secular spectrum was already present in the first, the immigrant generation (Liebman, 1965; Singer, 1967).

Another indication that most Eastern European Jewish immigrants were not committed to Orthodoxy is the paucity of Jewish education during this period. While the Jewish population in the United States in 1900 was estimated to be 1,085,135, with approximately 200,000 being children, "only 36,000 received any kind of organized Jewish instruction at any one time" (Winter 1966, 11). Of these, about 25,000 were enrolled in religious schools attached to synagogues, and the remaining 11,000 were enrolled in communal supplementary schools (ibid.). Although many presumably received their Jewish education from private teachers, it is apparent, nevertheless, that the majority of Jewish children did not receive any Jewish education.

The Eastern European Jews came not only for economic reasons but also because of harsh religious persecution. The pogroms and anti-Jewish legislation were, in fact, part of a long history of persecution in Europe. These Jews did not, therefore, consider Eastern Europe their home as, for example, the Italians considered Italy. When the Jews left Eastern Europe, they harbored no hopes of returning; their departure was final. They came to the United States to stay. They also had a reference group to whom they could look in their hopes for making a better life for themselves—their German-Jewish predecessors, who were rather successful. Jewish immigrants brought their wives and children with them or sent for them soon after their arrival. They were determined to stay and gain a security that was not possible in Eastern Europe, for themselves or at least for their children (cf. Sarna 1981, for a penetrating analysis of the exaggerated claims of a few Jews returning to Eastern Europe.)

Despite many hardships, the Eastern European Jews remained convinced that with hard work and a bit of luck their conditions would improve. Perhaps luck was on their side, for they arrived at a most propitious moment—the birth of the burgeoning clothing industry. Given the backgrounds and skills they brought and the fact that many of the industry's employers were German Jews, the immigrant Jews were presented with a unique opportunity. Many took advantage of it.

But it was not luck alone that enabled the immigrant Jews to gain a modicum of economic security. It also took many years of relentless sweat and toil, often in unsanitary and unsafe working conditions; frugality; and at times, organized conflict with employers. It was not wealth, nor even money per se, that they sought. Rather, after centuries of persecution and insecurity they yearned for a degree of security (if not for themselves, then for the children), that had been inconceivable in Europe. In a sense, it was another form of the same drive that impelled the pioneers of Zionism to create a Jewish homeland in what was then Palestine so that they could finally taste freedom. For many Eastern European Jewish immigrants, gaining freedom and economic security in America meant a national liberation. They foresaw the possibility of freedom and were determined to take advantage of it. Moreover, they had no intentions of giving up their religious and cultural heritage in order to enjoy the benefits of that freedom and security. Willing to make certain adjustments, they were convinced that they could have their cake and eat it too. They were convinced that they could gain economic security and at the same time maintain their own group identity.

As the period of the first generation—the Eastern European immigrant generation—came to a close, American Jewry had laid the foundation for the organizational structure that was to encompass the American Jewish community of the following generations. By and large, the immigrants had overcome the challenges of economic survival, and their children set out to take full advantage of the openness and opportunities they saw in American society. In these pursuits they Americanized Judaism and the American Jewish communal structure.

The transformation of the Jewish communal structure was enabled through the consequences of the well-known phenomenon of status inconsistency. This is common among middle- and upper-class minority group members who, understandably, wish to be treated in terms of their highest status, as middle or upper-middle class. But frequently they find themselves treated in terms of their lower, minority group status. This is a source of great frustration, and one of the typical ways for avoiding its consequences is to remain within the minority group. This is precisely what occurred with some economically well-to-do second-generation Jews, who found themselves treated as Jews, outsiders, despite their high socioeconomic status. Jewish communal workers provided them with the resolution by offering to help them construct a web of institutions that were parallel to those in the larger society but were all-Jewish, such as Jewish country clubs, Jewish Community Chests, and the like. The communal workers served as catalysts, or matchmakers, to bring together two segments of the community so that each could provide for the other's needs. In exchange for their financial support, the masses conferred the desired status on the wealthy, while the wealthy, in turn, provided the Jewish masses with the resources needed for an organizational structure of which they, the wealthy, would partake.

Despite the growth of a unique and complex communal structure there emerged signs of Americanization of the Jewish community and Judaism to the extent that by the third generation there were those who warned of the serious decline if not disappearance of the American Jewish community. The first empirical indications were highlighted by W. Lloyd Warner and Leo Srole (1945) in their analysis of "Yankee City." On the basis of field research conducted between 1930 and 1935, they suggested that "the progressive defection of successive generations of Jews from their religious system in a process apparently nearly completed among the children of the immigrants themselves" was much more apparent than the defections among other immigrant groups. It was their observation that "the religious subsystem of [the Yankee City Jewish] community is apparently in a state of disintegration" (199, 200), primarily because of the economic factor. If Jews were to successfully compete in the economic sphere, Warner and Srole argued, they had to break with traditional religious patterns, such as Sabbath observance, that restricted them. Although they readily dropped those religious traditions that inhibited their successful participation in the competitive race, Yankee City Jews did not opt for mass identificational assimilation, nor did their actions result in the disintegration of the Jewish community. As Warner and Srole observed, what developed was a basic change in the nature of the community: "[T]he process of change is one of a replacement of traditionally Jewish elements by American elements. In the religious system of the Jews there is no such replacement. The Jews are not dropping their religious behaviors, relations, and representations under the influence of the American religious system. There are no indications that they are becoming Christian. Even the $F^1$ generation [the native-born generation] can only be said to be irreligious" (202).

The Jewish community, according to them, was culturally assimilating but not disappearing. Even as Yankee City's Jews shed their traditional Jewish norms, they did not eliminate the religious element from the group self-definition. They did not cease to define themselves as a religioethnic group and proceed to become solely an ethnic group. Instead, they embraced Conservative Judaism, which they perceived as a progressive form of Judaism but also rooted in tradition. Conservative Judaism thus provided them with a framework within which they could behave as Americans while espousing an ideological commitment to tradition that maintained an explicit emphasis on the ethnic character of Judaism. In other words, their Judaism was basically an expression of ethnicity, not religion.

In his analysis of religion in the United States at mid-twentieth century, Will Herberg (1960) argued that the Americanization of Judaism "was characterized by a far-reaching accommodation to the American pattern of religious life which affected all 'denominations' in the American synagogue. The institutional system was virtually the same as in the major Protestant churches" (191).

Herberg (1960) then proceeded to provide a vivid portrait of that Americanization as it manifested itself in a variety of American Jewish religious patterns, including the organizational structure of the synagogue as well as the structure of the synagogue edifice itself, the patterns of worship, ritual observance, and Jewish education. He further suggested that "by mid-century, all three of the 'denominations' were substantially similar expressions of this new American Jewish religious pattern, differing only in background, stage of development, and institutional affiliation" (195).

Although different in important ways and although Herberg never mentions it, his central thesis about religion in America in general at midcentury is reminiscent of Durkheim's theory of religion and society ([1912] 1995) when, concurring with theologian Reinhold Neibuhr (1955), Herberg (1960) argues: "What Americans believe in when they are religious is . . . religion itself . . . what they seem to regard as really redemptive is primarily religion, the 'positive' attitude of *believing*. It is this faith in faith, this religion that makes religion its own object, that is the outstanding characteristic of contemporary American religiosity. . . . Prosperity, success, and advancement in business are the obvious ends for which religion, or rather the religious attitude of 'believing' is held useful" (265–66).

This kind of religion, Herberg argues is, in essence, not religion but crass secularism, in that it is worship not of God but of the goals and values of American society, the "American way of life." Thus, even though there were increases in the rates of religious identification and affiliation and increases in the percentage of Americans, including Jews, who placed importance on religion, it was not really religion and religious values but secular American social and cultural values that they were revering.

Herberg's (1989) critique may have been more theological than sociological and a reflection of his own personal spiritual transition from secularism to religion. But he was far from alone in deciphering the basic secularism of America's Jews, even as they continued to affiliate with American Jewish religious institutions. Thus, on the heels of the first edition of Herberg's work, Herbert Gans (1958), in his analysis of the acculturation and secularization of the Jews of Park Forest in line with Warner and Srole (1945), again portrayed the religion of America's Jews as actually an expression of ethnicity. As he saw it, the temple was the center of most of the community's activities but not because of its sacred status and the centrality of religiosity in the members' lives. Quite the contrary. The temple is the center because of ideological and institutional diffusion and because of its ability to adapt itself to the wishes and desires of its members. This is very much akin to what Peter Berger (1967) later portrayed as religious institutions being subject to consumer preferences. In the case of America's Jews, as Gans (1958) saw it, consumer preferences were essentially ethnic. That is, the temples, synagogues, and Jewish schools were, in the final analysis, manifestations "of the need and desire of Jewish parents to provide clearly visible institutions and symbols with which to maintain and reinforce the ethnic identification of the next generation" (247). For many, the problem was that it was very difficult to transmit an ethnic Jewishness without a substantive Judaism, and, as America's Jews faced the mid-1960s and beyond, serious questions about the future of American Jewry were heard, not only from pulpits and in scholarly writings, but in the mass media as well.

## Note

Some of this discussion is more fully developed in my book *America's Jews in Transition* (Philadelphia: Temple University Press, 1983).

## References

Berger, Peter L. 1967. *The Sacred Canopy: Elements of a Sociological Theory of Religion*. Garden City: Doubleday.

Glazer, Nathan. 1972. *American Judaism*, 2d ed.. Chicago: Chicago: University of Chicago Press.

Gans, Herbert J. 1958. "The Origin and Growth of a Jewish Community in the Suburbs: A Study of the Jews of Park Forest." In Marshall Sklare, ed., *The Jews: Social Patterns of an American Group*. New York: Free Press, pp. 205–48.

Herberg, Will. 1960. *Protestant–Catholic–Jew: An Essay in American Religious Sociology*, rev. ed. Garden City: Anchor Books.

Herberg, Will. 1989. *From Marxism to Judaism: The Collected Essays of Will Herberg*, ed. with an Introduction by David G. Dalin. New York: Markus Wiener.

Niebuhr, Reinhold. 1955. "Religiosity and the Christian Faith." *Christianity and Crisis* 14:24 (Jan. 24).

Sarna, Jonathan D. 1981. "The Myth of No Return: Jewish Return Migration to Eastern Europe, 1881–1914." *American Jewish History* 71:2 (Winter), pp. 256–68.

Sklare, Marshall. 1972. *Conservative Judaism: An American Religious Movement*, augmented ed. New York: Schocken.

Soltes, Mordecai. [1925] 1969. *The Yiddish Press: An Americanizing Agency*. New York: Arno Press.

Warner, W. Lloyd, and Leo Srole. 1945. *The Social Systems of American Ethnic Groups, Yankee City Series*, Vol. III. New Haven: Yale University Press.

Winter, Nathan H. 1966. *Jewish Education in a Pluralist Society: Samson Benderly and Jewish Education in the United States*. New York: New York University Press.

# 2 Carmel Ullman Chiswick

# Economic Adjustment of Immigrants

## Jewish Adaptation to the United States

### I. Introduction

Judaism is a relatively human-capital–intensive religion. Even in ancient times, Jewish parenting responsibilities emphasized the importance of Jewish education, not only through explicit study but also informally within the family and community and in the many opportunities provided by the observance of Jewish holidays.[1] This traditional emphasis on education reflects the high productivity of religious human capital in enhancing the quality of Jewish time (Iannaccone, 1990). Indeed, although it is possible to practice Judaism with very little prior investment, it is far more common for a newcomer (whether a "new" or a "returning" Jew) to feel a pressing need for study and learning to improve the quality of his or her Jewish observance.

Jewish skills complement and compete with other investments, whether work-related secular human capital or the various skills associated with leisure activities. Moreover, just as consumption patterns are influenced by the relative price (time and money) of Jewish goods and services, education patterns are affected by the relative rates of return to Jewish investments. Immigration is typically accompanied by an increase in the real wage, which has two consequences for religious observance. By raising the cost of time relative to purchased goods and services, it induces time-reducing change in religious practice as in all nonwork activities. A higher wage rate also raises rates of return to investment in work-related human capital, especially in country-specific market skills, and thus typically skews the human capital investment of immigrants toward the secular. Both of these effects have important implications for religious change in immigrant populations.

This essay considers some effects on American Jewish observance of the economic absorption of immigrants. The process is divided into four phases corresponding to the investment patterns typical of all immigrants. In the first phase,

Yiddish-speaking American Jewish immigrants invested heavily in country-specific secular human capital with correspondingly little allocation of time or money to Jewish religious life. As they moved into the second phase, with its high value of time and high rates of return to secular human capital, they continued to allocate few resources to religious human capital; and middle-class American Jewish observance became increasingly nostalgic and goods-intensive. As a consequence, the third phase, when the immigrants and their children had reached high levels of secular achievement and financial stability and were ready to turn their attention to religious investments, was characterized by low levels of Jewish human capital that would skew religious investments toward nonhuman rather than human capital. The fourth phase is associated with the maturing of the community into nonimmigrant status; incentives facing the middle-class grandchildren and great-grandchildren of immigrants, with their high levels of secular and low levels of Jewish human capital, led them to choose between increasing their Jewish investments or neglecting them entirely. This suggests that some of the observed instability of modern American Judaism may be a consequence of the community's past experience as an immigrant religion.

## II. Phase I: Immigrant Judaism

Although Jews have lived in the United States since colonial times, by far the largest numbers arrived from Russia and Eastern Europe during the period of mass immigration (1881–1914) (Kuznets, 1975; B. Chiswick, 1991).[2] The community formed by these immigrants would soon become the largest branch of world Jewry, with a distinctive role to play in Jewish history and culture.[3] Yet Jews have always been and continue to be a very small minority of the American population.[4]

Immigrant Jewish men and women were eager customers for all sorts of "Americanizing" education. If it seemed that Jews participated disproportionately in evening classes where English and "citizenship" were taught to new immigrants, surely this was an economic response to the high rate of return to investment in these country-specific forms of secular human capital. A popular Yiddish-language literature sprang up to educate consumers on the "modern" (American) way of cooking and nutrition, parenting, health care and hygiene, homemaking, matchmaking, and a host of other activities (Joselit 1994). Public schooling represented an investment with very high rates of return, and Jewish immigrant parents placed a high priority on their children's secular educational achievement. Indeed, Jewish immigrants wanted their children to avail themselves of the many opportunities, for leisure as well as work, that they themselves had been denied in the old country.

If the energies of new Jewish immigrants were intensely focused on assimilation in the secular sphere, religious change followed almost as an afterthought.

Much of the Jewish communal infrastructure (synagogues, kosher food sources, communal charities) transferred from Russia to the United States with relatively little stress, flourishing in the American environment of religious pluralism and tolerance.[5] In contrast, religious training and education had to compete for scarce time not only with secular pursuits but also with nonreligious Jewish activities.[6] Whereas religious human capital acquired by immigrants in old-country Jewish schools had been supplemented by informal training at home and in the community, less was available through these avenues to their new-country children.

Self-selected not only for high levels of entrepreneurship but also for low levels of religiosity, recent Jewish immigrants gave only perfunctory attention to investments in their children's religious human capital. Jewish schools in the immigrant neighborhoods were of uneven quality, and few were capable of providing religious human capital in a form suited to the middle-class American world in which the children would live as adults. If the immigrants were themselves self-selected from groups with relatively low levels of religious human capital, they passed on even less to their American children during the early postmigration years.

Synagogues in the immigrant neighborhoods tended to be small storefront affairs, sometimes organized around old-country communities *(landsmenshaftn)* to maximize familiarity (transferability of religious human capital acquired prior to migration). Their structure was often informal, with congregants taking turns at officiating and housekeeping chores and a teacher being hired to provide minimal training to the young.[7] Alternatively, a self-styled rabbi might readily establish his own *shul* (lit. study place, synagogue); those who did so ran the gamut from scholars of renown to pedestrian teachers.[8]

The substitution of goods for time generated by increased relative wages was reflected in these synagogues primarily by low attendance. New immigrants concentrated on acquiring country-specific secular human capital, with little energy left for religious change. For many Jews this neglect of religion would be temporary, part of their immediate adjustment process as immigrants, and religion would receive more attention after these early investments had paid off in the form of higher wage rates and incomes. Yet the dramatic changes in religious practice generated by higher wage rates would be adopted by synagogues in the new middle-class neighborhoods to which they moved. Meanwhile, synagogues in the old immigrant neighborhoods would lose their "market" and decline from inattendance and neglect, with no major change in religious practice.

## III. Phase II: An American Jewish Middle Class

The emphasis on secular investments in human capital among Jewish immigrants and their children would virtually transform the community in a very short time. Blue-collar laborers and craftsmen were 80 percent of the adult male Jewish work force in 1900 but only 25 percent by 1948; they would eventually decline to less than 10 percent by 1980 (B. Chiswick 1986, 1991). In contrast, managerial occupations (including self-employment) grew from 8 percent in 1900 to 45 percent in 1948. Professional occupations were also becoming more prevalent, predominantly in law, medicine, or college teaching. Indeed, by 1948 some 60 percent of American Jewish men worked in the high-level occupations associated with business and the professions, a proportion that would remain fairly stable throughout the second half of the twentieth century.

Thus, the first half of the twentieth century was a transitional period in which American Jewry was transformed from a community of low-wage, blue-collar immigrants to one of high-wage, white-collar suburbanites. The speed with which this was accomplished reflects the intensity of investment in secular human capital by Jewish men and women. Behaving as true partners in support of their husbands' specialization in the labor market, Jewish women took responsibility not only for family life but also for traditionally masculine jobs in Jewish communal services (usually on a volunteer basis) and in Jewish education. From fund-raising to social work to teaching in Jewish schools, women filled what would otherwise have become a vacuum in the Jewish community as men increasingly disengaged themselves from these activities as well as from the ritual of the synagogue.

The rituals, customs, and practices that gave texture to Jewish religious life during this period tended to be outside the synagogue, often related to the holiday calendar and the observance of major life-cycle events. These have been characterized as following two underlying trends: a growing "consumerism" and an increased emphasis on family traditions with a strong component of nostalgia (Joselit, 1994). The former is an obvious adaptation to an environment where time is costly and goods are relatively cheap. The latter is also an adaptation to high time prices, combining two time-intensive activities (religious observance and family life) in ways that enhance their mutual complementarity and reduce the total time devoted to both.[9]

## IV. Phase III: Developing an American Judaism

In contrast to the rapid economic transitions of the previous period, the second half of the twentieth century was one of economic stability. Higher education became the norm for Jewish youth, with about 40 percent of both men and women obtaining postcollege degrees, and high-level occupations accounted for about two thirds of all adult Jewish men throughout the period 1948–1990 (C. Chiswick 1995). Jewish demographic patterns reflected the high wage rates associated with these occupations: low birthrates; large investments in the health and education of children, girls as well as boys; late marriages; and (increasingly) two-career families. With the aging and retirement of first- and second-generation immigrants, managerial occupations had declined by 1990 to a mere 17 percent of the adult

Jewish male labor force. In contrast, professional occupations increased steadily to 27 percent by 1970 and 47 percent by 1990.[10]

Low levels of Jewish human capital and high wages made it both difficult and costly for the American-born generation of adults to participate in Jewish observance, even as increased levels of income and economic security increased their demand for religion. They could afford new buildings for synagogues and schools, often choosing to do so in magnificent style, yet few attended religious services with any frequency. The professional rabbinate grew in importance, substituting its hired skills for those provided directly by members of the congregation. Most synagogues operated afternoon Hebrew schools (complete with a building, teaching staff, and graded classrooms modeled after the public elementary school) to instruct children in the rudiments of Hebrew language and Jewish history.[11]

Yet a high opportunity cost of time stimulates not only timesaving innovations but also increases in the quality of time devoted to each activity. In fact, a perceived need to enhance the quality of religious activity is a salient characteristic of American Jewish experience. Although the timesaving practices shared by virtually all American synagogues are frequently noted, obvious quality-enhancing practices tend to be taken for granted: the availability of English translations for Hebrew readings, modern English as well as Hebrew in parts of the liturgy, sermons that emphasize "relevance" to contemporary American life, even the dependence on a professional rabbinate.

The development of American synagogue movements (primarily the Reform, Conservative, and Reconstructionist) was stimulated and reinforced by the perceived need to raise the quality of Jewish experience.[12] Although each movement has its own distinctive features, these tend to reflect different preferences as to the specifics rather than differences in basic approach: they all fundamentally accept the notion that Jewish observance must be adapted in order to compete for time with secular activities, and all seek to preserve the fundamental elements of Jewish religious tradition by enhancing compatibility with the current structure of economic incentives.

As immigrant Jews became middle-class suburbanites, most shifted their allegiance to these synagogue movements. By 1990 only 7 percent of American Jews identified themselves with the various Orthodox movements, while some 45 percent and 39 percent self-identified with the Conservative/Reconstructionist and Reform movements, respectively.[13] Moreover, the pattern varies by immigrant generation: the Orthodox account for fully 17 percent of foreign-born American Jews but only 2 percent of the native-born. (See table 2.1 for more detail.) Indeed, by the middle of the twentieth century, American Jews clearly identified with and were identified by these distinctive adaptations of an ancient religion to its new socioeconomic environment.

Another adaptation to problem of low Jewish human capital among the second-generation immigrants was a sort of generational division of labor. Older immi-

TABLE 2.1
Denominations of Jewish Adults, 1970 and 1990 (Percent Distribution)[a]

| | *1970/71 (Adults)* | | *1990 (Households)* | | | | | |
|---|---|---|---|---|---|---|---|---|
| *Synagogue Movement* | *All* | | *All* | | *Native*[b] | | *Immigrant*[b] | |
| All movements | 100 | (48) | 100 | (41) | 100 | (28) | 100 | (45) |
| Orthodox | 11 | (7) | 6 | (4) | 2 | (1) | 17 | (12) |
| Conservative[c] | 42 | (24) | 33 | (15) | 27 | (11) | 37 | (22) |
| Reform | 33 | (17) | 35 | (20) | 43 | (13) | 20 | (9) |
| None or other | 14 | (—) | 26 | (2) | 28 | (3) | 26 | (2) |
| Sample size | 5790 | | 1979 | | 1120 | | 162 | |

a. Percent of all respondents self-identifying with each movement. Figures in parentheses include only synagogue members.

b. "Immigrants" include all foreign-born persons. "Natives" include only those U.S.-born persons for whom both parents were also U.S.-born.

c. Includes Reconstructionist.

*Source:* Uzi Rebhun, "Trends in the Size of American Jewish Denominations: A Renewed Evaluation," CCAR Journal: A Reform Jewish Quarterly (winter 1993), p. 7.

grants, with both a lower value of time and more old-country Jewish human capital, effectively substituted for their children in adult Jewish roles. In a typical three-generation family it would be the grandparents who filled lay positions in the synagogue, who hosted family gatherings on Jewish holidays, who said the appropriate blessings and told stories to the children. Despite the irony of their own relative neglect of religion, immigrants became not only the custodians and teachers but the very benchmarks of Jewish religious tradition for their American grandchildren.

## V. Phase IV: Crisis and Instability

If a consequence of rapid economic success during the earlier period was that each generation had less Jewish knowledge and religious experience than the one before, the high-wage stability of this period is accompanied by continuing religious innovation and increased investment in Jewish human capital.[1] In part this reflects a consumption pattern associated with higher income levels, as children from financially secure, middle-class suburban families have displaced the immigrant generations. It also reflects the inherent economic instability associated with the combination of very low levels of religious human capital and very high levels of secular human capital.[15] There are two economic responses to this situation: a reallocation of time from low- to high-productivity activities and a reallocation of investments so as to raise the relative productivity of Jewish time. Hence, the "paradox" of American Judaism in the late twentieth century: rapid loss of members to assimilation and outmarriage even as the community as a whole exhibits a strengthening of religious life and cultural vibrancy.

The trend most easily documented and most visible to the non-Jewish world is the popularity of Jewish religious practices compatible with both low religious time inputs and low Jewish-specific investments in human capital. Many American Jews understand Judaism as an essentially secular ethnicity that they celebrate with cuisine, humor, a few Yiddish words, and family gatherings on holidays and life-cycle occasions with little religious content. Their understanding of Jewish belief focuses on Judaism as an ethical system, on the importance of social justice *(tikkun olam)*, and even on Jewish ecological values (e.g., the religious obligation to plant trees). By emphasizing such aspects of Judaism, which are fully compatible with the secular American liberal ideology that dominates the Jewish political agenda, and eschewing those aspects that would make them either visible or distinctive, they maximize the overlap between secular and religious investments and reduce the rate of return to investments in specifically Jewish human capital.

American Jews following this approach find the Reform synagogue movement most hospitable to their preferences, and Reform Judaism is expanding its share of American Jewry as religiously unskilled Jews shift their identities and affiliations away from the more demanding Conservative and Orthodox movements (Rebhun, 1993). This membership increase is especially noteworthy since, as the most "ecumenical" branch of American Judaism (i.e., with the least emphasis on distinct group boundaries), the Reform movement is also rapidly losing members to outmarriage and religious assimilation (Kelley, 1972).[16] Indeed, increases in religious out-marriage and the growth of Reform Judaism may both be understood as responses to a low level of religious human capital and hence as a lingering consequence of economic decisions made by Jewish immigrants and their children.

Another observable American response to low levels of Jewish human capital is a general upgrading of religious skills (for themselves and their children), a search for ways to enrich the quality of Jewish time and exploit complementarities between Judaism and other forms of human capital. Indeed, all American synagogue movements are characterized by continuing innovation and increased intensity of Jewish religious observance, an economic response that effectively raises the productivity of Jewish investments. Reform synagogues have restored to their ritual many holiday observances and synagogue practices (including especially the use of Hebrew, the wearing of *kipa* and *tallit*, and the Bar Mitzvah) deliberately excluded by earlier generations. The Orthodox movement has slowed its long membership decline with two (generally alternative) responses to the perceived need for more religious human capital, one of which develops strategies for combining a Jewishly observant lifestyle with a high-level secular occupation; the other emphasizes reviving *Yiddishkeit* and the old-country traditions of Russian Judaism.

Less picturesque but perhaps more significant has been the growth of Jewish human capital in Conservative synagogues, a movement that accounts for well over a third of all American Jews. The Conservative movement places the greatest emphasis on Jewish education, including adult education, for Americans with active secular lifestyles. Expanding Jewish schools and upgrading the Jewish content of their curricula, Conservative synagogue practice reflects a steady increase in expectations for the Jewish human capital of congregants. A recent survey of Conservative Bar/Bat Mitzvah celebrants and their families found that no fewer than 65 percent of the parents thought their children had more knowledge of Judaism at age thirteen than they had acquired at the same age, and fully 95 percent wished their children to be better educated in Jewish content than they themselves were (Wertheimer, 1996).[17]

Egalitarianism (that is, similarity of religious privileges and responsibilities for men and women) may also be understood as part of the pattern of innovations that adapt religious practices to the economic environment. Although it takes different forms in each of the synagogue movements, it is evident everywhere and has become the norm in most non-Orthodox synagogues. The high opportunity cost of women's time requires greater efficiency in the production of women's religious experience, an incentive to improve the "quality" of synagogue life from their perspective; this is the same incentive that leads to convergence in the investment patterns of American men and women in many family, consumption, and work activities. Jewish egalitarianism is also consistent with the development of complementarities between family and religion, a shift in the locus of Jewish family life from home to synagogue. Indeed, as it reinforces the family orientation of religious experience and a synagogue orientation for Jewish family life, egalitarianism is an effective innovation for raising the quality of Jewish time in a high-wage community.

Aside from strengthening and innovating observances associated with Jewish holidays and life-cycle events, popular support for (and participation in) Jewish education, music, art, travel, literature, and journalism have flourished in the United States to the point of shaping the American Jewish community's very definition of itself. This phenomenon has been further stimulated by some midcentury changes in relative prices that effectively reduced the cost of Jewish practice and learning. Certainly the decline of anti-Semitism has been important in this respect.[18] Much more important, however, has been the emergence of Israel as a sovereign Jewish state where a somewhat different portfolio of religious human capital (especially intensive in Hebrew language fluency) has been accumulating. For example, the efficiency of American Hebrew schools has been greatly improved by the development in Israel of teaching materials and teacher training programs, and their curriculum has been enriched by the popular culture of a Hebrew-speaking Israeli population.

## VI. The Demographic Future of American Jewry

Today's American Jewish community is dominated by the well-educated natives of a suburban middle class. Each year there are fewer who even have immigrant family members, and the immigrant experience of American Jews is becoming the stuff of history and museum exhibits. Yet the turn-of-the-century immigrants from the Czarist Russian Empire had a formative effect on American Jewish culture, and their economic decisions would have implications for generations to come. Much has been written about the many contributions made by these Jewish immigrants (and their descendants) in secular spheres of activity; this essay focuses on their contributions to Jewish civilization. The immigrants' pattern of investment in human capital has been shown to have implications for Judaism itself, contributing to the current demographic crisis as well as to the development in America of a major center of Jewish culture. Similarly, the level and shape of Jewish human capital in the next century will undoubtedly be affected by educational decisions made in the context of today's economic conditions.

### Notes

Paper presented at the annual meeting of the Social Science History Association, Washington, D.C., October 1997. The author is grateful to Stephen Warner for inspiration and encouragement in the development of this study. The current draft has benefited from comments by Barry Chiswick, Evelyn Lehrer, Oscar Miller, Dan Olson, Rima Schultz, and various participants in the Twelfth World Congress of Jewish Studies and the Chicago Area Group for the Study of Religious Communities (CAGSRC). The author assumes sole responsibility, however, for all remaining errors and omissions.

1. The obligations that devolve upon a father concerning his son are: circumcision, redemption (in the case of a firstborn son), teaching Torah, teaching an occupation, marriage, swimming. (Mishnah *Nashim: Kiddushin*) Three of these involve providing human capital: investments that augment productivity at work, in consumption (health?), and in religious expression.
2. Jews accounted for some 9.4 percent of the 22 million new immigrants arriving during this period: Kuznets reports that fully 76 percent of these Jews came from the Czarist Russian Empire, 19 percent from Austria-Hungary, and 4 percent from Romania.
3. By 1994 the American Jewish community (primarily descendants of these immigrants) represented some 45 percent of the world's Jewish population; another 35 percent lived in Israel and the remaining 20 percent in various other countries (Schmeltz & DellaPergola, 1996).
4. Statistics on the size of the American Jewish population vary greatly according to the definition chosen for identifying individuals as Jews. The 1990 National Jewish Population Survey (NJPS) enumerates all respondents who self-identify as Jewish by religion, by ethnicity, by parentage, or by upbringing, as well as any non-Jewish members of their households. Using a broad definition that includes all self-identified

Jews, Jews are no more than 2.1 percent of the 1994 population of the United States (Schmeltz & DellaPergola, 1996).

5. In part this was because Judaism was fully adjusted to its status as a minority religion that could be transported to different cultural settings. Immigrants practicing a state religion in their country of origin had a much more difficult transition to minority status (Warner, 1993).
6. Although Hebrew is the language of Jewish religious life, Yiddish (lit., Jewish) was the everyday language of the vibrant Jewish culture in America as in Europe. Spoken both at home and on the street, Yiddish was the language of informal Jewish education; hence, the irony that Jewish linguistic contributions to the American melting pot are invariably associated with secular pursuits (e.g., literature, entertainment, journalism, the labor movement, cuisine) rather than the religion by which Jews are identified.
7. Some congregations of this sort hired a cantor to sing the synagogue liturgy, especially on the High Holy Days. Indeed, one strategy for financing the larger synagogues involved selling tickets (presumably to nonregular attendees) for services sung by a well-paid cantor.
8. In most cases the poverty of the community combine with nonobservance to make this a particularly unremunerative line of work, and these rabbis acquired the reputation of being *luftmenschen* who couldn't keep a "real" job.
9. More subtle, perhaps, is that synagogue attendance in America became an activity in which families participate as a unit, enhancing the mutual complementarity of two intrinsically time-intensive activities. For example, family seating (that is, without separation of men and women) was one of the earliest American innovations in the synagogue, and the presence of children is typically the main impetus for joining a synagogue.
10. Jewish professionals also became less concentrated in their areas of specialization, diversifying beyond medicine and law into a wide variety of technical fields. They typically work in predominantly non-Jewish environments, where they are a small religious minority; even though a large proportion of Jews are professionals, only about 5 percent of all professionals are Jews. Most American Jews are quite comfortable with this situation and do not perceive religion be an important factor in their work environment.
11. Beginning at the age of eight or nine (fourth grade), Jewish children would attend twice a week after school (for about two hours) and on Sunday mornings. Few continued this schooling into their teens, the greatest attrition occuring after the Bar Mitzvah ceremony at age thirteen.
12. Although these synagogue movements may have roots elsewhere, they have developed during the twentieth century along distinctively American lines. Reconstructionism, although a branch of the Conservative movement for many years, was responsible for some important innovations during the period under discussion and continues to be influential; it has only recently become independent and is still very small but appears to be growing in popularity.
13. The remaining 9 percent identified themselves as without denomination, as secular Jews, or as having "no" religion (including atheists and agnostics). These figures come from the 1990 NJPS and include all Jews by birth, exclusive of converts to other religions.
14. The very term *assimilation* has changed its meaning during this process. In the first two phases it referred to occupational success in the non-Jewish world and to adopting

consumption patterns similar to those of other Americans. In contrast, today it almost always refers to the loss of Jewish religious identity.

15. Masked somewhat by the intergenerational division of labor, this imbalance became apparent as the immigrant generation aged and thus ceased to be available as a repository of religious knowledge. Although major events outside the United States further stimulated renewed interest in Jewish religious life, especially the destruction of European Jewry (Holocaust) and establishment of the modern State of Israel, economic forces suggest that the demand for Judaism in America would have been greater during the second half of the twentieth century than the first even in the absence of these influences.
16. According to the NJPS, some 38 percent of the first marriages of self-identified Reform Jews were to non-Jewish spouses; the figure is considerably higher if the population is limited to younger marital cohorts.
17. This survey of children who had been Bar/Bat Mitzvah in a Conservative synagogue in the United States or Canada during the Jewish year 5755 (1994–95) involved a telephone interview with 1,467 young people and one of their parents. It contains a wealth of information supporting the increased investment in religious human capital among Conservative Jews.
18. Whether overt or of the "gentlemen's agreement" variety, anti-Semitism in the United States was never as virulent or destructive as in Europe in general and Russia in particular. Despite its recent emergence in some possibly new forms, it is relatively unpopular, and most American Jews are sufficiently insulated from its effects that its influence on their religious practice is negligible.

## References

Azzi, Corry, and Ronald Ehrenberg. 1975. "Household Allocation of Time and Church Attendance." *Journal of Political Economy* 83:27–56.

Becker, Gary S. 1981. *Treatise on the Family*. Cambridge, Mass.: Harvard University Press.

Chiswick, Barry R. 1986. "The Labor Market Status of American Jews: Patterns and Determinants." In *1985 American Jewish Yearbook*, pp.131–53. New York: The American Jewish Committee.

———. Chiswick, Barry R. 1991. "Jewish Immigrant Skill and Occupational Attainment at the Turn of the Century." *Explorations in Economic History* 28:64–86.

Chiswick, Carmel U. 1995. "The Economics of American Judaism." *Shofar* 13(4), pp. 1–19.

———. Forthcoming. "Israel and American Jewry in the Year 2020: An Economic Analysis." (In Jewish Agency for Israel, *Master Plan for Israel in the Twenty-first Century* (Hebrew translation from the English). Haifa: Technion.

———. Forthcoming. "The Economics of Contemporary Jewish Family Life." In P. Medding, ed., *Families and Family Relations among Jews in the Twentieth Century*. Studies in Contemporary Judaism 14. New York: Oxford University Press.

Iannaccone, Laurence R. 1986. "A Formal Model of Church and Sect." *American Journal of Sociology* 94 (suppl.): S241–S268.

———. 1990. "Religious Practice: A Human Capital Approach." *Journal for the Scientific Study of Religion* 29:297–314.

Joselit, Jenna Weissman. 1994. *The Wonders of America: Reinventing Jewish Culture 1880–1950*. New York: Hill and Wang.

Kelley, Dean M. 1972. *Why Conservative Churches Are Growing*. New York: Harper & Row.

Kuznets, Simon S. 1975. "Immigration of Russian Jews to the United States: Background and Structure." *Perspective in American History* 9:35–126.

Meyerhoff, Barbara 1979. *Number Our Days*. New York: E. P. Dutton.

Rebhun, Uzi. 1993. "Trends in the Size of American Jewish Denominations: A Renewed Evaluation." *CCAR Journal: A Reform Jewish Quarterly*, winter, pp. 1–11.

Schmeltz, U. O., and Sergio DellaPergola. 1996. "World Jewish Population, 1994." In *American Jewish Yearbook 1996*, pp. 434–63. New York: American Jewish Committee.

Schultz, T. W., ed. 1974. *Economics of the Family: Marriage, Children, and Human Capital*. Chicago: University of Chicago Press for the NBER.

Warner, R. Stephen. 1993. "Work in Progress toward a New Paradigm for the Sociological Study of Religion in the United States." *American Journal of Sociology* 98:1044–93.

Wertheimer, Jack. 1996. *Conservative Synagogues and Their Members: Highlights of the North American Study of 1995–96*. New York: Jewish Theological Seminary of America.

# Part II

## Assimilation of the American Jewish Population

Changes within the American Jewish population are often most clearly recognized through the use of demographic and attitudinal surveys. When dealing with large groups or groups that span large distances, observation alone does not suffice. For this reason, other sources of data are used. Gathering these data, however, is both difficult and expensive, and most social scientists do not have the resources to undertake and conduct "pure" research on their own. Invariably, they must turn to institutions that have a pragmatic interest in the information. And invariably, the needs of the sponsoring organization will have a strong influence on the nature of the research undertaken.

Information about many groups within the U.S. can be obtained from the national census, but this is not the case with respect to America's Jews because they are officially defined as a religious group, and the doctrine of separation of church and state has been interpreted to preclude questions concerning religious affiliation in surveys conducted by the U.S. Bureau of the Census. In addition, since the bureau does not identify Jews as an ethnic group, its data cannot be utilized as a significant source of information about Jews.

For more or less current information on the Jewish population in the United States there are three main sources. The most widely used and quoted and probably the most reliable since the 1970s is the National Jewish Population Survey (NJPS), sponsored by the Council of Jewish Federations (CJF). The CJF's interest is, obviously, in finding out about the American Jewish population so that it can better serve and be served by that population. The NJPS surveys, probably the most scientifically valid national samples of American Jews ever obtained, have provided a wealth of previously unavailable information. However, a complete report of the 1971 findings was never published, and only a series of brief reports that summarized data of concern in community planning within local Jewish federations was issued. The 1990 survey has received much more extensive analysis, and all of the articles in this section use its findings.

Another source of information on the American Jewish population, used in this chapter, is the series of community and regional surveys periodically conducted by local Jewish federations. The quality of these surveys, in terms of social research techniques, varies widely, although it has improved greatly in recent years. Some questions have been raised about their representativeness, even for the local community involved, since in many cases only those Jews affiliated with local Jewish institutions are surveyed. Questions have also been raised about the degree to which a particular community is representative of American Jewry as a whole, although Goldstein's review of community surveys revealed surprisingly uniform patterns (Goldstein 1971).

A final source of information is the limited number of specialized studies conducted by social scientists and reported in academic journals. Many of these suffer from problems similar to those of community studies. In addition, since Jews are such a small percentage of the American population, the samples in these studies usually contain only a very small number of Jewish cases. Given the limitations of reliable data, as well as some of the other inherent problems of social scientific predictability, all projections of future trends should be taken as tentative. In some cases, however, when the data come from a variety of sources and findings are more or less similar, we assume the emerging picture is close to accurate and plan accordingly while recognizing the element of uncertainty that underlies the projections.

In both the 1970 and 1990 surveys, the most striking finding was the rising intermarriage rate. The 1970 survey found that for individuals married before 1925 it was less than 2 percent. Of those marrying between 1940 and 1960 the intermarriage rate rose to about 6 percent. For the 1960–64 marriage cohort, it rose to 12 percent and then to a high of 29 percent during the five years preceding the 1970 survey (Goldstein 1992, 125). The magnitude of the increase, along with future projections, alarmed the Jewish community; and results of the 1990 survey, which found a significantly higher intermarriage rate, did nothing to dispel their concern. According to the 1990 survey, before 1965 the intermarriage rate was 9 percent. From 1965 to 1974 the intermarriage rate rose to 25 percent. It climbed even higher for those married between the years 1975 and 1984, to 44 percent. Marriages from 1985 on had an intermarriage rate of 52 percent. This means that for every new couple consisting of two Jewish partners approximately two new couples were formed in which only one partner was Jewish (Kosmin, Barry, et al. 1991, 14).

However, it appears that intermarriage rates, like other behavioral patterns, vary by region of the country. For example, the results of the 1991 United Jewish Appeal–Federation of Jewish Philanthropies survey of the New York Jewish population, which included the five boroughs of New York City and Nassau, Suffolk, and Westchester counties, found that for marriages since 1985, Jews living in New York have approximately half the intermarriage rate of that of the rest of the nation (Horowitz 1993).

Statistics other than the rising intermarriage rate illustrate how much the relationship between the Jewish and non-Jewish populations has changed and provide clear evidence of the Americanization of Jews in America. In terms of population distribution, Jews have become more and more dispersed throughout the country. Fifty-seven percent of American Jewry lived in the Northeast in 1900. Immigration raised this percentage to sixty-eight (68) by 1930 at which time only 12 percent of American Jews lived in the combined southern and western regions of the United States. The 1970 to 1971 NJPS found that 64 percent of American Jews lived in the Northeast, but by 1990 this distribution showed significant change. In 1990 only 43.6 percent of the American Jewish population lived in the Northeast. In the South and West together, however, this population grew to 45 percent. Goldstein (1992) points out that "whereas almost half of the Jews by religion are concentrated in the Northeast, less than one-third of the secular Jews and those who are Jews by choice are located there" (97–98). In this volume, Rebhun, DellaPergola, and Tolts analyze factors such as fertility, mortality, and worldwide Jewish migration to project the changes & continuities in the American Jewish population between the years 1990 and 2020.

Family life has always been regarded as the core strength of Jewish continuity, and it is here that changes such as the rising intermarriage rate have the greatest long-term impact. For this reason we have included the article by Fishman on the contemporary Jewish family. Taking a more historical approach, Fishman finds that the American Jewish family looks more like that of comparable American families. However, given the specific needs of Jewish life, the below-replacement birthrate for baby boomers (Waxman 1994), and the increasing number of never married are areas of concern.

## References

Goldstein, Sidney. 1971. "American Jewry, 1970." *American Jewish Year Book* 72, pp. 3–88. New York: American Jewish Committee.

Goldstein, Sidney. 1992. "Profile of American Jewry: Insights from the 1990 National Jewish Population Survey." *American Jewish Year Book* 92, pp. 77–173. New York: The American Jewish Committee.

Hammond, Phillip E., and Kee Warner. 1993. "Religion and Ethnicity in Late-Twentieth Century America." *Annals of the American Academy of Political and Social Science*, 527. (May):55-61.

Horowitz, Bethamie. 1993. *UJA–Federation 1991 New York Jewish Population Study*. New York: United Jewish Appeal-Federation of Jewish Philanthropies of New York.
Kosmin, Barry, et al. 1991. *Highlights of the CJF 1990 National Jewish Population Survey*. New York: Council of Jewish Federations.
Waxman, Chaim I. 1994. "Families of Jewish Baby Boomers." In Steven Bayme and Gladys Rosen, eds., *The Jewish Family and Jewish Continuity*, pp. 103–15. Hoboken, N.J.: Ktav.

# 3 Uzi Rebhun, Sergio DellaPergola, and Mark Tolts

# American Jewry

## A Population Projection, 1990–2020

### Introduction

Despite the absence of a question on religious identity both in the United States census and in vital statistics records, there exist today alternative adequate sources to estimate the size of the American Jewish population. The most reliable data derive from the 1990 National Jewish Population Survey (NJPS), which was conducted under the auspices of the Council of Jewish Federations.[1] Based on a national random sample, the NJPS estimated the Jewish population at 5,515,000 persons in the summer of 1990. This "core" Jewish population[2] includes persons who defined themselves as Jews by religion or ethnic identity, as well as people born in another faith who joined the Jewish group either by formal conversion, or otherwise. The Jewish population figure based on this study is within a sampling error range of plus or minus 3.5 percent,[3] namely, a range between 5.3 and 5.7 million. The other source, with potentially larger error, is the ongoing yearly compilation project of local Jewish population estimates undertaken by a research team at the North American Jewish Data Bank (NAJDB). The NAJDB estimate of the U.S. Jewish population for 1990 was 5,981,000, 8.5 percent higher than that of the NJPS.[4] The gap between the national and aggregate-local figures is explained by differences in sampling methods and in the criteria used to define the target population. Likewise, the gathering of local estimates is liable to "a great many local biases and tend[s] to fall behind the actual pace of national trends. This is especially true in a context of vigorous internal migrations, as in the United States."[5] Nevertheless, the two sources coincide well with one another and provide updated information on the size of U.S. Jewry in 1990 as well as on some of its sociodemographic characteristics.

Much less agreement is found regarding the future size of U.S. Jewry. Several projections, which applied scientific methods with different assumptions about the future courses of the salient demographic factors, arrived at different results. Based on corrected figures of the first NPS, of 1970/71, Schmelz and DellaPergola suggested for the year 2000 a range of Jewish population between 4.64 million if only natural movement and assimilation are considered and 5.57 million when a strong positive migration balance is added.[6] According to Bergman, if the American Jewish population size was reliant solely on natural causes, it most likely would maintain the number at which it leveled off in 1970 (i.e., about 5.4 million). But when assimilation, a principal parameter of demographic change among American Jewry, is taken into account, the number is expected to decline to a level of less than 1 million by the year the United States celebrates its tricentenial in 2076.[7] Under conditions of stable fertility and improvement in mortality, Lieberman and Wienfeld anticipated an increase in the number of American Jews from 5.37 million in 1970 to 5.7 million by the year 2000, after which, according to their estimate, it would decline to slightly less than 4 million by 2070.[8] Should Jewish fertility recover to replacement level, the number would rise to 5.8 million in the next twenty to thirty years and would stabilize at 5.7 million by the year 2070. A least likely alternative is a decline in fertility, which, according to Lieberman and Wienfeld, would diminish the size of American Jewry to 5 million by the year 2000, to 4 million by 2025, and to 1.6 million in 2070.

Another assessment, made recently by Goldstein, anticipated stability at around the 5.5 million figure found in the 1990 NJPS; and in the absence of a sizable upswing in fertility or large upsurge in immigration, the core Jewish population is more likely to decline toward 5.0 million or even below in the early decades of the next century.[9] These studies cautiously emphasize that unforeseen political, economic, or social changes, either national and global, may invalidate even a wide range of scenarios.

The 1990 NJPS is not only a good scientific source for estimating the size of the American Jewish population, the data set provides, inter alia, updated age-sex distribution and allows computation of the current size of major components of demographic change, including patterns of fertility and levels of assimilation. Likewise, the period since the late 1980s was one of unpredicted strategic trends in the general geopolitical system of a few countries with large Jewish concentrations. We refer, first and foremost, to the former Soviet Union but also to the peace process in the Middle East, the transition of power from the white rulers to the African majority in South Africa, and the continuation of unstable political and economic conditions in a few South America countries. These developments significantly changed the world Jewish migration system in which the United States is a major country of destination. Hence, it is important to reassess the demographic future of American Jews.

Based on moderate assumptions of the continuation of the recently prevailing levels of the components of internal evolution and taking into account the changing patterns of migration balance, this chapter presents the results of a population projection for the American Jewish population for the period 1990–2020. Size is critical to any organized efforts to ensure the strength and vitality of the Jewish community. Further, population size and composition are basics for any policy and for communal planning such as day care centers, parochial schools, auxiliary groups, and institutional infrastructure for the elderly population; increase or decrease in the demand for different services due to changes in the absolute numbers of certain age groups may affect the allocation of a given budget or pose special efforts on the part of the Jewish community to search for additional financial resources.[10] There is also great relevance to the changing proportion of Jews within the general American population. If the direction or rhythm of Jews' demographic evolution differs from that of the total population or other minority groups, it may accordingly affect their social and economic power and thus also determine their self-confidence to operate as a strong and proud community.

Today, American Jews constitute the largest Jewish community in the world and have held this quantitative demographic status for most of the twentieth century. Will this still be true in the next century? The projection for American Jews will be discussed in a global Jewish context vis-à-vis the demographic future of world Jewry, Diaspora Jewry, and individual communities including Israel.[11]

## Internal Population Dynamics

### *Assumptions of Internal Factors*

The fertility patterns of American Jews have experienced sharp fluctuations over the past fifty years. The total fertility rate (TFR), a synthetic expression of the level of reproductivity in a given period, reached an all-time minimum of 1.3 children around 1935, climbed to 2.8 in the mid-1950s and declined again to 1.5 around 1970.[12] While these trends basically coincide with those among the total white population, Jewish fertility was consistently lower, reflecting a greater responsiveness to periodic societal changes that have stimulated the general upward and downward swings. More recently, the 1990 NJPS revealed the average number of children ever born to a Jewish woman 40–44 years old to be 1.6.[13] The subsequent group of ages 45–49, which is considered to be the end of the reproductive period, averaged 1.9 children; nevertheless, when the younger age group reaches ages 45–49, their fertility will presumably not have increased much from its current level, if at all, since they carry different fertility behavioral patterns. The average of 1.6 children observed among the women ages 40–44 can therefore be seen as complete or very nearly complete Jewish fertility.

Jewish fertility in 1990 was substantially lower than that of all white women in the United States. It continues to be similar to the general tendency toward smaller white American families; yet some unique factors among the Jewish population, such as their higher social and economic stratification, rapid increase in the proportion of women in the labor force, and preference for residing in large metropolitan areas, operate to reduce both their complete fertility and that of each individual age group. According to Sidney Goldstein, Jewish women aged 25–29 in 1990 averaged only 0.5 children, whereas all white women of the same ages had already had one child; at ages 40–44, the respective figures were 1.6 and 2.1.[14] Even more significant, the level of American Jewish fertility stands below the replacement level of an average of 2.1 children.

Jewish fertility is further affected by the proportion of Jewish children among all children of intermarried couples. Only 28 percent of the children of mixed couples were being raised Jewish at the time of the 1990 NJPS. To avoid a loss to the Jewish population, at least half of those children must be raised Jewish; however, some 41 percent were raised in a non-Jewish religion and the remaining 31 percent with no religion.[15] The possibility does exist that some of the latter will opt to identify as Jews when they reach adulthood. But growing up in a society composed mainly of non-Jews diminishes this option and suggests that there will be a net loss to the core Jewish population in the next generation. Assuming that there are no significant differences between the fertility levels of Jewish inmarriages and Jewish intermarriages, the combination of the recent levels of intermarriage (52% among the marriage cohort of 1985–90)[16] and the low proportion of children who are identified as Jews among them results in a diminution of approximately 10 percent of overall Jewish fertility. Thus, the "effectively Jewish" fertility of American Jews in 1990 is estimated at 1.44. This level is kept constant throughout the projection period of 1990–2020.

The most updated information on patterns of mortality and survival are available for Rhode Island Jews.[17] Information obtained from Jewish funeral homes on deaths was combined with population data from a communal survey undertaken in 1987 to construct life tables and to enable insights into life expectancies at different ages for males and females separately. Although the data derive from a single Jewish community, which constitutes a very small proportion of the entire American Jewish population (approximately 0.3%), we see no reason to believe that mortality here differs significantly from that of Jews in other parts of the country. Life expectancy at birth, which is the average number of years a person has to live, was of 76.3 years for Jewish males and 79.3 years for Jewish females. These levels are used as the life expectancies of American Jews for the base year of the projection. Thereafter, we assume a linear growth to 79.0 years for males and 83.0 years for females at the end of the projection period.

### *Projected Size from Internal Evolution*

If low effectively Jewish fertility continues at approximately its recent level, the outcome of natural increase will be negative despite high life expectancies at birth; this will result in a shrinkage of the American Jewish population from 5,515,000 in 1990 to 5,438,000 at the turn of the twenty-first century and down to 5,173,000 by the year 2020 (table 3.1). This change reflects an overall decrease of

TABLE 3.1
Medium Projection of U.S. Jewish Population, 1990–2020

| | *Internal Factors* | | *All Factors* | |
|---|---|---|---|---|
| *Year* | *Number (Thousands)* | *Index Number (1990=100)* | *Number (Thousands)* | *Index Number (1990=100)* |
| 1990 | 5,515 | — | 5,515 | — |
| 1995 | 5,502 | 99.8 | 5,675 | 102.9 |
| 2000 | 5,438 | 98.6 | 5,702 | 103.4 |
| 2005 | 5,357 | 97.1 | 5,703 | 103.4 |
| 2010 | 5,286 | 95.8 | 5,675 | 102.9 |
| 2015 | 5,236 | 94.9 | 5,668 | 102.8 |
| 2020 | 5,173 | 93.8 | 5,648 | 102.4 |

slightly more than 6 percent relative to the size at the starting year of the projection. The shrinkage in the number of American Jews is not equally dispersed throughout the quinquenniums (table 3.2); after a modest decline in the first five years, the negative natural movement reaches a peak of –81,000 in the interval 2000–2005; the loss of Jewish population slightly diminishes in the next two quinquenniums, but beginning 2015, it is expected to accelerate again.

These fluctuations largely result from the age composition of U.S. Jews, which in the late 1980s was characterized by large baby boom cohorts which were concentrated at ages 25–44. Despite relatively low levels of total fertility, the frequency of Jews in the most procreative ages had the potential for a temporary rise in the number of Jewish newborn. Shortly afterward, the peak childbearing ages were occupied by smaller cohorts, born since the beginning of the 1960s when fertility had declined drastically. A second echo effect of the baby boom will be seen around the years 2005 to 2015, when the large numbers of the children of the baby boomers will themselves reach reproductive ages, but these will be much smaller cohorts that can hardly mitigate the negative natural increase.

Table 3.2 shows the respective influences of natural increase and assimilation. The projected loss of 342,000 persons from 1990 to 2020 is equally divided between the two factors. The decline in the first quinquennium is entirely attributed to loss of children of intermarriages who are not identified as Jews; from 1995 onward both factors operate to diminish the size of American Jewry. The pattern of change of natural increase is somewhat inverse to that of assimilation: while the former has a U-shaped curve, the latter is more convex; beginning in 2015, the two factors will behave similarly toward intensification of the demographic decline of American Jews. Presumably, the increase in life expectancy will not compensate for the negative effect of low fertility and assimilation, indicating the inability of U.S. Jewry to ensure its own numerical stability.

TABLE 3.2
Factors of Change in the Size of U.S. Jewish Population, 1990–2020 (in Thousands)

| *Period* | *Total Change* | *Internal Factors* | | | *International* |
|---|---|---|---|---|---|
| | | *Total* | *Natural Increase* | *Assimilation* | *Migration*[a] |
| Total | +133 | −342 | −171 | −171 | +475 |
| 1990–1995 | +160 | −13 | +17 | −30 | +173 |
| 1995–2000 | +27 | −64 | −36 | −28 | +91 |
| 2000–2005 | +1 | −81 | −56 | −25 | +82 |
| 2005–2010 | −28 | −71 | −45 | −26 | +43 |
| 2010–2015 | −7 | −50 | −21 | −29 | +43 |
| 2015–2020 | −20 | −63 | −30 | 33 | +43 |

a. Including natural increase and assimilation among the immigrants.

## External Factors: The Effect of International Migration

The United States continues to play an important role in global Jewish international migration as a country of origin but more so as the one of major alternative destination. The most significant recent development is the renewal, in the late 1980s, of large-scale migration from the former Soviet Union. The first arrivals, from the beginning of 1989 and until mid-1990, are assumed to have been included in the NJPS enumeration. For the following five years, there are adequate records for estimating the ex-Soviet migrants in the United States as well as some of their major demographic characteristics. Accurate data for 1990–95 are also available on the number of Jews who emigrated from the United States to Israel. Hence, we shall update our figures on the size of U.S. Jewry for 1995 with a combination of hard retrospective evidences and pure educated guesses.

### *Update for 1990–1995*

Referring to migrants assisted by the Hebrew Immigrant Aid Society (HIAS), between mid-1990 and mid-1995 some 175,500 Jews and non-Jewish members of their families migrated to the United States. This estimate, gathered from HIAS's yearly statistical reports, excludes a small number of people (possibly a few hundred each year) who did not need resettlement assistance or were assisted by non-Jewish agencies.[18] There is no documentary evidence on the ethnoreligious identification of the ex-Soviet migrants to the United States. Some rough range can be made according to the known experience of the two major competing areas of destination, namely Israel and Germany.[19] According to data processed by the Israel Central Bureau of Statistics, the percentage of non-Jews among ex-Soviet immigrants whose religion was ascertained increased from 3.8 percent in 1990 to 32 percent in 1995, or a weighted average of 12 percent for the entire period. As to the share of non-Jews among ex-Soviet migrants to Germany, data on the number of people who entered the country in the framework of the Jewish quota was combined with the number of members of the local Jewish community organization (whose admission criteria are based on the Jewish law [Halachah]), resulting in 41 percent of non-Jews for the years 1990–95.

It stands to reason that the number of non-Jews among migrants to the United States fell somewhere between the levels mentioned above, and we adopted an average rate of about one-fifth for 1990–1995. This should be considered a minimal boundary if we bear in mind that under circumstances of social and financial absorption by Jewish organizations, people in mixed families, including children, may tend to identify with the Jewish group. In the United States, religious identification is not anchored in any legal framework, and it is the self-definition given by respondents that provides the basis for the current analysis of Jewishness. Of the total 175,500 ex-Soviet immigrants to the United States who were assisted by HIAS, the number of "core" Jews is estimated at 140,500.

The United States is likewise a principal destination for Israeli Jews and attracts both native-born and foreign-born Israelis. Based on data on migration and remigration by period of arrival for the late 1980s,[20] we estimate the yearly number of Israeli emigrants in the United States to be approximately 6,200, or 31,000 for the period mid-1990–mid-1995. During this same period, some 9,500 American Jews moved to Israel.[21] For this group we applied a retention rate of 62 percent[22] which is equivalent to an absolute number of approximately 6,000 migrants. Hence, the net migration between the United states and Israel for the 1990–95 period is estimated at 25,000. Further, based on many different sources of data and estimates, we suggest a yearly surplus of 1,500 immigrants over emigrants to the United States from other Jewish communities, or 7,500 for the entire quinquennium.

Since the completion of the recent NJPS, the United States gained some 173,000 Jews from the former Soviet Union, Israel, and other Jewish communities. With the projected figure of 5,502,000 Jews resulting from internal changes of fertility, mortality, and assimilation, we suggest an American Jewish population of 5,675,000 in mid-1995 (table 3.1). Net migration not only compensated for the internal negative evolution, but it brought about an increase of 2.9 percent above the 1990 level.

### *Projected Size, 1995–2020*

Unless unexpected political or economic events are evolving in the former Soviet Union, it is likely that Jewish emigration will continue, though at a much slower pace. In 1996 American policy regarding refugees changed, reducing the yearly quota for Soviet Jewish immigrants to a level of 20,000. By extrapolating further from the Israeli experience of the ongoing increase in the proportion of non-Jews among the new immigrants, we arrived at a total number of 50,000 Soviet Jewish immigrants to the United States for the period 1995–2000 and 40,000 during 2000–2005. Most of the Jews who wish to leave the ex-Soviet Union will probably do so within the next decade, after which emigration will sharply decline to marginal numbers each year.

We assume the continuation of Jewish migration from other Diaspora communities to the United States at an average level of 7,500 persons in each quinquennium of the projection period. For all the emigrants from Diaspora communities, fertility, assimilation, and mortality levels similar to those of their veteran American Jewish counterparts were assumed. For Israelis, we maintained a net gain of 24,000 per quinquennium. Fertility is expected to decline linearly from a TFR of 2.7 (which was the level for Israeli Jews in 1990) to 2.0 at the end of the projection period, reflecting a tendency for convergence to the fertility patterns of the local Jewish population. No assimilation is assumed among the first generation of Israeli emigrants. Mortality levels are expected to parallel those of total American Jews.

Given all the demographic parameters of change, the American Jewish population is expected to peak at 5,702 million in the year 2000; it will maintain this level for a quinquennium, after which a gradual decline is projected to 5,648 million by the year 2020 (table 3.1).[23] At the end of the projection period, the number of Jews will be 2.4 percent higher than it was in 1990. Net migration to the United States will account for an increment of almost half a million Jews over the thirty-year interval, totally offsetting the internal loss caused by low levels of fertility and assimilation (table 3.2). However, with the anticipated termination of the large wave of emigration from the former Soviet Union, migrations may not be sufficient to affect the intensified internal negative evolution, and shortly after the turn of this century the size of U.S. Jewry is expected to begin to decline.

## The Aging of American Jews

### *Understanding the 1990 Age Composition*

The recent age composition of U.S. Jews derives, first and foremost, from past fertility levels. The decline in natality during the Great Depression and World War II, from 1930 to 1945, is reflected in the relatively small number of people who in 1990 were 45 to 64 years old (table 3.3). Thereafter came the large cohorts of the baby boom, which in the United States extended from 1946 to 1964; this generation is now aged 30–44 and constitutes the largest cohort, slightly more than one-quarter of the total American Jewish population. Beginning in the 1960s, Jewish fertility declined significantly, a drop that was exacerbated by increasing losses of newborns as a result of mixed marriages. The recent increase in the size of the youngest cohort

TABLE 3.3
Medium Projection of U.S. Jewish Population, by Age, 1990–2020 (in Absolute Numbers and Percentages)

| | | Internal Factors | | | All Factors | | |
|---|---|---|---|---|---|---|---|
| *Age* | *1990* | *2000* | *2010* | *2020* | *2000* | *2010* | *2020* |
| *Absolute Number* | | | | | | | |
| Total | 5,515 | 5,438 | 5,286 | 5,173 | 5,702 | 5,675 | 5,648 |
| 0–14 | 1,048 | 915 | 676 | 686 | 970 | 759 | 780 |
| 15–29 | 1,036 | 908 | 1,045 | 726 | 966 | 1,126 | 827 |
| 30–44 | 1,413 | 1,211 | 863 | 1,033 | 1,273 | 955 | 1,144 |
| 45–64 | 1,072 | 1,493 | 1,762 | 1,410 | 1,545 | 1,840 | 1,517 |
| 65+ | 946 | 911 | 940 | 1,318 | 48 | 995 | 1,380 |
| Median Age | 37.3 | 41.5 | 45.7 | 47.4 | 41.2 | 45.0 | 46.3 |
| *Percentage* | | | | | | | |
| Total | 100.0 | 100.0 | 100.0 | 100.0 | 100.0 | 100.0 | 100.0 |
| 0–14 | 19.0 | 16.8 | 12.8 | 13.3 | 17.0 | 13.5 | 13.8 |
| 15–29 | 18.8 | 16.7 | 19.8 | 14.0 | 16.9 | 19.8 | 14.6 |
| 30–44 | 25.6 | 22.3 | 16.3 | 20.0 | 22.3 | 16.8 | 20.3 |
| 45–64 | 19.4 | 27.5 | 33.3 | 27.2 | 27.2 | 32.4 | 26.9 |
| 65+ | 17.2 | 16.7 | 17.8 | 25.5 | 16.6 | 17.5 | 24.4 |

(aged 0–14) is attributed to an echo effect of the baby boom, that is, to the arrival since the mid-1970s of large numbers of people into the most procreative ages.

The current age composition of U.S. Jewry is also affected by the large numbers of Jews who arrived in the United States during the mass immigration at the turn of the century. These Jews are concentrated in the oldest cohort, 65 years and over, and make up 17.2 percent of the total Jewish population. In 1990 the median age of American Jews was 37.3. This is approximately four years older than the median of 33.5 years in 1970, demonstrating a significant trend toward an aging population. These developments in age composition parallel similar ones among the general white population of the United States; yet at least as far back as the late 1950s, Jews have been consistently older than the average for the white population.[24]

## *The Continuation of Aging*

If only internal factors are taken into account, by the year 2000 the number of elderly Jews will have declined slightly because the weak cohorts born since 1930, which occupied the late-middle-age range in 1990, will be penetrating the old-age range, and this trend will continue into the first decade of the twenty-first century. Nevertheless, low levels of fertility and the progressing of the baby boomers into a later stage on the age ladder are anticipated to increase the median age of American Jews to 41.5 years in 2000 and 45.7 in 2010 (table 3.3).

The aging process will peak at the end of the projection period, when a substantial proportion of the baby boomers will constitute the oldest age cohort. The second echo effect of the baby boom, when the grandchildren of the original boomers reach the reproductive ages (beginning in 2010), will be much smaller than the first one; it is likely that they will fail to bring about a rise in the number of Jewish children and may only delay the trend of further decline. By the year 2020 the late-middle-age cohort (45–64 years old) and the elderly (65+) will each constitute approximately one-quarter of the entire American Jewish population, while the proportion of the two youngest cohorts (aged 0–14 and 15–29) are expected to approximate 13 percent and 14 percent, respectively. This anticipated age distribution will result in a median age of 47.4 years. The combined effect of low levels of fertility and declining mortality will inevitably produce an abnormal population pyramid with a narrow base and a relatively broad top.

The age profiles of Jewish immigrants to the United States differ according to their country of origin. The ex-Soviet migrants are an older population, whereas many of the Israeli immigrants are concentrated in the 20–35-year age brackets; the rest of the new arrivals are assumed to have an age composition that falls somewhere in between. The net gain of U.S. Jewry from international migration will increase the number of Jews in each age cohort but have only a minor effect on their overall age distribution and on their median age.

From the point of view of communal services, the most critical groups are children of school age and the elderly population. The data on children in table 3.4 are broken down into age groups that correspond, respectively, to preschool (including kindergarten), elementary school, junior high school, and senior high school. The different sizes of the various cohorts in 1990 once again show the effect of the past fluctuations in Jewish fertility behavior. Children aged 3–5 and 6–11 correspond to the birth cohort of 1979–87, when a substantial number of the baby boomers reached their most reproductive period. This is anticipated to increase the size of the cohorts of children aged 12 years and above at the turn of the century and to ensure an overall stability in the number of Jewish children at slightly less than 1 million. However, the transitory nature of this phenomenon is obvious: by 2010 the ages 20–44 will be occupied by weak cohorts, born since the mid-1960s, and the number of children is expected to decline markedly by more than quarter of a million from the starting point of our projection. The relatively large number of children among the new immigrants as well as their offspring who are expected to be born in America, will not change this trend but only slow it somewhat.

In the next twenty years, the number of Jews aged 65 and over will remain fairly stable at a level of slightly less than 950,000 (table 3.4). Between 2010 and 2020

TABLE 3.4
Medium Projection of Jewish School-age Children and of the Aged Population, 1990–2020 (in Thousands)

| | *Internal Factors* | | | |
|---|---|---|---|---|
| *Age* | *1990* | *2000* | *2110* | *2020* |
| Total 3–17 | 966 | 998 | 691 | 682 |
| 3–5 | 247 | 132 | 129 | 141 |
| 6–11 | 408 | 383 | 264 | 280 |
| 12–14 | 156 | 250 | 145 | 132 |
| 15–17 | 155 | 233 | 153 | 129 |
| Total 65+ | 946 | 911 | 940 | 1,318 |
| 75+ | 415 | 477 | 444 | 504 |
| *Change from 1990* | | | | |
| Total 3–17 | — | +32 | −275 | −284 |
| Total 65+ | — | −35 | −6 | +372 |
| Total 75+ | — | +62 | +29 | +89 |

many of the Jews who were born during the baby boom will enter the elderly cohort and are expected to bring about a sharp increase in the number of those who are 65 and older to about 1.32 million by the end of the projection period, slightly more if immigrants are included. More important perhaps is the future number of persons aged 75 and over, as they will constitute the segment most likely to need the health and social services offered by the organized Jewish community. Furthermore, given the extraordinarily high rates of geographic mobility among American Jews, the need for assistance on the part of these people might exceed what is anticipated, because many of them will be left with no close relatives nearby. In 1990 the number of Jews aged 75 and over was estimated at 415,000; although not linearly, this number will increase to approximately half a million by the year 2020, or to 534,000 if migration develops according to the projection assumptions.

## Comparative Perspectives

### *Jews among All Americans*

Shortly after the termination of the mass migration from Eastern Europe, American Jews constituted 4 percent of all whites in the United States (or 3.6 percent of the total population). The relative share remained fairly stable in the next decade, after which it began declining gradually to 3.7 percent in 1950, 3.1 percent

TABLE 3.5
Percentage of Jews among All Americans, 1930–2020

| | *Estimates*[a] | | | | *Medium Projection* | |
|---|---|---|---|---|---|---|
| | *1927* | *1950* | *1970* | *1990* | *2000* | *2010* |
| Jews among total population | 3.6 | 3.3 | 2.7 | 2.2 | 2.1 | 1.9 |
| Jews among total whites | 4.0 | 3.7 | 3.1 | 2.8 | 2.5 | 2.4 |

a. For calculation of these figures, the number of U.S. Jews for 1927 and 1950 were taken from the American Jewish Year Book, and for 1970 and 1990 from the NJPS of the same years. Data for the total American population derive from census publications of the U.S. Bureau of the Census.

in 1970, and to 2.8 percent in 1990 (table 3.5). For most of these years the absolute number of Jews increased, but it was at a much slower pace than that of the non-Jewish American population.

It is this trend that is expected to continue in the next three decades. Results of the medium projection for all whites in the United States are available from the Bureau of the Census, which generally assumes the continuation of current fertility and migration levels and an increase in life expectancy. The data suggest an overall increase of 22 percent in the number of white Americans between 1990 and 2020 (6 and 8 percent each decade).[25] This is a far higher level than that of the Jews when all demographic factors are considered. Hence, by the year 2020 the percentage of Jews will decline to 2.2 percent of all whites. It should be emphasized that these differences in the respective demographic evolution of the two populations are explained by the much greater aging of the Jews, their lower levels of fertility, and the assimilatory losses that have no parallel in the general population. On the other hand, the positive external migration balance, when translated to annual rates per 1,000 of population, was higher for the Jews.[26]

### *A Worldwide Jewish Perspective*

In table 3.6 we evaluate the demographic future of U.S. Jews compared with the Jewries of the Diaspora, Israel, and the world as a whole (according to a medium version that generally assumes the continuation of recent levels of the demographic factors).[27] Because of a younger age composition, U.S. Jews are expected to experience a more moderated change than the rest of Diaspora Jewry: based on internal dynamics, by the year 2020 they will decline to 94 percent of their size at the starting point of the projection, while the rest of the Diaspora will decline by nearly one quarter. This differential becomes more salient if migration is introduced into the projection equation because the aggregate geographic unit of the rest of the Diaspora will lose large numbers both to the United States and to Israel.

In 1990, American Jews constituted 43 percent of world Jewry, making them the world's largest Jewish community. By the year 2020 this proportion will decline

TABLE 3.6
Medium Projection of Jews in the U.S., the Diaspora, and the World, 1990–2020 (Percentage)

| | *Index Number 2020*[a] | | *Internal Factors* | | | |
|---|---|---|---|---|---|---|
| | *Internal Factors* | *All Factors* | *1990* | *2000* | *2010* | *2020* |
| World | 106 | 107 | 100 | 100 | 100 | 100 |
| Diaspora | 87 | 77 | 69 | 64 | 61 | 57 |
| U.S. | 94 | 102 | 43 | 42 | 40 | 38 |
| Other countries | 76 | 35 | 26 | 22 | 21 | 19 |
| Israel | 148 | 173 | 31 | 36 | 39 | 43 |
| U.S. and Israel | 116 | 132 | 74 | 78 | 79 | 81 |

a. 1990 = 100.

to between 38 and 41 percent, depending on migration. At the same time, Israel's relative share will increase, and around 2010 the numbers of Israeli and American Jews are anticipated to converge. This process of increase in the proportion of Israeli Jews and the decline in the proportion of U.S. Jewry will turn Israel into the largest Jewish community, and at a later stage, given continual large waves of migration, will allow it to constitute the absolute majority of world Jewry. The paramount factors responsible for the rapid growth in the Israeli Jewish population are the high levels of fertility and the absence of net assimilatory losses; the positive migration balance is only secondary.[28]

From the viewpoint of the geographic distribution of the world Jewish population, the combined effect of the differences in age composition of the base populations and the size of the demographic factors emphasize the Jewish spatial configuration of two centers of gravity: the United States and Israel. The joint share of these two communities is expected to increase from slightly less than three-quarters in 1990 to 81 percent in 2020 with no migration or to 91 percent if we assume migration. The latter percentage is largely based on a drastic diminution in the size of the ex-Soviet Jewish community due to outmigration. The fact that, at the time of this writing, more than half of Soviet Jews have already emigrated to other countries, mostly to Israel and the United States, strengthens our bipolar scenario.

## Summary and Conclusions

The future demographic dynamic of American Jews, like that of any other population, depends on the interplay between its structural profile in terms of the distribution by age and sex and the anticipated course of the events responsible for quantitative change. In 1990, the starting date of our projection, many of the Jews born during the baby boom were in their thirties and forties; despite low fertility (below the replacement level and further reduced by a loss of children through interfaith marriages), the fact that they occupied the most reproductive ages is likely to assure large cohorts of children for the next several years. A longer life span will somewhat moderate the diminution of the size of U.S. Jewry.

The evolution of the American Jewish population is also affected by the external factors of world Jewry. As a response to general political, social, or economic alterations in the host societies, the global Jewish international migration system has recently been very active, with the United States being one of the preferable countries of destination. This is expected to remain the case in the foreseeable future though at a somewhat lower pace. The overall estimate of excess of immigrants over emigrants for the next three decades is likely to compensate for the negative internal evolution and perhaps even bring about a slight increase relative to 1990 NJPS figures. Nevertheless, from a worldwide Jewish perspective, the number of Jews would be larger should American Jewry be able to guarantee its own demographic continuity.

What is expected to undergo a significant change is the age composition of American Jews. While our base population revealed a similarity in size of the two extreme cohorts on the age spectrum, different trends among them will presumably result in an elderly population of almost twice as large as the youngest cohort. The establishment of institutions and the planning of communal services are long-range processes that cannot always be adapted to temporary swings in number of potential constituencies. But the findings that emerge from this study suggest a clear structural change, which, in turn, should challenge the organized Jewish community to search for additional financial resources or, alternatively, to face painful choices in allocating money between educational program needs and health and social services. On a different level, the number of young adults is projected to decline, and this segment of the Jewish population is the major reservoir from which communal and organizational leadership can be drawn.

The analysis presented in this chapter focused on the national American Jewish scene. The results are an average of many communities of different size, age composition, religious identification, and other characteristics that determine demographic behavior. The demographic profile of individual communities will most likely be affected by residential mobility, be it intercity, interstate, or interregional move. It is apparent that internal migration is today "the major dynamic responsible for the growth or decline of many local Jewish communities and for the changing distribution of the Jewish population among regions of the country and among metropolitan areas."[29] Migration is associated with certain stages in the life cycle—going away to college, entering the job market, getting married, retirement; therefore, it is selective in age: disproportional numbers of young adults and to a lesser extent elderly people. Likewise, large metropolitan areas with dense Jewish populations are preferable to small and isolated towns as destinations for new arrivals from abroad. Services at the local level will further benefit from identifying the future trends of their specific communities; the imbalance between future needs and resources (including currently available fixed investments) may turn out to be even greater at the local community level than is apparent from watching the expected trends at the national level.

This projection is one of many alternative directions in which the American Jewish population can develop. We attach reserved caution to our results. American Jews are affected, first and foremost, by trends on the macro-level of the general social and political system and only in the second place as individuals who are sensitive to the Jewish communal subsystem. Jews today are successfully integrated into the societal American mainstream; they are concentrated in the upper strata of the social and economic ladder and hence are exposed to many social and normative changes. Judging by past experiences, they might react to them quickly and through large-scale and quite synchronic changes. Not less fluid and volatile is the world system under the impact of globalization processes that can alternately prompt or weaken the levels of Jewish international migration. Within these obvious constraints, we believe that a demographic projection of modest assumptions, which uses scientific tools, is a necessary quantitative framework for any serious attempt to evaluate current social and demographic changes among American Jewry and to assess their implications for the future.

## Notes

Materials presented in this chapter are part of an ongoing research at the Division of Jewish Demography and Statistics, the Avraham Harman Institute of Contemporary Jewry, The Hebrew University of Jerusalem. The project of new population projections for each of the major Jewish communities worldwide was initiated by the late Professor Uziel O. Schmelz, who actively participated in establishing the project's conceptual and technical framework. The project is currently supported by the Israel Humanitarian Fund. We gratefully acknowledge the encouragement of Marvin Sirota and Stanley J. Abrams. Thanks are due to the North American Jewish Data Bank in New York for providing the original database of the 1990 National Jewish Population Survey directed by Barry A. Kosmin and Sidney Goldstein. Judith Even helped in editing the text.

1. B. A. Kosmin, S. Goldstein, J. Waksberg, N. Lerer, A. Keysar, and J. Scheckner, *Highlights of the CJF 1990 National Jewish Population Survey* (New York: Council of Jewish Federations, 1991).
2. U. O. Schmelz, and S. DellaPergola, "World Jewish Population, 1989," in *American Jewish Year Book 1991* (Philadelphia: The Jewish Publication Society of America, 1991) p. 443.
3. Kosmin et al., *Highlights*, p. 39.
4. B. A. Kosmin, and J. Scheckner, "Jewish Population in the United States, 1990," in *American Jewish Year Book 1991*. (Philadelphia: The Jewish Publication Society of America, 1991), p. 204.
5. Schmelz and DellaPergola, "World Jewish Population, 1989," p. 454.
6. U. O. Schmelz, and S. DellaPergola, "The Demographic Consequences of U.S. Jewish Population Trends," in *American Jewish Year Book 1983*, (Philadelphia: The Jewish Publication Society of America, 1983), pp. 176–80.

7. E. Bergman, "The American Jewish Population Erosion," *Midstream* 23, no. 8 (1977), pp. 9–10.
8. S. S. Lieberman, and M. Weinfeld "Demographic Trends and Jewish Survival," *Midstream* 24, no. 9 (1977), p. 11.
9. S. Goldstein, "Profile of American Jewry: Insights from the 1990 National Jewish Population Survey," in *American Jewish Year Book 1992* (Philadelphia: The Jewish Publication Society of America, 1992), p. 124.
10. S. Goldstein, "The Demographics of American Jewry," in S. DellaPergola, and L. Cohen, eds.,*World Jewish Population: Trends and Policies*, Jewish Population Studies No. 23 (Jerusalem: Institute of Contemporary Jewry, The Hebrew University of Jerusalem, 1992), p. 61.
11. It should be emphasized already at this stage that a scientific demographic projection is not a prophecy. Rather, it is a computation of changes that are expected to occur in a population if it develops according to certain assumptions made in regard to the magnitude of the demographic factors. The projection presented here uses what we view today as "realistic" assumptions; they coincide with recent internal trends among American Jews as well as with external processes among world Jewry. Nevertheless, political, social, economic, or other processes in the global system are fluid and may suddenly change population behaviors in different parts of the world including that of Jews. This is especially true because our projection covers a relatively long span of thirty years into the future; the results are likely to be "reasonable for a few years ahead but then become progressively worse—margin of error increases." (C. Newell, *Methods and Models in Demography* [London: Belhaven Press, 1988], p. 181). We do believe, however, that the certitude of some trends and conclusions emerging from this study outweighs the uncertainty.

    We project the American Jewish population by using the demographic cohort-component method. The projection starts with the age-sex distribution of U.S. Jews by five-year age groups (base population) according to data from the 1990 NJPS. The assumptions regarding the course of the components of change—fertility, mortality, and migration—are then applied to the base population. In a case of a minority group, such as American Jews, an additional factor comes to play a role in determining population size, namely, the quantitative consequences of intermarriage. The 1990 NJPS found roughly equal numbers of people not born Jewish who had converted to Judaism and people who were born or raised Jewish but were currently following another religion; most of these accessions to and secessions from Judaism are likely to be by-products of interreligious marriage. Intermarriage also has a long-term effect on the number of newborns who are identified or raised Jewish. The gain or loss arising from the religious identification of children of intermarriage is introduced into the projection equation here via the component of fertility.

    While in practice the procedure of a population projection may become quite complex, the basic idea is simple and can be illustrated as follows:

| Population in $t+1$ | = | Population in $t$ | + | Natural increase (births – deaths) | + | Identificational change (accessions – secessions) | + | Net migration (immigration – emigration) |
|---|---|---|---|---|---|---|---|---|

In the context of our projection, the Jewish population at a time, $t+1$ is the Jewish population at an earlier point of time t, plus the numbers of Jewish newborns between $t$ and $t+1$ less the number of Jewish deaths, plus the number of accessions to Judaism less the number of secessions from Judaism, plus the number of Jewish immigrants to the United States less the number of Jewish emigrants from the country. While the duration of the projection is thirty years, the software package that was used here provides the results of the projection in five-year intervals (*PEOPLE: A User Friendly Package for Making National and Sub-National Population Projections* Versions 2.0, 1990).

We begin with the first part of the equation, which considers only internal evolution as determined by fertility, mortality, and assimilation. This will provide insights into the ability of the American Jewish community to ensure its own demographic continuity. External factors are then added, showing the effect of net international migration with other Diaspora communities and with Israel.

12. S. DellaPergola, "Patterns of American Jewish Fertility," *Demography* 17, no. 3 (1980), p. 263.
13. Golden, "Profile of American Jewry," p. 169.
14. Ibid.
15. Kosmin et al., *Highlights*, p. 16.
16. Goldstein, "Profile of American Jewry," p. 126.
17. S. Goldstein, "Changes in Jewish Mortality and Survival, 1963–1987," *Social Biology*, 43 no. 1–2 (1996), pp. 72–97.
18. HIAS, *Statistical Reports* (New York: The Hebrew Immigrant Aid Society (annual publications).
19. DellaPergola, S. "The Global Context of Migration to Israel," in: E. Leshem, and J. Shuval, eds., *Studies in Israel Society*, vol. 8 (New Brunswick, N.J.: Transaction, (forthcoming).
20. Y. Cohen and Y. Haberfeld, "The Number of Israeli Immigrants in the United States in 1990," *Demography* 34 (2) (1997), pp. 206–7.
21. Israel Central Bureau of Statistics, *Immigration to Israel* (Jerusalem, annual publications).
22. A. Dashefsky and B. Lazerwitz, "The Role of Religious Identification in North American Migration to Israel," *Journal for the Scientific Study of Religion* 22 (3), p. 265; Israel Central Bureau of Statistics, *Monthly Bulletin of Statistics*, Supplement D, January 1986, as cited in C. I. Waxman, *American Aliya: Portrait of an Innovative Migration Movement*. (Detroit: Wayne State University Press, 1989), p. 231.
23. If the U.S. government reduces significantly or abolishes, the quota for Eastern European refugees, a lower amount of immigration from the former Soviet Union would produce a result intermediate between this scenario and the one that considers only internal factors.
24. S. Goldstein, "Jews in the United States: Perspective from Demography," *American Jewish Year Book, 1981* (Philadelphia: The Jewish Publication Society of America, 1981) p. 44; Goldstein, "Profile of American Jewry," p. 105.
25. U.S. Bureau of the Census, *Population Projections of the United States by Age, Sex, Race and Hispanic Origin: 1993-2050*, Current Population Reports, Series P-25, no. 1104, 1993.

26. The older Jewish population is reflected in their median age as well as in the smaller proportion of children and higher proportion of elderly relative to the age profile of whites. As far as fertlity is concerned, the Bureau of the Census assumed a TFR of 2.1 for the middle series projection (holding constant age-specific fertility rates at the 1990 level). The average annual rates of migration per 1,000 population are as follows: 1990–95, 6.3 for Jews and 2.2 for total whites; 1995–2000, 3.2 versus 2.2; 2000–2005, 2.9 versus 2.1; 2005–10, 1.5 versus 2.0; 2010–15, 1.5 versus 2.0; and for 2015–20, 1.5 versus 1.9. This results in an overall difference for the entire projection period of 2.8 versus 2.1, respectively (for total whites); adapted from *Population Projections of the United States by Age, Sex, Race and Hispanic Origin: 1993–2050*).
27. S. DellaPergola, "The Jewish People towards the Year 2020: Sociodemographic Scenarios," in E. Gonen, and S. Fogel, eds., *A Blueprint for Israel in the 2000s* (Report No. 21). Haifa: The Technion: Israel Institute of Technology, April 1996, pp. 186–99 (in Hebrew).
28. DellaPergola, "The Jewish People towards the Year 2020, p. 192.
29. Goldstein, "Profile of American Jews," p. 95.

4

Sylvia Barack Fishman

# The Changing American Jewish Family Faces the 1990s[1]

Traditionally, the Jewish emphasis on marriage begins at birth. The male child, as he is ritually circumcised, and the female child, as she is named in the synagogue, each receives a blessing that they mature into marriage and good deeds and (for boys) the study of Torah. That blessing is repeated at each official milestone in the child's life, for Judaism views marriage not as a necessary compromise to human frailities but as the most productive state for adult human beings.

Informally as well, Jewish culture has reflected an emphasis on marriage which suffuses language, attitudes and behavior. Common Yiddish phrases expressed that preoccupation: If a five-year-old boy's ears protruded, his mother shrugged and remarked that "his bride will find him beautiful." If a twelve-year-old girl wore a mismatched skirt and blouse, a grandmother advised her to wear more appropriate clothing, for she was "almost a bridal girl." If a fifteen-year-old found unsavory friends, parents warned that she would "ruin her own marriage match."

Partially as a result of this overwhelming cultural bias, Jewish populations in the United States have, until very recently, achieved almost universal marriage—over 95 percent—by the time they were well into their reproductive years. Analyses based on the 1970 National Jewish Population Study (NJPS),[2] for example, show that, in 1970, 95 percent of American Jewish females were married by age 34, and 96 percent of American Jewish males achieved the same status by age 39. Although Jews married one to three years later, on average, than other whites in the United States, more of them ended up married.[3] Similarly, while American Jews have long had smaller families than other ethnic groups, until very recently children were cherished and deliberate childlessness was almost unheard of.

During the past two and one-half decades, however, the social climates of the United States has undergone dramatic changes, including a lively and much publicized "singles culture," later marriages, smaller families, increasing divorce rates, high geographical mobility, and chronological segmentation of populations. The behavior of the Jewish population has epitomized many of these changes.

For example, while four-fifths of Jewish households in 1970 consisted of married couples, most of whom had or intended to have at least two children, in 1990 fewer than two-thirds of Jewish households consisted of married couples, and very small families (one or no children) have become more commonplace, especially among those with high educational and professional status. The "singles" state, rather than being regarded as a mere prelude to marriage, has been adopted by some as an alternative lifestyle. Increases in divorce are seen, to lesser and greater extents, throughout Jewish-American society. In addition to later marriage, later family formation, and increased divorce, longer life spans among the elderly have meant that increasing numbers of Jewish "families" are composed of childless couples and unmarried individuals. For Jews, as for all Americans, the family has become increasingly unconventional.

Data from the 1990 National Jewish Population Study provide today's social scientists with information about Jews in the United States from coast to coast. These national data enable us, for the first time in twenty years, to engage in a systematic analysis of the status of contemporary Jewish households. When these national data are used in combination with studies conducted by almost two dozen individual Jewish communities, they reveal a picture both of sweeping national change and individual geographic variations (see table 4.1).

Table 4.1 shows the marital status of the Jewish population in the United States in 1990 and compares it with marital status of Jews in 21 cities in the 1980s, with marital status of Jews nationwide in 1970, and with U.S. census data on all Americans in 1970 and 1989. As table 4.1 illustrates, in terms of marital status the contemporary American Jewish community resembles the non-Jewish community far more than it resembles the American Jewish community of 1970. About two-thirds of today's Jews, like two-thirds of today's non-Jews, are married, compared to nearly four-fifths of Jews in 1970. As the 1990s began, fewer than two-thirds of Americans, both Jews and non-Jews, were married. More than one-fifth of Jews and non-Jews alike had never been married. Seven percent of Jews and 8 percent of all Americans were widowed, and 8 percent of both groups were currently divorced. When the national data are compared with the city studies, the populations of Jewish singles in six cities exceed the national average; the singles populations of another four cities equal or are within four percentage points of the national average. Only in cities which have large numbers of elderly Jews do the percentage of singles begin to approach the low of 6 percent singles found in the 1970 NJPS. In addition, the percentages of divorced or separated Jews are higher in a dozen cities than the 5 percent divorced Jews found in the 1970 study. Among all Americans in 1989 those who were divorced were 8 percent; Jewish divorced individuals exceeded that figure in five communities.

For American Jews, as for other Americans today, there is no one model of "the family." Jewish families reflect, in somewhat less extreme profile, an America in

TABLE 4.1
Marital Status of American Jewish Men and Women (Jewish Community Studies, 1970 and 1990 National Jewish Population Surveys, and White Americans, 1970 and 1989 Census Studies)

| *Location* | *Year Study Completed* | *Married* | *Single* | *Widowed* | *Divorced* |
|---|---|---|---|---|---|
| Atlantic City | 1985 | 67 | 13 | 13 | 6 |
| Boston | 1985 | 61 | 29 | 4 | 5 |
| Baltimore | 1985 | 68 | 19 | 9 | 5 |
| Chicago | 1982 | 65 | 23 | 6 | 6 |
| Cleveland | 1981 | 69 | 11 | 13 | 8 |
| Denver | 1981 | 64 | 23 | 4 | 9 |
| Kansas City | 1985 | 70 | 17 | 7 | 5 |
| Los Angeles | 1979 | 57 | 17 | 12 | 14 |
| Miami | 1982 | 61 | 7 | 23 | 8 |
| Milwaukee | 1983 | 67 | 14 | 9 | 10 |
| Minneapolis | 1981 | 66 | 22 | 7 | 5 |
| Nashville | 1982 | 70 | 17 | 8 | 5 |
| New York | 1981 | 65 | 15 | 11 | 9 |
| Phoenix | 1983 | 63 | 18 | 9 | 10 |
| Richmond | 1983 | 67 | 14 | 12 | 7 |
| Rochester | 1987 | 68 | 23 | 6 | 3 |
| St. Louis | 1982 | 68 | 9 | 17 | 6 |
| St. Paul | 1981 | 66 | 20 | 11 | 3 |
| San Francisco | 1988 | 69 | 19 | 4 | 7 |
| Washington, D.C. | 1983 | 61 | 27 | 4 | 7 |
| Worcester | 1987 | 69 | 14 | —18— | |
| NPS | 1990 | 64 | 21 | 7 | 8 |
| US Census | 1989 | 64 | 21 | 8 | 8 |
| NJPS | 1970 | 78 | 6 | 10 | 5 |
| US Census | 1970 | 73 | 16 | 9 | 3 |

which less than 15 percent of households conform to the model of father, mother-at-home, and children living together.[4] Jewish households in the United States include persons who have never married; the traditional, two-parent family with clearly differentiated masculine and feminine roles; the ultra-Orthodox two-parent family with many children; the dual-career two-parent family; divorced households without children; divorced and "blended" families; single-parent families; and elderly couples of widowed elder "singles."

## The Singles in Contemporary Jewish Communities

During the 1970s the singles state, for the first time in Jewish history, became an extended period in the adult life cycle rather than a short way station between childhood and adulthood. In every community a growing number of Jewish households could be designated as "single," a statistical category including several groups: young, middle-aged, and older people who have never married; young, middle-aged, and older divorcees; widows and widowers.

### *Never Married*

The recent trend toward postponement of marriage is nowhere more striking than in the advancing ages at which "universal marriage"[5] has occurred among Jews during the past fifteen years. In 1970 more than 95 percent of American Jewish women were married before age 34 and over 96 percent of American Jewish men before age 39. In the 1980s, however, universal marriage was achieved ten to fifteen years later, depending on location (see table 4.2).

Table 4.2 illustrates postponed marriage among Jews and non-Jews at the beginning of the 1990s. In the 1950s, three-quarters of American Jewish women were married by the time they reached age 25. Today, only 12 percent of Jewish women marry before age 25. In 1990, among American Jewish women ages 25 to 34, 30 percent had never been married, 62 percent were married, and 7 percent were divorced. Among those ages 35 to 44—once the most married of Jewish populations!—11 percent had never married, 74 percent were married, and 14 percent were divorced. For Jewish men, ages for first marriage are even later than they are for Jewish women, with 17 percent never married in the age 35 to 44 group.

Many unmarried Jews have gravitated toward cities reputed to offer a sophisticated and vibrant singles culture, such as Los Angeles, Denver, New York, and Washington, D.C. They appear to be primarily attracted by educational or job opportunities and by the presence of large numbers of singles, for few have families in the area. Friends often fill many family-like functions for singles, but the absence of actual family may be a factor in the length of time that passes before they marry.

TABLE 4.2
Marital Status of 1990 National Jewish Population Survey Respondents (Percentages Born or Raised Jewish by Age and Gender)[a]

| | *18–24* | | *25–34* | | *35–44* | | *45–54* | | *55–64* | | *65+* | |
|---|---|---|---|---|---|---|---|---|---|---|---|---|
| | *F* | *M* | *F* | *M* | *F* | *M* | *F* | *M* | *F* | *M* | *F* | *M* |
| Married | 12 | 2 | 62 | 46 | 74 | 73 | 75 | 77 | 77 | 87 | 57 | 82 |
| Never married | 88 | 96 | 30 | 50 | 11 | 17 | 7 | 9 | 2 | 6 | 2 | 3 |
| Divorced/separated | 1 | 1 | 7 | 3 | 14 | 10 | 14 | 11 | 14 | 6 | 4 | 3 |
| Widowed | — | — | 1 | — | 1 | 1 | 4 | 3 | 8 | 1 | 38 | 12 |

*1989 U.S. Census All Americans*[b]

| | *20–24* | | *25–29* | | *30–34* | | *35–39* | | *40–44* | | *45–54* | | *55–64* | |
|---|---|---|---|---|---|---|---|---|---|---|---|---|---|---|
| | *F* | *M* | *F* | *M* | *F* | *M* | *F* | *M* | *F* | *M* | *F* | *M* | *F* | *M* |
| Married | 35 | 21 | 29 | 49 | 72 | 66 | 76 | 74 | 75 | 80 | 75 | 81 | 68 | 83 |
| Never married | 63 | 77 | 62 | 46 | 17 | 26 | 10 | 15 | 6 | 8 | 5 | 7 | 4 | 6 |
| Divorced | 3 | 1 | 8 | 5 | 11 | 8 | 13 | 11 | 16 | 12 | 14 | 11 | 18 | 8 |
| Widowed | — | — | — | — | 1 | — | 1 | — | 3 | 1 | 6 | 1 | 9 | 3 |

*Sources:*

a. Sylvia Barack Fishman, *A Breath of Life: Feminism in the American Jewish Community* (New York: Free Press, 1993); 1990 NJPS data.

b. 1989 U.S. Census, U.S. Bureau of the Census, *Current Population Reports*, series P-20, No. 445.

Los Angeles had the smallest percentage of ever-married Jews in the 18–39 age category of any American city; more than one-third of Los Angeles Jewish respondents under 39 years old had never married, according to a 1980 study of households or "family types."[6] Similarly, Denver had a large number of young people: 43 percent of Denver's Jews are between the ages of 18 and 34, compared to 29 percent in this age group in Los Angeles. Just over half of Denver's Jews are married by age 29, and just under three-quarters of them by age 34. Universal marriage is not achieved until age 44.[7] The geographical mobility of the Jewish population, many of whom have moved to Denver recently, may delay readiness for commitment and the establishment of homes.

Washington, D.C., which has attracted numerous young professionals since the days of the New Deal, continues to host a large percentage (27 percent of the entire community) of Jewish singles, many of whom are attracted by and work in government-related positions. As Elazar notes, "given the revolving-door nature of federal employment, Washington is not a city that encourages people to sink roots. The effects are felt in the Jewish community, which is perhaps the most socially fragmented community in the United States, surpassing even Los Angeles and Miami, other contenders for the title."[8] The effects of this rootlessness and fragmentation are clearly seen in the city's ever-married figures. Less than 60 percent of Washington's Jews have ever been married by age 34; 92 percent have been married by age 44; and universal marriage is achieved by age 55, with 98 percent of Washington's Jews married.[9]

Manhattan, "the home of the never-marrieds," has the second-largest number of Jewish households in the New York area, following Brooklyn. In Manhattan in 1981, one-third of the population had never been married, 15 percent were divorced or separated, and 11 percent were widowed.[10]

While the figures are more dramatic in such cities, the Jewish singles phenomenon is also clearly visible in more family-oriented, "middle American" communities. A study of Milwaukee, Wisconsin, for example, showed that less than a third of all Jewish respondents were married by age 29 (30); 87 percent were ever-married by age 39; and not until the 40–49 age group did universal marriage occur, with 95 percent ever-married.[11]

For more than a decade, the singles culture was celebrated by the media as an exhilarating, vital way of life. Like others in their socioeconomic class, Jewish men born in the late 1940s and 1950s seemed uninterested in early commitments; when they did marry, they usually chose younger women, rather than choosing from the large number of unmarried women in their own age cohort. In addition, many more Jewish men than women intermarried, leaving a sizable proportion of Jewish women unmarried.[12]

A growing emphasis on feminist aspiration and achievement also contributed to later marriage and childbearing. The names of Jewish women were prominent among the roster of militant feminists, who exhorted women not to be lured into the twin slaveries of marriage and motherhood. Rather than viewing job skills as useful for earning money in cases of necessity, women began to see themselves acquiring professional education and careers in much the same way as men. Jewish women, who had always comparatively high educational levels and had married later than the general population, excelled in this new atmosphere of opening opportunities and often postponed marriage and family.[13]

By the 1980s, however, large numbers of unmarried Jews were openly searching for ways to combine the pleasures of achievement with the more traditional and companionable joys of family life and community participation. Singles and community leaders alike said that new methods had to be devised so that single Jews could meet each other and become involved in the Jewish community. Jewish dating services, both commercial and not-for-profit, have proliferated in major metropolitan areas. Some modern versions of the traditional *shadchan* utilize "computer matching" of eligible men and women. Some rely exclusively on the skills of human interviewers to combine like prospects for introductions, and some combine both methods.[14]

Homosexual households are newly visible in the Jewish community. Gay and lesbian congregations exist in Baltimore, Cambridge, Cleveland, Dallas, Miami,

Minneapolis, Montreal, Philadelphia, New York, San Francisco, Seattle, Washington, D.C., and elsewhere in North America.[15] In addition, most major college campuses have Jewish gay and lesbian societies.

Precise figures on the proportion of homosexuals in the Jewish community—as in the general American community—are difficult to obtain. Estimates as to the percentages of homosexuals in given communities have varied widely and are the subject of considerable disagreement. Recent estimates on the percentage of homosexuals are substantially lower than earlier estimates. No one knows exactly how many Jews now live as homosexual singles or in homosexual households, but there is no reason to assume that the percentage of homosexual Jews differs significantly from that in the general population. A proliferating number of books and articles on the subject of Jewish homosexuality indicates that the Jewish homosexual community includes many Jews who are extensively involved in Jewish life. Jewish homosexuals, whose group includes men and women, youths and senior citizens, whatever their other Jewish communal involvements, often establish alternative Jewish households, some of which include children.[16]

### *Divorced Jews*

Jews, like other Americans, experienced an increased divorce rate in the 1970s and 1980s. One may speculate that marriages broke up for traditional and not so traditional reasons. Men who were attracted to women outside the home may have been more willing to leave their families because of the putative attractiveness of freedom. Women who felt put upon by traditional roles may have been emboldened to leave them, both because they now had viable job skills and because the ideology of women's liberation encouraged independence rather than compromise.

Much in contemporary American culture contributes to the prevalence of divorce, not least the persistence of the youth culture and the pervasive pleasure principle in American society. One woman's husband left her "the year he turned 45 and the year his mother died." She says, "I guess his behavior is classic male mid-life crisis. But it's all so sordid!" A Jewish historian suggests that in "many instances, the divorce is a reassertion in middle age of youthful goals and dreams which have not been fulfilled in real life." Breaking the bonds of marriage is a last-ditch effort to "begin again," with presumably a more congenial and exciting partner, one more likely to gratify the fantasies still persisting from the past. In other cases, couples who married when they were young find that they have grown away from one another. One partner may have matured more than the other, developed new interests, or achieved a higher level of success. It cannot be denied that biological urges and socieconomic promptings such as these play a decisive role in the upsurge of middle-aged divorced in our times.[17]

Legal innovations such as no-fault divorce laws had the unpredictable consequence of making it easier for men to initiate divorce—often leaving the very women it aimed to defend in extremely difficult circumstances.[18] However, no-fault divorce laws have also often eased the way for women out of unhappy marriages. The net result of all this is increased rates of divorce.

Some contemporary divorces may be linked to the greater ambition of women today. Career goals may lead to stress with marriage and thus to divorce. About one-third of divorced Jewish women have master's degrees, compared to half as many married women with children at home. A surprisingly high proportion of divorced women in the general population have master's degrees. Women who obtained their master's degrees before marriage are not more likely than average to be divorced, whereas women who obtained their master's degrees after marriage are more likely to be divorced. Marriages which from their inception included a professional woman may be psychologically adjusted to weather the pressures of careers far better than those which began with more conventionally divided gender roles and later switched course.[19]

Both men and women today are often less committed to marriage as a permanent state and more interested in beginning a new life rather than making do with an imperfect situation. American societal norms, rather than supporting the couple who struggles to work out their differences and to grow together through episodes of conflict, often seem to support the individual in making a break with the past. Compromise is often presented by the media as antithetical to personal integrity and self-esteem. The idea that parents should make sacrifices in order to maintain the family unit is often seen as completely outmoded. Judith Wallerstein recalls Margaret Mead's troubled reflections on the rising rate of divorce: "There is no society in the world where people have stayed married without enormous community pressure to do so."[20]

And yet current studies demonstrate that the children of divorce often suffer more greatly from the breakup of the family than they did from the conflicts between their married parents. As Ari Goldman strongly asserts about his parents' divorce: "If they had tried, they could have learned to stop shouting and slamming doors. It might not have been easy for them—but it would have been easier than it was for me to learn how to live with divorce."[21]

Among other social movements, feminism has played its part in increased divorce. Given the economic skills to be self-supporting, women are far less likely to remain in an unhappy marriage simply to have a roof over their heads. In addition, some men, who expected a submissive wife, are outraged when their spouses grow into different roles. Moreover, feminist impatience with the compromises which most marriages require is also a factor in some breakups. Self-described Jewish Orthodox feminist and mother of five Blu Greenberg insists that "it goes without saying that feminism has had a powerful impact on the rising divorce rate in the Jewish community. As a young, divorced rabbi recently put it when asked why he divorced: 'My ex-wife got into this women's liberation thing, and I was too immature to know how to cope with it.' (He was being kind in not saying that his wife also did not know how to cope with it.) I am convinced that three-fourths of the marriages that succeed could have come apart at ten different points along the way," Greenberg adds, "and some three-fourths of the marriages that fail could have been put back together again at twenty points along the way. A great deal has to do with how one negotiates the inevitable impasses in an intimate relationship."[22]

The extent of Jewish divorce varies widely from community to community. In Los Angeles, for example, 9 percent of the Jewish population was currently divorced or separated in 1980, as opposed to 4 percent in 1968 and 2 percent in 1959. Thus, while substantially lower than the population as a whole, Jewish divorce rates in Los Angeles quadrupled in 21 years.[23]

Denver had a particularly high divorce rate: 68 percent of all Denver Jewish marriages in 1981 involved a second marriage for one partner; 14 percent were a second or third marriage for both partners; only 18 percent were a first marriage for both partners. One-fifth of Denver Jews between the ages of 40 and 49 were divorced.[24] This may be related to Denver's high rate of in-migration, for communities which attract large groups of immigrants also tend to have large percentages of divorced Jewish households: Los Angeles had 17 percent divorced/separated households in the 40–59 cohort;[25] Washington, D.C. had 12 percent in the 45–54 cohort;[26] Phoenix had 11 percent in the 40–49 cohort.[27]

Apparently, the newly divorced often find their singles state lonely rather than glamorous, for such high proportions of divorced Jewish men and women remarry that the true rate of divorce is effectively disguised in those studies which do not inquire about previous marriages. Several studies, however, have explored the relationship between divorce and remarriage. A 1982 St. Louis study, for example, reports that although less than 6 percent of the Jewish population is currently divorced or separated, an additional 12.5 percent of respondents and spouses were divorced and had remarried. The ever-divorced population of St. Louis would thus be 18.5 percent, a proportion far higher than it first appears.[28]

Table 4.3 presents the currently divorced, currently remarried, and ever-divorced rates in Denver, Miami, and Milwaukee by age cohorts. It illustrates the large number of divorces that are not apparent because of remarriage, especially among respondents in their 30s and 40s.

Those who emerge from marriage often join a singles culture very different from the one they had experienced before marriage. Lang describes women caught in a "cruel squeeze play": "Women's liberation offers vistas of growth, 'creative divorce,' and personal happiness, when the reality is often a long period of loss and mourning, and societal rejection of the middle-aged woman in favor of youth and good looks."[29] For men, too, the reality of divorce is often quite different from the fantasy of carefree bachelorhood. Men who joined a support group For Men Only at the Mid-Westchester Y.M.H.A. complained of loneliness, bitterness, and feeling of failure. They experienced difficulty in establishing new social networks.[30]

All denominations of Jewry have been influenced by the American propensity to divorce, but religious observance still has an inverse relationship to the number

TABLE 4.3
Currently Divorced/Remarried by Age Cohorts, Percent of Jewish Population in Denver, Miami, Milawaukee

| | Up to 29 | Up to 35 | Up to 39 | Up to 49 |
|---|---|---|---|---|
| *Denver* | | | | |
| Divorced[a] | 6 | | 13 | 21 |
| Remarried | | | 13 | 7 |
| Ever divorced | 9 | | 26 | 28 |
| *Milwaukee* | | | | |
| Divorced[a] | 4 | | 8 | 6 |
| Remarried | 3 | | 6 | 16 |
| Ever divorced | 7 | | 14 | 22 |
| *Miami* | | | | |
| Divorced[a] | | 11 | | 16 |
| Remarried | | 6 | | 9 |
| Ever divorced | | 17 | | 26 |

a. Indicates divorced and separated

of divorces, with unaffiliated Jews experiencing the greatest number of divorces. Brodbar-Nemzer found that Jews with a low rate of ritual observance are eight times as likely to be divorced at some time in their lives than Jews who have a greater commitment to traditional Jewish observance.[31] Nevertheless, the Orthodox Rabbinical Court *(Bet Din)* of New York reports that divorce rates are rising among Orthodox Jews and even among members of Hasidic sects.[32] It is not uncommon now for marriages even among the ultra-Orthodox to be "in trouble," partially because of the gap in the socialization of men and women. Young women have some acquaintance with secular culture and are encouraged to be perfectly groomed, while young men are expected to focus exclusively on the study of sacred literature, often leaving social graces to chance. Marital strain and divorce sometimes follow, although still far below the rates encountered in other Jewish denominations.

One study of divorced individuals shows that most of the women who initiated divorce did so prior to forming a romantic liaison, while all of the men who asked for a divorce were already involved with another woman before they initiated proceedings.[33] Perhaps most disturbing, Reform Rabbi Sheila Pelz Weinberg says that the traditional Jewish emphasis on the family stands in the way of communal response to the needs of women who do not fit the mold, because some fear that by supporting those who live in alternative households, "we are validating them."[34]

In most American cities, Jewish divorce primarily occurs among couples in their 30s and 40s. Young and middle-aged couples are not the only divorces, however; between 5 and 10 percent of Jewish respondents in their fifties and sixties were divorced in Denver, Miami, and Milwaukee.[35] Newspapers report that "an increasing number of couples who have been married for 20 or more years" are splitting up after their major responsibilities to their children have ended. Late-life divorces are most often initiated by men, often facing retirement or other intimations of mortality. They are probably also spurred on by the expectation of longer lives, by no-fault divorce laws, by isolation from extended family, and by unrealistic expectations from the marital relationship.[36]

Wives usually find such divorces a profound shock. For both younger and middle-aged female divorcees, a large part of that shock can be financial. In addition to the fact that women have traditionally gravitated toward lower-paying fields, the early years of marriage are often focused on the establishment of the husband's career while the wife's career is slowed by maternity, and husbands can emerge from a divorce with considerably more earning power than their wives have.

Table 4.4 compares the financial status of Jewish men and women in Rochester in the middle 1980s by their marital status. Total yearly household incomes of married men and women respondents are roughly equal. However, the financial status of divorced men and women is radically different: nearly two-thirds of Rochester divorced Jewish women make under $30,000 per year, while no divorced Jewish men make under $30,000 per year. More than half of Rochester divorced Jewish women have an annual family income of less than $20,000, and another 8 percent make between $20,000 and $30,000; 11 percent make $20,000 to $39,000; 24 percent make $40,000 to $49,000; and the highest income for

TABLE 4.4
The Effect of Termination of a Marriage on Financial Status of Males and Females, Rochester Jewish Population, 1987 (Percentages by Sex, Marital Status, and Yearly Income)

| *Income* | *Divorced (separated)* | | *Widowed* | | *Married* | |
|---|---|---|---|---|---|---|
| *by thousands* | *Women* | *Men* | *Women* | *Men* | *Women* | *Men* |
| Up to $20 | 54% | 0 | 67% | 60% | 6 | 5% |
| $20–$30 | 8% | 0 | 7% | 16% | 19% | 18% |
| $30–$39 | 11% | 47% | 7% | 0 | 19% | 16% |
| $40–$49 | 24% | 6% | 18% | 12% | 17% | 20% |
| $50–74 | 3% | 38% | 0 | 0 | 21% | 22% |
| $75–$100 | 0 | 0 | 0 | 0 | 10% | 11% |
| Over $100 | 0 | 9% | 0 | 12% | 8% | 7% |

divorced Jewish women, $50,000 to $74,000, is earned by only 3 percent. Nearly half the divorced Jewish men, on the other hand, make between $30,000 and $39,000 per year; another 44 percent of divorced Jewish men make between $40,000 and $74,000 per year; 9 percent make more than $100,000 per year.

Women in older age groups often have no professional life to turn to, and their social circles are being narrowed by illness and death. Most of them have shaped their entire lives and self-image around their husbands and view divorce, unlike widowhood, as a devastating shame. "Whatever he wanted I did it," said one sixty-four-year-old woman. "He wanted blintzes, I made blintzes. He wanted help in the store, I helped in the store. You name it, I did it. How does he say 'Thank you'? He lies; he cheats; and for an encore he defects."[37]

*Widows and Widowers*

A third group of unmarried Jewish adults is composed of widows and widowers. They are, as a group, older than the never-marrieds and the divorced, and thus both their options and their problems are significantly different from the younger group of "singles."

The elderly tend to be more polarized financially and geographically than any other age group. Older singles, for example, comprise approximately one-fifth of the Jewish populations of the Bronx, Brooklyn, and Manhattan but one-tenth or less of the Jewish populations of Staten Island, Nassau, Suffolk, and Westchester in New York.[38] Milwaukee provides a typical profile: elderly Jews in the inner city are older (many over age 75), less affluent, and the most likely to live with someone else. Jews in the most affluent North Shore include a number of very elderly, but the majority can afford to get help. Half of the elderly households in the North Shore, for example, have incomes of $30,000 or over.[39]

Despite the high rate of Jewish mobility, a significant proportion of elderly Jews live in the same geographical area as at least some of their children. Only one-quarter of the households over sixty in St. Louis, for example, report no children living in the St. Louis area. Only 11 percent have no other family living in the area. In addition, more than half of St. Louis elderly Jews surveyed said that they saw family members at least five times a month. Eighty-seven percent saw family members at least once a month, which roughly corresponds to the 89 percent who have children or other family members in the area.[40]

But large numbers of older singles live far from family. When they are lucky, they live close enough to persons similar to themselves to form family-like support networks. They may live in nearby apartment buildings or may find a congenial spot in a local library or Jewish community center to socialize. Barbara Myerhoff described such a family-like society of elderly Jews in Venice, California. For the elderly poor, a Jewish community center can become a kind of tribal meeting place, a locale in which lonely people can eat, talk, play cards, sing, get angry and argue, maintain deeply felt friendships and feuds, and care about each other.[41]

Affluent older persons have more flexibility; they are able to relocate to the more desirable sections of the urban areas they have always lived in or to spend part or all of the year in luxurious communities in the sunbelt. When they remain in their own communities, wealthy older Jews frequently make increased community work an effective substitute for waning family involvements. When they move to the sunbelt, however, they often choose to live in restricted communities with others of the same chronological and socioeconomic status. Like the poor inner city elderly Jews, the wealthy older Jews of the sunbelt thus socialize in homogeneous colonies. When given the choice, a number of elderly Jews evidently prefer to live in the tranquility of a child-free environment.

Some elderly Jews are not fortunate enough to find a community life of any kind. Left behind in decaying urban areas, they may be childless, or their children may have moved far away. Isolated from daily human contact, their physical and emotional health can deteriorate rapidly. Jewish community organizations in some cities actively search for such isolated persons and try to provide them with "friendly volunteers," who can bring quasi-family interactions back into their lies.

## Jewish Families with Children in America Today

### *Dual Career Jewish Families*

More than 20 years ago, David Reisman described "a few exceptionally energetic women, fortunate in their spouses and family situations, who appear to be omnicompetent and who as often arouse envy and admiration among other women."[42] Today, however, working Jewish wives and mothers are no longer an oddity and are less often considered as "omnicompetent" superwomen. Instead dual career families are a normative variety of contemporary nuclear family in the Jewish community.

Today's striking levels of higher education for Jewish women translate into shifting occupational profiles. The vast majority of Jewish college women today assume they will be labor force participants for most of their lives. They plan for that labor force participation and educate themselves for it; the days when college functioned as a kind of intellectual finishing school or exclusively as a preparation for intelligent motherhood seem to be past. Moreover, Jewish college women not only take for granted that they will work, they often assume that they have the right to choose and prepare themselves for work which will bring them maximal emotional and financial compensation. Thus, it is not at all unusual for middle-class Jewish college women to be directly ambitious for themselves, where they once would have been ambitious for their husbands, and only vicariously for themselves ("behind every great man . . .").

This ambition is reflected in the large numbers of Jewish women currently enrolled in professional programs. Silberman, for example, reports that "a 1980 national survey of first-year college students taken by the American Council on Education found that 9 percent of Jewish women were planning to be lawyers—up from 2 percent in 1969. The proportion planning a career in business management increased by the same amount, and the number planning to be doctors trippled, from 2 percent to 6 percent. In this same period the number of Jewish women planning to be elementary school teachers dropped . . . from 18 percent in 1969 to 6 percent in 1980; those choosing secondary school teaching plummeted from 12 percent to only 1 percent."[43]

Nearly 40 percent of contemporary wage-earning American Jewish women who fall into the following categories—childless women, mothers with children age 18 or under, and women age 44 and under—are employed in professional capacities. Indeed, viewing Jewish women by family formation and moving from the more mature family groupings to the youngest family groupings, the data indicate a dramatic decline in employment in clerical and technical capacities and a corresponding increase in those employed in professional capacities.

Employment in the generally more lucrative high-status professions, which have been accessible to women for the shortest period of time (physicians and dentists, lawyers and judges, professors, senior systems analysts, executive positions, etc.) increases from only 7 percent of Jewish women with children 19 and over to 11 percent of women with children 18 and under, and 15 percent of women who have not yet had children. Employment in the helping professions (teachers below the college level, social workers, librarians, middle-level engineers and programmers, nurses, etc.), many of which require master's degrees but are not usually as lucrative as the high-status professions, increases from 16 percent of women with children ages 19 and over to 28 percent of women with children ages 18 and under, and declines slightly among women with no children (24 percent); this decline may be significant, because teaching, social work, librarianship and nursing have traditionally been considered "women's professions," and the first two especially have historically been favored by American Jewish women. While percentages of women employed in managerial or service positions remain stable from one family grouping to another, women with children ages 19 or over are far more likely to be employed in clerical or technical positions—56 percent—than women with children ages 18 or under—37 percent.

Indeed, in many communities women with children under 18 are more likely to work than women with no children in the household. In Worcester, for example, nearly three-quarters of married women with children work full-time, part-time, or are students, and only one-quarter are full-time homemakers, compared to more than 40 percent of women without children at home who describe themselves as full-time homemakers.[44]

Until very recently, Jewish women were distinguished by the impact of family on their work lives—a pronounced plummeting pattern of their participation in the labor force. In 1957, only 12 percent of Jewish women with children under six worked outside the home, compared to 18 percent of White Protestants. As recently as 15 years ago, it was still true that Jewish women were likely to work until they became pregnant with their first child, and then to drop out of the labor force until their youngest child was about junior high school age.

Feminism and other social and economic factors have ensured that American Jewish women today are much more likely to be paid employees than American Jewish women at midcentury, and the majority of them continue to work for pay outside the home throughout their childbearing and child-rearing years. Among contemporary married Jewish women, 56 percent work for pay (44 percent work part-time and another 12 percent work full-time), one-quarter call themselves full-time homemakers, and 18 percent are unemployed or retired from labor force participation. Among American Jewish women ages 44 and under, 70 percent work for pay (59 percent work full-time and another 11 percent work part-time), only 17 percent are homemakers, 11 percent are students, and 4 percent are not employed (1990 NJPS Jewish female respondents). Today the labor force participation of Jewish women departs radically from patterns of the recent past. In most cities the majority of Jewish mothers continue to work even when their children are quite young. In Boston, Baltimore, San Francisco, and Washington, three out of every five Jewish mothers of preschool children are working (see table 4.5.)

Feminism is strongly bolstered by perceived economic need as factors encouraging a large proportion of Jewish women to work outside the home. As has been widely demonstrated in the general American population, for middle-class families today, two incomes are often needed in order to attain and maintain a middle-class standard of living; that is, purchase of a single family home in a desirable location; relatively new automobiles and major appliances; attractive educational options for one's children, including college and possibly private school and/or graduate school; and summer camp and vacation options. It is also true that perceptions of what comprises a middle-class lifestyle have been significantly revised upward, so that more income is needed by "middle class" families. These factors are especially significant for American Jewish families, who have traditionally had a strong ethic of providing their children with "everything."[45]

As the authors of the Cleveland study noted, "we are seeing a new generation of women who do not interrupt work or career even during child-bearing years. Their participation in the work force conforms to an entirely new pattern in society in general."[46]

Like other middle- and upper-middle-class American women, Jewish mothers face a series of decisions about how to balance the demands of careers and motherhood. They use a variety of strategies. Some sequence motherhood and career, by completing a portion of their schooling and/or career agenda, then dropping out of the labor force for a time to bear and raise their young children, and then returning to work when their children are school age. Others juggle the demands of work and home throughout the early childhood of their families. Part-time work is often an important strategy for both jugglers and sequencers. Jugglers often turn to part-time employment temporarily when their children are very

TABLE 4.5
Labor Force Participation by Location: Jewish Mothers of Children Under Six Years Old, Percentage Full-time and Part-time Employment

| | *Full-time* | *Part-time* | *Homemake* | *Other* |
|---|---|---|---|---|
| Boston | 29% | 36% | 33% | 2% |
| Baltimore | 27% | 38% | 35% | 1% |
| Kansas City | 28% | 21% | 44% | 7% |
| MetroWest | 22% | 26% | 49% | 4% |
| Milwaukee | 18% | 32% | 36% | 14% |
| Philadelphia | 23% | 14% | 59% | 3% |
| Pittsburgh | 29% | 25% | 42% | 4% |
| Phoenix | 26% | 21% | 50% | 3% |
| Rochester | 22% | 32% | 42% | 4% |
| San Francisco | 36% | 25% | 31% | 8% |
| Washington | 34% | 30% | 30% | 6% |
| Worcester | 15% | 34% | 51% | 1% |

*Source:* Adapted from Gabriel Berger and Lawrence Sternberg, *Jewish Child-Care: A Challenge and an Opportunity* (Cohen Center for Modern Jewish Studies, Brandeis University, Research Report No. 3, November 1988).

young, and sequencers may use part-time hours as a way of easing back into the job market. Part-time employment has the great advantage that it allows women to maintain their working skills and their visibility in the labor market while still enabling them to spend considerable amounts of time with their families. Disadvantages to the arrangement often include disproportionately lower salaries, job benefits, and prestige. Moreover, in certain fields part-time work is almost impossible to arrange.

Mothers who work part-time may need Jewish communal help in finding child care arrangements at least as much as mothers who work full-time because of the peculiarities of child care availability. Full-time workers often have more lucrative positions than part-time workers and thus are more easily able to find and afford good full-time, home-based child care, of either the live-in or live-out variety. When full-time workers have more than one child, they may opt to send the older child to an excellent preschool program even if it only operates for part of a day, because the full-time, home-based child care provider who watches their younger child(ren) can cover the rest of the needed hours. Part-time workers, on the other hand, are likely to use child care provisions outside of their homes.

It is important to note that the vast majority of all parents of children under six years old, whether they work full-time or part-time or define themselves as homemakers, state that they prefer Jewish-sponsored child care.[47] Moreover, studies indicate that families which enroll their children in Jewish-sponsored child care draw closer to Jewish practices as a family unit.[48]

In contrast to the conditions Reisman described, Jewish community disapproval no longer seems to be a salient factor in a woman's decision on whether or not to work. A recent survey found that only a third of Jewish women currently believe that nonworking women make better mothers than women who work, while close to half of non-Jewish women think that working women are less effective mothers and that children are more likely to get into trouble when both parents work.[49]

A Minneapolis survey of working Jewish mothers provided an interesting portrait of the group: on the whole, they tended to be young, highly educated, and professionally skilled. Thirty-nine percent were in the age 30–39 cohort. Almost 60 percent of the working Jewish mothers had B.A.s, master's degrees, or Ph.D.s, and almost 60 percent of them were employed in professional, technical, or administrative occupations. Only 12 percent of the at-home mothers in Minneapolis, on the other hand, had finished college or gone beyond.[50]

Studies have shown that women who are firmly grounded in Jewish life can enjoy great success both in wife-mother roles and in career roles.[51] Compromising and mutual supportiveness is typical of working families that work it all out: things are often less than perfect, but both spouses are firmly committed to their relationship and to their children, so they compromise, roll with the punches, and usually emerge with arrangements which are satisfactory for them both. In a study of nearly 500 married dual-career couples, researchers discovered that the character of the husband is the key to a successful dual-career marriage:

> The more supportive a husband is and the more supportive his wife perceives him to be, the higher the marital quality experienced by his wife. Examining the impact of "competitiveness, balance, gender-role identity, and support," these researchers found that "by far the most important factor affecting husbands' perceived marital quality is sensitivity. The stronger his sensitivity the more positive his perceived marital quality. The wife's perceived marital quality also rises with the increase in the husband's sensitivity. . . . The contemporary marriage is based on the emotional attachment of two persons, and that attachment is expressed by giving and receiving emotional support. People who lack the ability to form emotional attachments by expressing love and support obviously will experience a lower-quality marital relationship than people who have that ability.[52]

A study of ninety-seven Jewish career women with three or more children in the Washington, D.C. area,[53] for example, found that eighty-six women were members of Reform, Conservative, or Orthodox synagogues; three belonged to *havurot*; two were Reconstructionists; and only six had no religious affiliation. Over half the women invited to participate in the survey "said that Jewish beliefs and attitudes helped them to juggle their multiple obligations. . . . Several stated that religion and tradition 'held them together'" as the family worked through crisis situations. One-third of the respondents kept kosher homes, more than half had some form of Sabbath observance, and three-quarters sent their children to religious school—with one-fifth in day schools. Significantly, among these working women strong religious identification was not a factor of being closer to the immigrant generation: religious observance was more pronounced among younger than older respondents.[54]

Dual-career families do face significant practical problems in juggling their responsibilities to work and to each other, however, and these problems are often complicated by the decline in extended family units. Dual-career couples today are the predominant group among young and middle-aged families in every wing of American Judaism. Many are deeply committed to Jewish life. Such women say that their Jewish values and lifestyles have enhanced familial devotion, stability, and structure and increased the family's ability to weather dual-career stresses and strains. However, some say that the Jewish community, which supposedly wants to strengthen families and encourage larger families, is not doing its part. They feel that the local Jewish community is sadly failing Jewish dual-career families. They voice the complaint that "the Jewish community is urging us to have more children, but it isn't willing to help us meet the cost." The area of largest dissatisfaction is that of day care and Jewish education. Mothers of young children complain bitterly about the lack of Jewish day care centers. "Children should be raised in a Jewish environment, and day-care is part of that," said one. Others complain that Hebrew schools, day schools, and Jewish camps are unwilling to lower tuition fees for large Jewish families unless their income is very low. They assert that Jewish organizations retain the attitude that Jewish women should have more children *and* that Jewish women should bear the financial and psychological burden of raising those children.[55]

### *Traditional Jewish Families*

Traditional Jewish families—that is, children living with their own father and mother, with father as main breadwinner for the family, are a substantially represented family type in some middle-sized Jewish communities and in many suburban areas. While only 17 percent of American Jewish women under age 45 define themselves as full-time homemakers, the proportion focusing on homemaking and children is much higher in some particular communities. In Pittsburgh, one of the most demographically traditional communities, for example, more than half the Jewish mothers with children under 6 stayed at home full-time, and 42 percent of women with children under 18 were full-time homemakers.[56] The behavior of these families retains similarities to earlier American Jewish families.

A 1973 study by the National Opinion Research Center (NORC) compared cross-generated data among 12 ethnic groups in Michigan and found that Jewish families ranked unusually high "on scales measuring social support and warmth in the family environment," "parental compatibility," and "family intimacy," as well as on "scales measuring democracy and equality of decision making" compared to non-Jewish ethnic groups. Teenage children felt close to their parents and very much a part of the family decision-making process; they voiced their opinions easily and felt they were taken seriously. On the other hand, Jewish parents did not feel they were taken all that seriously by their teenage children; both parents and children assessed parental control of the family situation on a very low level. Additionally, Jewish fathers ranked far below the national average in "decision making power." The strong parent or disciplinarian is often the Jewish mother.[57]

Parents in traditional Jewish families still tend to treat children as extensions of themselves, as Marshall Sklare describes in *America's Jews*,[58] with the major change that they now place great stress on "independence training." Partially for this reason, the majority of Jewish children now participate in playgrounds, nursery school, or day-care programs. A 1984 study of the Pittsburgh Jewish community, for example, reported that even in this relatively traditional community, "child care usage for preschoolers is high. Eighty-three percent of all pre-school children are or will be in child care facilities, including both pre-school and day care programs. Two-thirds of them are using Jewish-sponsored facilities."[59]

A small but noteworthy and much-publicized trend is now emerging in which career women decide to leave or modify their careers in order to bear and raise children. Rejecting the pressures to be "superwomen," they opt, at least temporarily, for a more traditional nurturing role. Some leave work altogether when their children are small; others work part-time or at home, at times changing fields so they may have more flexible hours and access to their children. Many of these women become passionate advocates for the art of mothering and for the advantages of the traditional family.[60]

Mainstays of the traditional Jewish family are found among the Hasidim or ultra-Orthodox communities, largely located in self-defined enclaves in and around major American cities. Although life there proceeds in certain ways as it did in similar European communities, American mores and patterns have made significant inroads. In contemporary America, for example, it is extremely rare for even *shadchan*-matched Hasidic young men and women to come to the *chuppah* without having spent many hours with each other, although Hasidic "dates" are always in public places such as hotel lobbies or chaperoned situations.[61] Even more than other traditional families, ultra-Orthodox couples tend to be very close to their parents. Unlike other American Jews, Hasidic newlyweds are likely to choose residences in their parents' neighborhoods. Herz and Rosen describe the emotional hierarchy in which young Jewish couples persist in their parents' eyes as children:

Some couples seen by the authors have reflected the intensity of their family orientation in their conviction that they would always be children who, in their parents' view, would forever need to be cared for financially and otherwise. As might be expected, along with the very high value placed on the family is the emphasis upon geographical as well as emotional closeness between generations.[62]

This dependence may be fostered by the custom of young husbands studying for several years in a *kolel*, an institution for intensive Talmudic study, while the couple is supported by one or both sets of parents.

While highly traditional, many in the ultra-Orthodox community are two-paycheck families. Even in very Orthodox households, the working mother has often become a communal norm. In more modern Orthodox households, where levels of secular education among women are virtually indistinguishable from women who identify with other wings of Judaism, younger Orthodox women are almost as likely as their Conservative, Reform, and Just Jewish sisters to hold professional or managerial positions. The employment pattern differs somewhat among Orthodox women with lower levels of secular education, but Rubin cites figures showing that over half the Hasidic Satmar wives with children over six work outside the home. Rubin notes that the early assumption of responsibilities trains ultratraditional Satmar Hasidic girls for a life in which extensive child-rearing and work outside the home is the norm for women.[63]

Where strictly Orthodox facilities are available, such as in certain neighborhoods of New York which have city or federation-sponsored, religiously run day care, many Hasidic children are placed in day care facilities.

### *Single-Parent Jewish Families*

The number of Jewish single-parent families, like the number of divorces, seems deceptively small at first glance. Single-parent families occupy relatively small percentages in the number of Jewish *households* in each city, but, because of the generally low Jewish birthrate, they are a significant factor in the number of *households with children*. Nationwide, an estimated third of Jewish children live in homes which have been touched by divorce, with approximately 10 percent living in single-parent homes and approximately 20 percent living in homes in which at least one parent has been divorced. Although only 5 percent of Miami[64] Jewish households were headed by a single parent, for example, 18 percent of the households with children were single-parent families. In Pittsburgh,[65] 5 percent of all households were single-parent families, but 12 percent of households with children fell into that category. While Denver[66] Jewish households included only 4 percent single-parent families, one out of every seven Jewish families with children under 18 in Denver was a single-parent household. Thirty percent of New York's Jewish households fell into the traditional two parents with children configuration; only 4 percent were single-parent families—but that 4 percent translated into 27,300 single-parent households, hardly an insignificant number.[67]

These families have some unique problems, for Jewish life cycle celebrations can pull children of some single-parent or blended families in two directions. Children of single-parent families sometimes have difficulty dealing with the Jewish emphasis on family, particularly around holiday time.[68] In response, some Jewish institutions have begun to support programs to help broken families arrange life cycle celebrations with a minimum of trauma.

In the majority of cases, for Jews as well as non-Jews, the single-parent household is headed by a woman. Often this means that the financial base of the parent/child unit is severely diminished. As illustrated earlier, in table 5.4, divorced women usually have a much smaller annual income from earnings than divorced men do. While paternal child-care payments, when they are assigned and complied with, can help to alleviate low maternal earnings, national studies show that child-care payments usually are a small fraction of paternal earnings.[69] Single-parent mothers remain as a group among the least affluent members of the Jewish community, often even when they are working full-time.

Social and emotional factors as well as financial factors complicate life for the Jewish single-parent mother. In a sense, the Jewish emphasis on family works against those whose families are no longer intact by making it difficult for them to find a niche in the community and making them feel even more isolated. When the Jewish single parent reaches out to the Jewish community, she may have difficulty finding a supportive peer group. The call for responsiveness from the Jewish community is legion among single parents. Women in Oakland, California, complained that mothers emerging from divorce "should get help in finding affordable housing and day care—the same help immigrant families get. Single mothers are the new poor in the society."[70]

Single parenthood complicates not only the functioning of the fragmented nuclear family, but also the relationship between parents and grandparents. Divorced children may be less responsive to their aging parents, both emotionally and financially. In addition, as Hofstein points out, "The single parent is often thrown back into a dependency relationship with her own parents." He quotes Nehauer's observations that a divorced woman's "parents may add to her emotional burden by feeling sorry for her and worrying about her future. It is not uncommon for a parent to say to a daughter, 'Before I die, I would like to see you happily married again.'"[71]

### *Intermarriage*

For American Jews, who now face a shrinking Jewish population due to the twin forces of intermarriage and assimilation, concerns about the religious identity of children raised in Jewish homes is particularly pronounced today. Intermarriage between Jews and non-Jews in the United States is now commonplace. The propensity of Jews to marry non-Jews was extremely low until the mid-1960s, but rose sharply thereafter and continued to climb in the 1980s. As a result, in many Jewish communities, among those marrying in recent years, there are more outmarriages than inmarriages.

This change in the underlying social and religious structure of the American Jewish community has important implications. Marriage to non-Jews has increased partially because of the successful integration of Jews into American society and their achievement of a high level of social acceptance. However, intermarriage may reflect and contribute to the decline of Judaism in America.

The subject of intermarriage evokes considerable passion among Jews because it arouses fears about elemental issues of group survival. One aspect of the matter is quantitative: the offspring of intermarriage may not remain Jewish; within one or two generations there may be fewer Jews and a greatly weakened Jewish community. Another aspect is qualitative: even if intemarriage does not lead to a decrease in the physical number of persons living in households with a Jewish parent, questions remain as to their Jewishness, i.e., the intensity of their communal affiliation, ethnic identification, and religious practice.[72]

Observers differ widely in their perceptions of the consequences of the intermarriage phenomenon.[73] At one end of the spectrum are scholars who are comparatively pessimistic, some of whom predict the eventual disappearance of a distinctive Jewish community, seeing only the survival of the Orthodox. At the end of the spectrum are scholars who are relatively optimistic, who discern the transformation and even revitalization of the American Jewish community. Rising rates of intermarriage, the latter argue, provide an opportunity to strengthen the ranks of American Jewry through an infusion of new blood or "imports"— the born non-Jewish spouses and their children.

We do have certain numerical facts about the rates of intermarriage.

Although intermarriage increases dramatically among younger American Jews, rates of conversion fall. Mixed marriage is five times higher among Jews 18 to 34 than it is among those over 55. Almost one-third of Jews who married out in the 1970s have spouses who converted into Judaism, but only 13 percent of those who married out in the 1980s have spouses who are now Jews by choice.

The occurrence of intermarriage is not random. The likelihood that persons will marry out and will not be married to a Jew by choice follows certain patterns. Non-Jewish women are still far more likely than non-Jewish men to become Jews by choice. More than matrilineal descent is at work here. Jews who marry out—especially women who marry out, marry substantially later than Jews who marry in. Jewish women who marry Jewish men have a mean marriage age of 23.2 years; those who marry non-Jewish men have a mean age of 26 years. It seems very likely that conflicting feelings about marital choices may often enter into these later marriages.

A factor which is no longer salient to mixed marriage—or, to be more precise, is salient in the opposite ways than it used to be—is educational, occupational and income grouping. When men—and it was then mostly men—married out in the 1950s and 1960s, they were most likely to be the most highly educated, highly placed professionally, and affluent men. Marrying out was a way up the ladder of social mobility. Today, just the opposite is true. Now that Jews are largely highly educated, professional, and affluent, Jews who marry out are far more likely to be less educated, less professional, and less affluent. It is possible that they feel more accepted in non-Jewish than in Jewish social circles.

Intensive Jewish education is clearly associated with a reduced likelihood of marrying out. Persons receiving more than six years of either supplementary school education or day school education are dramatically less likely than persons receiving more minimal forms of Jewish education to marry a non-Jew. Day school education is associated with reduced likelihood of mixed marriage no matter in which branch of Judaism the person had been raised. The clear association between Jewish education and inmarried is strongest among younger American Jews. Overall, about one-fifth of Jews ages 25 to 44 who had received six or more years of day school education married non-Jews, compared to half of those who had received six or more years of supplementary school, and three-fifths of Jews who had received supplementary school or Sunday school. Two-thirds of those who received no Jewish education married non-Jews.[74] In addition, those who received extensive Jewish education were much more likely than those who had not to have spouses who converted to Judaism, rather than remaining non-Jews.

Moreover, the impact of Jewish education carries over to the next generation. Ninety-five percent of inmarried Jews provide their children with some Jewish education, as do 86 percent of conversionary families, while only 41 percent of married couples did so. Many Jews feel ambivalent about Judaism, but ambivalent is not the same as ambiguous. Whatever conflicts and/or hostilities a Jew carries vis-à-vis Judaism and/or the Jewish people, he or she feels at the core of being Jewish—not part Jewish and part Christian.

Today, group membership has become voluntary. Americans, living in an open society, are not compelled to remain tied either physically or emotionally to the ethnic and religious groups from which they derived. They may—and do—choose to move away from their group of origin by obtaining their schooling and their employment in a mixed environment, by living in a mixed neighborhood, by abandoning practices which distinguish and separate their ethnic or religious group, and by marrying persons who derive from a different heritage. Boundaries which in many societies seemed fixed are quite permeable in America today. While it is fashionable to celebrate "roots" and the maintaining of ethnic ties, powerful social forces act to diminish and even obliterate those very ties.

Nevertheless, many Jews do struggle to maintain ties with Judaism and the Jewish people. Being Jewish is very important to many individuals: they express considerable Jewish pride, are comfortable with their Jewishness, are happy that they were born Jewish, relate to other Jews as family, and want their children to remain Jewish. Popular religious observances—i.e., those relating to *rites de passage* and the holidays—continue to provide personal identity with its group aspects, a vehicle for expressing shared feelings in familial and communal contexts, which reinforce and heighten the positive emotional affect of group belonging at the core of personal identity. In the United States, being Jewish rather than Christian separates Jews. In Robert Bellah's words, "It is part of Jewish identity and the maintenance of the boundaries of the Jewish community to deny that Jesus is the Christ, the Messiah."[75] Paradoxically, as the religious aspects of Judaism have become relatively less central to the core of Jewish identity, and shared feelings have become more important, being *not* Christian has taken on greater salience as a defining element of Jewishness.[76]

Mixed marriage involves a very different situation. A mixed family creates an environment for identity formation that is founded on the competing heritages of the Jewish and the non-Jewish spouses, both of which enter into the child's core identity. Mixed marriage thus not only decreases the likelihood that an unambiguous Jewish identity will be formed, but also raises the possibility that no Jewish identity at all will emerge. As Nathan Glazer has explained, "Their children have alternatives before them that the children of families in which both parents were born Jewish do not—they have legitimate alternative identities."[77] They can incorporate the identity of the Jewish parent, that of the non-Jewish parent, that of both, or that of neither. Identifying wholly with one parent may prove traumatic to the extent that it involves the rejection of the other parent, as well as part of the self. Maintaining both identities simultaneously may create tensions and conflicts. The most commonly chosen solution is to identify with neither parent religiously and focus instead on shared general, secular values.

Since *not* being Christian is a major defining element of Jewish identity, the creation of an unambiguous Jewish identity entails the absence from the home of Christian symbols and practices, even if the level of Jewish identification is low. Inmarrieds shun Christian symbols: 98 percent do not have a Christmas tree. Among conversionary marrieds, 78 percent do not have a Christmas tree while 22 percent do. In contrast, among mixed-marrieds, 62 percent have a Christmas tree while 38 percent do not. Quite strikingly, more mixed-marrieds have Christmas trees than perform any single Jewish ritual.

## Geographical Concentration of Jewish Families

Today's American Jewish families are frequently physically divided along chronological and marital status lines into homogeneous colonies. This movement of specific Jewish populations into particular metropolitan areas represents a departure from earlier Jewish mobility. Jews have long been upwardly mobile, moving, often unidirectionally, from depresssed urban areas to more pleasant urban or suburban areas. The "Jewish" neighborhood typically traveled, with as many of its denizens as could afford the move, into outlying districts. The young, the middle-aged, and the elderly lived side by side, although the style and quality of their housing might vary considerably.

Contemporary Jewish communities, however, exhibit patterns of "specialization": single persons and childless dual-career couples occupy revitalized urban areas, families seek out suburban or exurban areas, and the elderly either move to communities specifically designed for their needs or are left behind in less desirable urban areas in neighborhoods largely devoid of Jewish youth.

As table 4.6 illustrates, for example, the 1981 New York Jewish population study, found dramatic divisions between population types in the eight counties. In the Bronx, which once had a vibrant Jewish population but which is now an economically depressed area, senior citizens comprised almost a third of the Jewish population, while less than one-fifth were two-parent families, and one-tenth were singles. In Brooklyn and Queens, long-standing residential communities with both apartment dwellings and private homes, nearly a third of the Jewish households were families, while approximately one-fifth were singles or young couples. Suffolk and Staten Island, the newest areas of settlement, had the highest proportion of dependent children, with approximately two-fifths of the Jewish population under the age of twenty. Only 3 percent of Staten Island's Jewish households were single, but 59 percent in Staten Island and 63 percent in Suffolk were two-parent families. In Nassau and Westchester, affluent residential communities, the under-20 population comprised 29 percent of the total Jewish community. Manhattan had a disproportionate number of singles and childless couples, with those two groups comprising almost half of the Jewish households. Forty percent of Manhattan's population were married, but only 16 percent had children under eighteen. Of those who have children, over half had one child and over one-third had two children, with less than 10 percent having three or more children.[78]

Cities that attract singles also tend to attract couples who have no children or very small families. While the number of Los Angeles Jewish never-marrieds fell to just under 4 percent in the 40–59 age category, for example, over 40 percent of Jewish households in the 40–59 cohort were married with no children under 18, and more than 15 percent were separated or divorced with no children. One can speculate that the atmosphere in many such communities stress both professional

TABLE 4.6
Geographical Concentration of Family Types in Greater New York

| *Household* | *Bronx* | *Brooklyn* | *Manhattan* | *Queens* | *Staten Island* | *Nassau* | *Suffolk* | *Westchester* |
|---|---|---|---|---|---|---|---|---|
| Young singles | 10 | 12 | 35 | 13 | 3 | 8 | 7 | 7 |
| Young couples | 8 | 9 | 12 | 9 | 13 | 6 | 10 | 9 |
| Conventional families | 18 | 28 | 13 | 25 | 59 | 50 | 63 | 42 |
| Singe parents | 3 | 5 | 3 | 4 | 4 | 4 | 5 | 4 |
| Mature couples | 34 | 28 | 16 | 35 | 13 | 28 | 12 | 28 |
| Mature singles | 21 | 18 | 21 | 14 | 8 | 4 | 3 | 10 |

achievement and enjoyment of the "good life" and offers little impetus for the sacrifice of either in order to maintain a marriage or raise a family. As the authors of the Los Angeles study comment:

> In general, one is struck by the overall absence of households with children. When all family types with children are combined overall, only 28.3 percent of all Los Angeles Jewish households have children under 18 in the household. Even in San Valley, which has the highest proportion of children, less than half (41.6 percent) of all the households include a child under 18. This is caused in part by delaying marriage, in part by delayed child bearing, and in part by some couples who have decided not to have children at all.[79]

A similar point might be made about Denver, a locale with many younger adults. When taken as a whole, nearly 60 percent of Denver Jewish households are married couples—but only one-quarter of these married couples have children under 18. Even in the 30–39 and 40–49 ages cohorts, less than half of Denver's married Jewish couples have children under 18.[80]

## Childbearing: The Contemporary Jewish Family and Fertility

Jewish communities across the country, concerned with the prognosis for Jewish family life in their area, have compiled figures on the number of children under 20 and on the sizes and configurations of Jewish households. Those community studies which ask respondents about the number of children in the household have generally asked how many children the couple *expects to have* and combined these figures with existing children for inclusion in the study (see table 4.7.)

Choosing parenthood is often correlated with the strength of a woman's Jewish connections and behaviors. Data from the 1990 National Jewish Population Study show that women who identify themselves as "Jewish by religion" are much more likely to have children than women who consider themselves to be secular Jews. Being a Jewish mother is also strongly associated with belonging to a synagogue, belonging to and working for Jewish organizations, making donations to Jewish charitable causes, having mostly Jewish friends, observing Jewish holidays, and seeing Judaism as a "very important" aspect of one's life. Women who call themselves Orthodox are more likely than others in the same age group to be married and have children; as a group, Orthodox women alone are currently having children above replacement (2.1 children per family) levels. Conservative women expect to have more children than Reform women, but among 35- to 44-year-old Conservative and Reform women few differences in actual family size exist.[81]

Despite differences between particular groups of women, there are sweeping changes in patterns of childbearing among large segments of the American Jewish population. With the exception that larger proportions of non-Jewish white women have children in their early twenties than do Jewish women, patterns of

TABLE 4.7
Family Formation Status of American Jewish Women, Percentages by Professional Status (Data Drawn from 1990 NJP Respondents Born or Raised Jewish)

| *Occupational Status Level* | *No Children* | *Children 18 or under* | *Children 19 or over* |
|---|---|---|---|
| High-status professionals | 15% | 11% | 7% |
| Helping professions | 24% | 28% | 16% |
| Managerial position | 13% | 13% | 14% |
| Clerical/technical | 35% | 37% | 56% |
| Service positions | 9% | 9% | 7% |
| Totals[a] | 96% | 8% | 100% |

a. Totals shown may be greater than or less than 100% because they are rounded.

*Source:* Sylvia Barack Fishman, *A Breath of Life: Feminism in the American Jewish Community* (New York: Free Press 1993).

childbearing among Jewish and non-Jewish women are similar.[82] Changes in marriage patterns have affected both the timing and the size of today's families. In 1990, 93 percent of Jewish women ages 18 to 24 had not yet had children. More than half of those ages 25 to 34 (55 percent) had no children. Among Jewish women ages 35 to 44, one out of four had no children. While almost all American Jewish women ages 45 or over reported having children, either biological or adopted, it is not clear that all or even most of the 24 percent of childless women in the 35 to 44 age group will in fact achieve the status of motherhood. As a result of delayed marriage and childbirth, the societal preference for smaller families, and unwanted infertility, most demographers now estimate the completed size of the contemporary Jewish family to average fewer than two children per married household.[83]

The vast majority of Jewish women still place an enormous value on having children. Jewish women are less likely than any other religious or ethnic group to state that they wish to remain childless.[84] Most American Jewish couples hope to have children "someday." Unlike women of other ethnic groups, where higher education is associated with lower expectations of childbearing, the more highly educated a Jewish woman, the more children she expects to have. Calvin Goldschieder and Francis Kobrin Goldscheider, relying on data which deal with expected family size, point out that among Jewish populations—unlike among Protestants and Catholics—"educational attainment is directly rather than inversely related to the fertility expectations." Thus, "Jews with doctorates expect 2.2 children and only 11 percent expect to be childless; Jews with 'only' college degrees expect only 1.8 children and 21 percent expect to be childless." In contrast, the reverse pattern is true of highly educated Protestants and Catholic women.[85]

However, highly educated Jewish women do not actually have as many children as they once expected to. Although Jewish career women are more committed to having families than any other group of career women, they are at least as likely as other white middle-class women to delay the onset of childbearing until they have reached what they consider to be an appropriate level of financial or occupational achievement. Expectations do not always give way to reality. Jewish women ages 16 to 26 years old who were interviewed in a national study in 1969–70 expected to have an average of 2.5 children; that cohort, today ages 35 to 44, have in fact borne an average of 1.5 children and expect an average of 1.7 children completed family size.[86] Contrary to the expectations of both women and demographers, "as education increases among both Jewish men and women, the proportion with no children increases." Indeed, "among those with a master's degree . . . Jews have significantly higher levels of childlessness than non-Jews."[87]

Recent data demonstrate that in many types of communities younger Jewish women are in fact beginning their families at measurably later ages than middle-aged women did. The ages at which today's mothers begin their families are similar to those of women ages 65 to 75, who married during the Depression.

Often, such childlessness is unintentional. When a couple conscientiously uses birth control as part of "family planning," they do not imagine that one day promoting conception rather than preventing it will be problematic. Despite insistence by some feminists that the specter of infertility has been exaggerated as part of an anti-woman "backlash,"[88] fertility is not an even playing field bounded on one side by menarche and on the other by menopause. For reasons still not clearly understood by the medical community, some women who easily conceive and carry pregnancies to term in their twenties have problems with conception and gestation in their later years. Moreover, even among those couples who would suffer from infertility at any age, beginning the process of trying to conceive earlier gives them and infertility specialists more time to work with and more chance of a successful outcome.

Additionally, the change in lifestyles inflicted by an infant upon older parents may be experienced as more disruptive than upon a more flexible younger couple. The classic comment of younger parents was that they "grew up" with their children. In contrast, an older mother of one interviewed in *The New York Times* cogently summarized the problem:

> There are all the problems of getting older. Running after a toddler in the street when I was in my late 30s didn't fit my image of myself at that age. And I used to force naps to compensate for my own loss of physical energy. . . . If I had it to do over again, I would probably have had one earlier in my 30s and at least one more right away.[89]

Under such circumstances, couples who had indicated that they wanted two children may decide they are better off with one.

## Conclusion

The "typical" American Jewish household today is more likely than not to be atypical in some way. Proportions of older, single, divorced, remarried, or dual-career households make up more of the Jewish population than intact young families with children. First, the elderly are the fastest growing cohort among the American Jewish population. Within this cohort, the young-old, aged 60–75, and the old-old, aged 75 and over, often comprise different kinds of "families" and have different effects on household structure. The great majority of older Jews, both couples and singles, live in their own households rather than with relatives: in Milwaukee, for example, less than 2 percent of Jewish households were composed of an elderly person living with children or other younger relatives.[90] In Los Angeles, 6 percent of persons over age 65 lived with others;[91] and in Phoenix, 5 percent of older Jews live with adult children.[92] As the frailer old-old population increases, however, this situation may change. Regardless of where they live, older couples and older singles will be increasingly prominent among American Jewish families.

The impact of changes in educational and occupational patterns on the American Jewish family appears to be continuing. Singles will probably maintain an important presence among Jewish families as young adults use their 20s and 30s to pursue career goals and self-development. In addition, it seems unlikely that American Jewish women will abandon educational and career opportunities; they will probably continue to marry later and bear their children later than earlier generations. As Jewish women retain career commitments even during their child-bearing years, the dual-career family may become even more normative.

No aspect of contemporary American life has aroused as much anxiety and debate in the Jewish community as changes in family formation. Many American Jews feel caught between two value systems, between an individualistic American ethos which gives priority to an individual's talents, strengths, and opportunities, and Jewish tradition, which gives priority to the needs of the family unit and the community first. The transformed Jewish family—like the transformed American family—has been influenced not only by feminism but by widespread cultural attitudes which stress individual achievement and pleasure; by materialistic expectations that elevate the perceived standard of what a "middle-class" lifestyle comprises; by a tightening economic market requiring dual incomes to maintain middle-class lifestyles; by the easy availability of contraceptive techniques and by the accompanying sexual revolution; and by patterns of chronological separation that split families by sending adolescents to far-off university campuses and grandparents to the sunbelt.

Individualism, with all the increased opportunities it has opened up, has not lessened the desire of American Jews to form families. Indeed, most American

Jews either have children or report that they hope to have children. Individualism has, however, changed the timing of childbearing, and has had a negative impact on the actual size of Jewish families. Rising rates of divorce, also part of our individualistic society, have created a situation in which one-third of Jewish children live in homes which have been touched by divorce: about 10 percent of Jewish children live in single-parent homes and 20 percent live in households in which at least one spouse has been divorced. Increasingly, moreover, the families which Jews form are not exclusively Jewish families. About one-third of children born to Jews today live in households in which one spouse does not consider him/herself to be a Jew.

The changed lifestyles of American Jewish men and women today have had a powerful, and probably permanent, impact on the character of the American Jewish family. And yet, despite the individualism which permeates American life, recent research indicates that Jews continue to value the creation of a happy home. Brodbar-Nemzer has shown that Jews are more likely than other ethnic groups to consider themselves successful human beings when they enjoy marital satisfaction and more likely to suffer a loss of self-esteem when they experience marital instability or divorce.[93] Jewish families have faced many challenges in the past—challenges which were usually evoked by adversity rather than prosperity. Today, however, Jewish families face the challenge of retaining their vitality and cohesion while responding to the opportunities of an individualistic and open society.

## Notes

1. This article, which is based on data from the 1990 National Jewish Population Survey and recent studies of Jewish populations in individual communities, also includes substantial information from my earlier essay on the subject, "The Changing American Jewish Family in the 80s," *Contemporary Jewry* 9, no. 2 (1988), pp. 1–33. Special thanks are due to my colleagues at the Maurice and Marilyn Cohen Center for Modern Jewish Studies at Brandeis University, especially to the following: Marshall Sklare, of blessed memory, who introduced me to the sociological study of the Jews; Gary Tobin and Lawrence Sternberg, for their ongoing support for and interest in my work on the Jewish family; research assistants Gabrielle Garschina and Miriam Hertz for their competent performance of a variety of tasks; and Sylvia Riese, executive secretary, who was of invaluable assistance in expediting the revisions of this essay.

   A portion of an earlier version of this essay, "The Changing Jewish Family of the 1980's," appeared in *Contemporary Jewry* 9, no. 2 (fall 1988): 1–33. The author is grateful for permission to reprint.
2. National statistics on the Jewish community in the United States are drawn from the 1990 National Jewish Population Survey, conducted under the auspices of the council of Jewish Federations. The first national study of American Jews undertaken since 1970, the 1990 NJPS studied some 6500 individuals in 2440 households, which were found after extensive screening through random digit dialing techniques. These households represent Jews across the country living in communities of diverse sizes

and composition. A summary of the findings is provided by Barry Kosmin et al., *Highlights of the CJF 1990 National Jewish Population Survey* (New York: Council of Jewish Federations, 1991). All nationwide figures for the American Jewish population in 1970 in this essay are derived from the National Jewish Population Study (NJPS). Unless otherwise noted, data from individual city studies are drawn from the following sources: Paul Ritterband and Steven M. Cohen, *The 1981 Greater New York Jewish Population Survey* (New York, 1981); Bruce A. Phillips, *Los Angeles Jewish Community Survey Overview for Regional Planning* (Los Angeles, 1980); Allied Jewish Federation of Denver, *The Denver Jewish Population Study* (Denver, 1981); Lois Geer, *1981 Population Study of the St. Paul Jewish Community* (St. Paul, 1981); Lois Geer, *The Jewish Community of Greater Minneapolis 1981 Population Study* (Minneapolis, 1981); Population Research Committee, *Survey of Cleveland's Jewish Population*, 1981 (Cleveland, 1981); Ira M. Sheskin, *Population Study of the Greater Miami Jewish Community* (Miami, 1982); Gary A. Tobin, *A Demographic and Attitudinal Study of the Jewish Community of St. Louis* (St. Louis, 1982); Bruce A. Phillips and William S. Aron, *The Greater Phoenix Jewish Population Study* (Phoenix, 1984–85); Bruce A. Phillips, *The Milwaukee Jewish Population Study* (Milwaukee, 1984); Nancy Hendrix, *A Demographic Study of the Jewish Community of Nashville and Middle Tennessee* (Nashville, 1982); Ann Shorr, Jewish Community Federation of Cleveland, and Jane Berkey and Saul Weisberg, United Federation of Greater Pittsburgh, *Survey of Greater Pittsburgh's Jewish Population*, 1984; Gary A. Tobin, Joseph Waksberg, and Janet Greenblatt, *A Demographic Study of the Jewish Community of Greater Washington* (Washington, D.C., 1984); Gary A. Tobin, *Jewish Population Study of Greater Baltimore*, 1986; Gary A. Tobin and Sylvia Barack Fishman, *Jewish Population Study of Greater Worcester*, 1987; Gary A. Tobin and Sylvia Barack Fishman, *Jewish Population Study of Greater Rochester*, 1988. Percentages in this paper have been rounded from .5 to the next highest number.

3. U. O. Schmeltz and S. DellaPergola, "The Demographic Consequences of U.S. Population Trends," *American Jewish Year Book* (1983), pp. 148–49.
4. Peggy Wireman, *Urban Neighborhoods, Networks, and Families: New Forms for Old Values* (Lexington, MA: Lexington Books, D.C. Health and Company, (1984), p. 6.
5. We define "universal marriage" to be 95 percent or over ever-married, regardless of the ultimate disposition of that marriage.
6. Bruce A. Phillips, *Los Angeles Jewish Community Survey Overview for Regional Planning* (Los Angeles, 1980), p. 11.
7. Allied Jewish Federation of Denver, *The Denver Jewish Population Study* (Denver, 1981), pp. 14, 40.
8. Daniel J. Elazar, *Community and Polity: The Organizational Dynamics of American Jewry* (Philadelphia: Jewish Publication Society of American, 1976), p. 236.
9. Gary A. Tobin, Joseph Waksberg, and Janet Greenblatt, *A Demographic Study of the Jewish Community of Greater Washington* (Washington, D.C., 1984), p. 45.
10. Paul Ritterband and Steven M. Cohen, *The 1981 Greater New York Jewish Population Study* (New York, 1981), p. II–11.
11. Bruce A. Phillips, *The Milwaukee Jewish Population Study* (Milwaukee, 1984), p. II–12.
12. William Novak, "Are Good Jewish Men a Vanishing Breed?" *Moment* 5, no. 2 (Jan./Feb., 1980), pp. 14–20.

13. See Sylvia Barack Fishman, *A Breath of Life: Feminism in the American Jewish Community* (New York: Free Press, 1993).
14. Among numerous newspaper articles and advertisements for Jewish dating services, see B. Drummond Ayres, Jr., "For Jewish Only: A Computer Dating Service," *The New York Times*, June 27, 1974; Judith L. Kuper, "2000 Singles Enrolled in Dating Service," *The Jewish Post and Opinion*, July 16, 1976; Yitta Halberstam, "Today's Shadchan: Popular and Expensive," *Jewish Week*, July 31, 1977.
15. Jewish Telegraphic Agency, *Community News Reporter*, April 11, 1986.
16. Christie Balka and Andy Rose, *Twice Blessed: On Being Lesbian and Gay and Jewish* (Boston: Beacon Press, 1989).
17. Robert Gordis, *Love and Sex: A Modern Jewish Perspective* (New York: Farrar, Straus and Giroux, 1978), p. 23.
18. Debra Renee Kaufman, *Rachel's Daughter: Newly Orthodox Jewish Women* (New Brunswick, N.J.: Rutgers University Press, 1991), p. 125.
19. Sharon K. Houseknecht, Suzanne Vaughan, and Anne S. Macke, "Marital Disruption among Professional Women: The Timing of Career and Family Events," *Social Problems*, February 1984, pp. 273–83.
20. Judith S. Wallerstein and Sandra Blakeslee, *Second Chances: Men, Women and Children a Decade after Divorce—Who Wins, Who Loses, and Why* (New York: Ticknor & Fields, 1989).
21. Ari L. Goldman, *The Search for God at Harvard* (New York: Times Books and Random House, 1991).
22. Blu Greenberg, "Zero Population Growth: Feminism and Jewish Survival," *Hadassah Magazine*, October, 1978, pp. 12–33, p. 29. Excerpted from *On Women and Judaism* (Philadelphia: Jewish Publication Society, 1979).
23. Bruce A. Phillips, *Los Angeles*, 1980, p. 9.
24. *Denver*, 1981, p. 44.
25. Phillips, *Los Angeles*, 1980, p. 44.
26. Gary A. Tobin et al., *Greater Washington*, 1984, p. 45.
27. Bruce A. Phillips and William S. Aron, *The Greater Phoenix Jewish Population Study* (Phoenix, 1983–1984), p. IV–7.
28. Gary A. Tobin, *A Demographic and Attitudinal Study of the Jewish Community of St. Louis* (St. Louis, 1982), p. 26.
29. Judith Lang, "Divorce and the Jewish Woman: A Family Agency Approach," *Journal of Jewish Communal Service* 54, no. 3 (1978), p. 12.
30. Thomas P. Ronan, "A Program for Men Facing the Traumas of Marriage's End," *The New York Times*, December 30, 1976; Andree Brooks, "When Older Men Divorce," *The New York Times*, October 12, 1984; Herme Shore, "Only for Men! Who've Been Hurt," *The Jewish Week–American Examiner*, June 17, 1979.
31. Jay Brodbar-Nemzer, "Divorce in the Jewish Community: The Impact of Jewish Commitment," *Journal of Jewish Communal Service*, 61 (winter 1984), pp. 150–59.
32. Rabbi Nahum Josephy, executive vice-president of the Rabbinical Alliance of America and secretary of its rabbinical court, quoted in Ben Gallob, "Divorce among Orthodox on Rise," *The Jewish Advocate*, July 17, 1975.
33. Wallerstein and Blakeslee, *Second Chances*.
34. Sheila Pelz Weinberg, "The Jewish Single-Parent Family," *Response* 14, no. 4 (spring 1985), pp. 77–84.

35. *Denver*, 1981, p. 31; Ira M. Sheskin, *Population Study of the Greater Miami Jewish Community* (Miami, 1981), p. 84; Bruce A. Phillips, *Milwaukee*, 1984, p. II–1.
36. Barbara S. Cain, "Plight of the Gray Divorcee," *The New York Times Magazine*, December 19, 1982; Sharon Johnson, "Expectations Higher; Many Long-Married Couples Are Divorcing," *The New York Times*.
37. *Ibid.*
38. Ritterband and Cohen, *New York*, 1981, p. II–9.
39. Phillips, *Milwaukee*, p. III–5.
40. Tobin, *St. Louis*, p. 44.
41. Barbara Meyerhoff, *Number Our Days* (New York: Simon and Schuster, 1978).
42. David Reisman, "Two Generations," *Daedalus* 92, no. 2 (spring 1964), pp. 711–35.
43. Charles Silberman, *A Certain People: American Jews and Their Lives Today* (New York: Summit Books, 1985), p. 123. See also Abraham D. Lavender, "Jewish College Women: Future Leaders of the Jewish Community," *The Journal of Ethnic Studies*, 52 (summer 1976).
44. Gary A. Tobin and Sylvia Barack Fishman, *Jewish Population Study of Greater Worcester*, 1987, pp. 70–71.
45. Marshall Sklare, *America's Jews* (New York: Random House, 1971), p. 88.
46. Population Research Committee, *Survey of Cleveland's Jewish Population*, 1981, p. 38.
47. Gabriel Berger and Lawrence Sternberg, *Jewish Child Care: A Challenge and an Opportunity*, Research Report No. 3 (Cohen Center for Modern Jewish Studies, Brandeis University, 1988), p. 21.
48. Ruth Pinkenson Feldman, *Child Care in Jewish Family Policy* (New York: American Jewish Committee, 1980).
49. Survey conducted by the Public Affairs Division of Market Facts, Inc., for B'nai B'rith Women, Inc., polled almost 1000 Jewish and non-Jewish women from across the U.S. Cited in "Jewish Women See Role Differently," *The Jewish Advocate*, Boston, June 20, 1985.
50. Lois Geer, *The Jewish Community of Greater Minneapolis 1981 Population Study*, Minneapolis, 1981.
51. See, for example, Aileen Cohen Nusbacher, "The Orthodox Jewish Professional Woman," M.A. thesis in the Department of Sociology, Brooklyn College, January 1977.
52. Dana Vannoy-Hiller and William W. Philliber, *Equal Partners: Successful Women in Marriage* (Newbury Park, London, and New Delhi: Sage Publications/Sage Library of Social Research 174, 1989), pp. 120–22.
53. Linda Gordon Kuzmack and George Salomon, *Working and Mothering: A Study of 97 Jewish Career Women with Three or More Children* (The National Jewish Family Center, The American Jewish Family Center, The American Jewish Committee, 1982). The research began with a questionnaire sent to 383 women selected from membership rosters of synagogues and Jewish community centers, lists of contributors to United Jewish Appeal and Federation, participants in Jewish education courses, and names suggested by early respondents to the questionnaire. Ninety-seven women completed the questionnaire, of whom thirty were later interviewed in depth.
54. Kuzmack and Salomon, *Working and Mothering*, p. 23.
55. See Rhea Karlin, "Challenges to the Jewish Family: A Jewish Single-Parent Family," American Jewish Committee Annual Meeting, November 1978; Weinberg, "The

Jewish Single Parent Family"; and Shirley Frank, "The Population Panic: Why Jewish Leaders Want Women to Be Fruitful and Multiply," *Lilith* 14 (winter/fall 1978), pp. 12–17.

56. Jane Berkey and Saul Weisberg, United Federation of Greater Pittsburgh, *Survey of Greater Pittsburgh's Jewish Population*, 1984, p. 27.
57. Andrew M. Greeley, "Further Commentary on the Michigan Cross-Generational Data," National Opinion Research Center for the Study of American Pluralism, October 31, 1973.
58. Marshall Sklare, *America's Jews* (New York: Random House, 1971), pp. 87–89.
59. United Federation of Greater Pittsburgh, p. 9.
60. See Anita Shreve, "Careers and the Lure of Motherhood," *The New York Times Magazine*, November 21, 1982; Arlene Rossen Cardozo, *Women at Home* (New York: Doubleday & Co., 1976), and *Sequencing* (New York: Macmillan Publishing Co., 1986); and Deborah Fallows, *A Mother's Work* (Boston: Hougton Mifflin, 1985).
61. Michael Graubart Levin, *Journey to Tradition: The Odyssey of a Born-Again Jew* (Hoboken, N.J., 1986).
62. Fredda M. Herz and Elliot J. Rosen, "Jewish Families," in McGoldrick, Pearce, and Giordano, eds., *Ethnicity and Family Therapy* (New York, 1982), p. 366.
63. Israel Rubin, *Satmar: An Island in the City* (Chicago, 1972).
64. Sheskin, *Greater Miami*, 1981, p. 91.
65. Berkey and Weisberg, *Pittsburgh*, 1984, p. 28.
66. *Denver*, 1981, p. 21.
67. Ritterband and Cohen, *New York*, 1981, p. II–9.
68. Sylvia Barack Fishman, "Challenge for Jewish Educators: Children of the Fragmented Family," *Ideas on Jewish Education* (June 1983), pp. 1–8.
69. See Gary A. Tobin and Ingrid Lomfors, "The Feminization of Poverty among Jews," unpublished manuscript, Center for Modern Jewish Studies; Lenore J. Weitzman, "The Economics of Divorce: Social and Economic Consequences of Property, Alimony and Child Support Awards," *UCLA Law Review*, no. 28 (November 1981); Ellen Max, "Divorce Is a Financial Disaster for Women and Children," *The Women's Advocate* (September 1982). Tobin and Lomfors write:

    > . . . the standard of living for women decreased by 73% during the first year after a divorce. At the same time, that standard of living for men increased by 42%. After divorce, the child support payments from the father are inadequate. Forty percent pay nothing and those who do pay average less than $2100 per year. Furthermore, in 1975 half the fathers who did pay support were contributing less than 10% of their income. In the cases where the child support payments were made, they decreased sharply after the first three years. (pp. 15–16)

70. "Single Parents Demand Services," *The Jewish Advocate*, May 3, 1984.
71. Saul Hofstein, "Perspectives on the Single Family," *Journal of Jewish Communal Service*, Spring 1978, p. 236.
72. Peter Y. Medding, Gary A. Tobin, Sylvia Barack Fishman, and Mordechai Rimor, "Jewish Identity in Conversionary and Mixed Marriages," *American Jewish Year Book 1992* (New York: American Jewish Committee and Jewish Publication Society, 1992) [chapter 12 in this volume].
73. Interpersonal relationships in intermarried households are explored in Paul and

Rachel Cowan, *Mixed Blessings: Marriage Between Jews and Christians* (New York, 1987) and in Susan Weidman Schneider, *Intermarriage: The Challenge of Living with Differences between Christians and Jews* (New York, 1989).

74. Sylvia Barack Fishman and Alice Goldstein, *When They Are Grown They Will Not Depart: Jewish Education and the Jewish Behavior of American Adults*, a joint publication of the Cohen Center for Modern Jewish Studies and the Jewish Educational Service of North America (Waltham, Mass.: Brandeis University CMJS Research Report, 1993).
75. Robert N. Bellah, "Competing Visions of the Role of Religion in American Society," in *Uncivil Religion: Interreligious Hostility in America*, eds. Robert N. Bellah and Frederick E. Greenspahn (New York, 1987), p. 228.
76. Medding et al., "Jewish Identity," p. 17.
77. Nathan Glazer, *New Perspectives in American Jewish Sociology* (New York: American Jewish Committee, 1987), p. 13.
78. Ritterband and Cohen, *New York*, 1981, p. II–2.
79. Phillips, *Los Angeles*, 1980, pp. 8–11.
80. *Denver*, 1981, pp. 16, 20, 43.
81. Frank Mott and Joyce Abma, "Contemporary Jewish Fertility: Does Religion Make a Difference?" *Contemporary Jewry*, Spring 1993.
82. U.S. Bureau of the Census, 1990. Current Population Reports, Series P-20 No. 436, *Marital Status and Living Arrangements: March 1989* (Washington, D.C.: U.S. Government Printing Office); and 1989, Current Population Reports, Series P-20 No. 436, *Fertility of Americans: June 1988* (Washington, D.C.: U.S. Government Printing Office); and 1988, Current Population Reports, Series P-20 No. 428, *Educational Attainment in the United States: March 1987 and 1986* (Washington, D.C.: U.S. Government Printing Office).
83. Uziel Schmelz and Sergio DellaPergola, Israeli demographers who study trends in the international Jewish population, estimate that married American Jewish women are having about 1.5 children; if unmarried Jewish women are included, they estimate 1.3 total fertility for American Jewish women over age 20 (U.O. Schmelz and Sergio DellaPergola, "The Demographic Consequences of U.S. Population Trends," *American Jewish Year Book, 1983* [New York and Philadelphia: American Jewish Committee and Jewish Publication Society of America, 1983], p. 154). They find marital fertility for the years 1970–76 to be 1.5 children per Jewish woman, with only a 1.3 total fertility rate for all Jewish women, regardless of marital status. However, it is very likely that Schmelz and DellaPergola's figures underestimate the completed fertility levels of American Jewish women, because they include women ages 20 and over. In contemporary American Jewish society, only tiny numbers of Jewish women marry before their mid-20s, except in right-of-center Orthodox circles. Thus, it may be valid to begin fertility estimates at age 20 among Jewish women in Israel or other more traditional societies, but among American Jewish women fertility statistics should probably begin with women not younger than age 24.
84. Calvin Goldscheider and Frances K. Goldscheider, "The Transition to Jewish Adulthood: Education, Marriage, and Fertility," paper for the 10th World Congress of Jewish Studies, Jerusalem, August 1989, pp. 17–20.
85. Calvin Goldscheider, *Jewish Continuity and Change: Emerging Patterns in America* (Bloomington: Indiana University Press, 1986), pp. 92–98.

86. Mott and Abma, "Contemporary Jewish Fertility."
87. Goldscheider and Goldscheider, "The Transition to Jewish Adulthood," pp. 17–20.
88. Susan Faludi, *Backlash: The Undeclared War against American Women* (New York: Crown Publishers, 1991), pp. 27–29.
89. Nadine Brozan, "Women Who Waited: Starting a Family after the Age of 30," *The New York Times*, September 23, 1977.
90. Phillips, *Milwaukee*, 1984, p. III–3.
91. Phillips, *Los Angeles*, 1980, p. 24.
92. Phillips and Aron, *Phoenix*, 1983–84, p. III–3.
93. Jay Brodbar-Nemzer, "Divorce in the Jewish Community: The Impact of Jewish Commitment," *Journal of Jewish Communal Service* 61 (winter 1984), pp. 89–98.

## References

*I. Jewish Population Studies*

Geer, Lois. *The Jewish Community of Greater Minneapolis 1981 Population Study*. Minneapolis, 1981.

———. *1981 Population Study of the St. Paul Jewish Community*. St. Paul, 1981.

Hedrix, Nancy. *A Demographic Study of the Jewish Community of Nashville and Middle Tennessee*. Nashville, 1982.

Phillips, Bruce A. *Los Angeles Jewish Community Survey Overview for Regional Planning*. Los Angeles, 1980.

———. *The Milwaukee Jewish Population Study*. Milwaukee, 1984.

Phillips, Bruce A., and William S. Aron. *The Greater Phoenix Jewish Population Study*. Phoenix, 1983–84.

Population Research Committee. *Survey of Cleveland's Jewish Population, 1981*. Cleveland, 1981.

Ritterband, Paul, and Steven M. Cohen. *The 191 Greater New York Jewish Population Survey*. New York, 1981.

Sheskin, Ira M. *Population Study of the Greater Miami Jewish Community*. Miami, 1981.

Shorr, Ann, Jewish Community Federation of Cleveland, and Anne Berkey and Saul Weisberg, United Federation of Greater Pittsburgh. *Survey of Greater Pittsburgh's Jewish Population*, 1984.

Tobin, Gary A. *A Demographic and Attitudinal Study of the Jewish Community of St. Louis*. St. Louis, 1982.

———. *Jewish Population Study of Greater Baltimore*. Baltimore, 1986.

Tobin, Gary A., Joseph Waksberg, and Janet Greenblatt. *A Demographic Study of the Jewish Community of Greater Washington*. Washington, D.C., 1984.

Tobin, Gary A., and Sylvia Barack Fishman. *Jewish Population Study of Greater Rochester*, 1987.

———. *Jewish Population Study of Greater Worcester*, 1987.

*II. Books and Articles Cited*

Ayres, B. Drummond, Jr. "For Jews Only: A Computer Dating Service. *The New York Times*, June 27, 1974.

Brodar-Nemzer, Jay. "Divorce in the Jewish Community: The Impact of Jewish Commitment." *Journal of Jewish Communal Service* 61 (winter 1984):150–59.

———. "Marital Relationships and Self-Esteem: How Jewish Families Are Different." *Journal of Marriage and the Family* 48 (February 1986): 89–98.

Brooks, Andree. When Older Men Divorce." *The New York Times*, October 12, 1984.

Brozan, Nadine. "Women Who Waited: Starting a Family after the Age of 30." *The New York Times*, September 23, 1977.

Cain, Barbara S. "Plight of the Gray Divorcee." *The New York Times Magazine,* December 19, 1982.

Cardozo, Arlene Rossen. *Women at Home*. New York: Doubleday & Co., 1976.

Elazar, Daniel J. *Community and Policy: The Organizational Dynamics of American Jewry*. Philadelphia: The Jewish Publication Society of America, 1976.

Fallows, Deborah. *A Mother's Work*. Boston: Houghton Mifflin, 1985.

Fishman, Sylvia Barack. "Challenge for Jewish Educators: Children of the Fragmented Family." *Ideas on Jewish Education*, June 1983, 1–8.

———. "The Changing American Jewish Family in the 80s." *Contemporary American Jewry*, fall 1988.

———. "Marginal No More: Jewish and Single in the 1980s." *Journal of Jewish Communal Service*, summer 1989.

———. "The Altered American Jewish Family." *USA Today*, Winter 1990.

———. *Jewish Households, Jewish Homes: Servicing Contemporary American Jewish Households*. Cohen Center for Modern Jewish Studies, Policy and Planning Paper 4 (Waltham, Mass.: Brandeis University, 1990).

———. "Into the Mouths of Babes: A Jewish Nursery School Education." *Trends in Jewish Education*, spring 1984.

Gallob, Ben. "Divorce among Orthodox on Rise." *The Jewish Advocate*, July 17, 1975.

Glazer, Nathan. *New Perspectives in American Jewish Sociology.* New York: American Jewish Committee, 1987.

Goldscheider, Calvin. *Jewish Continuity and Change: Emerging Patterns in America*. Bloomington: Indiana University Press, 1986.

Goldstein, Sidney. "Jewish Fertility in Contemporary America." In *Modern Jewish Fertility*, Paul Ritterband, ed., pp. 160–208. Leiden: E. J. Brill, 1981.

Greeley, Andrew M. "Further Commentary on the Michigan Cross-Generational Data." Chicago: National Opinion Research Center for the Study of American Pluralism, 1973.

Halberstam, Yitta. "Today's Shadchan: Popular and Expensive." *Jewish Week*, July 31, 1977.

Herz, Fredda M., and Elliott J. Rosen. "Jewish Families." In McGoldrick, Peace, and Giordano, eds. *Ethnicity and Family Therapy*, p. 366. New York: Guilford Press, 1982.

Holfstein, Saul. "Perspectives On the Jewish Single-Parent Family." *Journal of Jewish Communal Service*, spring 1978.

"Jewish Population Growth." *The William Petschek National Jewish Family Center Newsletter 4*, no. 1 winter 1984.

Jewish Telegraphic Agency. *Community News Reporter*, April 11, 1986. "Jewish Women See Role Differently." *The Jewish Advocate* (Boston), June 10, 1985.

Johnson, Sharon. "Expectations Higher: Many Long-Married Couples Are Divorcing." *The New York Times*, August 26, 1977.

Kosmin, Barry A., et al. *Highlights of the CJF 1990 National Jewish Population Survey.* New York, Council of Jewish Federations, 1991.

Kuper, Judith L. "2000 Singles enrolled in Dating Service." *The Jewish Post and Opinion*, July 17, 1976.

Kuzmack, Linda Gordon, and George Salomon. *Working and Mothering: A Study of 97 Jewish Career Women with Three or More Children.* New York: The National Jewish Family Center of the American Jewish Committee, 1980.

Lang, Judith. "Divorce and the Jewish Woman: a Family Agency Approach." *Journal of Jewish Communal Service* 54, no. 3 (1978).

Levin, Michael Graubart. *Journal to Tradition: The Odyssey of a Born-Again Jew*. Hoboken, N.J.: KTAV Publishing House, 1986.

Max, Ellen. "Divorce Is a Financial Disaster for Women and Children." *The Women's Advocate*, September 1982.

Mayer, Egon. *From Suburb to Shtetl: The Jews of Boro Park.* Philadelphia: Temple University Press, 1979.

Myerhoff, Barbara. *Number Our Days*. New York: Simon and Schuster, 1978.

Novak, William. "Are Good Jewish Men a Vanishing Breed?" *Moment* 5, no. 2 (Jan./Feb., 1980):1–20.

Nusbacher, Aileen Cohen. "The Orthodox Jewish Professional Woman." M.A. thesis, Brooklyn College, Department of Sociology January 197.

Reisman, David. "Two Generations." *Daedalus* 92, no. 2 (spring 1964): 711–35.

Ronan, Thomas P. A Program for Men Facing the Traumas of Marriage's End." *The New York Times*, December 30, 1976.

Rubin, Israel. *Satmar: An Island in the City*. Chicago: Quadrangle Books, 1972.

Schmelz, U. O., and S. DellaPergola. "The Demographic Consequences of U.S. Population Trends." *American Jewish Year Book* (1983):148–49.

Shore, Herme. "Only for Men! Who've Been Hurt." *The Jewish Week–American Examiner*, June 17, 1979.

Shreve, Anita. "Careers and the Lure of Motherhood." *The New York Times Magazine*, November 21, 1982.

"Single Parents Demand Services." *The Jewish Advocate*, May 3, 1984.

Sklare, Marshall. *America's Jews*. New York: Random House, 1971.

Tobin, Gary A., and Alvin Chenkin. "A Profile of the American Jewish Community: A Comparison of Selected Cities." *American Jewish Year Book* (1985): 154–78.

Tobin, Gary A., and Ingrid Lomfors. "the Feminization of Poverty among Jews." Unpublished manuscript, Center for Modern Jewish Studies, Brandeis University.

Weitzman, Lenore J. "The Economics of Divorce: Social and Economic Consequences of Property, Alimony and Child Support Awards." *UCLA Law Review* 28 (November 1981).

Wireman, Peggy. *Urban Neighborhoods, Networks, and Families: New Forms for Old Values*. Lexington, Mass.: Lexington Books, D.C. Heath and Co., 1984.

# Part III

## Cohesion and Conflict: Jews in American Society

In 1930, 68.3 percent of the Jewish population, compared to only 27.9 percent of the American population, lived in the northeastern region of the United States. This population included most of the 2.3 million Eastern European Jews who entered the United States during the Great Migration between 1880 and 1924 and settled in New York City. By 1971 the proportion of Jews in the Northeast had declined to 63.2 percent and in 1990 to 50.6 percent (Goldstein and Goldstein 1996, 38, table 2.2). The dispersion of the Jewish population across the country began in earnest with the move to the sunbelt cities of Florida and Los Angeles by World War II veterans (Moore 1994). In 1930 the South had only 7.6 percent of the American Jewish population and 30.7 percent of the population of the United States. By 1990 these numbers had changed to 19.3 percent and 34.4 percent, respectively. The Jewish population in the western part of the United States increased from 4.6 percent, in 1930, compared to 10 percent of the American population, to 18.8 percent and 21.2 percent, respectively.

In 1962, 46.5 percent of the national Jewish population lived in the New York–northern New Jersey–Long Island region. Today that region continues to have the largest Jewish population in the country, but their proportion has declined to 32.9 percent. Ten percent of the American Jewish population reside in the second most populous region, Los Angeles–Anaheim–Riverside in California. The Miami–Fort Lauderdale region is third with 6.5 percent (Kosmin and Scheckner 1995).

The significance of this dispersion is alluded to by Kosmin and Lachman (1993), who note that "it is only by having a critical mass in any one area that most small groups can maintain their viabilty over the generations. Unless there is geographical rootedness, the prospects for long-term survival of these small minority groups are dim" (67). The finding that intermarriage rates are significantly lower for Jews living within the New York City region than outside it (Horowitz and Solomon 1992) likewise supports the importance of population concentration for Jewish identity and continuity.

The effect of dispersion also becomes clearer when the Jewish identity of regional populations is examined. According to the 1990 National Jewish Population Survey (NJPS) (Kosmin et al. 1991), the Northeast continues to have the greatest proportion, 60.8 percent, of Jews who identify their Jewishness by religion. The West, on the other hand, has the greatest percentage, 20.8, of secular Jews, whereas only 10.6 percent live in the Northeast. The Midwest, which in 1900 had the second largest percentage of Jews, 23.7 percent, had only 11.2 percent in 1990. Among Jews in the Midwest, 43.9 percent identify by religion, 14.1 percent are secular Jews, and 4.8 percent have converted out. This latter figure is greater in the Midwest than in any other region of the country.

Except for the religiously observant Jew, the line of demarcation between Jew and non-Jew has become increasingly fuzzy and permeable. When asked in the 1990 NJPS whether being Jewish meant belonging to a cultural, religious, national, or ethnic group, the category receiving the overwhelming number of positive responses was "culture" (Kosmin et al. 1991, 28, table 13). Even Jews who identified as Jews by religion overwhelmingly answered yes to the cultural group identity. That the great majority of Jews identify being Jewish as belonging to a cultural group suggests that they continue to perceive a difference between Jewish culture and American culture. But of all the categories they could choose, culture is the broadest and therefore the hardest to define clearly and distinctly.

The different definitions of what being Jewish means is reflected in the 1990 NJPS. Eight separate population groups were identified as being part of the "American Jewish community," including Gentile adults living with the total Jewish population. They account for 16 percent of the total population in qualified households. A core Jewish population is defined as born Jews who identify their religion as Jewish, converts or Jews by choice, and persons who were born Jewish but currently have no religion, also called secular Jews. Secular Jews constituted 16 percent of the Jewishly identified population.

In their study of Jewish denominationalism, Lazerwitz et al. (1998) define secular Jews as Jews who have no denominational preference. This is significant in that they understand Jewish denominationalism as a structural characteristic that parallels other American religious groups. They note that "taking such 'Jewish stances' goes a long way toward expressing what the individual takes being Jewish to mean living in American society" (Lazerwitz et al. 1997, 127). To this extent, Jews who identify with a denomination are in conformity with the majority of the American population far more than secular Jews. In a 1989–90 survey of religion in America, 90 percent of Americans identified as religious, 2.3 percent refused to answer, and 7.5 percent answered "no religion" (Kosmin and Lachman 1993).

According to Klausner (1997) the characteristic of being born Jewish but having no religion, as is the situation for secular Jews, makes the person a candidate for conversion. He goes so far as to suggest that "a move away from steadfast Jewishness is associated with distancing from Jewish cultural settings (at home or in the school), a decrease in the salience of being Jewish and an adoption of a political attitude consistent with an opening of group boundaries followed by a more conservative one. All of these suggest that the candidates for conversion are those from the more open sectors of the Jewish community" (103).

Although individual variables are significant in and of themselves, it is perhaps, the composite measure of self-identity among Jews that best signifies the major change that has occurred in the American Jewish population. Jews typically regard being Jewish in multiple ways: Jewish as belonging to an ethnic, religious, national, and cultural group. And indeed, a compelling case can be made that Jewish identity consists of all of the above. Complicating this situation is the fact that in America personal identity, including one's religious faith, is regarded as chosen rather than ascribed. Whereas Americans regard ethnicity as an inherited identity, respondents to national polls overwhelmingly agree with the statement that "an individual should arrive at his or her own religious beliefs independent of any church or synagogue" (Hammond and Warner 1990, 60). Within the context of a pluralistic culture and a rising intermarriage rate for all religious and racial groups, this understanding of religion as a matter of personal choice makes it evident that the border that traditionally sheltered the Jewish population from erosion has become increasingly permeable.

Indeed, one of the more intriguing results of the 1990 NJPS is the self-reported change in what it means to be Jewish in America. Previously regarding themselves primarily as a religious or ethnic group, Jews now appear to define being Jewish as belonging to a cultural group. DellaPergola, the dean of demography, suggests that this change in identification is indicative of the "loosening" of the "primordial, exclusive, transmitted character of the Jewishness variable." In its place, culture, "a looser, subaltern concept . . . seems a residual category out of past, stronger Jewish identification" (1992:93).

In conjunction with the data on intermarriage and whether or not the children of these marriages are raised as Jews, the change in self-identity leads DellaPergola to conclude that the 1990 data, like the 1970 data, support the erosion model of the American Jewish community and not the revisionist or transformative model of change in the American Jewish population. Nevertheless, DellaPergola and others point to the persistence of a strongly identified Jewish core that is increasingly using the day school to ensure Jewish socialization for their children within multicultural America.

Originally, the nature and purpose of Jewish organizational structures was to mediate between the Jewish minority subculture and the majority Christian American culture, coordinate among Jewish communal and social structures, and respond to threats of anti-Semitism in America and abroad. Now, however, Jewish organizations must respond to demographic challenges like low fertility and high intermarriage rates, within the context of a denominational American structure that advocates pluralism, free choice, and voluntary affiliation and belonging. At the turn of the century, immigrants received assistance from Jewish communal organizations in their quest to Americanize, but today their primary goal must be to ensure a viable and vibrant Jewish religious identity in the American Jewish population and for recent immigrant groups, like those from the Soviet Union, who often come with little if any religious background.

In this part of the reader, Elazar traces the changing organizational structures of American Jews in terms of their varying functions. Chanes raises the interesting question of the relationship between what is traditionally defined as antisemitism and the perception of Jewish security. Continuing the discussion of the role of organizations within Jewish life, Bayme explores what the policy is and should be in response to the rising intermarriage rate among American Jews.

One of the clearest illustrations of the integration of Jews into American society is seen in the Jewish feminist movement, which began in the 1960s and 1970s when Jewish women were rebuffed by the international women's movement. At that time, Jewish members turned their analysis inward and began to examine critically the role of women in Jewish life. Since then, women's groups blossomed across the country in response to a need to share, experience, and discover the essence of a Jewish feminine spirituality. Reform and Conservative denominations of Judaism now ordain women as rabbis and train and hire women as cantors to lead Sabbath and Holiday services. In all denominations, women won the right to serve on previously all-male synagogue and temple boards. Religious schools of all the denominations, though not all groups within these denominations, teach Talmud to women. Women now author commentary and interpretation of traditional texts. However, leadership in Jewish social service and political organizations continues to be male-dominated even though women increasingly serve on the boards.

An important change, unconnected to either ritual or learning, is the increased presence of an *eruv* in observant Jewish communities. An *eruv* ritually encloses a community so that Orthodox Jews can carry on the Sabbath. This change is of special importance for women, who usually remain at home with the children, especially when nursing. The fact that it is rare to find an Orthodox community that does not have an *eruv* indicates the indirect though pervasive influence of the women's movement (Lipstadt 1995). Another important development, initiated by the feminist movement and generally accepted by all the denominations, though not by all segments within the denominations, has been the prenuptial agreement. Traditionally, it is the man who must grant the woman a divorce. The purpose of the prenuptial agreement is to provide a wife with additional legal recourse and thus prevent the man from refusing to give his wife a *get*, a Jewish divorce, which would prohibit her from remarrying.

In her essay, Sylvia Barack Fishman develops a conceptual framework to explain both the direction of change in different groups and the ideological source of conflict between groups. She organizes the transformations brought about by the feminist movement along a continuum of change, placing Halakhah, Jewish religious law, on the far right and the principle of egalitarianism on the far left. These principles provide both the goal and the guide to change.

Changes brought about by feminism for women closer to the "radical left" end of the change continuum, including Jews with minimal or no affiliation and affiliated Jews for whom Halakhah is not authoritative, include the acceptance and active participation of women in previously all-male domains, including the positions of rabbi and cantor and, ritually, participation in the minyan and acceptance of ritual honors such as *aliyah*, going up to the Torah. In addition, religious texts have been rewritten to eliminate the perceived gender bias, and ceremonies and prayers have been invented and composed to express specifically feminine experience of reality.

On the "radical right," which includes the most religiously observant Jewish communities, the authority of Halakhah governs all aspects of life and so provides the parameters for the actions of women (as well as for men). In these communities the study of traditional texts constitutes the highest expression of spirituality, and it is thus in the realm of study that the most significant changes have occurred. Because of their modesty, Orthodox women are traditionally more reticent to be publicly acknowledged. Change, however, is indicated in the acceptance by most Orthodox groups of the "bat mitzvah." Overall, Fishman finds that within the more Orthodox communities, as well as non-Orthodox communities that regard Halakhah as binding, the changing role of women has been associated with more intensive Jewish education for women, especially the study of Talmud.

## References

DellaPergola, Sergio. 1992. "New Data on Demography and Identification Among Jews in the U.S.: Trends, Inconsistencies, and Disagreements." *Contemporary Jewry* 12, pp. 67–97.

Goldstein, Sidney and Alice Goldstein. 1996. *Jews on the Move: Implications for Jewish Identity.* Albany: State University of New York Press.

Horowitz, Bethamie, and Jeffrey R. Solomon. 1992. "Why Is This City Different from Other Cities? New York and the 1990 National Jewish Population Survey." *Journal of Jewish Communal Service* 68, no. 4 (summer), pp. 312–20.

Klausner Samuel Z. 1997. "How to Think About Mass Religious Conversion: Toward an Explanation of the Conversion of American Jews to Christianity." *Contemporary Jewry* 18, pp. 79–129.

Kosmin, Barry A., Sidney Goldstein, Joseph Waksberg, Nava Lerer, Ariella Keysar, and Jeffrey Scheckner. 1991. *Highlights of the CJF 1990 National Jewish Population Survey.* New York: Council of Jewish Federations.

Kosmin, Barry A., and Seymour Lachman. 1993. *One Nation Under God: Religion in Contemporary American Society*. New York: Harmony Books.

Kosmin, Barry A., and Jeffrey Scheckner. 1995. "Jewish Population in the United States, 1994." In *American Jewish Year Book 1995*, edited by David Singer, pp. 181–206. New York: The American Jewish Committee.

Lazerwitz, Bernard J., Alan Winter, Arnold Dashefsky, and Ephraim Tabory. 1997. "A Study of Jewish Denominational Preferences: Summary Findings." In *American Jewish Year Book 1997*, edited by David Singer. New York: The American Jewish Committee.

Lazerwitz, Bernard J., Alan Winter, Arnold Dashefsky, and Ephraim Tabory. 1998. *Jewish Choices: American Jewish Denominationalism.* Albany: State University of New York Press.

Lipstadt, Deborah E. 1995. "The Impact of the Women's Movement on American Jewish Life: An Overview After Twenty Years." In Peter Y. Medding, ed., *Values, Interests and Identity: Jews and Politics in a Changing World, Studies in Contemporary Jewry, An Annual XI*, pp. 86–100. New York: Oxford University Press.

Moore, Deborah Dash. 1994. *To the Golden Cities: Pursuing the American Jewish Dream in Miami and L. A.* New York: The Free Press.

5 Daniel J. Elazar

# The Organization of the American Jewish Community

## Kinship and Consent: The Foundations of the Community

The Jewish community is a product of a unique blend of kinship and consent. The blend is already reflected in the biblical account of its origins: a family of tribes that becomes a nation by consenting to the Convenant. It continues to be reflected in subsequent biblical narratives. Postbiblical Jewish history gave the blend new meaning. The fact that Jews are born Jewish puts them in a special position to begin with, one that more often than not has forced them together for self-protection; yet sufficient opportunities for conversion, assimilation, or the adoption of a posture of simple apathy toward any active effort to maintain Jewish life have almost always been available as options. In the modern era, these options have expanded considerably in every respect. Today they stand at what is probably an all-time high, even though counterpressures have begun to reemerge.

Consequently, the maintenance of Jewish life can be understood as a matter of familial solidarity, but it must also be understood in the light of the active will of many Jews to function as a community. The "Jewish community" in the largest sense is defined as all those people born Jews or who have consciously and formally embraced Judaism though born outside the Jewish fold. Judaism itself is essentially a theopolitical phenomenon, a means of seeking salvation by constructing God's polity, the proverbial "city upon a hill," through which the convenantal community takes on meaning and fulfills its purpose in the divine scheme of things. While American civilization has influenced Jews to the extent that "being Jewish" is no longer an all-embracing way of life for most members of the Jewish community, nevertheless, the concept of and behavior involved in "being Jewish" remains far more broad-gauged in its scope and reach than the concepts of and behavior involved in "being Catholic" or "being Protestant." (Even the phrase, which is common enough in the language of modern Jewish discourse, is rarely found in Christian discourse. There are distinct ways in which different people are Catholic or Protestant, but they have to do with denominational and, more important, ethnocultural factors that shape the various Catholic and Protestant subcommunities. Traditional discussion of these matters in America have tended to ignore these distinctions and to assume that a certain universalism inheres in Catholicism or Protestantism that is undiluted by these more "mundane" factors and that is, ipso facto, absent from Judaism.)

In the end, while associational activity provides the motive thrust for the maintenance and continuation of Jewish life, the organic ties persist and tend to be strengthened when the survival of the community seems to be at stake. Jews, even very marginal ones, tend to have a "sixth sense" about threats to their security and survival as Jews. Since the Holocaust of World War II, when the Jewish people lost over one-third of their total number, this "sense" has been sharpened considerably.

Organizationally, American Jewry has made great strides in the twentieth century, and progress on that front seems to be continuing. Nevertheless, organizational matters must be treated in the context of the crisis of Jewish survival presently besetting the American Jewish community, whereby the gap between the intensive organizational life of the community and the lack of involvement of the majority of Jews within it seems to be growing to unmanageable proportions. The community's organizational successes may serve to obscure its failure to mobilize the great bulk of American Jewry. It should be borne in mind that the following discussion is presented with the knowledge that, while organization is vital and gives American Jewry much of its strength, organization alone cannot solve the problems of Jewish survival: assimilation, intermarriage, and negative population growth.

The American Jewish community is built on an associational base to a far greater extent than that of any other in Jewish history; that is to say, not only is there no unescapable compulsion, external or internal, to affiliate with organized Jewry, but there is no automatic way to become a member of the Jewish community. Nor is there even a clear way to affiliate with the community as a whole. All connections with organized Jewish life in America are based on voluntary association with some particular organization or institution, whether in the form of a synagogue membership, contribution to the local Jewish community federation—United Jewish Appeal (which is generally considered to be an act of joining as well as contributing)—or affiliation with a B'nai B'rith Lodge or Hadassah (the women's Zionist organization) chapter.

Indeed, the usual for affiliated Jews—like that of their fellow Americans—is one of multiple association, with memberships in different kinds of organizations reinforcing one another and creating a network of Jewish ties that binds the individual who chooses to become enmeshed in them more firmly to the community.

## The Federal Element in Jewish Organization

Since its emergence as an "organization" over three thousand years ago, the Jewish community has been organized on federal principles and has enhanced its survival power by applying them almost instinctively in changing situations. The very term *federal* is derived from the Latin *foedus*, meaning covenant. The utilization or application of federal principles, first applied in the federation of the twelve tribes, has undergone numerous permutations in the long course of Jewish history, but today, in an era of a-traditionalism, it is one tradition that is not being abandoned by Jews.

The congregation is the cornerstone of this federal structure, the first institution to be established when a sufficient number of Jews has gathered in one place to create an organized community (historically ten men, but in the United States today often counting women as well). The terms *congregation* and *community* are essentially synonymous in Hebrew. Jews have come together to form congregations wherever they have found themselves by formally consenting to articles of agreement or association that bind them together as a community in the manner defined by Jewish law and custom and/or recognized by the governing authorities.

Only in modern times did *congregation* and *synagogue* tend to become synonymous. While in the past every congregation included provisions for worship (a "synagogue"), it was not likely to begin and end with that function. On the contrary, since Jews do not need the institutional arrangements of a synagogue to pray, the organization of a congregation was more likely to come about when there was a need to structure the incipient community's social welfare or educational tasks through establishment of a cemetery or of institutionalized mechanisms for aiding the poor or for inauguration of a school. The traditional congregation was a very flexible device that could accommodate all those services and more, usually through a system of *hevrot* (fellowships) or committees, drawn from the congregational body as a whole.

As a community expanded, its organization necessarily became more complex, leading, particularly in modern times, to the founding of other congregations or organizations within the same locality. Ultimately, they would develop links with one another to create a more elaborate community structure. Under the impact of Emancipation (in Europe), Protestantism (both there and in the United States), and the sheer increase in Jewish population (in both places), this process was accelerated, leading to the emergence of the modern synagogue as essentially a place of worship though with ancillary functions to perform. Individual synagogues came to embody specific religious-ideological trends in Judaism (Reform, Orthodox, Conservative, etc.). Many of the functions formerly housed within congregations when they were entirely in the hands of volunteers were now "spun off," restructured in more elaborate ways, professionalized, and given separate organizational bases of their own within the overall community.

Thus, as the decision to be involved in Jewish life became increasingly voluntary for individuals the new voluntarism extended itself into the internal life of the Jewish community as well, generating pluralism, even within previously free but relatively homogeneous and monolithic community structures. This pluralism was increased by the breakdown of the traditional reasons for being Jewish and the rise of new and different incentives for Jewish association. It demanded new federal arrangements to achieve a degree of unity within a community, larger and far more diverse than any that Jews had confronted in their long history.

The pluralistic federalism that had emerged in the contemporary Jewish community substantially eliminates the neat patterns of communal organization that were frequently to be found in other times, the kinds that are easily presented on organization charts. Certainly, the model of a hierarchical organizational structure does not offer an accurate picture of the distribution of powers and responsibilities in the Jewish community today. There is no organizational pyramid in Jewish life. National organizations are unable to issue directives to local affiliates, and no local "roof" organization is able to order others within its "jurisdiction" into line.

The structure of the contemporary Jewish community is best understood as a mosaic, a multidimensional matrix that takes the form of a communications network, a set of interacting institutions that, which preserving their own structural integrity and filling their own functional roles, are informed by shared patterns of culture, activated by a shared system of organization, and governed by shared leadership cadres. The character of the matrix and its communications network varies from community to community. In some cases, the network is connected through a common center that serves as the major (but rarely, if ever, the exclusive) channel for communication. In others, the network forms a matrix without any real center, with the lines of communication crisscrossing in all directions.

The pattern itself is inevitably a dynamic one. Since the community is a voluntary one, persuasion rather than compulsion, influence rather than power, are the only tools available for making and executing policies. This, too, works to strengthen its character as a communications network since the character, quality, and relevance of what is communicated and the way in which it is communicated frequently determine the extent of the authority and influence of the parties to the communication.

## Four Orders of Organization

Institutions and organizations playing at least four kind of roles are to be found in every fully functioning and completely organized Jewish community, as follows:

1. Government-like institutions, whether roof organizations or separate institutions serving discrete functions, that play roles and provide services on all planes (countrywide, local, and where used, intermediate) that,

under other conditions, would be played, provided, or controlled predominantly or exclusively by governmental authorities (for instance, external relations, defense, education, social welfare, and public—that is, communal—finance).

2. Localistic institutions and organizations that provide a means for attaching people to Jewish life on the basis of their most immediate and personal interests and needs.
3. General-purpose, mass-membership-based organizations, operating on all planes, that function to *(a)* articulate community values, attitudes, and policies; *(b)* provide the energy and motive force for crystallizing the communal consensus that grows out of those values, attitudes, and policies; and *(c)* maintain institutional channels of communication between the community's leaders and "actives" ("cosmopolitans") and the broad base of the affiliated Jewish population ("locals") for dealing with the problems and tasks facing the community in the light of the consensus.
4. Special-purpose organizations that, by serving specialized interests in the community on all planes, function to mobilize concern and support for the various programs conducted by the community and to apply pressure for their expansion, modification, and improvement. The first two of these types are essentially embodied in the institutions that form the structural foundations of the community and the last two essentially in organizations that function to activate the institutional structure and give it life.

Institutions of the first type are easily identifiable in most communities. They include the Jewish community federations and those institutions and organizations dedicated to serving community-wide needs that are associated with them. In a typical local community they will also include a Jewish community center, a central agency for Jewish education, a Jewish community relations council, various social welfare institutions to deal with problems ranging from adoption to aging, a Jewish hospital (until recently, when changing health needs and unhindered Jewish access have rendered them redundant), a welfare fund, and various cultural societies claiming community-wide appeal.

The most important localistic institutions are the synagogue, which, by their very nature, are geared to be relatively intimate associations of compatible people. Even the very large American synagogues that have lost any sense of intimacy remain localistic institutions in this sense, within the overall community context. (Indeed, the contradictions between the size and function may lie at the root of the problem of the contemporary American synagogue.) The most important localistic organizations other than synagogues are lodges, *landsmanshaften* (associations of immigrants from the same town in the "old country"), and occasional secular societies that function as synagogue surrogates for those who actively proclaim their nonbelief. By and large, the latter are declining at present, leaving the field to synagogues and *havurot*.

In the United States, B'nai B'rith and Hadassah, with lodges or chapters in virtually every organized Jewish community from Maine to Alaska, come closest to performing the functions of organizations in the third category. They are supplemented by a number of small countrywide organizations, such as the American Jewish Committee, American Jewish Congress, National Council for Jewish Women and the various Zionist groups (of which Hadassah is formally one).

While the special interest organizations are best identified on a local basis, there are some common patterns countrywide. Certainly, the various groupings of synagogues, with their men's clubs, sisterhoods, and youth groups, and the Anti-Defamation league represent the major examples in this category. In addition, local groups serving such diverse interests as support of Jewish institutions of higher learning, Jewish-sponsored hospitals and medical centers, vocational training programs for Jews in other countries, and a variety of Jewish cultural institutions, abound.

It is conceivable that in the smaller Jewish communities the four kinds of roles may be compressed with fewer institutions and be filled incompletely as a consequence. In any case, the functions themselves must be institutionalized somehow in order for an organized community actually to exist.

American Jewry organizes itself to be active in five spheres:

1. The religious-congregational sphere
2. The educational-cultural sphere
3. The community relations–defense sphere
4. The communal-welfare sphere
5. The Israel-overseas sphere

Table 5.1 schematically summarizes the spheres and the organizations within each.

### *Religious-Congregational Sphere*

The religious-congregational sphere is that most closely resembling the American religious sphere as a whole. It consists primarily of synagogues and synagogue movements, the latter essentially countrywide confederations of like-minded congregations. Jewish religion as we know it is congregational in its foundations. Any group of Jews who desire to may organize themselves into a congregation, choose a rabbi to their liking, and maintain a range of Jewish activities centered on religious worship but far from confined to that. This freedom to organize into congregations exists even where there are more firmly established Jewish frameworks beyond the congregational.

This congregational system, which was borrowed by Christianity two thousand years ago and made the organizational core of American Protestantism, not only

TABLE 5.1

Spheres, Institutions, and Organizations

| | Institutions and Organizations | | |
|---|---|---|---|
| | *Local* | *Countrywide*[a] | *Worldwide* |
| Religious-congregational | Synagogues<br>Rabbinical associations<br>Boards of rabbis<br>Rabbinical courts<br>*Kashruth* councils<br>Orthodox enclaves | Synagogue confederations and the men's, women's, and youth affiliates<br>Seminaries and yeshivas<br>Rabbinical associations | Israeli rabbinate<br>Israeli Knesset<br>International synagogue confederations<br>Joint Distribution Committee (JDC) |
| Educational-cultural | Synagogues<br>Communal, secularist, and day schools<br>Colleges of Jewish studies<br>Central agencies of Jewish education<br>Jewish studies programs in universities<br>Local cultural institutions and groups<br>Jewish community centers<br>Jewish federations | Coalition for the Advancement of Jewish Education (CAJE)<br>National Center for Learning and Leadership (CLAL)<br>Jewish Educational Services of North American (JESNA)<br>National Foundation for Jewish Culture-Joint Cultural Appeal<br>Torah Umesorah<br>Jewish Welfare Board<br>B'nai B'rith Hillel Foundations<br>Jewish colleges and universities<br>Scholarly associations<br>Educators' associations<br>Jewish cultural institutions and organizations<br>Jewish foundations | Jewish Agency and subsidiaries<br>Memorial Foundation for Jewish Culture<br>Joint Distribution Committee (JDC)<br>Jerusalem Center for Public Affairs |

TABLE 5.1
Spheres, Institutions, and Organizations (*continued*)

| | *Institutions and Organizations* | | |
|---|---|---|---|
| | *Local* | *Countrywide*[a] | *Worldwide* |
| Community relations | Jewish community relations councils<br>Local chapters or offices of American Jewish Committee, Anti-Defamation League, American Jewish Congress, Jewish War Veterans, Jewish Labor Committee | Jewish Council for Public Affairs (JCPA)<br>Presidents' Conference<br>Council of Jewish Federations (CIF)<br>American Jewish Committee<br>Anti-Defamation League<br>American Jewish Congress | World Jewish Congress<br>Israeli government<br>International Jewish Committee for Interreligious Consultation (IJCIC)<br>Simon Weisenthal Center |
| | Jewish federations | Jewish Labor Committee<br>Jewish War Veterans<br>Professional associations<br>Special-purpose groups (e.g., for Soviet Jewry) | |
| Communal welfare | Jewish federations<br>Social service agencies<br>Jewish Community Centers<br>Local Jewish press<br>Hospital health care | CIF<br>Jewish Community Centers Association (JCCA)<br>B'nai B'rith<br>American Jewish Committee<br>United Hebrew Immigration Aid Center (HIAS) Service<br>National Association of Jewish Family and Children Services | Israeli government<br>Jewish Agency for Israel (JAFI)<br>International professional/ functional associations<br>Joint Distribution Committee (JDL)<br>Jerusalem Center for Public Affairs |

TABLE 5.1
Spheres, Institutions, and Organizations (*continued*)

| | *Institutions and Organizations* | | |
|---|---|---|---|
| | *Local* | *Countrywide*[a] | *Worldwide* |
| Israel-overseas | Jewish federations | Presidents' Conference | Israeli government |
| | Local Zionist chapters | CIF | Jewish Agency |
| | Local Zionist offices | United Jewish Appeal (UJA) | Jewish National Fund |
| | Local "friends" chapters | Zionist organizations | Organization for Rehabilitation and Training (ORT) |
| | | Israel bonds organization | Claims Conference |
| | | United HIAS Service | World Jewish Conference |
| | | "Friends of Israel" or overseas institutions | Conference of World Jewish Organizations (COJO) |
| | | American-Israel Public Affairs Committee (AIPAC) | JDC |
| | | JCCA | Otzar HaTorah |
| | | B'nai B'rith | Jewish Center for Public Affairs |
| | | American Jewish Committee | World synagogue bodies |

For the most complete available listing of countrywide institutions and organizations, local Jewish federations, and the Jewish press, see the annual directories in the *American Jewish Year Book*.

has been ideal for the American environment, where it fits in with the "free market" of American religious expression, but has offered Jews an unsurpassed way to fit into that environment. Hence, from the first it became the nuclear form of Jewish life in America. Indeed, between 1654 and 1795, American Jewry consisted of congregational communities; that is to say, each city in which there was a sufficient number of Jews for self-organization organized one congregation that served all Jews in the area and provided all services—religious, ritual, educational, and welfare—that Jews sought to provide for themselves. It was not until 1795 in Philadelphia that a second congregation was established in the same city, and that was not repeated elsewhere until a second congregation was organized in New York some thirty years later.

Today all but the smallest Jewish communities normally have two or more congregations, and the larger communities have many, reflecting not only the different branches of Judaism but the nuances within each and the different worship styles that different groups of Jews choose for themselves. Still, for most Jews, the congregation still remains the nucleus of Jewish religious and communal life.

The vast majority of American Jews who affiliate with synagogues are either Reform or Conservative. The two movements are approximately equal in size, and each represents about 40 percent of the affiliated. The major Reform synagogue association is the Union of American Hebrew Congregations, and the major Conservative association is the United Synagogue of Conservative Judaism. Approximately 10 percent are Othodox, whose congregations are either in the Union of Orthodox Jewish Congregations, in Young Israel, or associated with one or another of the ultra-Orthodox groups that include followers of the Lithuanian yeshivot (academies for Torah study) or one or another of the Hassidic movements, of which there are perhaps half a dozen that "count." Much smaller are the Reconstructionist movement, the Union for Traditional Judaism, and various "New Age" fellowships. With the exception of the various ultra-Orthodox movements, which have significant power lodged in their national (indeed, in some cases internal) leadership, in all of the other movements the real repository of authority and power remains in the individual congregations; the national movements are merely confederations of their respective affiliated congregations.

### *The Educational-Cultural Sphere*

Because of its character as a text-based religion, one must study the sacred texts, including the Bible, the Talmud, the great codes, and the religious commentators on all of the above to be considered a truly educated Jew capable of fulfilling the religious commandments properly. The task of doing so is compounded by the fact that these texts should be studied in their original form, and the originals are written in Hebrew and Aramaic. Hence, Jewish education takes up a large proportion of the involvement time of Jews relative to other religions. Traditionally, textual study is considered as important as prayer, if not more so. After a period in which the drive for Americanization reduced the amount of textual study that Jews undertook to the barest minimum, it is once again becoming fashionable for committed Jews of all stripes to engage in such study, whether in Hebrew and Aramaic or in English translation. Indeed, one of the achievements of American Jewry in recent decades has been the translation of much of the vast corpus of a textual tradition that goes back over three thousand years.

Jewish education in the United States has three principal components: *(a)* basic education for the young, *(b)* academic education, and *(c)* continuing education.

1. Education for children and teenagers is mostly carried out through supplementary schools conducted in each congregation, meeting on Sundays and one or two weekdays after the hours of public school. Jewish day schools that provide both general and Jewish studies have been growing in importance. They now enroll some 25 percent of students receiving a basic Jewish education, most in six- to eight-year elementary frameworks and some in high schools. The major Jewish religious movements maintain day schools, and the Jewish community as a whole maintains some community day schools as well. Orthodox Jews have the highest percentage of their membership enrolled in day schools, all of which emphasize textual study in the original. The Reform movement has the lowest percentage of its members enrolled in day schools since it has only recently begun to advocate day school education as a means of providing a more enriched Jewish education than is possible in the supplementary schools.
2. Since the late 1960s, courses in Judaic studies at general colleges and universities have become a major vehicle for the Jewish education of young adult Jews. These courses can be taken while Jewish students are enrolled in programs designed to give them a general education and to prepare them for their careers and are taught on an academic level. Most Jewish students enrolled in these courses take only one or two survey courses or courses on such contemporary topics as the Holocaust or women in Judaism and rarely acquire much Jewish textual knowledge. A smaller number pursue majors in Jewish studies at the undergraduate level or prepare for careers in Jewish life at the graduate level and sustain more elaborated programs in Judaic studies, which do bring them into contact with a wider segment of the corpus of Jewish civilization.

   In addition, there are some colleges and universities under Jewish auspices that offer more substantial programs, usually based on a knowledge of Hebrew. These are mostly communal and nondenominational in orientation. For the ultra-Orthodox and those attracted to that way of life there are higher yeshivot that serve as academies for Torah learning. Students in these programs often become the leaders and standard-bearers in the Jewish community as a whole and in its several religious subcommunities.

3. Adult continuing education is less formal than either of the first two and includes many home and synagogue study groups and courses that meet weekly to provide Jewish learning in a somewhat social setting. For most American Jews, it is in these settings that contact with the core of the tradition is facilitated. While many of the groups are also devoted to text and language study, they have become the setting where most of the intellectual trends that affect contemporary Jewry reach their best audiences.

There are also Jewish cultural institutions and activities ranging from local Jewish theater in Jewish community centers to major publication programs and serious cultural expressions of all kinds. Most of the latter serve a limited audience within the community and are rarely seen as religious in orientation. Needless to say, these normally reflect the current myths, interests, and learnings of the community or "challenge" them by carrying them even further than their contemporary community consensus.

Capping all of the above are the serious academic and rabbinical study programs of a handful of major institutions, mostly under Jewish sponsorship. These institutions have programs that have produced world-class scholars in every field of Jewish study and have given American Jewry a firm place in Jewish intellectual history. Paralleling them in a certain way in the cultural sphere are the various "gurus" who, coming from a religious background, endeavor to teach a spiritual Judaism and Jewish culture to interested Jews of all stripes. These people, especially the more profound thinkers among them, have developed a distinctive American Jewish thought to accompany the increasingly distinctive American Judaism.

### *The Community Relations–Defense Sphere*

The organizations in this sphere are those most engaged in American public life on behalf of the Jewish community. The long Jewish experience with anti-Semitism and Jewish fears that serious anti-Semitism might develop in the United States led the Jews to develop a number of Jewish community relations organizations beginning at the turn of the century, when American (indeed Western) racism was at its height. Among them are the American Jewish Committee, the Anti-Defamation League, the American Jewish Congress, the Jewish Labor Committee, the Jewish War Veterans, local Jewish community councils, and the umbrella organization that to a greater or lesser degree involves them all, the Jewish Council for Public Affairs.

These organizations cover the ideological spectrum of the Jewish communal consensus, which means that all are ideal-oriented. Over the years they have moved from competition with one another to specialization in various community relations tasks based on their strengths and constituencies. These bodies are all secular in character although they may include religious organizations and individuals in their membership. Indeed, it is reasonable to assume that almost all of those active in such organizations are also synagogue members, although their synagogue membership has no direct connection with their community relations activity.

Most of the time these are the organizations called upon to represent the Jewish community in the American public square on issues of religious significance, often in relation to the representatives of Catholicism, Protestantism, and other religious communities who are directly connected with their respective churches or church movements. For many years the majority of these organizations were staffed by the most secular Jews active in the Jewish community, whose basic liberal commitments led them into community relations work, especially as community relations and defense were defined to mean Jewish organizational cooperation with other groups, religious and secular, of goodwill in the struggle against discrimination and racism in its various forms. This could have been an embarrassment to the Jewish community, and indeed was often presented as such within the community by the community's religious representatives, except for the fact that Judaism is so all-encompassing that the same ethical and moral positions expressed in the most socially conscious synagogues were expressed and even featured by these community relations organizations. One need only look at the joint action program issued by the Jewish Council for Public Affairs every other year to represent the consensus of views in these organizations as the community consensus on matters of community relations, defense against anti-Semitism, and social policy. Recently, as the secular left has disappeared as a force, more and more of those involved in the professional leadership of these groups are drawn from the more religiously committed, even Orthodox, Jewish population. Still, even our latest surveys show that the leadership of these groups remains further away from Jewish religious concerns or observance than any of the religious movements.

### *The Communal-Welfare Sphere*

In the days when there was no more than one congregation per city, all communal and welfare matters were handled within the congregational framework. Those days are long gone, but the traditional Jewish concern for providing support for those within their community who need it and for functioning collectively as a community remains strong. As local Jewish communities grew larger in the United States, they first developed separate charitable societies for various tasks and then, at the time of the Civil War, began to federate those functional associations into bodies that bore names like United Jewish Charities or United Hebrew Benevolent Association or some equivalent.

After 1880 and the beginning of the mass immigration of Jews from Eastern Europe, those relatively simple charitable unions needed to be supplemented by more massive efforts to assist the immigrants in their resettlement and integration into the United States and to provide for the other concerns of the Jewish community, such as recreation, culture, and education. In response, Jewish communities throughout the country organized what are today the Jewish community federations. In the last one hundred years, what began as federations of charities have evolved into the closest thing that the Jewish community has to a framing institution or common address. As such they have federated all the major service agencies, schools, and community centers of the local community—in short, organizations in all of the other spheres except the religious-congregational.

The individual synagogues have remained outside of formal linkage with the local federations for historic reasons. They regard themselves as religious institutions, and the federations began by regarding themselves as civic or secular institutions designed to handle functions outside of the purview of the synagogues. That distinction is an artificial one; from the very first the federation leadership often included the same people who played significant roles in their congregations wearing different hats. Over the past twenty years, closer connections have developed between federations and synagogues in community after community, with the federations subsidizing educational activities provided by synagogues on an ever-broader basis. The two sets of institutions are developing especially close ties around the issue of "Jewish continuity."

Countrywide, the local federations are confederated through the Council of Jewish Federations, an umbrella organization headquartered in New York City. Each of the major constituent agencies of the federations has its own national league or confederation.

### *The Israel-Overseas Sphere*

The federations began their work of relief and rescue of Jews outside the United States in the days of World War I. At that time the various organizations dealing with rescue, relief, and rehabilitation in the United States organized themselves into the American Jewish Joint Distribution Committee (JDC). The federations were involved in that effort at least indirectly from the first. After World War I, the JDC continued its work with federation support. At the end of the 1930s, federations forced the integration of JDC with fund-raising for rebuilding Jewish life in what was then Palestine, conducted by what is now the United Israel Appeal (UIA). The two organizations came together and formed the United Jewish Appeal, the main fund-raising arm of the Jewish community for Israel and overseas activity.

The federations actually raise the money locally for transmission to the UJA, where it is divided between JDC, UIA, and United HIAS, the countrywide body for absorbing Jewish immigrants into the United States. Today this structure is undergoing reorganization that will bring about a "back room" merger of CJF and UJA; that is to say, a unification of their housekeeping functions. There are promises to be some measure of reorganization of UIA and JDC as yet undetermined.

While UJA is seen as the major fund-raiser for Israel and overseas activities, the truth is that by the 1990s at least an equal amount of money was being raised by other organizations independent of it. They included Zionist organizations such as Hadassah, the women's Zionist organization, a major provider of support for health care and other services in Israel. The other Zionist organizations comprise a myriad of "Friends" associations, whose primary purpose is to raise money for one institution or another in Israel, ranging from the various Israeli universities to shelters for battered women, severely disabled children, and the Israeli equivalent of the USO. In recent years the JDC has been joined by important Jewish foundations to provide support and activities for rebuilding Jewish life in the former Communist bloc.

In addition to these five spheres a major new set of actors on the American Jewish scene are the Jewish foundations, both great and small, including such major foundations as those endowed by people like Bronfman, Mandell, Milken, and Wexner but also including medium-sized and smaller ones, many of which are managed by the federation endowment funds attached to all the major federations. These foundations, which are not formally part of the organized Jewish community but rather are the private initiatives of their founders and funders, play an increasingly important role in the community and its activities, especially since their founders are themselves leaders in the community and have strong views as to how their money should be used.

What is important to note in all of this is that "religion" or religious institutions cannot be segregated from the entire communal corpus. The so-called secular organizations and institutions of the community not only speak out on religious matters for the community but view themselves as operating within the spirit, if not the letter, of Judaism in its religious sense. Moreover, while the explicitly religious institutions have, from time to time, tried to challenge this situation, inevitably they have failed. One of the reasons that this is so is that the religious groups are seriously divided ideologically and organizationally, while the Jews as a whole want to maintain their collective unity, at least to the outer world, and it is easier to do so through the present arrangements.

## The Development of Jewish Organization in America

The United States, with close to six million Jews (over half of all the Jews in the diaspora and nearly half of all the Jews in the world today) stands in a category (as well as a class) by itself. The combination of a very large, fully modern society built from the first on individualistic principles, pluralistic in the full sense of the word, and settled by several significantly different waves of very adventurous Jewish immigrants who shared one common commitment, that of seeking new lives as individuals, was not conducive to the development of sufficient homogeneity to permit the emergence of a neat communal structure. Consequently, every effort to create even so much as a single nationwide "address" for American Jewry has failed.

Nor is this situation without precedent. No Jewish community approaching the size of the American Jewish community has ever succeeded in building a neat structure for itself, complete with roof organization and all the other accoutrements. The vaunted *kehillot* (organized Jewish communities) of other times and climes were all developed for much small communities. Since Roman times, probably none exceeded a few hundred thousand population, and most were far smaller than that. The urban regions with the largest Jewish populations in the United States, those centered around New York, Los Angeles, Philadelphia, Chicago, Boston, and Miami, are themselves larger than all but a handful of countrywide communities that have existed over the long history of the Jewish people.

The roots of the present system lie in the response of the Jews already established in the United States at the time of the mass immigration, roughly between 1880 and 1920, to the needs of the new immigrants as they perceived them, as modified by the organizational demands generated by the latter for and by themselves. Their response led to the founding of organizations of all four types: welfare federations, defense agencies, congregational roof organizations, and seminaries in the first category; Orthodox, Conservative, and Reform synagogues, *landsmanshaften*, and fraternal organizations in the second; organizations such as B'nai B'rith (actually expanded from its earlier form), the American Jewish Congress, and the Zionist groups in the third; and a welter of "national" and local groups in the fourth. The defense organizations were the first to organize in the countrywide arena. In the late nineteenth century, B'nai B'rith took responsibility for fighting anit-Semitism at home and abroad, but it remained a secondary task. At the turn of the century its role was challenged by the notables of the century; in 1906 they organized the American Jewish Committee, whose thrust was toward quiet diplomacy. Seeking a more militant approach in the wake of the Leo Franke case, B'nai B'rith organized the Anti-Defamation league as a separate organization under its aegis in 1913. Five years later an American Jewish Congress was convened with the intention of capturing the community for the Zionist movement and its supporters. Although it failed, it gave birth to a continuing organization of the same name.

Finally, beginning in Boston in 1891, Jewish welfare federations were established, linking local health, welfare, and educational agencies, principally for federated fund-raising to reducing the number of separate campaigns. By World War II every major Jewish community had such a federation. At the same time, the connections between these multifarious organizations and groups were minimal, if not competitive, or simply nonexistent. No real communications network existed on either the countrywide or local plane.

World War I brought the first real steps toward the creation of such a network in the countrywide arena. The unification of overseas welfare activities under the newly formed Joint Distribution Committee was the first successful effort to link old-line (i.e., "German"), Orthodox, and secularist elements into a common framework. The war also produced abortive attempts to create Jewish unity on a mass basis countrywide through the 1918 American Jewish Congress. In the aftermath of its failure new efforts were generated on the local plane to link the diverse elements in the community for at least limited welfare and defense purposes. During the 1920s the welfare federations and community councils, the institutions that best embodied these efforts, took root locally and began to coalesce on a countrywide basis. The Council of Jewish Federations was founded in 1932 as the Council of Jewish Federations and Welfare Funds and instituted an annual General Assembly, today the most important gathering of American Jewry.

The demands placed on the American Jewish community in the 1930s led to a growing recognition of the need to reconstitute the community's organizational structure at least to the extent of rationalizing the major interinstitutional relationships and generally tightening the matrix.

In 1938, in response to Kristallnacht, the United Jewish Appeal was established, uniting Zionist, JDC, and fund-raising efforts for local needs through the annual UJA campaign, conducted by the local welfare federations. In 1942 the American Jewish community united around the idea of establishing a Jewish state in Palestine. In 1944 the Council of Jewish Federations and Welfare Funds initiated the MacIver Report, which, while not implemented per se, led to a greater rationalization of functions among the defense organizations. Locally, the 1930s brought the establishment of local Jewish community councils, leagues of local congregations and organizations that claimed to speak in the name of the community in matters of Jewish concern.

These efforts at reconstitution received added impetus from the changes in American society as a whole (and the Jews' place in it after 1945). They signaled the abandonment of earlier chimerical efforts to create a more conventional organizational pyramid in imitation of foreign patterns, which would have been quite out of place, given the character of American society as a whole.

## Trends in Jewish Organization after World War II

The aftermath of World War II brought with it new conditions. American Jewry had become the foremost Jewish community in the world, ten times larger than its nearest functioning counterpart.

Within it was located the bulk of the wealth that world Jewry could mobilize to undertake the tremendous tasks of relief and reconstruction confronting it as a result of the Nazi Holocaust, tasks that were to be increasingly concentrated in the foundation of the new State of Israel as the initial demands of postwar relief were satisfied.

At the same time, American Jewry confronted a new situation at home, in which the barriers against full participation in American society rapidly fell away, to be replaced by what Will Herberg was to call the "triple melting pot," or the recognition of Judaism and Catholicism along with Protestantism as "legitimate" American faiths. Finally, the opening of the metropolitan frontier, with the resultant suburbanization of America, saw the Jews in the vanguard of the movement to the suburbs or, at the very least, out of the old neighborhoods to suburban-like areas within the central cities, requiring institutional adaptations to new lifestyles.

All these factors influenced the course of Jewish organizational development between the end of the war and the mid-1960s. In the first place, the community federation movement began to frame or, at last, properly link the government-like functions undertaken by the Jewish community. The major impetus behind this gain was its emergence as the dominant fund-raisers in the Jewish community.

Pioneering in "single drive" fund-raising in the style of the United Fund, the federations became the powerhouses behind an unprecedented voluntary effort. The exciting tasks of raising funds for postwar relief and the rebuilding of Israel, which captured the imaginations of American Jews and raised the bulk of the money from them, stimulated a phenomenal increase in the amount of money contributed for all Jewish communal purposes. The impetus provided by Israel redounded to the benefit of domestic Jewish needs as well, since the larger sums forthcoming from the coordinated drives were so allocated as to increase their resources too.

The federations did not (and for the most part still do not) subsidize synagogues or those functions that had come under the synagogues' wing. By common agreement, congregations were left to raise their own funds and did so with remarkable success. Nevertheless, though large amounts of money were raised for the construction and maintenance of synagogues in the same period, synagogue fund-raising had neither the excitement nor the demands for continuity that abetted the annual federation drives. Their great efforts were necessarily one-shot affairs, and their annual needs remained relatively limited and seemingly parochial as well.

The substantive quality and the recurring nature of the federations' tasks served to strengthen their hands in other ways. They attracted leadership, both voluntary and professional, of the highest caliber available to the Jewish community. In time that leadership, at least partly because of the nature of the tasks that confronted it, began to see Jewish communal problems as connected with one another. Federation leaders began to concern themselves with the broad range of Jewish needs, not simply with overseas relief or with the welfare functions that had been traditional to the federations in the pre–World War II period.

By 1960, most of the major Jewish federations were engaged in community planning of some sort; were supporting Jewish educational and cultural programs as well as welfare, defense, and overseas services; and were beginning to think of themselves as the central bodies for Jewish communal endeavor within their respective areas of jurisdiction. Increasingly after 1960, federations began to define the range of their interests as embracing virtually the total Jewish community, excluding only the synagogues themselves. At the same time, on the countrywide plane, the Council of Jewish Federations and Welfare Funds began to strengthen its position, often providing the impetus for local federations to become involved in one area or another that had previously been defined as outside their purview. Alongside it, the UJA became the most visible of all Jewish organizations, attracting the really big money of American Jewry for overseas relief and rescue and building Israel.

During this period, there was also a sorting out of roles among the previous existing countrywide organizations, many of which had previously aspired to the central role being assumed by the federation movement. Thus, the Zionist organizations declined precipitously in size and influence after 1948. The American Jewish Congress, the American Jewish Committee, and the Anti-Defamation League concentrated on their community relations functions. B'nai B'rith began to edge away from the tasks of actually providing government-like services to redefine itself as, purely and simply, a mass-based social and educational organization. It was, in effect, to influence the federations and the public affairs agenda of the American Jewish community.

The one set of organizations willing to challenge the federation movement were the three synagogue movements—in their congregations as discreet movements and in combination through the Synagogue Council of America. The decade of the 1950s was a particularly propitious time for them to assert themselves. The apparent redefinition of Jewishness as an exclusively religious phenomenon obviously strengthened the hands of those who claimed to be the spokesmen for Judaism as a religion.

The synagogues' position was enhanced by the impact of the metropolitan frontier. The Jews who settled in the great cities during the heyday of the urban frontier had settled in neighborhoods where their organic links were as strong as, if not stronger than, their associational ones. This was as true of the more assimilated Central European Jews "uptown" as of the Eastern European immigrants in the great ghettos. Whether one formally joined a synagogue or not, in those neighborhoods a Jew was surrounded by family and friends, businesses and institutions, all operating within an essentially or substantially Jewish milieu. The move to the suburbs broke up the old neighborhoods and, with each successive move outward from them, lessened the proximity of Jews to one another and weakened the extent to which the immediate environment was "Jewish." Under such conditions, Jews had to seek more formal associational ties simply to keep those relationships alive. The local synagogue offered the easiest and most acceptable (in the American context) means of making the transition.

The resurgent synagogues capitalized on their position by reaching out to embrace functions not inherently "cosmopolitan." They became the primary custodians of Jewish education, establishing synagogue schools on their premises as means of attracting additional members, adapting those schools to the new conditions of suburbia, and creating an ideology to justify the new trends they initiated, virtually eliminating the private and communal Hebrew schools of the previous era. They became the primary organizers of the youth, either on a congregation basis or through their national organizations, virtually replacing both the Zionist organizations and B'nai B'rith. They began to undertake recreational and social service functions that had been the province of the Jewish community centers and the local Jewish welfare agencies. In order to play their expanded role, synagogues had to become larger institutions, often with memberships of over one thousand families. Indeed, synagogues with fewer than five hundred families came to be considered less than viable.

While this was occurring on the local plane, the national synagogue bodies—Orthodox, Conservative and Reform—were also laying claim to a special importance in American Jewish life that transcended their earlier efforts to foster congregations of their respective "persuasions" in a rough competition for the unaffiliated, challenging all other national bodies in the process. Though their challenge was only marginally successful, it did represent a continuing area of contention within American Jewish life.

The struggle between the federations, with their constituent agencies, on the one hand, and the national synagogue bodies, with their constituent congregations, on the other was a classic manifestation of the cosmopolitan-local dichotomy. The former, dominated by the cosmopolitans of the Jewish community, had their eyes focused on typical cosmopolitan interests ranging from those of the local community as a whole to those of world Jewry as a whole. The focus of the latter was equally and typically localistic, whether in reference to immediate congregations or to the interests of the separate branches (a term used here to describe the denominations that are not as full or final as those separating the Protestant denominations) in their competition with one another and with the extra-synagogue elements in the overall community.

## The Bases of American Jewish Organization Today

By the 1960s, then, the American Jewish community had developed certain organizational patterns that were more or less replicated in over eight hundred communities—framed within over two hundred community federations—and countrywide as well. The patterns were all derived from the associational basis of American Jewish life described above.

While certain of its organizations have succeeded in developing from the top down, the basic institutions of the American Jewish community are essentially local and, at most, are loosely confederated with one another for very limited purposes. The three great synagogue movements are excellent cases in point. All three are essentially confederations of very independent local congregations linked by relatively vague persuasional ties and a need for certain technical services such as professional placement, the organization of intercongregational youth programs and the development of educational materials. The confederations function to provide the requisite emotional reinforcement of those ties and the desired services for their member units. They have almost no direct influence on crucial congregational policies and behavior, except insofar as the congregations themselves choose to look to them as guides because, short of expulsion from the movement, they have no devices to exercise any authority they might claim.

The other great countrywide institutions of American Jewry are similarly organized. The Council of Jewish Federations (CJF) is an equally loose confederation of the 235 local Jewish federations that have emerged as the most powerful institutional forces in organized Jewish life. The role of the CJF (it shortened its name in 1979 to better reflect the changed purposes of its constituent community federations) is definitely tributary to that of its constituents, who do not hesitate to give it direction, an informal league of the largest federations, known colloquially as the "big nineteen." The power of the CJF flows from its ability to provide services to the local affiliates and manage the flow of professionals. So, too, the National Jewish Welfare Board (JWB) is the service agency of the clearly autonomous local Jewish community; the American Association for Jewish Education, since reorganized as the Jewish Education Service of North America (JESNA), the service agency of the local bureaus of Jewish education; and the National Jewish Community Relations Advisory Committee (NCRAC), the service agency for the local Jewish community relations councils.

With the exception of a few institutions of higher education (and once upon a time a few specialized hospitals, now nonsectarian), all Jewish social, welfare, and educational institutions are local in name and in fact. Those that claim national status and have no local or movement base soon find themselves without a constituency. In the postwar years, these organizations declined, and their roles were transferred to the federations and their constituent agencies.

On the other side of the ledger, the Conference of Presidents of Major Jewish Organizations was founded in 1955 as a vehicle for coordinating American Jewish lobbying on behalf of Israel. It was not until after the Six-Day War (1967) that it came into its own as the principal channel for Israeli government communication of its views to the American Jewish leadership. Today it has more than fifty members (itself a telling statement about American Jewish community organization) and is the American Jewish community's principal spokesman for Israel-related external affairs.

American Jewish unity on a federative level is very different from unity on a hierarchical one. What emerges in front of the viewer's eye is not a single pyramidal structure, not even one in which the "bottom" rules the "top," as in the cases of the Jewish communities with representative boards in other parts of the world, but a three-dimensional matrix consisting of a bundle of institutions and organizations tied together by a crisscross of membership, shared purposes, and common interests, whose roles and powers vary according to situation and issue.

## The End of the First Postwar Generation

The trends of the postwar period reached their culmination in the early 1960s. The ostensible religious revival came to an end; membership in synagogues, as in the churches, stabilized and then, by the late 1960s, began to decline, with new challenges emerging to threaten the established organizations. By the end of the 1960s the trends toward sorting out the various elements in the organizational structure of the Jewish community and harmonizing them within a common communications network had taken another step forward, partly through the decline of one segment of the structure and partly through the redefinition of the other.

A series of external events robbed the synagogues of much of the basis of their claim to primacy. First, the changed American attitude toward organized religion and the use of "ethnicity" to replace it made the Jewish champion of organized religion—namely, the synagogue—far more vulnerable to outside criticism, especially from the ranks of youth. Second, the emergence of a disaffected segment of the youth population, which drew disproportionately from Jewish ranks, led to direct challenges to the synagogue as an instrument of the "establishment." Finally, the Six-Day War, in June 1967, made it clear for all Jews to see that it was not simply a common concern with religious affiliation that bound Jews together so much as it was a sense of a common fate as a people, symbolized and reaffirmed by the Israeli-Arab crisis.

By the mid-1970s, the synagogues had passed through their period of crisis, membership had stabilized, and synagogues began to resume their role in the community. They did so within the framework established by the local federations, but they had the great advantage of being the only institutions in the community that regularly assembled significant numbers of Jews who had not otherwise chosen to commit themselves to Jewish activity. In other words, the federations may have had the money, but the synagogues had the "troops." Together the two sets of institutions emerged as the twin pillars of American Jewish life, increasingly in alliance, albeit at times an uneasy alliance.

After 1960 the federations developed a deepening concern for Jewish education and culture and wider interest in community planning. All of this tended to strengthen the hands of the federations as the framing institutions of Jewish communal life. At the same time, the federations became more mindful of traditional Jewish practices. They began to embrace the public observance of Jewish religious practices in their own programs and to encourage traditional and observant Jews to involve themselves in their ranks, thereby building bridges into those segments of the Jewish community that had previously been outside their normal purview. The decade culminated with the federations taking the most effective action toward developing a means to reach out to the disaffected Jewish youth.

The federation movement reached its peak between 1970 and 1985. During that period it was like the proverbial "500-pound canary" that could rest itself wherever it chose. After the mid-1980s, however, the federation movement began to lose power and authority. A combination of trends ranging from the growth of privatism in American life, which led people away from organization activity and commitments, to the greater desire for "hands-on" giving, where the donors could choose the objects of their support directly and follow them personally; the general decline of federation giving in the United States, which can be seen as the unraveling of the achievements of the Progressive era at the beginning of the twentieth century, of which the Jewish community federations were a major part; and new divisions in the Jewish community with regard to Israel and religious matters. All combined to weaken the ability of the federations to draw in their former share of the voluntary funds raised in the community and, to a lesser extent, to exercise the power that flowed from those funds. By the mid-1990s the federations, while still powerful as framing institutions, especially locally, faced more competition outside the local arena and perceived themselves to be embattled.

At the same time, new organizational and functional patterns emerged in response to the dissatisfactions. Those young Jews who sought an authentic religious experience were searching for new ways to organize their religious life. The development of *havurot* (fellowships) and the increase in the number of small congregations devoted primarily to worship and fellowship were features of Jewish religious organization and innovation in those years.

In most respects, those innovations represent a return to traditional standards though in new format. Thus, the pioneers of this reaction to the forms of American Judaism were traditionally minded Jewish academics and scientists, who in the late 1950s and early 1960s began to create their own synagogues, which were both Orthodox and traditional; that is to say, while committed to the meticulous observance of Jewish law, they also involved a revival of the style of congregational organization common before the day of the large synagogue. That organization emphasized small membership composed of families highly committed to one another and seeking a great deal of interpersonal interaction aside from that built around the worship experience proper.

By the late 1960s this pattern was taken up with considerably more fanfare by Jewish academics and intellectuals from Conservative and to some extent Reform backgrounds, primarily through *havurot* and "underground" seminaries. In their peak period they infused a certain dynamism into religious life that has carried over beyond the confines of their fellowships and seminaries, although by the mid-1970s their movement had lost its momentum. By that time the *havurah* system had become routinized in a number of different ways, but it had its own network and its "market share," which was neither increasing nor declining.

Organization for defense took on new forms in the post–World War II era. In most Jewish communities, local action against anti-Semitism was replaced as the major defense function by efforts to assist Jews in subjugated communities overseas and, overwhelmingly, by assistance to Israel. In effect, American Jewry, understanding that the threat of local anti-Semitism had substantially diminished, saw its primary defense task as the maintenance of Israel, not only as a place of Jewish refuge or a haven for Jewish refugees but also as the symbol of the new and improved Jewish status in the world.

As is usual with the defense function in any community, that took the highest priority in Jewish organizational life, with the support of Israel standing above everything else in the hierarchy of organizational goals. After 1967 this trend was reaffirmed and the priority assigned to it raised even higher, if possible. In the 1980s, however, it was openly challenged by those opposing Israeli government policies. For most of the community, however, dissatisfaction or doubts about Israeli government policies have not led to challenges so much as disaffections; that is to say, the vast majority of American Jewry remained sympathetic and concerned about Israel, but the Jewish state occupies a lesser place in their lives, even in the constellation that defines their Jewishness. The two Jewish concentrations have been growing apart as each becomes more preoccupied with its internal problems than with interrelationships.

Defense of the State of Israel will continue to dominate the concerns of American Jewry in the foreseeable future whenever Israel is perceived as threatened. Indeed, the feelings of isolation generated in the period immediately preceding the Six-Day War and subsequently, as a result of Israel's apparent lack of allies other than World Jewry, heightened American Jewry's sense of solidarity with Israel and even its sense of "apartness" from non-Jews, thereby reversing the whole trend of the 1950s and 1960s, which had led to a well-nigh universal belief that those differences had lessened.

Organization for external relations has always been tied in very closely with the defense function. In fact, at one time the two were essentially inseparable, with the fight against anti-Semitism at the center of both. The trend after World War II was to lessen the intensity of the fight against anti-Semitism, primarily because overt anti-Semitism had declined as a result of the world's reaction to the Holocaust. Defense on that front became a matter of fighting social discrimination, seeking rapprochement with the churches, and resisting atavistic elements rather than waging a full-fledged battle. Jewish concern with external relations in the United States then turned toward general participation in the struggle for the extension of human rights, with the organized Jewish community in the forefront of the civil rights movement. Symbolizing this change was the shift to referring to the erstwhile defense agencies as community relations agencies. The beginning of that period had witnessed some degree of rationalization of the organizational structure for external relations; its end witnessed a serious, if limited, assault on the very existence of such organizations by those who felt that they were no longer needed. This situation was turned around in the late 1970s as new challenges on the American and world scenes and organizational adaptation to the new situation combined to reawaken interest in the national community relations organizations.

The Six-Day War brought an abrupt end to that era of relative calm. Jewish human relations professionals found that they still had to do battle for Jews. In the aftermath of the war, anti-Semitism again became somewhat respectable, particularly as the New Left began attacking organized Jewry under the rubric of "anti-Zionism," thereby encouraging the reemergence of right-wing anti-Semites, who had previously remained quiet for fear of public rejection. Moreover, the more militant blacks rejected Jewish assistance in their own struggle and, indeed, identified with anti-Jewish elements in the Israel-Arab conflict. Jewish external relations once again came to revolve around the defense of more straightforward Jewish interests, leading up to a strengthening of Jewish organizational capabilities in that direction.

In other aspects of external relations, new organizations emerged to claim a role. After a period of jockeying for position with regard to expressing American Jewry's interests in Israel and other international problems, the President's Conference emerged as the body uniting all the major Jewish organizations in a common front expressly for external relations purposes.

While this was happening, there also emerged for the first time in many years, if not ever, a group of Jewish neoconservatives, who dissented from the established liberal views of the overwhelming majority of American Jews. While these neoconservatives often reached their positions on the basis of their Jewish understandings, they also reflected changes in the larger American community. By the mid-1990s the majority of Jews remained liberals and had become outliers on the American scene as a whole, similar to blacks but not to any other major American groups. Indeed, it could be said that as American Jews acculturated and then began to assimilate into American society, it was in their liberalism that they were most distinguished from other Americans.

The trends in educational organization were more problematic, since education involves and exposes all the ambivalences of contemporary Jewish life—the desire for survival in conflict with the desire for full integration into the general society or, perhaps more accurately, into the new worldwide cosmopolitan culture that is so attractive to the American Jewish middle and upper classes, particularly the students and intellectuals among them. On the one hand, the trend in Jewish education between the end of World War II and the mid-1960s involved an increase in enrollment in Jewish schools, with a concomitant decline in the number of hours of instruction and the breadth of the curriculum. This trend was stimulated by the transfer of Jewish education to the synagogue, which made the teaching of "synagogue skills" and loyalties primary, to the exclusion of more substantive materials.

Enrollment in Jewish schools peaked around 1962 and has been declining since, though it may now have stabilized once again. The continued diffusion of the Jewish population into outer suburbia and the increased demands of the public schools on their students have made supplementary Jewish schooling more difficult, thereby encouraging further reductions in hours and content.

On the other hand, the drive for intensive Jewish education among a minority of Jews had taken the form of the development of a substantial day school movement, a sharp departure from the thrust of American Jewish interests during the modern epoch, when Jews tried desperately to break down all barriers that might keep them out of general schools and were even willing to sacrifice the Jewish education of their children on behalf of integration. No group in the United States has been more fervent in its support of the public schools than the Jews, who perceived that free, nonsectarian public education was the ultimate fulfillment of the Jews' emancipationist and integrationist dreams. Today, however, one quarter of all Jewish students attend all-day schools, and every Jewish community of several thousand population has at least one such school within its precincts. Moreover, the Jewish federations, which for years avoided extending any assistance to such schools, have now made them significant beneficiaries, if not constituent agencies in many cases.

The day school movement was clearly strengthened by the fact that many Jews were caught in changing neighborhoods, where the public schools deteriorated before they were ready to move. Faced with the problems that this presented, they determined to send their children to private schools, whereupon they chose Jewish private schools over others as a matter of preference.

The 1960s and 1970s also witnessed the development of programs of Jewish studies in secular institutions of higher learning. Originally masked under titles like Near Eastern Studies or Semitic Languages and Literatures, these programs were pushed into the limelight at the end of the decade as a result of the blacks' struggle for programs of their own. As blacks began to demand Black Studies programs in the universities, young Jews countered by demanding more extensive Jewish studies programs under that explicit label, with no masks. Whatever the format, this has led to an increase in the number of college-age Jews exposed to Jewish education, often for the first time in a systematic way, and it also created a market for scholars of Judaica, American-born and -trained. A generation later, no American university that aspires to be up-to-date is without some form of Jewish studies, with major programs at the major universities adding a whole new dimension to Jewish education opportunities throughout the country.

Overall, the trend in Jewish educational organization seems to be toward the enhancement of day schools and Jewish studies programs, with an additional element added to the latter. Whereas the 1960s saw a rejection of independent programs in higher Jewish education, conducted under Jewish auspices, the 1970s and 1980s saw a return to such programs, alongside of or in conjunction with programs in the secular universities, as Jews seek to sharpen their sense of independent identity.

Through the 1970s the welfare state became more deeply rooted and expanded. Functions formerly performed by private or public nongovernmental agencies became beneficiaries of government support at ever higher levels. Functions performed by the Jewish community were no exception. Jewish welfare organizations were increasingly financed from non-Jewish (usually governmental) sources and, by the same token, were increasingly providing their services on a nonsectarian basis. Indeed, Jewish hospitals, once developed to provide Jewish doctors with places to practice medicine when other hospitals would not have them, now represent a major Jewish contribution to the service of the inner city in many communities. Specifically Jewish welfare services took on two forms: (1) increasing attention to the treatment of middle-class ailments, primarily psychiatric ones, and (2) the provision of services to the aged and to people left behind in changing neighborhoods, who for one reason or another are unable to leave.

This pattern was partially reversed by the Reagan-Bush cutbacks in the 1980s and the "devolution revolution" of the 1990s. As the federal government cut back its social welfare expenditures, not only the states but also the public nongovernmental agencies had to pick up an ever larger share of the costs. This pressed hard on Jewish institutions, especially as federation contributions stabilized or decreased, causing an increase in the share of funds raised locally that were kept locally rather than being transmitted for Israel or overseas needs. The transformation in health services to health maintenance organizations also led many Jewish communities to sell their hospitals to the HMOs and remove themselves from the hospital management business.

The enforcement of community norms has undergone great changes in the Jewish community. The enforcement of traditional Jewish law, which was always voluntaristic to some extent, has now become entirely so, and the organized Jewish community is not really actively engaged in that today. Between 1967 and 1987 new norms developed that subtly enforced the community's organizational network. They revolved around support for Israel and "giving," that is to say, assuming one's share of the financial obligations of the community. Israel became the primary norm of an increasingly secularized Jewish community, with virtually all Jewish organizations sharing in the task of enforcing those norms that relate to it and that, in a sense, took the place of the old halakhic or God-centered norms, even in many of the synagogues. At times these new norms approached "Israelolatry." Then in the 1980s there was an abrupt reversal of this trend. In its place, "spirituality" began to assume an ever more important role in Jewish communal life. As a religious phenomenon, this was distinctively nonhalakhic, emphasizing as it did personal fulfillment through individual experience rather than through collective norms. Nevertheless, because of its religious character, there was a turn toward reconsideration and even refamiliarization with halakhah and mitzvot, more as suggestions than as requirements, many of which were seen as adding to personal self-fulfillment and hence endorsed on that basis.

Since some common norm seems to be necessary for the maintenance of a voluntaristic community, it is expected that norm enforcement will continue to be a task in Jewish organizational life. After three hundred years of secularization and assimilation, there is strong evidence that a revived concern with Jewish tradition is leading to its acceptance as another norm. While different groups within Jewry will be entitled to define Jewish tradition in various ways, identification with that tradition and acceptance of the responsibility for maintaining, fostering, and extending it seems to be reemerging as a central norm in Jewish life, one that is embraced by all Jewish organizations and enforced by them. This also is reflected in the rise of Orthodoxy to the fore in organized Jewish life and in a wider segment with Orthodox expressions of Jewish tradition among the Jewish leadership.

The least change is to be expected in the realm of Jewish public finance. Jews must rely on voluntary giving to maintain their organizational structure and activities. In recent years all major Jewish organizations have made increased demands on the members of their community to meet expanded needs at home and abroad. There is no reason to believe that these demands will not continue at a very high level. The question has been raised as to whether Jewish response to those demands is diminishing. There was a sharp acceleration in giving as a result of the 1967 crisis and its aftermath. A new and higher "floor" was established, and that has been maintained even under less tense circumstances. Nevertheless, federated giving has not grown substantively to keep pace with inflational dollar devaluation. In that sense, campaigns are essentially flat or declining. At the same time, new channels of Jewish giving have developed, much of it more hands-on in nature.

The thrust of the modern epoch, beginning in the mid-seventeenth century and accelerating thereafter, was to fragment world Jewry. The tight communal organization of the Middle Ages was the first to give way. It was followed by the abandonment of life according to Jewish law on the part of a growing number of Jews (a majority by the twentieth century). In the past two generations even traditional ties to the community were abandoned by a majority of Jews as they sought full integration as individuals into the larger society, leading to what seemed to be the ultimate fragmentation of world Jewry. In all of this, American Jewry was in the vanguard. Traditional communal organization never existed in America because it never had any legal support. Life according to Jewish law was never the style of the majority, nor was life according to Jewish tradition. Pursuit of individual goals was always far more possible in the New World than anywhere else.

Then, in the twentieth century, when fragmentation had reached new heights, a movement to reintegrate around new vehicles and norms began to gain momentum. The Holocaust opened the door to a reconsideration of the need for Jewish unity and, together with the sheer passage of time, contributed to the postmodern breakdown of the rigid ideologies that divided Jews in the last third of the modern epoch (mid-nineteenth to mid-twentieth centuries). Finally, and most important, the creation of the State of Israel gave Jews a new and compelling focus that continues to enhance the interest of many in being Jewish. Israel's crucial role as a generator of Jewish ties, regardless of other differences, was effectively demonstrated at the time of the Six-Day and Yom Kippur wars.

Accompanying this rediscovery of community among Jews has been a reintegration of the organizational components of the Jewish community, leading to the emergence of a more clear-cut structure and communications network linking them. More important, there has been an increase in the commitment of organizations of different kinds to the essential wholeness of the Jewish way of life. The rediscovery itself is clearly rooted in the acceptance of a new pluralism in Jewish life, one that is reflected in the organizational structure of the Jewish community. Pluralism, organized in a more or less permanent structural arrangement, leads to federalism, and federalism has been the traditional way that Jews have maintained their organizational structures in the face of the various internal and external pressures they have confronted. As we have seen, contemporary Jews are no exception.

Given a new growth in the will to be Jewish among a significant segment of American Jews, the Jewish community of the 1970s and 1980s pursued this reintegration, extending it to include the reintegration of American Jewry with world Jewry as its central organizational thrust. Organizationally, the American Jewish community may well have discovered a pattern for itself that can meet the challenges that confront it. Organizational advances, however, will not solve the problem of the individual who must decide whether to be or not to be seriously Jewish. All institutions can do is to facilitate that decision in its positive aspects. And it is clear that the decision itself remains in doubt for most of American Jewry.

# Antisemitism and Jewish Security in Contemporary America

## Why Can't Jews Take Yes for an Answer?

Nothing endures like change.
—Heraclitus

The times they are a-changin'.
—Dylan

As we approach the new millennium, antisemitism continues to confound and puzzle American Jews. There is a profound paradox—"the riddle of the defensive Jew" in the words of Jewish communal leader Earl Raab—that plays itself out within the American Jewish community when it comes to the question of antisemitism.[1] On the one hand, Jews, when questioned in surveys, consistently aver that they feel "comfortable" in America. Yet some eight of ten American Jews believe that antisemitism is a "serious" problem in the United States. In 1985, in the San Francisco Bay Area, approximately one-third of those questioned[2] said that Jewish candidates could not be elected to Congress from San Francisco, citing anti-Jewish bias or prejudice. Yet three of the four congressional representatives from that area, as well as the two state senators and the mayor of San Francisco, were, in fact, well-identified Jews *at the time the poll was conducted.* (The population of San Francisco was approximately 97 percent non-Jewish, mirroring the national average.)

The question most Jews, indeed many Americans, are really asking, in parody of that sentimental old song, is "Will you hate me in 2000 as you did in 1930?" Consider some appalling events and developments during the 1990s: the Crown Heights (Brooklyn) riots in which blacks attacked Jews in August 1991, the candidacies of former Klan leader David Duke, the outrages of journalist and sometime political candidate Patrick J. Buchanan, the continuing swirl of activity surrounding the Nation of Islam's virulent Minister Louis Farrakhan, former President George Bush's 12 September 1991 press conference in which he characterized Jewish grass-roots advocacy as "powerful political forces" (was that antisemitism, asked many Jews), City College of New York professor Leonard Jeffries's contention that Jews were behind the slave trade, continued suggestions of Holocaust "revisionism"—the denial of the reality and extent of the destruction of European Jewry. All these have given American Jews heartburn and worse and raise serious questions, particularly with respect to evaluating data on antisemitism and interpreting those data in terms of threats to Jewish security. Clearly, these and other developments indicate that certain taboos long thought to inhere in the society may be at risk.[3] At the same time, American Jews ask how are we to parse data that assert that antisemitism across the board is in fact on the decline?

Further, these developments and questions must be viewed through the lens of deep communal angst, of a specter that haunts the American Jewish community—that of a community whose organizations are shrinking, whose agencies are weakened, whose funding is collapsing, whose agendas are increasingly irrelevant—all of this precisely at a time when the creative continuity of the community is being called into question.

These observations, the data from behavioral manifestations, and statistics from polls and surveys pose a fundamental question: How do the data on antisemitism and our corresponding view of antisemitism affect the larger picture of *Jewish security* in America?

Interpretation of data on antisemitism is often a Rashomon-like exercise. Perception and interpretation have as much to do with psychological dynamics as with the technical stuff of the sociologists. While I do not want to enter here into "shrink-time," I will nonetheless return to some of the social-psychological dynamics involved in the perception of antisemitism,[4] notwithstanding what the data show.

A number of specific questions guide the analysis. First, what do we know? What are the current available data on antisemitism in the United States? What is really happening out there, and just as important, what is *not* happening?

Second, why did antisemitism in fact *not* take firm root in the United States, whatever manifestations—some very serious—there may have been? What is the historical context for the relative dearth of antisemitism in America?

Third, how do we explain perceptions within the Jewish community of an antisemitism ascendant, even as data along a broad range of evaluative criteria tell us that antisemitism in America has declined and probably continues to decline? Jewish perceptions of antisemitism: In 1983, in a survey conducted among American Jews by the American Jewish Committee, approximately one-half of the respondents disagreed with the statement "Antisemitism is currently not a serious problem for American Jews." By 1988 the proportion had risen to 76 percent. And 1990 National Jewish Population Survey numbers show 83 percent of American Jews either are "strongly" or "somewhat" agreeing that antisemitism is a serious problem in the United States. How can nine of ten Jewish Americans say they "feel at home in America," in a country they think is rife with antisemitism?[5] What accounts for the perception among most Jewish people that antisemitism is a serious problem in America and that the status and security of Jews is at risk?

If things are so good out there, why do so many Jews think that things are so bad?

Fourth, and related to the last question, when Jews say that antisemitism is a serious problem, what do they mean? What are they talking about?

Fifth, antisemitism emanating from the black community has clearly become a major source of Jewish concern. What do we know—and what do we *not* know—about antisemitism in the African American community?

Sixth, what ought we be doing about antisemitism? What are the most efficacious means of counteracting antisemitism, and which means are "feel-good" activities but may be a waste of communal time, energy, and dollars?

Seventh, what areas of study and research are indicated in areas of antisemitism about which we know very little?

Finally, what happens in a society such as that of the United States, in which antisemitism in its various forms continues to wither away and the fear of a different threat to Jewish security—assimilation—is widespread?

This article addresses these and other questions and, in so doing, explores the question of the level of security enjoyed by Jews in the United States. The picture that emerges challenges some conventional wisdom and raises a fundamental question: why can't Jews take yes for an answer?

First, of course, there is the question of definition. What is antisemitism? There have been many efforts aimed at defining antisemitism. One view, on the extreme end of the continuum, is the traditional Jewish rabbinic formulation—"An established principle: Esau hates Jacob"—is the classic representation of antisemitism: Babylonia, Rome, Christendom as "Edom," the antisemitic descendants of Esau—antisemitism incarnate, antisemitism universal, antisemitism unending, antisemitism eternal, antisemitism immutable.

There have been many other efforts to define antisemitism, from the elaborate formulations reflected in attitudinal surveys—and we will come back to this—to the question: can antisemites be converted, *is* antisemitism immutable? And to the classic one-liner, an elaboration of the "Esau-hates-Jacob" locution: an antisemite is one who dislikes Jews more than is absolutely necessary. And even this tired old saw tells us something about the nature, irrationality, and unpredictability of hatred of Jews. For the purpose of this discussion, however, we suggest a simple and stark definition of antisemitism: antisemitism is all forms of hostility manifested toward the Jews throughout history.

Sometimes the best approach, paraphrasing former U.S. Supreme Court Justice Potter Stewart in his comment about obscenity, is "I can't define it, but I know it when I see it."[6] However, this approach poses one problem: all too often incidents or expressions are characterized as antisemitism when they are really not. The gut feeling—what I call the *kishke* factor—is important; it tells us something about perceptions. But gut reactions are not the same as hard data.

What is the *kishke* factor? My mother's favorite story: Two Jews in post-*Anschluss* Vienna are walking through an antisemitic neighborhood. They see that they are being followed by two Nazi thugs. One of the Jews says to his friend, "We better make a run for it. There are two of them, and we are all alone." The *kishke* factor.

However one defines antisemitism, one point must be kept in mind: *antisemitism presupposes that the Jews are radically "other."* This simple central point is a universal, timeless characteristic of antisemitism.

## "America Is Different!": A Historical Context

America is different! A review of antisemitism in the United States must take place in the singular context of democratic pluralism, associationalism, and American exceptionalism. What makes America "different" are those constitutional protections, particularly those in the Bill of Rights and the separation of church and state, that inform a society of democratic pluralism. The genius of American democratic pluralism is that rights of majorities *and* minorities, of groups *and* individuals *and* of the state are protected. It is the rich soil of pluralism that has been inhospitable for the nightshade of antisemitism to take firm root, whatever manifestations of antisemitism there have been and continue to be.

Antisemitism in America, like other dynamics in the American Jewish experience, has been informed by this singular nature of American society, a society based on the principles of democratic pluralism and nurtured by the Bill of Rights protections. The experience of two-hundred-plus years has shown that American society, for all of its flaws and imperfections, is among diaspora societies the one that is best suited for Jewish continuity and survival, for individual and communal Jewish life.

Overall, the historical record shows that there has been *relatively* little manifestation of antisemitism in America, certainly as compared with the European experience. The key point to bear in mind is that in this country antisemitism has not been embedded in the institutions of power, often the formal institutions of power, as it was in Europe over the course of many centuries. This factor is absolutely central and must be recalled especially by those who would equate the conditions of America in the 1990s with those of Germany in the 1920s.

Why does the history of the Jewish encounter with America evidence little in the way of antisemitism? There are four structural differences between the United States and Europe that collectively account for American exceptionalism and uniqueness and for the fact that antisemitism did not take firm root in America.

1. The separation of church and state tautologically meant that Jews were not living in a "Christian" society or in *any* kind of religious society. It was church-state separation that lifted pluralism from being a conceptual or philosophical ideal and made it a *legal* obligation.[7] In the United States, from the very beginning of the American polity, the public sphere was viewed, by legal fiat, as being a neutral place. Church-state separation therefore asserted that Jews (and other minorities and individuals) would not be merely tolerated but *accepted.* Maintaining a firm line of separation between church and state, therefore, is central to religious voluntarism and to religious freedom; by extension, it fosters the distinctive survival and creativity of religious groups, including Jews.
2. American society was a post-Emancipation society from its very beginnings. This reality was most crucial in ensuring that political antisemitism of the kind that arose in nineteenth-century Europe did not come to be in the United States. Before the late eighteenth century, Jews everywhere in Europe were legally defined as outsiders in society and therefore alien to the polity. The opening for Jews to become citizens came as a result of the Enlightenment; the French Revolution acted as the engine for Enlightenment ideas, with the result that Jews began entering the mainstream of European societies.

   America did not carry the European pre-Enlightenment baggage. The bulk of American Jewish history begins after the Declaration of Independence and the Constitution were drafted, with the result that Jews no less than any others were entitled to equal status in the body politic.
3. The United States was a new nation, a frontier society, made up people of diverse backgrounds, without "insiders" and "outsiders." In contrast, in Europe, Jews had to cope with the fact that the nation-states in which they were citizens as result of the Emancipation had historical memories, deriving from a Christian context, going back centuries and that they, the Jews, were not part of these memories except as aliens and enemies.
4. The United States, as a nation of immigrants, was inherently pluralist. Indeed, even when the ideology of choice was the "melting pot," the reality was always cultural and democratic pluralism; and pluralism became a uniquely American way of positioning oneself as a member of American society, even as that person (or group) retained religious and ethnic identity. An important by-product of a pluralist society was that it removed the onus under which Jews had been compelled to live in many other societies.

The sum result of these four dynamics is that antisemitism did not reside in the formal institutions of power, as it did in Europe.

## What Do We Know about Antisemitism in America?

To the set of questions raised:

First, on the question of the nature and extent of antisemitism—in the United States, there are some fairly concrete data. To paraphrase the political commentator Ben Wattenberg, the good news is that the bad news isn't all bad.

There are two kinds of antisemitism—two kinds of anything, when it comes down to it, following the "Merton model"—behavioral and attitudinal. There is a crucial relationship between what people *think* and what people *do*, between *attitudinal* and *behavioral* antisemitism. Antisemitism of both kinds is assessed along a broad range of evaluative criteria.[8] The data on antisemitism, along these criteria, indicate that both behavioral and attitudinal antisemitism have declined in the United States over the past forty years, even as we must watch and concern ourselves with recurring danger signals. This finding, of course, is no great revelation; it is amply confirmed by evidence both anecdotal and research-generated and fully explored by a number of essayists in this volume. Nonetheless, the finding calls for some analysis in terms of both behavioral and attitudinal manifestations.

Behavioral antisemitism is manifest, of course, in different ways, from swastika daubings to "JAP" jokes to political rhetoric. The reality is that behavioral antisemitism "where it counts" is simply no longer a factor in American life. Such behavioral antisemitism includes large-scale discrimination against Jews; the cynical use of antisemitism in political rhetoric in order to achieve political gains (arguably the most virulent form of antisemitism), and most important, the inability or reluctance of the Jewish community to express itself on issues of concern because of anti-Jewish animus. This kind of antisemitism, the kind that makes a difference in terms of the security and status of American Jews, has declined steadily and dramatically over the past four decades and more.[9]

It follows, therefore, that in any analysis of antisemitism in the United States, a crucial distinction must be made. There is a need to distinguish between *antisemitism*, which does exist and must be monitored, repudiated, and counteracted, and *Jewish security*, which is strong. Jewish security is strong largely because of a history and tradition of constitutional protections and institutions that inform democratic pluralism, as noted above. While antisemitism and Jewish security are concentric circles and therefore obviously related, the distinction between them is important when discussing the issue in the context of America in the 1990s.

Attitudinal antisemitism is where the issue of data interpretation is best addressed, and some exploration is therefore called for.[10]

It comes as a surprise to many that attitudinal antisemitism in the United States has been a relatively little studied phenomenon over the past three decades. In an age when social scrutiny seems to extend into the most obscure corners of our experience, we learn that antisemitism, an enduring social phenomenon and, needless to say, one of special significance in our own time, has received scant attention from America's social scientists until recently. Most comprehensive, indeed landmark, studies were conducted during the 1960s. Notable among these were the Anti-Defamation League's *Patterns of American Prejudice*, the "Berkeley studies," which developed a scale of antisemitic beliefs of non-Jews and articulated the now classic reverse correlation that the higher the education level, the less likely are non-Jews to hold antisemitic beliefs.[11]

On the narrow question, what do Americans think about Jews, there are fairly conclusive findings. The cumulative data of attitudinal surveys conducted by a range of researchers over the years have consistently substantiated the view that the level of conventional antisemitic beliefs has continued in its forty-year decline. Simply put, there are fewer Americans who profess unfavorable images of Jews.

The usual explanation for this transformation is generational. As analyst Earl Raab and others have put it, it is not that the antisemites are being converted but that each succeeding age group tends to display fewer antisemitic attitudes than the preceding generation of that age group. Committed antisemites are swayed to virtue neither by events nor by prejudice-reduction programs. Earl Raab puts it best: antisemites do not fade away; they simply die. Research findings clearly, strongly, and consistently suggest that a younger, better educated, more affluent population is less antisemitic. This pattern, a negative correlation of education level and antisemitism, obtains across the board, including among blacks.[12]

While attitudinal surveys are in some ways suspect, the lack of a truly comprehensive study since the American Jewish Committee's 1981 Yankelovich poll greatly hindered the examination of present-day antisemitism in America.

There have now been five studies in 1990s: the University of Chicago's National Opinion Research Center (NORC) 1990 General Social Survey, a comprehensive survey of fifty-eight ethnic groups commissioned by the American Jewish Committee (AJC) and conducted by NORC's Tom W. Smith;[13] a 1992 survey of American attitudes toward Jews conducted for the Anti-Defamation League (ADL) by Marttila and Kiley;[14] a 1992 intergroup relations study of New York City done by the Roper Organization for the AJC;[15] a 1993 ADL/Marttila and Kiley survey on racial attitudes in America;[16] and most recently, a 1994 comprehensive study (commissioned by the AJC) by NORC's Tom W. Smith, confirming and synthesizing the findings of previous studies.[17] It is particularly instructive to analyze and compare the AJC/NORC and ADL/Marttila studies.[18]

The NORC 1990 General Social Survey provided data on fifty-eight ethnic groups, including one fictitious group, the "Wissians" (NORC found that significant numbers of Americans hold negative attitudes toward the "Wissians"). These data were analyzed by NORC's General Social Survey director Tom W. Smith for the AJC in order to elicit specific information about anti-Jewish attitudes.

The NORC data related to six areas.[19] Among the AJC/NORC's general findings was, most generally, that antisemitism and negative attitudes are at a low point. Specifically, only few members of certain minority groups harbor some negative attitudes toward Jews, and conflict between Jews and non-Jews is less serious than are clashes between many other ethnic groups. NORC also found that latent sources of antisemitism are not closely connected and therefore are not likely to sustain one another. And the behavioral antisemitism that exists in one area is almost always unconnected to that in another area. These important findings suggest a pattern different from that which existed in America fifty years ago.

Particularly intriguing were AJC/NORC's findings on Israel and antisemitism. It has long been known that anti-Israel and antisemitic attitudes are linked, that antisemitic attitudes are more common among those with negative attitudes toward Israel, and that anti-Israel attitudes are stronger among those with antisemitic beliefs. According to NORC, this linkage is not especially strong. Attitudes toward Israel may be related to causes other than antisemitic attitudes, such as oil, Arabs, a particular worldview, and so on.

Also instructive is the question of how Jews were perceived, in terms of social standing, relative to other groups. Among religions, Jews come in tenth of twenty religious groups, below Protestants and Catholics but above Mormons, Greek Orthodox, Christian Scientists, Unitarians (an interesting finding), Spiritualists, and Jehovah's Witnesses.

A most significant area of the AJC/NORC study, as in any poll of attitudes toward Jews, is that of perceived power and influence. The "Jewish power" question is one to which significant import is given, and therefore it merits some analysis. The way in which the question is asked makes a difference. If the question is open-ended—as in "Which groups have too much power?"—Jews will consistently come out low. If the question is closed-ended and contextual—"Which groups from the following list have too much power?"—Jews still come out relatively low. If the question is completely closed-ended—"Do Jews have too much power in the United States?"—the numbers are higher.

The Jewish-power question was asked by NORC not as "Do Jews have too much power in the United States?," and it should never be asked in this way because the data would not tell us much. It was asked as a contextual question: "Which of the following groups [twenty-three were listed; e.g., Arab oil nations, the media, labor unions, Orientals, blacks, the Catholic Church, the banks] have too much influence and power?" Jews come out way down; about the only ones lower than Jews were Hispanics.

Seymour Martin Lipset and others suggest that with regard to this issue, people are not antisemitic, they are antipower.[20] That is, the issue is power, not Jews. People think that many groups have too much power in this society. But even this requires further nuance, which is illumined in the Marttila poll discussed below.

Antisemitism in America is neither virulent nor growing, concluded the AJC/NORC study, consistent with the data from earlier polls. But NORC cautioned that antisemitism in America is not a spent force, that Jews are yet recognized as an ethnic or religious outgroup and are often accordingly judged and treated in a distinctive manner. Antisemitism has not disappeared; it has become dormant, and latent antisemitism does have the potential to become actualized. And antisemitic incidents do occur. Furthermore, antisemitic political groups may exist as isolated entities in the lunatic fringe. Fringe elements are tautologically "fringe" and rarely enter the mainstream. But lunatics can be dangerous.

While the AJC/NORC study is almost a decade old, it is hardly stale. The data are yet relevant and highly instructive.

A survey conducted by the polling firm Marttila and Kiley for the ADL in 1992 proves significant as well, but in a different way from the AJC/NORC study. For NORC, Tom Smith massaged general data in order to generate information about attitudes toward Jews. The ADL/Marttila study is the first comprehensive study, *specifically* of attitudes toward Jews, since the Yankelovich poll of 1981 and once again used the criteria for antisemitism (the "index") first developed by the Berkeley Studies and used by Yankelovich. This study is almost a decade old, but the findings remain important. Moreover, Marttila's methodology suggests a number of significant questions about attitudinal surveys in general that are of import to social scientists.

ADL/Marttila generally corroborated everything that has been known for many years and most of the things that were suspected about attitudinal antisemitism. Marttila's central investigative device consists of an eleven-item scale, the "Index of Antisemitic Beliefs," consisting of questions designed to detect antisemitism.[21] Six or more yes answers render a person "most antisemitic"; two to five yeses result in a rating of "middle"; one or two yes answers: "not antisemitic."

ADL/Marttila's general findings were that 20 percent of Americans answered yes to six or more questions; they are therefore characterized as "most antisemitic." Forty-one percent were "middle," and 39 percent were "not antisemitic."

Further, the survey results showed a continuing pattern of decline, albeit a slow one, along a range of antisemitic beliefs. The negative correlation of "education and other social/economic indicators up, antisemitism down" holds for all groups in the society, including blacks. Age is a factor. Americans over sixty-five are twice as likely as those under sixty-five to fall into the "most antisemitic" category. Important data in ADL/Marttila were those linking antisemitism and racism. Individuals who are "most racist" are likely to be "most antisemitic," and vice versa. One cautionary note in ADL/Marttila concerned the Jewish-power question. The numbers there are slightly up, between 24 and 31 percent, depending on the question asked.[22]

Perhaps the most surprising finding in the ADL/Marttila survey was the refutation of conventional wisdom that the more contact a person has with Jews, the less antisemitic that person will be. Marttila's findings indicate that this is not so and require further study.

One other fascinating finding of the study, taken, let us recall, during the last months of the Likud/Shamir government in Israel, is that criticism of Israel is no predictor of antisemitic attitudes. Indeed, many critics of Israel are well educated and embrace tolerant, pluralistic attitudes. As a point of fact, there are some Jews who are anti-Israel and many Jews (perhaps a majority of American Jews according to some polls), who opposed the policies of the Likud government under former Prime Minister Shamir.[23]

The ADL/Marttila poll is valuable, even though it did not reveal much that was new.[24] With respect to data analysis and interpretation, ADL/Marttila serves as a case study for data analysis. It is in this respect that I would suggest four questions about the ADL/Marttila poll, questions that illumine issues about the study of antisemitism in general:

The first question has less to do with the study and everything to do with the way in which data on antisemitism are presented and interpreted. "Twenty percent of Americans are strongly antisemitic," asserted the ADL when it released the Marttila findings. Was this bad news or good news? Although 20 percent is hardly a trivial number—30 million antisemites out there is nothing to be laughed at—the news was not all that bad. The first questions any social scientist asks about any such assertion is "Compared to *when*, and compared to *what*?" The 20 percent reported was down from the 29 percent of the 1964 ADL/Berkeley Studies. Further, with respect to the "compared to what" question, ample data exist from any number of sources that indicate that 20 percent, or more, of any group hates any other group. So: good news or bad?

Second, some of the questions in the index may not have been perceived by respondents as reflecting negatively on Jews; they indeed may not measure antisemitism. A classic example of this type of flaw in questioning is illustrated in the 1986 poll of evangelical Christians in America conducted by the ADL. At the height of what was known as the "Christianization of America," the ADL asked this question: Are fundamentalists more antisemitic than the general population? Is it antisemitism that informs their agenda? The ADL found that fundamentalists factor out in levels of antisemitism about the same as everyone else, approximately 20 percent.

In the course of the survey, the ADL in effect asked the following question: "Are Jews tight with their money?" A significant percentage of the respondents answered, "Yes, Jews are tight with their money." To many that is antisemitism. But then, the follow-up question was asked: "Is this good?" Most answered, "Yes, this is a good trait; Jews are thrifty, etc." Now is that antisemitism? The lesson is that a number of questions in the "Index of Antisemitic Beliefs" may not be measuring antisemitism per se but some other beliefs or feelings, which may indeed represent some anti-Jewish animus or they may in fact be reflective of *positive* attitudes toward Jews.

Third, and a more serious issue: attitudes are much more nuanced than the three groupings "most antisemitic," "middle," "not antisemitic."[25] There is a basic ambiguity in most responses that should be noted. A respondent who answered yes to six or seven, some of which questions may in fact *not* measure antisemitism, as was just indicated, has been just fine on four or five. Even among the "most antisemitic," therefore, there exist identifiable pro-Jewish attitudes. Among the "not antisemitic," the reverse is true; they may very well hold anti-Jewish attitudes. A more sophisticated conceptual scheme is clearly needed, one that takes into account these ambiguities.

Fourth, and most troubling: ADL/Marttila and, indeed, attitudinal surveys in general are leading *Jews* toward a new definition of antisemitism, namely, attitudes toward Jews that *Jews* find distasteful; attitudes that Jews wish "they" (i.e., non-Jews), would not have, rather than the classic definition of antisemitism as expressed hostility toward Jews.

For example, the increase in numbers on the Jewish-power question is indeed troubling. But Jews in America *are* a power group. Is it unreasonable for some people to ask whether Jews have too much power? The question is, how do individuals who hold such views *act* on those views? *The* fundamental question in antisemitism anywhere, at any time, is what the relationship is between *attitude* and *behavior.*

Mention ought be made of two other studies. One, conducted by Louis Harris for the National Conference (formerly the National Conference of Christians and Jews) and released in 1994, evaluated the state of intergroup relations in the United States and provided a further context for the study of antisemitism.[26] With respect to prejudicial attitudes in general, the study found that members of minority groups are more likely than are whites to agree to negative stereotypes about other minority groups. In terms of antisemitism, the National Conference/Harris survey data revealed disturbingly high numbers in the responses to the Jewish-power and dual-loyalty questions, among both whites and minority group members. Forty-three percent of blacks and 22 percent of whites said that Jews "have too much control over business and the media." Forty-seven percent of blacks and 24 percent of whites responded that Jews "are more loyal to Israel than to America."

The most recent study, *A Survey of the Religious Right: Views on Politics, Society, Jews and Other Minorities*, was conducted by the Gallup International Institute and analyzed by Tom W. Smith of NORC for the AJC and was released by the AJC in 1996. Again, no surprises with respect to attitudes toward Jews. On the positive side, those aligned with the "religious right" are more supportive of Israel and the special biblical status of Jews than are other Americans; on the negative side, religious-right adherents are more likely to raise objections to Jews "on religious grounds." For example, 22 percent (as compared with 8 percent of other Americans) think that Jews must still answer for killing Christ. The interesting news from the AJC poll is that in terms of social and political acceptance, those on the religious right differ little from most Americans. Seventy-nine percent would vote for a Jew as president, and 88 percent do not believe that Jews have too much influence in American society.

There are, of course, inherent problems with any survey data. Respondents may be disingenuous: "I may *think* it; I can't *say* it." Or questions may be flawed, not sufficiently probing, or without good follow-up. Recall if you will the ADL questions of the fundamentalists.

In sum: notwithstanding the problems with comparing the two large surveys owing to the many differences between them, some conclusions with respect to broad trends are called for. There is a steady, albeit slow, lessening of expressed negativity toward Jews, with a possible exception of the stereotypes of Jewish power; a smaller percentage of the population scores as antisemitic; there is a more widespread acceptance of positive statements about Jews. The dual-loyalty numbers may have remained more or less constant over the years, but other statistics, exhibiting positive attitudes, have evidenced dramatic change: in 1958, 61 percent of Americans said they would vote for a Jew for president; in 1987, 89 percent of Americans said they would so vote.[27]

So much for attitudinal data. One further general observation about antisemitism in America should be indicated. This is followed by some specific concrete issues that go to the core of data interpretation.

Cogent lessons should be learned about antisemitism from recent experiences. Often not what happened that matters but what did *not* happen. One way of measuring antisemitism is by looking at responses to "conflict" situations, namely, situations that could tend to polarize society—with the expectation that antisemitism will increase. When the whole range of conflict situations over the past four decades is observed—from the Rosenbergs in the 1950s to the oil crises of 1973–74 and 1979 (remember the "Burn Jews, Not Oil" bumper stickers that nobody saw?); the Iran/Contra affair, with its Israeli connection; the conviction during the 1980s of Jewish public officials in New York and Maryland; the Ivan Boesky insider-trading case; the farm crisis in the mid-1980s;[28] the *intifada*; and most dramatically, the Pollard spy case, invoking clearly the question of dual loyalty—it is a history replete with situations that everyone confidently expected would trigger expressions of antisemitism. In fact, none of these resulted in an increase of antisemitic expression or attitude in the United States. The response to conflict situations is most instructive.[29]

While the response over the years to conflict situations has been fairly standard, not resulting in increased antisemitic expression, mention ought be made of two events during the 1990s that suggest that some inhibiting factors may be weakening somewhat. At his 12 September 1991 news conference, then-president George Bush referred to pro-Israel activists who had converged on Washington to press for loan guarantees, characterizing the Jewish grass-roots advocacy as "powerful political forces." Those comments were a direct response to a conflict situation and were very troubling to many American Jews. Was it antisemitism? In my view, the answer is no. Was it on the margin, signifying the breakdown of a taboo against political antisemitism? Certainly.

Serious concern was expressed as well over the 26 August 1990 (and subsequent) remarks of columnist Patrick J. Buchanan: "There are only two groups that are beating the drums of war in the Middle East—the Israeli Defense Ministry and its 'amen' corner in the United States." Buchanan's amen-corner remarks, characterized by *New York Times* columnist A. M. Rosenthal as a "blood libel,"[30] were in direct response to a conflict situation, namely, the developing Gulf crisis, and were very troubling.

The context of Buchanan's remarks, of course, was the journalist's questionable history with respect to Jews, very different from that of George Bush, whose remark might be considered sui generis. In both his syndicated columns and on television, Buchanan had over the years evidenced significant hostility to Israel and to many Jewish concerns. He questioned the validity of continued American support of the Jewish state, proclaimed the innocence of suspected Nazi war criminal John Demjanjuk, and supported the presence of the Carmelite convent at the Auschwitz/Birkenau death camp.

## Antisemitism in the Black Community

The most difficult questions with respect to data interpretation in the United States have to do with antisemitism in the black community, arguably the main source of angst among Jews. A focus on so-called black antisemitism is justified by three considerations. First, black America is one of the few places, probably the chief place in the United States, where visible and vocal antisemitism can still be observed. Second, the black community is among the few sites where antisemitism of an extremist or fringe nature is making a serious bid for communal acceptance and legitimacy in the mainstream institutions of the society. This danger is illustrated by the activities of Louis Farrakhan in the political arena, certainly a mainstream institution; and of City College of New York professor Leonard Jeffries Jr. in the arena of higher education. What American Jews most fear—the "mainstreaming" of antisemitism, something that has not taken place in this country, whatever the problems American Jews may have—has threatened to occur in these cases. Jeffries and Farrakhan represent something more than disturbing but isolated incidents of antisemitism. They demonstrate the danger that African American antisemitism could spread from individual racists to infect broad segments of academe, the civil rights movement, and even the political arena. Gauging the reality of the threat requires an analysis not of manifestations by Farrakhan but of the attitudes of blacks in general toward Jews.

The third consideration is the history and tradition of American Jewish involvement in the struggle for civil rights, which was the regnant item on the Jewish communal agenda from the early 1950s to the mid-1960s, and the relationship between black antisemitism and black-Jewish relations.

The fact is that we know very little about the nature and extent of antisemitism among blacks.[31] There has never been a comprehensive study of black attitudes toward Jews, an issue complicated by black attitudes toward whites in general. The data that we do have are limited and fragmentary and mostly old. Until the 1960s the question of black views was sidestepped completely. Since then there have been some limited pieces of evidence from Charles Herbert Stember, Daniel Yankelovich, Gary Marx, some from Marttila, and a large amount of anecdotal evidence.[32]

Two observations should be noted. First, conventional wisdom about black antisemitism is mostly unfounded. For example, the view that as education levels rise in the black community so does antisemitism and that the best-educated blacks are the most antisemitic enjoys popular currency. Recall that in the general community the relationship between educational level and antisemitism is inverse; as education levels go up, antisemitism goes down.

But in fact, there are almost no data to justify the assertion that in the black community, as education goes up, so does antisemitism.[33] What can be said, based on the little that is known with certitude, is that the level of antisemitism drops steeply for both whites *and* blacks as education level rises, but less so for blacks; the reverse correlation exists but is weaker. The ADL/Marttila and Kiley survey, in one of its most important findings, indeed confirms this fact. Blacks do continue to be relatively more antisemitic than whites at any given education level. But this is very different from saying that they become more antisemitic as they become better educated and achieve higher economic status. In point of fact, they become less antisemitic, as do other members of the society.

But whatever the data reveal or fail to reveal, the reality exists that many blacks, for whatever the reason, may not be constrained in their venting of antisemitic sentiment. Various polls taken over the years have substantiated the fact that the black population, which has always lagged well behind the general population in a range of economic and social indicators, is the only group in which the reservoir level of anti-Jewish feeling has not dropped and may have increased in some areas and in which the taboos against expression of antisemitism have eroded. Additionally, blacks are less reluctant to repudiate antisemitism in their midst. For many American Jews this pattern is the tough reality of black antisemitism.

This form of black antisemitism requires analysis as well. Is failure to repudiate antisemitic statements *antisemitism*, or is it the reflection of other dynamics at work?

Indeed, it was the failure of black leaders to repudiate antisemitism that was at the heart of a number of experiences during recent years. This was exemplified by the unhappy and highly instructive Cokeley affair in 1989. The obscene antisemitic (and anti-Christian) utterances of Steven Cokeley, black aide to then Chicago mayor Eugene Sawyer, including the appalling shocker that Jewish doctors were injecting black babies with AIDS, were awful enough; they were made even more so by the fact that Sawyer, instead of firing Cokeley within the hour that the story broke, temporized for five days. Equally disturbing was the fact that the black leadership of Chicago, including even Sawyer's black political rivals, did not immediately and vigorously denounce and repudiate Cokeley. The experience once again followed a pattern all too evident in recent years. More immediate and equally obvious examples: the failure of many black leaders to repudiate Nation of Islam minister Louis Farrakhan and his virulently antisemitic statements.

The pattern exemplified by the Cokeley affair and the numerous Farrakhan experiences reflects the interpretation by each group of its priorities in light of its separate past. Blacks focus on *unity* and *solidarity*, which they indeed learned in part from the Jewish community, and argue that it was black disunity that simplified slavery and helped prevent black advancement in the century following emancipation. American Jews focus on and perhaps are even obsessed with *denunciation* and *repudiation*. Jews would argue and rightly so that repudiation of antisemitism and of its practitioners by non-Jews and the willingness of those in leadership positions to speak out are key components in the counteraction of antisemitism. Jews argue that it was the failure to denounce Hitler's early evils that opened the way for the Holocaust.

It is important for Jews to understand that often, when black antisemitism is invoked, what is being described may not be the attitude of the black population in general toward Jews—we do not know very much about that—but very different dynamics indeed, those of repudiation and solidarity. And this may be even more significant in terms of the tactics and strategies of our communal organizations. Denunciation and repudiation of antisemitism *are* key elements in the counteraction of antisemitism. Courageous black leaders have repudiated antisemitism and must continue to do so. But Jews ought not recklessly scapegoat the broader black population when hard data on that population are not in hand.

With respect to the riots in Crown Heights, an event that continues as a flash point between blacks and Jews in New York, there is no question that a serious antisemitic outburst occurred in August 1991. There is no question that an antisemitic murder was committed. But in analyzing the conditions in Crown Heights that led to the tragic events, a nuanced approach is indicated. The key question with respect to Crown Heights is whether Crown Heights is sui generis: Can we and ought we extrapolate Crown Heights to the black population in general or to other communities around the country?

The August 1991 events in Crown Heights had more to do with long-standing "tribal rivalries," to use the words of sociologist Jonathan Rieder—rivalries of real estate, power, culture—than with a deep-seated antisemitism that indeed may not be present in a hardly monolithic black population in that neighborhood.[34]

Further, and this goes to the heart of data interpretation, is the question of whether the antisemitism of the black street kid yelling "Kill the Jew!" is the same as the antisemitism of Louis Farrakhan or Leonard Jeffries? Is it the same as that of the white skinhead in Jersey City or of Holocaust deniers? We will not know very much about what goes on in neighborhoods like Crown Heights, where "Kill the Jew!" is directed at the most visible manifestation of white power, until we are ready to mount a serious ethnographic study on the street. Most important, it seems clear that the causes and events of Crown Heights would not be replicated elsewhere, and this is the key issue.[35]

Further, consider another neighborhood, the Williamsburg section of Brooklyn. Williamsburg has many of the same ingredients as did Crown Heights, such as "tribal" rivalries over land and power, a well-organized and politically savvy Hasidic group (in this case, the Satmar Hasidim), and a minority group that feels it has been given the short end of the stick. It is a tinderbox that could explode. Same situation as Crown Heights, only in Williamsburg there are no blacks; there are Hispanics. It was not black antisemitism that caused Crown Heights; it was tribal rivalry, primarily over land, exacerbated by individuals who exploited a tense situation.

As the United States increasingly becomes a multiethnic society, the patterns of antisemitism unfortunately reflect those of increasing ethnic strife. We are not in an era of antisemitism in this country; we are in an era of ethnic conflict. The problem is that in large measure ethnic groups sometimes are not affirming their unity by affirming the positive values of their heritages. For ethnic groups the only truly valid principle is this *positive* affirmation. Many groups are instead defining their unity in negative ways: either by the memory of their hurts (for the Jews, the Holocaust and pogroms, to which blacks say, "You don't have a monopoly on the Holocaust; we had slavery," etc.) or by focusing on The Enemy. What comes out of these projections is anger, which generates counter-anger, which generates . . .

Neither group, blacks nor Jews, has anywhere to go in this kind of battle; and the traditional coalition that believes that bettering the conditions of society will lessen bias (including antisemitism), which is a well-proven thesis, will split, as it has done. But if and as members of minority groups move into the system, as they become better educated and economically upwardly mobile, they become less antisemitic. The anger decreases. The attitudes, for individuals, may not have changed; the conditions have changed.[36]

## The Perception Gap in Antisemitism: Perceptions and Reality

Let us return to the questions with which this chapter began, specifically to what explains the perception gap between the grass roots and the data with respect to antisemitism.

First, it is necessary to understand what Jews *are* saying when they say that antisemitism is a serious problem. On this question there are some data. A study conducted by Brandeis University's Perlmutter Institute for Jewish Advocacy revealed that when asked about specific areas of "seriousness" of the antisemitism they were reporting, most respondents did not pinpoint economic, power, or political areas but rather incidents of vandalism or Israel-related activity. Or they are saying "I heard from my neighbor that he heard on the radio . . ."[37]

So what explains the perception gap between the Jewish grass roots and the data? At bottom, it is clear that much of the anxiety felt by many American Jews is obviously related to the historical experience of the Jews, particularly the Holocaust. History has made Jews unusually sensitive, and it is a sensitivity worth maintaining. This gut reaction, the *kishke* factor, is a response not to antisemitism but to a foreboding that latent antisemitism will become actual. Recall the classic definition of a Jewish telegram: "Start worrying. Letter follows." The 80 to 90 percent who are responding yes to the question "Is antisemitism a serious problem?" are responding not to antisemitism but to the Jewish telegram.

Earl Raab, who has articulated much of the vocabulary of the Jewish community relations field,[38] has written about this foreboding at length. Raab suggests that the foreboding felt by most Jews is that of an antisemitism that is latent among many in the society, requiring some radical social dislocation to cause its actual expression This foreboding is useful. It keeps Jews on their toes. But Raab suggests that it will not help much if anti-Israel activity is seen as only the latest version of atavistic Jew hatred. At best, the foreboding leads to an understanding that the best fight against latent antisemitism is the fight to strengthen positive American self-interest attitudes toward Jews.[39]

But there is more to the gap between the perception of antisemitism and the reality of Jewish security than just the foreboding of latent antisemitism. Social scientists should pay attention to their own numbers. Sociologist Steven M. Cohen has found that more than half of all American Jews continue to hold traditional negative stereotypes of non-Jews.[40] Whatever the data on antisemitism's actual decline, these negative images resonate in the perception of an antisemitism reemergent. And this dynamic reinforces itself: the perception that non-Jews are hostile may very well lead Jews to avoid non-Jewish intimacies and associations. In turn, the absence of such contact sustains the negative image of the non-Jew and reinforces Jews' fear of non-Jews—in a word, of antisemitism.

Further, the perception of antisemitism found among many American Jews may be a vestige of a time when antisemitism in America was very real and when every Jew was insecure vis-à-vis non-Jews. If these outmoded social and cultural perceptions of the non-Jew persist, it may be too soon to measure the reactions of American Jews to questions about Jewish security against the *true* state of Jewish security.

Further, there is the inevitable intrusion of issues from the public affairs agenda into the consciousness of many American Jews. The Christian religious right and the notion of America as a Christian nation[41] and the related attack on the separation of church and state as a quick fix for the dearth of values in the "public square" (witness the unending debates over prayer in the public schools)—all threats to Jewish security—suggest to some Jews a renewed wafting of antisemitic odors. Questions with respect to the religious right went beyond and deeper than the debate over public policy issues. The controversy over the assertions found in the writings of the Reverend Pat Robertson, leader of the Christian Coalition, portraying a worldwide conspiracy of international bankers,

Communists, and Freemasons—code words all for classic antisemitica—further suggests that there remains a reservoir of antisemitism that may inform much of the activity of the religious right. At the very least, the apocalyptic vision that underlies much of the support by the religious right for the State of Israel is in essence conversionary and not especially friendly to Jews. Robertson has expressed his "sincere regrets" for his statements. But whatever one makes of his apologia, it is certainly true that Pat Robertson has chosen to fish in some very dirty waters.

There are additional obvious influences on the perceptions of antisemitism by American Jews. Antisemitic activity in Europe has a psychological effect on Americans. American Jews also cannot discount the effects of traumas such as Crown Heights. Most important is the effect of intergroup tensions in general in the United States. The source of anxiety for most American Jews may not be antisemitism but the rise of intergroup conflict across the map. The relationship of intergroup tension to antisemitism in America is an area that requires significant study.

## New and Newer . . .

Although this article is not a report on developments on the antisemitism front, I will nonetheless flag an item that may be noteworthy as we approach the close of the decade. The dissemination of racism, specifically antisemitism, via the global telecommunications network has increased in recent years. The Internet has emerged as an uncontrollable, unpoliceable, and decentralized zone, where any voice, however objectionable, can "speak" and be heard—the number of Internet users in the United States alone is in the millions. Among the manifestations, the Internet is increasingly becoming a primary communications tool for the extremist fringe, including being used as a vehicle for the dissemination of Holocaust-denial materials.

Mention ought be made as well of another dynamic in the way in which Jews are viewed by some non-Jews. The reality in 1998 is that, as I have repeatedly suggested, we are not in an era of antisemitism. At best (or worst), we are in an age of "countersemitism," to use the phrase coined by *National Review* columnist Joseph Sobran, himself no mean anti-Jew. Sobran, a "Christian-America" radical isolationist, characterizes his views thus: "[I am] against just about everything the Jewish community advocates for America. But I certainly don't wish Jews any ill." An illustration of what countersemitism is all about was the flap that developed over an op-ed article in the *New York Times* [42] by conservative commentator William F. Buckley Jr. in which Buckley took pains to defend Dartmouth College, one of the eight Ivy League colleges, from allegations of an antisemitic past. Dartmouth, a paragon of Ivy Leaguism, has a history, as do the other Ivy

League colleges and many colleges around the United States, of anti-Jewish quotas. There is nothing new in this. The Dartmouth quotas became news, however, on 8 November 1997, when James Freedman, the college's president, a Jew himself, used his speech at the dedication of the new campus Jewish center as a vehicle for reading documents from the college archives that complained that Dartmouth had "too many Jews" and that something had to be done about this and was in fact being done. Enter Buckley, who, with respect to the Jewish community, made his name by purging antisemites from the American political right, thereby stripping antisemitism of its last bastion of respectability. Buckley said, in effect, "It's not so bad." If a college wanted to spread Christianity, that was a legitimate goal. Quotas? It's not antisemitism, suggests Buckley. The larger issue, averred Buckley in his *New York Times* piece, is that the new America is a-borning with a boldly Christian majority culture, and if Jews are "outsiders to some extent," that is just too bad.

The Buckley stance, not exactly antisemitism, is countersemitism. Buckley has, as have Sobran and others, articulated these views this many times before. What is noteworthy at this point is the fact that the view was expressed in the pages of the *New York Times*. This event is illustrative of a larger matter. There is a move toward re-Christianized America that would welcome, once again, the marginalization and indeed a re-ghettoization of Jews. The question for the American Jewish polity is that of the seriousness of this move and whether it is embraced by sizable numbers of people in the American body politic.

The issue of countersemitism must be placed in the context of the overall assessment of antisemitism in the United States as we approach the twenty-first century. Hostility toward Jews continues at a far lower level than hostility toward other groups in American society. There are precious few signs in the United States of institutional or political antisemitism, arguably the most virulent form of antisemitism. The threshold for Jewish security, the ability of Jews and of the Jewish polity to participate fully at every level of society, has not been crossed, nor will it be crossed.

This analysis is in sharp contrast to that offered by other analysts, notably those associated with the Tel-Aviv University's Project for the Study of Anti-Semitism. In the Project's *Anti-Semitism Worldwide 1995/6*,[43] produced by the Anti-Defamation League and the World Jewish Congress, the emphasis for the United States is, as has traditionally been the case, on the activities of antisemitic extremist organizations and hate groups, on the annual Anti-Defamation League "bean count" of incidents of antisemitic vandalism, and on Holocaust denial. While none of these areas is to be trivialized (antisemitism on the Internet is of special concern, in my view), the reporting on and analysis of American antisemitism is much more nuanced than the traditional trotting out of extremists who, tautologically, *are* extremist, representing a tiny cadre without any influence in the larger society and indeed are repudiated by the larger society.

## Who Are the Antisemites? Questions for Study and Research

All of the above suggests not the question, "Who are the antisemites?" but who are those who are *not* antisemites? There are three types of people: philosemites, non-antisemites, and anti-antisemites.[44] The security of Jews does not depend on people being non-antisemites; for most people in the United States, Jews are simply not an issue.

And indeed, in the 1991 gubernatorial campaign in Louisiana, 55 percent of the white vote went to former Klan leader David Duke not *because* of his racial views but *despite* those views; when self-interest is a factor, non-antisemites may ignore the antisemitism or racism of a candidate. According to exit polling, 27 percent of voters supported Duke because of his views on the state's economy, 39 percent because of government corruption, and only 12 percent because of Duke's views on racial issues.[45] This response to Duke strongly suggests that many in the non-antisemitic group will support an antisemite if some other area of self-interest is invoked.[46] A more recent and more dramatic example of this dynamic was the Million Man March convened by the Nation of Islam and its leader Louis Farrakhan on 15 October 1995. Most of the 800,000 or so blacks who gathered in Washington on that day were there not because of Farrakhan's virulent message but despite that message.

There is a substantial number of people who do not care about the Jews one way or another but who are unconstrained enough to support an antisemite if such support appears to serve their needs. These are the non-antisemites. The dynamic at work in non-antisemitism lies at the interface of the social control and trigger mechanisms.

The real security of Jews lies in people being *anti*-antisemites, for whom antisemitism is totally illegitimate and must be repudiated. A relatively small number of people fall in the anti-antisemite category, and not much is known about the taboo that informs anti-antisemitism. It is clearly an area for study.

Finally, What *don't* we know about antisemitism in America? What ought be our research agenda?

First, we need to know more about the taboos and controls surrounding expression of antisemitism that cause non-antisemites to become anti-antisemites. With respect to triggers of antisemitism, it is not enough to mouth the simple formula "bad times equals increased antisemitism." Bad economic times can be the background; they do not constitute the trigger. What is required is a combination and interaction of *background* and context, antisemitic *attitudes* of the population that are measured, and *trigger*.[47]

Second, there are forms of antisemitism that are difficult to observe and measure, namely, hidden and latent antisemitism. Additionally, traditional, cruder forms of antisemitism may not have been eliminated but may have been revamped and repackaged for a new generation. This "new" antisemitism, articulated in a different, perhaps less blatant manner, more subtle and nuanced, calls for study. The difficulty is that while new forms of antisemitism may be open and observable, compared with hidden and latent antisemitism, they are often encrypted.[48]

Third, and related, is the question of threshold. The different points at which individuals *perceive* antisemitism should be probed. What yardstick are people using when they measure situations that they themselves perceive or experience as antisemitism? Should survivors of the Holocaust, on the one hand, and college students who never experienced behavioral antisemitism until they reached the campus, on the other hand, be categorized in the same manner? Both groups, from opposite ends of the spectrum, have very low thresholds for perceiving antisemitism.[49] This is a difficult and sensitive area.

Fourth: research and study of the nature and extent of antisemitism in the black community. As suggested earlier, relatively little is known about antisemitism among blacks.

Fifth: a new look at the surveys. The surveys, which may be either antiquated or irrelevant, should be retooled.

Sixth: a hierarchy of antisemitism must be developed. This is extremely important. Not all forms of antisemitism carry equal weight. It is ridiculous to equate political antisemitism, a most virulent form of antisemitism, with the telling of a "JAP" joke. No one would want to minimize any form of antisemitic expression; any person who is at the receiving end of such expression is an abused person. But until some serious weighting system is developed, we will be at the mercy of those who would exploit antisemitism.

Seventh: the relationship of bigotry in general and antisemitism. The ADL/Marttila data are extremely valuable in this regard and call for follow-up analysis.

Eighth, and most crucial: what is the relationship between attitude and behavior? This question has been around for decades and has bedeviled the research psychologists as much as the sociologists.

And finally, how do we assess not antisemitism but Jewish perceptions of antisemitism? My speculations and those of others in this area need more comprehensive analysis. What are the specific factors that influence or inform our perceptions? Why do American Jews respond more to the Jewish telegram than to realities? Why can't Jews take yes for an answer?

Until fifty years ago, antisemitism was perfectly normal, indeed normative, in Jewish history.[50] In our own day, however, one might say that Adolf Hitler gave antisemitism a bad name, as did Father Coughlin and Gerald L. K. Smith in the United States. But once again, taboos against expressions of antisemitism, against racism and bigotry in general, appear to be breaking down. Not many years ago, expression of antisemitism was not considered to be legitimate. But as the American Jewish Committee's David Singer has said, "Jesse Jackson was the first to show [in our day] that there is life after antisemitism."

Further, what is troubling about antisemitism in America today is not the reality of antisemitism; after all, antisemitism is always a reality. What appears to be different today is the fact that the efforts to introduce what was until now considered fringe or extremist manifestations of bigotry into the mainstream institutions of society as legitimate expression have increased. Items: Leonard Jeffries and higher education, Louis Farrakhan and the political arena, Holocaust denial and the academy and the press. A note on this last point: however few are the adherents to Holocaust revisionism, and by all accounts they are few indeed, Holocaust denial is a new vehicle for antisemitism that exploits the free discussion and the "two sides to the question" sense of fair play ideal traditional to most Americans.

Are there more negative dynamics at work today than there were ten years ago? Yes. Are there clouds in what five or ten years ago was a cloudless sky? Yes. Are they storm clouds? No, because the qualitative difference between a pluralistic America of 1998 and the Europe of 1928 and 1938 remains, and this is a very significant difference.

What about counteraction of antisemitism?

The organized Jewish community, traditionally viewing antisemitism as a key item on the intergroup relations agenda, has counteracted antisemitism in a number of ways. Popular among Jewish "defense" agencies has been the use of a variety of prejudice-reduction programs, although there are limited data that such programs result in the diminution of attitudinal antisemitism among members of the broad population. Legislative and judicial remedies—"hate crimes" laws, for example—are important to the extent that the message that the government will not tolerate bigoted behavior is sent but will not result in a decrease in antisemitic or racist expression. The most efficacious counteraction of antisemitism, in my view, is the improvement of social and economic conditions. The data, without fail, assert that in any population, in any geographic area, at any time, in which the conditions of society are improved, bigotry and racism decrease.[51] This verity holds true across racial lines as well. Transcending all of these approaches, of course—and this goes not to the question of *antisemitism* but to *Jewish security*—is the enhancement of constitutional protections, chiefly those embodied in the First Amendment to the U.S. Constitution and most centrally the separation of church and state. There is no surer guarantor of the security of Jews and of the Jewish polity in the United States than the strength of constitutional institutions.

And last: The American Jewish community has been hypnotized by antisemitism. It monitors it, measures it, chases after antisemites. But ultimately the important issue is not antisemitism; it is Jewish security. There are any number of things in America that have nothing to do with antisemitism that are terribly destructive to Jews. Noteworthy among these are attacks on church-state separation. And there are many things in this country that could be fairly characterized as antisemitism that are superficial, that pose little or no danger to the Jewish polity or to individual Jews. Why can't American Jews take yes for an answer? And more basic, how, ultimately, can we measure Jewish security?

This article was largely based on judgments arising out of survey data, and it closes with a view that challenges this approach. The late historian Lucy Dawidowicz, writing in *Commentary* magazine in 1970, asked a simple question: "Can Anti-Semitism Be Measured?"[52] Dawidowicz suggested that survey analysis, which presents a picture frozen in a moment in time, is by its nature unequipped to investigate the historic images and themes that yet flourish even in America; it is certainly unequipped to trace the passage of these themes from one culture to another. How much more difficult to locate a specific variety of antisemitism within a meaningful historical continuum and translate this form of antisemitism in a responsible way for our communities? It is this last question that, ultimately, is our charge in interpreting antisemitism and interpreting what we mean by Jewish security.

## Notes

1. Portions of this chapter appeared in Jerome A. Chanes, "Antisemitism and Jewish Security Today: Interpreting the Data," chap. 1 of Jerome A. Chanes, ed., *Antisemitism in America Today: Outspoken Experts Explode the Myths* (New York: Carol Publishing/Birch Lane Press, 1995), 3–30; and in "Redefining the Protocol for the Study of Antisemitism in the United States," forthcoming in *Patterns of Prejudice*. On the spelling and usage of "antisemitism": the use of a hyphen and upper case (as in "anti-Semitism") emphasizes a fictitious and imaginary "Semitism," characterizing a racially defined (rather than linguistic) Semitic group. Such a usage gives the antisemites a victory right off the mark. Throughout this article, therefore, the word will be spelled "antisemitism."
2. Jews affiliated in some manner with the Jewish community were surveyed.
3. Historian Robert Wistrich suggests a parallel development in Europe. It is of interest to compare the American with the European situation in terms of similarities and differences. See Robert S. Wistrich, *Anti-Semitism in Europe since the Holocaust* (New York: American Jewish Committee, 1993), p. 19.
4. Among those who address the psychological dynamics of antisemitism is psychoanalyst Martin Bergmann. See Bergmann, "Antisemitism and the Psychology of Prejudice," in Jerome A. Chanes, ed., *Antisemitism in America Today*, pp. 100–115.
5. See Earl Raab, "Taking the Measure of Anti-Semitism on the 21st Century" (paper presented to the 1992 plenary session of the National Jewish Community Relations Advisory Council. The author expresses his appreciation to Earl Raab for his guidance and counsel.
6. *Jacobellis v. Ohio* 378 U.S. 184, 196 (1964).
7. The Bill of Rights—the First ten Amendments to the U.S. Constitution—includes, in the first amendment, the "religion clauses": "Congress shall make no law respecting an establishment of religion, or prohibiting the free exercise thereof." Analysts note that, while there are occasional tensions between "establishment" and "free exercise," the two clauses are not in competition but complement and reinforce one another.
8. Among the criteria for assessing antisemitism developed by the National Jewish Community Relations Advisory Council (NJCRAC, now the Jewish Council for

Public Affairs, JCPA) are prevailing attitudes toward Jews; acts of aggression, covert or overt, toward Jews; discrimination against Jews; expressions of antisemitism by public figures; expressions of antisemitism by religious figures; response to conflict situations; official reactions to antisemitism; antisemitic "mass" movements; personal experience with antisemitism; and anti-Zionist manifestations in which the legitimacy of the State of Israel—and therefore the legitimacy of the peoplehood of the Jews—is questioned (this does not include criticism of the policies of the Israeli government). *NJCRAC 1985–86 Joint Program Plan* (New York: NJCRAC, 1986).

9. Other behavioral manifestations are certainly present in the United States, some disturbingly so. For example, the number of incidents of antisemitic vandalism, as monitored by the Anti-Defamation League's annual "Audit of Anti-Semitic Incidents," increased each year from 1987 to 1991, although the number of such incidents declined during the mid-1990s. Analysts suggest that the ADL's audit must be evaluated in the context of the total number of bias- and prejudice-related incidents reported around the country and assessed in terms of the nature of the incident and the identity of the perpetrator (for example, the Skinhead, who expresses hate against many groups, including Jews; the teenage swastika dauber, and so on).

10. For a survey of the data and a useful bibliography on attitudinal antisemitism through 1995, see Renae Cohen, "What We Know, What We Don't Know, about Antisemitism: A Research Perspective," in Jerome A. Chanes, ed., *Antisemitism in America Today*, pp. 59–83.

11. *Patterns of American Prejudice* was published as a seven-volume series based on the University of California (Berkeley) Five-Year Study of Anti-Semitism in the United States, designed by the Survey Research Center at Berkeley and carried out by the University of Chicago's National Opinion Research Center under a grant from the Anti-Defamation League of B'nai B'rith. The eleven-item antisemitism scale developed by Gertrude Selznick and Stephen Steinberg for the Berkeley Studies was the model for subsequent surveys, including the 1981 Yankelovich, Skelly, and White poll commissioned by the American Jewish Committee and the 1992 Marttila and Kiley survey conducted for the Anti-Defamation League (see below). While there are numerous differences in the samples, study designs, and execution in the three surveys, the antisemitism scale used is substantially the same in all three. This has raised serious questions among researchers. See Tom W. Smith, "The Polls — a Review: Actual Trends or Measurement Artifacts? A Review of Three Studies of Anti-Semitism," *Public Opinion Quarterly* 57 (fall 1993): 380–93, for an exploration of these questions.

    An earlier, landmark study, *The Authoritarian Personality*, by T. W. Adorno, Else Frenkel-Brunswik, Daniel J. Levinson, and R. Nevitt Sanford (New York: Harper and Row, 1950), explored the personality of prejudice. In this American Jewish Committee study an earlier antisemitism scale was developed.

12. See, for example, the findings from the Anti-Defamation League/Marttila and Kiley survey.

13. *What Do Americans Think about Jews?* (New York: American Jewish Committee, 1991).

14. *Highlights from an Anti-Defamation League Survey on Anti-Semitism and Prejudice in America* (New York: Anti-Defamation League, 16 November 1993).

15. Carolyn E. Setlow and Renae Cohen, *1992 New York City Intergroup Relations Survey* (New York: American Jewish Committee, 1992).

16. *Highlights from an Anti-Defamation League Survey on Racial Attitudes in America* (New York: Anti-Defamation League, June 1993).
17. *Anti-Semitism in Contemporary America* (New York: American Jewish Committee, 1994).
18. The American Jewish Committee Intergroup Relations Survey of New York, while containing valuable data, is a local study; the Marttila racial attitudes survey addresses the question of prejudice in America generally and calls for its own discrete treatment.
19. The six areas examined by AJC/NORC are (1) the perceived social standing of Jews, compared to other ethnoreligious groups; (2) the images that people have of Jews, compared to those of other ethnoreligious groups; (3) the perceived influence and power that Jews have, compared to other groups; (4) the warmth or closeness that people feel toward Jews, compared to other groups; (5) social interactions between Jews and non-Jews in the areas of friendship and intermarriage; and (6) the perceived loyalty of Jews and the connection between anti-Israel and anti-Semitic attitudes.
20. Personal conversation with the author.
21. The eleven items in the "Index of Antisemitic Belief": Jews stick together more than other Americans, Jews always like to be at the head of things, Jews are more loyal to Israel than to America, Jews have too much power in the U.S. today, Jews have too much control and influence on Wall Street, Jews have too much power in the business world, Jews have a lot of irritating faults, Jews are more willing than others to use shady practices to get what they want, Jewish businessmen are so shrewd that others don't have a fair chance in competition, Jews don't care what happens to anyone but their own kind, Jews are [not] just as honest as other businessmen.
22. The Jewish-power question was asked both as an objective question and as a contextual question.
23. Cf. the AJC/NORC findings, above.
24. Indeed, social scientists and Jewish defence agencies may wish to think about getting off the antisemitism polling fix and explore other areas. Political scientist Seymour Martin Lipset, to cite one example, would prefer that social scientists study philosemitism: why do some people have an unusual affinity for—*like* or *love*—Jews?
25. On this issue, see Gary E. Rubin, "A No-Nonsense Look at Anti-Semitism," *Tikkun*, May–June 1993, pp. 46–48, 79–81.
26. *Taking America's Pulse: The National Conference Survey on Inter-Group Relations* (New York: The National Conference, 1994).
27. The apparent contradiction between a decline in attitudinal antisemitism and an increase over some of the years surveyed in the number of antisemitic incidents can be easily explained: among those relative few who profess antisemitic attitudes: in recent years there has been a greater propensity to act out their beliefs in various forms of expression, consistent with the general erosion of traditional societal taboos that has been noted in the United States.
28. In some ways the farm crisis is the most significant of these conflict situations, in that there was severe economic and social dislocation in the Plains states during the period of the crisis, and the heretofore universally accepted notion of "economic crisis triggers antisemitism" was tested. See below on triggers of antisemitism.
29. A comparison of the European and American experiences with respect to conflict situations is instructive. Do the same patterns obtain? Or is there more likely to be an antisemitic response to conflict situations in Europe?

30. 14 September 1990.
31. An essay on this issue that is dated but nonetheless worth reading is Leonard Dinnerstein's "Black Antisemitism," in *Uneasy at Home: Antisemitism and the American Jewish Experience* (New York: Columbia University Press, 1987), 218–54. Dinnerstein's essay offers a capsule review of such events as New York's Ocean Hill–Brownsville school board turmoil and other events of the 1960s and early 1970s, including early manifestations of "affirmative action." Caution, however: while Dinnerstein's essay is valuable, the polling data cited are woefully out of date.
32. For a valuable review of the data on black antisemitism, see Jennifer L. Golub, *What Do We Know about Black Anti-Semitism?* (New York: American Jewish Committee, 1990).
33. The only data that I could find are those from Ronald Tadao Tsukashima's study of Los Angeles, "The Social and Psychological Correlates of Anti-Semitism in the Black Community" (Ph.D. diss., University of California, Los Angeles, 1973).
34. Jonathan Rieder, "Reflections on Crown Heights: Interpretive Dilemmas and Black-Jewish Conflict," in Jerome A. Chanes, ed., *Antisemitism in America Today*, pp. 348–84.
35. A NJCRAC survey of twenty-five communities of significant Jewish and black populations confirms this judgment. (Telephone interviews conducted by Jerome A. Chanes of the National Jewish Community Relations Advisory Council, September 1991; unpublished findings.)
36. For a full exploration, see Arthur Hertzberg, "Is Anti-Semitism Dying Out?" *New York Review of Books*, 24 June 1993, pp. 51–57.
37. Unpublished findings, 1991.
38. See Earl Raab, "Can Antisemitism Disappear?" in Jerome A. Chanes, ed., *Antisemitism in America Today*, pp. 84–99.
39. "Taking the Measure of Anti-Semitism in the 21st Century" (paper presented to the plenary session of the National Jewish Community Relations Advisory Council, 16 February 1992).
40. Steven M. Cohen and Charles S. Liebman, *Two Worlds of Judaism: The Israeli and American Experiences* (New Haven, Conn.: Yale University Press, 1990).
41. Revealing was the observation of Senator Howell Heflin (D-Alabama), who, in his opening remarks in Senate subcommittee hearings in 1994 on language on religious harassment in the workplace for Equal Employment Opportunity Commission guidelines, averred, "We have [in this country] Americans, Jews, and others." Heflin thought he was being a nice guy.
42. 18th November 1997.
43. Tel Aviv, 1996. See chapter on United States of America by Marc Caplan of the Anti-Defamation League (pp. 215–27).
44. Philosemitism is a social-psychological phenomenon that calls for a discrete study.
45. *Exit Poll Cross Tabulations, Louisiana Runoff 1991* (New York: Voter Research and Surveys, 1991), photocopied. The raw data were interpreted by Mark Mellman of Mellman and Lazarus, Washington.
46. The question of whether there was receptivity to Duke's racist message even as his overt Klan connection was rejected or ignored is addressed by Mellman and others. Mellman points out that there are data to suggest that responses such as "reform the welfare system," conventionally considered to be code words for racism, are in fact nothing of the sort. Indeed, most Americans, when queried, respond that most people

on welfare are white and that welfare is an issue of being responsible for one's own actions, not one of race.

47. Earl Raab, "Taking the Measure of Anti-Semitism," explores this area.
48. For a comprehensive discussion of hidden, latent, and "new" antisemitism, see Tom W. Smith, *Anti-Semitism in Contemporary America*, pp. 19–22.
49. I thank Dr. David Singer of the American Jewish Committee for suggesting this example.
50. This is not to say that Jewish history is the history of antisemitism; it is not. What historians Cecil Roth and Salo Baron characterized as "the lachrymose theory of Jewish history" is a misrepresentation of the history of the Jews. Roth and Baron's point that antisemitism is but one aspect, albeit a significant aspect, of Jewish history is right on the mark.
51. See, for example, data from studies conducted over the past decade by the National Conference of Christians and Jews, Marttila and Kiley, Yankelovich, and the General Social Survey of the National Opinion Research Center.
52. "Can Anti-Semitism Be Measured?" July 1970, pp. 36–43.

**7** Steven Bayme

# Jewish Organizational Response to Intermarriage

## A Policy Perspective

American Jewry today is debating how to secure its future continuity. Some, proclaiming that the battle against intermarriage is over, call for a fundamentally new, more liberal and inclusive attitude toward mixed marriage and broader outreach to mixed-married couples. Others claim the sole hope for American Jewry lies in a renewed commitment to Jewish religion and tradition.[1] The release of the 1990 National Jewish Population Study (NJPS), however, signaled the demise of civic Judaism and constituted a clarion call to the Jewish community to address its internal religious and cultural life. Assimilation, it seemed, posed a far greater threat to the security and well-being of Jews than anti-Semitism.

The 1990 NJPS was surprising in several respects. First, intermarriage had risen to the historically high rate of 52 percent. But perhaps more surprising was that conversion, once regarded as the appropriate antidote to mixed marriage, had not increased with the rise in mixed marriages. This finding strongly suggests that as intermarriage became more pervasive in American society, it no longer appeared necessary to modify one's religious affiliation to have a single-faith household. Dual-faith households appeared no more problematic than other family models in an America in which family life was endangered in any case and seemed so welcoming of the prospect of marriage with Jews. Moreover, the decision by the liberal Jewish religious movements to accept patrilineal descent as a criterion for Jewish identification removed one of the major stimuli to conversion to Judaism. In other words, the message of patrilineality was that one need not be a Jew to raise Jewish children.

To be sure, this story of Jewish assimilation coexisted with a narrative of Jewish renewal. High rates of mixed marriage and low rates of conversion, synagogue affiliation, and childbearing accompanied smaller, yet by no means insignificant, numbers of Jews who had enriched their lives Jewishly in ways their parents or grandparents could never have imagined. Certainly, American Jews had greater opportunities to lead creative Jewish lives than at any time in American Jewish history. The question was whether they would avail themselves of those opportunities. In short, it was the best of times and the worst of times simultaneously.[2]

More particularly, the debate rages as to how to secure the Jewish future. Several themes are already discernible and must be confronted realistically in any discussion of Jewish continuity. First, the acceptability of mixed marriage must be addressed. No generation of Jewish leaders in history has failed to resist mixed marriage. However, we hear today, for the first time, calls for a "fundamentally new attitude" in which we define mixed marriage no longer as a threat to the Jewish future but as an opportunity for Jewish renewal. In short, one question in the current debate over Jewish continuity is the desirability of a new attitude toward mixed marriage. Others suggest that the new attitude reflects more wishful thinking than sober diagnosis of contemporary Jewish realities.[3]

Second, in terms of numbers, we must confront the reality that some losses are virtually inevitable. These will often be painful, for they may involve the personal families of communal leaders dedicated to the Jewish communal enterprise. Yet a realistic look at the demographics does not suggest the disappearance of the Jews. On the contrary, those committed to leading a Jewish life are doing so in ways that are incredibly vibrant by Jewish historical standards. Smaller numbers will, to be sure, lead to a decline both quantitatively and qualitatively. Fewer Jewish institutions will connote decreased potential for a Jewish cultural elite. Smaller is by no means greater. Yet, that said, the second major demographic conclusion is that the core of the Jewish community, those committed to renewing Jewish life, represents a powerful resource and reservoir of energy. A community declining from 5.5 million to 4 million is clearly a likely if not an inevitable forecast.

Yet 4 million Jews still represent a critical mass capable of sustaining much, albeit by no means all, of the current Jewish communal enterprise. To date, the demographic strength of the Jewish community has been fairly constant since 1950, at 5.5 million American Jews. By comparison with American society generally, Jews have shrunk as a portion of the American population, which has increased from 150 million in 1950 to 265 million today. Despite continued low birthrates, American Jews preserved their numbers by virtue of a temporary baby boom until the mid-1960s and some immigration from abroad through the 1980s. Moreover, the effects of intermarriage, which has risen only in the past twenty years, have not yet been felt numerically by the Jewish community—meaning that although only 20 percent of mixed-marrieds raise their children exclusively as Jews, Jewish partners in mixed marriages continue to self-identify as Jews. Therefore, the numbers have held steady for over two generations. Some losses for the future are likely, given that so few mixed-marrieds are raising their children exclusively within the Jewish faith. Yet if we forecast a Jewish community of 4 million, we would do well to remember that vibrant Jewish societies have been built with far fewer demographic and economic resources.

Third, what is in question is whether the broad middle range of Jews interested in Jewish continuity but lacking the wherewithal to provide it to their children and grandchildren can be empowered by the community to transmit Jewish heritage and identity. If losses are virtually inevitable among the 20 percent at the periphery and Jewish life remains strong among the 20–25 percent at the core, the debate rages concerning the broad middle of 50–55 percent who want Jewish grandchildren but lack the knowledge and capacity to transmit a meaningful sense of identity to their progeny. Jewish continuity initiatives at present appear to be targeted toward these "middles" of Jewish life. The optimists of the 1990s do not believe that Jewish continuity in America is in question. For them, what is in question is the future quality of Jewish life. Pessimists, however, worry that if intermarriage continues unchecked it will have a spiraling effect, whereby rates of intermarriage can approximate 90 percent, further opening the door to assimilation and erosion.[4]

At the core of efforts to enhance Jewish continuity lies the centrality of religion and religious institutions. For American Jews there can simply be no continuity absent commitment to Judaism. Pockets of energy and renewal exist within each of the religious movements, but none is lacking for problems and challenges. Although the Orthodox are generally doing well by standards of Jewish continuity, their actual demographic numbers are smaller today than a generation ago. Whereas in 1970 Orthodox Jews constituted 11 percent of the American Jewish population, today Orthodoxy stands at 6–7 percent. To be sure, among Jews under age twenty-five, 10 percent identify as Orthodox, signaling reservoirs of strength in the future. More to the point, the predictions of the demise of Orthodoxy, so common in the 1950s, appear stale and hollow in the 1990s. Orthodoxy is succeeding in retaining its young and has demonstrated great capacity for the future. Perhaps the most telling symbol of contemporary Orthodoxy was the *siyum hashas* in Madison Square Garden. The idea of Jews setting aside time for the study of Torah on a daily basis represents a powerful symbol for American Jewry. If we are to learn lessons from Orthodox experiences with Jewish continuity, it will require equal dedication on the part of the non-Orthodox movements toward strengthening Jewish education and preserving Jewish family life.

The cultural battles within Orthodoxy are perhaps more disturbing. The past forty years have witnessed the ascendancy of ultra-Orthodox groupings and the eclipse of Modern Orthodoxy as the dream of a creative and vital synthesis between Jewish tradition and modern culture. The power of ultra-Orthodoxy is particularly felt in Jewish education circles. Modern Orthodox educators routinely complain that they are forced to hire *haredi* instructional personnel. Moreover, the one-year program in Israel that has become normative for graduates of Orthodox high schools has had an enormous effect on the culture of Orthodoxy here in the United States. Students returning from the program with renewed commitment to Israel, to Jewish observance, and to the Jewish people often see little value in the ideology of Modern Orthodoxy which calls for a creative engagement with secular culture.

Perhaps the greatest challenge to Orthodoxy lies in the question of Jewish communal relations. As Orthodox Jews become more self-confident about their future and more skeptical of the continuity of the non-Orthodox movements, Orthodox triumphalism becomes expressed in ever more abrasive and contemptuous terms. The gulf between Orthodoxy and non-Orthodoxy widens, both with respect to the capacity for cooperation within American Jewry and with respect to the breach between religious and secular in Israel. Demonstrated Orthodox successes in ensuring Jewish continuity, while justly hailed by all concerned with the Jewish future, runs in tandem with continued Orthodox triumphalism and dismissal, if not outright contempt, for non-Orthodox expressions of Judaism.[5]

Conservative Jewry similarly conveys a dual image of strength and weakness. Approximately 47 percent of Jews affiliated with synagogues today are found in Conservative synagogues. Numerically, therefore, it is the largest of the Jewish religious movements. The recent study of Conservative Jews reports continued low rates of mixed marriage for current members of Conservative synagogues. Moreover, approximately 86 percent of current Conservative members believe it is important to marry other Jews. That percentage, however, declines to 32 percent among current Conservative teenagers. What Jack Wertheimer, director of the study, refers to as the "soft core" of Conservative Jewry points to significant challenges for the future of the movement and how it defines itself in the spectrum of Jewish life. At present, it is probably fair to say that most Conservative Jews do not define themselves as halakhically observant. However, they do perceive the Conservative synagogue as a wholly Jewish institution and framework in which they can lead full Jewish lives and raise Jewish families. Whether they will succeed in doing so for the future remains, as per the Wertheimer study, very much an open question.[6]

The picture of the Reform movement is considerably different yet in some respects similar. The Reform movement reports enormous numerical strength. More Jews call themselves Reform than any other denomination. However, many of these are wholly self-defined as Reform Jews, without any significant commitment to a particular Reform synagogue. In other words, part of the reason for the numerical success of Reform Judaism is that many Jews who wish, at most, a minimal connection with Jewish life define themselves as Reform. Thus, where some 38 percent of American Jews call themselves Reform, far fewer are actually members of Reform congregations.

Within Reform temples, considerable tension exists between the imperatives of in-reach to those committed to lead a Jewish life and outreach to mixed-marrieds. The current leadership of the Reform movement is signaling renewed efforts at enhancing Judaic literacy. The president of the Hebrew Union College and his counterpart at the Union of American Hebrew Congregations articulate a language of "Torah Torah Torah." Yet philosophically, real tension exists between personal autonomy and commitment to Jewish peoplehood and tradition. In effect, two trends are occurring simultaneously within the Reform movement. A trend of serious Jewish education and effort to define Reform Judaism in a language of norms, values, commitment, and demands is paralleled by a trend toward more inclusive outreach to those with the most minimal attachments to Reform Judaism. Whether the Reform movement can succeed in navigating both trends simultaneously is questionable. Already, Reform rabbis often report that the inclusion of mixed-marrieds within Reform synagogues makes it difficult, if not impossible, for the rabbi to discourage interfaith marriage.[7]

All of this points to some definite policy directions for the future. First, within all of the Jewish religious movements a renewed commitment to serious expressions of Judaism and Jewish identity is needed. Jews who are informed, literate, and knowledgeable about Jewish tradition are most likely to be committed to preservation and enhancement of the Jewish community. Thus, the test for the future should lie not so much in who is a Jew but, rather, are we the possessors of a serious Judaism?

As a minority religion in America, it is essential to declare both what is and what is not a serious Judaism. The boundary in contemporary America between Jew and Gentile is incredibly fluid. Efforts to enhance Jewish continuity cannot be limited to transmittal of what Judaism is, as important as that may be, but must also acknowledge that aspects of American culture that otherwise might be quite positive, such as the triumph of romantic love, may often be dissonant with the imperatives of Jewish continuity, which emphasizes marriage between Jews.[8]

Third, we ought to acknowledge the plurality of Jewish expression in America as resource and asset rather than as a threat and danger. That is where so many of the contemporary religious polemics in Jewish life are hurtful to the cause of Jewish continuity. Different Jews will require different avenues of expression of their Jewishness. The success of Jewish continuity rests very much with the success of all the religious movements to retain their current members and attract new adherents.

Finally, what of the vexing problem of communal responses to mixed marriage itself? A single statistic has dominated discussion on the extremely rich and comprehensive portrait of American Jewry, emanating from the NJPS of 1990: 52 percent of American Jews who married between 1985 and 1990 chose unconverted Gentile partners. Though this finding evoked wide and profound concern, it was not at first explored in depth, nor were its implications for communal policy examined carefully. Responses took a polarized form. On the one hand, some argued that "the battle against intermarriage is over," suggesting that a skyrocketing level of intermarriage was inevitable in the open society and that the only appropriate Jewish communal response was outreach to intermarried couples. Others argued that an exclusive focus on outreach based on an assumption of the inevitability of accelerating intermarriage was a serious mistake and that the outreach itself had the effect of validating intermarriage from a Jewish communal perspective. They pointed out that mixed marriage was not randomly distributed among American Jews. While intermarriage had become normative in some sectors of American Jewry, it remained uncommon in others. This suggests that efforts to lower the incidence of intermarriage were not doomed to failure; they should be pursued more energetically and deserved a larger portion of communal resources.[9]

A recent study by Bruce A. Phillips, commissioned by the American Jewish Committee and the Wilstein Institute of Jewish Policy Study, suggests some directions for communal policy with respect to mixed-marrieds. One interesting, though preliminary, finding in this study indicates that the rate of intermarriage has leveled off and may even be declining. Phillips speculates that this development may be related to the fact that communal leaders, rabbis, and parents have begun to speak more clearly and forcefully about the value of marrying within the faith. Jewish communal efforts to reinforce the norm of endogamy are particularly significant in view of the overwhelming acceptance by non-Jews of the prospect of their children marrying Jews, a finding reported on as early as 1983 in a Gallup survey.[10]

An important section of Professor Phillips's study demonstrates in detail the impact of Jewish education on rates of intermarriage. Among other conclusions, he challenges the widely held assumption that only day school education will lower the rate of intermarriage. All Jewish education during the adolescent years is particularly crucial, whether formal or informal. It is clear from this study that the Jewish community's continued investment in education for its teenagers—apart from the core reason of creating Jewishly literate Jews—will have an impact in reducing the incidence of intermarriage. The adolescent years demand this special focus because it is at that point that questions of dating, marriage, and family become critical. Jewish education during the high school years nurtures Jewish dating patterns, and these are probably the strongest predictors of Jewish inmarriage. Generally, those who date Jews in high school are most likely to do so as adults. Establishing patterns of Jewish dating during adolescence and inculcating norms of endogamy, therefore, appear to be critical in Jewish communal efforts to lower the incidence of intermarriage. Youth groups and overnight Jewish camps are identified as particularly significant in this regard.

One specific example of wise communal policy is the landmark resolution, adopted in 1991 by the Conservative movement's United Synagogue Youth (USY), urging its members to refrain from interdating and barring officers of the movement from doing so. The resolution was criticized by some who saw it as a violation of individual autonomy and as undermining future efforts at outreach to mixed-married couples. But Phillips's study reaffirms the wisdom and appropriateness of the USY resolution.

In its discussion of outreach to mixed-married couples, the study focused on the intermarrieds' openness to outreach efforts. It did not attempt to evaluate the effectiveness of these efforts in bringing about conversion or encouraging Jewish education for the children. By dividing intermarrieds into subgroups based on the religious patterns of the two spouses, Phillips was able to identify those intermarrieds who expressed the most interest in outreach efforts. The painful reality, however, is that the overwhelming majority of mixed-marrieds are not interested. The most promising target of outreach is what Phillips calls the "Judaic mixed marriage" in which Judaism remains the sole faith practiced in the home. Only about 14 percent of mixed marriages currently fit this profile. Those divorced from mixed marriages constitute a second target for outreach initiatives. Therefore, even the most enthusiastic advocate of outreach should acknowledge that the community must deal with difficult questions in assessing outreach efforts and deciding on the allocation of resources to provide them. How much effort should be devoted to pursuing intermarrieds who show little interest in outreach efforts? What are appropriate objectives for outreach efforts, and how should their effectiveness be evaluated? How should the community respond to interest on the part of some intermarrieds in outreach programs that will help them raise their children in two faiths? Are such efforts compatible with Jewish communal interests? What are appropriate Jewish communal responses and policies that will enable the community to deal with the current intermarriage crisis?

Frequently, policy discussion is colored by well-intentioned desires to provide human consolation to those affected. These, to be sure, are noble sentiments but constitute a disastrous base on which to formulate communal policy. Overall, the Jewish community must continue to pursue a multitrack and nuanced approach, consisting of prevention, conversion, and continued outreach to the mixed-married.

There are at least four reasons for pursuing a policy of prevention. First, we do it because we must. Throughout history, no generation of Jewish leaders has ever failed to resist intermarriage. Therefore, no matter how unsuccessful prevention policies may prove to be, it remains our historical mandate to continue to encourage Jewish in-marriage.

Second, were we to abandon prevention policies, the results would be even more disastrous. A climate in which there are no constraints against intermarriage would result in even higher intermarriage rates since Jews are a mere 2.5 percent of the total U.S. population. It is precisely because we have continued to maintain the Jewish communal preference for in-marriage that intermarriage rates have not risen even further. Italians and Irish already experience out-marriage rates in excess of 60 percent, while Lutherans and Methodists marry outside their respective faiths at rates exceeding 70 percent.

Third, it must be acknowledged that certain forms of prevention *do* work. We know, for example, that intermarriage rates are lower among those who have gone to graduate or professional school. This runs counter to traditional assumptions that intermarriage increases as social and educational attainments increase. But in fact the concentration of Jews is greater in graduate schools than in undergraduate colleges. There is a clear policy implication here: send our children to colleges where a significant proportion of the students are Jewish.[11]

Fourth, there is a real question of who will articulate the message of in-marriage if Jewish organizations do not. Jonathan Sarna has argued that if Jews are serious about resisting intermarriage, they must recognize that they are unique in American society.[12] The difficulty in making this point is illustrated in an article in *Moment* magazine by Rabbi Rachel Cowan, a prominent advocate of outreach to mixed-married couples. A woman approached her at the conclusion of a weekend program and expressed gratification that her son had been unable to attend. Had he been present, the woman said, he would have heard from Cowan only the message of outreach and nothing at all about the importance of marrying a Jewish partner. Cowan writes that she considered the subject and the woman's thoughts but concluded that, were she to do it over again, she would say exactly the same things.[13]

The second pillar of Jewish communal policy toward intermarriage is conversion to Judaism. This has been our primary response to the reality of intermarriage. The policy imperative appears clear: to overcome remaining barriers that may inhibit conversion. In this regard, there appear to be at least three initiatives that may be undertaken. First, we must underscore the Jewishness of the Jewish partner. When the Jewish side of the family cares about Jewish identity, the likelihood of the non-Jewish partner's converting to Judaism is all the greater.

Second, there is the issue of the communal reception of converts to the Jewish faith and fold. Our tradition here is very clear—make no distinction between those who are born Jews and those who have accepted the Jewish covenant. A policy that is serious about conversion must encourage the Jewish community to adopt a receptive and positive attitude toward converts to Judaism.

Finally, serious discussion is necessary concerning the absence of a uniform conversion procedure acceptable to the various religious movements in North America. In the absence of a uniform procedure, we are creating both personal and communal tragedies when people converting to Judaism in good faith find their conversion invalidated by other sectors of the community. The failure to develop a uniform procedure signals that the traditionally primary response to intermarriage—namely, conversion—can never really succeed. To be sure, there are questions concerning conversion. The 1990 NJPS refers to "self-declared converts"—30 percent of those currently practicing Judaism but not born Jews did not undergo any official conversion ceremony or procedure. It is hard to avoid skepticism about the commitment of such self-declared Jews.

Similarly, we have concerns regarding "one-generation converts." Joseph Tabachnick and Brenda Forster, in a study of converts to Judaism in the Chicago area, underscored the weakness of Jewish identity among converts to Judaism in their failure to oppose the intermarriage or interdating of their own children. Fewer than 50 percent of the Jews by choice in the Chicago area sample placed importance on their children marrying within the Jewish faith. Only 28 percent felt that it was important for their children to limit their dating to other Jews. Tabachnick and Forster rightly conclude that a serious conversion policy must explain to those entering the Jewish fold the importance of marriage to other Jews and the building of Jewish families. Otherwise, conversion only postpones the ultimate dissolution of Jewish identity through the out-marriage of one's children and grandchildren.[14]

The most sensitive and difficult area is that of continued outreach to mixed-married couples. Questions have been raised concerning the effectiveness, appropriateness, and priority level of outreach programming to mixed-married couples. First, there is the question of respective costs and priorities. Is more to be gained by working with those who are outside the community or by attempting to enrich those who are already committed to leading a Jewish life? It is not enough to say that we must do both. In an age of limited resources, serious questions arise as to what is the most effective channeling of the resources available to us.

Second, we must ask whether the community really has the capacity to reach mixed-married couples. Do they wish to be chased by us? Or do we waste valuable communal resources in a vain pursuit of people who have no desire for contact with the Jewish community? Actually, we do not even know if our costly advertising to mixed-marrieds even reaches its intended audience.[15]

Third, we must address the question of tension between outreach efforts and efforts designed to ensure the conversion of the non-Jewish spouse. Rabbi Alexander Schindler, in an important address to the UAHC biennial in November 1991, criticized the tendency of outreach efforts to become neutral toward conversion. Very often, in a well-intentioned desire to build bridges to mixed-marrieds, outreach advocates do not make strong cases for conversion to Judaism. When mixed-married couples tell the community they want involvement but not conversion, a serious question arises as to how effective outreach has been.[16]

Finally, there is the question of the sustaining power of outreach. Absent conversion, can outreach sustain the Jewish identity of the mixed-married family in the second and third generations? Thus far, the evidence is negative. Research conducted by Peter Medding of the Hebrew University points to the importance of an "unambiguous Jewish identity" in preserving the Jewishness of the home. The Jewish identity of a mixed-marriage home is often highly ambiguous, due to the presence of Christian symbols and the observance of Christian holidays. It should come as no surprise, therefore, that, absent conversion to Judaism, mixed-marriages result in "terminal Jewish identity" by the third generation.[17] Medding's research corroborates the earlier findings of Egon Mayer in research undertaken by the American Jewish Committee in 1983.[18]

Given these questions, it still remains necessary to advocate outreach on both human and demographic grounds. On the human level, these are all members of our families, and the Jewish community clearly is not about to turn its back on them. On the demographic level, mixed marriage poses serious dangers of significant demographic losses within a generation.

Therefore, outreach must be carefully targeted to those mixed-marrieds who are interested in leading a Jewish life. Steven Cohen's analysis of the Jewish community differentiates between the 20–25 percent who are core activists, the 15–20 percent who are totally uninterested, and the 50–55 percent who form the "middles" of Jewish life—those who are interested in Jewish continuity in the form of Jewish grandchildren but are unsure how to attain it. Cohen, as well as Jack Ukeles, has argued that outreach efforts ought be targeted to those middles—to those who have already expressed some interest in leading a Jewish life. Our goal ought be to enlarge the core by shrinking the middle.[19]

To be sure, that route presupposes that some losses become inevitable. Moreover, it is probably only a minority of mixed-married couples that actually fall among the middles. The majority have already signaled, by their decisions to raise their children outside the Jewish faith, that they have little interest in the Jewish community. Here again it becomes a question of how we utilize limited resources to the best effect.

Moreover—and this is of equal sensitivity—outreach must be appropriately designed so that the overall message of the Jewish community regarding Jewish marital values, the importance of building a Jewish home, and the importance of finding Jewish mates is clearly communicated. Our task, while respecting the personal choices of individuals, must be to articulate communal norms that are seen as being the preferred model for Jews generally. To quote Charlotte Holstein, past chair of the AJC's Jewish Communal Affairs Commission: "Certainly, on a personal level, I felt touched by the new research findings and revised policies. However, it was necessary to draw the distinction between what I felt emotionally and what rationally was good for the survival of the Jewish community as a whole. . . . The basic question was at what point do one's personal experience and one's communal responsibility blend or act in concert and when do they conflict or cause tension?"[20]

To be sure, that distinction is difficult to make and will often get lost. Failure to make the distinction, however, runs the risk of communicating a vision of intermarriage as simply one acceptable option among others. It is at that point that we have abandoned our responsibility as Jewish leaders and have fallen into a trap of moral relativism that anything that Jews happen to do automatically becomes legitimate.

Some initiatives indeed have been launched that address these concerns. The Memorial Foundation for Jewish Culture has started programs in the Metro–West New Jersey and the St. Louis federations focusing on outreach to "underaffiliated" Jews, including mixed-marrieds, within a broader population of those who are only marginally affiliated.[21] Those programs wisely identify the underaffiliated rather than the mixed-married as the problem. They target outreach to those who have expressed some desire to lead a Jewish life. And by including mixed-marrieds within a broader outreach program they do not blur the crucial message of endogamy.

In conclusion, we face four pressing tasks, and we must confront them with candor and honesty: First, let us acknowledge that this is a disaster in the making.

Left unchecked, intermarriage will dilute both the quantity and quality of the Jewish community. Pretending that this is not a problem will succeed only in providing false comfort to some. Second, Jewish leaders must distinguish between their personal needs and those of their families and the good of the community for which they have responsibility. Comforting statements are important, but they are a poor basis for framing communal policy. Third, the community of social scientists must realize that what they say and do creates a cultural climate and communal norms affecting intermarriage. Statements of "pure" social science often get translated as prescriptive advocacy and can prove harmful. The Talmud's advice to sages, "Watch your words," is no less applicable to contemporary social scientists.

Finally, outreach advocates must lower their sights, avoiding messianic claims and focusing on what is doable and realizable rather than holding out false visions to the community. Statements to the effect that outreach will "transform the intermarriage crisis into the greatest opportunity of modern Jewish history"[22] are simply irresponsible. We must acknowledge that the core of the Jewish future is not likely to come from the ranks of the mixed-marrieds. Nevertheless, we should pursue outreach with the objectives of preserving Jewish identity and enabling mixed-married couples to incorporate a sense of Jewishness within their homes.

American Jewry, in short, as it enters the twenty-first century confronts significant challenges, not to its status as Jews in America but rather to its identity as American Jews. All Jewish organizations are continually faced with the challenge of transforming their agendas so as to advance the all-inclusive goal of Jewish continuity. Whether American Jewry and its leadership succeed in realizing that goal remains very much an open question. The currents of renewal coexist with the currents of assimilation. Whether American Jews envision their future as empowered and enriched by Judaic heritage or as overwhelmed and demoralized by the reality of assimilation will, in many ways, determine the course of future Diaspora history.

## Notes

1. See the contrasting viewpoints in Alan M. Dershowitz, *The Vanishing American Jew* (Boston: Little, Brown, 1997), esp. pp. 42–44, 320–24; and Elliott Abrams, *Faith or Fear* (New York: The Free Press, 1997), chap. 5.
2. Samuel C. Heilman, *Portrait of American Jews* (Seattle: University of Washington Press, 1995), pp. 5–7.
3. Steven Bayme, in *Approaches to Intermarriage* (New York: American Jewish Committee, 1993), pp. 9–15.
4. Steven M. Cohen, *Content or Continuity?* (New York: American Jewish Committee, 1991), pp. 40–42, 51–52.
5. Steven Bayme, "On Orthodoxy and Non-Orthodoxy," *Jewish Week*, May 2, 1997, p. 26.
6. Jack Wertheimer, ed., *Jewish Identity and Religious Commitment* (New York: Jewish Theological Seminary, 1997), pp. 15–16, 61–62.

7. Stephen Fuchs, "A Reform Jewish Response to the Intermarriage Crisis," in *The Intermarriage Crisis: Jewish Communal Perspectives and Responses* (New York: American Jewish Committee, 1991), pp. 51–53.
8. Jack Wertheimer, Charles Liebman, and Steven M. Cohen, "How to Save American Jews," *Commentary* 101, no. 1 (January 1996), pp. 47–51.
9. Steven Bayme, "Enhancing Jewish Identity: Form and Content," in David M. Gordis and Dorit P. Gary, eds., *American Jewry: Portrait and Prognosis* (West Orange, N.J.: Behrman House, 1997), pp. 394–403.
10. An earlier version of this section appeared previously as the preface, jointly authored with David M. Gordis, to Bruce A. Phillips, *Re-examining Intermarriage* (New York: American Jewish Committee and the Susan and David Wilstein Institute of Jewish Policy Studies, 1997), pp. vii–x. See also Tom W. Smith, *What Do Americans Think about Jews?* (New York: American Jewish Committee, 1991), pp. 16, 56.
11. Steven M. Cohen, *Alternative Families in the Jewish Community* (New York: American Jewish Committee, 1989), pp. 9–10, 30.
12. Jonathan Sarna, "Interreligious Marriage in America," in *Intermarriage Crisis* (New York: American Jewish Committee, 1991), p. 4.
13. Rachel Cowan, in *Moment*, April 1992, p. 14.
14. Brenda Forster and Joseph Tabachnick, *Jews by Choice* (Hoboken, N.J.: Ktav, 1991), pp. 100–102. See also Jonathan Sarna, "Reform Jewish Leaders, Intermarriage, and Conversion," *Journal of Reform Judaism*, winter 1990, pp. 1–8, which also raises the specter of "one-generation converts."
15. Jacob Ukeles, "Does Outreach Justify Investment? Alternatives to Outreach," in *Intermarriage Crisis*, pp. 17–19.
16. Alexander Schindler, "The Reform Jew: Values, Practices and Visions" (paper presented to the 61st General Assembly of the Union of American Hebrew Congregations, Baltimore, November 2, 1991).
17. Peter Medding et al., chapter 12 in this volume.
18. Egon Mayer, *Children of Intermarriage* (New York: American Jewish Committee, 1982).
19. Steven M. Cohen, *Content or Continuity: The 1989 National Survey of American Jews* (New York: American Jewish Committee, 1991), pp. 51–52.
20. Charlotte Holstein, "When Commitments Clash: One Leader's Personal Dilemma," in *Intermarriage Crisis*, p. 35.
21. Steven Bayme, *Outreach to the Unaffiliated: Communal Context and Policy Direction* (New York: American Jewish Committee, 1992), p. 15.
22. See, for example, David W. Berlin, "Confronting the Intermarriage Crisis with Realism and Effective Action," in *Intermarriage Crisis*, p. 39.

8 Sylvia Barack Fishman

# Negotiating Egalitarianism and Judaism

## American Jewish Feminisms and Their Implications for Jewish Life

### Introduction: Jewish Feminisms in a Post-Feminist Age

Today's American Jewish culture can arguably be said to have reached a postfeminist state. During the last quarter of the twentieth century the lives of American Jews as individuals, in family groups, and in communal settings have undergone sweeping changes vis-à-vis gender role construction. However, many of these changes have come to seem so commonplace that their revolutionary status and flavor has been virtually lost. Feminism and its impact on American Jewish life seems to some observers a nonissue, concerning just those few women who combine fervid Jewish and feminist concerns. Indeed, in the recent *Portrait of American Jews*, by a preeminent ethnographer of American Jewish communities, the author dismisses Jewish feminism as affecting only "the minority of those American Jews who chose to be actively Jewish."[1]

Despite the camouflage of familiarity, however, a broad variety of feminisms flourish in American Jewish life today and continue to produce change across the spectrum of mainstream environments. Observing large Jewish organizations and the cultural artifacts they produce can provide useful demonstrations of both the grass-roots nature and the diversity of continuing Jewish feminist sensibility in the United States. The national president of Hadassah proudly declares that Hadassah women have "returned to our Jewish feminist roots," and the June/July 1996 issue of *Hadassah* magazine features the following feminist-influenced political, cultural, and religiously oriented articles: "Letter from Washington: Synergy and Harmony," by Hanita Blumfield, described as follows: "Jewish women are finding that the strength they give to the women's movement can provide benefits for the Jewish agenda as well"; "Nice Jewish Girls," by feminist journalist

Marlene Adler Marks, described thus: "Cultural stereotypes run about two generations behind, but the images of American Jewish women are catching up with a new reality"; "World of Our Mothers," by Rahel Musleah, an illustrated essay on Jewish women painters who "defied the stereotypes of their generation"; and "Late Mitzvas," by Barbara Trainin Blank, about geriatric female prayer leaders and *b'not mitzvah*.[2] Among the subjects discussed in this most middle-class, middlebrow publication are the Jewish Caucus in Beijing, the importance of grooming a new generation of Jewish feminist leaders, the resentments of nursing home residents toward traditional Jewish restrictions on women, wife abuse in Jewish homes, and the spiritual fantasies of pre–Bat Mitzvah girls. The articles search for "heroines . . . who go beyond the boundaries life sets up for them."[3] As one author unequivocally states, "Hadassah has a place at the feminist table."[4]

Diverse varieties of American Jewish feminism are interesting not only in and of themselves but because they provide a useful vantage point from which to view religious subgroups in American Jewish societies. Both in those areas of life that are unique to Judaism and those that Jewish women share with their non-Jewish neighbors, feminism has had and continues to have powerful impact. This essay is concerned with Jewish feminisms that focus on Judaism, rather than on political or social agendas; thus, the discussion addresses religious, personal, and organizational/institutional areas such as bringing women to the center of synagogue worship by increasing participatory roles for women in public Judaism, creating woman-centered rituals that celebrate women's life cycle events, creating gender-neutral and/or woman-affirming liturgies, providing increased levels of Jewish education for girls and women of all ages, breaking the glass ceilings that keep women out of positions of decision making and power in Jewish communal life, and promoting feminist scholarship and literature that reclaims the history of historical Jewish women and interprets the experiences of contemporary Jewish women.

Notwithstanding the Judaic focus of this essay, it is important first to take note as well of the many Jewish feminisms that are not exclusively Jewish in their concerns. Some feminisms center on personal aspects of life: women's health issues, friendship circles, erotic liaisons, marriage, family relationships, fertility, childbearing, and child rearing. Others are concerned with professional development: education, vocational choice, and career advancement. While Jewish women share these areas of feminist impact with other American women, their attitudes are sometimes influenced by Jewish communal norms and values. For example, in their feminist enterprises, Jewish women can draw on the cultural biases toward competence, articulateness, and assertiveness in women, which were common in traditional Jewish societies, rather than docility and decorative value.[5] Jewish cultural biases favoring women who blend marketplace activism[6] with familial passion may be reflected in the fact that among Jewish women, unlike women in other religious and cultural subgroups, higher levels of education and occupational achievement are accompanied by higher levels of expected fertility.[7]

American Jewish women as a group display a remarkably liberal "package" of personal, social, and political beliefs and attitudes. Not only in the bicoastal major metropolitan areas but even in midwestern communities, Jewish women are passionately in favor of personal and reproductive choice and value independence for themselves and their daughters.[8] Although literature, film, and popular culture still often portray Jewish women as militant traditionalists, in terms of demographic realities and personal ideals, ethnic boundaries have been relocated among contemporary American Jewish women. The contemporary normative "nice Jewish girl" has dramatically transformed expectations from those of her predecessors.

Regardless of which variations of feminism engage a particular American Jewish woman, American Jewish feminisms are organized along two continuums of sacred values that profoundly affect many aspects of Jewish experience. Running from radical right to radical left, these continuums include (1) the authority of rabbinic law, including but not exclusively determined by denominational preference, and (2) commitment to egalitarian principles. Using examples of transformations of Judaic aspects of women's lives to illustrate diverse forms of Jewish feminism, this essay explores the placement of American Jewish feminisms along the axes of those contiuums and discusses the ways in which the diversity of Jewish feminism reflects the pluralistic character of American Jewish religious communities.

## Two Primary Principles: Egalitarianism and Halakhah

In preemancipation Diaspora Jewish communities, rabbinic law, Halakhah, transcended religious activity and was a basic organizing factor of life, affecting all aspects of personal, familial, and communal behavior. For Orthodox and traditional Conservative Jews in the United States today, rabbinic law still enjoys hegemonic status, at least in theory, although for most American Jews it has far less impact on daily life than in earlier historical periods. For those American Jewish women and men who acknowledge the authority of rabbinic law, all religious change must take place within halakhic parameters. For those whose interpretive framework relegates the halakhic system to a more or less permeable guideline, rather than a strict boundary for behavior, however, social and religious changes have been more dramatically achieved, although not without their own struggle and conflict.

American Jews are affected not only by the traditional guidelines of Halakhah but also by American principles and traditions. Egalitarianism is a value with deep and important roots in American life that has gained increased salience in the wake of civil rights efforts and the feminist transformation of American society. For many American Jews, egalitarianism is a sacred principle, and for some it has greater spiritual relevance and power than does rabbinic law.

If we place Halakhah and egalitarianism on a continuum and look at their manifestations in American Jewish societies, we see that they often (but not always) occupy a chiastic relationship. At two extremes stand the radical right and the radical left, ideological positions occupied in reality by relatively small groups of people in comparison with the great middle ground of American Jewish life. However, although the radical right and radical left are numerically small groups, they have an impact and a mythic significance in American Jewish life that goes far beyond their numbers. Indeed, it is not uncommon for normative Jewish subgroups to measure their own dedication to Torah Judaism or to liberal ideals against the extremes of right or left, respectively.

The radical right is defined by a communal interpretive framework in which the Halakhah stands unique and unmitigated as a moral and behavioral guideline, and considerations extrinsic to rabbinic law have little authority. The radical right is unabashedly hierarchical in its ideological organization. In some radical right groups rabbinic leaders and their families occupy near divine status, and lines between even right-wing religious groups are sharply maintained. Small groups on the radical right support the training of descendants of the biblical priestly class, *kohanim*, to perform sacrifices and make plans to re-create the Temple on the Temple Mount in Jerusalem. Irrelevant in this framework are such diverse concerns as the nonegalitarian nature of the priestly class or the potential outcry against animal sacrifice by animal rights activists or the political realities of Israel's relationships with her Arab neighbors. When other persons on the radical right oppose these ideas, they do so because they believe they transgress some halakhic ruling, not because they are "wrong," using guidelines external to the Halakhah to judge the situation.

Similarly, persons on the radical left of the continuum use egalitarianism as the principle by which all other things are judged. The radical left proposes remaking Judaism as a completely egalitarian civilization, leveling traditional hierarchies of person, place, and time and reincorporating woman-centered spiritual elements that have been rejected by historical Judaism. Some on the radical left are primarily theological in their attentions; they advocate bringing goddess language or imagery or rituals derived from pagan rites or witchcraft into a transformed Judaism, claiming that "paganism" and "witchcraft" are words used by a repressive patriarchal religious hierarchy to disenfranchise and demonize powerful women. As feminist writer Kim Chernin approvingly expresses this goal, "Can it be that the initiation process occurring among women today is part of an historic moment in which the Great Goddess of the ancient world is hastening back to redress the patriarchal imbalance in our culture? . . . . When a woman seriously asks herself what it means to be a woman, she is pulling at a thread that can unravel an entire culture."[9] Others on the radical left are primarily political in their focus, insisting that relationships between women worldwide have far more salience than racial or ethnic distinctions, which are putatively used to artificially divide women from each other. For such feminists on the radical left, the demands of Jewish history and tradition can make few claims against the sacred principle of human equality.

TABLE 8.1
Model of a Continuum: Egalitarianism and Halakhah

| | | | *Normative Religious Groups* | | |
|---|---|---|---|---|---|
| *Radical Left* | *Normative Reconstructionist* | *Normative Reform* | *Normative Conservative* | *Normative Orthodox* | *Radical Right* |
| Remake Judaism as completely egalitarian belief system. Reject hierarchies of gender, status, socioeconomic factors. Remake Judaism as woman-friendly, species-friendly, earth-friendly religion. Re-incorporate woman-centered elements rejected by patriarchal, monotheistic, hierarchical Judaism. | Egalitarianism sacred principle. Reject most hierarchies: status, gender, religious functionaries. Regard Halakhah as system created by men, with considerable historic inspirational interest but not binding. Reject outright paganism and witchcraft. | Egalitarianism of gender accepted and priestly class not factor, but status differences exist for institutional needs. Marked differentiation between religious functionaries and congregants. Socioeconomic status can make difference. Halakhah object of study and respect: can provide options but not binding. | Egalitarianism of gender accepted by most but not all. Women may be required to live up to higher standards to "qualify" for religious or congregational leadership positions. Hierarchy of religious functionaries. Most don't distinguish priestly class. Socioeconomic hierarchies matter institutionally. Halakhah cherished guideline for religious life; however, Judaism is viewed as organically developing and responsive to changing social conditions. | Egalitarianism of gender not an official value. Halakhah binding. Liberalization of gender rolls only through legal precedents. Many halakhic hierarchies accepted; priestly class distinctions part of worship service. Separation of men and women during prayers. Religious functionaries respected but share values and lifestyles with congregants. Socioeconomic hierarchies matter, but learning provides alternative status. Many reject pluralism and are mistrustful of interaction with non-Orthodox. | Hierarchies desirable and continually reinforced. Egalitarianism seen as anathema destructive to historical Jewish lifestyles. Goals: rebuild Temple, reinstate priestly class, reinforce gender role distinctions. Reject expanding women's roles even within rabbinic guidelines. Utterly reject pluralism; draw lines between differing grades of Orthodox Jews. |

Between these two extremes of radical right and radical left stretches the broad expanse of normative American Jewish life: Normative Reform, Reconstructionist, Conservative, Traditional, Left and Centrist Orthodox communities, in which the principles of Halakhah and egalitarianism exercise rival claims (see Table 5.1). At the left edge of normative Reform, egalitarianism has far more authority than does Halakhah; at the right edge of normative Orthodox, Halakhah occupies a category of authority totally different from egalitarianism. But at every point in the normative continuum, negotiations between the two continue.

## Aspect of Women's Lives Affected by Feminisms, Egalitarianism, and Halakhah

The complexity of negotiations between egalitarianism and halakhah and the placement of American Jewish feminisms are best illustrated by looking at specific areas of feminist change. Indeed, by exploring the changes that have occurred as a response to the feminist challenge, we learn a great deal about the way in which each wing of Judaism has responded to change during the last decades of the twentieth century. We also acquire a deeper understanding of the peculiarly American intersection between Judaism and modernity.

In American Jewish communities, feminisms affecting the most women in the most Jewish ways are connected to the synagogue, Jewish education, and the sacralization of women's life cycle events. The vast majority of the American Jewish population, including substantial numbers of Jews who believe themselves to be on the right segment of the halakhic continuum, now find it appropriate to provide women with some life-cycle event celebrations (such as *Shalom Bat* or Bat Mitzvah), with formal Jewish education, and with some public communal prominence. Similarly, across the denominational spectrum, female attendance at prayer services is seen as appropriate. The roles women play in the synagogue, however, differ from denomination to denomination.

### *Separateness and Equality in Public Religious Settings*

Institutionally, the most visible, critical, and sometimes controversial focus for Jewish feminist activity has been the placing of women at the center of public Jewish religious life by counting them toward the prayer quorum, having them lead the congregation in prayer, calling them to the public reading of the Torah, and ultimately having them serve the congregation in a rabbinical or cantoral capacity. In traditional Jewish societies only males were encouraged to pray at three specific times daily in a public quorum—a minyan—of ten men. Only men were obligated in prayer by the time-bound format, only men could be counted toward the quorum, and thus only men comprised—or could lead—the praying congregation, the *tzibbur*.[10] Nevertheless, the image of women praying is not a new invention. Jewish law obligated women to pray daily in private, as their family responsibilities permitted them.[11] However, the assumptions and the language of Judaism, its narratives, laws, and liturgy—with a number of noteworthy and deeply significant exceptions—have largely been framed in the language of men to reflect the experiences of men.

Feminism is a point of pride within the Reform movement, which was from its inception committed to the idea that an inferior position for women is an immoral, outmoded aspect of a non-Western, Oriental mind-set. Nevertheless, women did not occupy truly equal status with men in the earliest days of Reform Judaism's origins in Germany. Separate seating remained in force, and the leadership of Reform congregations was exclusively male.[12] In the United States, the movement of women into egalitarian modes went forward somewhat more easily. Much discussion was devoted to women's participation in choirs at the dedication of the Bene Israel synagogue in Cincinnati in 1852. Those who opposed female participation said that, according to Jewish custom, it was inappropriate to hear female voices in the public services. However, American Reform Judaism gradually succeeded in eliminating many of the inequalities that had separated men and women in Jewish prayer. Reform congregations introduced mixed choirs, abolished the women's gallery, built temples with family pews, and substituted the confirmation ceremony for boys and girls in place of Bar Mitzvah for boys alone.[13] Although the leadership for Bat Mitzvah ceremonies must accurately be assigned to the Conservative movement, the Reform movement was the first to ordain a practicing woman rabbi in 1972, and the increasing presence of Reform female rabbis and cantors changed the American Jewish religious environment. Today, many Reform Jews garner considerable satisfaction from the trend-setting role the Reform movement has played in giving women high-profile positions in public Judaism.

However, it is important to remember that full participation in prayer services has been limited not only because of gender issues but also because of the hierarchical structure of formal worship in most mainstream Conservative and Reform congregations. In Reform congregations, for many decades paid religious functionaries provided the active leadership during services, with congregants, both male and female, playing largely passive, audience-like roles. To the extent that a given congregation provides prayer leadership roles to persons who are neither rabbis, cantors, nor choir members, most contemporary Reform congregations allow women to perform in equality with men. Although Reform female rabbis have yet to attain proportionately high status, lucrative job placements, many feel that professional opportunities are moving in a more positive direction for women. Today, the Reform cantorate is disproportionately female, and women seem to have few difficulties in obtaining high-status positions as cantors.

Feminism occupies a more complicated position within Conservative Judaism because of the movement's commitment to the guidelines of Halakhah. As Judith Hauptman points out, "Today, the Conservative Movement is home to those Jews who . . . accept *halakhah* as binding, and yet recognize that as ethical and social thinking becomes more refined, it becomes necessary to modify religious practices."[14] Looking back at the expansion of women's roles within the Conservative movement, several rabbinic rulings contributed to incremental modifications. The Conservative Committee on Jewish and Standards, the official halakhic body of the movement, included a statement permitting women to be called to the Torah in 1955, prior to the development of a full-fledged Jewish feminist movement but about the same time that Bat Mitzvah celebrations were being launched in some congregations.

By late 1971, Jewish women's prayer and study groups were being formed. Women from the New York Havurah joined with like-minded friends to explore the status of women in Jewish law. This group evolved into Ezrat Nashim, a particularly influential although small organization, composed primarily of women who identified as Conservative Jews, including many who were quite liturgically literate and had attended the Hebrew-speaking Ramah camps sponsored by the Conservative movement. Members of Ezrat Nashim appeared at the convention of the Conservative Rabbinical Assembly (RA) in 1972 and had a powerful influence on many rabbis. In 1973 the Committee on Jewish Laws and Standards passed an independent statement that women could be counted equally with men in a minyan; in 1974 they passed a series of proposals that allowed women to participate fully in synagogue rituals, in the role of prayer leader, for example. The issue of rabbinical ordination of women was wrestled with in 1973 and 1974, and the decision was made to grant ordination to appropriate female candidates.[15] In 1987 the movement officially endorsed the idea of female cantors. The first Conservative female rabbi was ordained in 1985;[16] prior to that time, several Conservative women had sought ordination at the Reconstructionist Rabbinical College because it was unavailable to them at the Jewish Theological Seminary (JTS).

The issue of egalitarian behavior is not completely settled within all Conservative congregations. While the great majority of congregations associated with the Conservative United Synagogue or organization come close to full equality, a minority continue to struggle with conflicting approaches by differing factions within the congregation and within the leadership cadre. Some United Synagogue congregations have undertaken lengthy study sessions to enable congregants to reach an amicable consensus on the topic of women's public religious roles. For these congregations, traditional halakhic considerations often seem at odds with feminist, egalitarian considerations.

For members of the Union of Traditional Congregations, the feminist issue of female religious leaderships proved the modernist straw that broke the organizational camel's back: traditionalists within the Conservative movements had been actively writing and lobbying to try to prevent JTS ordination of women. A report by two scholars, warning that the true soul of Conservative Judaism was found among its most observant, most anti-women's-ordination segments, articulated the credo of a small but determined group.[17] After the JTS made the commitment to prepare women for rabbinical ordination, a dissenting group of Conservative scholars, pulpit rabbis, and laypersons broke off from JTS and the RA to form a new organization, called first the Union for Traditional Conservative Judaism and then the Union for Traditional Judaism (UTJ).

Current leaders of the UTJ insist that they are far from a one-issue organization and that their goal is to upgrade halakhic observance in general, not to object solely to female rabbis. The movement has its own rabbinical school, rabbinical organization, and member congregations. The organization places great stress on many aspects of rabbinic law, including Sabbath and Kashruth observance. The UTJ's newsletter, *Hagahelet*, emphasizes the movement's mutual commitment to tradition and modernity, to laws of personal and communal piety and those of social action.[18]

Nevertheless, the UTJ has yet to take a proactive stance on women's issues through such innovations as creating a credentialed category of leadership roles for women. Ironically two New York Orthodox congregations created para-rabbinical internship positions for women in 1998, and Israeli Orthodox feminists and their rabbinical supporters had already succeeded in creating a cadre of female *to'anot*, legal advocates, who assist women in difficult divorce cases, but the UTJ had not yet at that time, six years after its inauguration, devised any new policies vis-à-vis women and leadership. Although it consistently hires women for the executive director position and has published carefully researched responsa literature on women's issues, which clarify a generally positive and supportive attitude toward women studying rabbinic texts and participating in Jewish life in areas that are not prohibited by Halakhah, the UTJ is still widely perceived by outsiders as having arisen in a negative response to feminism and the ordination issue.

The Reconstructionist movement has played a significant role in the egalitarianizing of the American Jewish community, especially through the Havurah movement, which emerged in the 1960s and 1970s primarily out of Reconstructionist environments. Havurah worship and study groups were informal in their organization, and they encouraged participation by individuals in the group rather than paid professionals. Initially, the egalitarianism of most Havurah groups was an equality of males only; men worshipped and studied and women occupied a familiar, enabling stance. As the Havurah movement developed and its women acquired more liturgical skills, however, it became the locale for the most complete incorporation of women into public prayer and leadership.[19] The Reconstructionist Rabbinical College (RRC) welcomed female candidates early in its history; it graduated the first Reconstructionalist female rabbi in 1974. The RRC was the first to regard alternative lifestyles as complementary to, rather than antithetical to, Judaism; and lesbian and gay rabbinical candidates have found their first and most welcoming environment in the RRC. The movement has an ongoing task force on women's issues, and it continues to provide important Jewish feminist leadership to the American community as a whole.

Feminism is most feared and suspected in the Orthodox world but nevertheless has had significant impact upon American Orthodox life. In 1997 and 1998, the first and second International Conference on Feminism and Orthodoxy brought together one thousand and two thousand participants, respectively, in Manhattan for two days of numerous study sessions and plenary discussions. Participants ranged from bewigged Hasidic women to *talit*-wearing feminists from the left-most segments of Orthodox life, but the vast majority came from established modern and centrist Orthodox communities. A large proportion of conference participants were also members of the Women's Tefillah Network, a countrywide coalition of all-female *tefillah* (prayer) groups, in which women have the opportunity to lead prayers and read the Torah, to be vital participants in a context in which for millennia they were nonessential auxiliaries. Such *tefillah* groups have been operating in scattered communities in the United States since the early 1970s but became more numerous in the 1980s and 1990s.

Members of a new hybrid community, Orthodox Jewish feminists are in many ways a heterodox group, spanning a wide spectrum of ages and religious and educational backgrounds. Their ranks include a dozen forward-looking Orthodox rabbis who research legal precedents for expanding women's spiritual expression and work with women, both individually and in groups, to implement their findings.[20] In Orthodox settings, conformity with Jewish values and behaviors are intermixed with conformity with American values and behaviors. *Tefillah* groups are the embodiment of a consciousness that has coalesced Jewish and American values in complicated ways.[21] From traditional Judaism comes the value of daily prayer (Maimonides, Nachmanides, and other religious authorities prescribe private daily prayer for women);[22] however, traditional Judaism does not envision women as members of a congregation or as needing participatory group settings for prayer. Many Orthodox women will not recite the 20 percent of the prayer service reserved for a quorum of ten men unless they receive permission to do so by a recognized male rabbinical *posek* (person recognized as a competent formulator of Jewish law). Still, the consciousness of women as a spiritual group, rather than spiritual individuals, is drawn from contemporary American feminist cultural values, and the desire of women to work together to change their own destiny is derived from the most cherished American beliefs in self-sufficiency and the responsiveness of fate to individual courage and resourcefulness.

Ethnographically, the behavior of *tefillah* group participants is symbolic of the juxtaposition of modernity and tradition in the lives of American Orthodox Jews. Women's *tefillah* group participants have conformed in significant ways to the communal expectations of Orthodox Jewish life. When Orthodox women began to organize women's prayer meetings, from the early 1970s onward, most of them looked for a rabbinic *posek* who would give them "permission" *(heter)* to pursue their group their agendas by creating religious rulings in their favor. It has been typical of Orthodox women's *tefillah* groups to ask one particular rabbi to be their group's regular and official *posek* and to refer all ritual questions affecting the group to him. In doing so, they are acting within a religious framework that is nonegalitarian in ways not directly connected to gender. Within traditional Jewish communities, the rabbi whom the community takes on as its regular spiritual leader *(morah d'asrah)* is the ultimate authority on religious questions. The organic development of the body of religious law is due to the fact that traditional Jewish individuals and communities continue to approach rabbinic authorities with large and small questions. As in any legal system, the rabbi who has been asked a question researches rabbinic legal literature for precedents and discussions and bases his answer *(p'sak)* on his best understanding of rabbinic law and the particular circumstances of the supplicant. Within the spiritual symbolism of the halakhic system, each rabbinic adjudicator reflects a divinely inspired authority, passed on from Moses through the great rabbinic sages of the talmudic and medieval periods.

The protocols of traditional rabbinic decision making are hierarchical, and in their unameliorated form they fly in the face of such democratic, egalitarian principles as the rule of the majority or consensus building. When a rabbi delivers a halakhic decision, it is under ideal Orthodox conditions, regarded not as a suggestion on which the congregation votes but as a legal ruling. Members of the community need not ask the rabbi for his judgment, but once they have asked him to adjudicate a religious question, they must abide by his answer whether or not they are happy with the answer. Traditional Jews sometimes "shop around" *before* they ask a rabbi to render a decision, and it is common for people to ascertain what the answer is likely to be before they ask a particular rabbi. However, once a *posek* has been asked, especially if the adjudicator is a rabbi and a *morah d'asrah*, his answer to the supplicants is, quite literally, Jewish law. For this reason, Jewish law often differs in its details from community to community and even from congregation to congregation.

However, *tefillah* group participants are often *perceived* as behaving transgressively by some Orthodox leaders and co-religionists. Despite the enormous care taken by Orthodox women's *tefillah* group participants to find acceptable religious authorities for their activities, their very existence has often antagonized rabbinic and lay segments of the Orthodox community. The fact that most prayer sessions of women's *tefillah* groups involve handling and reading from a Torah scroll has proved a source of great controversy in the Orthodox community, despite the fact that women are not proscribed by Jewish law from handling or reading from a Torah scroll at any time in their reproductive cycles.[23] Although menstruating women are not prevented by Jewish law from doing so, communal customs have grown up over the centuries that view females touching the Torah scrolls as a highly nonnormative event.

Responding to the issues of women conducting their own Torah service, as well as to the correctly perceived feminist influence in the evolution of prayer groups, for over two decades rabbis as individuals and in groups have issued statements prohibiting or permitting participation of Orthodox women in *tefillah* groups.[24] At times these rabbinic pronouncements have escalated into communal scandals, attracting heavy press coverage, with verbal and written invective used as a weapon against burgeoning women's participation. Ironically and perhaps counterintuitively, contemporary rabbinic prohibitions often have a sociological rather than a halakhic basis: prayer group participants have been accused of lacking appropriately pure motivation, of looking for power rather than for spiritual expression, of rejecting their foremothers or Jewish notions of femininity, and of having been influenced by the "licentiousness of feminism." In contrast, rabbinic defenders of women's *tefillah* groups usually eschew ideological arguments and set forth the halakhic precedents for each element of the prayer groups' activities.

### *Bat Mitzvah Ceremonies*

Some observers have been surprised by the determination of feminists who focus on women's rituals and ceremonies. Their activities should be placed in the context of the apparent human need for ritual. Every civilization, society, and religion has devised rituals and ceremonies to mark passages in the lives of its citizens and adherents. Participants find such observances meaningful for many reasons. Perhaps most important, they confirm the communal importance of personal experience; they assure the individual that s/he does not celebrate or mourn alone, because the community as a whole shares the joy and the grief. Ceremonies legitimate not only the life-cycle event itself but, by extension, the individual who celebrates and mourns as well. The message of a life-passage ritual to the individual is "Your happiness and your sorrow are real; your friends rejoice and grieve with you; your life and its events are important to all of us." In addition, when the ritual or ceremony is part of a religion, it has another layer of significance—it is sanctified and is marked as an event that is important to God as well as to human beings.

Although Judaism has historically provided ceremonies to sanctify the life-cycle events of Jewish males, Jewish women have found many of the most profoundly moving events of their lives unmarked and unsanctified. For much of Jewish history, female life-cycle events have largely passed without formal communal, ceremonial responses and even without provision for personal rituals that might express the sacredness of the moment as the individual woman herself experienced it. It is a mark of how thoroughly the principles of egaltarianism have been absorbed into American Jewish societies that this is no longer the case.

Perhaps the most widespread sociological result of the religious efforts of Jewish feminism is the popularity of the Bat Mitzvah celebration. Reconstructionist founder Mordecai Kaplan, who was also closely associated for many years with the JTS, is considered the first to suggest the concept of Bat Mitzvah,[25] and Conservative Judaism made popular the actual celebration of this event. At first, few families chose to celebrate the Bat mitzvah,[26] and during the 1950s and 1960s many Conservative synagogues limited the celebration to the less problematic Friday night services, when the Torah is not read. Moreover, Reform congregations did not take the lead in mainstreaming Bat Mitzvah ceremonies because at the time when they were gaining popularity, many Reform congregations had substituted the concept of Confirmation ceremonies at the completion of Sunday school studies for the concept of Bar Mitzvahs. It was not until some time later, when the Reform movement was reincorporating a number of more traditional rituals into its services, that it also reincorporated the Bar Mitzvah ceremony—and with it the Bat Mitzvah as well. By the late 1980s, however, most Conservative and almost all Reform and Reconstructionist congregations had made Bat Mitzvah and Bar Mitzvah ceremonies virtually identical, including calling girls to the Torah. Today, the vast majority of American girls aged twelve and up and women aged eighteen to twenty-four have had Bat Mitzvah celebrations.

Once nearly unthinkable in Orthodox settings, the celebration of Bat Mitzvah now also crosses American denominational lines. Orthodox practitioners have slowly responded to the pressure to celebrate a girl's religious majority. Some congregations have established a format for celebrating Bat Mitzvah on Sunday morning or Shabbat afternoon at a special *seudat sh'lisht*, the traditional festive "third meal." At these occasions the girl typically delivers a *d'var torah*, a homiletic address marking the seriousness of the occasion. Other congregations leave the mode of celebration up to the discretion of the child and her parents. These celebrations have become commonplace in many Orthodox circles, with families sometimes traveling great distances to be at a Bat Mitzvah, just as they would for a Bar Mitzvah. Much feminist commentary on this phenomenon has tended to concentrate on the disparity between limited Orthodox forms of Bat Mitzvah, on one hand, and egalitarian Conservative, Reform, and Reconstructionist modes of Bat mitzvah on the other; however, Orthodoxy has in fact traveled farther than other wings of Judaism in breaking away from previously prevailing norms.

Girls interviewed in a study of Orthodox Bat Mitzvahs differed greatly in their attitude toward the event, depending on the seriousness with which the family and community treated the accompanying ceremony.[27] One of the girls interviewed said she looks forward to using her skills at future women's prayer groups, which take place on the premises of her Orthodox synagogue: "We have the women's Torah reading on Simchat Torah, and I *layned* there. Each time, it's something so special that it makes me wish that I could do this more often." Significantly, this Orthodox Bat Mitzvah girl stated firmly that she does not want to pursue these activities in an egalitarian setting: "To become Bat Mitzvah in a way that is not approved by the Torah defeats the whole object."[28]

The impact of Bat Mitzvah celebrations is not limited to children: Sisterhood Sabbaths at suburban temples have housewives spending months preparing Torah readings in Hebrew, with cantilation. Even elderly women are rediscovering a heritage that they thought, for most of their lives, was forever closed to them. One woman interviewed by a journalist was the last in her family to have a Bat Mitzvah, after "my two daughters and two granddaughters celebrated their bat mitzvah." Women in nursing homes, remembering a time when "women were nothing in the religious service," are now "changed from being negative and frightened to being positive"; as one puts it, "I never expected this, but it feels incredibly good."[29] In what was perhaps the world's largest known Bat Mitzvah ceremony, with over 1,000 women in attendance, 122 adult women at the Hadassah National Convention participated in a group Bat Mitzvah on July 15, 1996, at the Fountainblue Hotel in Miami Beach, Florida.

### *Jewish Education for Women*

The ubiquitousness of the Bat Mitzvah has had a critical and not always acknowledged side effect: the celebration of Bat Mitzvah among American Jewish females over the past two decades has virtually erased the gender gap in Jewish education. Before the Bat Mitzvah became popular, one-third of American Jewish women used to receive no formal Jewish education whatsoever; today, the fact that girls, like boys, must prepare for Bat Mitzvah has brought them into supplementary schools and day schools at nearly the same rates as their brothers and has virtually erased the gender gap in Jewish education. Thus, Bat Mitzvah is the link to the formal Jewish education which has emerged as the true "Jewish connection" for American Jewish women today. Data from the 1990 National Jewish Population Survey (NJPS) show that women who have received six or more years of supplementary school or dayschool are the most likely to marry Jewish men, belong to and attend synagogues, volunteer time for and give money to Jewish causes, practice Jewish rituals in their homes, visit and feel attached to Israel, and have children and provide them with a Jewish education—regardless of the wing of Judaism in which they were raised.

Although many opinions in rabbinic law state that intensive formal Jewish education is inappropriate for females, high-level Jewish education for women was actually initiated on a wide scale a century ago in a daring response to the challenges of secular modernity. Observing that in enlightened societies Jewish women who lacked deep knowledge of Judaic texts might more easily drift away from Jewish lifestyles, Sara Schnirer, a pious Eastern European woman who had been well educated in Germany, established the Bais Yaakov movement, which revolutionized Jewish education for girls. In 1917 she opened a school with 25 girls; the school expanded rapidly, and new branches were established. In 1937–1938, 35,585 girls were enrolled in 248 Bais Yaakov schools in Poland alone.[30] Although the original Bais Yaakov movement's vitality in Europe was brutally cut off during World War II, along with millions of lives and an irreplacable, richly diverse cultural heritage, the basic assumptions underlying the formation of the Bais Yaakov schools has now been accepted by even the most ultra-Orthodox groups in the United States: the education of girls is widely viewed as a necessity for the preservation of a traditional Jewish way of life.

In day schools ranging from the Satmar school, Bais Rochel, which eliminates the twelfth grade to make sure its graduates cannot attend college, to coeducational Orthodox schools such as Ramaz in New York and Maimonides in Boston, which provide outstanding secular education and teach their boys and girls Talmud together, the crucial necessity for providing girls with a Jewish education has become an undisputed communal priority. During the past decade, it has also become increasingly popular for Orthodox young women to spend a year of religious study in Israeli yeshivot between high school and college. A broad spectrum of seminaries for girls and women have prospered in Israel and in major American metropolitan areas, in response to ever-increasing interest in high-level Jewish education for females: Drisha Institute for Jewish Education in New York is one such noteworthy educational setting. Stern College for Women, an undergraduate school of Yeshiva University, now offers courses in Talmud, as do a growing number of Orthodox synagogues.

The fact that Lubavitch schools still assiduously avoid teaching Talmudic texts to girls masks the little publicized fact that the late Lubavitcher Rebbe stated that women should be taught the Gemara in order to preserve the quality of Jewish life and in order that the tradition should be passed down from generation to generation. In a Hebrew article he urges that women be taught the oral Torah so that they, who provide the most consistent presence in the home, can supervise and guide their children's religious studies. They should study subjects with their husbands, even including the "fine, dialectical" points of law which most previous rabbis posited as being inappropriate for women. These study sessions are necessary, Rabbi Schneerson said, because without them women can easily be seduced by the charms of secular studies. He wrote: "It is human nature for male and female to delight in this kind of study. Through this there will develop in them (the women) the proper sensitivities and talents in the spirit of our Holy Torah."[31] Indeed, today in every wing of Judaism, from the traditional right to the creative left, advanced schools of Jewish education that either cater to women or are coeducational are flourishing.

### *Jewish Women's Scholarship*

In a parallel development, Jewish women's scholarship has developed into a full-fledged field in colleges and universities across the United States. Recent research has revealed that formal Jewish education is the key differential in creating new generations of committed American Jews. However, when males and females sit together in a Jewish studies classroom, the texts they read and the issues they discuss may not be equally relevant to both genders. Unless the curriculum has been composed with a consciousness of gender equity within the framework of Jewish schooling, most or all of the texts studied frequently are androcentric in their focus; female students may be absorbing something besides a strong Jewish identity. In the worst case scenario, some say they "learn" that women do not really count in Jewish history, culture, or life.

Scholars interested in analyzing the connections between gender, religion, social and historical change, and cultural milieu have explored the history of women in Jewish societies from the Bible onward and have produced scores of pioneering works on Jewish women in the fields of Bible studies, rabbinics, history, literature, sociology, psychology, and popular culture. These scholarly works have had a significant impact on individual departments, on particular fields, and on Judaic studies as a whole. Thousands of students each year take college courses, taught by feminist scholars, that focus on women in Judaism. Moreover, not only college and university students have been affected by the ground-breaking writing of several generations of Jewish feminist scholars.[32] The insights of female academics are slowly being incorporated into Jewish studies curriculums for children, teenagers, and adults as well.

Institutional responses to the growth of Jewish feminist scholarship have flourished in recent years. In 1997 the International Research Institute of Jewish Women (IRIJW) was established by Hadassah at Brandeis University; the IRIJW incorporates Jewish women's historical and contemporary experiences in diverse interdisciplinary contexts by holding conferences, creating a monograph series, and promoting scholarship in a broad spectrum of subject areas relevant to studying Jewish women. In the same year, the Jewish Women's Archive was established in Brookline, Massachusetts, for the purpose of retrieving and publicizing the history of Jewish women. In addition, 1997 saw the publication of *Jewish Women in America: An Historical Encyclopedia* in two massive volumes, edited by Paula Hyman and Deborah Dash Moore and featuring 800 biological and 110 topical entries.[33] Numerous resource books and bibliographies are continually published in areas related to Jewish women's studies, including a critical sourcebook on Jewish American women writers[34] and many others.

Jewish women's studies programs have been established at Brandeis University, the Jewish Theological Seminary, the Reconstructionist Rabbinical College, and elsewhere. Academic women are organized into a Women's Caucus at the Association for Jewish Studies conference, which enables them to attend more closely to each other's works and to supportively share their experiences in the field. Each of the major religious groups has devoted time at recent conferences to discussion of incorporating gender issues and women's studies into their religious school curriculums, and Brandeis University Women's Studies Program held a conference on "Gender in the Day Schools" (February 1996), which has been expanded into an ongoing national initiative. On a more popular level, intellectual and social issues and books of interest to Jewish women are publicized by Jewish feminist magazines such as *Lilith*, which premiered in 1976, in addition to the house organs of various Jewish women's organizations, many of which have become decidedly more feminist in their orientation as the years pass.

### *Birth-related Ceremonies*

Beyond the Bat Mitzvah and formal Jewish education, the sacralization of women's life-cycle events is often limited to smaller, more Jewishly involved groups of women, in contrast to the situation of rituals marking the life-cycle events of Jewish men from birth. Ceremonies surrounding the birth of a son are extensive, long sanctified by Jewish law and community custom.[35]

In contrast to the communal joy and profound feelings evoked by the circumcision and other male birth ceremonies, ritual responses to the birth of a girl were minimal in the past. Jewish feminists have frequently talked and written about their determination that the lives of Jewish girls and women should be accorded deep spiritual significance as well. The creation of sacred rituals, however, is a complex task and one that often touches on sensitive issues. Suggestions for new ceremonies or liturgical responses to such events as the birth of a daughter, the onset of menses, a girl's religious coming of age, childbirth, miscarriage or abortion, or menopause can seem to some observers to be alien intrusions into an ancient tradition. Some Jewish feminists are very alert to religious sensitivities, well educated in Jewish texts and attitudes, and careful to make use of materials that are clearly in the spirit of Jewish tradition. Others, however, freely incorporate materials from other cultures, which serve as additional irritants to those who oppose Jewish feminist innovation. Opponents of such Jewish feminist innovations sometimes accuse Jewish feminists of criticizing and rejecting two thousand years of Jewish religious observance, history, and thought through the introduction of woman-oriented ceremonies and prayers.

Since Jewish feminists who focus on sacralizing women's life-cycle events are clearly involved in "inventing tradition," one of the great challenges facing them is to ground innovative ceremonies in the traditions of the past so that they will evoke a sense of deep connections with historical Jewish women and communities. Today the birth of a Jewish girl in Jewishly active circles across denominational lines is likely to be the occasion for meaningful ceremonies and celebrations. The Sephardic custom, *seder zeved habat*,[36] "celebrating the gift of the daughter," has been adapted in many communities into the more commonly entitled *shalom bat*, "welcoming the daughter," or *simhat bat*, "rejoicing in the daughter." Once a little-known concept, the *shalom bat* has become popular in many Jewish communities. In the home or synagogue, with mother and daughter present, friends gather to listen to talks, eat, sing, and celebrate together. It is very common to announce the child's name at this ceremony and to discuss the origin of the name. Time is often devoted to recalling and honoring the person after whom the daughter has been named.

Some parents use traditional Sephardic prayers; others compose new prayers for the occasion; still others make use of printed materials that have been written and disseminated in liberal Orthodox, Conservative, Reform, and Reconstructionist circles.[37] Roslyn Bell, reviewing the many methods now in use for welcoming a Jewish daughter, notes that "the Reform movement includes a 'Covenant of Life' ceremony in its *Gates of the Home* prayer book for home usage. There is also a naming prayer in the Reconstructionist prayer book. The Conservative Rabbinical Assembly has a printed certificate that can be presented upon the birth of a daughter . . . and some Orthodox synagogues, such as Lincoln Square Synagogue and Kehilath Jeshurun of Manhattan, have printed procedural suggestions for a *simhat bat*."[38]

The ritual invisibility of the Jewish mother—except as her presence affects her husband—has absorbed the attention of some Jewish feminists. Today, Jewish women are reclaiming and composing sacred ceremonies that celebrate their unique roles in the reproductive process. Many of these ceremonies make use of ancient blessings, quotes, and other materials. In many traditional synagogues today the mother recites aloud *birkat hagomel*, the traditional prayer of thanksgiving for deliverance from a potentially dangerous situation, when the Torah is read at the first Sabbath service after childbirth. The mother recites the prayer either standing at her place after her husband's Torah reading (in Orthodox synagogues) or after she herself receives an *aliyah* (in non-Orthodox services). This custom of a woman coming to synagogue and saying the *birkat hagomel* marks a feminist change from the past, when new mothers led more restricted lives and the husband recited this prayer on his wife's behalf because a woman's voice was seldom raised for herself in a public setting.

Across the spectrum, Jewish feminists are actively involved in composing, re-creating, and reclaiming blessings in an attempt to fill that vacuum. In the Orthodox world there is great resistance to creating new blessings, and some authorities feel that such creations are actually prohibited. Most acceptable to Orthodox women are prayers rendered acceptable by the passage of time: some blessings are a century or more old, examples of the Yiddish *tekhinnes*, Yiddish prayers for women—and sometimes authored by women—passed down from mother to daughter, which were earlier attempts to fill the lacunae of Jewish women's spiritual experiences.[39] Among women in the more liberal wings of Judaism there is use of original, recently authored women's blessings which also often draw heavily on biblical and traditional materials.[40]

### *Women and Their Weddings*

The one event of Jewish women's lives that has been vigorously celebrated for hundreds of years in both Ashkenazi and Sephardic traditional societies is the transformation of a girl into a bride. The *kallah*, bride, for a short but glorious time is a special person indeed. Contemporary normative-right Jewish feminist brides often add to traditional practices events of an overtly spiritual or scholarly nature. Thus, some Orthodox and right-wing Conservative brides have adopted egalitarian principles into the traditional wedding format: Some prepare a prenuptial scholarly talk, the result of some months of study, to be delivered at an engagement party on a Sabbath before the wedding (sometimes in combination with a bridal *aliyah* to the Torah) or in a bridal room that more closely parallels events in the groom's room *(hatan's tisch)* before the traditional veiling ceremony. Indeed, within centrist to left-wing Orthodox and traditional Conservative communities, it is now quite common for the bride to have a full-fledged *kallah's tisch*, or bride's table, at which female relatives and friends enjoy scholarly talks, refreshments, singing, and dancing before the wedding ceremony commences. This event is supplementary to or replaces the traditional *Shabbat kallah* on the Saturday before the wedding, during which time the bride's friends keep her company while her bridegroom is called up to the Torah *(ufruf)* in another worship community.

Within normative Conservative and Reform Judaism, the traditional *ketubach*, the wedding contract, is sometimes adapted so that it is more reciprocal. Some brides and grooms change the English format only; at some weddings changes extend to the Hebrew contract and liturgy as well. Double-ring ceremonies, in which both bride and groom make declarations to each other, are common. Passages from the biblical Songs of Songs are sometimes sung by women and men as part of the expanded liturgy; this new custom incorporates traditional materials into a very nontraditional setting and implementation.

However, for some Jewish feminists, the traditional wedding contract, the *ketubach*, seems irredeemably flawed, because in terms of its language it is basically a purchase agreement in which the groom promises the bride financial, social, and emotional security in exchange for the exclusive rights to her sexual (and by implication reproductive) capacities.[41] Some within the Jewish feminist community dispense with traditional marriage materials altogether and compose their own original ceremonies of union. For Jewish lesbians who attend the weddings of heterosexual friends, traditional ceremonies often seem especially exclusionary, and some have urged wholesale revisions more inclusive to alternative lifestyles. Some have urged the Jewish sanctification of partnering commitments, while others reject the concept of marriage as inherently flawed and inappropriate for persons living in alternative family units.

### *Divorce and* Agunot

The sweep of diverse Jewish feminisms is felt in divorce proceedings as well as marriages. According to rabbinic law, in order for a woman to remarry she must receive an official Jewish divorce document, a *get*, from her husband. The *get* is seen as a necessary step in dissolving a Jewish marriage: just as the marriage was begun by a religious contract, it must be terminated by the appropriate religious contract. If a man does not issue a *get*, he can still remarry, according to religious law, but a civilly divorced or abandoned woman remains an *agunah*, a chained woman, until she receives a *get* or her marriage is annulled. Observers have estimated that *agunot* in the United States number in the many hundreds, and those in Israel in the many thousands. Should an *agunah* remarry without benefit of a *get*, a child of the new marriage is considered illegitimate, a *mamzer*, and cannot marry another Jewish person except one who is also a *mamzer*. (According to Jewish law, children born of premarital sexual unions are legitimate; only the child of a married woman and a man not her husband is illegitimate.)

In the Reform community, many rabbis advise congregants in the words of a publication by the Union of American Hebrew Congregation's Committee on the Jewish Family: "Reform Judaism in the United States has interpreted divorce as a purely civil action to be dealt with in the secular courts. It eliminated the *get* as anachronistic and therefore unnecessary."[42] This is seen as an advantage by some Jewish feminists, who believe that the procedures connected with a traditional Jewish divorce are demeaning to women. Others, however, feel that this "liberal" approach was devised to meet the needs of Reform men in liberating themselves more easily from first wives. Exclusive dependence on the civil divorce may potentially complicate the lives of first wives who later wish to remarry more observant men. It is also potentially creating a class of Jewish children who are, unbeknownst to themselves, considered illegitimate according to Jewish law and who will not be able to marry spouses from the Conservative and Orthodox communities.

The Conservative movement devised a clause before the emergence of Jewish feminism, authored by the late Professor Saul Lieberman in 1953, which is meant to be added to the *ketubah* and arranges for an automatic *get* in the case of a civil divorce.[43] The movement has since suggested other strategies to be used if the Lieberman clause has not been inserted into the *ketubah*, including a Conservative *p'sak* (rabbinical decree) approving of nullification of the original wedding contract.

The Orthodox world continues to struggle with the *get* issue. Several organizations have been formed that help individual women and publicize the plight of chained women, including Agunah, Inc., G(et) E(quitable) T(reatment), and others. In Israel, a small cadre of women have been trained to be *to'anot*, legal advocates for women dealing with recalcitrant husbands in Jewish courts of law. A special *bet din*, rabbinic court, which specializes in utilizing marriage annulment as a strategy to deal with uncooperative, abusive, or mentally disturbed husbands, has been created in Israel as well. Nevertheless, much of the Orthodox community continues to deal with each case on an ad hoc basis. Some rabbis make use of the nullification technique, ruled as an Orthodox *p'sak* by the late Rabbi Moses Feinstein, and some insert a conditional divorce clause, or *t'nai*, into the original wedding contract. The Orthodox rabbinate is regularly urged by Orthodox Jewish feminists and by the families of *agunot* who are trapped by often callous, abusive, vindictive, or apathetic ex-husbands to find and implement an effective class action solution.

### *Mikveh: New and Old Uses for the Ritual Bath*

Rabbinic law requires brides and married women to bathe thoroughly and then to immerse themselves in the *mikveh* following menstruation and seven "white" days, prior to initiating or resuming sexual activity. Much to the surprise of older American Jews, many of whom regarded the *mikveh*—if they thought of it at all—as a quaint relic of outmoded attitudes and lifestyles, interest in the *mikveh* has had a renaissance of sorts in feminist circles. The traditional halakhic prenuptial visit to the *mikveh* has been championed by many Jewish feminists on the left side of the halakhic continuum, most of whom have no intention of regularly maintaining the family purity laws after marriage. A key factor was Rachel Adler's positive discussion in the first *Jewish Catalogue*.[44] Feminists exploring Jewish women's spirituality and religious expression, together with well-educated younger generations of Orthodox women who take religious obligations seriously and newly observant women who seek the structured environment and sexual limits of Orthodoxy, have revitalized *mikvehs* in many communities. Two female rabbis, graduates of the Reconstructionist Rabbinical College, wrote an article while they were students about how *mikveh* ties into their search for Jewish feminist spirituality: "It appeals to the individual on the many levels of her spiritual existence and relationships. First, it addresses her relationship with her future husband—that intimate, binding relationship of two people who at times fuse in body and soul. Next, it addresses her relationship with other Jewish women, who have ancient and current ties to her through water. Finally, it addresses her relationship with all Jews, through Torah and its folkways."[45]

In addition, the *mikveh* has taken on importance as the locus of new, specifically feminist ceremonies, such as ceremonies for healing after rape, miscarriage, or abortion.[46] These events are often powerfully significant to women, and they yearn for the acknowledgment and amelioration that religious rituals and ceremonies can offer.

### *Death-related Rituals*

Some personal life-cycle events revolve around the lives and deaths of others. The death of a parent, in particular, is a momentous life-cycle event for surviving children. Traditional Jewish law treats mourning sons and daughters identically in many ways. Both men and women are required by Jewish law to exhibit public and private mourning behavior: during the period of shiva (for seven days after the funeral) they are expected to wear torn clothing, to avoid bathing, to cover their mirrors, to sit on low stools, and to avoid commerce or daily tasks such as food preparation. The practical effect of the latter prohibition is that even the mother of a large young family is prohibited from kitchen tasks during the week of shiva. These tasks must be assumed by nonmourners, thus allowing the female mourner to confront her grief with the same intensity as a male mourner. For a month after the funeral it is customary for neither men nor women to cut their hair. For a year after the funeral, avoidance of joyous celebrations (except for their own children's weddings and bar/bat mitzvahs), particularly those with live music, is equally incumbent upon both males and females.

However, in many traditional Jewish circles only men are assumed to be required to recite the kaddish prayer in memory of their parents. The recitation of the kaddish prayer (which is actually a paean to God's greatness and does not refer to death) has attained a powerful symbolism for many, perhaps most Jews.[47] For most American Jews, the kaddish is significant because it is a way to publicly honor and show devotion to a departed parent and to express one's commitment to the totality of the Jewish people, linking the values of the past with an as yet unknown future. Even Jews who are in many other ways rather removed from formal prayers and religious rituals are often punctilious about reciting the kaddish during the mourning period and on the *yarzheit*, anniversary of a parent's death.

In articles and interviews[48] many women say they remember being deeply offended by their exclusion from public prayer after the death of a parent. Because Orthodox or traditional Conservative synagogues are those most likely to have daily prayers, many women who otherwise worship in liberal Conservative, Reconstructionst, or Reform congregations on Sabbath or holidays have sought opportunities to recite the kaddish in more observant prayer communities. They have often discovered that some synagogue regulars regard the daily prayer services as kind of privileged male turf, regardless of that particular congregation's official stand on female participation in Sabbath morning services. Such exclusions during a time of extreme vulnerability evoke strong feelings among many women. Indeed, experiences around the issue of saying kaddish for a parent are among the most universal, transdenominational factors in the radicalizing of women and the formation of Jewish feminist commitments.

It is noteworthy, however, that social change is underway. In many congregations, feminism has quietly changed the socioreligious culture. Women showing up in the early dawn hours to say kaddish in modern Orthodox or Conservative synagogues are no longer a complete rarity. Their needs are usually accommodated with some small show of graciousness or at least grudging silence. Thus, although right-wing practitioners usually assume that kaddish is a ritual for men only (in some circles rabbinical students are hired to say kaddish for a person so "unfortunate" to have only daughters), in the rest of the American Jewish world daughters also work through the complexities of their grief in the public recitation of this ancient prayer.

## Conclusion: Feminisms Mainstreamed in American Jewish Life

As this overview demonstrates, despite the fact that American Jewish women, like many other middle- and upper-middle-class women, are likely to begin sentences with "I'm not a feminist, but . . . ," their lives have been transformed by feminism according to virtually every sociological measure. Whether spurred by personal experience or other motivations, the creative exploration of Jewish lifecycle celebrations for females has affected huge numbers of American Jewish women. Even women who are not directly involved in the more intensive forms of Jewish feminist spirituality have a different relationship with their own religious and ethnic heritage in an environment in which women have increasingly become public Jews.

The attitude of American Jews toward women has been sweepingly more liberal than that of other American ethnic groups and than that of Jews in some other areas of the world, such as Israel and Latin America. American Jews, for example, are overwhelmingly committed to equal educational and occupational opportunity for women and to reproductive choice. Thus, in the realm of personal choice, marriage, and family planning, the American community has by and large relocated its ethnic boundaries. Rather than being defined as a community that is highly prescriptive in its gender role construction, American Jewish men and women today, especially outside Orthodox communities, tend to be characterized by more permeable gender role constructions than those found in many other groups.[49]

In the religious realm as well, American Jewish life has been deeply affected by goals. Feminists with diverse backgrounds, attitudes, and agendas within the American Jewish community have been struggling for the past three decades to make American Judaism more feminist in its structure and liturgy. Those reformers who actively work to bring women into positions of power and public prominence in worship services or synagogue politics or who attempt to change Jewish liturgy so that it incorporates biblical women, reflects women's experiences, uses gender-neutral language are quite conscious of the fact that they are working with two distinct belief systems. Wherever they can, they try to find precedents to lend traditional legitimation to their activities, but outside the Orthodox world, even in the absence of such traditional precedents, most of them see the feminist moral imperative as being so compelling that they must and should proceed with change.

For some Jewish women across the denominational spectrum, these feminist strivings are an active enterprise and the subject of passionate concern. For many more, feminist change has become part of the everyday texture of life and thus does not seem to them to be specifically feminist in resonance. Just as contemporary young women may not think of feminism when they attend Ivy League schools, acquire professional training, or rise through the corporate ranks, women may not think of feminism when they attend a girl's yeshiva to study Talmud in Jerusalem, celebrate their own or their daughter's Bat Mitzvahs, are called to the Torah, or are voted synagogue president—but feminism has made these behaviors possible and continues to do so. In addition, role models affect the larger population in a plethora of overt and subtle ways; even the most passive female congregant who looks up from her prayer book and sees a female rabbi, cantor, synagogue president, or Bat Mitzvah celebrant has different feelings about her own role in the Jewish community.

In strictly numerical terms, behaviorally practicing American Jewish feminists far outnumber either practicing Orthodox or Reconstructionist Jews. While few active feminists would declare their struggles over or their battles entirely won, in American Jewish life today feminist change has effected great change in the lives of individual Jews, their families, their organizations, and their places of worship and socialization. Ironically, it is the very domestication of Jewish feminisms, their incorporation into the lives of millions of American Jews, that demonstrate their success—and account for their perceived invisibility.

## Notes

1. Samuel C. Heilman, *Portrait of American Jews: The Last Half of the Twentieth Century* (Seattle: University of Washington Press, 1995), p. 94.
2. Marlene Post, "President's Column: Soul Talk," *Hadassah* 77, no. 10 (June/July 1996), pp. 4, 6.
3. Rahel Musleah, "The Arts: World of Our Mothers," *Hadassah* 77 (June/July 1996), pp. 53–57.
4. Hanita Blumefeld, "Letter from Washington: Synergy and Harmony," *Hadassah* 77 (June/July 1996), p. 20.
5. Paula Hyman, Charlotte Baum, and Sonya Michel, *The Jewish Woman in America* (New York: Dial Books, 1986), a pioneering work in exploring the Jewish cultural bias toward competent women.
6. Hasia Diner, "Jewish Immigrant Women in Urban America" (paper presented for the Mary I. Bunting Institute, Radcliffe College, 1979).
7. Frank C. Mott and Joyce Abma, "Contemporary Jewish Fertility: Does Religion Make a Difference?" *Contemporary Jewry* 13 (1992), pp. 74–94.
8. Sid Groeneman, "Beliefs and Values of American Jewish Women" (report by Market Facts, Inc. presented to the International Organization of B'nai B'rith Women, 1985). The data were drawn from 956 questionnaires roughly divided between Jewish and non-Jewish informants. They showed that Jewish women in the Midwest had political and personal attitudes fundamentally like those of Jewish women in New York and California, whereas midwestern non-Jewish informants were far more conservative than those on either coast.
9. Kim Chernin, *Reinventing Eve: Modern Woman in Search of Herself* (New York: Times Books, 1987), p. 25. See also Barbara Walker, *The Woman's Encyclopedia of Myths and Secrets* (New York: Harper & Row, 1983); and Merlin Stone, *When God Was a Woman* (New York: Harcourt Brace Janovich, 1978) for the theories that some left-wing Jewish feminists have incorporated into their own feminist theology.
10. Avraham Weiss, *Women at Prayer: A Halakhic Analysis of Women's Prayer Groups* (Hoboken, N.J.: Ktav Publishing House, 1990), pp. 43–46, documents such opinions as the comments of the Meiri (Provence, 1249–1316), who notes that the *Kahal*, the congregation, excludes women, *Beit ha-Behirah* to *Berakhot* 47b, and many other sources for the concept that "men carry out public responsibilities; women's role is private."
11. Jewish tradition indicates that each woman, like each man, has her own personal connection with her Creator. Indeed, the biblical Hannah's heartfelt prayer was considered by talmudic sages to exemplify correct and effective communication with God (*Berakhot* 30b–31a).
12. Sally Preisand, *Judaism and the New Woman* (New York: Behrman House, 1975), pp. 30–35.

13. David Philipson, *The Reform Movement in Judaism* (New York: Ktav Publishing House, 1907/1976), pp. 377, 485n.
14. Judith Hauptman, "Women and the Conservative Synagogue," in Susan Grossman and Rivka Haut, eds., *Daughters of the King: Women and the Synagogue* (Philadelphia: The Jewish Publication Society, 1992), pp. 159–181, quotation on p. 170.
15. An extended discussion of the process through which Conservative Judaism moved toward more inclusive roles for women can be found in Sylvia Barack Fishman, "Praying with Women's Voices," in *A Breath of Life: Feminism in the American Jewish Community* (New York: Free Press, 1993), esp. pp. 150–53.
16. See Simon Greenberg, ed., *The Ordination of Women as Rabbis: Studies and Responsa* (New York: Jewish Theological Seminary, 1988).
17. Charles S. Liebman and Saul Shapiro, "A Survey of the Conservative Movement and Some of Its Religious Attitudes" (survey sponsored by the Jewish Theological Seminary of America in cooperation with the United Synagogue of America, September 1979, unpublished).
18. Information on *Hagahelet* and the UTJ's other publications can be obtained by writing to Union for Traditional Judaism, 811 Palisade Avenue, Teaneck, New Jersey 07666.
19. Riv-Ellen Prell, *Prayer and Community: The Havurah in American Judaism* (Detroit: Wayne State University Press, 1989), pp. 273–315.
20. Those interested in researching this issue further should look for publications by Rabbis Avraham Weiss, Saul Berman, Joel Wolowelsky, Simcha Krauss, Emanuel Rackman, Aryeh Frimer, and David Silber, among others.
21. See Sylvia Barack Fishman, *Negotiating Both Sides of the Hyphen: Coalescence, Compartmentalization, and American-Jewish Values* (Cincinnati: University of Cincinnati Judaic Studies Program, Lichter Lecture Series, 1997); see also Fishman, *American Jewish Lives in Cultural Context* (Albany: SUNY Press, forthcoming).
22. Maimonides (1135–1204), *Mishneh Torah, Tefillah* 1:1–2, 4–5. For a complete discussion of this issue, see Avraham Weiss, *Women at Prayer: A Halakhic Analysis of Women's Prayer Groups* (Hoboken, N.J.: Ktav, 1990).
23. The Palestinian *Tosefta* states that women may study the Torah even when they are menstruating or have recently given birth (*Tosefta Berakhot*, chap. 2, para. 12); the Babylonian Talmud disagrees, insisting that women may not study Torah (Babylonian Talmud *Berakhot* 22a) except in the case of exceptional women; however, it does not link the prohibition to ritual impurity but instead to the putative intellectual poverty of females.
24. For a fuller discussion of this phenomenon, see Sylvia Barack Fishman, "Praying with Women's Voices," pp. 158–70.
25. Carol Kessner, "Kaplan on Women in Jewish Life," *Reconstructionist*, July–Aug. 1981, pp. 38–44.
26. Marshall Sklare, *Conservative Judaism: An American Religious Movement* (New York, 1972), pp. 154–55.
27. Those who had Bat Mitzvah celebrations in the context of a Torah reading in a women's prayer group described the experience as profoundly spiritual and moving. Perhaps the most eloquent was an Orthodox day school student:

    I know on *Shabbes* when I was *davening* [praying—here, leading the female group in prayer] and I was *layning* [chanting the portion of the week from the Torah], I felt when people talk about being close to *Hashem* [the Name, respectful Hebrew euphemism for God], this is what they mean. I felt awe. It was really a wonderful feeling that I'm doing something here that I don't usually get to do, but it's still a meaningful thing. . . . A Bat Mitzvah's about taking a new role in Jewish society. Since then, I've been a lot more aware of what I should and shouldn't do. It used to be that I wouldn't care too much if what I did was right and wrong. Now I know that this is my responsibility, not anyone else's. No one else is watching me, no one's going to fix my mistakes. It's become more important to me to do the right thing, both to be nice and kind, and also to look at the Torah more carefully, to learn, and to fulfill all the commandments. (Nicky Goldman, "The Celebration of Bat Mitzvah Within the Orthodox Community in the United States Today," unpublished Master's thesis, Hornstein Program in Jewish Communal Service, Brandeis University, Waltham, Spring 1991, 14–15)

28. Ibid.
29. Barbara Trainin Blank, "Family Matters: Late Mitzvas," *Hadassah* 77 (June/July 1996), pp. 25–27.
30. See Menachem Brayer, *The Jewish Woman in Rabbinic Literature: A Psychological Approach* (Hoboken, N.J.: Ktav, 1986), vol. 2, pp. 79–80.
31. Contradicting much classical Jewish thought, Rabbi Schneerson asserts that all women are capable of learning the Oral Law. He notes that in the past the group of women who did in fact study the Oral Law was limited because it was entirely voluntary. Today, however, he urges, women may and should be taught the complete range of talmudic texts. Rabbi Menachem Schneerson, *Me-Sichat Shabbat Parshat Emor, Erev Lag B'Omer* 5770: *Al Devar Hiyyuv Neshei Yisrael Be-Hinukh Limud ha-Torah*, May 1990.
32. Those interested in researching this area further should look for publications by Jewish feminist scholars such as Tikvah Frymer-Kensky, Ross Kraemer, Nehama Aschkenasy, Carol Meyers, Susan Niditch, Judith Hauptman, Judith Bas-kin, Paula Hyman, Marion Kaplan, Hasia Diner, Shulamit Reinharz, Joyce Antler, Sara Horowitz, Rochelle Millen, Norma Baumel Joseph, Chava Weissler, Marcia Falk, Deborah Dash Moore, Ellen Umansky, Judith Plaskow, and Riv-Ellen Prell, to name just a few representative scholars among scores of actively publishing academics. Within each field the list of feminist scholars is long, diverse, and growing.
33. Paula E. Hyman and Deborah Dash Moore, eds., *Jewish Women in America: An Historical Encyclopedia* (New York: Routledge, 1997).
34. Ann R. Shapiro et al., eds., *Jewish American Women Writers: A Bio-Biographical and Critical Sourcebook* (Westport, Conn.: Greenwood Press, 1994).
35. The first Friday night after the birth of a son, Ashkenazi fathers traditionally host a *shalom zachor*, wishing good health, peace, and welcome to the male in an informal, festive after-dinner gathering at their homes, at which songs are sung, homilies set forth, and refreshments served. Eight days after the birth of a son, the *brit milah*, ritual circumcision, provides an occasion at once solemn and festive for communal celebration and sanctification of the child's birth. In addition, if the first child is a male, thirty days after his birth his father participates in a *pidyon haben* ceremony, "buying back" his son from the service the child would otherwise be obligated to render to the priestly class, according to biblical law. The ritual circumcision, with both religious and nationalistic overtones, conveys the male child into the historical destiny of the Jewish people, not only by duplicating the "mark upon his flesh" first practiced by Abraham but also by evoking the concept of the chosenness of the Jewish people. At

the ceremony, parents are blessed with a wish that they may be privileged to escort their son as he matures into the study of the Torah, the marriage canopy, and doing deeds of lovingkindness.

36. The full text of the *zeved habat* ceremony can be found in the Sephardi De Sola Poole Prayer Book.
37. For a listing of printed materials on shalom bat cermonies, see Susan Weidman Schneider, *Jewish and Female: Choices and Changes in Our Lives Today* (New York: Simon and Schuster, 1984), pp. 121–29.
38. Roselyn Bell, "Thank Heaven for Little Girls," in *The Hadassah Magazine Jewish Parenting Book* (New York: The Free Press, 1989), pp. 19–24.
39. A century-old prayer for the birthing mother, for example, reads: "Oh, my God! Soon approaches the great hour when I shall give birth to another human being, according to thy wise ordination. . . . I call upon Thee, from the depths of my soul. Fortify me with strength and courage in the hour of danger, God of Mercy! Grant that the life of my child may not be my death! . . . . Convert, O God, my pain into delight at the lovely sight of a living, well-formed and healthy babe, whose heart may be ever dedicated to Thee (prayer for the onset of labor, 1878). Fanny Neuda, "Prayer on the Approach of Accouchement," *tekhine* translated by M. Mayer and published in *Hours of Devotion* (Vienna: H. L. Frank, 1878; repr. Henny Wenkart, *Sarah's Daughters Sing: A Sampler of Poems by Jewish Women* [Hoboken, N.J.: Ktav, 1990], pp. 140–41).
40. Thus, one modern prayer for a woman who has just given birth—"Blessed art Thou, our Creator, for making me Thy partner in the creation of a new Jewish soul"—is actually based on the biblical Eve's declaration when she had just given birth to Cain: "I have acquired a man-child with the help of God" (Gen. 4:1).
41. For a feminist deconstruction of the traditional *ketubah*, see Laura Levitt's article in Miriam Peskowitz and Laura Levitt, *Judaism since Gender* (New York: Routledge, 1997).
42. Sanford Seltzer, *When There Is No Other Alternative: A Guide for Jewish Couples Contemplating Divorce* (Boston: Union of American Hebrew Congregations, Committee on the Jewish Family, 1998).
43. Edward M. Gershfield, "The Problem of the Agunah: The Current Situation," *United Synagogue Review* (spring 1994): 30–31.
44. Rachel Adler, "Tumah and Taharah—Mikveh," in *The Jewish Catalogue*, comp. and ed. Richard Siegel, Michael Strassfeld, and Sharon Strassfeld (Philadelphia: Jewish Publication Society, 1973), pp. 167–71.
45. Barbara Rosman Penzer and Amy Zweiback-Levenson, "Spiritual Cleansing: A Mikveh Ritual for Brides," *Reconstructionist*, Sept. 1986, pp. 25–29.
46. See, for example, Laura Levitt and Sue Ann Wasserman, "Mikvah Ceremony for Laura," and Penina Adelman, "The Womb and the Word: A Fertility Ritual for Hannah" and "A Ritual of Loss," all in Ellen M. Umansky and Dianne Ashton, eds., *Four Centuries of Jewish Women's Spirituality: A Sourcebook* (Boston: Beacon Press, 1992), pp. 321–25, 247–56.
47. In Eastern European culture, a male child was often referred to as a *kaddish'l*, a guarantee that the kaddish would be recited after one's death. According to some strands in Jewish tradition, survivors reciting the kaddish aid the soul of the departed as it attempts to rise from a limbo-like state into heavenly existence; when no male survivor was available, a (preferably pious) male was paid to recite the prayer.

48. The author interviewed 120 women across the United States. The full results of that research are reported on in Sylvia Barack Fishman, *A Breath of Life: Feminism in the American Jewish Community* (New York: Free Press, 1993). In this essay, all references to interviews that are not otherwise cited are taken from this data.
49. Sid Groeneman, "Beliefs and Values of American Jewish Women" (report by Market Facts, Inc., presented to the International Organization of B'nai B'rith Women, 1985). The data were drawn from 956 questionnaires roughly divided between Jewish and non-Jewish informants.

# Part IV

## Constructing a Modern Jewish Identity

The 52 percent intermarriage rate recorded in the 1990 National Jewish Population Survey has given special urgency to understanding the nature of contemporary Jewish identity. The question of how one's being Jewish is understood, defined, and expressed in American society is not easily answered. For many, their Jewish identity is shaped by the experience of the Holocaust and what it symbolizes—namely, persecution for no other reason than that they are Jewish. (See Bershtel and Graubard [1992] for an extreme example of this form of Jewish identity.) For others, a sense of Jewish identity is shaped by support for the State of Israel, which provides a sense of security as well as a sense of victory over all efforts at extinction. For secular and Reform Jews in America, the pursuit of a social and politically liberal agenda seems to constitute a central motivating force in the expression of their Jewishness. A 1988 *Los Angeles Times* survey found that 54 percent of the persons interviewed answered that a commitment to social equality was most important to their Jewish identity. Sixteen percent in that survey specified support for Israel, and another 15 percent said that religious observance was most important. For religious observant Jews, Jewish identity is defined in their observance. These mitzvot include an attachment to and desire to settle in the Land of Israel. For many others there is no particular meaning they can cite as the source of center of their Jewish identity. Rather it is just there, a part of them. They *feel* Jewish.

In Eastern Europe, where the ancestors of the great majority of American Jews lived, Jewishness was indelibly imprinted on the minds, hearts, and souls of the inhabitants. Jews lived and breathed as Jews, without need for formal training or education. This is not to say that Jews did not receive formal education and training, just that it was not so essential in instilling a sense of what it meant to be

Jewish. The Eastern European shtetl was, in Soloveitchik's term, a *mimetic* culture (this volume). This holistic, unself-conscious definition of one's identity worked in part because Jews often lived apart and were treated differently from the majority population. Being Jewish encompassed culture, nationality, and religion. Thus, it constituted the core of an integrated personal identity that was reinforced by the fact that Jews lived in their own communities, largely governed and organized in accordance with Jewish law (Katz 1993, Wirth 1928/1956). In Eastern Europe, in other words, an external definition supported and was supported by an internalized sense of one's indelible Jewish self.

Many of the Eastern European Jews who arrived in America at the turn of the century were poorly educated, religiously as well as generally. The Jewish scholars and teachers of Jewish life generally stayed in Europe until they were forced to flee, thinking it not possible to remain a kosher Jew in *treife* (non-Kosher) America, Thus, in the early part of the century there were few religious teachers and few religious schools in America. The lack of a strong institutional structure, combined with the widely held view that Jewishness was an intrinsic, innate aspect of being that one did not need work to retain, led to minimal organized efforts to educate the young. And given the conditions of extreme poverty under which most Jews in Eastern Europe lived, it was understandable that the primary concern of the immigrant generation was to achieve economic security for their children. There is no question that the immigrant generation wanted and expected their children to retain a Jewish identity, but whereas they worked very hard to achieve economic advancement, they did not work as hard to achieve the former (Chiswick, this volume).

In general, Jews took their Jewish identity for granted and "reasonably" assumed that, after a two-thousand-year history of surviving as a frequently persecuted people living in the Diaspora, it was something with which they did not need to be overly concerned. A scene in the movie *Hester Street* expresses this sentiment. Jake, a recent immigrant, goes on a picnic in the park with other immigrants, two of whom are more educated in and intent on remaining within the Jewish tradition. Jake is seen in profile; he stands, wearing American clothes, with one hand on his hip, the other hand curling his stylish mustache. "There, don't I look like a Jew?" he asks. No one answers because there really is nothing about him that looks Jewish, and so he answers: "Of course. How could I not look like a Jew? A Jew is a Jew, no?"

Although Jewish identity throughout the ages had, to a considerable extent, been shaped by the negative threat of persecution, being Jewish in America was thought to be different (Halpern 1983). In large part this was because of the lack of governmental support for anti-Semitic ideology and behavior. Jews were not singled out any more than were other immigrant groups, and the Jewish communities that formed in America generally assumed a pattern similar to that of other immigrant groups. There was a Little Italy and a Chinatown, each with an immigrant population comparable to that found among Jews on the Lower East Side of

New York. Nevertheless, the forces of modernity in America led to a greatly diluted Jewish identity.

It is perhaps paradoxical that the greatest threat to Jewish identity in America came from the same source that allowed it to flourish. The fact that, in America, roles and identities are achieved rather than ascribed implies that with hard work and diligence a person can become whatever he or she chooses. That some aspects of one's life are necessarily inherited is recognized. But the realms that are usually central to one's personal identity, such as belief, faith, and religious affiliation, are regarded as a matter of personal choice. In their study, Hammond and Warner 1993, 60) found that 77 percent of Americans supported the statement that "an individual should arrive at his or her own religious beliefs independent of any church or synagogue." This openness and fluidity of personal religious identity is an exceptionally compelling idea, making it clear to Jews and other groups in America that there are no firm boundaries, existential, psychological, or concrete, within which one lives. The doors are open; one may enter and exit as one pleases.

Because of this openness, traditional informal group controls have a greatly lessened power to keep people attached to a community. This is true even within communities that seek separation from secular life and thus function with a relative degree of independence. Hassidic communities found in Williamsburg, Borough Park, Monroe, and Monsey, New York, are examples. In these, as in all Orthodox communities, there is a high degree of social interaction around the overlapping and multiple dimensions of ritual observance, including attendance at daily prayer services, religious schooling, adult learning groups, and celebrations. In these communities, religious observance constitutes the core of one's life, and there is an integration of personal belief, action, and community. Overlapping bonds created by continuous communal involvement are perhaps the most effective means of achieving group maintenance, in that ties of ethnicity, culture, and religious belief and practice all come together within a geographically defined space. Nevertheless, participation in any group in America remains voluntary. And a multiplicity of alternative ways of being Jewish are accepted as part of the American creed. With only unofficial censors to control behavior, incompatible and unexamined beliefs and ideas from the secular world can easily break through the barriers erected to separate these communities from outside influences.

The primacy of personal choice in America suggests that commitment to a strong Jewish identity, which most studies seem to point to as emerging from a "religious" identity or affiliation, requires not the traditional "push" factor of anti-Semitism but rather, a clear and positive "pull" factor. There must be, in other words, the sense that a strong Jewish identity offers something of value, something that will be worth the social and economic costs of commitment, worth the radical change in lifestyle and affiliation and perhaps most dramatically, worth the change in authority. This is precisely where the role of education is found to be so significant. Today education is regarded as the key, the cornerstone of a strong Jewish identity, which can no longer lack consciousness and intentionality but rather must be conscious, intentional, and more than ever before, an educated choice.

What are the constituent parts that go into making this choice? Issues pertaining to the continuity of the Jewish people focus on the question of what constitutes a Jewish identity and, second, on the process whereby one forms and maintains a strong Jewish identity. To this extent the issue of Jewish identity is central to understanding Jewish continuity. The traditionally integrated Jewish identity found in the Eastern European shtetl community is no longer a relevant model and is nearly impossible to replicate under conditions of modernity. Just the fact that we can identify and separate out religious beliefs and behavior from other activities in our lives is, according to Sharot (1991), indicative of the effects of seculariztion.

Within a largely secularized culture, Jewish identity is inevitably going to be differently defined and understood from the way it had been in Eastern Europe. Indeed, Medding et al. (this volume) note that in the past the common denominator of Jewish identity was a community of belief based on a system of shared prescriptive values. Now they find that Jewish identity constitutes a community of shared individual feelings. This diminution, if not complete disappearance, of the communal realm in Jewish identity leads to a very different set of relationships and a very different experience and understanding of what being Jewish is about, both existentially and communally. It is a result of the individualized perception of modern religious belief (Bellah 1985, Berger 1967, Luckmann 1967) that intermarriage can be perceived as *not* affecting one's own religion and religiosity. Although the sense of belonging to a religious community was, until now, compromised by intermarriage, this too is changing as groups form and books are published on how to deal with and respond to situations created as a result of intermarriage. New definitions and strategies of adjustment emerge within a culture that values personal choice and change more highly than community stability and continuity.

## References

Bellah, Robert N., Richard Madsen, William M. Sullivan, Ann Swidler, and Steven M. Tipton. 1985. *Habits of the Heart: Individualism and Commitment in American Life*. New York: Harper and Row.

Berger, Peter. 1967. *The Sacred Canopy: Elements of a Sociological Theory of Religion*. Garden City, N.Y.: Doubleday & Co.

Bershtel, Sara, and Allen Graubard. 1992. *Saving Remnants: Feeling Jewish in America*. New York: The Free Press.

Halpern, Ben. 1983. "America Is Different." In *American Jews: A Reader*, edited by Marshall Sklare, pp. 25–45. (West Orange, N.J.: Behrman House.)

Hammond, Phillip E., and Kee Warner. 1993. "Religion and Ethnicity in Late-Twentieth-

Century America." *Annals of the American Academy of Political and Social Science* 527 (May): 55–66.

Katz, Jacob. 1993. *Tradition and Crisis: Jewish Society at the End of the Middle Ages.* New York: Schocken Books.

Luckmann, Thomas. 1967. *The Invisible Religion: The Problem of Religion in Modern Society.* New York: Macmillan.

Sharot, Stephen. 1991. "Judaism and the Secularization Debate." *Sociological Analysis* 52(3):255–75.

Wirth, Louis. 1928/1956. *The Ghetto.* Chicago: The University of Chicago Press.

9 Charles S. Liebman and Steven M. Cohen

# Jewish Liberalism Revisited

It is a truism embraced by countless spokesmen for American Jews and by no small number of observers: Jews are more liberal than their fellow Americans, *and* their liberalism derives from loyalty to Jewish "values" or, more specifically, to the Jewish religious tradition. "Jews are the most liberal group in the country," wrote the sociologist Nathan Glazer over forty years ago, in a statement with which few have had occasion to quibble. And as for the reason why, here is Albert Vorspan, who served for many years as the leading spokesman for the "social-action" program of Reform Judaism: "A commitment to social justice is inherent in Judaism. . . . [A] Judaism without keen involvement in the struggle for human decency is a contradiction, a denial of the deepest elements of the Jewish spirit."

But is either part of the truism true? To answer this question, we examined evidence from a survey of American social attitudes conducted almost annually between 1973 and 1994 by the National Opinion Research Center (NORC). What the data reveal is that Jews do indeed differ from non-Jews in terms of their own self-image: a full 48 percent of the former, versus only 27 percent of the latter, define themselves as liberal. And Jews also tend to *be* more liberal than other Americans on at least three defining issues: a commitment to the welfare state and to some redistribution of income; a concern for oppressed minorities, especially American blacks; and a passion for individual freedom, especially freedom of speech. On still other issues, especially having to do with sexual morality and with the separation of church and state, they are more liberal still.

We will have occasion below to qualify these statements significantly. But let us pause to note a deep problem, right at the start, with the standard explanation for Jewish political attitudes. For if, as many contend, political liberalism is somehow embedded in Jewish tradition ("inherent in Judaism," in Vorspan's words), those Jews who are closest to the religious tradition should be the most liberal, and those farthest away should be the least liberal. In fact, however, the opposite is the case. Frequent synagogue attendees register views in the NORC survey that are consistently *less* liberal on almost every issue than those who attend synagogue infrequently or not at all or who are intermarried.

This pattern holds true not only on such matters as aid to the poor or to blacks, or on the government's role in reducing income differences, or on freedom of speech but—dramatically—on sexual and social matters as well. For example, 58 percent of intermarried Jews say that homosexual sex is not wrong, in contrast to 10 percent of those who attend religious services at least twice a month (the comparable figure for the vast majority in between is 49 percent). The only exception to the pattern concerns church-state issues and specifically prayer in the public schools: here, religious, less religious, and nonreligious Jews alike are all opposed, in almost equal numbers.

That exception aside, however, if we judge by the religious *behavior* of American Jews, there is little support for the notion that Jewish liberalism derives from an attachment to the Jewish religious tradition.

Nor should that really come as a surprise. Jewish religious values, as expressed in the Bible, the Talmud, and later rabbinic literature, are ethnocentric rather than universalistic. In most traditional sources, Jews are commanded to assist the Jewish poor but not necessarily the non-Jewish poor, to return the lost objects of their fellow Jews but not the lost objects of non-Jews, and so forth. What is more, the Torah imposes restraints on freedom of speech, is far more sensitive to questions of individual rights, and envisions a society of laws to regulate the private conduct of individuals. True, the tradition enjoins the practices of compassion, concern for others, and even a measure of justice; but, with notable exceptions, these injunctions are intended to regulate relations among Jews, not between Jews and non-Jews.

When it comes to sexual morality, the gulf between the clear teaching of Jewish tradition and contemporary liberalism is much wider still. The Ten Commandments flatly proscribe adultery. As for homosexuality, the biblical passages prohibiting it, along with such other "abominations" as incest and bestiality, were deemed so central that the ancient rabbis decreed they be read aloud in the synagogue on Yom Kippur, the holiest day of the Jewish calendar. The tradition's continuing concern with the proper channeling of sexual appetites is evident in the relatively strict codes of dress and in proscriptions on relations between the sexes that characterize millennia of Jewish law and practice. In short, no credible case can be made that a permissive attitude toward extramarital or homosexual sex represents the Jewish tradition. Quite the contrary.

Of course, those who trace Jewish liberalism to Judaism have a fallback position and one worth considering seriously. What really motivates American Jews, they say, are certain ingrained attitudes which, though ultimately derived from the religious tradition, by now transcend it and exist independently of specific religious behavior like synagogue attendance. The Jewish tradition, they concede, may not be unambiguously liberal in the contemporary sense, but that is not the point. After all, even the authors of the American Constitution presupposed the institution of slavery and made no provision to ensure women the right to vote. But if, within the *spirit* of that same Constitution, slavery could be abolished and women granted suffrage, it is similarly possible to maintain that no inversion of the Jewish tradition is involved in applying to society at large the virtues of compassion and social justice which the tradition mandates in connection with Jews.

If we accept this line of reasoning, it makes perfect sense that non-Orthodox Jews (who incidentally far outnumber the Orthodox in America) should tend to be more liberal. After all, it was Reform Judaism that, starting in the nineteenth century, consciously set out both to discard Jewish practices it found outmoded and, at the same time, to universalize what it took to be the core Jewish values. According to the mandates of their own religious tradition, non-Orthodox Jews *ought* to be more liberal.

Unfortunately, however, this too does not get us very far. For one thing, while an insistence upon compassion, a demand for social justice, and even (according to the scholar Moshe Greenberg) freedom of speech may have roots in the tradition, a commitment to any or all of these does not necessarily lead in a straight line to the particular positions of many contemporary liberals. A concern for the equal treatment of minorities, for example, need hardly translate into support for what today travels under the banner of affirmative action; a belief in freedom of speech need not require one to adopt a tolerant attitude toward the spread of pornography (an issue that, as it happens, has split the liberal and feminist communities). In each of these cases and in many others like them, one could argue that contemporary liberalism, far from fulfilling the spirit of traditional Jewish values, traduces both spirit and letter alike.

For another thing, legitimate interpretation of the tradition has its limits, and no tradition can survive if it is infinitely malleable. Many of the same Jewish liberals who appeal to the tradition in defending their zeal for "social justice" tend simply to ignore or radically distort its teachings with regard to relations between the sexes. Nor, finally, can any tradition be legitimately interpreted except by those who understand it—something that cannot be said of many who presume to speak in the name of Jewish values.

Here, indeed, is where the major qualification we mentioned at the outset becomes relevant. For the most striking result of our examination of the NORC data is this: when Jews are compared not with other Americans in general but specifically with other Americans *who resemble them*—in age, education, income, and pattern of residence—the vaunted Jewish "deference" all but disappears.

Thus, on the question of whether the government should spend more on welfare, Jews are only four percentage points more liberal than their non-Jewish peers and only two percentage points more liberal on the issue of whether the government should act to reduce income gaps between rich and poor. Similarly, Jews are no more likely than their social and economic peers to favor greater government aid to American blacks, and only three percentage points more likely to attribute the disadvantaged position of blacks to discrimination. Finally, when it comes to freedom of expression, Jews are only three percentage points more likely than their non-Jewish peers to be in favor of atheists or Communists speaking in their communities or teaching at universities.

To be sure, Jews do still take decidedly more liberal (not to say libertine) positions on sexual morality than even those non-Jews who share their age, education, income, and residential patterns. This is a phenomenon noted by Earl Raab in "Are American Jews Still Liberal?" and we can confirm it on the basis of a much larger sample over a longer period of time. Thus, holding constant for socioeconomic factors and residence patterns, we found that 24 percent more Jews than non-Jews approve of abortions for any reason; 21 percent more approve of legalizing marijuana; 7 percent more are opposed to banning pornography; 7 percent more assert that premarital sex is not wrong at all, 15 percent more that extramarital sex is not always wrong, and 26 percent more that gay sex is not wrong at all. An analogous gulf divides Jews from similarly situated non-Jews when it comes to church-state relations: 37 percent more of the former oppose prayer in the public schools—and as we noted earlier, this opposition cuts across denominational lines.

In the end, though, these may be the only discrepancies that still need explaining. American Jewish liberalism does not, it turns out, nowadays comprise a *special* sympathy for African Americans or for the poor, nor does it feature an extraordinary attachment to civil liberties. As for those issues on which the Jewish position is still distinctive, on at least one set of them, namely, relations between church and state, that position might arguably be traced to a perception of group self-interest: since America is (still) a Christian country, prayer in the public schools would tend to take on a Christian character, thus implicitly posing a threat to a religious minority like the Jews. Similar fears, real or imagined, may also lie in part behind Jewish permissiveness in those sexual matters on which Christian churches have taken a strongly conservative position.

But whether this sufficiently explains the anomaly or not, one thing we can say with confidence: whatever the source of the—selective—liberalism of American Jews may be, there is little if any evidence to support the notion that it reflects the impact of Jewish values or of the Jewish tradition.

Jerome S. Legge Jr.

# Understanding American Judaism

## Revisiting the Concept of "Social Justice"

This article uses the 1991 Survey of New York Area Jews to reexplore the "social justice" concept developed by Sklare and Greenblum. It is supportive of Sklare and Greenblum, who noted the tendency of Jews to have a broad concern for humankind and secular causes but to focus their behavior concerning social justice primarily on Jews. Bivariate analysis indicates that the Orthodox identify most strongly with the concept, although their view of social justice is "inward" and directed primarily at fellow Jews. This finding is confirmed in a multiple regression analysis. The level of charitable contributions is used as a surrogate for social justice. In contrast, denomination is of no explanatory value in explaining philanthropic contributions to secular charities. Rather, the dependent variable is predicted most strongly by income.

Among the more provocative questions raised by Sklare and Greenblum (1979) in their study of "Lakeville" is the issue of what characteristics constitute a "good Jew." Like "Christianity," the concept of Judaism has multiple meanings, and the unity of religious belief has always been blurred somewhat by divisions both within and between the Orthodox, Conservative, and Reform denominations. But underneath all the complexity, two basic themes have dominated the literature which describes the relationship between Jews and their religion. On the one hand, a person may be a "good" Jew because an individual follows a religious model of behavior, emphasizing beliefs and practices. In contrast, one may obtain the goal by taking an active role in society and following a model of "social justice." While it is common sociological knowledge that the Orthodox and other traditional Jews are more active in practicing purely religious *mitzvot* (commandments), less attention has been paid to which Jews especially identify with social justice and in fact practice it. In this article we focus on the social justice concept and explore it with bivariate and multivariate analysis.

Within Judaism, the performance of righteous deeds is somewhat difficult to separate from beliefs, prayer, and ritualistic behavior, at least with regard to virtuousness. It is often asserted that Judaism is a religion of action and deeds as opposed to beliefs; charitable actions toward fellow citizens are just as much *mitzvot* as more formal worship. *Both* concepts play a role in the lives of all religious Jews, regardless of denomination. But the "religious beliefs and practices" concept holds that the Jew best fulfills obligations to the faith by a strict adherence to Halakha (religious law). It is the "good" American Jew who fulfills religious obligations and responsibilities to humankind through study of the Torah, strict observance of the Sabbath and religious holidays, and observance of *kashruth* (the dietary laws).

Within the United States, the social justice aspect of being a "good Jew" has been prevalent for some time. Partially because of the complexity of Jewish worship and prayer and the difficulty of maintaining a lifestyle strictly within the parameters of religious law, many American Jews have defined their relationship to their religion within social justice (Stone, 1994).

While "rabbinic" Judaism tends to emphasize the importance of Halakha, social justice has its roots in "prophetic" Judaism. Prophets such as Isaiah tended to emphasize the importance of righteousness as a religious concept, with a special emphasis on *tzedakeh*. Broadly interpreted, the concept holds that the poor are entitled to some share of wealth from the more fortunate as a matter of right (Fuchs, 1955). The prophetic concept tends to emphasize the universalistic aspects of Judaism, with a special emphasis on obligations to all of humankind, not just fellow Jews (Fein 1988, 164).

It is this broad concern with humankind which has marked the behavior of so many Jews in America. It helps explain extensive Jewish involvement in philanthropy, both within and outside the Jewish community as well as Jews aiding in the struggle of African Americans for civil rights and in the advocacy of civil liberties (Kristol 1990).

The most prominent academic work which compares religious practice to social justice is that of Sklare and Greenblum (1979). In this study, survey respondents were requested to list those characteristics which described a "good Jew." The qualities most often named, significantly, consisted primarily of attributes which would be considered "social justice." The most important qualities mentioned included leading "an ethical and moral life," promoting humanitarian causes, and improving the community; in contrast, more religious activities such as synagogue membership and observing dietary laws trailed far behind.

Reform Judaism has been identified more closely with ethical concerns as opposed to emphasizing religious ritual and Halakha (Seltzer 1980, 762–63). This is not to suggest that the denominations which have more ritualistic behavior at the core are unconcerned with social justice. Rather, the matter is one of emphasis. With other factors being equal, we might expect greater sympathy for social justice among Reform and secular Jews, while it is anticipated that adherents to

Orthodoxy and Conservatism would be more favorably inclined toward religious beliefs and practices. We first explore the extent to which American Jews identify with either mode of behavior.

## Data and Sample

The data consist of a stratified sample of New York area Jews, and the questionnaire and survey design are similar to the National Jewish Population Survey (1990).[1] The counties included are the five boroughs of New York City (Manhattan, the Bronx, Brooklyn, Queens, and Staten Island) as well as the suburban counties of Nassau and Suffolk on Long Island and Rockland and Westchester counties. The vast majority of interviews were conducted in English; however, a small minority utilized Russian, Yiddish, and Spanish.

While past research has sought simply to define the characteristics of a "good Jew," the questions in the New York survey are slightly more encompassing regarding the meaning of being Jewish in America. During the course of the interview, respondents were asked two questions which parallel the two approaches to Judaism we have discussed thus far. Specifically, respondents were asked to state levels of agreement or disagreement with the following statements:[2] (1) "Being a good American Jew means living in accordance with religious beliefs and practices." (2) "Being a good American Jew means advocating Jewish values of social justice and concern for the poor."

Unlike Sklare and Greenblum, whose sample contained a low number of Orthodox Jews, approximately 15 percent of the individuals in the New York data set list their current denomination as Orthodox, with approximately 28 percent indicating it as the denomination of upbringing. In addition, initial research on this sample indicates that while New York Jews are highly similar to U.S. Jews in general in demographics, they tend to identify more closely with Judaism both religiously and socially. Horowitz (1994, 20) attributes this fact to a "climate which makes it easier for Jewish people to identify with Jews and Judaism, in contrast to the social forces which may work against such identification elsewhere in the nation." The variations in denomination and the more robust Jewish religious and social activities in New York allow us to determine more convincingly how the social justice concept is perceived.

Based upon the literature, we expect that the most religiously committed Jews would most likely identify positively with "religious practice," while those of the Reform denomination and secular Jews would be more apt to express positive sentiments toward social justice. The reasons for these hypotheses are rooted in the sociological literature of Judaism, which suggests that denomination is an important determinant of social and political, as well as religious, behavior (Harrison and Lazerwitz 1979, 1982). As the Reform denomination places less emphasis on religious law and more on social justice and the Orthodox have shown opposite tendencies and at times conservative political and social leanings (Heilman and Cohen 1989), these hypotheses appear sound. We test these propositions using bivariate and multivariate analyses in the next section and then focus more exclusively on social justice.

## Findings

### *Bivariate Analysis*

A first objective of the data analysis is to examine the distributions of the two primary variables of interest: the social justice and the religious practice variables. In performing a bivariate analysis we are interested first in two items of information. First, how do the majority of respondents view the concept of a "good" American Jew? Is it in line with the "social justice" findings of Sklare and Greenblum (1979), or is "religious practice" more in evidence? A second question concerns the relationship between this variable and the denominations. After examining the initial relationships between denomination and mode of observance, we analyze the relationship between denomination and different practices of social justice, conceptualized as organizational and charitable activities. We conclude the study with a multivariate analysis, linking the amount of charitable contributions to denomination, income, and the importance of being a Jew; along with a number of other control variables.

For purposes of conserving space, we list only those who "agree strongly" with the measures of religious practice or social justice.[3] One obvious finding is that with some exception for the Orthodox, Jews regardless of denomination are much more accepting of the social justice notion of citizenship (see table 10.1). Less than 20 percent of the Conservative Jews and approximately 10 percent of the Reform and secular Jews agree strongly with the religious beliefs and practices position; in contrast, the number agreeing with social justice is in the range of 45–55 percent, depending on denomination and whether we are considering upbringing or the respondent's current affiliation. In this sample, the "good American Jew" is clearly a person who pursues social justice.

The surprising findings concern the Orthodox. There are differences when one considers whether an individual was raised Orthodox or is currently Orthodox in embracing the religious practice model. This is to be expected, and there is a 30 percentage point difference on the variable. But the unexpected finding is how high the Orthodox rate social justice. Regardless of current denomination, those who were raised Orthodox view the social justice model as being much more important than religious practice, and while those currently Orthodox view the practice variable as being more important, they surpass the other denominations by a wide margin in embracing social justice. Regardless of whether one considers denomination of upbringing or current denomination, rough linear patterns

TABLE 10.1
Respondents Who "Strongly Agree" with "Religious Beliefs and Practices" and "Social Justice" by Denomination of Upbringing and Current Denomination

| | *Religious Beliefs and Practices* | | | |
|---|---|---|---|---|
| | *Orthodox* | *Conservative* | *Reform* | *Secular* |
| Upbringing | 47.0% | 18.2% | 10.3% | 12.5% |
| | (486) | (254) | (91) | (43) |
| | *gamma* = –.362 ($t$ = –18.87; $p$<.001) | | | |
| Current | 77.1% | 21.1% | 9.4% | 9.4% |
| | (430) | (291) | (131) | (35) |
| | *gamma* = –.545 ($t$ = –30.21; $p$<.001) | | | |

| | *Social Justice* | | | |
|---|---|---|---|---|
| | *Orthodox* | *Conservative* | *Reform* | *Secular* |
| Upbringing | 65.4% | 50.2% | 46.3% | 50.9% |
| | (673) | (699) | (410) | (172) |
| | *gamma* = –.183 ($t$ = –8.18; $p$<.001) | | | |
| Current | 66.5% | 55.7% | 49.5% | 46.0% |
| | (359) | (773) | (683) | (169) |
| | *gamma* = –.182 ($t$ = –7.85; $p$<.001) | | | |

N's are in parentheses and refer to the entire cross-tabulation.

are evident, with the Orthodox being most concerned with social justice, followed by the Conservative, Reform, and Secular.

The fact that the Orthodox perform religious *mitzvot* to a greater extent than others is well established and demands no further analysis in this paper.[4] But a second and more important task in the bivariate analysis is to determine how members of the different denominations behave in terms of social justice. While the New York data set is voided of items which measure social justice in a political sense (such as support for civil rights and liberties and reproductive freedom), if we are prepared to accept organizational activity and charitable contributions as surrogates for social justice, the results are interesting. Overall, table 10.2 confirms that the Orthodox clearly live a life of social justice as contrasted to members of the Conservative and Reform denominations and secular Jews if we look at specific behaviors. But the table reveals also that social justice for the Orthodox is "inward" and directed more specifically at Jews. For example, while a far greater percentage of Orthodox volunteer for organizational work in general compared to others, the relationship is reversed when only non-Jewish organizations are considered. The Orthodox contribute to Jewish charities far more than others and give at the highest levels. The relationship is again reversed when secular charities are considered alone. Interestingly, the Orthodox are more likely than others

TABLE 10.2.
Cross-tabulation of Charity *Mitzvot* and Behavior with Current Denomination

| | *Orthodox* | *Conservative* | *Reform* | *Secular* |
|---|---|---|---|---|
| Volunteer work past year | 61.2% (565) | 40.6% (1430) | 38.0% (1439) | 31.3% (403) |
| | *gamma* = −.229 ($t$ = 8.98; $p$<.001) | | | |
| Volunteer only Non-Jewish organizations | 2.6% (567) | 10.2% (1427) | 14.4% (1434) | 18.7% (401) |
| | *gamma* = .295 ($t$ = 13.17; $p$<.001) | | | |
| Contributed Jewish charity | 91.8% (564) | 72.7% (1408) | 62.6% (1397) | 45.8% (393) |
| | *gamma* = −.437 ($t$ = −16.99; $p$<.001) | | | |
| Contributed $5,000+ Jewish charity | 13.8% (478) | 2.8% (1285) | 1.0% (1324) | 1.0% (381) |
| | *gamma* = −.420 ($t$ = −22.08; $p$<.001) | | | |
| Contributed secular charity | 58.0% (552) | 72.3% 1408) | 75.6% (1416) | 65.9% (393) |
| | *gamma* = −.117 ($t$= −4.04; $p$<.001) | | | |
| Contributed $5,000+ secular charity | 1.4% (524) | 1.1% (1298) | .7% (1298) | 1.3% (380) |
| | *gamma*= .089 ($t$=4.30; $p$<.001) | | | |
| Strongly agree funds needed Jewish causes | 47.3% (491) | 31.6% (1170) | 26.6% (1099) | 22.4% (268) |
| | *gamma* = −.181 ($t$ = −7.50; $p$<.001) | | | |
| Strongly agree most give Jewish charity | 53.4% (506) | 18.2% (1019) | 13.1% (986) | 10.5% (267) |
| | *gamma* = −.464 ($t$ = −21.81; $p$<.001) | | | |
| Strong agree Jewish organizations aid general community | 18.3% (496) | 15.4% (1230) | 16.3% (1290) | 13.4% (336) |
| | *gamma* = −.002 ($t$ = .123; $p$>.05) | | | |

N's are in parentheses and refer to the entire cross-tabulation.

to contribute $5,000 or more to secular charities, but when the relationship as a whole is considered, Conservative, Reform, and secular Jews are more likely to donate funds.

The Orthodox express a strong level of agreement that more funds are needed for Jewish programs than was the case five years ago. Consistent with Horowitz's (1994) belief that New York fosters a community which encourages strong identification with Judaism, more of the Orthodox, by a very high margin, have friends who contribute to Jewish charities. A final and interesting question is whether

Jewish organizations should give to the general community. Surprisingly, the Orthodox express the strongest agreement with the statement but when the entire table is examined (data not shown), the gamma statistic indicates that the relationship drops to near zero. While the Orthodox are inclined to agree strongly with the statement, they also are the most likely of the denominations to disagree strongly.

*Multivariate Analysis*

A final exercise was to examine if the importance of denomination was maintained in explaining social justice if other relevant social and demographic variables were regressed along with it in a multivariate analysis. For the dependent variables, we chose contributions to both Jewish and secular charities as surrogate variables for social justice and included as regressors gender, age, education, income, and "importance of being a Jew," along with three denominational dummy variables (Orthodox, Conservative, and Reform).

Each of the denominational variables were coded "1" if the respondent identified with that particular branch of Judaism and "0" if otherwise. The reference category consisted of the secular Jews. Thus, the importance of being either Orthodox, Conservative, or Reform is contrasted against Jews declaring no preference.[5] Results are presented in table 10.3.

Table 10.3 reveals important differences between those who give to Jewish, as opposed to secular, charities. First, with the exception of the "importance of being a Jew" variable, the control variables affect the dependent variables in the same direction and at approximately the same magnitude within each equation. There are no significant differences between men and women in the level of charitable contributions, but the greater the level of income and education and the older the individual, the higher the contribution. We should not be surprised with these findings. As the measure for charitable contributions is an ordinal one which is not based on a per capita measure, one would think that the greater the amount of money an individual has, the more likely they would give to either a secular or religious charity with all other factors being equal. Similar, it stands to reason that those with higher educations would have a greater level of income and more prestigious occupations, which also would be associated with charitable giving and organizational membership. With regard to age, the results indicate that it is the older Jews who are most inclined to give. The finding is in line with previous research in New York and Boston, which found charity to decrease with each succeeding generation (Cohen 1988, 44–45; Dashefsky 1990). Also, many older Jews reached early adulthood and middle age at a time (the 1950s and early 1960s) when less emphasis was placed on the rituals of worship and more attention was given to social activism (Sklare and Greenblum 1979).

The final control variable, the "importance of being a Jew," is interesting. In the Sklare and Greenblum work (1979) most respondents believed that pride in being a Jew and not hiding one's Jewishness was essential in being a "good Jew."

TABLE 10.3
Standardized Regression Coefficients of Charitable Contributions with Controls and Denominations

| | *Jewish Organizations* | *Secular Organizations* |
|---|---|---|
| Controls | | |
| Gender | −.01 | −.02 |
| Age | .18[a] | .16[a] |
| Education | .09[a] | .17[a] |
| Income | .29[a] | .37[a] |
| Importance | .14[a] | −.01 |
| Denomination | | |
| Orthodox | .45[a] | .00 |
| Conservative | .14[a] | .01 |
| Reform | .04 | .04 |
| Summary Statistics | | |
| $R^2$ | .33 | .21 |
| *F*-value | 212.82[a] | 115.36[a] |
| *N* | 3,436 | 3,436 |

a. Significance at .001 or better.

The coefficient is insignificant when secular contributions are considered yet significant when the equation estimates donations to Jewish organizations. This finding stands to reason as well. The importance that an individual places on being Jewish would seem to be a logical predictor of how much will be given to Jewish organizations. In addition, those who place a great deal of importance on Jewishness would be among the most likely to support such organizations. In contrast, the finding for the secular organizations may indicate that the limited resources many committed Jews possess force individuals to channel their contributions strictly to Jewish organizations. Examining the standardized coefficients for the secular organizations, income itself (ß=.37) is a stronger predictor of giving than it is for the Jewish organizations (ß−.29).

With the use of the above controls, the denominational variables confirm the cross-tabular findings with regard to the greater social justice of the Orthodox as well as to their "inwardness." With all other variables held constant, the Orthodox are far more likely than either members of the Conservative or Reform denominations to give to Jewish organizations. The influence of income on charitable contributions is far stronger than that of denominational identification among those who identify as Conservative or Reform Jews, but not among those who identify as Orthodox. This finding suggests that Orthodoxy itself is a greater aid in explaining the dependent variable than income. The Orthodox are far more likely than others to contribute *regardless of income level.* While Conservatives also are more likely than others to give, the ß coefficient for Orthodox is more than three times the size of the Conservative coefficient. The size of ß for the Reform denomination does not meet the criteria for statistical significance and is extremely small.

Cross-tabular analysis also demonstrated that members of the Reform denomination were more likely to contribute to secular charities, followed by the Conservatives and the Orthodox. The secular equation demonstrates that this still is the case, but none of the denominational coefficients are significant when considered with the controls. Again, Jewish donations to secular charities are best viewed as a function of income which has more than twice the impact of either education or age in impacting secular contributions. Neither denominational affiliation nor the importance which one holds in being Jewish helps very much in predicting secular charitable contributions. Winter (1993) also finds that variables measuring such concepts are of use primarily in understanding contributions to Jewish related charities. It is possible, as Winter suggests, that the secular charities are so varied and mutually incompatible (contributions to the NRA are not distinguished from those to the ACLU) that whatever influence denomination or the importance of being Jewish has is cancelled out, leaving income as the most important variable.

## Discussion

In several respects our findings reinforce those of Sklare and Greenblum. For example, these scholars make the observation that while a large majority in Lakeville (67 percent) believed that it was "essential" to support "all" humanitarian causes, only 39 percent had a similar belief regarding Jewish philanthropies. Yet in actual practice, only 19 percent gave to other than Jewish charities (Sklare and Greenblum 1979, 329–30). They go on to raise the question as to whether "future generations [will] be prepared to live with the dichotomy . . . [of] a universal humanitarianism as the prime value in combination with the practice of giving priority to Jewish causes. . . . May they not conclude that their humanitarian aspirations dictate that they place the accent on the general rather than the Jewish?"

In this essay we have demonstrated that the vast majority of Jewish respondents in New York openly embrace the social justice concept but, like Sklare and Greenblum, found the direction of social justice continues to be "inward." This is especially true of the Orthodox, who view the concept most favorably. With the continuing fears of assimilation, fueled by the 1990 National Jewish Population Survey, religious leaders, and the Jewish popular media, this finding should not be a surprise. As Sklare and Greenblum (1979, 330) hint, the need for survival and group identity seem to outweigh the broader concern for humanity or social justice in general when put to the test of philanthropy.

Another important finding of this research is the impact of denomination in explaining social justice. While social justice is a concept which is stressed perhaps most heavily by the Reform denomination, both the bivariate and multivariate analyses indicate that in terms of financial contributions this group is least likely to practice it. It may be that Reform Jews in New York express their concern for social justice along other political and social measures which are not present in this survey (e.g., support for civil liberties, feminist rights, etc.) Instead, social justice seems to be coupled with denominations which demand a heavier degree of religious observance. Rather than a conflictual relationship, the analysis suggests that social justice is most likely to be present when individuals also place a great importance on religious beliefs and practices as well. This central finding does not contradict Sklare and Greenblum but does add to their work, since these scholars had so few practicing Orthodox with which to test the different concepts of American Judaism.

## Notes

1. The 1991 Survey of New York Area Jews was sponsored by the Council of Jewish Federations and the United Jewish Appeal in cooperation with the City University of New York. The data utilized in this study were made available by the North American Jewish Data Bank, Center for Jewish Studies, Graduate Center, City University of New York. The data were collected originally by Marketing Systems Group of Philadelphia. Neither the original collectors of the data nor the NAJDB bear any responsibility for the analyses or interpretations presented in this paper.
2. While Sklare and Greenblum (1979) asked about the characteristics of a "good Jew," the inclusion of the word "American" gives the question a slightly broader context. The coding for both the "religious beliefs and practices" and "social justice" variables is 1 = strongly disagree, 2 = disagree, 3 = somewhat agree, 4 = strongly agree.
3. The gamma statistics and their associated probabilities are calculated for the entire cross-tabulation. For the entire sample, 82.7 percent "strongly agreed" or "agreed" with social justice versus 58 percent with religious beliefs and practices.
4. Simple cross-tabular analysis (not shown) indicates that the Orthodox are more likely to be involved in all aspects of religious practice.
5. The coding for the other variables in the model is the following. Education was coded 1 = less than high school; 2 = high school graduate; 3 = some college; 4 = college degree; 5 = some graduate school; 6 = masters degree; 7 = doctoral degree; gender, 1 = female, 0 = male; the importance of being a Jew, 1 = not important, 2 = not very important, 3 = somewhat important, 4 = very important; income, 1 = less than $7500, 2 = $7500–$12499, 3 = $12500–$19999, 4 = $20000–$29999, 5 = $30000–$39999, 6

= $40000–$40999, 7 = $50000–$59999, 8 = $60000–$79999, 9 = $80000–$124999, 10 = $125000–$149999, 11 = $150000–$199999, 12 = $200000 and over; amount contributed to Jewish and secular charities, 0 = did not contribute, 1 = under $100, 2 = $100–$499, 3 = $5000–$999, 4 = $1000–$4999, 5 = $5000–$9999, 6 = $10000 or more.

## References

Cohen, Steven, M. 1988. *American Assimilation or Jewish Revival?* Bloomington: Indiana University Press.

Dashefsky, Arnold. "Sources of Jewish Charitable Giving: Incentives and Barriers." *In American Pluralism and the Jewish Community*, edited by Seymour Martin Lipset, pp. 203–26. New Brunswick, N.J.: Transaction.

Fein, Leonard. 1988. *Where Are We?* New York: Harper & Row.

Fuchs, Lawrence W. 1955. "American Jews and the Presidential Vote." *American Political Science Review* 49:385–401.

Harrison, Michael, and Bernard Lazerwitz. 1979. "American Jewish Denominations: A Social and Religious Profile." *American Sociological Review* 44:656–66.

———. 1982. "Do Denominations Matter?" *American Journal of Sociology* 88:356–77.

Heilman, Samuel C., and Steven M. Cohen. 1989. *Cosmopolitans and Parochials: Modern Orthodox Jews in America.* Chicago: University of Chicago Press.

Horowitz, Bethamie. 1994. "Findings from the 1991 New York Jewish Population Study." *Contemporary Jewry* 15:4–25.

Kristol, Irving. 1990. "The Liberal Tradition of the American Jews." In *American Pluralism and the Jewish Community*, edited by Seymour Martin Lipset, pp. 109–16. New Brunswick, N.J.: Transaction.

National Jewish Population Survey. 1990. North American Jewish Data Bank, Center for Jewish Studies, City University of New York Graduate Center.

Seltzer, Robert M. 1980. *Jewish People, Jewish Thought.* New York: Macmillan.

Sklare, Marshall, and Joseph Greenblum. 1979. *Jewish Identity on the Suburban Frontier*, 2nd ed. Chicago: University of Chicago Press.

Stone, Ira F. 1994. "Worship and Redemption: Receiving Our Spiritual Vocabulary." *Judaism* 43:66–77.

Winter, J. Alan. 1993. "Not by Bread Alone: A National Replication of Refinement of a Study of Income, Identity, Household Composition, and Jewish Involvements." *Journal of Jewish Communal Service* 69:75–81.

11 Chaim I. Waxman

# Center and Periphery

## Israel in American Jewish Life

The Six-Day War is widely seen as having had major impact on American Jewry, including its relationship with Israel.[1] Whether the changes brought about in that relationship were "revolutionary," as suggested by some,[2] is another question. In any case, there is considerable evidence that Israel moved from the periphery to the center in the structure and culture of the American Jewish community.

Viewed from the perspective of the institutional structure of American Jewry, Israel undoubtedly plays a central role in American Jewish life, and much of that role developed as a result of the Six-Day War. In the *American Jewish Year Book*'s annual listing of national Jewish organizations, for example, contains more than eighty organizations specifically devoted to Zionist and pro-Israel activities; and for many others, objectives and activities such as "promotes Israel welfare," "support for the State of Israel" and "promotes understanding of Israel," appear with impressive frequency. In addition, more than fifty of the largest and most active of these national Jewish organizations are affiliated with the Conference of Presidents of Major American Jewish Organizations, for which Zionist and pro-Israel activity is the major emphasis. The Conference of Presidents shares an address with the U.S. headquarters of the Jewish Agency and World Zionist Organization, and virtually all of its chairmen have had long records of extensive activity on behalf of Israel.

Israel became central to the American Jewish philanthropic structure as a result of the Six-Day War, as Menahem Kaufman has indicated, to the point where leaders of the United Jewish Appeal are supportive of almost every decision of almost every Israeli government, at times becoming actual lobbyists for Israeli government policy.[3] The leadership acts in this manner out of its own convictions and also with the tacit support of a broad cross section of the American Jewish population. For example, in 1990 more than 70 percent of American Jewish baby boomers agreed with the statement "The need for funds for services and programs in Israel is greater now than five years ago."[4] Although that figure has probably decreased somewhat as the result of the widely publicized assertion by Israel's deputy foreign minister, Yossi Beilin, that Israel is a modern, growing society and no longer needs American Jewish charity,[5] there is every reason to assume that Israel still plays a major role within the American Jewish philanthropic structure.

In terms of the overall pro-Israelism of the American Jewish community, the empirical evidence indicates very strong support for Israel among the community's leadership. For example, a 1989 survey conducted by Steven M. Cohen that included "key professionals and top lay leaders from some of the most influential organizations in American Jewish life," as well as a small number of academics who are involved with Israel, found that 99 percent of the respondents had been to Israel at least once and 84 percent had been there three times or more. Moreover, 78 percent identified themselves as Zionists, and 54 percent had "seriously considered living in Israel." When asked, "How close do you feel to Israel?" 78 percent responded "very close" and 19 percent "fairly close." Only 2 percent stated that they feel "fairly distant," and none stated "very distant."[6] Jewish communal leaders not only feel close to Israel and identify with Zionism in the American sense of that term (i.e., pro-Israelism),[7] they also appear to subscribe to the Zionist tenet of the centrality of Israel. Thus, in response to the statement "Jewish life in America is more authentically and positively Jewish than Jewish life in Israel," 81 percent of Cohen's sample disagreed and only 10 percent agreed.[8] The ways in which Jewish organizations have been strongly involved in defense activity for Israel have been amply documented.[9]

Israel has also become increasingly central in the realm of American Jewish education. In 1968, Alvin Schiff found that Israel was taught as a separate subject in 48 percent of all Jewish schools, including all-day, weekday afternoon, and one-day-a-week schools under Orthodox, Conservative, Reform, communal, and secular auspices;[10] by 1974, as Barry Chazan found, 63 percent of the school curricula listed Israel as a separate subject, and "a general increase of attention paid to Israel in all subject-areas as compared with 1968."[11] Although there are no more contemporary empirical data, anecdotal "evidence" and personal observation convey the strong impression that this pattern has only intensified over the years. As for the role of Israel in American Jewish education, its increased importance is evidenced in a wide variety of ways, not the least of them being that Israel is today a major source for curriculum materials in the field of Jewish education. In certain respects, the biblical vision, *ki mitzion tetzei tora* (From Zion shall Torah flow) has been realized, for example, in the publication of Judaica and a wide variety of Jewish curriculum materials.

Israel also has become an integral part of the synagogue service of American Jewish denominations. As David Ellenson and I have indicated, almost all of the standard American Jewish prayer books now incorporate some prayers for the State of Israel as a part of the weekly service. Thus, the official prayer book of the American Reform Movement, *Sha'arei Tefillah* (Gates of Prayer), published in 1975, is radically different from its predecessor, the Union Prayer Book, in many ways, not the least being its inclusion of a prayer for the State of Israel as part of the weekly and holiday service. The movement's holiday liturgy, as set down in *Gates of the Seasons* (1983), incorporates Israel's Independence Day, Yom Ha'atzmaut, into the religious calendar and the ritual service. Although the most popular edition of the Orthodox Art-Scroll *Siddur* does not contain any reference to the State of Israel, there is an abundance of data to substantiate that the Orthodox have the most extensive and deepest attachments to Israel.[12]

Perhaps even more dramatic is the impact of the Six-Day War on the culture of the American Jewish community. In their assessment of the extent to which Israel has become central within the American Jewish community since the Six-Day War, published in the *Encyclopaedia Judaica* in 1971, Eventov and Rotem indicated that Israel now occupies "an important place in synagogue activities, sermons, and various religious celebrations," including Israel Independence Day. They continued: "The Israel flag is frequently displayed in synagogues and community centers. In many synagogues, prayers for the welfare of the State of Israel and world Jewry are recited on Sabbaths and holidays following that for the welfare of the United States. . . . Hebrew songs and Israel folk dances have become American Jewish popular culture: at weddings, bar mitzvot, and on many college campuses."[13]

Although Israel has become part of the religious behavior of American Jews, as Charles Liebman observed,[14] or even *the* religion of American Jews, as Nathan Glazer observed,[15] it is nevertheless the case that America's Jews are a "nonreligious" group, even though they might define themselves as a religious group. Understanding this requires a recognition of the difference between the American Jewish community and the American Jewish population. They are certainly not one and the same. In fact, a majority of American Jewish baby boomers are not affiliated with the American Jewish community. They are not members in any Jewish organization; they do not subscribe to any Jewish publication, and they are not members in any synagogue or temple—even the ones they don't attend.

A careful examination of the evidence on the behavior and attitudes of American Jewish baby boomers strongly suggests that the impact of the Six–Day War is actually significantly less than a look at American Jewish communal life might indicate. The data presented below underscore a basic fact of American Jewish life, namely, that there is a vast difference between the American Jewish community and the American Jewish population.

The population with which we are concerned—American Jewish baby boomers—is composed of those who were born between the years 1946 and 1964 and who, when asked in the 1990 National Jewish Population Survey (NJPS), "What is your current religion?" identified themselves as Jewish. This age group was selected for analysis because it represents those currently ascending to leadership and dominance in a variety of institutional spheres in American society. Thus, for example, the election of Bill Clinton as U.S. president was widely seen as symbolic of the ascendancy of the baby boom generation to political dominance.

Without getting too technical about it, it is important to know that the NJPS sample consists of 2,441 respondents. Each of the respondents provided the information for himself or herself and also for each member of their household. Thus, the survey obtained information on almost three times as many people as the actual number of respondents, or 6,514 individuals. The resulting data were subsequently statistically weighted, so that the sample of Jewish households would then represent more than three million American households nationally.

The question "Who is a Jew?" is an important one, not only on the Israeli political scene but also for social scientists studying Jews and Jewish communities. The problem may be even more difficult for social scientists in that they can not resort to ideological definitions; they can only follow the empirical evidence. Moreover, people may define themselves as Jewish by different criteria. That is, some may define themselves as Jewish by religion, some as Jewish by ethnicity, some as Jewish by birth, and others as Jewish by emotion (i.e, they "feel Jewish").

Since the vast majority of those who identify as Jewish say that they are Jewish by religion, and since the vast majority of those who identify as Jewish but say that they are not Jewish by religion manifest very low levels of Jewish identity and identification, I selected for analysis only those who when asked, "What is your current religion?" responded, "Jewish." Thus, the NJPS sample selected for analysis consists of 801 Jewish baby boomer respondents. There are several reasons that only actual respondents were selected for analysis. In general, I have problems with relying on data obtained from anyone but the actual respondent. Even more important in terms of this article is the fact that many of the questions probing Jewish identity were asked only of respondents.

Since there has been something of a debate among the social scientists most directly involved with NJPS as to exactly which, if any, weighting procedure should be used in many instances[16] and especially when dealing with Jewish cultural issues, all of the tables presented below are of three sets: one consisting of unweighted percentages, one using an alternative weighting procedure suggested by Steven M. Cohen (SMC), and one using the NJPS weights (POPWGT). Although the figures differ depending on which set is used, the most important findings are not the very specific percentages but the patterns; and in the patterns there are no basic differences between sets.

It should be emphasized that the figures in table 11.1 are for the national American Jewish population, and there are regional differences. A major study of the New York Jewish population found that New York Jews rank higher in their ties with Israel, as well on most indices of Jewish identification and identity, than do Jews nationwide. Thus, among New York Jews aged 18–34, 40 percent stated that they had been to Israel; among those aged 25–49, 37 percent did. [17]

How one interprets these figures is obviously a matter of perspective. To those who accepted the figures frequently bandied about by representatives of the Jewish

TABLE 11.1
Number of Times Jewish Baby Boomers Have Been to Israel

| | *Unweighted* | *SMC Weight* | *POPWGT* |
|---|---|---|---|
| Once | 15.0 | 15.7 | 12.8 |
| Twice | 5.0 | 5.5 | 4.8 |
| Three times | 1.5 | 2.2 | 1.9 |
| 4–9 times | 3.5 | 4.3 | 3.3 |
| 10+ times | 0.5 | 0.4 | 0.4 |
| Born in Israel | 1.1 | 1.5 | 1.4 |
| Never | 73.4 | 70.4 | 75.3 |

Agency and/or the World Zionist Organization—to wit, that only about 10 percent of America's Jews have ever visited Israel—the data may be good news. However, if one considers the facts that Israel is supposedly a key component of American Jewish identity and that America's Jews are relatively well off socioeconomically and presumably travel considerably, the figures would appear to suggest something quite different.

The meaning of the baby boomer figures takes on additional significance when we compare their rates of visits to Israel with those of what may be called "middle agers," those who were 45–65 in 1990 (see table 11.2).

It might be suggested that the reason most American Jewish baby boomers have not visited Israel is the fact that they are busy with their families, especially their children, and at this stage in their lives have too many financial obligations to visit Israel (even though they do find the time and money to visit elsewhere).

TABLE 11.2
Number of Times Been to Israel, Baby Boomers and Middle-Agers

| | *Ages 26–44* | *Ages 46–64* |
|---|---|---|
| Once | 12.8 | 19.8 |
| Twice | 4.8 | 5.0 |
| Three times | 1.9 | 1.5 |
| 4–9 times | 3.3 | 3.2 |
| 10+ times | 2.0 | 2.0 |
| Born in Israel | 1.4 | .3 |
| Never | 75.3 | 68.3 |

Instead, it may be more revealing to look at feelings about Israel rather than actual visits. However, when we look at the data on the emotional attachments of American Jewish baby boomers to Israel, the picture is not all that different. Some 70 percent say that they are either "not attached" or "somewhat attached," and only about 30 percent say that they are either "very attached" or "extremely attached" (see table 11.3).

Here again, we find that the baby boomers' levels of emotional attachment to Israel are lower than those of the middle-agers (see table 11.4). Since emotional attachments do not, in and of themselves, cost money, the lower levels are indeed significant.

America's Jews are highly pro-Israel. Indeed, 85 percent of those sampled in a 1988 *Los Angeles Times* survey favor strong U.S. support for Israel.[18] Such a high percentage of pro- Israelism is obviously a manifestation of Israel as an important factor in American Jewish identity.[19] However, to place this in proper perspective, it must be recalled that Americans as a whole are quite favorably disposed toward Israel.[20] One should also be cautious in interpreting the significance of the sharp rise in pro-Israelism among American Jews in 1967. It was probably not as clear a reflection of the centrality of Israel in American Jewish identity as some have suggested.[21] It was also a reflection of the *Americanization* of America's Jews, in that many of them felt by then comfortable enough as Americans to express their support for Israel, especially since the United States supported Israel; whereas in earlier times (e.g., 1956 and 1948) they were less comfortable doing so lest they be viewed as less than complete Americans. That support for Israel is today completely compatible with being American is evident from a remark made recently by a 55-year-old (slightly older than baby boomer) New York Jewish "radio personality," who said about Israel: "I'm glad it's there. I viscerally support them in their wars with the various Arab states, but I'm an American and I'm going to live and die in America most likely."[22]

A number of observers have suggested that the Six-Day War conjured up fears of another Holocaust.[23] Accordingly, ties to Israel are, in part, related to feelings of security in the United States. In fact, the condition of American Jewry is unprecedentedly positive. Perhaps Charles Silberman captured it best when, about eight years ago, he called them "a *certain* people."[24] American Jews have made it

TABLE 11.3
Emotional Attachments of Jewish Baby Boomers to Israel

| | *Unweighted* | *SMC Weight* | *POPM1WGT* |
|---|---|---|---|
| Not attached | 19.6 | 17.7 | 24.2 |
| Somewhat attached | 49.8 | 48.6 | 47.0 |
| Very attached | 20.1 | 22.0 | 18.2 |
| Extremely attached | 10.5 | 11.7 | 10.6 |

TABLE 11.4
Emotional Attachments to Israel of Baby Boomers and Middle-Agers

| | *Ages 26–44* | *Ages 46–64* |
|---|---|---|
| Not attached | 24.2 | 15.0 |
| Somewhat attached | 47.0 | 38.0 |
| Very attached | 18.2 | 33.2 |
| Extremely attached | 10.6 | 13.7 |

into American society in ways that could not have been predicted even as recently as midcentury. Although much publicity was given to a recent ADL report showing that one in five, or 20 percent, of Americans hold anti-Semitic beliefs and attitudes, what was not given notice was that this reflects a decrease in anti-Semitism. Indeed, all studies since World War II indicate a rather steady and consistent decrease in anti-Semitic beliefs and attitudes by white Americans.[25] Does this mean that there is no anti-Semitism in the United States or that we shouldn't be concerned about it? Certainly not! It does exist, as the ADL report indicates, and it is greater in some parts than in others. For example, it seems fair to assume that in cities such New York, where the economy suffers substantially and where there is the greatest competition between Jews and blacks, hostilities will be greater. Moreover, Jews are disproportionately urban, so there is an even greater probability of such competition. And if there is one lesson that history has taught us, it is that we must constantly be vigilant to anti-Semitism, no matter how unrepresentative of the society it appears to be.[26]

Also, although surveys of non-Jewish Americans consistently indicate a decrease in anti-Semitic attitudes, most Jews continue to believe that anti-Semitism is a serious problem in the United States. For example, approximately 82 percent of American Jewish baby boomers stated that the believed anti-Semitism to be a serious problem in the United States (table 11.5).

Anti-Semitism has long been a force in maintaining Jewish group identity and in maintaining ties to Israel, and one might assume that, with such a high

TABLE 11.5
Respondent: Anti-Semitism Is a Serious Problem in USA

| | *Unweighted* | *SMC Weight* | *POPM1WGT* |
|---|---|---|---|
| Strongly disagree | 2.5 | 2.2 | 3.4 |
| Somewhat disagree | 14.9 | 15.1 | 14.3 |
| Somewhat agree | 33.5 | 30.7 | 34.9 |
| Strongly agree | 49.2 | 52.1 | 47.4 |

TABLE 11.6
Respondent Personally Experienced Discrmination

| | *Unweighted* | *SMC Weight* | *POPM1WGT* |
|---|---|---|---|
| Yes, getting job | 1.2 | 1.8 | 1.3 |
| Yes, promotion | 2.8 | 2.9 | 2.6 |
| Yes, both | 2.0 | 2.1 | 1.6 |
| Yes, other | 2.4 | 2.4 | 2.3 |
| No discrimination | 91.2 | 90.3 | 91.5 |
| Did not try for job | 0.4 | 0.5 | 0.6 |

level of perception of anti-Semitism, the bonds will continue to remain firm.

However, when we look at those who say that they personally experienced discrimination because of their Jewishness, the percentages drop radically (table 11.6), with more than 90 percent of Jewish baby boomers stating that they have never experienced discrimination. And although the percentages were somewhat lower, when asked whether for their agreement or disagreement with the statement "In a crisis, Jews can only depend on each other," approximately 60 percent disagreed "somewhat" or "strongly" (see table 11.7).

There is ample evidence that Jews are making it into spheres of American society that were traditionally closed to them. Evidence from studies of occupational patterns indicate that Jews can now be found in virtually every occupational sphere and at the highest levels. Even more, they are able to reach these spheres and levels without denying their Jewishness. They don't have to change their names and make a secret of their Jewishness.[27]

However, the "symbolic" rather than ideological and/or structural nature of their Jewishness is evident in a variety of manifestations. To cite but one example, when we look at the character of the neighborhoods in which American Jewish baby boomers live, we find an interesting paradox. On the one hand, a majority say that the Jewishness of their area is either somewhat or very important (table 11.8). On the other hand, when we look at the actual Jewish character of

TABLE 11.7
In Crisis Jews Can Only Depend on Each Other

| | *Unweighted* | *SMC Weight* | *POPM1WGT* |
|---|---|---|---|
| Strongly disagree | 30.5 | 28.6 | 31.6 |
| Somewhat disagree | 30.5 | 28.6 | 30.0 |
| Somewhat agree | 14.5 | 16.1 | 14.6 |
| Strongly agree | 24.5 | 26.7 | 23.8 |

TABLE 11.8
Respondent's Assessment of Importance of Neighborhood Jewishness

| | *Unweighted* | *SMC Weight* | *POPWGT* |
|---|---|---|---|
| Not important | 19.9 | 17.7 | 21.7 |
| Not very important | 25.8 | 24.4 | 25.0 |
| Somewhat important | 38.2 | 39.2 | 38.2 |
| Very important | 16.0 | 18.7 | 15.1 |

their neighborhoods as they describe them, we find that more than 60 percent state that their is little or no Jewish character to their neighborhood (table 11.9).

The age of the "melting pot," in which being ethnic was a stigma, is over. The change from an ideology of the melting pot to that of cultural pluralism took place during the 1960s. One of its first manifestations was the election of a Catholic, John F. Kennedy, to the presidency. Not only was JFK a Catholic, he was Irish; and when he visited Ireland he spoke proudly of his Irish homeland. In earlier times that would have been heresy! To be president one has to be actually born in the United States. As Theodore Roosevelt once said, hyphenated Americans are unacceptable. And then comes JFK and proclaims his Irish heritage.

The change to cultural pluralism was quickly picked up by Madison Avenue, and the late Pan Am Airlines had an ad campaign that proclaimed that all Americans have two homelands, the USA and that from which they or their parents emigrated; that you should visit your other homeland; and that when you do, of course, you should fly Pan Am. Or to cite one more example from the world of advertising, during the mid-1960s, Rheingold Beer had an ad campaign on television in which they would show a series of ethnic festivities, one for each ad spot—an Italian wedding, for example. They showed ethnic songs and dances, and at one point, all the people would lift their glasses of beer—Rheingold, of course—in blessing, salute, or what have you. The point is, this ad campaign was a clear public celebration of ethnicity, something that earlier would have been "un-American."

When I moved to New Haven in 1965, it was extremely rare to see a *kippa* at Yale. Today, that is not so rare, and one sees *kippot* on the heads of prominent

TABLE 11.9
Jewish Character of JBB's Neighborhood

| | *Unweighted* | *SMC Weight* | *POPWGT* |
|---|---|---|---|
| Not Jewish | 31.2 | 28.5 | 33.0 |
| Little Jewish | 31.8 | 31.2 | 32.1 |
| Somewhat Jewish | 28.3 | 30.7 | 27.0 |
| Very Jewish | 8.7 | 9.6 | 7.9 |

doctors in major hospitals, in Wall Street offices, law offices, and even, several years ago, worn by the chief of the public defender's office in Los Angeles in the television series, *The Trials of Rosie O'Neal*. And frequently, no mention is made and no attention paid to the *kippa*. It's very natural.

That Jews have made it into American society is also evident in the fact that increasing numbers of Jews are running for public office on the national level, and they serve while retaining their Jewish affiliation. Senator Joseph Lieberman of Connecticut is one outstanding example, and there are more.

One final manifestation of Jews having made it into American society is, much as it causes us pain, the significant rise in intermarriage. As the NJPS clearly shows, intermarriage today is basically different from what it was in the past in that the Jewish spouse is no longer expected to renounce his or her Jewishness. On the contrary, the non-Jewish spouse frequently finds the spouse's Jewishness attractive. This, again, is reflected in the media. Remember Michael and Hope on *"Thirtysomething"*? In a sense, it's in to be Jewish today. Several years ago, Joel, the doctor from New York on *Northern Exposure*, a very popular prime-time weekly televison show, proclaimed, "I am not white. I'm Jewish." And you can be sure he was not looking for a Jewish wife in Alaska! In fact, the next season he proposed to his colleague, Maggie O'Connell.

Nor is it only with respect to mate selection that Jews are increasingly bonding with non-Jews. Approximately two-thirds of the Jewish baby boomer respondents said that none or few of their closest friends are Jewish (table 11.10).

Again, New York Jews are significantly different. Among those between the ages of 18 and 34, 57 percent stated that most of their close friends are Jewish, and among those between the ages of 35 and 49, 61 percent did.[28]

What we are dealing with is what Herbert Gans calls "symbolic ethnicity."[29] Traditional ethnicity meant submerging the individual self to the demands of the group. The group has strong social control. Today, the group has no control, and the individual does not submit. Symbolic ethnicity is modern; it is an attempt to synthesize individualism with what Robert Nisbet referred to as the "quest for community"[30]—but not community in the traditional sense of power over the individual. Rather, it is a community with which one chooses to identify emotionally. It is, perhaps, a psychological community but not a sociological one. Even in

TABLE 11.10
JBB's Closest Friends Who Are Jewish

| | *Unweighted* | *SMC Weight* | *POPWGT* |
|---|---|---|---|
| None Jewish | 5.9 | 4.7 | 6.3 |
| Few or Some Jewish | 58.4 | 53.1 | 60.4 |
| Most Jewish | 26.7 | 31.4 | 24.3 |
| All Jewish | 9.0 | 10.8 | 9.0 |

choosing to identify with an ethnicity, the individual picks and chooses that which he can accept and that which he rejects. Symbolic ethnicity is "pick and choose" ethnicity, much as modern religion has become pick-and-choose religion. Charles Liebman also suggests that much of American Judaism is of a symbolic nature.[31]

James Davison Hunter has analyzed the "culture wars" raging in the United States today.[32] A number of the speakers at the opening session of the Jerusalem conference[33] pointed to a somewhat similar series of culture wars in Israel. In the United States the more traditional element is much more involved with Israel. How that will play itself out if the less traditional element in Israel moves farther away from the "civil religion" of Israel remains to be seen. Likewise, the greater the strength of the *Haredi* element in Israel becomes, the more it is likely to alienate the American Jewish nontraditionalists as well as a smaller but significant percentage of those in the traditional fold. Again, what will emerge from such developments is difficult to predict.

What seems clear is the nature of the American Jewish-Israeli relationship has undergone substantial change since the Six-Day War. There is no solid evidence, despite suggestions to the contrary by both American Jewish communal leaders and others,[34] that visits to Israel are the *causal* factor in intensifying Jewish identity and identification. There is evidence that Israel plays an important part in American Jewish identification, and the American Jewish community needs Israel much as Israel needs the American Jewish community. However, as the evidence presented indicates, fewer Jews now identify with the organized American Jewish community and with Israel.

Yet it might be argued, that perhaps there actually has not been any dimunition in American Jewish attachments to Israel, despite the evidence that there has. The data presented relate, primarily, to formal, institutional connections with Israel. Perhaps those have declined simply as a result of the broader decline in American Jewish attachments to what might be called the "public Judaism" of the organized American Jewish community. Some have argued that despite the decline in these type of attachments, there has been no decline—indeed, some suggest an increase—in "private Judaism," that is, informal as well as formal Judaism within the private sphere, especially family, without the formalized institutional connections.

Reassuring as that hypothesis sounds, the evidence does not appear to support it. With respect to attachments to Israel, in particular, the data presented relate to "private" as well as "public" spheres. Emotional attachments are most certainly the private sphere and, as table 11.4 indicates, they have declined among baby boomers. Furthermore, if it were only the attachments to Israel in the public, formal institutional sphere that have declined, we might have expected that, for example, the rate of aliya among baby boomers at least remained constant. Aliya, after all, is "doing" rather than "joining." Hard data on recent American aliya is meager. What is evident is that, although the median age of American immigrants to Israel, *olim*, remains in the 25–29-year-old cohort, as it has for at least several decades, there was a steady decline in the number of American *olim* during the

1980s, and the 1990 figures were the lowest since the 1960s.[35] So there does not appear to be anything in the Israel-related evidence, of a private sphere or public-sphere nature, to suggest that the diminishing of Jewish identification and identity is of only a limited nature. Although there may be sporadic and short-lived surges of manifestations of "symbolic Judaism," especially with respect to episodic American Jewish attention to Israel, there has been a decline in attachments that are socially meaningful and significant—that is, involving the individual for any length of time in ways that can be empirically demonstrated. An important question then becomes whether those weakening ties will strengthen those in Israel who already wish to distance themselves from the American Jewish community and what impact such a trend may have on both the American Jewish community and Israel.

## Notes

Paper presented at the conference on "The Six-Day War and Communal Dynamics in the Diaspora," Institute of Contemporary Jewry, The Hebrew University, Jerusalem, December 20, 1994.

1. Arthur Hertzberg, "Israel and American Jewry," *Commentary* 44 (2) (August 1967), pp. 69–73.
2. Menahem Kaufman, "From Philanthropy to Commitment: The Six Day War and the United Jewish Appeal," *Journal of Israeli History* 15 (2) (summer 1994), p. 161.
3. Ibid., pp. 161–91.
4. The data are from the National Jewish Population Survey. Specifics on the population involved are discussed below.
5. *Long Island Jewish World*, Feb. 11–17, 1994, p. 2.
6. Steven M. Cohen, *Israel-Diaspora Relations: A Survey of American Jewish Leaders* (Ramat-Aviv: Israel Diaspora Institute [Report No. 8], 1990), pp, 26–28.
7. Chaim I. Waxman, *American Aliya: Portrait of an Innovative Migration Movement* (Detroit: Wayne State University Press, 1989), pp. 105–18.
8. Cohen, *Israel-Diaspora Relations*. If it were based solely on this statement, Cohen's interpretation of the responses to this question as a measure of Zionism would be somewhat questionable. Those who responded negatively may not have been affirming the centrality of Israel. Perhaps they merely do not subscribe to the centrality of America; that is, they may hold Israel and America as of equal importance. That would be in line with the findings of a study of Reform Jewry's national leadership in which an almost identical percentage disagreed with the statement "It is easier to lead a fuller Jewish life in Israel than in the U.S." (Mark L. Winer, Sanford Seltzer, and Steven J. Schwager, *Leaders of Reform Judaism: A Study of Jewish Identity, Religious Practices and Beliefs, and Marriage Patterns* [New York: Research Task Force on the Future of Reform Judaism, Union of American Hebrew Congregations, 1987] pp. 63–64). However, in light of the responses of Cohen's sample to other Israel-related questions, his interpretation does seem appropriate for the majority.
9. See, e.g., Daniel J. Elazar, *Community and Polity: The Organizational Dynamics of*

*American Jewry* (Philadelphia: Jewish Publication Society, 1976), p. 288; Jonathan S. Woocher, *Sacred Survival: The Civil Religion of American Jews* (Bloomington: Indiana University Press, 1986), pp. 76–80.

10. Alvin I. Schiff, "Israel in American Jewish Schools: A Study of Curriculum Realities," *Jewish Education* 38(4) (October 1968), pp. 6–24.
11. Barry Chazan, "Israel in American Jewish Schools Revisited," *Jewish Education* 47(2) (summer 1979), p. 10.
12. David Ellenson, "Envisioning Israel in the Liturgies of North American Liberal Judaism," and Chaim I. Waxman, "The Changing Religious Relationship: American Jewish Baby Boomers and Israel," in Allon Gal, ed., *Envisioning Israel: The Changing Ideals of North American Jews* (Detroit: Wayne State University Press, 1996); also see Chaim I. Waxman, ed., *Israel as a Religious Reality* (Northvale, N.J.: Jason Aronson, 1994).
13. *Encyclopaedia Judaica*, 16:1147.
14. Charles S. Liebman, *The Ambivalent American Jew* (Philadelphia: Jewish Publication Society, 1973), pp. 88–108.
15. Nathan Glazer, "American Jews: Three Conflicts of Loyalties," in Seymour Martin Lipset, ed., *The Third Century: America as a Post-Industrial Society* (Stanford, Calif.: Hoover Institution Press, 1979), p. 233.
16. For example, see Steven M. Cohen, "Why Intermarriage May Not Threaten Jewish Continuity," *Moment* 19(6) (December 1994), pp. 89ff.
17. Bethamie Horowitz, *The 1991 New York Jewish Population Study* (New York: UJA-Federation, 1993), table 2.2, p. 52.
18. Robert Scheer, "The Times Poll: U.S. Jews for Peace Talks on Mideast," *Los Angeles Times*, April 12, 1988.
19. Chaim I. Waxman, "All in the Family: American Jewish Attachments to Israel," in Peter Y. Medding, ed., *A New Jewry? America since the Second World War*, Studies in Contemporary Jewry, vol. 8 (New York: Oxford University Press, 1992), pp. 134–49.
20. A good analysis is that of Peter Grose, *Israel in the Mind of America* (New York: Knopf, 1984).
21. For example, Eli Eyal, in his address at the opening session of the conference, "The Six-Day War and Communal Dynamics in the Diaspora," The Hebrew University, Institute of Contemporary Jewry, Jerusalem, December 1994.
22. Quoted in Jon Kalish, "The Roots of Radio," *The Jewish Week*, Queens edition, Oct. 14–20, 1994, p. 25.
23. Chaim I. Waxman, *America's Jews in Transition* (Philadelphia: Temple University Press, 1983), p. 114.
24. Charles E. Silberman, *A Certain People: American Jews and Their Lives Today* (New York: Summit Books, 1985).
25. Leonard Dinnerstein, *Anti-Semitism in America* (New York: Oxford University Press, 1994).
26. For a thoughtful challenge to the thesis of "American exceptionalism" as it pertains to anti-Semitism, see Benjamin Ginsberg, *The Fatal Embrace: Jews and the State* (Chicago: University of Chicago Press, 1993).
27. For example, see Samuel Z. Klausner, *Succeeding in Corporate America: The Experience of Jewish M.B.A.'s* (New York: American Jewish Committee, Institute of Human Relations, 1988).

28. Horowitz, *The 1991 New York Jewish Population Study*, table 2.2, p. 52.
29. Herbert J. Gans, "Symbolic Ethnicity: The Future of Ethnic Groups and Culture in America," in Herbert J. Gans, Nathan Glazer, Joseph R. Gusfield, and Christopher Jencks, eds., *On the Making of Americans: Essays in Honor of David Riesman* (Philadelphia: University of Pennsylvania Press, 1979), pp. 193–220.
30. Robert A. Nisbet, *The Quest for Community* (New York: Oxford University Press, 1970).
31. Charles S. Liebman, "Ritual, Ceremony, and the Reconstruction of Judaism in the United States," in Ezra Mendelsohn, ed., *Art and Its Uses: The Visual Image and Modern Jewish Society*, Studies in Contemporary Jewry, vol. 6 (New York: Oxford University Press, 1990), pp. 272–83.
32. James Davison Hunter, *Culture Wars: The Struggle to Define America* (New York: Basic Books, 1991).
33. "The Six-Day War and Communal Dynamics in the Diaspora," The Hebrew University, Institute of Contemporary Jewry, Jerusalem, December 1994.
34. For example, see David Mittleberg, *The Israel Visit and Jewish Identification* (New York: American Jewish Committee, American Jewish-Israel Relations Institute, 1994).
35. Chaim I. Waxman, "In the End Is It Ideology?: Religio-Cultural and Structural Factors in American Aliya," *Contemporary Jewry* 16 (1995), pp. 50–67.

**12** Peter Y. Medding, Gary A. Tobin, Sylvia Barack Fishman, and Mordechai Rimor

# Jewish Identity in Conversionary and Mixed Marriages

Intermarriage between Jews and non-Jews in the United States is now commonplace. The propensity of Jews to marry non-Jews was extremely low until the mid-1960s but rose sharply thereafter and continued to climb in the 1980s. As a result, in many Jewish communities, among those marrying in recent years, there are more out-marriages than in-marriages.

This change in the underlying social and religious structure of the American Jewish community has important implications for the present and future state of that community. On the one hand, marriage to non-Jews may indicate the successful integration of Jews into American society and their achievement of a high level of social acceptance. On the other hand, intermarriage may betoken and contribute to the decline of Judaism in America.

The subject of intermarriage evokes considerable passion among Jews because it arouses fears about elemental issues of group survival. One aspect of the matter is quantitative: the offspring of intermarriage may not remain Jewish; within one or two generations there may be fewer Jews and a greatly weakened Jewish community. Another aspect is qualitative: even if intermarriage does not lead to a decrease in the physical number of persons living in households with a Jewish parent, questions remain as to their Jewishness—that is, the intensity of their communal affiliation, ethnic identification, and religious practice.

This article[1] focuses on the qualitative aspects of Jewish intermarriage in the United States. It presents a theory of Jewish identity that provides a framework for the systematic empirical analysis of Jewish identification and behavior in households representing three basic marriage types: in-marriage (between two born Jews), conversionary marriage (between a born Jew and a born non-Jew who converts to Judaism), and mixed marriage (between a born Jew and a born non-

Jew who does not convert to Judaism). Although, as we will show, they differ greatly, the latter two categories are often referred to collectively as intermarriage or out-marriage.

It has been notably difficult for researchers to assess the quality of Jewish life in intermarried families or to make the kinds of meaningful comparisons between conversionary and mixed-married families that could help to gauge the potential for future Jewish commitment. Among the specific issues calling for clarification are the following: What are the characteristics and extent of Jewish behavior and identification in conversionary and mixed-married households? To what degree do the offspring of conversionary and mixed marriages receive formal Jewish education? To what extent are non-Jewish identities maintained in conversionary and mixed-married households?

In an effort to better understand the relationship between marriage type and level of Jewish identification, this study employs a typology for categorizing patterns of Jewish identification and behavior. The typology makes it possible to clarify whether and under what conditions Jewish identity is maintained in such marriages and to evaluate the character and content of that Jewish identity.

The article begins with a review of the recent literature on intermarriage, indicating how the present analysis goes beyond previous work in the field. It then provides a detailed description of the data set and methodology used in the analysis. Following a discussion of background variables, the article presents a new theory of Jewish identity and a typology of conversionary and mixed marriages. Empirical analysis of the Jewish identification and behavior of the various marriage types follows. This establishes the basis for the construction of an overall index of Jewish identification that makes it possible to quantify the various categories in the typology. The typology is then expanded to include a category we call dual-identity households. These households incorporate Jewish and Christian identities simultaneously. The concluding section takes note of the major findings and their implications.

## Review of the Literature

Numerous books and articles in the past decade have discussed the effects of the escalating rate of Jewish intermarriage on the character and vitality of individual Jewish identity and the continuity and survival of the American Jewish community as a whole. Observers differ widely in their perceptions of the consequences of the intermarriage phenomenon.[2] At one end of the spectrum are scholars who are comparatively pessimistic, some of whom predict the eventual disappearance of a distinctive Jewish community, seeing only the survival of the Orthodox. At the other end of the spectrum are scholars who are relatively optimistic, who discern the transformation and even revitalization of the American Jewish community.

Rising rates of intermarriage, the latter argue, provide an opportunity to strengthen the ranks of American Jewry through an infusion of new blood or "imports"—the born non-Jewish spouses and their children.

During the past ten years the optimists have dominated the discussion of Jewish intermarriage in the United States. Thus, Egon Mayer, who has written extensively on the subject, derives encouragement from the fact that contemporary intermarried couples tend to feel closer to Judaism than to Christianity. What is more, he argues, the generally higher educational and occupational status of the Jewish spouse enhances this leaning toward Judaism.[3]

Another scholar who leans toward the optimistic view is Steven M. Cohen. He argues that the "concentration of intermarriage among the Jewishly peripheral means it is less threatening to Jewish continuity." He also takes a positive view of conversionary marriages, which "in all likelihood . . . are both quantitative and qualitative assets to the Jewish population." However, Cohen is somewhat less sanguine about the impact of mixed marriages. On the plus side, he observes that "most mixed-married Jews report not one, but several sorts of attachment to Jewish people and Jewish ritual and, less frequently, to organized Jewry." On the negative side, he asserts that "the marriages of Jews to born non-Jews vastly increase the chances that the partners will be less involved in various aspects of Jewish life," even if the Jewish spouse was peripherally involved to begin with. On the whole, Cohen maintains, intermarriage does not present a "grave threat to the Jewish continuity of large numbers of American Jewry."[4]

A significant scholarly exchange on the subject of intermarriage appeared in *Studies in Contemporary Jews*, volume 5. Israeli demographers Sergio DellaPergola and U. O. Schmelz interpret not only rising rates of intermarriage but also trends toward postponement of marriage and nonmarriage, low fertility rates, increasing divorce, and the like as pointing to the "decline of the conventional Jewish family." Reviewing the available survey data, they argue that "as a result of more frequent out-marriage, particularly mixed marriage, Jewish identity is generally weakened, often amalgamated with the ethnocultural heritage of an originally non-Jewish spouse or parent and frequently lost in the longer run."[5]

Aiming to refute this position, Calvin Goldscheider asserts that "there is currently about a 20 percent gain of Jewish adults through conversion relative to total in-marriages."[6] Goldscheider argues that the "growing acceptance of intermarriage and the intermarried into Jewish life" and the "increasing similarity between the intermarried and the nonintermarried in measures of Jewishness" make for a situation in which a relationship between intermarriage and Jewish discontinuity is "weak and growing weaker." Goldscheider concludes: "Concerns over the demographic implications of Jewish intermarriage for survival of the group seem exaggerated."[7]

In this debate about its quantitative implications, the impact of intermarriage on the nature and intensity of Jewish identification and behavior has been relatively neglected. Thus, while Mayer, Goldscheider, and Cohen[8] all have data showing that persons living in intermarried households are generally less Jewishly involved than those in in-married households (except for conversionary marrieds in matters of religious performance), these qualitative aspects of intermarriage have not been subjected to systematic and detailed analysis.

This study focuses directly on the nature and intensity of Jewish identification and behavior in conversionary and mixed marriages. The analysis highlights two significant factors that elsewhere have gone unnoticed: the Jewish denominational identification of the various types of households and the simultaneous presence within them of Christian symbols and practices. Moreover, the large size of the sample used in this study[9] permits a more in-depth statistical analysis of qualitative data than ever previously undertaken.

## Methodology

This article is based on data collected in eight different Jewish communities in the United States: Baltimore; Boston; Essex and Morris counties in New Jersey; Providence, Rhode Island; and Worcester, Massachusetts, all in the eastern United States; Cleveland in the Midwest; Dallas in the Southwest; and the San Francisco Bay area in the West.[10]

These eight communities were selected from the many Jewish population surveys on file at the Cohen Center for Modern Jewish Studies at Brandeis University on the basis of four criteria. They reflect the current regional spread of American Jewry, the samples were fully representative, the data were collected between 1985 and 1988, and the questions relating to key variables were mostly identical, which permitted the files to be merged.

The analysis focuses on married couples, who are also referred to as households. In constructing a merged data set, therefore, the first step was to remove all unmarried respondents—the widowed, the divorced, the separated, the singles—from the data files of each of the eight communities. Following this, a consecutive merged file was constructed via the SPSSX Data Analysis System. Consecutive merging of the variables was facilitated by the identical or almost identical wording of the questions, relating to the items (variables) that were included in the merged file.

In each of the individual community surveys a weighting factor had been applied to enable projections to be made corresponding to the estimated numbers of individuals and households in a particular community. The merged file is based on these projected totals. Consequently, the weight applied to each community in the merged file is determined by its projected Jewish population, not by the actual numbers in the original sample used in each community survey. As such, the merged file is fully representative of the eight communities.

No attempt has been made to weight or correct the merged file further in order to make it representative of the actual proportions of these communities within

American Jewry as a whole. However, the same basic trends, relationships, and patterns relating to marriage types are found in each of the individual communities. As a result, merging the file does not erase nor average out contradictory trends and patterns in the different communities.

The total projected number of households in the merged file is 197,078, representing a total Jewish population in the eight communities of over 433,104 individuals in in-married households, 35,266 in conversionary households, and 106,163 individuals in mixed-married households—in all, 574,533 individuals, or about 9.75 percent of American Jewry. All percentage calculations have been made on the basis of these projected numbers.

The present analysis focuses on differences between marriage types, as reflected in the pattern of identification or behavior of the household as a unit. Occasionally, however, the analysis focuses on the attributes or achievements of the individual Jewish spouse or spouses, as, for example, is the case with most of the background variables (except for income, which is a household attribute). Thus, the incidence of the various types of marriage within the different age groups, for example, is arrived at by counting each individual Jewish spouse as a single unit.

The sum of the individual Jewish spouses in all marriage types will always be greater than the sum of couples or households. Put simply, one marriage of each type (in-marriage, conversionary, mixed) adds up to three marriages. However, the sum of born-Jewish partners in these three marriages is four (two in the in-marriage and one in each of the other types).

Household intermarriage rates—the percentage of intermarried couples as a proportion of all couples, households, or marriages—are always higher than individual rates: the percentage of born Jews in intermarriages as a proportion of the total of married Jewish individuals. Thus, in the example above, the individual intermarriage rate is 50 percent (two of four Jews are in intermarriages), whereas the household intermarriage rate is 66 percent (two of three marriages are intermarriages). Or to take actual figures: for the decade 1980–89 the individual rates shown—62 percent in-marriage, 5 percent conversionary marriage, and 33 percent mixed marriage—have computed equivalent household rates of 45 percent in-marriage, 7 percent conversionary marriage, and 48 percent mixed marriage.

## Background Characteristics and Marriage Types

### *Rates of In-marriage and Intermarriage*

The distribution of marriage types varies by community. For example, approximately 80 percent or more of marriages in Baltimore, Boston, Cleveland, Essex/Morris counties, and Providence are in-marriages, whereas in San Francisco and Dallas the proportions are 60 percent and 66 percent, respectively. In the merged sample, 73 percent of all marriages are in-marriages, 5 percent are conversionary, and 21 percent are mixed marriages.

### *Decade of Marriage*

The overall distribution of marriages in the merged sample shows a consistent increase in the incidence of intermarriage since 1960. Almost 94 percent of Jewish individuals who married prior to 1960 are in-married; only 2 percent are in conversionary marriages and 5 percent in mixed marriages. The proportion in-marrying declines by about 10 percent in the 1960s and by another 10 percent in the 1970s. This process becomes accelerated in the 1980s, when the rate of in-marriage declines by a further 13 percent. Conversely, the proportion entering into mixed marriages rises dramatically over time. By the 1980s, 33 percent of Jewish individuals are entering into mixed marriages.

Significantly, since the 1960s the proportion of individuals entering into conversionary marriages has remained fairly steady at about 5 percent. Despite what some have claimed, converts do not constitute an increasing proportion of the intermarried. To the contrary, the figures show that they constitute a rapidly declining proportion of the intermarried, from 28–29 percent before 1970 to 13 percent in the 1980s.

### *Age and Generation*

The basic pattern with regard to intermarriage is confirmed by examining marriages within age and generation. The incidence of in-marriage declines steadily with age, from well over 90 percent among Jews aged 55 and older to 70 percent among those aged 18–34. There has been a fivefold increase in the incidence of mixed marriage among younger age groups; 5 percent of those in the two oldest age groups are mixed-married, as compared with 25 percent of those aged 18–34. At the same time, the incidence of conversionary marriage more than doubles, rising from about 2 percent for those aged 55 and older to 5 percent for those under age 44.

Tabulation of marriages by generation produces a similar but even more pronounced pattern. While 93 percent of first-generation Jews are in-married, only 56 percent of the fourth generation are. At the same time, the proportion of Jews entering into conversionary marriages increases threefold, from 2 percent in the first generation to 6 percent in the fourth. However, the proportion of those in mixed marriages increases more than sevenfold—from 5 percent in the first generation to 38 percent in the fourth.

### *Gender*

In the past, Jewish men were much more likely than Jewish women to intermarry. Although rates of intermarriage and mixed marriage for both men and women have risen steadily over time, Jewish men are still more likely than Jewish women to intermarry. Overall, 82 percent of Jewish men are inmarried, compared with 90 percent of Jewish women. The proportion of in-marriages among Jewish men declined by 35 percent in three decades, from 90 percent for the period before 1960 to 55 percent in the decade of the 1980s. For Jewish women, the proportion of in-marriages declined by 28 percent during the same period, from 98 percent to 70 percent. Significantly, since the 1960s, the decline in the proportion of in-marriages for the two sexes has proceeded apace, with a 23 percent decline among Jewish men and a 21 percent decline among Jewish women. Apart from the fact that both groups are subject to the same societal influences, the two rates are also integrally connected to each other: as increasing proportions of Jewish men intermarry, there will be fewer available Jewish males for Jewish women.

In all decades of marriage, Jewish men are consistently more likely than Jewish women to be involved in conversionary marriages, indicating the greater propensity of non-Jewish women to convert to Judaism, compared with non-Jewish men married to Jewish women. Over three decades, the proportion of mixed marriages among Jewish women increased from 2 percent to 28 percent; among Jewish men it increased from 8 percent to 38 percent.

### *Multiple Marriages*

Intermarriages are more common in subsequent marriages than in first marriages. While 86 percent of first marriages are in-marriages, the proportion drops to 70 percent in second marriages and 54 percent in third or subsequent marriages. Conversely, rates of mixed marriage rise with the number of marriages, but conversionary marriages remain fairly static. Other data indicate that individuals under the age of 45 are more likely to have multiple marriages than those over age 45. Nevertheless, when controls for age are introduced, mixed marriages are still more common in the case of multiple marriages. Multiple marriage, it appears, lowers the likelihood of choice of Jewish marriage partners, possibly because religiously suitable partners are less readily available. In addition, factors related to starting and raising a family may no longer be relevant, which may also influence these trends.

### *Age at First Marriage*

For the entire sample, the mean age is 25 years. In-married men have a mean age of 25.9 years; for women it is 23.2 years. The mean age jumps to 27.8 years for males and to 25.7 years for females in conversionary marriages, and to 27.9 years for males and 26 years for females in mixed marriages. The tendency of conversionary and mixed marriages to occur at a later age than in-marriages suggests that a substantial proportion of never-married individuals currently in their thirties and forties are likely to marry non-Jews.

*Children at Home*

The distribution of marriage types among households with children at home more or less mirrors that of the whole sample. If anything, there are slightly more mixed-married households with children at home than the proportion of mixed-marrieds in the total sample, reflecting the increased incidence of mixed marriage among the younger age groups. Overall, 24 percent of households with children at home are mixed marriages, and 4 percent are conversionary marriages. Thus, nearly three in ten families with children at home have one spouse who was not born Jewish, and the vast majority of these constitute mixed marriages.

*Education, Occupation, Income*

Marriage type is related to socioeconomic status but in ways that defy conventional wisdom, which associates intermarriage with high socioeconomic achievement and integration. The data reported here indicate the opposite: higher socioeconomic status is associated with lower levels of mixed marriage, higher rates of conversion, and higher rates of in-marriage. Education, occupation, and income alone are weakly associated with marriage-type variation, but these associations are stronger when age group is introduced as a variable. Generally, lower socioeconomic status is associated with higher rates of intermarriage and much higher rates of mixed marriage. This is particularly noticeable in the 18–34 age group. For example, 74 percent of those with a graduate degree in that age group are in-married, compared with 69 percent of those with a college degree, 63 percent of those with some college, and 59 percent of those with a high school diploma or less. Conversely, 41 percent of those with a high school education are in mixed marriages but only 19 percent of those with graduate degrees. There are also differences in the incidence of conversionary marriages. In the 18–34 age group, 7 percent of those with graduate degrees are in conversionary marriages, compared with under I percent of those with a high school diploma or less. Overall, similar but less pronounced marriage patterns appear for the 35–44 age group but are not present among those aged over 45 years.

Again, in the 18–34 age group, between 72 percent and 75 percent of those in professional, executive, and sales positions are in-married, compared to 61 percent of those in clerical positions, and 54 percent of those in blue-collar and service occupations. Conversely, while the proportion of mixed-marrieds is about 20 percent in the three highest occupational categories in the 18–34 age group, it climbs to 45 percent in the lowest occupational category. As with education, these patterns are apparent but less so in the 35–44 age group; for the most part they are not present in the older age groups.

This general picture is further corroborated by the household income data. While the data indicate that the proportion of mixed marriages is at its lowest where income is highest (i.e., among those earning over $150,000), the opposite does not appear to be true, and there does not appear to be any association between lower income and higher rates of mixed marriage. However, when broader income categories are used, lower income does turn out to be associated with mixed marriage. Overall, 26 percent of those with incomes below $75,000 are mixed-married as compared with 18 percent of those earning over $75,000. The picture is sharpened further when we control for age.

The data demonstrate clearly that there is a strong association between lower income and higher rates of mixed marriage among those under 45 but that it does not exist at all among those over 45. Thus, in the under 45 age group, 37 percent of those earning under $30,000 and 33 percent of those earning between $30,000 and $75,000 are mixed-married, while 21 percent among those earning over $75,000 are. Conversely, 56 and 59 percent, respectively, of the two lower income groups are in-married, compared with 72 percent of those earning over $75,000. Turning to those over 45 years, the differences between the rates of mixed marriage of the three income groups are extremely small. The rate of mixed marriage is slightly higher in the middle income group (17%) than among the lower and higher income earners (12% and 15%, respectively).

In all, greater proportions of younger Jews than of older Jews are better educated, in more prestigious occupations, and earn higher incomes. Why they are more likely to in-marry than those young people who do not achieve these educational, occupational, and income levels and why the latter are more likely to marry out is not clear from our data. One possible explanation is that within a community in which high levels of achievement are the norm, low achievers will be less attractive marriage partners and more limited in their choices than high achievers. Conversely, low achievers in terms of Jewish norms may still be relatively high achievers by the norms of American society as a whole and may seek to maximize these assets outside the Jewish community rather than compete within it against higher achievers.

### *Jewish Education*

The data relating to Jewish education seem to indicate that individuals who have had some Jewish education and those who have had none at all are almost equally likely to be involved in conversionary and mixed marriages. However, closer examination of the data does reveal differences based on duration of Jewish education, particularly so in younger age groups. In general, going from older to younger age groups, there is a linear increase in the proportion of individuals receiving more than six years of Jewish education, strikingly so among women. Thus, 45 percent of women aged 18–34, as against 21 percent of women over 65 years of age, received six or more years of Jewish education; the comparable figures for men are 46 percent and 35 percent. Similarly, the proportion of women receiving no Jewish education at all declines markedly, from 45 percent of those aged 65 and over to 25 percent of those in the 18–34 age group. By way of contrast, the proportion of men of all age groups with no Jewish education at all is consistently much lower—in the range of 11 percent to 20 percent—and there is no linear relationship with age.

While Jewish women are both less likely than Jewish men to have received any Jewish education at all and to have received it for more than six years, older Jewish women are also less likely to intermarry. This suggests a complex relationship between Jewish education and the propensity to intermarry. To control for these factors, the figures for years of Jewish education were broken down by both age and gender. A comparison of those with more than six years of Jewish education and those with less or none at all confirms that Jewish education is clearly associated with higher rates of in-marriage and lower rates of mixed marriage. While this holds true for both men and women in all age groups, the association between more than six years of Jewish education and in-marriage is strongest in younger age groups—especially among men aged 35–54, and it is also weakly present in the 18–34 age group. For women it is strongest among those under age 45 (particularly in the 18–34 age group).

Among those with less than six years of Jewish education, there does not appear to be a consistent relationship between number of years of Jewish education and the propensity to in-marry. In only two of ten cases, Jewish males aged 35–44 and Jewish males aged 45–54) is there a clear linear relationship between the two, with those having up to five years of Jewish education more likely to be in-married than those without any Jewish education. In four other cases the opposite is true—those who have not received any Jewish education are more likely to be in-married than those with up to five years of Jewish education. In yet another four cases there is little or no difference at all.

In general, the association between in-marriage and a lengthy period of Jewish education appears strongest at a time when the incidence of intermarriage is relatively high, as can be seen among younger men and women, and appears weakest when the incidence of intermarriage is relatively low, as in the case of older men and women. Clearly, the relationship between these two elements is not linear but is mediated by other powerful social and psychological factors, most especially the character and salience of personal Jewish identity at the time of marriage.

These background data have been concerned with the question of which Jews have a greater or lesser propensity to intermarry. Overall, they indicate that age, generation, and gender are more highly associated with intermarriage than are the other background factors. Intermarriage rates are highest among younger and fourth-generation American Jews, particularly males. The data also show an increased incidence of mixed marriage over time, with the rates of conversionary marriage remaining fairly stable.

By the 1980s just under half of the marriages involving Jews were mixed, forming families in which one spouse was Jewish and the other was a non-Jew. Consistently, the incidence of mixed marriage was found to be highest in the younger age groups, among whom it was only slightly lowered by long exposure to Jewish education. Thus, in the youngest age cohorts, even those who received more than six years of Jewish education manifest a relatively high rate of mixed marriage, peaking at 25 percent among males aged 18–34 years.

This finding of increasing mixed marriage even among strongly identified Jews suggests a hitherto unappreciated and intriguing possibility: the increasing incidence of mixed marriage may be associated with underlying changes in the nature of Jewish personal and group identity. These changes, in turn, have led to expectations or hopes that Jewish identity can still be maintained and transmitted in mixed marriages.

Given the increasing incidence of intermarriage, how these hopes and expectations play themselves out—in short, what happens to Jewish identity in conversionary and mixed marriages—is a particularly crucial question for investigation. We begin with a theoretical analysis of the nature of contemporary Jewish identity, the underlying changes within it, and the implications for different marriage types.

## Contemporary Jewish Identity and Intermarriage

Jewish identity is located at the core of personal identity, which Herbert Kelman defines as "the enduring aspects of the person's definition of himself . . . the individual's conception of who he is and what he is over time and across situations." Included in this is "the child's cultural and ethnic heritage—the groups into which he is born." These form "an inherent part of his identity . . . by virtue of the fact that the group[s] to which he belongs are usually an inevitable part of his life experience." Thus, Kelman notes, an individual's ethnic and cultural heritage "enters into who and what he is, just as his biological heritage does." The individual, therefore, "must somehow take his cultural as well as his biological heritage into account if he is to develop a firm personal identity." The group's definition of itself—its own conception of its basic values—enters into the individual's personal identity as an ongoing cultural heritage that exists independently of the individuals that bear it. It is expressed in written documents, oral traditions, institutions, and symbols.[11]

### *A Partial Community of Shared Feelings*

In the past, the common denominator of Jewish identity was a community of belief based on a system of shared prescriptive values.[12] Over the past century, however, this has shifted in the direction of a community of shared individual feelings. The community of belief constituted a total system that controlled the individual's environment with a detailed pattern of prescribed actions and fixed roles. Group membership was thus clearly defined. In contrast, the contemporary community of shared individual feelings is a voluntary and partial community of personal choice, with unclear boundaries and undefined membership. It is characterized by emotions and attachments that, while often deep, are not always clearly articulated.

This shift in Jewish identity is paralleled and reinforced by the trend in American society in the direction of what Richard Merelman has called "the decline of group belongingness and the rise of individualization." Merelman notes that in contemporary America, "many people continue to be members and identify with groups, [but] they believe their group identities to be matters of individual choice, which can be changed without stigma. Group membership thus becomes voluntary, contingent, fluid, not 'given,' fixed and rigid."[13] The process that Merelman is describing shows itself in the fact that many American Jews give strong expression to feelings of Jewishness as a central component of their personal identity even when they fail to uphold major Jewish religious beliefs and rituals. As documented in many studies, being Jewish is very important to such individuals: they express considerable Jewish pride, are comfortable with their Jewishness, are happy that they were born Jewish, relate to other Jews as family, and want their children to remain Jewish.

Despite the shift away from the community of shared belief, the religious value system remains a distinctive defining characteristic of the Jewish group at the normative and cultural levels. Popular religious observances—those relating to *rites de passage* and the holidays—continue to provide personal identity with its group aspects, even though the practices may have been selectively detached from a coherent and consistent whole. They serve as a vehicle for expressing shared feelings in familial and communal contexts, which reinforce and heighten the positive emotional affect of group belonging at the core of personal identity.

At the same time, religion differentiates and separates Jews from other groups. This implies, first and foremost, a rejection of the dominant Christian culture.[14] In Robert Bellah's words, "It is part of Jewish identity and the maintenance of the boundaries of the Jewish community to deny that Jesus is the Christ, the Messiah. This is to claim, however tacitly, that Christianity is a false religion."[15] Paradoxically, as the religious aspects of Judaism have become relatively less central to the core of Jewish identity and shared feelings have become more important, being *not* Christian has taken on greater salience as a defining element of Jewishness.[16]

In the partial community of shared individual feelings, Jewishness forms part of the core of self-identity. As such, it can be significant without requiring the individual to raise it constantly to the level of conscious awareness. But there are also occasions in the life of the individual that do characteristically raise the issue of Jewish identity to the level of conscious awareness, for example, when choosing a marriage partner, at the birth of a child, and when making decisions about whether and how to transmit an ethnic heritage to the children. Similarly, events that affect the larger Jewish group, such as episodes of prejudice and discrimination—rejection of the group by others—may be experienced as personal rejection. Such rejection threatens all members of the community of shared individual feelings, constituting an attack on the core of personality, whether or not the attack is directed at them personally and however tenuous their own ties with the group.

*Segmented and Unambiguous Jewish Identity*

The Jewishness of the community of shared feelings in contemporary American society has become segmented in a number of different ways.

First, Jewishness constitutes only one segment of personal identity; it exists alongside others, such as those deriving from being an American, college-educated, a high-income earner, or a social and political liberal, for example. Needless to say, the various aspects of personal identity inform and shape each other. Thus, the trait of Jewishness plays a part in how Jews act out their various roles in American society, and their various roles in American society influence their Jewish identity.

Second, the multiple aspects of identity coexist independently rather than coalescing to form a larger, integrated whole. The result is what might be termed a pluralistic personality. The significance and salience for the individual of any particular segment of his or her personal identity will vary with particular circumstances—personal, societal, historical, and so forth.

Third, neither the extent nor the intensity of the Jewish segment of personal identity is fixed. The Jewish segment may be very broad, taking in many aspects of contemporary Jewish group identity (such as religion, Israel, philanthropy, culture, group defense, friendship) or only one or a few aspects. At the same time, involvement in even a single, narrow segment of Jewishness may be very intense, whereas simultaneous involvement in a number of aspects may be attenuated.

Although contemporary Jewish identity is segmented in these various ways, the core of Jewishness remains unambiguous, in the sense that it is perceived by both Jews and others to be exclusively connected with the Jewish group's cultural and ethnic heritage. Thus, in families in which both parents are Jewish and continue to identify as such, the Jewish ethnic and cultural self-identity imparted to their children is unambiguous, even when it is weak or generates ambivalence. They are Jewish and nothing else. The Jewish self-identity of these individuals defines both who they are and who they are not, irrespective of the extent and intensity of its particular form. The process of unambiguous Jewish identity formation is reinforced by values in American society encouraging individuals to build on their own cultural roots for purposes of self-esteem, individual happiness, and positive intergroup relations. Under these conditions, an unambiguous ethnic identity provides the foundation for a secure personal identity.[17]

*Segmented Jewish Identity and Mixed Marriage*

The existence of a segmented and unambiguous Jewish identity encourages Jews who enter into mixed marriages to assume that this will not prevent them from continuing to affirm and maintain the Jewish element at the core of their personal identity. (By the same token, their non- Jewish spouses, if they so choose, will be able to maintain a culturally different personal identity.) They see Jewish identity as a personal issue and are convinced that participation in a mixed family is compatible with strong personal expressions of Jewishness: to feel part of the Jewish people, to be proud of one's Jewishness, to attend synagogue, to perform Jewish rituals, to support Israel. The experience of diversity and pluralism within the family may be deemed personally enriching. The rationale of mixed marriage, therefore, is that neither partner's personal identity need impinge on the other.

The structural realities of American Jewish life predispose young American Jews to meet, date, and marry non-Jews. The segmented and unambiguous character of their Jewish identity often leads them to assume or hope that intermarriage will have little effect on their Jewish feelings and commitments. Many also believe that their children will likewise be Jewish and that mixed families are not a bar to the transmission of a Jewish personal identity. These expectations are not always realized, however, and indeed run counter to the fundamental dynamics of mixed families in America. Thus, an unambiguous Jewish identity in the parental generation may turn out to be a terminal Jewish identity in the next. To understand why this is so, it is necessary to examine the identity dynamics in mixed and conversionary marriages.

### *Identity Dynamics in Conversionary and Mixed Marriages*

Conversionary and mixed marriages reflect very different hopes and goals and set in motion opposing processes. Conversion to Judaism generally indicates a desire to create an environment for identity formation that avoids competing and conflicting identities within the family and thereby increases the chances of developing an unambiguous Jewish identity in the children. Conversion to Judaism, however, is a process, not an act, and as such it is by no means easy, quick, or inexorable. Some who convert may not proceed very far along the road, may stop, or go backward, while others do indeed reach the final destination. Conversion involves a change of personal and group identity by the non-Jew, necessitating, on the one hand, distancing, disaffiliation, and cutting off ties with the usually Christian spiritual heritage and identity of the family into which the individual was born and the adoption of Jewish symbols, behavior, and identity, on the other.

Conversion to Judaism may trigger a number of difficulties. In the first place, a Christian core identity may prove resistant to change and may therefore manifest or reassert itself on symbolic occasions during the cycle of the year or at critical junctures of the life cycle unless it is consciously rejected. Second, it is often not clear what becoming Jewish entails in terms of the Jewish partner's desires and expectations. If it entails conversion to Judaism as a religion, then it is clear what that means and how it can be achieved. But if Jewishness involves an ethnic dimension—a relationship in blood, membership in a people characterized by shared feelings and history—it is not so clear how this may be attained, even after formal religious conversion. It may take time and experience before the convert to Judaism "feels" Jewish.

Mixed marriage involves a very different situation. A mixed family creates an environment for identity formation that is founded on the competing heritages of the Jewish and the non-Jewish spouses, both of which enter into the child's core identity. Mixed marriage thus not only decreases the likelihood that an unambiguous Jewish identity will be formed but also raises the possibility that no Jewish identity at all will emerge. As Nathan Glazer has explained, "Their children have alternatives before them that the children of families in which both parents were born Jewish do not—they have legitimate alternative identities."[18]

In mixed-married families, the absence of agreement about fundamental matters of identity confronts the children with a choice between four alternatives: they can incorporate the identity of the Jewish parent, that of the non-Jewish parent, that of both, or that of neither. Identifying wholly with one parent may prove traumatic to the extent that it involves the rejection of the other parent, as well as part of the self. Maintaining both identities simultaneously may create tensions and conflicts that prevent the development of an integrated personal identity. Thus, the most commonly chosen solution may turn out to be identifying with neither parent and focusing on shared, general, secular values.

The range of possible Jewish identity outcomes from both conversionary and mixed marriages can be presented in the form of a typology with six cells or subtypes, as shown in table 12.1. The cells are based on the intersection of Jewish identification and marriage type. As there are three levels of Jewish identification (low, medium, and high) and two marriage types (conversionary and mixed) this results in six subtypes, three for each marriage type.

At this point, this typology does not take account of the possible simultaneous presence within the various marriage types and subtypes of a Christian identity, assuming an inverse relationship between Jewish identity and Christian elements. The existence of marriages in which Jewish and Christian identities are both maintained will be examined at a later stage and will result in an expanded typology.

Having established a theoretical framework for the examination of Jewish identity in mixed and conversionary marriages, let us now turn to the empirical data.

TABLE 12.1
Conversionary and Mixed-Marriage Typology

| | *Jewish Identification Level* | | |
|---|---|---|---|
| *Marriage Type* | *Low* | *Medium* | *High* |
| Conversionary | LC | MC | HC |
| Mixed | LM | MM | HM |

## Marriage Type and Jewish Identification

### *Denomination*

Jewish identity is formed not only within the family but also within formal religious structures, such as synagogues and schools, that are generally affiliated with organized Jewish religious movements. These denominations, as they are known, represent alternative normative patterns of Jewish belief and behavior, each having different standards and expectations on a whole range of matters, including conversion to Judaism and mixed marriage.

It was argued above that, in the community of shared feelings, the religious aspect of Jewish identity continues to be central to the core of individual and group identity. One expression of this is the overwhelming extent to which American Jews think of themselves as being Orthodox, Conservative, or Reform Jews even when they are not formally affiliated with a synagogue or temple.[19] (In the survey files, there is an additional category of "Just Jewish." Sometimes it is a specific denominational alternative; when not, it is a residual category for all who give some other broad general term of Jewish identification.) In all, denomination is likely to be strongly associated with differences in the pattern of individual Jewish identification and behavior.

The need to control for denomination is underscored by the differential distribution of the four denominations within each marriage type. Thus, Conservative Jews constitute over one-third of the total sample but only 12 percent of the mixed-marrieds. Conversely, those who identify as Just Jewish represent less than 14 percent of the total sample but make up over one-third of the mixed-marrieds. Finally, Reform Jews represent 45 percent of the total sample but constitute 57 percent of the conversionary marrieds.

These patterns of discrepant representation are a result of the clear relationship between denominational identification and marriage type. In the case of the in-marrieds, the rank order is Orthodox, Conservative, Reform, and Just Jewish, while in the case of the mixed-marrieds it is the reverse. About nine in ten Orthodox and Conservative Jews are in-married, as against seven in ten Reform Jews, and five in ten of the Just Jewish. Conversely, nearly half of the persons calling themselves Just Jewish are mixed-marrieds, as are over one-fifth of those identifying as Reform Jews, but only one in 15 of those calling themselves Orthodox and Conservative Jews. The overall level of conversionary marriages is low among all denominational groups—ranging between 2 percent and 7 percent—with the rank order being Reform, Conservative, Just Jewish, and Orthodox. (The very small number of Orthodox conversionary and mixed-marrieds in our sample necessitates their exclusion from all further statistical analyses involving denominations, leaving only Orthodox in-marrieds).

It is clear, then, that persons identifying themselves with different wings of American Judaism exhibit very different marriage profiles. While Orthodox and Conservative Jews are predominantly in-married, among those who identify as Reform three in ten are either conversionary marrieds or mixed-marrieds, as are half of the Just Jewish. It must be emphasized, however, that these denominational figures are based on current self-identification, and their relationship to family of origin is unknown. Thus, a person who grew up in an Orthodox home and married a convert might decide that he or she would be more comfortable affiliating with a Conservative or Reform congregation. One cannot draw any conclusions from these data about possible linkages between the denomination of the family of origin and the propensity to engage in conversionary or mixed marriages.

*Religious Affiliation and Identification*

Synagogue membership and attendance give public expression to religious affiliation and identification. On a more private, familial level, ritual practice plays the same role.

The overall data for marriage types show that the differences between in-marrieds and conversionary marrieds are very narrow and not unidirectional. In-marrieds are slightly more likely than conversionary marrieds to belong to synagogues, but conversionary marrieds are more likely than in-marrieds to attend synagogue regularly. Thus, 60 percent of in-marrieds belong to synagogues and 28 percent attend regularly; among the conversionary marrieds the figures are 56 percent and 34 percent, respectively. In-marrieds and conversionary marrieds perform Jewish rituals with almost identical degrees of frequency: 87 percent of both groups attend a Passover seder, 85 percent and 84 percent light Hanukkah candles, 68 percent fast on Yom Kippur, and 38 percent and 32 percent, respectively, light Sabbath candles.

The most striking feature of the data is the marked difference between in-marrieds and conversionary marrieds, on the one hand, and mixed-marrieds on the other. For all three measures, mixed-marrieds score 30 percent to 40 percent lower than the in-marrieds and the conversionary marrieds: 15 percent of mixed-marrieds belong to a synagogue; 6 percent attend synagogue regularly (53% never attend); 52 percent participate in a seder; 52 percent light Hanukkah candles; 34 percent fast on Yom Kippur; and 3 percent light Sabbath candles.

For all three marriage types, the same denominational rank order from highest to lowest—Orthodox, Conservative, Reform, Just Jewish—is evident. Thus, 36 percent of Conservative mixed-marrieds are synagogue members, as against 21 percent of Reform mixed-marrieds and 5 percent of Just Jewish mixed-marrieds. The comparable figures for regular synagogue attendance are 75 percent, 63 percent, and 25 percent, respectively. The practice of all the Jewish rituals follows a similar pattern. For example, 76 percent of Conservative mixed-marrieds fast on

Yom Kippur, as against 40 percent of Reform mixed-marrieds, and 17 percent of Just Jewish mixed-marrieds. The three apparent exceptions to this pattern do not alter this basic finding.[20]

Comparison of the different marriage types within denominations shows that Conservative and Reform conversionary marrieds are less likely than their in-married counterparts to belong to synagogues but are more likely to attend synagogue. The differences in synagogue membership are greatest among Conservative Jews: 68 percent of Conservative in-marrieds belong to synagogues but only 54 percent of Conservative conversionary marrieds do; 59 percent of Reform in-marrieds and 57 percent of Reform conversionary marrieds belong. With regard to synagogue attendance, in both denominations the margin in favor of conversionary marrieds is about 10 percent: 42 percent of Conservative conversionary marrieds attend synagogue regularly, as do 32 percent of Conservative in-marrieds; among Reform Jews the equivalent figures are 33 percent and 22 percent. However, no clear pattern emerges for ritual performance: in both denominations, in-marrieds and conversionary marrieds are variously higher on different rituals. Moreover, the margins between them are very narrow, usually a few percentage points.

In contrast, Just Jewish conversionary marrieds consistently score higher, sometimes much higher, than Just Jewish in-marrieds on all three measures of religious affiliation and identification. Thus, 49 percent of Just Jewish conversionary marrieds belong to synagogues, compared with 23 percent of Just Jewish in-marrieds; 66 percent of the conversionaries attend synagogue at least a few times a year, but only 43 percent of the in-marrieds do so. Again, 86 percent of Just Jewish conversionary marrieds light Hanukkah candles and 60 percent fast on Yom Kippur, compared with 52 percent and 33 percent, respectively, of Just Jewish in-marrieds. The differences between the two groups indicate an underlying secular orientation among Just Jewish in-marrieds and a more religious orientation on the part of Just Jewish conversionary marrieds, even when this is not accompanied by current denominational identification. (There may, of course, have been some denominational affiliation in the past, during the conversion process.) Given the relatively small actual numbers of Just Jewish conversionary marrieds, however, all findings relating to them must remain somewhat tentative and will therefore be excluded from further analysis.

The considerably lower levels of religious involvement of mixed-marrieds are maintained within the various denominations. On average, mixed-marrieds are 25 percent lower than the other two marriage types on all measures of religious identification and affiliation. Thus, 36 percent of Conservative mixed-marrieds, 21 percent of Reform mixed-marrieds, and 5 percent of Just Jewish mixed-marrieds belong to a synagogue, compared to 68 percent, 59 percent, and 23 percent, respectively, of comparable in-marrieds. Similarly, 76 percent of Conservative mixed-marrieds, 68 percent of Reform mixed-marrieds, and 35 percent of Just Jewish mixed-marrieds light Hanukkah candles, while 95 percent, 86 percent, and 52 percent of equivalent in-marrieds do so.

Mixed-marrieds calling themselves Conservative are more likely to belong to synagogues (36%) than Reform mixed-marrieds (21%). This is true despite the Reform movement's recognition of patrilineal descent and greater Conservative ideological opposition to mixed marriage.

Denominational identification is closely associated with level of religious involvement. Conservative and Reform mixed-marrieds are on average about 30 percent more likely than Just Jewish mixed-marrieds to have current synagogue membership, to attend synagogue, and to participate in ritual practice. Clearly, among mixed-marrieds a denominational self-definition is associated with a higher level of religious involvement, while Just Jewish as a self-definition indicates conscious distancing from Jewish religious identification.

The strength and stability of the relationship between marriage type and religious affiliation and identification were tested by controlling for the effects of age and family type. For age, the sample was divided into two groups: under 45 years of age and over 45 years of age. For family type, the sample was divided into two groups: couples with no children at all and couples with unmarried children, whether living at home or not. These controls were applied to the questions relating to synagogue membership, synagogue attendance, and ritual practice, for the three marriage types, both by themselves and within denomination. The results indicate that although both age and family type are themselves influential, the impact of marriage type and denomination are still clearly evident within age groups and family types. In general, the expected age-related and life-cycle-related influences do not diminish the strength of the association between denomination and marriage type on the one hand and Jewish religious affiliation and identification on the other.

Two aspects of the relationship between marriage type and Jewish religious identification and affiliation are particularly noteworthy. The first is the extent to which conversionary marriages are like in-marriages, both as a whole and within denomination. Clearly, conversion often leads to the maintenance of Jewish religious practices. At the same time, a significant proportion of conversionary marriages are low in their levels of Jewish religious practice, which raises questions about the quality and meaning of such conversions. The second aspect is the low overall level of Jewish religious affiliation and practice of mixed-marrieds, although these levels are slightly higher among those who are denominationally identified. Mixed marriage clearly militates against Jewish religious affiliation and practice.

### *Organizational Membership and Ties to Israel*

The broad pattern of organizational membership for the three marriage types generally parallels that for synagogue membership. Indeed, the same rank order is evident—in-marrieds, conversionary marrieds, and mixed-marrieds. At the same time, there are some significant variations.

The data for marriage types as a whole show that in-marrieds and mixed-marrieds respond uniformly to both organizational and synagogue membership but with one fundamental difference: in-marrieds are uniformly quite high in their membership levels, while mixed-marrieds are uniformly low. Thus, 57 percent of in-marrieds belong to Jewish organizations and 60 percent to synagogues, whereas 16 percent of mixed-marrieds belong to Jewish organizations and 15 percent to synagogues. In contrast, however, among conversionary marrieds the level of Jewish organizational membership is significantly lower than that for synagogue membership—45 percent belong to Jewish organizations and 56 percent to synagogues.

When the data for membership in synagogues and other Jewish organizations are combined, it is found that 40 percent of in-marrieds belong to both and 24 percent to neither, 31 percent of conversionary marrieds belong to both and 30 percent to neither, and 5 percent of mixed-marrieds belong to both and 75 percent to neither.

From the data it would appear that conversion to Judaism in the sense of religious integration proceeds faster than communal integration. Apparently it takes longer to acquire and develop Jewish communal ties than it does to adopt new religious beliefs and practices. At the same time, the obstacles placed by mixed marriage in the path of Jewish self-identity seem to apply equally to both the religious and communal dimensions.

Ties to Israel were probed by means of a question asking whether any member of the household had ever made a trip to Israel. The data replicate the rank order seen previously: in-marrieds, conversionary marrieds,and mixed-marrieds. Overall, 47 percent of in-marrieds have visited Israel, compared to 39 percent of conversionary marrieds and 21 percent of mixed-marrieds.

When the denominational factor is taken into account, some noteworthy exceptions emerge. On the one hand, the expected rank order for both organizational membership and visits to Israel—Orthodox, Conservative, Reform, and Just Jewish—maintained. However, with regard to visiting Israel, differences between the Just Jewish and the other denominations are rather small; indeed, only 2 percent separates Reform Jews and the Just Jewish in this regard. For Orthodox, Conservative, and Reform Jews, the level of synagogue membership is higher than the level of organizational membership, which in turn is higher than the level of Israel visits. For the Just Jewish, however, the reverse is true: the level of Israel visits is highest (34%), followed by organizational membership (26%), with the level of synagogue membership (16%) lowest. These data further demonstrate the underlying secular orientation of the Just Jewish in all marriage types.

When marriage types within denominations are examined, there is a striking exception to the expected pattern: Conservative conversionary marrieds are almost as likely as Conservative in-marrieds to belong to Jewish organizations (56% vs. 59%) and more likely to visit Israel (55% vs. 47%). On the basis of this finding, the earlier suggestion that conversionary marrieds generally have a lower level of ethnic and communal identification compared to their religious identification must be revised, since it holds only for Reform, not for Conservatives. The explanation may lie in the interaction between denomination and conversion, perhaps in the differing standards and expectations of Conservative and Reform conversions, combined with a process of self-selection among those undertaking conversion.

Within each denomination, mixed-marrieds are consistently less likely than other marriage types to belong to Jewish organizations and to visit Israel. Moreover, their levels of participation are lower than their already low levels of religious affiliation and identification. Thus, 33 percent of Conservative, 17 percent of Reform, and 7 percent of Just Jewish mixed-marrieds belong to Jewish organizations; the comparable figures for visiting Israel are 16 percent, 20 percent, and 24 percent.

When controls are introduced for age, the results clarify further the differential processes at work among Conservative and Reform conversionary marrieds. While both Conservative and Reform inmarrieds and mixed-marrieds over the age of 45 are much more likely to have visited Israel than those under the age of 45, with Conservative and Reform conversionary marrieds the situation is reversed. Among Conservative conversionary marrieds under the age of 45, 61 percent have visited Israel, compared to 34 percent of those over the age of 45; among Reform conversionary marrieds, 27 percent of those under the age of 45 have visited Israel, compared to 18 percent of those over the age of 45.

It would appear that the increasing centrality given to Israel in contemporary Jewish life has in recent years found direct expression in visits to Israel as part of the conversion process, whether formally or informally. This seems particularly evident in the case of young Conservative conversionary marrieds. This process is augmented within the Conservative movement by membership in Jewish organizations: 63 percent of Conservative conversionary marrieds under the age of 45 belong to Jewish organizations, compared to 39 percent over the age of 45. In contrast, among Reform conversionary marrieds, membership in Jewish organizations is slightly lower for those under the age of 45 than for those over the age of 45.

### *Jewish Philanthropy*

Researchers have consistently found that contributing to Jewish causes is highly correlated with other measures of Jewish identification.[21] According to Jonathan Woocher, philanthropy constitutes one of the central tenets of American Jewry's civil religion of "sacred survival." And indeed, in the study described here, some 80 percent of respondents report that their households contribute to Jewish causes.

The pattern of giving to Jewish causes follows the rank order of the marriage types previously encountered for other measures of Jewish identification: inmarried (86%), conversionary married (81%), and mixed-married (57%). Similarly, the denominational rank order replicates the standard pattern: Orthodox

(87%), Conservative (86%), Reform (83%), and Just Jewish (65%). However, the differences between Orthodox, Conservative, and Reform Jews with regard to philanthropy are narrower than for any of the other measures. Moreover, the level of participation of the Just Jewish in Jewish philanthropy is higher than for all other items of religious and communal identification. When marriage type is combined with denomination, the same pattern of relationship between marriage type and Jewish philanthropy is maintained.

By way of comparison, 72 percent of households report that they give to non-Jewish or nonsectarian causes, which is slightly lower than the overall rate of Jewish giving. Differences between marriage type and denomination and between combinations of the two are much narrower for general philanthropic giving than for donations to Jewish causes. When giving to both types of causes is compared, within all denominations in-marrieds are more likely to give to Jewish than to non-Jewish causes, whereas the opposite is the case with mixed-marrieds.

### *Friendship Patterns*

Jewish religious identification and communal affiliation are reinforced by primary groups such as family and close friends. Thus, it is important to examine the relationship between marriage type and the ethnic character of friendship groups.

The patterns of friendship of the three marriage types were analyzed in two categories: a predominantly Jewish friendship pattern, in which two or all of one's three closest friends are Jewish, and a predominantly non-Jewish friendship pattern, in which only one or none of one's three closest friends are Jewish.

The figures indicate an extremely strong relationship between marriage type and friends, with each marriage type maintaining its own distinctive pattern of friendship. Exactly three-quarters of the in-marrieds have predominantly Jewish friends, whereas one-quarter have mainly non-Jewish friends. Among the conversionary marrieds, exactly half mix with predominantly Jewish friends, and the other half have mainly non-Jewish friends. The friendship pattern of the mixed-marrieds is more or less the reverse of that of the in-marrieds: about seven in ten have predominantly non-Jewish friends, and three in ten have predominantly Jewish friends.

A somewhat more complex picture of friendship patterns emerges when denomination is taken into account. Overall, the familiar denominational rank order is evident: the Orthodox have the highest proportion of predominantly Jewish friends, followed by Conservative Jews, Reform Jews, and the Just Jewish. It is worth noting that when marriage types are compared within and across denominations, the expected distance between Conservative and Reform in-marrieds is virtually erased. However, the major deviation from the expected rank order occurs among the conversionary marrieds: Conservative conversionary marrieds are less likely to have predominantly Jewish friends (41%) than are both Refom conversionary marrieds (54%) and Conservative mixed-marrieds (49%).

When controls for age are introduced, the expected denominational and marriage-type rank orders are reinstated for those aged 45 and older. In this age group, 84 percent of Conservative conversionary marrieds have predominantly Jewish friends, compared with 63 percent of Reform conversionary marrieds and 65 percent of Conservative mixed-marrieds. But among those under 45 years of age, the previously noted deviations from the expected denominational and marriage-type rank orders are even more marked. Only 34 percent of the younger Conservative conversionary marrieds have predominantly Jewish friends, compared with 54 percent of Reform conversionary marrieds and 43 percent of Conservative mixed-marrieds.

The low proportion of predominantly Jewish friends among younger Conservative conversionary marrieds is consistent with the general relationship between age and friendship patterns: for every combination of denomination and marriage type (except the Orthodox in-marrieds) those under the age of 45 are less likely to have predominantly Jewish friends than those over age 45. However, the difference between the two Conservative conversionary married age groups—50 percent—is twice that of the age groups for other denominational marriage types. Why this is so, since younger Conservative conversionary marrieds score relatively high on all other dimensions of Jewish identification, is not clear.

### *Jewish Education for the Children*

There is a relationship between marriage type and the provision of formal Jewish education to children during the key period, ages 10-13. Among the in-married, formal Jewish education for children in the pre–bar/bat mitzvah years is almost universal (95%), and its incidence is only slightly lower among the conversionary marrieds (84%). However, the proportion receiving Jewish education drops to 41 percent among the children of mixed marriages.

This rank order among marriage types remains intact when denomination is taken into account, but some striking variations are apparent. First, among all marriage types the differences between Conservative and Reform Jews in the provision of Jewish education are minimal. Second, within both denominations the differences between the in-married and the conversionary marrieds, on the one hand, and the mixed-marrieds, on the other, are greatly reduced; among the Just Jewish the gap between them is increased to the maximum. Among Conservative Jews the difference between the mixed-marrieds and the other two marriage types in providing children with formal Jewish education is 19 percent; among Reform Jews it ranges from 12 to 14 percent, but among the Just Jewish it is 100 percent. While all the Just Jewish in-marrieds provide their children with formal Jewish education, no Just Jewish mixed-marrieds do so.

Denominational identification is closely related to the provision of Jewish education to the children of mixed marriages. Over 80 percent of mixed-marrieds who identify with a denomination give their children Jewish educations, but mixed-marrieds without a denominational identification do not. In all likelihood, this relationship is two-directional: attendance at Jewish schools that are denominationally affiliated usually entails formal synagogue or temple affiliation, thus providing children with a clear denominational identification. Conversely, denominational self-identification facilitates formal synagogue or temple membership, which in turn encourages the provision of Jewish education for the children.

Three main conclusions may be drawn from the foregoing analysis of the relationship between marriage type and various aspects of Jewish identification. First, there is a strong, direct relationship between marriage type and all measures of Jewish identification. Second, within the marriage types themselves, there are recurring variations that point to the existence of separate subtypes. Third, these patterns continue to show themselves even when account is taken of the strong and consistent influence of denomination, which variously mutes or reinforces the impact of marriage type but never overrides it completely. This is even more the case when the weaker and less consistent influences of family type and age are considered.

### *Index of Jewish Identification*

Taking the analysis a step further, an index of Jewish identification was constructed, making it possible to identify the different marriage subtypes as well as to determine the relative weight of each within the broader marriage type, within the denomination, and within the total sample.

The index of Jewish identification was constructed by combining all the various elements of Jewish identity into a single numerical score on an additive (Likert) scale. Ten items were included: synagogue membership, synagogue attendance, Sabbath candle lighting, participation in a Passover seder, fasting on Yom Kippur; lighting Hanukkah candles, membership in a Jewish organization, donating to a Jewish charity, visiting Israel, and having predominantly Jewish close friends. In each case one point was assigned for a positive response, except for synagogue attendance, where one point was given for attendance on the High Holy Days and a few times a year and two points for attending monthly or weekly. To avoid problems of standardization, only respondents who answered all of the questions were scored, thus excluding those in communities in which not all of the questions were asked and those who, for whatever reason, did not answer particular questions. As a result, the total number of respondents was reduced by about one-third. The range of possible scores is 0–11, and following the shape of the frequency distribution, it is divided into three categories: low Jewish identification, 0–4 points; medium Jewish identification: 5–8 points; and high Jewish identification, 9–11 points.

It should be noted that the index does not include items indicating higher levels of Jewish identification, such as strict Sabbath and festival observance, keeping kosher, and daily synagogue attendance. Although the original Jewish population surveys contain such data, these and similar items that reflect traditional standards of Jewish religious identification were excluded to reduce the range of the index, thereby lowering the threshholds for the medium and high levels. The net effect, therefore, is to include within these two categories many individuals who would not otherwise have been included.

Measured by the index of Jewish identification, 25 percent of all respondents score high; 45 percent, medium; and 30 percent, low. When divided according to marriage type, the data show the same relationship between marriage type and Jewish identification for the overall index as for the individual items—there is little difference between in-marrieds and conversionary marrieds on the index, but the gap between them and mixed-marrieds is quite wide.

These data also serve as the basis for identifying and locating the various marriage subtypes in the typology of conversionary and mixed marriages and assessing their relative weights. Thus, the vast majority of conversionary marrieds (83%) are to be found at the middle and upper levels of Jewish identification. One-third of them (33%) are "high-Jewish-identification conversionary marrieds," indicating the considerable value and identity change, if not total transformation, that has resulted from conversion. Half of the total (50%) are "medium-Jewish-identification conversionary marrieds." The smallest group, about one-sixth (17%), are "low-Jewish-identification conversionary marrieds," for whom conversion may be described as nominal or pro forma because it has resulted in little or no change in identification or behavior.

The pattern for mixed-marrieds is strikingly different. Indeed, judging by these figures, mixed marriage represents an almost insuperable bar to the achievement of a high level of Jewish identification. Thus, only 1 percent are high-Jewish-identification mixed-marrieds, who have created a family environment in which a strong Jewish identity is being maintained and transmitted. The largest single group by far, just under seven in ten (69%), are at the opposite end of the scale, low-Jewish-identification mixed-marrieds. In these households, Jewish identification and behavior are peripheral. Finally, three in ten mixed marriages (30%) are medium-Jewish-identification mixed-marrieds, mainly households that emphasize ritual home practices rather than communal or ethnic ties.

Taking denomination into account sharpens the picture even further. Looking first at differences within denomination, Conservative conversionary marrieds score somewhat higher than Conservative in-marrieds, while the pattern within Reform is dichotomous: Reform conversionary marrieds are represented more at the high and low levels of Jewish identification and less at the medium level than are Reform in-marrieds. Mixed-marrieds among all the denominations score much lower than do the other marriage types.

Turning to differences across denominations, just under half (48%) of Conservative conversionary marrieds, but only a little more than a quarter of Reform conversionary marrieds (27 percent), exhibit high levels of Jewish identification. Conversely, very few Conservative conversionary marrieds (3%) show low levels of

Jewish identification, compared with nearly a quarter (23%) among Reform conversionary marrieds. The largest groups in both denominations are those with medium Jewish identification; they represent about half of all conversionary marrieds.

The differences between Conservative mixed-marrieds and Reform mixed-marrieds, in contrast, are narrower and are concentrated at the lower and middle levels of the Jewish identification index. Very few Conservative mixed-marrieds or Reform mixed-marrieds exhibit high Jewish identification, but 53 percent of Conservative mixed-marrieds are at the medium level, compared with 41 percent of Reform mixed-marrieds. At the bottom of the scale the situation is reversed: 57 percent of Reform mixed-marrieds show low Jewish identification, compared with 42 percent of Conservative mixed-marrieds. However, the largest differences are between Conservative and Reform mixed-marrieds, on the one hand, and the Just Jewish mixed-marrieds on the other. There are no Just Jewish mixed-marrieds with high Jewish identification, and only 13 percent are at the medium level; the vast majority (87%) are at the low level.

### *Identification with Non-Jewish Cultural and Religious Symbols*

The foregoing discussion analyzed the extent and strength of key aspects of Jewish identification in different marriage types. Our theory of Jewish identity posited that being *not* Christian was a major defining element of Jewish identity. The creation of an unambiguous Jewish identity entails, at the very least, the absence from the home of Christian symbols and practices, even if the level of Jewish identification is low. Empirically, we can then hypothesize that Jewish identification and the incorporation of Christian practices and symbols in the home will vary inversely. Thus, in homes with medium and high levels of Jewish identification we would not expect to find Christian symbols and practices; such symbols would be present only when Jewish identification had disappeared completely or was at a low level.

This hypothesis is explored by means of a question about having a Christmas tree at home. While this single question serves clearly to identify those who have introduced a central Christian symbol into the home, it does not indicate whether it is an isolated practice or the tip of the iceberg—part of a more extensive incorporation of Christian symbols and values into the home. However, the surveys contain no further questions that might resolve this issue.

It is clear that in-marrieds shun the practice: 98 percent do not have a Christmas tree. Such an unequivocal response strongly supports our theory that, among in-marrieds at least, there exists an unambiguous Jewish identity, in which being *not* Christian is a defining element. Among conversionary marrieds, 78 percent do not have a Christmas tree, and 22 percent do. In contrast, among mixed-marrieds, 62 percent have a Christmas tree, and 38 percent do not. Quite remarkably, more mixed-marrieds have Christmas trees than perform any single Jewish ritual. (The most widely practiced rituals are attending a Passover seder and the lighting of Hanukkah candles, which are engaged in by 52% of the mixed-marrieds.)

The expected denominational rank order remains firm in this area. Overall, 3 percent of Orthodox Jews have Christmas trees, as do 4 percent of Conservative Jews, 18 percent of Reform Jews, and 33 percent of the Just Jewish. The same rank order is maintained when marriage types are compared across denomination. Thus, 8 percent of Conservative conversionary marrieds, as against 33 percent of Reform conversionary marrieds, have Christmas trees; among mixed-marrieds the comparable figures are 41 percent and 63 percent, and 66 percent for the Just Jewish.

Introducing controls for age, family type, and the ethnic character of friendship groups does not alter the above patterns. Indeed, family type itself is seen to have a marked impact: within every denomination and marriage type (particularly among mixed-marrieds), those who have children are consistently more likely to have a Christmas tree than are those who have no children. Where marriage type, denomination, and family type are mutually reinforcing, the proportion having a Christmas tree reaches a peak. Thus, 81 percent of Just Jewish mixed-marrieds with a child at home have a Christmas tree. When controls for age are introduced, the impact of marriage type, denomination, and family is clearly apparent, both among those under 45 and those over 45. In contrast, the impact of close friends is less clear-cut. While Conservative conversionary marrieds and Conservative mixed-marrieds with predominantly non-Jewish friends are more likely to have a Christmas tree than those with predominantly Jewish friends, this is not the case among Reform conversionary marrieds and Reform mixed-marrieds.

### *Dual-Identity Households*

As we have seen, virtually all in-married households manifest a single, unambiguous Jewish identity by virtue of the fact that Christian symbols are barred, irrespective of the level of Jewish identification. Thus, in-married Jews, including those with a low level of Jewish identification and those without denominational identification, overwhelmingly reject the practice of having a Christmas tree in the house.

Among intermarrieds, however, the situation is more complex. Conversionary and mixed marriages constitute arenas within which various theoretically possible identity resolutions or outcomes that come to characterize the household work themselves out. Unambiguous Jewish single-identity households are one possible identity outcome, as are Christian single-identity households, secular-identity (religiously and ethnically neutral) households, and dual-identity households. A *dual-identity* household is one in which both Jewish and Christian symbols and identification are maintained side by side, even when Jewish identification is at a medium level or higher. Indeed, under certain circumstances, Christian symbols and practices are more likely to be found in such households when Jewish practices are present than when they are absent.

The existence of single-identity and dual-identity households among conversionary and mixed marriages makes it necessary to expand the typology presented above. Each of the previously specified subtypes can now be divided into those that have a Christmas tree and those that do not.

Among conversionary marrieds, dual low-Jewish-identification conversionary-marriage households represent a partial or incomplete conversionary process, one that has not resulted in an unambiguous Jewish identification, even at a low level, due to the simultaneous retention of a Christian identification. Dual medium-Jewish-identification conversionary-marriage households represent a conversionary process that involves a moderate, if not modal, acceptance of Jewish identification and values yet is bivalent to the extent that it also incorporates certain Christian elements in the home. In dual high-Jewish-identification conversionary-marriage households the value and identity transformation is still not fully achieved, since Christian symbols show themselves. The existence of a dual identity where Jewish identification is high will in all likelihood create considerable dissonance within the family.

Among mixed-marrieds, the combination of low Jewish identification and a Christmas tree in the house—dual low-Jewish-identification mixed marriage households—points to people on the margins of two heritages, perhaps even marginal in the classic sociological sense of not quite belonging to either. As against this, dual medium-Jewish-identification mixed-marriage households exhibit a marked degree of religious syncretism. The dual high-Jewish-identification mixed-marriage household cell is empty, as a result of the absence of a dual-identity subtype that both maintains and transmits a high level of Jewish identification and simultaneously incorporates Christian symbols.

The data indicate 62 percent of all mixed-marrieds to be in dual-identity households, compared with 20 percent of conversionary marrieds. Most of the conversionary marrieds in the dual-identity category exhibit medium and high levels of Jewish identification, while most of the mixed-marrieds are at the low level. Taken together, among all conversionary and mixed marriages, dual-identity households outnumber single-identity households 54 percent to 46 percent.

When denomination is examined, it becomes clear that the formation of dual-identity households is closely related to the standard denominational rank order. Thus, among conversionary marrieds, 7 percent of Conservative Jews and 30 percent of Reform Jews are in dual identity households; among mixed-marrieds, 33 percent of Conservative Jews, 65 percent of Reform Jews, and 69 percent of the Just Jewish are in that category. Overall, 20 percent of all Conservative conversionary and mixed-marrieds are in dual-identity households, compared with 56 percent in the Reform denomination. The small proportion of dual high-Jewish-identification conversionary-marriage households are all found among Reform Jews; there are none in the Conservative denomination.

Higher levels of Jewish identification are generally associated with single-identity households. Over two-thirds of all conversionary marrieds with medium or high Jewish identification, and 90 percent of the Conservative Jews among them, are not in dual-identity households. At the opposite end of the scale, 35 percent of the Reform and 63 percent of the Just Jewish low-Jewish-identification mixed-marrieds are in dual-identity households.

At the same time, a not insubstantial number of households at reasonably high levels of Jewish practice maintain Christian practices simultaneously. Thus, in the medium- and high-Jewish-identification categories, 14 percent of Conservative mixed-marrieds, 23 percent of Reform conversionary marrieds, and 29 percent of Reform mixed-marrieds are in dual-identity households. In the case of the latter, the dual-identity outcome is by far the most popular, outnumbering the single-identity households by a ratio of more than two to one.

Introducing controls for age provides a clear indication of the direction of these trends among the mixed-marrieds. Three features stand out when those under age 45 are compared with those over age 45. First, Reform identification is far more prevalent within younger mixed-married households than older ones. Thus, while 40 percent of mixed-marrieds over age 45 call themselves Reform, 60 percent of those under age 45 do so. This increase has come at the expense of the nondenominationally identified Just Jewish mixed-marrieds, whose proportion is 49 percent in the older age group and 31 percent in the younger one.

Second, the proportion of Reform mixed-marrieds in dual-identity households has increased dramatically. While just over half (54%) of those over 45 are in dual-identity households, nearly three-quarters (73%) of those under 45 are. (Among the Just Jewish mixed-marrieds, the equivalent proportions decline from 76% to 68%.)

Third, much higher proportions of younger than of older Reform Jews with medium and high Jewish identification are in dual-identity households. Among Reform mixed-marrieds, 34 percent of those with medium and high Jewish identification under age 45 are in dual-identity households, compared with 19 percent of those over age 45. The equivalent figures for medium- and high-Jewish-identification Reform conversionary marrieds are 29 percent and 9 percent, respectively, indicating an even greater movement in the direction of dual-identity households.

The total extent of this change is clearly shown in a comparison of the distribution of marriage types in the two age categories. Nearly one-quarter of all households (23%) in the under-45 age group are dual-identity intermarried households, and about one-sixth (16%) are single-identity intermarried households, as against 8 percent and 7 percent, respectively, in the over-45 age group. Conversely, in-marriages, which constitute the overwhelming majority of households in the older group (85%), represent only six in ten (61%) in the younger group.

## Conclusion

The data reported above demonstrate and quantify the dramatic changes in the marriage choices of American Jews in the past four decades. With every passing generation and the coming of age of every younger cohort, more Jews have been marrying non-Jews, and mixed marriages represent an increasingly larger proportion of married couples. While males are more likely than females to marry non-Jews, the greatly heightened propensity of Jewish women to do so has narrowed the difference between them. Rates of intermarriage are consistently higher among those with lesser socioeconomic achievement, as measured by education, occupation, and income, than among those with greater achievement.

The finding that intensive Jewish education alone has not acted as a bar to intermarriage suggests that the increase in the propensity of Jews to marry non-Jews and to establish mixed families is associated with the nature and quality of contemporary Jewish identity. It was argued that the core of Jewish personal and group identity is distinguished less by "shared beliefs" and more by "shared feelings." This has led to the development of a Jewish personal identity that is both secure and unambiguous and at the same time is segmented, individualistic, pluralistic, and varied in intensity and salience.

A Jewish identity of this nature can facilitate mixed marriage by permitting Jews to marry non-Jews in the hope or assumption that they will be able to maintain their personal Jewish identity. That is to say, they will not be called upon to surrender part or all of the religious core of their personality or to deny their ethnic heritage (neither will their non-Jewish spouses), and they will be able to transmit that Jewish identity to their offspring. How these hopes and assumptions actually turn out—how Jewish identification fares in conversionary and mixed marriages—constitutes the central focus of this study. In what follows, the key findings relating to it are briefly summarized and linked to our theoretical framework, and their implications for future trends are discussed.

### *Conversionary Marriages*

Overall, Jewish identification fares well in conversionary marriages, or at least as well as in in-marriages, if the identical proportions of both marriage types at each level of Jewish identification are the criterion. Indeed, the Jewish identification of conversionary marrieds fares even better when they are denominationally connected: the overall level of Jewish identification among Conservative and Reform conversionary marrieds turns out to be higher than that of their respective in-marrieds.

However, conversionary marriages do not fare so consistently well in developing an unambiguous Jewish identity. Here denominational differences are decisive. While very few Conservative conversionary marriages result in dual-identity households, nearly a third of Reform conversionary marriages do so.

In sum, these findings indicate that conversion usually leads to the achievement of medium and high levels of Jewish identification, and more often than not brings about a qualitative identity transformation that results in the acquisition of an unambiguous Jewish identity by the convert and the establishment of a single-identity household. At the same time, the existence of significant proportions of conversionary marrieds who remain at low levels of Jewish identification and those who maintain dual-identity households suggests that conversion "does not always work." Clearly, there are different types and levels of conversionary marriage, and in differentiating among them, greater attention must be paid to the content and character of the conversion process and its denominational auspices. Similarly, the effect of the actual timing of conversion—whether it takes place before or after marriage, about which we had no data—is an issue meriting further analysis.

*Mixed Marriages*

Despite the hopes and assumptions, Jewish identification does not fare well in mixed marriages. The overall level of Jewish identification among the overwhelming majority of mixed-marrieds is low and in only one case (Conservative mixed-marrieds) are less than a majority in the low-Jewish-identification category. In all, the data indicate that mixed marriage and the level of Jewish identification are strongly negatively related. So few mixed-marrieds manifest a high level of Jewish identification, and denominational connection makes so little impact in this regard, that mixed marriage must be regarded as a virtual bar to the achievement of a high level of Jewish identification.

Predominantly, Jewish identification in mixed marriages is accompanied by the presence of symbols of Christian identification, resulting in dual-identity households at all levels of Jewish identification. Contrary to what might have been expected, among Reform mixed-marrieds there was clear evidence of a positive relationship between the level of Jewish identification and the incorporation of Christian symbols. That is to say, as the level of Jewish identification rises to medium, so too does the proportion of dual-identity households. This tendency has increased over time and reaches its peak in the younger age groups.

Overall, the chances of a mixed marriage resulting in a single-identity household at any level of Jewish identification are extremely slim, and the chances of it resulting in a single-identity household at a high level of Jewish identification are infinitesimal. Under these circumstances, the likelihood of creating an unambiguous Jewish identity, should such indeed be the intention or the desire, is virtually nil.

Dual-identity households are segmented and pluralist, responding to the individual needs of both partners in an intermarriage and catering to their different if not competing religious and ethnic heritages. The longer-term viability of such marriages and the actual identity resolutions arrived at by the children in these households, the bearers of both traditions, are at present unknown. If the theory of personal identity and of the unambiguous character of Jewish identity elaborated above is correct, then the least likely resolution of all is the development of a new synthesis of Judaism and Christianity, a modern version of the ancient Judeo-

Christians, or Christian-Jews. It is more likely that, over time, choices will have to be made between being either Jewish or Christian or neither. The low level of Jewish identification in these households to begin with, the pull of the majority, and the strength and attraction of common secular and general values do not augur well for the choice of an unambiguous Jewish identity. Rather than meeting the hope of being able to transmit Jewish identity, mixed marriages may prove to be terminal for Jewish identity.

However these choices turn out in the future, one thing is certain. The American Jewish community as we know it, formerly based on a heavy predominance of in-marriage that transmitted an unambiguous Jewish identity—even if the latter was not always strong and was sometimes the source of ambivalence—is rapidly being transformed. The increased rate of mixed marriage has already produced an age cohort under 45 whose marriage profile is very different from that of the cohort over 45. As we have noted, only six in ten of all households under 45 are in-marriages, and about a quarter are dual-identity households.

If the rate of mixed marriage continues to increase and present trends continue, the already low overall level of Jewish identification is likely to fall further, and dual-identity households may eventually rival if not outnumber single-identity households. Unambiguous Jewish identity may become the mark of a minority. Whether such a Jewish community can command the will and resources to support the network of Jewish institutions, causes, and activities within the community, in American society and politics, and abroad, is an open question. But the answer to it will determine the future of American Jewry.

It can be argued that current trends and patterns are neither inexorable nor irreversible and may be influenced by changes in individual attitudes and communal policies. Both individual Jews and communal leaders may take a passive or more active response to the issues. The critical differences between conversionary and mixed-married households are clearly revealed by the data and suggest that a more activist approach to conversion, including conversion after marriage, could have a considerable impact on future developments. By the same token, the ambiguous character of mixed-married households provides opportunities for activist policies aimed at encouraging a degree of identity transformation that might lead to conversion rather than result from it.

Moreover, the quality of Jewish life of the core of the Jewish community—the in-married couples—may be enhanced or diluted as time goes on. Such changes will directly affect the intermarried Jewish population as well. Thus, the strength and viability of the American Jewish community will be affected at least as much by the strength and growth of the most deeply committed Jewish groups as by its success in drawing less committed groups closer to Judaism.

The size of the Jewish population, the vitality of Jewish life, and the future of the American Jewish community all depend on a clear understanding of these phenomena and on appropriate actions taken by individual Jews, scholars, and communal leaders.

## Notes

1. This article provides a more extensive and intensive analysis and theoretical treatment of data originally discussed in Sylvia Barack Fishman, Mordechai Rimor, Gary A. Tobin, and Peter Medding, *Intermarriage and American Jews Today: New Findings and Policy Implications—Summary Report* (Waltham, Mass.: Brandeis University, Maurice and Marilyn Cohen Center for Modern Jewish Studies, 1990).

   In addition, Cohen Center researchers have explored aspects of intermarriage in Research Notes (Maurice and Marilyn Cohen Center for Modern Jewish Studies): Larry Sternberg, *Intermarriage: A First Look* (1988); Mordechai Rimor, *Intermarriage and Conversion: The Case from the Boston Data* (1988); Mordechai Rimor, *Intermarriage and Jewish Identity* (1989); Mordechai Rimor, *Feelings and Reactions to Intermarriage* (1989).
2. Interpersonal relationships in intermarried households are explored in Paul and Rachel Cowan, *Mixed Blessings: Marriage between Jews and Christians* (New York, 1987) and in Susan Weidman Schneider, *Intermarriage: The Challenge of Living with Differences between Christians and Jews* (New York, 1989).
3. Egon Mayer, "Processes and Outcomes in Marriages between Jews and Non-Jews," *American Behavioral Scientist* 23, no. 4 (Mar./Apr. 1980), pp. 487-518.
4. Steven M. Cohen, "Reason for Optimism," in Steven M. Cohen and Charles S. Liebman, *The Quality of Jewish Life: Two Views* (New York: American Jewish Committee, 1987), pp. 13–17, 2–27.
5. Sergio DellaPergola and Uziel O. Schmelz, "Demographic Transformations of American Jewry: Marriage and Mixed Marriage in the 1980s," and "American Jewish Marriages: Transformation and Erosion: A Rejoinder to Calvin Goldscheider," in *Studies in Contemporary Jewry*, vol. 5, ed. Peter Y. Medding (New York and Oxford: Oxford University Press, 1989), pp. 169–200, 209–14; at 193.
6. Calvin Goldscheider, "American Jewish Marriages: Erosion or Transformation?" in *Studies in Contemporary Jewry*, 5, ed. Peter Y. Medding, pp. 201–8, at 204.
7. Calvin Goldscheider, *Jewish Continuity and Change: Emerging Patterns in America* (Bloomington: Indiana University Press, 1986), p. 28.
8. Egon Mayer and Carl Sheingold, *Intermarriage and the Jewish Future: A National Study in Summary* (New York: American Jewish Committee, 1979); Egon Mayer, *Love and Tradition* (New York, 1985); Goldscheider, *Jewish Continuity and Change*; Steven M. Cohen, *American Assimilation or Jewish Revival?* (Bloomington: Indiana University Press, 1988).
9. Thus, Goldscheider's sample of the Boston community contained 934 cases, Cohen's study of New York was based on 1,566 cases, and Mayer and Sheingold's sample totaled 446 cases. As will be explained below, the present study includes 6,673 households.
10. The eight studies are as follows: *Jewish Population Study of Greater Baltimore*, prepared for Associated Jewish Charities and Welfare Fund (data collected during 1985), principal investigator: Gary A. Tobin. *Jewish Population Study of Greater Boston*, prepared for the Combined Jewish Philanthropies (data gathered during 1985), principal investigator: Sherry Israel. *Jewish Population Study of MetroWest, New Jersey*,

prepared for the United Jewish Federation of MetroWest (data gathered during 1985 and 1986), principal investigator: Gary A. Tobin. *Jewish Population Study of Greater Worcester*, prepared for the Worcester Jewish Federation (data gathered during 1986), principal investigator: Gary A. Tobin. *Jewish Population Study of Greater Cleveland*, prepared for the Jewish Community Federation (data gathered during 1987), principal investigator: Ann Schorr. *Jewish Population Study of Rhode Island*, prepared for the Jewish Federation of Rhode Island (data gathered during 1987), principal investigators: Calvin Goldscheider and Sidney Goldstein. *Jewish Population Study of the Bay Area*, prepared for the Jewish Federations of San Francisco, Oakland, and San Jose (data gathered during 1986), principal investigator: Gary A. Tobin. *Jewish Population Study of Greater Dallas*, prepared for the Jewish Federation of Greater Dallas (data gathered during 1988), principal investigator: Gary A. Tobin.

11. Herbert C. Kelman, "The Place of Jewish Identity in the Development of Personal Identity." Working paper prepared for the American Jewish Committee's Colloquium on Jewish Education and Jewish Identity, Nov. 1974, mimeo, pp. 1–3.
12. The next two sections further develop the theory first propounded in Peter Y. Medding, "Segmented Ethnicity and the New Jewish Politics," in *Studies in Contemporary Jewry*, 3 ed. Ezra Mendelsohn (New York and Oxford: Oxford University Press, 1987), pp. 2–45.
13. Richard M. Merelman, *Making Something of Ourselves: On Culture and Politics in the United States* (Berkeley: University of California Press, 1984), p. 30.
14. As Ben Halpern puts it, "America is really a Christian country." See the illuminating discussion in his *Jews and Blacks: The Classic American Minorities* (New York, 1971). The citation is on p. 60.
15. Robert N. Bellah, "Competing Visions of the Role of Religion in American Society," in *Uncivil Religion: Interreligious Hostility in America*, ed. Robert N. Bellah and Frederick E. Greenspahn (New York, 1987), p. 228.
16. Psychologist Joel Crohn, who has worked in marital counseling and ethnotherapy groups with ethnic and religious intermarriages, reports that "Christian symbols were often perceived by the Jewish partners as unwelcome and even dangerous reminders of the dominance of the Christian world." Some "perceived irreconcilable differences between the Jewish and Christian worlds." One intermarried Jewish subject in such a group, when asked by another group member, "Do you feel like learning about Christianity is somehow betraying who you are—like it's entering the bowels of the demon?" replied, "Yeah. I feel like it's a big betrayal." See Joel Crohn, *Ethnic Identity and Marital Conflict: Jews, Italians and WASPs* (New York: Institute for American Pluralism, American Jewish Committee, 1986), pp. 33, 36.
17. See Perry London and Barry Chazan, *Psychology and Jewish Identity Education* (New York: American Jewish Committee, 1990), p. 9, who cite the theory of Henry Tajfel and John Turner that "feeling positive toward one's group is a major factor in enhancing one's self-image and self-esteem," and that "strong group identity promotes a positive sense of self."
18. Nathan Glazer, *New Perspectives in American Jewish Sociology* (New York: American Jewish Committee, 1987), p. 13.
19. See Jack Wertheimer, "Recent Trends in American Judaism," *AJYB* 89 (1989), pp. 63–162, for a broad-ranging analysis of denominationalism in American Jewish life. Denominational self-identification in twenty-seven recent community studies ranged

between 70 and 95 percent. In the same communities, between 26 and 84 percent were currently synagogue members.

20. On two cases (higher figures for seder attendance and Hanukkah candle lighting by Conservative in-marrieds than Orthodox in-marrieds and higher synagogue membership among Reform conversionary marrieds than among Conservative conversionary marrieds), the percentage differences are marginal. In the third case (higher levels of ritual performance by Just Jewish conversionary marrieds than by Reform conversionary marrieds), the actual numbers of Just Jewish conversionary marrieds are so small that these results must be treated with caution.
21. See, for example, Mordechai Rimor and Gary A. Tobin, "Jewish Giving Patterns to Jewish and Non-Jewish Philanthropy," in *Faith and Philanthropy in America*, ed. Robert Wuthnow and Virginia A. Hodgkinson (San Francisco, 1990), pp. 13–64.

**13** Steven M. Cohen

# The Impact of Varieties of Jewish Education upon Jewish Identity

## An Intergenerational Perspective

This study assesses the impact of several forms of Jewish education upon composite measures of Jewish identity for teenagers and for their parents. The analysis controls for each generation's parents' Jewishness as well as for other factors. All forms of Jewish education, except Sunday school, are associated with higher levels of Jewish identity in both generations. The putative effects of day school, including non-Orthodox day schools, are especially pronounced. Among adults, all forms of Jewish education, except Sunday school, are associated with lower rates of intermarriage. The likely impact of youth groups and Israel travel on intermarriage rates is rather small.

Like other American religious and ethnic groups, American Jews have developed a multifaceted educational system embracing both schools and programs of nonformal education. The more widely used instruments of children's Jewish education include Sunday schools, afternoon schools, day schools, summer camps, youth groups, and Israel travel programs. In their entirety, these institutions employ tens of thousands of educators and support staff, at an annual cost sometimes estimated at two billion dollars (Commission on Jewish Education in North America 1990).

If for no other reason, the sheer size of this endeavor prompts one to ask: To what extent does this voluntary, sectarian educational system succeed in what many regard as its chief purpose, that of transmitting, shaping, and strengthening Jewish identity among its students as they mature? In simple terms, does Jewish education make a difference, and, if so, how, and in what ways, and for whom?

Obviously, this question has direct implications for the future of American Jewry—in particular, its prospects of remaining a distinctive and cohesive ethnic and religious group. Recent reports of high and mounting rates of Jewish-Gentile marriage (Kosmin, Goldstein, Waksberg, Lerer, Keysar, and Scheckner 1991) have led many to speculate that large numbers of American Jews—or, more precisely, their offspring—will fail to identify as such or will do so in only the most superficial fashion. In response, many Jewish parents and the organized Jewish community are pinning their hopes for "Jewish continuity" on the Jewish educational system.

Well before the most recent wave of attention to an increased intermarriage rate, American Jews had become less concerned about obtaining acceptance as Americans and more concerned about their families' Jewish continuity (Cohen and Fein 1985). As a result of the increasing concern with Jewish group continuity and diminished anxieties about self-segregation, Jews came to increasingly use more intensive forms of Jewish education such as day schools and Israel youth travel, both of which maintain significantly higher rates of participation than in the mid-1960s. In this context, the effectiveness of this education system bears directly on the question of the very ability of American Jewry to maintain its demographic size and its cultural distinctiveness.

On a larger plane, this question also speaks to our understanding of American ethnicity and American religious life. With regard to ethnicity, much of the recent social scientific literature casts doubt on whether middle-class white ethnic groups will persist as culturally distinctive and socially cohesive communities (see Alba 1985, 1990; Lieberson and Waters 1988). Gans (1979) has advanced the widely cited notion of "symbolic ethnicity" (and, most recently, "symbolic religiosity" [Gans 1994]), which sees American white ethnics as maintaining only a symbolic but not substantive link to their particular ethnic subcultures and subcommunities.

In contrast, in the 1960s and 1970s, several scholars had suggested that American ethnic groups manage to sustain and reinvent ethnic cultures in ways suitable to contemporary America (Glazer and Moynihan 1963, 1975; Greeley 1974; Novak 1971). The validity of this "cultural pluralist" perspective (or others close to it) ultimately rests on current directions now underway among white, economically comfortable ethnic groups, among which Jews are a critical case in point.

Unlike many white ethnic groups who have experienced what may be called ethnic erosion, American Jews have seemingly resisted assimilatory trends, at least until recently. Signs of ethnic dissolution among American Jews—as would be embodied in evidence of a failing Jewish educational system—would certainly strengthen the case of "melting pot" and "symbolic ethnicity" theorists; for if the Jews cannot persist as a socially cohesive and culturally distinctive group, how likely is it that Poles, Italians, and others will do so?

With respect to American religious life, the recent literature points to a quarter century of decline in the more liberal churches (Roof and McKinney 1987, Finke and Stark 1992). It can be argued that these sorts of churches resemble Reform and Conservative Judaism, the two most populous branches of American Judaism. If the trends of the larger society do, in fact, embrace American Judaism, then we would expect to witness declines in Jewish religious practice and affiliation as well as an increasingly ineffective religious education system.

To assess the impact of various forms of Jewish education on group identity (a term used in an intentionally loose fashion throughout this article), this study examines two contemporary groups of American Jews: younger to middle-aged adults and, where available, their teenage children. With respect to these individuals, it explores the extent to which instruments of Jewish education have generally produced the results widely sought after by various stakeholders in the Jewish educational system.

A noteworthy handful of quantitative, empirical studies of American Jewry over the last quarter century have explored the impact of Jewish education on Jewish identity (or portions thereof) in fairly similar ways (Bock 1976, 1988; Dashefsky and Shapiro 1974; Fishman 1987; Fishman and Goldstein 1993; Himmelfarb 1974, 1979; Lipset 1994; Mayer 1993; Rimor and Katz 1993). They developed quantitative measures of current Jewish identify among adults, related them to previous Jewish schooling, and controlled for relevant background factors, in particular, the Jewishness of the home (i.e., the respondents' parents). Taken in their totality, these studies agree on some key issues, disagree on others, leave some critical questions unanswered, and generally suffer from a particular and consequential methodological shortcoming.

Consistent with Greeley and Rossi's influential research on American Catholic schooling (1966), most of these studies agree that the Jewish involvement of the home or the parents exerts more influence than the school upon levels of Jewish involvement as an adult. Some social scientists and educators have argued that with respect to Jewish values and commitment, schools usually can do little except to reinforce that which has been fostered by Jewishly involved parents.

The second key point of consensus entails the intensity of Jewish schooling. All studies on the matter agree that more Jewish schooling, whether measured in terms of years or total number of hours in Jewish studies, is associated with higher levels of subsequent adult Jewish involvement.

One key area of disagreement concerns the effectiveness of part-time Jewish schools (those meeting in the weekday afternoons and on Sunday mornings). Several studies concluded that controlling for parental Jewish involvement, alumni of part-time Jewish schooling hardly differed, if at all, from those with no Jewish schooling on most measures of adult involvement (e.g., Bock 1976, Himmelfarb 1974, 1979).

In contrast, analysis of the 1981 Greater New York Jewish Population Study, a data set similar in structure and content to those used in previous studies of Jewish schooling, demonstrated that failure to control for sex obscures the impact of part-time Jewish schooling (Cohen 1988). To elaborate, in the earlier decades of the twentieth century, many Jewish daughters from stronger Jewish home and community environments received no formal Jewish schooling. (The gap between the

Jewish educational experiences of girls and boys has closed considerably since then.) As a result, the no-school group for Jewish adults who were children prior to 1950 contains a good number of Jewishly involved women. Their presence elevates the measures of Jewish involvement for this group, effectively obliterating the differences with the alumni of part-time schools. Separating the men from the women allowed for the emergence of a moderate impact of part-time schools when compared with no-education groups of the same sex. Of all the half dozen or so studies in the field, this is the only one that argues in favor of the presence of generally effective part-time schools. Obviously, the question of their effectiveness remains open.

Although several studies have examined the impact of Jewish schools, hardly any have touched upon the parallel effects of informal Jewish education. Few, if any, quantitative studies have sought to examine the long-term impact of summer camps, youth groups, and travel to Israel by young people on adult Jewish identity (for an exception, see Horowitz 1993; also see Goldstein and Fishman 1993). This gap in the research literature is all the more glaring in the case of the "Israel experience" (organized trips by adolescents to Israel, generally for four to eight weeks during the summer months). Israel youth travel has increased policy significance in just the last few years. American Jewish philanthropists and their agencies have placed increasing emphasis on this particular educational instrument as a way of diminishing future rates of intermarriage and assimilation among today's Jewish young people. No study has yet examined the assumption that trips to Israel eventually strengthen Jewish involvement generally or that they increase the chances that participants will marry Jews, more specifically.

Even were the previous studies conclusive, concurring and comprehensive, the extend of change in American Jewry and in Jewish education calls into question the relevance of prior research for understanding the recent or current impact of Jewish education. Among the notable changes in Jewish education are the growth in day school enrollment and consequent change in the character of day school students. Once day school referred almost exclusively to Orthodox-sponsored institutions serving youngsters from Orthodox homes. Today the number of youngsters who at some point receive some day school education outside of Orthodoxy now roughly equals the number who ever attend Orthodox yeshivas and day schools (see table 13.1 for the rates in the two generations in this study). Whereas travel to Israel prior to 1968 was a relatively rare occurrence for a Jewish adolescent, the last quarter century has seen thousands of such youngsters participate in well-established, highly structured, and highly supervised organized programs offering a wide range of activities and ideological frameworks. Since most of the adults in this study had attained age sixteen by 1968, it is not all that surprising to learn that 14 percent of them had visited Israel in their youth; reflecting the rise in adolescent Israel travel, an even greater proportion (19%) of their children ages sixteen and seventeen had been to Israel. (Horowitz [1993] also finds a clear rise in Israel travel among younger New York area Jews.)

TABLE 13.1
Percentage of Participation in Schools and Informal Programs for Adults and Teenagers

| *Most Intensive Form of Jewish Schooling* | *Adults* | *Teenagers* |
|---|---|---|
| Orthodox day school: 5+ years | 6 | 6 |
| Other day school: 5+ years | 1 | 6 |
| Part-time school: 3+ years | 40 | 41 |
| Sunday school: 3+ years | 25 | 21 |
| None or only tutoring | 28 | 25 |
| Youth group | 58 | 55 |
| Israel travel[a] | 14 | 19[b] |

a. Includes travel to Israel under private auspices as well as in organized groups.
b. Calculated only for teenagers 16–17 years old.

One of the most significant relevant developments in the last quarter century is the sharp rise in Jewish-Gentile marriage. The proportion of Jews marrying non-Jews who do not convert to Judaism has risen from over 20 percent in late 1960s to over 40 percent in most recent years (see Cohen [1994] and Kosmin et al. [1991] for alternative estimates of the recent mixed marriage rate in the National Jewish Population Study data), bearing implications for Jewish education on several levels. Conceivably, the environment of a high rate of intermarriage may limit the effectiveness of Jewish education. For those who intermarry, the presence of a non-Jewish spouse may make it all but impossible for the former participants in Jewish schools, camps, youth groups, and Israel trips to put their education into practice; and for the entire population, the awareness of a high intermarriage rate may subtly undercut and delegitimize the distinctive and sometimes particularistic teachings of Judaism and Jewish education.

Given the sharply lower rates of Jewish involvement on the part of mixed-married as contrasted with in-married Jews, any contemporary analysis of the impact of Jewish education must consider the two populations separately, as the impact of Jewish education may well be limited to the in-married. Moreover, and not least, is the question of whether Jewish education directly affects the chances of marrying within the group.

A methodological complication has justifiably limited the readiness of previous researchers to claim that they have demonstrated a discernible impact of childhood Jewish education upon adult Jewish identity. Several of the previous studies had at their disposable relatively little information regarding the childhood home of the respondents. The data sets analyzed certainly contained a large number of items on adults' current Jewish involvement, as well as adequate information on their childhood Jewish schooling. But many studies have been forced to rely on only a few questions pertaining to their parents' Jewish involvement.

One case in point is the 1990 National Jewish Population Study (NJPS), the widely cited random-sample survey of American Jews sponsored by the Council of Jewish Federations (Kosmin et al., 1991). In just two years, these data generated at least five studies of Jewish education (Fishman and Goldstein 1993, Goldstein and Fishman 1993, Lipset 1994, Mayer 1993, Rimor and Katz 1993). This highly authoritative source of data on contemporary American Jews contains only two critical pieces of information on respondents' parents: whether they were both Jewish (asked of only a third of the sample) and their Jewish denomination (Orthodox, Conservative, Reform, etc.).

In exploring the impact of different sorts of Jewish schooling on adult Jewish involvement, the recent NJPS-based studies did their best to factor out parents' involvement. To do so, they used the items on parents' in-marriage and denomination raised to statistically assume that the alumni of all types of Jewish schools, in effect, shared parents with equal levels of Jewish involvement. Given the limitations of the NJPS data, this assumption translates into the claim that the home environments of in-married Conservative parents who chose day schools, part-time schools, Sunday schools, or no schools for their children are functionally equivalent. In point of fact, Conservative in-married couples range across a wide spectrum of Jewish involvement, one that relates strongly to choice of Jewish school for one's children. Conservative parents who sent their children to Jewish day schools in the 1960s or earlier were among a very small minority whose youngsters went to schools of Orthodox sponsorship (the prevalent form of day school at the time). In this, they clearly differed from their counterparts who sent their children to part-time schools sponsored by their Conservative synagogues.

The extent of differences among in-married Conservative parents can be illustrated by some results from this study. Of current adults who went to day schools and were raised by in-married Conservative parents, 66 percent reported that their parents scored "high" on an index of parental Jewish involvement (details on index construction are provided below); in contrast, of the alumni of part-time schools, only 35 percent reported highly involved parents, as did just 16 percent of those who went to Sunday schools. Clearly, even though all were raised by in-married Conservative parents, the extent of their parents' Jewish involvement varied dramatically by intensivity of Jewish education.

Inaccuracies in measuring parental Jewish involvement in these studies tend to produce *over*-estimates of the impact of more intensive forms of Jewish education. To illustrate, since day schools tend to draw students from more Jewishly involved homes, failure to properly extract the impact of their greater home involvement leaves day schools artificially picking up the "credit" for producing Jewishly involved graduates that properly should be attributed to their homes.

To be sure, researchers have been well aware of these limitations and, by careful choice of words, have avoided making explicit causal inferences. Fishman and Goldstein (1993) provide an apt illustration when they conclude (italics added):

> The 1990 NJPS data show us the strong *correlation* of Jewish education and enhanced Jewish identification. . . . Extensive Jewish education is definitively *associated* with higher measures of adult Jewish identification. Even after adjusting for denomination of Judaism in which a person is raised, extensive Jewish education is *related* to a greater ritual observance [and other aspects of Jewish identification]. (12)

With more comprehensive measures of parental Jewish involvement, we can feel more confident about making the types of causal inferences that are more implicit that explicit in the previous studies. This study aims to build upon and extend the previous research, addressing questions that the prior studies could not and resolving discrepancies in their findings.

The main empirical questions addressed here are the following:

1. Most broadly and most fundamentally, does Jewish education during childhood affect Jewish identity, even after more fully controlling for the levels of parents' Jewish involvement and other confounding factors? To what extent do the results for adults and for teenagers confirm (or contradict) one another?
2. What are the effects of part-time Jewish schools on Jewish identity? Are they in fact negligible as previous studies have claimed?
3. Is the influence of Jewish day schools limited to the Orthodox variety that dominated in the past, or does it extend to today's increasingly popular non-Orthodox full-time schools as well?
4. Does informal Jewish education—particularly the Israel travel experience—strongly influence subsequent Jewish involvement, as some educators and volunteer leaders have asserted?
5. How does Jewish education interact with marital choice? Does it indeed influence chances for marrying within the group? Beyond any possible influence upon choice of marriage partner, does Jewish education influence Jewish identity more among the in-married than among mixed married Jews?

## Data

The data for this study were collected via mail-back questionnaires administered in 1993 to a national sample of Jewish parents ($N = 1{,}464$) of 4–17-year-old children and their teenage children, ages 13–17, where present ($N = 615$), by the Washington office of Market Facts, Inc. This company maintains a Consumer

Mail Panel which, at the time, consisted of over a quarter million respondents who have agreed to participate in consumer research surveys.

Adult members of the Jewish subsample had identified their religion as Jewish on a previous screener questionnaire administered periodically. Adults received an eight-page questionnaire, and teenagers, where available, completed a two-page instrument. In both instances (parents and teenagers), approximately 70 percent of those receiving questionnaires returned them. Of these, a few were excluded from the analysis for reasons of ineligibility; either they failed to identify as Jews, or in the case of the teenagers, a few were out of the specified age range.

Samples drawn from lists of individuals who have agreed to take part in frequent social surveys demand scrutiny. To what extent do we find evidence of systematic bias? To address this question, we compare the Consumer Mail Panel sample with a subsample drawn from the 1990 NJPS, which may be used as a benchmark. The households selected from the NIPS for comparison met two criteria. First, a 4–17 child was present. Second, either the respondents said their current religion was Jewish or identified their spouse as such, in line with the way Market Facts identified eligible respondents for this study.

Tables 13.2a and 13.2b present key characteristics for this sample (CMP refers to the Consumer Mail Panel) and for the comparable NJPS households. The NJPS findings are weighted in two ways: by weights supplied by the survey research company (ICR, Inc.) to take into account sample biases related to major sociodemographic characteristics; and to replicate the CMP sample design, households with teenagers present were assigned weights such that they constituted one half the sample (as they do, approximately, in the CMP sample). For gender-specific frequencies on age, education, and marital status (where information was available on respondent and spouse), no further weights were needed. However, the two samples differ in that all Jewish individual adults had an equal chance (theoretically) of entering the CMP sample, while the NIPS sample, when weighted, represents households, not individuals. Thus, to convert the NIPS subsample's results reported only by respondents (e.g., attendance at a Seder) to individual level statistics, the analysis multiplied the weights enumerated above by the number of Jewish household heads (one or two). In a manner of speaking, NJPS households with two adult Jews present voted twice; those with only one (primarily mixed-married and single-parent households) voted only once.

Notwithstanding some noticeable differences, the sociodemographic and Jewish identity characteristics of this sample generally resemble those for the NJPS subsample. Among the smaller differences are those relating to region of the country, men's education, men's marital status, income, lighting Hanukkah candles, Passover seder attendance, Yom Kippur fasting, lighting Sabbath candles, synagogue membership, belonging to a Jewish organization, having traveled to Israel, and religious denomination. Somewhat larger differences are found elsewhere: more CMP women have a graduate degree; fewer CMP members went to day school, and more attended once-a-week Sunday schools; more CMP women

TABLE 13.2A

Comparison of NJPS Subsample with Consumer Mail Panel Sample on Selected Variables: Percentage Distributor[a]

| *Region* | *NJPS* | *CMP* |
|---|---|---|
| Northeast | 47 | 47 |
| Midwest | 12 | 12 |
| South | 19 | 21 |
| West | 21 | 21 |

| | *Men* | | *Women* | |
|---|---|---|---|---|
| *Age* | *NJPS* | *CMP* | *NJPS* | *CMP* |
| 50+ | 9 | 13 | 5 | 7 |
| 40–49 | 50 | 61 | 43 | 54 |
| 30–39 | 37 | 25 | 48 | 37 |
| Under 30 | 3 | 1 | 5 | 2 |

| | *Men* | | *Women* | |
|---|---|---|---|---|
| *Marital status* | *NJPS* | *CMP* | *NJPS* | *CMP* |
| Married | 97 | 95 | 96 | 80 |
| Divorced/sep | 3 | 4 | 3 | 17 |
| Widowed | 0 | 1 | 1 | 3 |

| | *Men* | | *Women* | |
|---|---|---|---|---|
| *Education* | *NJPS* | *CMP* | *NJPS* | *CMP* |
| Graduate degree | 45 | 47 | 31 | 39 |
| B.A. | 32 | 27 | 21 | 26 |
| Less | 24 | 26 | 39 | 36 |

a. Respondents eligible for NJPS subsample (unweighted $N = 381$) consisted of those who answered "Jewish" for their current religion or that of their spouses and who reported the presence in the household of a child 4–17. All results here are weighted, using the "household weights" supplied by the data collection company. In addition, results for individuals which are not broken down by sex have been weighted by the number of Jewish adults in the household. To illustrate, table 13.2b reports that 88% of Jewish adults in this NJPS subsample were in homes that usually lit Hanukkah candles, a figure somewhat higher than the proportion of homes that did so.

TABLE 13.2B

Further Comparisons of NJPS Subsample with CMP Panel Sample on Selected Variables: Percentage Distributor[a]

| | NJPS | CMP |
|---|---|---|
| *Household Income* | | |
| $80,000+ | 27 | 30 |
| $60,000–79,999 | 22 | 22 |
| $40,000–59,999 | 27 | 28 |
| Under $40,000 | 25 | 19 |
| *Jewish schooling as a child* | | |
| Day school | 14 | 8 |
| Part-time school | 40 | 40 |
| Sunday school once a week | 20 | 25 |
| None or just tutoring | 25 | 28 |
| *Married to a Jew* | 70 | 64 |
| *Most friends Jewish* | 50 | 41 |
| *Always or usually:* | | |
| Lights Hanukkah candles | 88 | 93 |
| Participates in Passover Seder | 82 | 81 |
| Fasts Yom Kippur | 67 | 61 |
| Lights Sabbath candles | 31 | 25 |
| Has meat and dairy sets of dishes | 16 | 17 |
| *Synagogue member* | 60 | 60 |
| *Attends High Holiday services* | 73 | 75 |
| *Attends services monthly or more* | 37 | 31 |
| *Jewish organization member* | 34 | 30 |
| *Been to Israel* | 25 | 28 |
| *Denomination of respondent* | | |
| Orthodox | 9 | 6 |
| Conservative, Reconstructionist | 33 | 32 |
| Reform | 45 | 37 |
| Other | 14 | 25 |

a. See note to table 13.2a.

were divorcees, and fewer were married; more CMP members were mixed-married, and fewer reported mostly Jewish friends. The most significant difference between the two samples is that CMP members are older—more are in their forties and fewer are in their thirties. The age difference helps explain why more CMP women are divorced.

In sum, in terms of Jewish identity characteristics, this sample is about as involved as the NJPS subsample or, in a few instances (intermarriage most prominently), somewhat less involved. Some demographic differences are noticeable, especially with respect to age where the CMP sample is a few years older.

The extent to which these demographic variations affect the results is unknowable. In other areas of research, sampling variations and biases tend to have less impact on correlations and relationships between variables than on frequencies. Moreover, no compelling theory suggests why the sorts of differences noted here should affect the key concern of this paper, i.e., the impact of Jewish education. For example, the older and younger members of this sample report nearly identical patterns of results with respect to the impact of Jewish education on Jewish identity. In addition, where the results here overlap with those reported in the earlier studies, the findings here, in their substance, replicate rather than contradict them.

Clearly, from a sampling point of view, these data are less than ideal. If we take the NJPS as authoritative, the number of variations at least raises the possibility of some unknown bias. On the other hand, these data do offer the possibility for undertaking analyses that are impossible with the limited but certainly more representative NJPS data set. The results here, then, can be seen as valuable but should be treated with caution.

The adult respondents reported on their parents' Jewish involvement, their own childhood Jewish education, their current involvement as Jewish adults, and their children's Jewish education. The teenagers' questionnaire included a small number of questions on current Jewish involvement.

By linking the teenagers' responses with those of their parents, the analysis examines three generations of Jews: the parents of the adult respondents, the adults themselves, and the teenagers. To be clear, the analysis of adults reports on all the adults, including parents of younger children. The portion focusing on the teenagers includes only their own parents, constituting less than half the adult sample.

The large number of cases within the relevant age groups permits analyses of certain critical subgroups (e.g., graduates of non-Orthodox day schools). In addition, the data set contains excellent and comprehensive information on parental variables. In the case of the adults, we have a very large battery of questions on their mothers and fathers. In the case of the teenagers, we have their own parents answering direct questions on their practices, affiliations, and attitudes.

The design allows us to examine whether findings concerning the impact of education can be generalized beyond one period or generation. Given all the changes over the last thirty years, researchers have exercised extreme caution about generalizing from the patterns among today's adults (whose childhood Jewish education took place at least 20 years ago) to the likely impact of current Jewish education 20 years from now. From a policy point of view, the ideal study would reveal the impact of today's Jewish education upon adult Jewish identity in the distant future. Obviously, that study lies beyond the realm of the feasible. Short of that ideal, we can examine the two most relevant generations simultaneously: today's younger adults and their teenage children. That is, we can examine the long-range impact of Jewish education experienced in the distant past, and the short-range impact of Jewish education experienced quite recently. Should the results for the two generations coincide (as we shall see they do), we can feel more confident in drawing inferences about the likely impact of today's Jewish education in the future.

## Measures and Methodology

The analysis developed summary measures of Jewish involvement for three generations of individuals: the teenagers, the adults (the teenagers' parents plus parents of younger children), and the adults' parents (i.e., the grandparents of the teenagers and younger children of their generation). The teenagers and adults reported on themselves. The information on the adults' parents (the so-called grandparents) derived from reports of the adult respondents. Presumably, self-reports by the adults and teenagers on their own current behavior and attitudes are more reliable than the adults' reports on their parents' behavior and attitudes some twenty to forty years ago.

Students of modern Jewish identity have not come to a clear-cut consensus on the meaning of Jewish identity. However, this lack of conceptual clarity has not prevented quantitatively oriented social scientists from developing what has become a traditional set of measures of Jewish identity (see, for example, Cohen 1983, 1988; Goldscheider 1986; Goldstein and Goldscheider 1968). The measures used here fit within the general parameters of that research tradition.

The items included in the composite indices of Jewish involvement for the adults and their parents overlap to some extent. The parents' index contains items pertaining to attending a Passover Seder, lighting Hanukkah candles, using separate dishes for meat and dairy, lighting Sabbath candles, not having a Christmas tree, and belonging to a Jewish organization. In addition, the index incorporated parents' denomination, awarding more "points" for more denominational traditionalism (Orthodoxy = 3; Conservatism = 2; Reform = 1; other = 0).The composite index of adult respondents' Jewish involvement included questions on: attending a Passover Seder, lighting Hanukkah candles, using separate dishes for meat and dairy, lighting Sabbath candles, fasting on Yom Kippur, attending High Holiday services, attending service monthly, not having a Christmas tree, not celebrating Christmas in any way, attachment to Israel, planning to visit Israel in three years, stated importance of "being Jewish . . . in your life," belonging to a synagogue, belonging to a Jewish Community Center, attending JCC programs and having mostly Jewish friends.

The teenagers' index of Jewish involvement incorporated six questions: the importance of being Jewish, attachment to Israel, attending High Holiday services, fasting on Yom Kippur, having mostly Jewish friends, and commitment to dating mostly Jews.

Each index was constructed by adding a single point for each item (except with respect to parents' denomination). Preliminary analyses used standardized versions of these indices as the principal dependent variables. The final results presented below present dichotomized measures, that is, the percent scoring high on Jewish involvement for adults and for teenagers.

"High" for teenagers was set equivalent to scoring on four or more of the six items. As a result, of the high group, 97 percent fasted on Yom Kippur, 83 percent date mostly or only Jews, 82 percent say being Jewish is very important to them, 73 percent had mostly Jewish close friends, 62 percent felt very or extremely attached to Israel, and 48 percent attended religious services several times a month or more.

Among the adults defined as "high," on the Jewish involvement index, over 90 percent reported synagogue membership, always having a Seder, always lighting Hanukkah candles, attending High Holiday services, fasting on Yom Kippur, and never having a Christmas tree (or celebrating Christmas in any other way). At least two-thirds had mostly Jewish friends, attended synagogue monthly, usually lit Sabbath candles, and belonged to a Jewish organization.

Substantively, almost all results for the dichtotomous dependent variables replicate those using the standardized version; the former (percent scoring high) were retained below for ease of interpretation and presentation. (The one exception—entailing the impact of the Israel trip—is noted and explained below.) When incorporated in the Multiple Classification Analysis, parents' (i.e., the "grandparents") and the current adults' involvement were recoded into 7- and 6-point indices, respectively.

As noted earlier, denominational upbringing and parental in-marriage alone (the two parent-related variables available on the NJPS) cannot adequately represent parental Jewish involvement. Indeed, for adult respondents in this study, these two variables explain just 11 percent of the variance in the composite measure of Jewish involvement as opposed to 18 percent when using the parental index of Jewish involvement constructed out of the five ritual items, organizational membership, as well as denomination. (On the other hand, adding parents' rituals to denomination raised does nothing to increase the ability to predict the likelihood of intermarriage.) Denomination raised is a very powerful predictive variable, possibly the most valuable single variable of its kind. Nevertheless, the addition of other information on parents' household can, in some cases, dramatically improve the ability to predict certain Jewish identity characteristics.

Clearly, previous studies that relied on such limited information about respondents' parents were understating the influence of parents' Jewish involvement (since it was so poorly measured) and overstating that of Jewish schooling (since it, in a sense, illegitimately inherited the unmeasured influence of parental Jewish involvement). Logically, the superior measures of parental Jewish involvement here diminish the extent to which education is falsely credited with impact that properly must be attributed to the parental home. Any remaining random errors in measuring parental involvement—which cannot be ruled out entirely—lead to overestimates of the impact of Jewish education.

The analysis examines the impact of two dimensions of Jewish education: schooling and informal education. With respect to schooling, respondents were classified according to the most intensive form of Jewish schooling they received, provided they attended a minimum number of years (five years for day schools, three for other schools). This procedure yields five groups: those who attended (1) Orthodox day schools, (2) non-Orthodox day schools, (3) part-time schools, (4) Sunday schools, and (5) those who had no schooling. (The final analysis—results are presented below—ignored the impact of private tutoring, an educational experience typically associated with preparation for the Bar or Bat Mitzvah ceremony. Preliminary analyses demonstrated little or no impact of tutoring net of parental involvement and other forms of Jewish education.)

The main branches of informal Jewish education in the United States include Israel travel, youth groups, and educationally intensive summer camping sponsored by religious institutions and Zionist youth movements. Owing to a defect in the questionnaire design, the analysis was forced to exclude camping. The single survey question on Jewish summer camping did not successfully distinguish those who attended camps with large Jewish enrollments and only a smattering of Jewish programming from those who attended the handful of educationally intensive Jewish camps. As a result, the impact of Jewish camping could not be addressed in this study.

Several tables below examine the relationship between Jewish education and Jewish involvement. These are presented for parents and teenagers, both before and after adjusting for parental Jewish involvement and other control variables. The latter (adjusted) figures represent the extent to which high Jewish involvement scores (or the likelihood of intermarrying) for a particular type of schooling differ from the omitted category, those with no Jewish schooling; in the case of the dichotomous variables (youth group and Israel travel), the entries represent the difference in Jewish involvement between participants and nonparticipants.

In addition to variables noted above, the analyses control for age, region (living in the western United States), and socioeconomic status (SES), as measured by a composite of adult respondents' education and income). Generally, older adults were more Jewishly involved, as were those who live outside the West and those with higher SES.

## Findings

The Jewish involvement scores of adults and teenagers are arrayed in an order almost uniformly corresponding to intensity of Jewish education (table 13.3). Among the categories of Jewish schooling, Orthodox day school alumni (or students) score the highest by far, followed by the non-Orthodox day school group, those who attended part-time schools, the Sunday school students, and those with no schooling. (The one exception: adults who attended Sunday School score lower than those who attend no school.) Similarly, for both adults and teenagers, participation in youth groups and Israel travel are each associated with higher levels of Jewish involvement. Intermarriage frequencies, which are obviously available for adults but not for teenagers, show similar relationships with education: more Jewish education is associated with lower rates of intermarriage.

These simple tabulations replicate those found in previous studies of this phenomenon: more Jewish education (except for Sunday school attendance by adults)

TABLE 13.3
Percent Scoring "High" on Jewish Involvement Indices[a] for Adults and for Teenagers and Percent Mixed-Married for Adults by Type of Jewish Schooling and by Informal Jewish Education

| *Type of Jewish Schooling* | *None* | *Sunday School* | *Part-Time* | *Non-Orthodox Day* | *Orthodox Day* |
|---|---|---|---|---|---|
| *High on index* | | | | | |
| Adults | 15% | 14% | 32% | 50% | 83% |
| N | 371 | 330 | 529 | 20 | 81 |
| Teenagers | 7% | 17% | 31% | 59% | 97% |
| N | 153 | 157 | 253 | 39 | 37 |
| Mixed-marrieds adults | 45% | 52% | 23% | 21% | 9% |
| N | 338 | 303 | 497 | 19 | 78 |

| *Informal Jewish Education* | *Youth Group* | | *Israel Travel* | |
|---|---|---|---|---|
| | *No* | *Yes* | *No* | *Yes* |
| *High on index* | | | | |
| Adults | 19% | 31% | 22% | 50% |
| N | 581 | 810 | 1,262 | 202 |
| Teenagers | 4% | 40% | 22% | 60% |
| N | 252 | 354 | 521 | 88 |
| Mixed-marrieds adults | 40% | 33% | 37% | 27% |
| N | 476 | 747 | 1,061 | 185 |

a. The indices for adults and for teenagers consist of different items.

TABLE 13.4
Percentage Distributions of Jewish Schooling, Youth Group Participation, and Israel Travel by Parents' Jewish Involvement for Adults and for Teenagers

| | Adults | | |
|---|---|---|---|
| *Their parents' Jewish involvement:* | *High* | *Mod* | *Low* |
| Day school | 25 | 3 | 0 |
| Part-time | 57 | 52 | 28 |
| None and Sunday | 18 | 46 | 72 |
| Youth group | 73 | 72 | 50 |
| Israel travel | 24 | 17 | 10 |
| N | 271 | 431 | 629 |
| | *Teenagers* | | |
| *Their parents' Jewish involvement:* | *High* | *Mod* | *Low* |
| Day school | 33 | 4 | 3 |
| Part-time | 49 | 48 | 18 |
| None and Sunday | 18 | 48 | 79 |
| Youth group | 79 | 60 | 22 |
| Israel travel | 34 | 8 | 3 |
| N | 179 | 282 | 144 |

is seemingly linked with higher levels of Jewish involvement. Of course, we cannot readily attribute causality to this simple association without first taking into account significant confounding factors, of which parental Jewish involvement is the most influential.

Indeed, the patterns of Jewish education vary closely with the level of the respective parents' Jewish involvement (table 13.4). Those from more Jewishly involved homes experienced more intensive Jewish schooling. To illustrate, of adults whose parents were the most involved in Jewish life ("High" in table 13.4), almost a quarter attended day schools, as contrasted with hardly any among those who reported only moderate or low levels of Jewish involvement on the part of their parents. Among those with moderately involved parents, just over half report more than Sunday school or no education, as contrasted with only 28 percent of those whose parents scored low on Jewish involvement.

As with schools, so with youth group participation and Israel travel; participation rates in both are also closely associated with parental Jewish involvement. Those adult respondents whose parents had high involvement were much more likely than those with the least involved parents to report participation in youth groups (73% vs. 50%), and they were over twice as likely to report having visited Israel as a youngster (24% vs. 10%). Adult respondents with moderately involved parents reported intermediate frequencies of participation in youth groups and Israel travel.

The association between parental Jewish involvement and intensivity of Jewish education is even stronger among the teenagers. Moving from low, to moderate, to high levels of parental Jewish involvement, we find that day school utilization rises from 3 percent to 4 percent to 33 percent; youth group participation jumps from 22 percent to 60 percent to 79 percent; and Israel travel surges from 3 percent to 8 percent to 34 percent.

In light of the close connection between parents' Jewishness and their children's education, and in light of the substantial impact of parental Jewish involvement on the child's involvement, a major portion of the association between childhood Jewish education and current involvement must be attributed to the link between parental involvement and intensivity of Jewish education. We cannot estimate the impact of Jewish education on current Jewish involvement without first extracting the influence of parental Jewish involvement that underlies, influences, and chronologically precedes both factors.

Using Multiple Classification Analysis, we can take account of the confounding influences of parental involvement as well as other related factors (e.g., age, sex, SES, and region). With respect to youth groups, the analysis also controls for type of Jewish schooling, an event which typically precedes teenage participation in youth groups. For similar reasons, the computation of the net impact of adolescent Israel travel (which usually takes place at age 16 or 17) controls for both schooling and youth groups. (Almost all Israel travelers belonged to youth groups, and a disproportionate number attended day schools. The estimate of the impact of the Israel experience needs to remove the confounding of these prior educational experiences as well.)

Overall, when compared with the simple cross-tabulations presented earlier, the findings point to a significantly diminished impact of Jewish education as a result of controlling for these factors (table 13.5). Significantly, the patterns for adults and teenagers generally resemble one another.

The scores of Sunday school students (−1 point for adults) suggest little if any impact of this type of Jewish education upon Jewish identity. (A score of −1 means that, all other things being equal, those who attended Sunday schools were one percentage point less likely to emerge as highly involved Jewish adults than were those with no Jewish education.) In contrast, the part-time school graduates display a modest positive impact of their schooling (10 points for the adults and 10 for the teenagers). The non-Orthodox day schools score far higher (31 and 32 points for adults and teens respectively). The Orthodox day school alumni substantially outscore the others: 48 for the adults, and 55 for the teenagers. In other words, the net impact of Sunday schools on high Jewish involvement as an adult is

TABLE 13.5
The Impact of Jewish Education on Jewish Involvement: Percent Scoring High on Jewish Involvement by Type of Jewish Schooling and by Informal Jewish Education for Adults and for Teenagers, Adjusting for Their Parents' Jewish Involvement, Age, Sex, SES, Region (West), and Prior Jewish Educational Experience[a] (Multiple Classification Analysis)

| *Impact of Type of Jewish Schooling (vs. None)* | *Sunday* | *Part-Time* | *Non-Orthodox Day* | *Orthodox Day* |
|---|---|---|---|---|
| Adults | −1 | 10 | 31 | 48 |
| Teenagers | 7 | 10 | 32 | 55 |

| *Impact of Informal Jewish Education* | *Youth Group vs. None* | *Israel Travel vs. None* |
|---|---|---|
| Adults | 7 | 15 |
| Teenagers | 9 | 14 |

Note: The numerical entries represent the differences between the particular category and those with no Jewish school, or no youth group participation, or no Israel experience. For example, the far right number in the top row means that graduates of Orthodox day schools have a 48% higher chance of reporting high levels of Jewish involvement today as compared with no Jewish schooling, after controlling for differences that one would anticipate on the basis of parental Jewish involvement, SES, age, and other control variables.

a. Results for youth group also adjust for type of Jewish schooling. Results for Israel travel also adjust for type of Jewish schooling and youth group participation. Schooling entries are deviations from the mean of those with no formal Jewish schooling. Youth group and Israel travel entries represent the adjusted differences between those reporting and not reporting these experiences. The indices for adults and for teenagers consist of different items.

negligible; that of part-time schools, on average, is slightly positive; that of non-Orthodox day schools, substantially greater; and of Orthodox day schools, even greater still.

Beyond schools, both youth groups and adolescent Israel travel are associated with increments in Jewish involvement, even after controlling for parents' Jewish involvement, Jewish schooling, and other factors. Controlling for those factors, youth group participation increases the chances of high involvement in Jewish life by 7 points for adults and 9 points for teenagers. The Israel visit in one's youth seems to bring with it a 15 percent increment in the chances of scoring high on Jewish involvement, above and beyond the home, Jewish schooling, youth groups, and other factors. The teenagers' net Israel travel effect amounted to a nearly identical 14 percent points.

The results in table 13.5 may exaggerate the impact of Israel experience. Here the results suggest that the Israel experience is clearly more influential than part-time schools, though less than non-Orthodox day schools. In point of fact, more detailed analysis (not shown) of the individual items in the Jewish involvement

TABLE 13.6
The Impact of Jewish Education on Intermarriage: Percent Married to Non-Jews by Type of Jewish Schooling and by Informal Jewish Education for Adults and for Teenagers, Adjusting for Their Parents' Jewish Involvement, Age, Sex, SES, Region (West), and Prior Jewish Educational Experience[a] (Multiple Classification Analysis)

| *Impact of Type of Jewish Schooling (vs. None)* | *Sunday* | *Part-Time* | *Non-Orthodox Day* | *Orthodox Day* |
|---|---|---|---|---|
| | 8 | −11 | −19 | −20 |

| *Impact of Informal Jewish Education* | *Youth Group vs. None* | *Israel Travel vs. None* |
|---|---|---|
| | −5 | −5 |

Note: Entries are differences between the particular category and those with no Jewish school, or no youth group participation, or no Israel experience.

a. Results for youth group also adjust for type of Jewish schooling. Results for Israel travel also adjust for type of Jewish schooling and youth group participation. Schooling entries are deviations from the mean of those with no formal Jewish schooling. Youth group and Israel travel entries represent the adjusted differences between those reporting and not reporting these experiences.

indices demonstrated that Israel travel affects Israel attachment much more than ritual practice, communal affiliation, and association (a pattern borne out in the results for intermarriage presented in table 13.6). In addition, use of standardized versions of the dependent variables (i.e., adults' and teenagers' Jewish involvement scores) demonstrated that the impact of the Israel experience drew even with that of part-time schools and youth groups. When combined with the findings in table 17.5), this pattern may mean that Israel trips work well to foster entry into the upper reaches of Jewish involvement but that it does less to raise overall levels of involvement.

To summarize the key findings thus far, relative to those with no Jewish education, almost all forms of Jewish education contribute to higher levels of Jewish involvement. Sunday school is the one clear exception to this generalization. The part-time school, youth group, adolescent Israel travel, each make modest contributions to subsequent Jewish involvement. Day schools, Orthodox or not, typically exert much greater impact than that of the other instruments.

Beyond whatever impact Jewish education may exert upon Jewish involvement generally is the question of whether and to what extent it influences the likelihood of intermarriage in particular. Controlling for parents' Jewish involvement, age, sex, social status, and region (Jews in the West report higher rates of intermarriage), several forms of education do appear to diminish the chances of intermarriage. (The mixed-marriage rate in this sample is 35%.) Controlling for other factors, alumni of part-time schools were eleven percentage points less likely to intermarry than those with no Jewish schooling (table 13.6). Alumni of day schools were even more likely to marry within the faith (a net difference of 19 points for non-Orthodox day schools and 20 points for the Orthodox). Again, Sunday schools stand out as an exception. Those with a Jewish education no more intensive than the Sunday school actually report 8 percent more frequent intermarriage than do those with no Jewish schooling.

To understand this counterintuitive finding, we must recall that Sunday schools in the previous generation were most often associated with the Reform movement. Affiliates of this movement then, as now, tend to reside in areas where the Jewish population is relatively more sparse and where in-marriage rates are lower. As a result, attendance at a Sunday school is, in all likelihood, associated with residence in areas of low Jewish density, which are in turn associated with reduced chances of Jewish-Jewish marriage.

Youth groups and Israel travel exerted far less influence upon in-marriage probabilities than did Jewish schooling. Youth group participation, net of other factors (including parents' involvement and Jewish schooling) diminished intermarriage chances by only five percentage points, the same as travel to Israel. In contrast with results for Jewish involvement, where informal education exerts a stronger impact than part-time schools, intermarriage seems to be affected more by schooling than by youth group participation or Israel travel.

Mixed-married Jews are far less active in conventional Jewish life than the in-married (see, e.g., Medding, Tobin, Fishman, and Rimor 1992). The relationship established above between Jewish education and intermarriage suggests the possibility that the impact of Jewish education on Jewish involvement is largely a

TABLE 13.7

The Impact of Jewish Education on Jewish Involvement among In-married and Intermarried Adults: Percent Scoring High on Jewish Involvement by Type of Jewish Schooling and by Informal Jewish Education for In-married and Intermarried Jewish Respondents, Adjusting for Their Parents' Jewish Involvement, Age, Sex, SES, Region (West), and Prior Jewish Educational Experience[a] (Multiple Classification Analysis)

| *Impact of Type of Jewish Schooling (vs. None)* | *Sunday* | *Part-Time* | *Non-Orthodox Day* | *Orthodox Day* |
|---|---|---|---|---|
| In-married | 2 | 10 | — | 49 |
| Mixed married | −1 | 1 | — | — |

| *Impact of Informal Jewish Education* | *Youth Group vs. None* | *Israel Travel vs. None* |
|---|---|---|
| In-married | 8 | 18 |
| Mixed married | 3 | 7 |

a. Results for youth group also adjust for type of Jewish schooling. Results for Israel travel also adjust for type of Jewish schooling and youth group participation. Schooling entries are deviations from the mean of those with no formal Jewish schooling. Youth group and Israel travel entries represent the adjusted differences between those reporting and not reporting these experiences.

function of its impact on intermarriage. That is, we need to examine whether higher levels of Jewish education are still associated with higher levels of Jewish involvement, even after controlling for type of marriage (by dividing the sample into in-married and mixed-married subsamples). Perhaps the influence of education on involvement operates primarily through choice of spouse.

Table 13.7 presents the differences in the percentage scoring high on indices of Jewish involvement, controlling for parents' Jewish involvement and other variables, for in-married and mixed married adults, tabulated separately. The results point to the persistence of the sorts of effects seen earlier for the in-married. However, among the mixed-marrieds, the seeming impact of Jewish education, both formal and informal, is markedly reduced.

## Conclusions

The evidence supports the view that most instruments of Jewish education raise subsequent levels of Jewish involvement. Sunday schools, possibly because of the minimal amount of time and commitment they entail, are the single exception to this generalization. At the other extreme, Orthodox day schools seem to produce the most marked net increase in Jewish involvement of any form of Jewish education. Clearly, even non-Orthodox day schools "work," but Orthodox day schools work even better.

Why Orthodox day schools excel is a matter for speculation. Their exceptional impact might be due to stronger parental involvement or to longer hours and years in Jewish school characteristic of the Orthodox population, or to still other factors that are distinctive to Orthodoxy and its schools. These data cannot satisfactorily distinguish among these alternative explanations. Almost all the Orthodox day school students attend(ed) through high school; almost all the others ceased their Jewish day school studies before then.

Contrary to earlier studies, the findings here support the view that even part-time schools that meet more than once a week exert a moderate impact on Jewish involvement. In addition, youth groups and Israel trips as an adolescent also seem to be associated with increments in Jewish involvement, although they have little impact on the chances of marrying within the group.

These effects of Jewish education persist beyond marriage. It increases the chances that Jews will marry Jews; and if they marry Jews (but not Gentiles), Jewish education elevates the likelihood that as adults they will be more involved in Jewish life.

The conclusions drawn here regarding the effectiveness of Jewish education can be taken with a greater degree of confidence than those emerging from earlier studies for a number of reasons. One consideration is that this data set permits more precise, accurate, and comprehensive measures of parents' Jewish involvement, a major confounding factor whose influence on their children's Jewish involvement may well have been mistakenly attributed to Jewish education in previous studies. In addition, this study drew upon analyses of two generations—younger to middle-aged adults and teenagers. The similarity in the findings for both generations suggests greater reliability in the substantive conclusions. Moreover, the large number of cases allowed for distinguishing between Orthodox and non-Orthodox day schools, further clarifying an issue that had been muddied in the past.

Truth be told, the estimates derived here for the impact of Jewish education on Jewish identity are both too high and too low. They are too high in the sense that even these data do not permit a complete control of parental and community influences. In theory, the analysis held constant the parents' interest and involvement in Jewish life. In reality, even after controlling for holiday celebration, ritual involvement, Israel attachment, in-marriage, denomination, and so on, one still has to suspect that parents who send their children to more intensive forms of Jewish education (such as day school) are somehow more Jewishly committed than those who do not. Moreover, parents' Jewish schooling choices also reflect something about the communities in which these schools are available, as well as the parents themselves. Parents who choose more intensive forms of Jewish education have also chosen to live in communities with a sufficient number of Jews interested in supporting intensive forms of Jewish education.

For these and other reasons, those children who experienced more intensive forms of Jewish education bring with them unmeasured (and possibly unmeasurable) parental and communal Jewish resources lacking in their counterparts. These unmeasured advantages may well explain some of the gaps between, say, day school and part-time school students (or between participants in Israel trips and youth groups versus those who participated in neither). In short, even in the best of circumstances we cannot fully control for antecedent and confounding factors, and therefore we cannot guarantee a totally level statistical playing field in which to assess the true net impact of Jewish education on Jewish identity.

At the same time, this analysis may well have underestimated the impact of Jewish school or, perhaps more precisely, its potential impact. These results measured only the average influence of each major form of Jewish education. We had no information on the quality associated with each type of education. The analysis contained no information on issues related to teachers, curriculum, parental involvement in education, administrative excellence, school resources, community support and numerous other factors that the "school effects" literature have shown to influence academic achievement. Presumably, this principle extends to the realm of Jewish education, although no systematic quantitative studies have related Jewish educational quality to outcome measures. Logically, those Jewish youngsters who attended weaker schools experienced, on average, a less profound impact on their Jewish identity than those who went to "better" schools, however "better" is defined. Thus, the true measure of the impact of Jewish education needs to take into account not only the choice of major forms of Jewish education (the only feature of education available here) but its quality as well. Clearly, by itself, the quantitative, retrospective approach embodied in this study is ill-suited to the important task of understanding how value-oriented education aiming at long-term impact succeeds or fails in its central mission.

Finally, evidence that many forms of Jewish education can be effective in developing Jewish identity and involvement as an adult speaks to the larger questions raised earlier regarding American ethnicity and American religious life. This evidence suggests that the persistence of ethnic attachment among an upper-middle-class white ethnic group and/or the intergenerational transmission of religious commitment among American liberal religious groups are at least feasible endeavors, though certainly still difficult. As such, this evidence serves to undermine the claim of those who would assert the near inevitability either of the melting pot model for American ethnic groups or of the continuation of the decline in more liberal religious groups experienced over the past quarter-century.

## Notes

This research was supported by a grant from the Joint Authority for Jewish-Zionist Education of the WZO and the JAFI. I express my gratitude to Sylvia Barack Fishman, Alice Goldstein, and Susan Wall for their helpful comments on an earlier version of this article.

## References

Alba, Richard. 1985. *Italian Americans: Into The Twilight of Ethnicity*. Englewood Cliffs, N.J.: Prentice-Hall.

———. 1990. *Ethnic Identity: The Transformation of White America*. New Haven, Conn.: Yale University Press.

Bock, Geoffrey. 1976. "The Jewish Schooling of American Jews: A Study of Non-cognitive Educational Effects." Ph. D. dissertation, Harvard University, Cambridge, Mass.

Cohen, Steven M. 1974. "The Impact of Jewish Education on Religious Identification and Practice." *Jewish Social Studies* 36: 316–26.

———. 1983. *American Modernity and Jewish Identity*. New York: Methuen.

———. 1988. *American Assimilation or Jewish Revival?* Bloomington: Indiana University Press.

———. 1994. "Why Intermarriage May Not Threaten Jewish Continuity." *Moment*, December, pp. 54ff.

Cohen, Steven M., and Leonard J. Fein. 1985. "From Integration to Survival: American Jewish Anxieties in Transition." *Annals of the American Academy of Political and Social Science* 480:75–88.

The Commission on Jewish Education in North America. 1990. *A Time to Act*. Lanham, Md.: University Press of America.

Dashefsky, Arnold, and Howard M. Shapiro. 1974. *Ethnic Identification among American Jews*. Lexington, Mass.: Lexington Books.

Finke, Roger, and Rodney Stark. 1992. *The Churching of America*. New Brunswick, N.J.: Rutgers University Press.

Fishman, Sylvia Barack, and Alice Goldstein. 1993. *When They Are Grown, They Will Not Depart: Jewish Education and the Jewish Behavior of American Adults*. Research Report #8. Waltham, Mass.: Brandeis University, Cohen Center for Modern Jewish Studies.

Gans, Herbert J. 1979. "Symbolic Ethnicity: The Future of Ethnic Groups and Cultures in America." *Ethnic and Racial Studies* 2:1–20.

———. 194. "Symbolic Ethnicity and Symbolic Religiosity: Towards a Comparison of Ethnic and Religious Acculturation." *Ethnic and Racial Studies* 17:576–92.

Glazer, Nathan, and Daniel P. Moynihan. 1963. *Beyond the Melting Pot*. Cambridge, Mass.: MIT Press.

———, eds. 1975. *Ethnicity: Theory and Experience*. Cambridge, Mass.: Harvard University Press.

Goldscheider, Calvin. 1986. *Jewish Continuity and Change*. Bloomington: Indiana University Press.

Goldstein, Alice, and Sylvia Barack Fishman. 1993. *Teach Your Children When They Are Young: Contemporary Jewish Education in the United States*. Research Report #10. Waltham, Mass.: Brandeis University, Cohen Center for Modern Jewish Studies.

Goldstein, Sidney, and Calvin Goldscheider. 1968. *Jewish Americans*. Englewood Cliffs, N.J.: Prentice-Hall.

Greeley, Andrew M. 1974. *Ethnicity in the United States: A Preliminary Reconnaissance*. New York: John Wiley & Sons.

Greeley, Andrew M., and Peter Rossi. 1966. *The Education of Catholic Americans*. Chicago: Aldine.

Himmelfarb, Harold. 1974. "The Impact of Religious Schooling: The Effects of Jewish Education upon Adult Religious Involvement." Ph. D. dissertation, University of Chicago.

———. 1979. "Agents of Religious Socialization." *The Sociological Quarterly* 20:477–94.

Horowitz, Bethamie. 1993. *The 1991 New York Jewish Population Study*. New York: UJA-Federation.

Kosmin, Barry A., Sidney Goldstein, Joseph Waksberg, Nava Lerer, Ariella Keysar, and Jeffrey Scheckner. 1991. *Highlights of the CJF 1990 National Jewish Population Survey*. New York: Council of Jewish Federations.

Lieberson, Stanley, and Mary Waters. 1988. *From Many Strands: Ethnic and Racial Groups in Contemporary America*. New York: Russell Sage Foundation.

Lipset, Seymour Martin. 1994. *The Power of Jewish Education*. Los Angeles: Wilstein Institute of Jewish Policy Studies.

Mayer, Egon. 1993. "Jewish Education and Intermarriage among American Jews: Some Demographic and Sociological Insights from the 1990 NJPS." Paper presented at the January 1993 meeting of the International Steering Committee of the Association for Demographic Policy of the Jewish People.

Medding, Peter Y., Gary A. Tobin, Sylvia Barack Fishman, and Mordechai Rimor. 1992. "Jewish Identity in Conversionary and Mixed Marriages." In *American Jewish Year Book* 3–76. Chapter 12 in this volume.

Novak, Michael. 1971. *The Rise of the Unmeltable Ethnics*. New York: Macmillan.

Rimor, Mordechai, and Elihu Katz. 1993. *Jewish Involvement of the Baby Boom Generation: Interrogating the 1990 National Jewish Population Survey*. Jerusalem, Israel: The Louis Guttman Israel Institute of Applied Social Research.

Roof, Wade C., and William McKinney. 1987. *American Mainline Religion*. New Brunswick, N.J.: Rutgers University Press.

14 Roberta Rosenberg Farber

# Creative Decision Making and the Construction of a Modern Jewish Identity

As a consequence of modernity the center of Jewish identity shifted from an externally imposed to a voluntary internally determined one. This understanding places the act of choice, as well as an implied process of decision making, at the center of the construction of a Jewish identity. In a postmodern society an individual chooses whether or not to identify as a Jew. A person also determines what type of Jew he or she will be. Personal choice, in other words, is the fulcrum of a modern Jewish identity. This contrasts with the traditional Eastern European culture in which Jewish identity was formed by a mix of socialization, formal and informal education, and a host culture that typically restricted the activity and livelihood of Jews. For a person brought up, educated, and socialized as a Jew, it is often the richness of family and friendship relationships, in addition to one's religious education, that forms and structures a Jewish identity. In a way, this background would seem to lessen the aspect of choice. Nevertheless, the very fluidity of boundaries between groups and the emphasis on change and choice that permeates all of American society makes it a clear option.

The finding that an extensive Jewish education is a critical determinant of a strong Jewish identity and serves as a deterrent to intermarriage indicates the importance of acquiring a personal understanding of why and how a person is Jewish, as well as providing cultural and social ties and the context within which to be Jewish. For persons raised within a Jewish context the emphasis on personal choice is not likely to be as extensive an influence as for persons raised as secular Jews. Lacking outside constraints and combined with a culture that emphasizes personal choice, freedom, and self-actualization, a modern or postmodern Jewish identity becomes completely dependent on an individual's decision to define him or herself as Jewish, to live Jewishly, and to raise one's children as Jews. One lens through which to view this decision process is the choice of *ba'alei teshuvah* to be religiously observant of Orthodox Jewish law.

This essay examines the nature of the change process experienced by *ba'alei teshuvah*, using in-depth interviews conducted during 1985–86 in New York City and Jerusalem. Fifteen persons were interviewed: nine women and six men, whose ages at the time ranged from twenty-four to fifty-four years, with an average age of thirty-six. Five respondents had master's degrees, and all but one completed college. Thirteen respondents were married, one was divorced, and one person expected to marry soon. All had children except an unmarried man and a woman who was then expecting her first child. All respondents but one had been born in the United States; the exception was a woman from England. Eleven interviews were conducted in New York City and four in Jerusalem, all in English.

The snowball method was used to achieve a random sample in both Jerusalem and New York City. In-depth interviews were conducted with each of the respondents. In most cases the interviews took place in the respondent's home, although office settings, the interviewer's home, and public settings such as a café or hotel lounge were also used. Interviews lasted from one and three-quarters hours to approximately four hours, using two sessions when required. All interviews were taped, and most have been transcribed. To ensure the presence of radical change in both consciousness and behavior, only persons who became religiously observant of Orthodox Jewish law were included in the study. Because of the potential for backsliding, only persons who had been living a religiously observant lifestyle for at least five years were chosen. Five years seemed a sufficient amount of time to ensure that a person was settled in her or his new way of life.

According to tradition, a *ba'al teshuvah* is someone raised within Orthodoxy who goes away and then returns. Of the fifteen persons interviewed, only one fit this category; in other words, she was raised in an Orthodox family setting. Seven interviewees, five men and two women, were raised in Traditional or Conservative families. One person had a Reform background, and six came from secular Jewish households. Eight respondents came from families with fairly strong connections to the Jewish world and six came from families with far more tenuous Jewish connections, including one family in which the parents were Yiddish Bundists and another in which the parents were Trotskyites.

After beginning an interview one woman mentioned that she was really a convert, not a *ba'alot teshuvah* as most people assumed. I decided to keep this interview to see if her story differed in any significant way from the others. It didn't, although as expected, several of the issues she raised were not addressed by the others. Most respondents were second- or third-generation Americans or some combination of the two. A few were fourth-generation. The Holocaust played an essential role in the journey of one *ba'alot teshuvah* and of the convert.

Because meanings emerge out of the particular context of a person's life and must be seen within this context, I felt it essential that people tell their stories in their own words. In this way, the framing of the story conveys the meaning of actions taken and choices made (Langer 1942, 1953; Bruner 1990). Thus, interviews were conducted with as little interference as possible. After ascertaining basic information, I asked the respondent to tell the story of how she or he became religious. Pseudonyms are used for all the interviewees.

Lazerwitz et al. (1998, 81) find that 10 percent of Jews who have no denominational preference, that is, secular Jews (Kosmin et al. 1991), have switched to Orthodox Judaism. This means that they have chosen to live a life ruled by Orthodox observance of Halakhah, Jewish religious law, which governs the smallest to the largest details of a person's life. Having been raised as secular Jews, these *ba'alei teshuvah* are unlikely to have strong Jewish ties, either social, familial, or organizational. They are also likely to lack a Jewish education. Thus, they may clearly be said to have made a radical life change. Because of the radical nature of this change, within the literature on the sociology of religion their change process is regarded as a conversion (Davidman 1991, and others).

Eight percent of Jews raised as Conservative have also switched to the Orthodoxy (Lazerwitz et al. 1998). It is assumed that in most cases their change was neither as extensive nor as radical as the aforementioned 10 percent. That is to say, from a Jewish knowledge and observance point of view, they knew more and are more than likely to have observed a greater number of Jewish rituals and to have observed them with greater frequency than the first group. In addition, their change is not likely to have been as socially isolating because, having been raised as Conservative Jews, they are more likely to have established contacts within a Jewishly oriented and organized world. However, given the current flexibility of observance within non-Orthodox denominations (Wertheimer 1993), *ba'alei teshuvah* raised as Conservative Jews can also be expected to redefine their worldview and establish new social and organizational contacts. Thus, some will properly be regarded as having undergone a conversion process, whereas others are perhaps more appropriately defined as having "switched" denominations (Lazerwitz et al. 1998, chap. 5).

In both cases, however, the type of Jewish identity, or affiliation, and how and what this identity expresses is a consequence of a personal choice. The choice of *ba'alei teshuvah* is partly so interesting because it would appear to move in the opposite direction of "modernity," signifying a return to the particularity of the Jewish People and away from the universality and subjectivity characteristic of postmodern belief systems. Inglehart (1990, 1997) notes that concern with spirituality and the meaning of one's life is characteristic of the postmaterialist values that dominate postmodern societies. A return to religion can be regarded as an expression of such concern.

Nevertheless, the multiple constraints and regulations of Orthodox Judaism to which *ba'alei teshuvah* return seems excessive and contradictory since the decision appears to limit rather than expand choice. Literature in the sociology of religion, however, suggests that the more demanding religious groups like evangelicals and fundamentalists, are increasing their membership (though these may be persons who rejoin) and, because they employ more commitment mechanisms (Kanter 1972), have a higher rate of retention. Others explain religious preferences differently (Finke and Stark 1992).

Still, a person who chooses a belief system and way of life that seems to contradict the culture and education of his or her upbringing raises many fascinating questions, not the least of which is how a stable and coherent sense of self is maintained throughout the change. How does a person raised with one set of values, who radically transforms his or her life to reflect another set, retain a coherent inner core and self-image? The fact that the action is voluntary, motivated, and achieved as a consequence of personal choice suggests that the decision to change emerges from an inner perception of a need and/or desire. But for what? What is the motive of the change and how is it expressed? Is there a motif, a theme to the change, and if so, what is it? Might not this motif provide both the motive to change and the coherence of self needed for authentic self-definition and expression?

Kaufman (1993) found that women returnees reinterpret the values, regulations, and constraints of Orthodox Judaism in feminist terms, thus linking the "old" and "new" cultural frameworks. Davidman (1991) found comparable results in her study of *ba'alei teshuvah*. Interestingly, a similar observation about the return to Catholicism in Cuba is made by Lorenzo Albacete (1998), a reporter for *The New Yorker*. He writes:

> we were introduced to half a dozen novices, who had been born under the Revolution. All of them had come from nonbelieving families and were college-educated. Each told us basically the same story: she had met Catholic students at the university, had been struck by their sense of social mission, and had ended up deciding to devote her life to social service through contemplation in the cloister. "It became clear to me that the strength of revolutionary ideology was weakening—that it could no longer demand the kind of sacrifices it once did," one of the novices, a former sociology student, said. "I became fascinated by the notion of an absolute that inspired people to help others." Indeed, every time I spoke with young Cuban Catholics, even the seminary students in Havana, they used this sort of revolutionary language to describe their faith. (36)

These studies suggest that what appears to be a radical contradiction in lifestyles is perceived by the individual as continuous in terms of a core set of values, ideals, or ideas. In the change process particular ideals or ideas are abstracted out from one context or conceptual framework and placed into one thought to offer a more effective actualization framework. Thus, the change process can be conceptualized as the consequence of a classically defined rational decision (Simon 1957) in which the effectiveness of one framework for action is evaluated for its ability to accomplish an intended mission and found lacking. The new framework is adopted specifically because it provides a more effective framework within which to implement core values and ideals.

Placed in this context, the quest motivating a *ba'al teshuvah* to act can be seen as one of self-actualization. This would be consistent with postmaterialist values, such as a concern with the meaning of life, prevalent in a postmodern society. What is so interesting in the case of *ba'alei teshuvah*, as well as in the examples given by Albacete, is that the move is from a system in which the goal of self-actualization is defined by a subjective, individual judgment to a system in which self-actualization, though still central, proceeds in accordance with carefully structured guidelines. The authority structure, in other words, changes very dramatically and very radically.

If one visualizes this change, it is as though a person transposes core values from the center of one circle and places them in the center of another. If we understand this center as constituting a person's central or fundamental life motif, it means that the core center remains; but in order to be more effectively actualized, it is placed within a radically different framework of action. The center remains, in other words; what changes is the framework or context within which action occurs. It is, of course, appropriate to argue that, once placed within a different framework for action, the ideal itself is transformed and or redefined. Nevertheless, from an individual perspective this core meaning can be seen to constitute the connection, the link, between the new framework of action and belief system and an authentic sense of self. This center links the underlying motivation of the change with its destination, guides the person through the change process, and provides a measure against which to evaluate whether or not the original goal has been fulfilled as a result of the change.

The nature of the change, as outlined above, is analogous to processes of creative development and also to the process found in adult development. Creative development is motivated by an inner vision or knowledge intuited by the artist or scientist. This inner vision provides the motive for the creation, guides its process of development, and determines whether or not the final work accurately expresses the inner vision. The philosopher of aesthetics Susanne K. Langer (1953) calls this inner vision the "commanding form" of the work. Referring to the development of a musical composition she writes:

> Music is an occurrent art; a musical work grows from the first imagination of its general movement to its complete, physical presentation, its *occurrence*. In this growth there are, however, certain distinguishable stages—distinguishable, though not always separable.
>
> The first stage is the process of conception, that takes place entirely within the composer's mind (no matter what outside stimuli may start or support it), and issues in a more or less sudden recognition of the total form to be achieved. I say "more or less sudden," because the point of this revelation probably varies widely in the typical experience of different composers and even in the several experiences of any of them. . . . But however the total *Gestalt* presents itself to him, he recognizes it as the fundamental form of the piece; and henceforth his mind is no longer free to wander irresponsibly from theme to

theme, key to key, and mood to mood. This form is the "composition" which he feels called upon to develop. (It is significant, at this point, that one speaks of "composition" in painting in an analogous sense; the basic form of the picture, which is to be developed, and by which every line and every accent is controlled.)

. . . Yet in the whole process of subsequent invention and elaboration, the general *Gestalt* serves as a measure of right and wrong, too much and too little, strong and weak. One might call that original conception the *commanding form* of the work. (121–22)

Other kinds of creative work confirm this same process of development, in which an inner knowledge motivates, guides, and evaluates its construction (Ghiselin 1952). The perceptual structure of such inner knowledge, like the *commanding form*, is nondiscursive (Langer 1942, 1953). This means that its meaning is holistically perceived, its parts intricately related to one another, and that the parts cannot be taken out from the whole without losing their meaning. Nor can the meanings of this perceptual form be generalized. The creative development process can then be said to begin with a nondiscursive type of knowledge. In the process of making that knowledge a concrete reality, discursive knowledge is used as the composer, artist, or scientist experiments with and analyzes the effectiveness of various possibilities. The process then returns to the initial conceptualization to guide the choice process. According to Langer (1953) it is in the sensing of an intuitive click that the composer confirms a match with the commanding form.

The idea of a nondiscursively structured knowledge that inspires and guides a person throughout his or her life is used by Daniel Levinson in his study of adult male development (1978). He calls this form the Dream and describes it in terms strikingly similar to Langer's (1953) description of the commanding form.

. . . In the course of our study, we have discovered another factor that plays a powerful and pervasive role in early adulthood. This factor, often portrayed in mythology and literature, is rarely considered in academic research. We call it "the Dream." (We use the initial capital to identify and emphasize our specific use of the word.)

In its primordial form, the Dream is a vague sense of self-in-adult-world. It has the quality of a vision, an imagined possibility that generates excitement and vitality. At the start it is poorly articulated and only tenuously connected to reality, although it may contain concrete images such as winning the Nobel Prize or making the all-star team.

Whatever the nature of his Dream, a young man has the developmental task of giving it greater definition and finding ways to live it out. It makes a great difference in his growth whether his initial life structure is consonant with and infused by the Dream, or opposed to it. If the Dream remains unconnected to his life it may simply die, and with it his sense of aliveness and purpose. (91–92)

As Levinson suggests, not everyone fulfills or actualizes and concretizes the Dream in his or her life. Its very presence, however, affects one's life in that it provides a standard against which the accomplishments of a person are measured. Like the commanding form in the creative decision-making process, a consequence of experiencing "the Dream" is the responsibility to actualize it, to give it concrete form. The close analogy between the commanding form and the Dream suggests that the use of a nondiscursive presentational structured knowledge to guide personal identity construction and life development is not unusual. In fact, it may be its absence that requires explanation.

For *ba'alei teshuvah* this Dream, or commanding form, is found to be best fulfilled when living an Orthodox Jewish life. Since the development process of *ba'alei teshuvah* leads to a new life, I would expect a life motif to emerge from the stories of *ba'alei teshuvah* that works in the same way as the commanding form and the Dream. This life motif, in other words, will motivate, guide, and evaluate the process of change. Once it is perceived, a person must then strive to express the motif in the concrete forms of his or her everyday life. Making this happen is never an easy task. An inner struggle ensues because of the dissonance between everyday reality and a desire to give this goal a concrete reality.

The motif is first known as a nondiscursive perceptual form. This means it cannot be clearly articulated and requires that the individual struggle to understand it. Understanding, however, is achieved primarily or even exclusively by giving it concrete form, which for *ba'alei teshuvah* requires the experiencing of alternative lifestyles or other life commitments until finding the one that matches the governing life motif. The sense of "coming home" and familiarity that *ba'alei teshuvah* often note when encountering Orthodoxy, whether at a Sabbath meal or when learning in a yeshiva, can be explained in terms of Langer's sensing of an intuitive click. There is a sense of recognition that makes the situation or event familiar even though experienced for the first time.

Davidman and Greil (1993, 87–88) endorse the use of the term *conversion* in their study of *ba'alei teshuvah*, even though the reference is to persons who may be said to convert to their own religion. This is because a Jewish Orthodox lifestyle is radically different from all other Jewish or secular lifestyles. The nature of the change a *ba'al teshuvah* experiences is both attitudinal and behavioral. Within the sociology of religion the definition of conversion generally follows that of William James (1929): "To say a man is 'converted' means . . . that religious ideas, previously peripheral in his consciousness, now take a central place, and that religious aims form the habitual centre of his energy" (193).

Contemporary studies of conversion within the sociology of religion focus on the rationality and intentionality of a convert's action. This is a major change from the earlier conversion model, which derived from the experience of Paul on the way to Damascus. In this model, conversion is conceptualized as a passive response to the miraculous presence of God, inexplicable and indescribable in normal, everyday terms. The actor has no choice but to conform to the requirements made clear in his or her vision. The process of change, in other words, lacks independent analysis and thought. It is this model that governed the perception of persons who converted to cults as being brainwashed. Closer investigation, however, suggested the actor to be neither passive nor brainwashed but rather searching and making choices (Richardson 1985)—thus, the theoretical shift to a focus on the intentionality and rationality of the person who converts.

The format of a search followed by choice suggests that a rational decision model is appropriate but problematic since, as a consequence, the role of nonrational ways of knowing in the conversion process are rejected. Important life choices like conversion are rarely, if ever, achieved through a discursively based cost-benefit analysis or a listing of pros and cons. Instead, choice is usually based on the intuitive "gut feeling' one gets after a discursive analysis. This is not unlike the sensing of an "intuitive click" to which Langer (1942) refers. It would seem to point to an inner perception of the way in which our lives should unfold—not the events, over which we often have little if any control, but something more basic, something closer to what Taylor (1991) defines as one's authentic self.

It is my thesis that this authentic self is what *ba'alei teshuvah* seek to actualize in their process of change. Thus, the process of change proceeds in accordance with and is governed by this intuitively known self. Langer's analysis finds that the meanings of a nondiscursive symbolism or expressive form, like the commanding form or Levinson's Dream or the life motif I suggest, is known through feeling, which she understands to be, like thinking and analysis, a rational way of knowing (1942). It seems reasonable to assume that the reference to what "feels right" or "feels like me," which is often made by *ba'alei teshuvah* to explain their pace of change, is a reference to a nondiscursive perceptual understanding of this inner authentic self.

Indeed, in interviews with *ba'alei teshuvah*, I found that they use not only the thinking and analytic processes, as advocated by the rational decision model, but use and may even rely on insight, inspiration, feelings, and mystical and or spiritual experiences as well. All of these latter forms of knowing are traditionally conceptualized as nonrational. Using Langer's (1942) conceptualization, however, these ways of knowing are understood as rational. It is important, however, to note that in order to communicate the meanings of these nondiscursive ways of knowing, the knowledge must be expressed in occurrent form. A process of development, in other words, must attend this type of knowledge if it is to be shared with others. It is my understanding that this is the process by which *ba'alei teshuvah* become religiously observant of Orthodox Jewish law. Examples from the interviews are given below.

Leah said she came from a very Conservative upbringing but always wanted to be more religiously observant. At summer camp, when she was thirteen years old, she had

> a very strong sense of God's presence. . . . I had never thought much about God before that but now I knew there was some kind of force or whatever in the universe and the experience made a very strong impression on me. . . . I was sitting on a bench and recall feeling totally at peace with myself. A little later, while I was sitting on the grass I wrote a poem. I

was quiet and still, even though everything was going on around me. Camp had started; the kids were up. I wrote about knowing. Knowing, knowing, knowing. Not in terms of thinking about HaShem [God] specifically, but like knowing there was a certain purpose in life. The strong feelings of contentment and being at peace with myself came from knowing there was a purpose to the world. That I was being taken care of and had a certain destiny in my life. That feeling stayed with me for a long time but once I was home, gradually even that was lost and I remember feeling neither calm nor content. But I know it made a really big impression on me because when I returned home I wanted to be back in camp so I could have those feelings again. It was like this experience had become a real place for me. And as I got older I always referred back to it in my mind as something I wanted to achieve—that feeling of peace and contentment. But I didn't know how to achieve it or in which sense; I wasn't sophisticated enough to define the feelings. And even when I got older, I didn't know what it meant until I became *frum* (religiously observant). What I did know was that I had touched something in myself I wanted to return to.

The above beautifully expresses the idea of a life motif, an experience that constitutes a commanding form or life Dream, which then provides the direction and goal for a person's life. The challenge is how to actualize it. It might be assumed that since Leah came from what she described as "a very Conservative upbringing," it would be easy for her to translate the experience into intensified religious observance. But for various reasons, articulated in the interview, she didn't. Instead, among other things, Leah gets involved in college campus politics, then drops out of college and works in an abortion clinic, and then becomes seriously involved with a non-Jewish man. A rabbi and a friend persuade her to break off the relationship. A series of other experiences gradually lead her to Israel, where she attends a yeshivah. There she has great difficulty in accepting the teachings. It is only after struggling with issues that highlight the conflict between her secularly based ideas, mostly concerning the role and behavior of women, that she comes to accept the Orthodox approach. Here is what she says: "For me the abortion question was all tied up in the meaning of a woman's identity. As I learned about Halakhah [Jewish religious law] and the role of a Jewish woman, I saw it was true. That this way of life was true woman's liberation and that the other was just a woman fighting against her nature, her true purpose in life. It wasn't just a question of having children. I mean, there's much more than that. Gradually, I understood how it all fit into place. This happened over a long time."

This second stage involves the struggle to concretely express the initial intuition, which she had when she was thirteen, of her life purpose, her life motif. It is only after a great deal of trial-and-error experimentation in how she should live and then the working through of the ideas and how they affect her life that she is able to see how all the parts fit into place. The search for purpose guided her path of return and, importantly, provided a measure against which she could evaluate whether or not her goal was achieved.

A very different story is told by Linda, a Yale graduate. Brought up in New Jersey by "non-practicing Reform Jews," Linda went Christmas caroling, decorated Christmas trees, and wished she "could be a born-again Christian though, intellectually, I knew I never could." But interestingly, the life motif occurs to her at an age similar to Leah's. In Linda's second stage of development she works in various social activist movements and organizations; she travels through Europe and then to Israel. In Israel she attends yeshivah where she, like Leah, confronts the conflict in the ideas between the secular world she knows and Orthodox Judaism. Here's what she says close to the conclusion of her story:

> I knew that just as there's a physical order in the world, there must be a moral order as well. It's possible to establish a logical basis for this idea but my feeling about it was purely intuitive. In other words, I didn't formulate this idea in terms of a physical order because I'm not a scientist. I didn't believe that because everything else in the physical realm interacts so perfectly, the human being should do the same. Rather, I felt that our purpose is to create a moral harmony to parallel the harmony found in the physical realm, taking into account the profound difference between the two realms: in the physical world there are rules, whereas in the moral realm we have choices. In the physical world, gravity is gravity, and you can't choose in or out of it, but you do choose whether or not to conform to an existing moral law. . . .
>
> I really always felt that way, but I first became aware of this thought when I was about fifteen years old and applied it to the idea of littering. . . . but when I came of age and could consciously choose, like at fifteen, I remember saying that I wanted to be the kind of person who, if everybody did what I did, the world would be a better place. . . . My parents tell me I said this all through my teens. Then I started to feel this way about all of my actions. Like I wouldn't be able to live with myself if somebody, by imitating me, if the whole world imitated me, the whole world would be worse. Littering is a minor thing, but it was symbolic of how an individual's actions have the potential to transform an entire society, an entire world.
>
> So really, I was always searching for the right structure within which to become a good person. The key to the structure working was that it had to account for and acknowledge the importance of personal action. It had to recognize that as a result of personal action, society could be transformed. Intuitively I knew this structure existed. I was looking for it when I worked for those organizations after college, but I didn't know where to find it. So from that perspective, I can say that all my life I've been searching for Torah, I just didn't know it.

We see that Linda has an initial vision of the way things should be that functions as her life motif. It establishes a goal, which she seeks to implement and actualize in her everyday life. Searching for it, Linda becomes involved in various organizations and movements that she eventually rejects because they fail to measure up to her standards as defined in her life motif. This trial-and-error experimentation eventually leads her to learn in a yeshivah in Israel. But only when she struggles with the Torah perspective and encounters people who are living a Torah life does she feels that she's found that for which she had always been searching.

Naomi was already in her fifties when she became a *ba'alot teshuvah*. Her background was that of "a completely absorbed, assimilated British Jew; so absorbed that I knew Christmas and I knew Easter. And I only knew about Judaism that I was Jewish; that I was different. I knew I was different because in school they told me I was different. For instance, 'Would Jewish girls please leave the hall until the prayers are over.' And if they hadn't told me I was different, I probably wouldn't even have known it. So every school I ever went to, we Jewish girls always walked out. That made me feel pretty good. I don't know why but it made me feel pretty good." She describes an unexplainable attraction to being Jewish, expressed while she is still a young girl: "And whenever I went past a synagogue my soul was tugging. I could feel it. It was yearning. It was a yearning to go in. And whenever I came across anything Jewish, a challah in a shop window for instance, this soul would activate itself and I would feel hungry. Not physically hungry, but spiritually hungry, like I've got to go in because that belongs to me. Not as if I'm starving hungry, no. Rather, this is mine; this is me. But I couldn't have it because we didn't observe Shabbat."

The feelings described above constitute Naomi's life motif. It engenders a search to move closer to Jewish observance, but because of various obstructions, like marrying someone who came from a religious family but didn't want to be observant, the search continues most of her life. Once her children are grown, she finds a path that takes her to a yeshivah in Israel, where she learns how to observe Jewish law and make it the basis of her everyday life. Only in so doing, she states, was she able to appease the restlessness of her soul that caused her great hardship and pain throughout most of her life.

In another example, David, who was thirty-two at the time of the interview, was brought up in a Conservative home in which his mother lit candles every Friday night, but after having a nice meal, "things went back to normal." Although his parents weren't as observant as he would have liked them to be, he did live in a religious neighborhood and remembers seeing people walk back and forth from the synagogue on the Sabbath and holidays. He remembers wanting to be like them.

David traces his desire to be religiously observant to a Sunday school experience in which he and one other boy in his class said they wanted to wear *tzitzis*, the fringed garment that all Orthodox men wear—usually, but not always, under their shirts. In retrospect, David understands this as a clear indication that he always wanted to be religiously observant, but his family, whose nominal denomination was Conservative, did not. This thwarted desire is expressed in his behavior with his tefillin, the phylacteries worn by men during their morning prayers once they have reached the bar mitzvah age of thirteen.

Contrary to the required practice, after his bar mitzvah, David never put on his tefillin again until he became Orthodox. Instead, he did put his tefillin into a dresser drawer, and every year he took them out to look at them, promising that once he moved out of his parent's house he would become observant. This became a life motif for David in that part of the significance in the donning of tefillin when a boy reaches the age of bar mitzvah is that this is the age when he becomes responsible for what he does and doesn't do in his life. This same meaning is attached to leaving one's parents' home. David promised himself that when he left his parents' home he would become religious. This didn't happen until he was twenty-eight years old.

Because he stayed home, the second stage of the development process did not include the searching and trying out of alternatives we saw in the earlier stories. Instead, David lives the life he sees his parents living (this is the alternative he tries out) and becomes more and more convinced that becoming a *ba'al teshuvah* is the right choice for him.

I said to myself, I've got one life, so I might as well live it as a Jew. You know, it's like sort of a buried treasure in my backyard. All I have to do is dig it up. I figured out there's such a small percentage of Jews in the world, it's such a miracle and it's such a waste to go through your life living like a non-Jew when you have these riches. That's the way I feel. You're just wasting your life if you don't live it the way you're supposed to. . . .

So, young people start really looking and questioning; is that what I'm going to be doing for the rest of my life? It's a crazy game where me and two million other people on the train are all going to the same place to get money to go home to buy food and strengthen ourselves so we can go to work. And people start thinking, people start really thinking as the months turn into years, start thinking that there's got to be more to life than three meals a day, going to work, watching Johnny Carson, going to sleep.

To take responsibility for his life, David makes the radical change of becoming observant of Orthodox Jewish law. In this way he demonstrates the fact that he has considered the options, found the path of his parents wanting, and identified another way, which he finds more purposeful and therefore more personally rewarding. His sense of personal responsibility extends to his role in the community; he desires to give back as well as take. In this he must find his place. A piano tuner by trade, he finds out about a local volunteer organization that delivers food for the Sabbath and the holidays to poor people and volunteers to work for them.

It's a tough job. It's up to the guys from the street, the guys who grew up in the street like me who could lift the thirty-, forty-pound boxes and lug them upstairs. I find that if guys like me can't do that, nobody could. You have to do what you can. I might not be able to give as much charity as I want. I might not be able to learn the way I want. But at least let me use my physical ability—you know, my ability to drive, my ability to lug heavy stuff upstairs. Let me use that and let the other *frum* people do what they do best. Let them, you know, if they don't get into such physical work, let them not. I find that job has to be for the guys that don't mind dirty work, like me, so I feel that it's my duty to do it.

We see in all these cases the connection between a life motif, often envisioned when a young person, that is carried over as the central idea or ideal in the person's commitment to his or her new Jewish life. It is this central motif that lends continuity in a process of radical change and transformation, thus providing the important coherence of self. This central meaning then becomes the focal point for expressing one's Jewish identity.

What is so very interesting are the multiple meanings through which people become attached to and assume an Orthodox Jewish identity. Whereas this multiplicity of meanings that are central in the formation of a Jewish identity was probably always present, its significance is one of the consequences of modernity. The emphasis on self and freedom of choice, the openness to alternatives and pluralistic values, that characterize postmodern societies suggest that meanings must derive primarily from within and that they will inevitably revolve around one's own sense of self. In the study of Jewish identity this suggests the importance of understanding the multiple meanings that constitute the focal point of a person's Jewish commitment, even within the same denomination. In terms of policy implications, the importance of education cannot be overstated. For without exposure to the multiple dimensions and meanings of Judaism and Jewish life, it cannot be chosen as the central focus of personal identity.

It is easy to think that persons turn to Orthodoxy because it offers a simpler worldview, one in which many choices do not seem to be available. However, the fact that all Jewish identity emerges from an inner consciousness and understanding means that there will be many paths by which persons connect. To this extent, the process is closest to that of creative development, and each person can be thought of as an artist who must construct his or her own Jewish identity. The process, as outlined above, is analogous to the process of creative development in that the motive and motif emerge from an inner knowledge, which is then used to guide a person's life journey, to evaluate alternative ways of actualizing this life motif, and to determine when and how it is correctly expressed. The processes of becoming religious, developing creatively, and constructing a modern Jewish identity all seem to share these same characteristics.

Clearly, not everyone will go through such a process. Some persons will be content to stay where they are, follow in the footsteps of their parents, or embark on a path that retains the same conceptual and action framework. But for those who do take the option of choice to fashion a life of their own choosing, this format will most likely be the one they will follow. The motive and motif come from an inner source, and it is this inner source that must be satisfied with the form that is chosen. Only then is the search concluded.

## Note

This is a revised version of a paper presented at the Twelfth World Congress of Jewish Studies in Jerusalem, Israel, August 1997.

## References

Albacete, Lorenzo. 1998. "The Poet and the Revolutionary." *The New Yorker*, January 26, pp. 36–41.

Bruner, Jerome. 1990. *Acts of Meaning*. Cambridge, Mass.: Harvard University Press.

Davidman Lynn. 1991. *Tradition in a Rootless World: Women Turn to Orthodox Judaism*. Berkeley: University of California Press.

Davidman, Lynn, and Arthur L. Greil. 1993. "Gender and the Experience of Conversion: The Case of 'Returnees' to Modern Orthodox Judaism." *Sociology of Religion* 54 (spring), pp. 83–100.

Finke, Roger, and Rodney Stark. *The Churching of America 1776–1990: Winners and Losers in Our Religious Economy*. New Brunswick, N.J.: Rutgers University Press.

Ghiselin, Brewster, ed. 1952. *The Creative Process: A Symposium*. New York: New American Library.

Inglehart, Ronald. 1990. *Culture Shift in Advanced Industrial Society*. Princeton, N.J.: Princeton University Press.

———. 1997. *Modernization and Postmodernization: Cultural, Economic, and Political Change in 43 Societies*. Princeton, N.J.: Princeton University Press.

James, William. 1929. *The Varieties of Religious Experience: A Study in Human Nature*. New York: Modern Library.

Kanter, Rosabeth Moss. 1972. *Commitment and Community: Communes and Utopias in Sociological Perspective*. Cambridge, Mass.: Harvard University Press.

Kaufman, Debra Renee. 1993. *Rachel's Daughters: Newly Orthodox Jewish Women*. New Brunswick, N.J.: Rutgers University Press.

Kosmin, Barry, Sidney Goldstein, Joseph Waksberg, Nava Lerer, Ariella Keysar, and Jeffrey Scheckner. 1991. *Highlights of the CJF 1990 National Jewish Population Survey*. New York: Council of Jewish Federations.

Langer, Susanne K. 1942. *Philosophy in a New Key: a Study in the Symbolism of Reason, Rite, and Art*. New York: New American Library.

———. 1953. *Feeling and Form: a Theory of Art Developed from Philosophy in a New Key*. New York: Charles Scribner's Sons.

Lazerwitz, Bernard, J. Alan Winter, Arnold Dashefsky, and Ephraim Tabory. 1998. *Jewish Choices: American Jewish Denominationalism*. Albany: State University of New York Press.

Levinson, Daniel. 1978. *The Seasons of a Man's Life*. New York: Ballantine Books.

Richardson, James T. 1985. "The Active vs. Passive Convert: Paradigm Conflict in Conversion/ Recruitment Research." *Journal for the Scientific Study of Religion* 24 (2), pp. 119–236.

Simon, Herbert A. 1957. *Administrative Behavior: A Study of Decision-Making Processes in Administrative Organization*, 2nd ed. New York: The Free Press.

Taylor, Charles. 1991. *The Ethics of Authenticity*. Cambridge, Mass.: Harvard University Press.

Wertheimer, Jack. 1993. *A People Divided: Judaism in Contemporary America*. New York: Basic Books.

# Part V

## Religion and Spirituality: Denominational Responses to Postmaterialist Values

The advent of modernity brought about a major transformation in the concept and practice of religion. This was inevitable, in that religion had been the defining cultural force in traditional societies. Religion was the center around which a community formed. It was the source of the moral and ethical values that infused all sectors of society and the basis of stability and continuity. It provided the stories that integrated the multiple dimensions of life and helped a person make sense of life's joys and sorrows. Although most communities were homogeneous, even in heterogeneous communities social boundaries were rarely crossed. Authority was vested in the religious hierarchy, heretical expression condemned. This centrality of religion contrasts sharply with its contemporary role in advanced industrial societies.

With modernity came the freedom to choose, not only whether to observe the religion into which one was born but also the freedom not to be religious and the freedom to change one's religion. Status is no longer ascribed but rather achieved. This means that personal identity could be constructed throughout one's lifetime. The ethic of pluralism, prevalent in countries like the United States, means that all religions and cultures are regarded as of equal value. This implies they are interchangeable, leading individuals to mix and match from a "salad bar" of ritual, ceremony, and beliefs in constructing a personal identity. Generally lacking a shared mediating framework, like that previously provided by religion, it is the government in a pluralistic society that provides a political structure intended to mediate value and authority conflicts between groups. Thus, from a communal and societal perspective, religion no longer provides the coherent and integrative framework to guide action. And from a personal perspective we find religious expression and commitment to be but one aspect of a continually forming identity and, in most cases, not its integrative force.

Implicit in these changes is a transformation in the way in which a person who lives a religious life is conceptualized. In traditional societies people were religious because "everyone was religious." Religion was the culture; the background to everyone's lives. But in advanced industrial societies, like America, a person has the right to choose whether or not to be religious and also the way in which to express religiosity. This aspect of choice implies a decision process and thus is understood to conceptually endow a person's action with an intentional rationality (Dawson 1990, Richardson 1985). In making a choice it is assumed that a person acts in his or her best interest. But people change over time, and this means that one's needs also change. Commitment to a particular path is then regarded as unnecessarily restrictive. Rather than service to a greater spiritual power or higher truth, religion is now conceptualized as something to be used in the attainment of personal goals. Indeed, any commitment undertaken is generally perceived as intended to meet personal needs.

It is easier to understand the tensions and conflicts that exist between and within the different denominations of Judaism in terms of the radical change in the way in which religion is conceptualized. Guided by Halakhah, Orthodox Judaism retains many, if not all, of the traditional conceptualizations of the role and purpose of religion and the way in which it should be practiced. The Conservative and Reform denominations, on the other hand, are much closer to American cultural values, like egalitarianism, as noted by Fishman (in this volume) with regard to feminism in Jewish life. This conflict, played out in the relationships between and within the denominations of Judaism is also expressed within American society, in what Hunter (1991) calls the "culture wars."

The shift from a traditional to a modern to a postmaterialist society did not happen all at once, and while undergoing this transformation, Eastern European Judaism, as practiced on American soil, was becoming more and more Americanized. One of the first changes was in the nature and style of worship (Wertheimer 1987). Synagogues, once small, informal, and communal, became more similar to the American style of worship, which was, of course, primarily Christian. Elaborate and large temples were built. Services were shortened, often recited in English rather than the traditional Hebrew, and were conducted with greater formality, more emphasis being given to decorum. Most ritual observances were dropped; "only those that could be integrated within the framework of American cultural values were retained" (Waxman 1983, 88). These changes had dramatic consequences for the entire fabric of Jewish communal life (Farber 1995). An example is the Sabbath, the observance of which within the Orthodox denomination prohibits driving a car or using any other mode of transportation. To observe the Sabbath means that Orthodox persons must live within walking distance of a synagogue. Though this prescription limits residential options, it also assures the presence of a community: wherever they move, at least some, if not most or all, of the other members of the synagogue community will also live within walking distance. As a result, Orthodox Jews do not experience many of the problems that mobility often entails for the rest of the society. They do not experience the struggle to develop roots in a community to which they have recently moved, since, by virtue of the Sabbath, it is given that one will live within walking distance of the synagogue, and invariably, others will too. Orthodox Jews do not have to worry about where they will meet people in their new neighborhood; they know that they will meet them in the synagogue on the very first Sabbath there. They also know that there they will probably meet children with whom their own children will socialize and, in many cases, with whom they will also go to school. Thus, for at least one day a week, they are engaged in a more intensive "Gemeinschaft-like" existence than is much of the rest of modern society. When the Conservative denomination removed the prohibition not to drive on the Sabbath and holidays, this close relationship that forms between geographic proximity and community ended. Being Jewish became a discrete part of one's life; the intricate interweaving of religion with the chores and cycles of everyday life all but disappeared.

Whereas Conservative Judaism arose out of a desire to retain one's Jewishness in the process of becoming an American, Reform Judaism, which began in Germany, responded to modernity by instituting fundamental changes in Jewish law, belief, and practice. During the period of peak immigration from Eastern Europe (1880–1926), Reform Judaism was not the preferred branch of Judaism for the immigrants and their children. But as their knowledge and understanding of traditional Judaism disappeared and they became increasingly Americanized, Reform Judaism became more attractive. Like other Americans, Jews wanted to retain a religious affiliation, and Reform was found to be most conducive to meeting this need (Gans 1979, Herberg 1955, Sklare 1972; Waxman 1983). Will Herberg (1955) writes about the third generation: "Religion has become a primary symbol of 'heritage,' and church membership the most appropriate form of 'belonging' under contemporary American conditions" (57). Gans (1979) called this type of belonging "symbolic ethnicity."

During the 1960s and 1970s many of the younger generation turned away from traditional religious practice and toward Eastern meditation and spiritual techniques in their quest to achieve a sense of peace and oneness with the universe. Some Jewish youth who chose to remain within their own tradition pioneered the development of *havurot*. These were small groups, some of which were devoted to a personal and creative approach to prayer and ritual, while others extended the religiously based communities of synagogues and temples to recreation and family gatherings. Some Orthodox leaders responded to the alienation of Jewish youth with a new outreach approach that developed into a *ba'al teshuva* or "returnees" movement. Initiated by the Lubavitch Hasidic movement, Yeshiva University, and others, this approach provided an alternative religious experience within the domain of Orthodoxy and, in turn, provided an impetus to the revival of Jewish Orthodoxy (Danzger 1989).

The change in the perception of Orthodox Judaism, from being an old-fashioned relic to a lifestyle that accomplished and educated youth might freely choose, was initially puzzling (Sklare 1972). America was viewed as a secular society, and American Jewish youth were among the most secular. Indeed, some scholars of American religion predicated the virtual disappearance of institutionalized religion by the end of the century (*"A Bleak Outlook"* 1968). However, disappointment in the ability of science to solve critical human problems left a void in what to believe. In addition, Ronald Inglehart (1990) points out that postmaterialists, having experienced economic security in their formative years, are no longer concerned with issues of physical and economic security. Rather, they are concerned with issues of meaning and purpose in life, which had traditionally been the province of religion. In this context, the return to Jewish life and belief, albeit different in the different denominations, made sense.

Significant as that phenomenon is, however, it does not reflect the dominant experience of America's Jews. For the overwhelming majority of the American Jewish population, the ideological positions of a pluralistic, postmaterialistic culture have replaced the traditionally integrative and unifying role of traditional Judaism, which is understood as incompatible with pluralistic, postmaterialist, and democratic values.

Perceiving a conflict between the larger culture in which they live and a desire to retain and transmit at least some, if not all, of the traditional Jewish values and way of life, a small and perhaps growing percentage of Jews began to intensify their own observance of Jewish ritual and commitment to Jewish life and to provide their children with more intensive formal Jewish education, as well as sending them to Jewish camps and on trips to Israel. The return to the study of traditional texts provided a specifically Jewish dimension to the meaning and purpose of everyday life actions. Organizations began to act on the premise that continuity required money and resources to make it happen. Jewish identity, in other words, was no longer taken for granted, and it was acknowledged that Judaism was the core of this identity.

One significant implication of the culture shift for Jewish religion and spirituality is that they must be responsive to postmaterialist concerns to be viable. In times of economic hardship, as in European Jewish communities, spirituality and religion provided an antidote to the ever-present deprivation and persecution. For persons who experience economic security in their formative years, living within a society in which anti-Semitism is not a major problem, both spirituality and religion must respond to the more abstract and higher human needs for belonging and meaning in life. Some Jews meet these needs through an integration of spiritual and religious practice. Others find it by increasing the spiritual dimension in their life, irrespective of the source. For example, in response to the growing intermarriage rate and the needs of the modern world, some Reform leaders sought to create a Jewish spiritual identity divorced from the notion of peoplehood by blending traditional Jewish sources with traditions of Eastern meditation (Cowan

1997). A question raised by this trend is whether one can divorce spirituality from the practice of Jewish religious ritual and still practice Judaism, especially since the need for meaning overlaps with the quest for community. The increased frequency with which the different denominations are turning to traditional texts for inspiration and guidance suggests that all branches of institutionalized Judaism believe that Jewish life must be rooted in a knowledge and practice of Judaism. At the same time, there is a growing division between the denominations as each asserts its exclusive authenticity as the way of being Jewish.

## References

"A Bleak Outlook Seen for Religion." *New York Times*, Feb. 25, 1968.

Cowan, Rachel. 1997. Liberal Judaism Flourishing." *Moment*. December, 37.

Danzger, M. Herbert. 1989. *Returning to Tradition: The Contemporary Revival of Orthodox Judaism*. New Haven, Conn.: Yale University Press.

Dawson, Lorne. 1990. "Self-Affirmation, Freedom, and Rationality: Theoretically Elaborating 'Active' Conversions." *Journal for the Scientific Study of Religion* 29(2), pp. 141–63.

Farber, Roberta Rosenberg. 1995. "Those 'New York Jews.'" *Tradition* 29(4).

Gans, Herbert. 1979. "Symbolic Ethnicity: The Future of Ethnic Groups and Culture in America." In Herbert J. Gans, Nathan Glazer, Joseph R. Gusfield, and Christopher Jencks, eds., *On the Making of Americans: Essays in Honor of David Riesman*, pp. 193–220. Philadelphia: University of Pennsylvania Press.

Herberg, Will. 1955. *Protestant—Catholic—Jew: An Essay in American Religious Sociology*, rev. ed. New York: Anchor Books.

Hunter, James Davison. 1991. *Culture Wars: The Struggle to Define America*. New York: Basic Books.

Inglehart, Ronald. 1990. *Culture Shift in Advanced Industrial Society*. Princeton, N.J.: Princeton University Press.

Richardson, James T. 1985. "The Active vs. Passive Convert: Paradigm Conflict in Conversion/Recruitment Research." *Journal for the Scientific Study of Religion* 24(2), pp. 119–236.

Sklare, Marshall. 1972. *Conservative Judaism: An American Religious Movement*, augmented ed. New York: Free Press.

Waxman, Chaim I. 1983. *America's Jews in Transition*. Philadelphia: Temple University Press.

Wertheimer, Jack, ed. 1987. *The American Synagogue: A Sanctuary Transformed*. Hanover, N.H., and London: Brandeis University Press.

**15**

Charles S. Liebman

# Ritual, Ceremony and the Reconstruction of Judaism in the United States

Until very recently, observers of American Jewish life have noted a steady decline in ritual observance. This observance has been challenged in recent years[1] and was one of the points of contention in two recently published papers on the quality of Jewish life in the United States.[2] Each author assumed that the question of whether Jews were observing more, the same or less Jewish ritual than they had in the recent past was a critical dimension in assessing the quality of Jewish life in the United States. I wish to argue that the issue was improperly formulated. In the first place, insufficient account was taken of the distinction between ceremony and ritual. Second, too much emphasis was given to whether a particular ritual (or ceremony) was performed and inadequate attention was paid to the context in which it was performed and, therefore, the manner in which it is understood.

## Ceremony and Ritual

Although the terms "ceremony" and "ritual" are used interchangeably in popular discourse, many students of religion distinguish between them.[3] Such a distinction is very relevant for understanding the religious behavior of American Jews. For our purposes, the comment by Zuesse in *The Encyclopedia of Religion* is especially appropriate. He notes that "some social anthropologists distinguish between 'ritual'—stylized repetitious behavior that is explicitly religious"—and ceremony, which "is merely social even in explicit meaning." Ritual not only involves "intentional bodily engagement,"[4] which is necessarily more stylized than ceremonial behavior, but it is also believed to be efficacious. It is directed toward a particular goal and becomes, among other things, a mechanism for achieving those goals. Religious ritual connects the participant to some transcendent presence. It provides a bridge to God by engaging the participant in an act that God has commanded. At the very least, it is efficacious in the sense that it is pleasing to God or avoids God's displeasure. But it only produces the desired results when performed correctly.

In ceremony, aspects of the social and cosmological order find representation. Participation in the ceremony affirms the individual's membership in this order. But since the ceremony is not deemed to be commanded by God, it need not be performed in as precise or stylized a manner as ritual. Because it is a consciously social act and a representation of a social order, it is more amenable to change than ritual. Precisely because it is not perceived as preordained, those in charge are held responsible for its suitability and appropriateness.

Ceremony is symbol. It, too, may be cloaked in an aura of mystery—participants may derive a variety of meanings from the ceremony, and the specific connections between the ceremony and the social order it represents may be sensed rather than articulated. But even the "sense" of the participants allows them to judge the content of a ceremony as unsuitable or inappropriate or poorly done. Ritual is both more resistant to change (though by no means invulnerable), and less amenable to criticism of its content.

In Judaism, it seems to me, most *mitzvot* (sing.: *mitzvah*: commandment), fit the definition of ritual. They are believed to be commands, ordained by God, that the Jew must perform in a prescribed manner. For example, before Jews eat bread, they must recite a blessing. Before reciting this blessing they must wash their hands and recite a blessing over this act. Even the manner in which the hands are to be washed is prescribed—the kind of utensil to be used, the order in which the hands are to be washed and the number of times each hand is to be washed are clearly spelled out. Within the Jewish tradition, questions are raised about whether the individual who performs a ritual in an improper manner has fulfilled his obligations. But indifference to the manner in which the ritual is performed is certainly inappropriate. It may render the blessing one recites prior to performing the mitzvah a "superfluous blessing," which itself is sinful. Ritualism, as Mary Douglas has observed, therefore, is the opposite of ethicism, which attributes primary importance to intention and devalues the precise manner in which an act is performed. "The move away from ritual is accompanied by a strong movement towards greater ethical sensitivity," she observes,[5] although her own study indicates how ultimately self-defeating this may become. If we understand ritual in this respect, there can be little question that there is an increase in ritual behavior among Orthodox Jews in the United States[6] and a decline among the non-Orthodox. The latter comprise close to ninety percent of American Jews.

On the other hand, ceremonial behavior flourishes. This is most noticeable within the Reform movement, which has embraced Jewish symbols and encourages its members to partake of ceremonial activity that it often (mistakenly in our terms) calls ritual. Its synagogues are far richer in Jewish ceremony than they were in the past. But this, too, should not be confused with ritual. The Sabbath service in a Reform synagogue may not include reading from the Torah (the central point of the traditional Sabbath service) or may include reading only a few lines rather than the entire weekly portion, but it will include a rather elaborate ceremony in which the Torah scrolls are taken out of and returned to the highly ornamented ark in which they are kept. A bar mitzvah ceremony in a Reform synagogue might have the rabbi removing the Torah scroll from the ark and handing it to the parents of the youngster whose bar mitzvah is being celebrated. The parents, in turn, hand the Torah, in this case a symbol of the Jewish tradition, to the bar mitzvah celebrant. In traditional Judaism, the only purpose for taking the Torah scrolls out of the ark is to read from them. Indeed, Jewish law is rather strict in proscribing other uses of the scrolls because of their sanctity. Hence the elaboration of the ceremonial in which the Torah scrolls are handled is certainly "ritually" inappropriate. But we are dealing with ceremony rather than ritual. The congregants do not believe that what they are doing was commanded by God, that it must only be performed in a prescribed manner or that its proper performance is efficacious. They are partaking of ceremonial behavior, that is, symbolic behavior, whose social nature in this case seems fairly explicit. The ceremony symbolizes the ties between parent and child in a Jewish context; the centrality of generational continuity and the special role of the parent-child relationship in transmitting the Torah (i.e., tradition); the almost proprietary rights Jews have with respect to the Torah; and the central role of the rabbi. The ceremony clearly projects a certain representation of the Jewish social order and affirms the participants' membership in this order.

The ceremonial service need not necessarily be contrary to ritual in order for us to appreciate what is and what is not being celebrated. A good example is the recent flourishing of *havdalah* services. At the close of the Sabbath, but as late as midweek if he forgets to do so, a Jew is commanded to recite three blessings that distinguish the Sabbath from the rest of the week. The *havdalah* service, as performed by most Orthodox Jews, is recited immediately on conclusion of the Saturday evening prayers. Its recital takes no more than two or three minutes. There is hardly a Jewish meeting, conference, seminar or event of any kind that has taken place during the last decade held on the Sabbath that has not included the *havdalah* ceremony. Indeed, among the non-Orthodox this ceremony tends to be far more elaborate than among the Orthodox. The ceremony may conclude with all those present forming a large circle, holding hands, singing together and, quite often, kissing one another. While most of the participants are unlikely to perform *havdalah* in their own homes, they seem to look forward to the ceremony when performed under organizational auspices. The ceremony may be performed in a ritually correct manner, but from the point of view of Orthodox Judaism, it is not acceptable to conduct a *havdalah* service while omitting the evening prayers that precede it. It seems reasonable to suggest that the *havdalah* service described here is more appropriately defined as ceremony than as ritual.

The popularity of *havdalah*, along with other ceremonials we have mentioned, suggests a ceremonial renaissance among American Jews. Even this would not have been anticipated by students of Jewish religious life in the United States a generation ago. Those observers suggested that the steady decline in ritual and ceremonial behavior among American Jews (the two forms of behavior were not distinguished) foretold their approaching assimilation. That may or may not be true. But the situation is more complex than was suggested. American Jews are not abandoning Jewish ceremonies, nor are they substituting non-Jewish for Jewish ritual. Instead, they are transforming Jewish patterns of behavior into American ones. The very emphasis on ceremony and de-emphasis of ritual illustrates this pattern. Ceremony, in addition, lends itself—far more than ritual—to reconstruction, and it is this reconstruction that is so critical to understanding contemporary developments in the religious life of American Jews.

## Religious Reconstruction

In his study of Jewish life in a wealthy suburban community first published in 1967, Marshall Sklare detected a development that is now identifiable as a major trend in American Jewish life. "I feel Judaism is changing," says one of Sklare's suburban respondents. "Some people only think of religion in terms of ritual. I don't."[7] How then do Jews think of Judaism? I suggest four central components, really two sets of two components each, that distinguish the manner in which American Jews conceive of their religious tradition and represent the tools for reconstructing that tradition. These are: personalism and voluntarism as one set of components, universalism and moralism as the other. They are all interrelated but, for heuristic purposes, are best discussed separately.

### *Personalism and Voluntarism*

Personalism is a philosophical perspective in which "person is the ontological ultimate and for which personality is thus the fundamental explanatory principle."[8] Personalism is reflected in the observation by Sklare that "the modern Jew selects from the vast storehouse of the past what is not only objectively possible for him to practice but subjectively possible for him to 'identify' with."[9] Sklare is referring to the performance of mitzvot, or Jewish ritual, but personalism is imposed on all aspects of the religious tradition. Personalism refers to the tendency to transform and evaluate the tradition in terms of its utility or meaningfulness to the individual. "The best assurance of Jewish survival," Cohen and Fein say, "is the development of a community that offers its members opportunities for personal fulfillment not easily found elsewhere";[10] that is what American Jews appear intent on doing with their religious tradition.

Voluntarism refers to the absence or devaluation of *mitzvah,* or commandment. The individual is urged, encouraged, cajoled into performing certain acts of a ceremonial nature and is constantly reassured that what one does is legitimate if that is what one chooses to do. Personal choice is endowed with spiritual sanctity and is in all cases (contrary to past tradition) considered more virtuous than performing an act out of one's sense of obedience to God. While subtle distinctions exist between personalism and voluntarism, they are interrelated, and the examples offered here illustrate both these principles.

The new Conservative prayer book, *Siddur Sim Shalom,* includes among its selected readings a statement by Edmund Fleg (1874–1963), the French author and essayist, who only affirmed his Jewishness in mid-life. He wrote, "I am a Jew because [among other reasons] Judaism demands no abdication of my mind." This statement was reprinted and formed a central reading in a Sabbath prayer service at the Conservative movement's Pacific Southwest convention of synagogues in 1986. (We shall return to Fleg's affirmation because his formulation of "Why I am a Jew" foreshadows many aspects of contemporary Judaism.) Prayer, as it is transformed by personalism, ceases to become a medium of communication between people and God. Rather, asks one writer, "How, practically, can Jewish prayer function to help one confront anger and utilize it for personal transformation and social change?"[11] Another author says, "As we begin to focus on issues of importance to us, perhaps our Jewish traditions will evolve in ways to help us sustain our efforts. We have learned over the past 5000 years that things do not change overnight. But we have also learned that if we do nothing, they do not change at all."[12]

What we have here is the belief that tradition should be made compatible with the needs of the individual Jew. This, given the emphasis on voluntarism, is hardly surprising. Personalism and voluntarism are incompatible with ritual, that is, behavior performed in a specified, stylized manner undertaken because this is believed to be God's command. It is not, however, incompatible with ceremonial.

*Siddur Sim Shalom,* first published in the mid-1980s, offers a number of alternative services or prayers for different occasions. It has been argued that each of the alternatives in the Conservative prayer book, unlike the Reform prayer book, has a basis in Jewish law. However, the Union for Traditional Conservative Judaism, representing the more traditionalist wing within the Conservative movement, has published a responsum (legal opinion of Jewish law) that concludes, "although *Siddur Sim Shalom* may be used as a resource work, it should not be used for the purpose of fulfilling one's prayer obligations" because, among other reasons, some of the alternatives are not the services that the tradition prescribes.[13] Whatever the case, offering the worshipper a variety of choices reflects the spirit of personalism and voluntarism to which we have alluded.

The Conservative Temple Beth Ami in Reseda, California, proud of its efforts to encourage what it takes to be "ritual observance," prepared a booklet on the topic that it distributed to other Conservative congregations. The program was conceived and developed by a faculty member of the University of Judaism, the West Coast rabbinical seminary and institution of higher education of the Conservative movement. The synagogue program is built around a voluntary group patterned on Weight Watchers. Each member of the group undertakes to perform certain "rituals" and to report back to the monthly meeting of the group on his or her progress. Members fill out a "12-Month Goal Sheet" in which "they should determine which rituals they would like to involve themselves in during the coming year. The members should understand that the goal of this program is not to make them become any more Jewish than what they will be comfortable with."[14]

No less interesting is that a number of these "rituals" have no great significance in Jewish law, others are customs rather than mitzvot and still others are probably contrary to Jewish law. However, their functions are quite obvious in contributing to a sense of family harmony and personal fulfillment. For example, among the eighteen Sabbath rituals we find: "playing shabbat music to set mood," "blessing children," "blessing wife," "blessing husband," "have a special Shabbosdick meal," "using a white tablecloth and good dishes" and "singing shabbat songs around the table."

Consistent with our understanding of personalism and voluntarism, we would expect that the definition of who is a Jew and the boundaries between Jew and non-Jew would become increasingly flexible. Jews, in keeping with these principles, are those who choose to call themselves Jews, and they are free to incorporate into their religious behavior whatever it is within a broadly and freely defined Jewish tradition that they find personally fulfilling. It would be an overstatement to say that the majority of American Jews affirm the applications of these principles in their extreme form, but it would not be an exaggeration to say that some of them do so and that most of them seem to be moving closer to, rather than further away from, the more extreme applications of these principles.

The recent decision of the Reform movement to include within the definition of a Jew someone whose mother is non-Jewish but whose farther is Jewish is one such effort. This decision simply legitimated practices that have been employed for many years in many, if not most, Reform synagogues. This, in turn, is attributable to the rising number of mixed marriages (the marriage of a Jew and a non-Jew when neither partner converts to the other's religion) and, no less important, the desire of the couple to affiliate with a synagogue and raise their child within a Jewish framework. In other words, what we are witnessing is a process whereby the Jewish spouse, married to a non-Jew who may remain a believing Christian, not only demands legitimacy of Jewish status for himself/herself and children but even, to some extent, for the Christian partner. As the authors of a study on conversion point out, over half of the non-converts in their sample "felt that one could be part of the Jewish people and community without undergoing a formal conversion process."[15] The point is brought home in articles by converts to Judaism who remain married to non-Jews, a condition facilitated by an increasingly tolerant Jewish community.

Thus, a potential convert to Judaism writes, "*Chanukah* and Christmas will probably both be observed, simply because the family ties my husband associates with the mid-winter holiday are too significant to abandon."[16] And another says:

> I am very fortunate because my husband supports my decision to convert to Judaism. . . . His main concern was that I might expect him to convert also, or that the rabbi might expect it. [Apparently the rabbi did not.] Tom is a very spiritual person and I had no expectations that he would have to take the same journey. I knew that we could still share much of Judaism as a couple and as a family.[17]

And later, describing her synagogue:

> At Beth Shalom there are many non-Jewish spouses and so there is a great deal of concern that these non-Jewish family members feel accepted and a part of the community. Our religious school also is very supportive of the children who have a non-Jewish parent or relative and every effort is made to make those children feel that they belong.[18]

And:

> I refuse to let my religious choice cause strife in my family. I made a personal religious choice and if I expect people to honor my choice then I must honor theirs.[19]

Or, as another writer says:

> As for the synagogue and community involvement, I do not see a need for the gentile spouse to feel excluded. While there are definite honors from which one would be excluded, there are plenty of meaningful opportunities to involve the non-Jew in synagogue life and congregations should do that. Though these people may not be Jewish, that does not mean they do not want our synagogue and organizational activities to be successful. Because their families are involved, they do want to see us reach our goals.[20]

A recent book entitled *Raising Your Jewish Christian Child: Wise Choices for Interfaith Parents* is advertised as "how to give your children the best of both heritages" and urges readers to "act now to enrich your children's spiritual lives. This year's holidays can be the richest, most harmonious ones your family has ever celebrated."[21]

A book on the topic, even when published by a large commercial house, is only a straw in the wind. But the book, advertised in *Commentary* magazine, carries a blurb written by the then-president of the Association for the Sociological Study of Jewry, who calls the book "an endearing message on a thorny subject . . . both a ray of hope and a helping hand to families such as her own, who wish to celebrate the duality of faith and culture."

*Universalism and Moralism*

Universalism refers to the sense that the Jewish tradition has a message for all people, not only for Jews, and that it is also open to the messages of other traditions and cultures. As we have seen, Judaism can even be construed at times as open to non-Jews who may develop a variety of partial affiliations with the Jewish people. The *Commentary* ad that suggests how the child of an interfaith marriage can benefit from the "best of both heritages" is a good illustration. *Moralism* is another term borrowed from Sklare. He defines it as the notion that "religious man is distinguished not by his observance of rituals but rather by the scrupulousness of his ethical behavior."[22] Recent emphases in American Jewish life (as already suggested) continue to invoke the term *ritual* but convert ritual to ceremonial and reinterpret its meaning in moralistic terms. Jewish symbols are retained in their particularistic form, but the referent or meaning is explained as a moral or ethical imperative. Since ethics are generally viewed as universal, examples of universalism and moralism tend to overlap.

One of Edmund Fleg's reasons for being a Jew—"because the promise of Judaism is a universal promise"—suggests moralism as well as universalism. At the 1986 Conservative synagogue convention referred to earlier, a second selection, entitled "The Essence of Judaism," was read immediately before the recital of the *Sh'ma*, a central point in the religious service. The selection (author unknown) begins by affirming that Jews are united by a four-thousand-year-old bond that has "sensitized the Jewish individual to the needs of the group" and then states, "From one group to one humanity has been our goal. From our early teachings came the ideas of a society where individuals will treat each other with dignity and respect. These ideas are the essence of Judaism."[23]

Thus, the essence of Judaism is contained in three ideas: group (i.e., Jewish) needs, the integration of the group into one humanity, and the treating of all individuals with dignity and respect.

The meaning of universalism and moralism is also illustrated in a newspaper article by a Conservative rabbi who writes on the topic *Golus* (or *Galut*), which means exile. He refers to the exile of the Jewish people from the Land of Israel. Within the Jewish tradition, especially its mystical wing, one can also find a metaphysical meaning attributed to the term. But it is strange to find a rabbi writing:

> While *Golus* is a Jewish word it is not only a Jewish issue. It is a human issue as well. *Golus* in 1986 is children going to sleep hungry night after night. It is approximately 30 armed conflicts ranging around the globe. It is the continuing deterioration of our habitat and ecosystem. . . . And most alarmingly, it is thousands of nuclear warheads ready at this moment to annihilate us all.[24]

In a sophisticated and carefully balanced discussion of the topic of Biblical particularism and universalism, Jon D. Levinson makes the following statement, which is very relevant to our concerns:

For Jews in the post-Enlightenment West, where ideas of human equality and democratic government hold sway, there is a temptation to stress the instrumental dimension of Jewish chosenness and to deny or ignore the self-sufficient dimension. We are sometimes told that the "chosen people" means the "choosing people," as if passive and active participles were not opposite in meaning. Judaism is presented as a commitment to some rather amorphous "Jewish values," which, on inspection, turn out to be *universal* values, in which Jews and gentiles alike ought to believe. Convenant, if it is mentioned at all, appears only as the basis for a warm, meaningful community life. The fact that the Covenant distinguishes sharply between insiders and outsiders—although both are God's—is ignored.

In large measure, such attitudes are dictated by the exigencies of living as a minority in a mixed society with a high degree of openness. It is simply not prudent to affirm a distinctiveness of ultimate significance based on heredity, and what is not prudent to express publicly often loses credibility, becoming peripheral or taboo even in private discourse. In addition, the contemporary theology in question represents a cognitive surrender to a Kantian theory of ethics in which morality entails universalability: if the behavior cannot be advocated for everyone, it cannot be moral. On Kantian principles, Jewish ethics—a norm for one group only—is a contradiction in terms. Hence the common substitution of ethics for Torah. "Ethics," writes Michael Wyschogrod, "is the Judaism of the assimilated."[25]

The moralization of Judaism is most pronounced on the Jewish political Left. Arthur Waskow is a major representative of this tendency. He serves as executive director of the Shalom Center located at the Reconstructionist Rabbinical College (but with a board of directors and advisory council that includes three Orthodox rabbis). Here, for example, is an excerpt from a recent fund-raising letter:

Across the US, Jews will celebrate the harvest festival of Sukkot from October 17 to 25 as *Sukkat Shalom*—the Shelter of Peace. The fragile Sukkah, open to wind and rain, is the exact opposite of a fallout shelter or of a "laser shield." It symbolizes that in the nuclear age, all of us live in a vulnerable Sukkah. *Our only real shelter is making peace.*

The theme of Sukkat Shalom is "From Harvest Booth to Voting Booth." Urge your congregation or Jewish group to press your members of Congress *to end all nuclear testing.*

Rosh Hashanah is the birthday of the world. As the new year turns and returns, *let us look our children and all the world's children in the eye and say–*

*"We did our best to choose life for you and us this Rosh Hashanah!"*

Universalism and moralism is not, however, confined to the Jewish Left. In his book *Sacred Survival*, Jonathan Woocher demonstrates how moralism comprises a basic component of what he calls the "civil religion" of American Jews, although what he actually describes is the civil religion of the Jewish lay leadership. He quotes one Jewish leader as saying, "Charity and working for social justice—Tzedakah and Mitzvos—are not options for Jews. They have the force of articles of faith. They are duties and requirements."[26]

What is remarkable in this quotation is the assumption that the terms "Mitzvos" and "Tzedakah" are accurately translated by the term "working for social justice," although both have a technical meaning within halakhic tradition. But this is a commonplace among American Jews, at least among their leaders. As another leader says, "For us, social justice—Tzedakah in its full meaning—has always been indivisible—for all." And yet another proclaims, "It has always been Jewish doctrine that social justice cannot be limited to Jews alone: Jews are dedicated to social justice for all mankind. 'Love the stranger as thyself,' the Bible taught."[27] The citation, taken out of context, confers on the passage a meaning that Bible scholars would find somewhat forced. Be that as it may, in the conception of American Jews (or at least their leaders), as long as Jews remain a people committed to these values, "Jewish survival is not a chauvinistic conceit, but a requisite for the continued fulfillment of the Jewish role as an exemplar of human values."[28]

Moralism, universalism and even a dash of personalism are reflected in contemporary American Jewish transformations of the holiday of Purim. Purim is unique among the holidays of the Jewish calendar. It is a holiday of joy and laughter in which drinking (even to excess) and revelry are encouraged. Despite its location within the catalogue of "religious" festivals, Purim is generally considered the most secular of holy days. It has been suggested by traditional rabbis as well as anthropologists that it is an inversion of Yom Kippur, the most sacred of all Jewish holidays. During Yom Kippur the community celebrates its relationship to God and locates itself as part of the sacred order.[29] Purim, on the other hand, reaffirms the secular order through the mitzvah of exchanging gifts among peers and of giving charity to the needy, thereby identifying one's social place. In addition, the popular custom (rather than mitzvah) of satirizing community leaders, including scholars, reflects the practice that anthropologists refer to as "inversion." This is another device to reaffirm the social order by permitting and marking off its periodic violation. In keeping with the spirit of the holiday, there is a remarkable degree of flexibility in its celebration. Customs include masquerading (most often as characters from the biblical book of Esther) and the production of skits and plays of a humorous and satirical nature. The prescribed *mitzvot* include the two we have mentioned—charity to the poor and gifts to one's friends—and, in addition, partaking of a Purim feast and hearing a ritual reading of the story of Esther from a scroll. The story of Esther, after recounting how Mordechai and Esther save the Jews (God makes no appearance whatsoever in this rather extraordinary tale located in ancient Persia), goes on to tell of the punishments inflicted on the Jews' enemies. Haman—the archvillain of the story and the prototype of all anti-semites—and his sons are hanged by order of the gentile king. In addition, multitudes of other non-Jews are killed by the Jews with permission of the king.

The holiday (as I indicated) has undergone an interesting transformation in the United States. Masquerading and public revelry are activities ill-suited to a minority group living as part of, rather than segregated from, a majority culture in which it seeks acceptance. Until recently, Purim, if celebrated at all, tended to be celebrated within the synagogue itself or in the home. It was, however, generally devalued among American Jews. This is less true today. Part of the reason, no doubt, rests on the insistence of many Orthodox Jews in displaying Jewish traditions to the general public. But the fact is that the non-Orthodox have acquiesced in this display, participating in it rather than shunning it. This, itself, may be a function of the increased legitimacy accorded to ethnicity in the United States. The reasons, however, are not of primary concern here. The question is, what have American Jews done with the festival in the last few years?

For one thing, although they now publicize Purim, it ceases to be an exclusively Jewish celebration. Rather, non-Jews are invited to partake as well, in which case, as we shall see, the holiday assumes somewhat different dimensions. According to a report in the *New York Times*, 1987 was the first year in which a sidewalk Purim parade was organized in Manhattan. But, says the writer:

> Its organizers hope that someday it will grow into an event like the Queens parade, which last year drew some 50,000 people.
>
> In Queens on Sunday, more than 10 blocks of Main Street will be closed for the parade . . . It is a fully ecumenical event, according to Mitchell Mann, the chairman of the parade, and includes Jewish groups of every branch as well as Roman Catholic school marching bands and black cowboys on horseback. . . . Among the others marching are: mounted police and motorcycle escort, the United States Marine Corps Color Guard, St. Benedict's Fife and Drum Corps and the Mitzvah tank of the Lubavitcher Hasidim.
>
> At the end of the march, there will be a street fair and concert. . . . Among the attractions on the street will be a ferris wheel, rides on elephants and camels, a petting zoo and a wide variety of foods, both Jewish and not-so-Jewish.[30]

Universalizing the celebration of Purim involves not only changing who participates but also what the holiday comes to represent. So, according to Orthodox rabbi and popular hasidic singer Shlomo Carlebach, as quoted in the same article, "Purim is a holiday of children." But he goes on to say, "this doesn't mean you have to be a child to enjoy it, just that you have to begin to believe in the world again like on the first day you opened your eyes." Implied, although unstated in this description of Purim, is that you certainly don't have to be Jewish.

Overtones of "personalism" mix a universalism of style in the following report of a Purim celebration at a Conservative synagogue in Connecticut. According to the rabbi:

> The Hebrew text will be wrapped around with song, dance and narrative in musical revue format—a folk art pageant involving the entire congregation. . . . We present Purim in this way in order to bring out its ever-current as well as its ancient meaning. . . . A point like this is brought out through the songs of such composers as Spike Jones, Cole Porter and George Landry, late voodoo chief of New Orleans.[31]

An explicit example of the transformation of Purim in moralistic terms is its celebration at the largest Conservative synagogue in the New Haven area. The Congregation printed a pamphlet called *Purim Service* for its members. The

*Purim Service* is read aloud as a replacement of, rather than addition to, the Biblical story of Esther. It is an abbreviated version, almost entirely in English, organized in the form of responsive readings, a style designed to involve the audience. What is especially striking about the reformulated story is the excising of any violence. Haman is not hanged on a gallows. Instead, "When the King found that Haman plotted against the people of Esther, the Queen, he removed him from office and appointed Mordekhai in his place." The moral of the story is thus formulated as: "Our story is important because it is about people who had courage and who risked their lives to help others. That's what we celebrate on Purim."[32]

## Conclusion

The failure by scholars to distinguish between ritual and ceremonial has resulted in an inadequate understanding of developments taking place among Americans Jews. It would appear that the former is declining while the latter may even be on the rise, a development indicating the Americanization of American Judaism. The term "Americanization," however, may be a misnomer because colleagues have observed similar developments taking place among Jews of Western Europe. Furthermore, these developments in the United States are not peculiar to Judaism. William D. Dinges, for example, notes that opposition to the radical change in Catholic liturgy in the 1960s, aside from charges of mistranslations, focused on the shift in understanding of the Mass from "propitiatory sacrifice" to "communal meal," in diminishing emphasis on the "Real Presence" and on tendencies "emphasizing love of neighbor and edification of the laity and on the new liturgy's alleged 'Protestant' and 'ecumenical' character."[33] The opposition, in other words, was disturbed by the very same trends we find taking place among American Jews.

Two sets of central values, I believe, animate the reconstruction of Judaism taking place in the United States: personalism and voluntarism is one and universalism and moralism the other. These values, by themselves, are the antitheses of ritual; it is no surprise, therefore, that their ascendancy also marks the decline of ritual observance. None of these aspects or values are entirely new, much less alien to Judaism: all of them are to be found within the tradition itself. What is new is the emphasis they have received and the fact that together they have become major dimensions or instruments through which American Jews interpret and transform the Jewish tradition.

## Notes

1. Steven M. Cohen, *American Assimilation or Jewish Revival?* (Bloomington, Ind., 1988).

2. Steven M. Cohen and Charles S. Liebman, *The Quality of Jewish Life in the United States: Two Views* (New York, 1987).
3. Bobby C. Alexander, *The Encyclopedia of Religion*, vol. 3, s.v. "Ceremony," 179–83.
4. Evan M. Zuesse, *The Encyclopedia of Religion*, vol. 12, s.v. "Ritual," 405–6.
5. Mary Douglas, *Natural Symbols* (New York, 1973), 41.
6. Charles S. Liebman, *Deceptive Images: Toward a Redefinition of American Judaism* (New Brunswick, N.J., 1988).
7. Marshall Sklare and Joseph Greenblum, *Jewish Identity on the Suburban Frontier*, 2d ed. (Chicago, 1979), 77.
8. John H. Lavely, *The Encyclopedia of Philosophy*, vol. 5, s.v. "Personalism," 110.
9. Sklare and Greenblum, 48. *Jewish Identity*.
10. Steven M. Cohen and Leonard J. Fein. "From Integration to to Survival: American Jewish Anxieties in Transition," *Annals of the American Academy of Social and Political Science* 480 (1985), 88.
11. Jeffrey Dekro, "Prayer and Anger," *Response* 46 (1984), 73.
12. Rebecca Alpert, "Sisterhood Is Ecumenical: Bridging the Gap between Jewish and Christian Feminists," *Response* 46 (1984), 15.
13. Union for Traditional Conservative Judaism, *Tomeikh kahalakhah: Responsa of the Panel of Halakhic Inquiry* (1986), 12.
14. Temple Beth Ami, "Hevrt Mitzvah Program" (n.d.).
15. Egon Mayer and Amy Avgar, *Conversion among the Intermarried* (New York, 1987), 9.
16. Amy Richard, "I Wish to Be a Jew; My Husband Doesn't," *Sh'ma* 17, no. 326 (1987), 41.
17. Anne Anderson, "My Support Is Real—So Are My Memories," *Sh'ma* 17, no. 326 (1987), 42–43.
18. Ibid.
19. Ibid.
20. Sharon Haber, "Gaining a Faith but Not Losing My Family," *Sh'ma* 17, no. 327 (1987), 51.
21. *Commentary* 84 (1987), 78.
22. Sklare and Greenblum, 89. *Jewish Identity*.
23. United Synagogue of America, Pacific Southwest Region. *Supplementary Prayer Book "Guardian of Israel*" (1986).
24. Cited in Liebman, *Deceptive Images*.
25. Jon D. Levinson, *Jewish Perspectives: The Universal Horizon of Biblical Particularism* (New York, 1985), 12.
26. Jonathan S. Woocher, *Sacred Survival: The Civil Religion of American Jews* (Bloomington, Ind., 1986), 85.
27. Ibid.
28. Ibid.
29. Shimon Cooper, "Inversion and Paradox in Purim Celebration" (paper delivered at the 1987 meeting of the American Anthropological Association).
30. *New York Times*, 13 March 1987, C34.
31. *Connecticut Jewish Ledger*, 12 March 1987, 13.
32. Congregation B'nai Jacob, *Purim Service* (n.d.).
33. William D. Dinges, "Ritual Conflict as Social Conflict: Liturgical Reform in the Roman Catholic Church," *Sociological Analysis* 48 (1987), 144.

# Rupture and Reconstruction

## The Transformation of Contemporary Orthodoxy

This essay is an attempt to understand the developments that have occurred within my lifetime in the community in which I live. The orthodoxy in which I and other people my age were raised scarcely exists anymore. This change is often described as "the swing to the Right." In one sense, this is an accurate description. Many practices, especially the new rigor in religious observance now current among the younger Modern Orthodox community, did indeed originate in what is called "the Right." Yet in another sense, the description seems a misnomer. A generation ago, two things primarily separated Modern Orthodoxy from what was then called ultra-Orthodoxy, or the Right: first, the attitude to Western culture, that is, secular education; second, the relation to political nationalism, that is Zionism and the State of Israel. Little, however, has changed in these areas. Modern Orthodoxy still attends college, albeit with somewhat less enthusiasm than before, and is more strongly Zionist than ever. The ultra-Orthodox, or what is now called the *haredi*[1] camp is still opposed to higher secular education, though the form that the opposition now takes has local nuance. In Israel the opposition remains total; in America the utility, even the neccesity of a college degree is conceded by most, and various arrangements are made to enable many *haredi* youths to obtain it. However, the value of a secular education, of Western culture generally, is still denigrated. And the *haredi* camp remains strongly anti-Zionist, at the very least, emotionally distant and unidentified with the Zionist enterprise. The ideological differences over the posture toward modernity remain on the whole unabated—in theory certainly, in practice generally. Yet so much *has* changed, and irrecognizably so. Most of the fundamental changes, however, have been across the board. What had been a stringency peculiar to the Right in 1960, a

"Lakewood or Bnei Brak *humra*," as—to take an example that we shall later discuss—*shiurim* (minimal requisite quantities) had become, in the 1990s, a widespread practice in modern Orthodox circles, and among its younger members, an axiomatic one. The pheonomena were, indeed, most advanced among the *haredim* and were to be found there in a more intensive form. However, most of these developments swiftly manifested themselves among their co-religionists to their left. The time gap between developments in the *haredi* world and the emerging modern Orthodox one was some fifteen years, at most.

It seemed to me that what had changed radically was the very texture of religious life and the entire religious atmosphere. Put differently, the *nature* of contemporary spirituality has undergone a transformation; the ground of religiousity had altered far more than the ideological positions adopted thereon. It further appeared that this change could best be studied in the *haredi* camp, for there it takes its swiftest and most intense form. With this in mind, I read widely in the literature of the *haredim*, listened to their burgeoning cassette literature, and spent more time than was my wont in their neighborhoods. I tried my best to understand what they were doing in their terms and what it meant in mine. And the more I studied them, the more I became convinced that I was, indeed, studying myself and my own community. I uncovered no new facts about them or us but thought that I did perceive some pattern to the well-known ones. As all these facts are familiar to my readers, the value of my interpretation depends entirely on the degree of persuasive correspondence that they find between my characterizations and their own experiences.

If I were asked to characterize in a phrase the change that religious Jewry has undergone in the past generation, I would say that it was the new and controlling role that texts now play in contemporary religious life. And in saying that, I open myself to an obvious question: What is new in this role? Has not traditional Jewish society always been regulated by the the normative written word, the Halakhah? Have not scholars, for well over a millennium, pored over the Talmud and its codes to provide Jews with guidance in their daily round of observances? Is not Jewish religiousity proudly legalistic, and isn't exegesis its classic mode of expression? Was not "their portable homeland," their indwelling in their sacred texts, what sustained the Jewish people throughout its long exile?

The answer is, of course, yes. However, as the Halakhah is a sweepingly comprehensive regula of daily life—covering not only prayer and divine service but equally food, drink, dress, sexual relations between man and wife, the rhythms of work and patterns of rest—it constitutes a way of life. And a way of life is not learned but rather absorbed. Its transmission is mimetic, imbibed from parents and friends, and patterned on conduct regularly observed in home and street, synagogue and school.

Did these mimetic norms—the culturally prescriptive—conform with the legal ones? The answer is, at times, yes; at times no. And the significance of the no may best be brought home by an example with which all are familiar—the kosher kitchen, with its rigid separation of milk and meat—separate dishes, sinks, dish racks, towels, tablecloths, even separate cupboards. Actually little of this has a basis in Halakhah. Strictly speaking, there is no need for separate sinks, for separate dish towels or cupboards. In fact, if the food is served cold, there is no need for separate dishware altogether. The simple fact is that the traditional Jewish kitchen, transmitted from mother to daughter over generations, has been immeasurably and unrecognizably amplified beyond all halakhic requirements. Its classic contours are the product not of legal exegesis, but of the housewife's religious intuition imparted in kitchen apprenticeship.

An augmented tradition is one thing, a diminished one another. So the question arises: did this mimetic tradition have an acknowledged position even when it went against the written law? I say "acknowledged" because the question is not simply whether it continued in practice (though this too is of significance) but whether it was accepted as legitimate? Was it even formally legitimized? Often yes; and, once again, a concrete example best brings the matter home. There is an injunction against *borer*—sorting or separating on Sabbath. And we indeed do refrain from sorting clothes, not to speak of separating actual wheat from chaff. However, we do eat fish, and in eating fish we must, if we are not to choke, separate the bones from the meat. Yet in so doing we are separating the chaff (bones) from the wheat (meat). The upshot is that all Jews who ate fish on Sabbath (and Jews have been eating fish on Sabbath for at least some two thousand years)[2] have violated the Sabbath. This seems absurd, but the truth of the matter is that it is very difficult to provide a cogent justification for separating bones from fish. In the late nineteenth century a scholar took up this problem and gave some very unpersuasive answers.[3] It is difficult to imagine he was unaware of their inadequacies. Rather his underlying assumption was that it *was* permissible. There must be *some* valid explanation for the practice, if not necessarily his. Otherwise hundreds of thousands, perhaps, millions of well-intending, observant Jews had inconceivably been desecrating the Sabbath for some twenty centuries. His attitude was neither unique nor novel. A similar disposition informs the multivolumed *Arukh ha-Shulhan*, the late-nineteenth-century reformulation of the *Shulhan Arukh*.[4] Indeed, this was the classic Ashkenazic position for centuries, one which saw the practice of the people as an expression of halakhic truth. It is no exaggeration to say that the Ashkenazic community saw the law as manifesting itself in two forms: in the canonized written corpus (the Talmud and codes), and in the regnant practices of the people. Custom was a correlative datum of the halakhic system. And, on frequent occasions, the written word was reread in light of traditional behavior.[5]

This dual tradition of the intellectual and the mimetic, law as taught and law as practiced, which stretched back for centuries, begins to break down in the twilight years of the author of the *Arukh ha-Shulhan*, in the closing decades of the nineteenth century. The change is strikingly attested to in the famous code of the next generation, the *Mishnah Berurah*.[6] This influential work reflects no such reflexive justification of established religious practice, which is to say that it condemns received practice. Its author, the Hafetz Hayyim, was hardly a revolutionary. His instincts were conservative and strongly inclined him toward some post facto justification. The difference between his posture and that of his predecessor, the author of the *Arukh ha-Shulhan*, is that he surveys the entire literature and then shows that the practice is plausibly justifiable in terms of that literature. His interpretations, while not necessarily persuasive, always stay within the bounds of the reasonable. And the legal coordinates upon which the *Mishnah Berurah* plots the issue are the written literature and the written literature alone.[7] With sufficient erudition and inclination, received practice can almost invaribly be charted on these axes, but it is no longer inherently valid. It can stand on its own no more.

Common practice in the *Mishnah Berurah* has lost its independent status and needs to be squared with the written word. Nevertheless, the practices there evaluated are what someone writing a commentary upon *Shulham Arukh would* normally remark on. General practice as such is not under scrutiny or investigation in the *Mishnah Berurah.* It is very much so in the religious community of today.

One of the most striking phenomena of the contemporary community is the explosion of halakhic works on practical observance. I do not refer to the stream of works on Sabbath laws, as these can be explained simply as attempts to determine the status, that is to say, the permissibility of use, of many new artifacts of modern technology, similar to the spate of recent works on definition of death and the status of organ transplants. Nor do I have in mind the halakhic questions raised by the endless proffer of new goods in an affluent society. I refer rather to the publications on *tallit* and *tefillin*, works on the daily round of prayers and blessings in synagogue and home, tomes on High Holiday and Passover observance, books and pamphlets on every imaginable topic. The vast halakhic corpus is being scoured, new doctrines discovered and elicited, old ones given new prominence, and the results collated and published. Abruptly and within a generation, a rich literature of religious observance has been created, and—this should be underscored—it focuses on performances Jews have engaged in and articles they have used for thousands of years.[8] These books, moreover, are avidly purchased and on a mass scale; sales are in the thousands, occasionally in the tens of thousands. It would be surprising if such popularity did not indicate some degree of adoption. Intellectual curiosity per se is rarely that widespread. Much of the traditional religious practice has been undergoing massive reevaluation and by popular demand or, at the very least, by unsolicited popular consent. In Bnei Brak and in Borough Park and to a lesser, but still very real extent, in Kiryat Shmuel and Teaneck, religious observance is being both amplified and raised to new, rigorous heights.

Significantly, this massive, critical audit did not emerge from the ranks of the left or centrist Orthodoxy, some of whose predecessors might have justly been suspect of religious laxity,[9] but from the inner sanctum of the *haredi* world, from the ranks of the Kolel Hazon Ish and the Lakewood Yeshivah. It issued forth from men whose teachers and parents were beyond any suspicion of ritual negligence or causalness. Morever, it scarcely focused on areas where remissness had been common, even on the left. Indeed, its earliest manifestations were in spheres of religious performance where there had been universal compliance. The audit, rather, has encompassed all aspects of religious life, and its conclusions have left little untouched. The best example and also one of the earliest ones, is *shiurim* (minimal requisite quantities). On Pesach evening one is obliged to a minimal amount of *matzah*—a quantity equal to the size of an olive. Jews have been practicing the Seder for thousands of years, and no one paid very much attention to what that *shiur* was. One knew it automatically, for one had seen it eaten at one's parents' table innumerable Passover eves; one simply did as one's parents had done. Around the year 1940, R. Yeshayahu Karelitz, the *Hazon Ish*, published an essay in which he vigorously questioned whether scholars had not, in effect, seriously underestimated the size of an olive in talmudic times. He then insisted on a minimal standard about twice the size of the commonly accepted one.[10] Within a decade his doctrine began to seep down into popular practice and by now has become almost de rigeur in religious, certainly younger religious circles.[11]

This development takes on significance when placed in historical perspective. The problem of "minimal requisite quantities" (*shiurim*) has been known since the mid-eighteenth century, when scholars in both Central and Eastern Europe discovered that the *shiurim* commonly employed with regard to solid food did not square with the liquid-volume *shiurim* that we know in other aspects of Jewish law. The ineluctable conclusion was that the standard requisite quantity of solid food consumption should be roughly doubled. Though the men who raised this issue, the GRA and the Noda Beyehuda,[12] were some of the most famous Talmudists of the modern era, whose works are, to this day, staples of rabbinic study, nevertheless, their words fell on deaf ears and were without any impact, even in the most scholarly and religiously meticulous circles.[13] It was perfectly clear to all concerned that Jews had been eating *matzot* for thousands of years and that no textual analysis could affect in any way a millennia-old tradition. The problem was theoretically interesting but practically irrelevant.

And then a dramatic shift occurs. A theoretical position that had been around for close to two centuries suddenly begins, in the 1950s, to assume practical significance and within a decade becomes authoritative. From then on, traditional conduct, no matter how venerable, how elementary, or how closely remembered, yields to the demands of theoretical knowledge. Established practice can no longer hold its own against the demands of the written word.

Significantly, this loss by the home of its standing as religious authenticator has taken place not simply among the modern Orthodox, but first, indeed foremost, among the *haredim* and in their innermost recess—the home. The zealously sheltered hearth of the *haredi* world can no longer validate religious practice. The authenticity of tradition is now in question in the ultra-Orthodox world itself.

This development is related to the salient events of Ashkenazic Jewish history of the past century.[14] In the multiethnic corporate states of Central and Eastern Europe, nationalities lived for hundreds of years side by side, each with its own language, its own religion, its way of dress and diet. Living together, these groups had much in common, yet at the same time they remained distinctly apart. Each had its own way of life, its own code of conduct, which was transmitted formally in school, informally in the home and street—these are the acculturating agencies, each complementing and reinforcing one another. Equally significant, each way of life seemed inevitable to its members. Crossing over, while theoretically possible, was inconceivable, especially when it entailed a change of religion.

These societies were traditional, taking their values and code of conduct as a given, acting unself-consciously, unaware that life could be lived differently. This is best epitomized in the title of one of the four units of the *Shulhan Arukh*. The one treating religious law is called *Orah Hayyim* (The Way of Life). And aptly so. In the enclaves of Eastern Europe, going to *shul* (synagogue) in the morning, putting on a *tallit katan* (fringed garment), and wearing *pe'ot* (sidelocks) were for centuries the way of life of the Jew. These acts were done with the same naturalness and sense of inevitability as we experience in putting on those two strange Western garments, socks and ties. Clothes are a second skin.

The old ways came, in the closing years of the nineteenth century and the early ones of the twentieth, under the successive ideological assaults of the Socialist and Communist movements and that of Zionism. In the cities there was the added struggle with secularism, all the more acute as the ground there had been eroded over the previous half century by a growing movement of Enlightenment. The defections, especially in urban areas, were massive; traditional life was severely shaken, though not shattered. How much of this life would have emerged unaltered from the emergent movements of modernity in Eastern Europe, we shall never know, as the Holocaust, among other things, wrote finis to a culture. There was, however, little chance that the old ways would be preserved by the "surviving remnant," the relatives and neighbors of those who perished, who earlier had embarked for America and Israel. These massive waves of migration had wrenched these people suddenly from a familiar life and an accustomed environment and thrust them into a strange country where even stranger manners prevailed. Simple conformity to a habitual pattern could not be adequate, for the problems of life were now new and different.[15] What was left of traditional Jewry regrouped in two camps: those who partially acculturated to the society that enveloped them and those who decisively turned their back on it, whom we, for lack of a better term, have called *haredim*. They, of course, would define themselves simply as Jews—Jews resolutely upholding the ways of their fathers.

They are that indeed. Resolve, however, is possible only in a choice, and ways of life that are upheld are no longer a given. Borough Park and Bnei Brak, not to speak of Riverdale and Teaneck, while demographically far larger than any shtetl, are, as we shall see, enclaves rather than cultures. Alternatives now exist, and adherence is voluntary. A traditional society has been transformed into an orthodox one,[16] and religious conduct is less the product of social custom than of conscious, reflective behavior. If the *tallit katan* is worn not as a matter of course, but as a matter of belief, it has then become a ritual object. A ritual can no more be approximated than an incantation can be summarized. Its essence lies in its accuracy. It is that accuracy that religious Jews are now seeking. The flood of works on halakhic prerequisites and correct religious performance accurately reflects the ritualization of what had previously been routine acts and everyday objects. It mirrors the ritualization of what had been once simply components of the given world and parts of the repertoire of daily living. A way of life has become a *regula*, and behavior, once governed by habit, is now governed by rule.

If accuracy is now sought, indeed deemed critical, it can be found only in texts. For in the realm of religious practice (*issur veheter*), custom, no matter how long-standing and vividly remembered, has little standing over and against the normative written word. To be sure, custom may impose an added stringency, but when otherwise at variance with generally agreed interpretation of the written law, almost invariably it must yield.[17] Custom *is* potent, but its true power is informal. It derives from the ability of habit to neutralize the implications of book knowledge. Anything learned from study that conflicts with accustomed practice cannot really be right, as things simply can't be different than they are.[18] Once that inconceivability is lost, usage loses much of its force. Even undiminished, usage would be hard pressed to answer the new questions being asked. For habit is unthinking and takes little notice of detail. (How many people could, for example, answer accurately: "How many inches wide is your tie or belt?") When interrogated, habit replies in approximations, a matter of discredit in the new religious atmosphere.

There is currently a very strong tendency in both lay and rabbinic circles towards stringency (*humra*).[19] No doubt this inclination is partly due to any group's need for self-differentiation, nor would I gainsay the existence of religious one-upmanship. It would be unwise, however, to view this development simply as a posture towards outsiders. The development is also immanent. Habit is static; theoretical knowledge is dynamic and consequential, as ideas naturally tend to press forward to their full logical conclusions. "Only the extremes are logical" remarked Samuel Butler, "but they are absurd." No doubt. What is logical, however, is more readily agreed upon than what is absurd. When the mean is perceived as unconscionable compromise, the extreme may appear eminently reasonable.

It is one thing to fine-tune an existing practice on the basis of "newly" read books; it is wholly another to construct practice on the basis of books. One confronts in Jewish law, as in any other legal system, a wide variety of differing positions on any given issue. If one seeks to do things properly (and these "things" are, after all, God's will), the only course is to attempt to comply simultaneously with as many opinions as possible. Otherwise one risks invalidation; hence the policy of "maximum position compliance," so characteristic of contemporary jurisprudence, which in turn leads to yet further stringency.

This reconstruction of practice is futher complicated by the ingrained limitations of language. Words are good for description, even better for analysis, but pathetically inadequate for teaching how to do something. (Try learning, for example, how to tie shoelaces from written instructions.) One learns best by being shown, that is to say, mimetically. When conduct *is* learned from texts, conflicting views about its performance proliferate, and the simplest gesture becomes acutely complicated.[20]

Fundamentally, all the above—stringency, "maximum position compliance," and the proliferation of complications and demands—simply reflect the essential change of the nature of religious performance that occurs in a text culture. Books cannot demonstrate conduct; they can only state its requirements. One then seeks to act in a way that meets those demands.[21] Performance is no longer, as in a traditional society, replication of what one has seen, but implementation of what one knows. Seeking to mirror the norm, religious observance is subordinated to it. In a text culture, behavior becomes, inevitably, a function of the ideas it consciously seeks to realize.

No longer independent, religious performance loses, then, its inherited, fixed character. Indeed, during the transitional period (and for some time after), there is a destabilization of practice, as the traditional inventory of religious objects and repertoire of religious acts are weighed and progressively found wanting. For many of those raised in the old order, the result is baffling, at times infuriating, as they discover that habits of a lifetime no longer suffice. Increasingly, they sense that their religious past, not to speak of that of their parents and teachers, is being implicitly challenged and, on occasion, not just implicitly.[22] But for most, both for the natives of the emergent text culture and its naturalized citizens alike, the vision of perfect accord between precept and practice beckons to a brave new world. And as ideas are dynamic and consequential, that vision beckons also to an expanding world and of unprecedented consistency. The eager agenda of the religious community has, understandably, now become the translation of the ever increasing knowledge of the Divine norm into the practice of the Divine service.

So large an endeavor and so ambitious an aspiration are never without implications.[23] Translation entails, first, grasping an idea in its manifold fullness and then executing it in practice. This gives rise to a performative spirituality, not unlike that of the arts, with all its unabating tension. What is at stake here, however, is not fidelity to some personal vision, but to what is perceived as the Divine Will. Though the intensity of the strain may differ between religion and art, the nature of the tension is the same, for it springs from the same limitations in human comprehension and implementation. Knowledge rarely yields finality. Initially, thought does indeed narrow the range of interpretation by detecting weaknesses in apparent options, but almost invariably, it ends with presenting the inquirer with a number of equally possible understandings, each making a comparable claim to fidelity. Performance, however, demands choice, insistent and continuous. Whatever the decisions, their implementation is then beset by the haunting disparity between vision and realization, reach and grasp.

A tireless quest for absolute accuracy, for "perfect fit"—faultless congruence between conception and performance—is the hallmark of contemporary religiousity. The search is dedicated and unremitting; yet it invariably falls short of success. For spiritual life is an attempt, as a great pianist once put it, to play music that is better than it can be played. Such an endeavor may finally become so heavy with strain that it can no longer take wing, or people may simply weary of repeated failure, no matter how inspired. The eager toil of one age usually appears futile to the next, and the performative aspiration, so widespread now, may soon give way to one of a wholly different kind, even accompanied by the derision that so often attends the discarding of an ideal. Yet this Sisyphean spirituality will never wholly disappear, for there will always be those who hear the written notes and who find in absolute fidelity the most sublime freedom.

In all probability, so ardous an enterprise would not have taken so wide a hold had it not also answered some profound need. "The spirit blows where it listeth" is often true of individuals, rarely of groups. The process we have described began roughly in the mid-1950s,[24] gathered force noticeably in the next decade, and by the mid-1970s was well on its way to being, if it had not already become, the dominant mode of religiosity. The shift of authority to text, though born of migration. did not then occur among the immigrants themselves but among their children or their children's children.[25] This is true even of the post-Holocaust immigration. *Haredi* communities had received a small, but significant, infusion after World War II, which had strenghtened their numbers and steeled their resolution. Unlike their predecessors, these newcomers came not as immigrants but as refugees, not seeking a new world but fleeing from a suddenly beleaguered old one. And they came in groups rather than individually.[26] However, equally unlike their predecessors, they did not hail from the self-contained shtetl or the culturally isolated ghettos of Poland and the Pale. Few from those territories escaped the Holocaust. These refugees came from the more urbanized areas of Central Europe, especially Hungary, and their arrival in America was not their first encounter with the contemporary world.[27] The rise of the text culture occurred only after a sustained exposure to modernity, in homes some twice removed from the shtetl.

This exposure finally made itself felt, as the century passed its halfway mark, not in willful accommodation, God forbid, but in unconscious acculturation, as large (though, not all)[28] segments of the *haredi* enclave, not to speak of modern Orthodoxy, increasingly adopted the consumer culture and its implicit values, above all the legitimacy of pursuing material gratification.[29] Much of the *haredi* community took on an increasingly middle-class lifestyle. The frumpy dress of women generally disappeared, as did their patently artificial wigs. Married women continued, of course, to cover their hair, as tradition demanded, but the wigs were now fashionably elegant, as were also their dresses, which were, to be sure, appropriately modest but now attractively so. Elegant boutiques flourished in Borough Park. Ethnic food gave way to culinary pluralism, and French, Italian, Oriental, and Far Eastern restaurants blossomed under the strictest rabbinic supervision. Dining out, once reserved for special occasions, became common. Rock music sung with "kosher" lyrics was heard at the weddings of the most religious.[30] There had been no kosher jazz or kosher swing, for music is evocative, and what was elicited by the contemporary beat was felt by the previous generation to be alien to a "Jewish rejoicing" (*yidishe simche).* This was no longer the case. The body syncopated to the beat of rock, and the emotional receptivities that the contemporary rhythm engendered were now felt to be consonant with the spirit of Jewish rejoicing. Indeed, "Hasidic rock concerts," though decried, were not unheard of. The extended family of the old country (*mishpokhe*) gave way considerably to the nuclear one. Personal gratification, here and now, and individual attainment became increasingly accepted values. Family lineage (*yikhes*) still played an important role in marriage and communal affairs, but personal career achievement increasingly played an equal, if not a greater one. Divorce, once rare in religious circles, became all too familiar. The divorce rate, of course, was far lower that that of the surrounding society, but the numbers were believed to be sufficiently large and the phenomenon sufficiently new to cause consternation.[31]

Even the accomplishments of Orthodoxy had their untoward consequences. The smooth incorporation of religious practice into a middle-class lifestyle meant that observance now differentiated less. Apart from their formal requirements, religious observances also engender ways of living. Eating only kosher food, for example, precludes going out to lunch, vacationing where one wishes, and dining out regularly as a form of entertainment. The proliferation of kosher eateries and the availability of literally thousands of kosher products in the consumer market,[32] opened the way to such pursuits, so the religious way of life became, in one more regard, less distinguishable from that of others. The facilitation of religious practice that occurred in every aspect of daily life was a tribute to the adaptability of the religious and to their new mastery of their environment; it also diminished some of the millennia-old impact of observance.

Not only did the same amount of practice now yield a smaller sum of difference, but the amount of practice itself was also far less than before. A mimetic tradition mirrors rather than discriminates. Without criteria by which to evaluate practice, it cannot generally distinguish between central and peripheral, or even between religious demands and folkways. And the last two tended to be deeply intertwined in Eastern Europe, as ritual, which was seen to have a physical efficacy, was mobilized to ward off the threatening forces that stalked man's every step in a world precariously balanced between the powers of good and evil (*sitra ahara).* The rituals of defense, drawn from the most diverse sources, were religiously inflected, for the Jew knew that what lay in wait for him was not goblins, as the peasant thought, but *shedim*, and that these agents of the *sitra ahara* could be defeated only by the proven weapons of traditional lore. Prophylactic ritual flourished as it served the roles of both religion and science. Its rites were thoroughly intertwined with the normative ones and, to most, indistinguishable from one another. Joined in the struggle for health, for example, were amulets, blessings, incantations, and prayers.[33] In the world now inhabited by religious Jewry, however, the material environment has been controlled by a neutral technology and an animistic, value-driven cosmos replaced by a mechanistic and indifferent one. Modernity has thus defoliated most of these practices and stripped the remaining ones of their signifiance. People still gather on the eve of circumcision but as an occasion of rejoicing, not as a nightwatch (*wachnacht*) to forestall the forces of evil from spiriting away the infant.[34] A Jewish hospital differs from a Catholic one in the symbols on its walls and in the personal religion of its staff but not in any way in the procedures of health care. As religion ceased to be called upon to control directly the natural world, many vital areas of activity lost their religious coloration and, with it, their differentiating force.

It would be strange, indeed, if this diminution of otherness did not evoke some response in the religious world. They were "a nation apart," and had lived and died for that apartness. Their deepest instincts called for difference, and those instincts were not to be denied. Problems of meaningful survival were not new to religious Jews, and they were not long in evolving the following response:

> If customary observances differentiated less, more observances were obviously called for. Indeed, they always had been called for, as the normative texts clearly show, but those calls had gone unheeded because of the power of habit and the heavy hand of custom. The inner differences of pulse and palate may well have been leveled, and the distinctive Jewish ideals of appearance and attractiveness may equally have been lost. This was deplorable, and indeed our religious leaders had long railed against the growing pursuit of happiness.[35] But small wonder, for people had failed to take stock in the New World. They had turned to habit and folklore for guidance rather than to study, and despite the best of intentions, their observances had been fractional. Even that fraction had been less than it seemed, for superstition had been confused with the law and on occasion had even supplanted it. Religious life must be constructed anew and according to the groundplan embedded in the canonized literature and in that literature alone. While this reconstruction was going on, the struggle for the inner recesses of the believer would continue as before, only now it would be bolstered by the intensification of religious practice. And there was hope for the outcome, for our moralists (*hakhmei ha-mussar*) had always insisted that "the outer affects the inner," that constantly repeated deeds finally affect the personality. As for the so-called stringency, some of it was simply a misperception based on the casual attitude of the past, much only legal prudence. As for the remainder—if there was one—that too was for the good, for there could not be too much observance when dwelling amid the fleshpots of Egypt.

An outside spectator, on the other hand, might have said that as large spheres of human activity were emptied of religious meaning and difference, an intensification of that difference in the remaining ones was only natural. Moreover, the more pervasive the influence of the milieu, the more natural the need of a chosen people to reassert its distinctiveness and to mark ever more sharply its identity borders. As the inner differences erode, the outer ones must be increased and intensified, for, progressively, they provide more and more of the crucial otherness. In addition, the more stable and comprehensive the code of conduct, the less psychologically threatening are the subtler inroads of the environment. The narrowing of the cultural divide has thrust a double burden on religious observance, as ritual must now do on its own what ritual joined with ethnicity had done before. Religious practice, that spectator might have added, had always served to separate Jews from their neighbors; however, it had not borne alone that burden. It was now being called on to do so, for little else distingushed Jew from Gentile, or the religious Jew from the nonreligious, for that matter.

But then, there always is a dissimilarity between what is obvious to the participant and what is clear to the observer.

Both participant and observer, however, would have agreed that it was the mooring of religion in sacred texts that enabled this reassertion of Orthodoxy's difference. And for those who sought to be different and had something about which to be genuinely different,[36] the 1960s in America were good years, as were the decades that followed. The establishment lost much of its social and cultural authority.[37] Anglo-conformance now appeared far more a demeaning affectation than part of the civilizing process by which the lower orders slowly adopt the refinements of their betters. The "melting pot" now seemed a ploy of cultural hegemony and was out; difference, even a defiant heterogeneity, was in. Not only in, but often it even told in Orthodoxy's favor. The repugnance in many quarters with the emergent permissive society stood the religious community's difference in good stead, and Orthodoxy's dissent from contemporaneity gained stature from the widespread disenchantment with modernity and with the culture that had brought it to pass.[38]

Not that the collapse of the WASP hegemony led to Orthodoxy's resurgence; rather, the new climate of inclusion reduced the social and psychological costs of distinctiveness; and in the new atmosphere, the choices of their parents seemed ever more problematic. What had appeared, at the time, as reasonable adjustments, now appeared as superfluous ones, some verging even on compromise.[39] This only strengthened the new generation's quiet resolve that in the future things would be different, which, together with a respectful silence and a slightly bemused deference, often accompanies the changing of the guard in a traditional society or in one that still takes its reverence seriously. To the children and grandchildren of the uprooted, the mandate was clear; indeed, it had been long prefigured. Judaism had to return now, after the exile from Eastern Europe and its destruction, as it had returned once before, after the Exile and destruction of the Second Temple, to its foundational texts, to an indwelling in what the Talmud had termed "the four cubits of the Halakhah."[40]

As separate as religious Jews may feel themselves to be from their irreligious and assimilated brethern and as different as they may be from them in many of their ways, nevertheless, they are historically part of the larger American Jewish community, and their reassertion of difference was one facet of that community's wider response to the conjunction of third-generation acculturation with the civil rights movement and with the decline of the WASP ascendancy. The rapid emergence of the text culture in the late 1960s and 1970s and its current triumph should be viewed alongside two parallel developments; the sudden centrality, almost cult, of the Holocaust, an event that had prior to the 1960s been notable by its absence in American Jewish consciousness,[41] and the dramatic rise in intermarriage that occurred in these same years. Intermarriage, which, until the mid-1950s, had been extraordinarily low and stable for close to a half century (4–6%), quadrupled in a dozen years (1968) to some 23 percent, and within the next two decades approached, if it did not pass, the 50 percent mark.[42]

Most of the children of the immigrants had decisively turned their backs on the old ways of their parents. Many had even attended faithfully the chapel of Acceptance, over whose portals they saw inscribed *Incognito Ergo Sum,* and which, like most mottoes, was both a summons and a promise.[43] Whether that promise was more real than illusory may never be entirely known, for only rarely could the summons be fully met. Most Jews had imbibed from their immigrant parents' home far too many culturally distinctive characteristics for them to be indistinguishable from the rest, not to speak of being joined with other ethnic groups in so intimate an enterprise as marriage. For the second generation, this sense of otherness was reinforced by the social and career exclusions they experienced at home and the growing crescendo of persecutions they witnessed abroad.

In the late 1950s and 1960s, however, otherness collapsed from both within and without. A third generation, raised in American homes, came of age just at the time when the civil rights and Black Power movements were discrediting racism in many circles. With this uprising, America discovered that it had been born, indeed, had long lived in, sin; and the establishment's sudden awareness of its centuries-long unawareness shook its confidence in its monopoly of virtue, a necessary illusion of any ruling class. Its agony and confusion over foreign policy, long an area of special establishment accomplishment, induced a further loss of nerve. The center ceased to hold; meanwhile, ethnic barriers were crumbling among the grandchildren of the immigrants, as were the enforced solidarities of discrimination. This was especially true on the campuses, where young Jews were found in inordinate numbers. Many of them no longer saw nor found any bar to intermarriage. Others now sought their uniqueness outside themselves, in the unspeakable deeds of the Nazis. What had been previously known as "the destruction of European Jewry" became simply "the Holocaust," a word that now resonated with new and singular meaning. Admittedly, the astonishing victory of the Six-Day War may have had to occur before Jews could dwell on their past victimization without fearing that it might be seen as a congenital defect. And probably only a new generation, unburdened by the complicity of silence, could bear aloft the memory of a frightful and premonitory past. But what is memorable, even inviolable, is not necessarily unique. The sudden, passionate insistence that the suffering of one's people was sui generis and incomparable with that of any other nation in the long and lamentable catalog of human cruelty betokens, among other things, an urgent need for distinctiveness, which must be met but cannot be satisfied from within, from any inner resources. Finding one's inimitability in the unique horrors that others have committed against oneself may seem a strange form of distinction, but not if there remains a powerful urge to feel different at a time when one has become indistingushable from the rest.

One can respond to a loss of identity borders by intermingling, by finding a new source of difference or by re-creating the old differences anew. And much of American Jewish history of the past generation has been the intertwined tale of these conflicting reactions. People respond to situations according to their temperaments and backgrounds. At the time, they appear divided by the different positions they adopt, as indeed they often deeply are. In retrospect, however, they also appear united by the shared burden of the need for reponse and by their common confinment to the solutions that lay then at hand.

Just as the religious response of difference should be seen not only in its own terms but also horizontally, as part of wider, contemporary developments, so too should its acculturation be viewed vertically: plotted on the long curve of the history of Jewish spirituality. The growing *embourgeoisement* of the religious community, repercussive as it was in itself, was also a final phase of a major transformation of values that had been in the making for close to a century, namely, the gradual disappearance of the ascetic ideal that had held sway over Jewish spirituality for close to a millennium.[44] While there was sharp division in traditional Jewish thought over the stronger asceticism of mortification of the flesh, the milder one of distrust of the body was widespread, if not universal.[45] The soul's control over the flesh was held to be, at most, tenuous; and without constant exercises in self-denial, there was little chance of man's soul triumphing over the constant, carnal pull. Certain needs and propensities had indeed been sanctioned and in the instance of martial relations even mandated by the Law. Sanction and mandate, however, do not mean indulgence, and the scope of what was seen as indulgence was broad indeed.[46] Natural cravings, if not closely monitored, could turn easily into uncontrolled desires; and while they need not be negated, they should be reduced to a minimum. To be sure, states of joy were encouraged by some, appropriate moments of rejoicing advocated by all; but joy, unlike pleasure, is preeminently a state of mind, for unlike pleasure it reflects not simply the satisfaction of a natural impulse but of a coming together of such a satisfaction with the experience of a value. Through a millennium of ethical (*mussar*) writings runs a ceaseless warfare between will and instinct, as does the pessimistic feeling that the "crooked timber of humanity" will never quite be made straight.

Little of all this is to be found in the moral literature of the past half century.[47] There is, to be sure, much criticism of hedonism; restraint in all desires is advocated, as is a de-emphasis of material well-being. However, what is preached is "plain living and high thinking," rather than any war on basic instinct. The thousand year struggle of the soul with the flesh has finally come to a close.[48]

The legitimacy of physical instinct is the end product of Orthodoxy's encounter with modernity that began in the nineteenth century, as the emergent movements of the Enlightenment, Zionism, and socialism began to make themselves felt in Eastern Europe; and the current, widespread acceptance of physical gratification reflects the slow but fundamental infiltration of the this-wordly orientation of the surrounding society.[49] This metamorphosis, in turn, shifts the front of religion's incessant struggle with the nature of things: the spiritual challenge becomes less to escape the confines of the body than to elude the air that is breathed. In a culturally sealed and supportive environment, the relentless challenge to the religious vision comes from within, from man's bodily desires. In an open but culturally antagonistic environment, the impulses from without pose a far greater danger than do those from within. On the simplest level, the risk is the easy proffer of mindless temptation; on the deeper level, the risk is cultural contamination. The move from a self-contained world to a partially acculturated one engenders a transformation of the religious aspiration, as the quest becomes not so much to overcome the stirrings of the flesh as to win some inner deliverance from the osmosis with the environment. Purity, as ever, is the goal. However, in a community that chooses, or must choose, not flight from the world, as did once the monasteries and as do now the Amish, but life within the larger setting, the aspiration will be less to chasteness of thought than to chasteness of outlook, more to purity of ideology than of impulse.

Religion has been described as "another world to live in." Of nothing is this more true than of the enclave, with its inevitable quest for unalloyed belief and unblemished religiosity. And the other world in which the religious Jews seek now to dwell and whose impress they wish to bear is less the world of their fathers than that of their "portable homeland," their sacred texts, which alone remain unblighted by the contagion of the surroundings.

But could the world that was emerging from these sacred texts be seen as differing from that of their fathers, whose ways the *haredim* so strove to uphold? Such a perception would have undermined the entire enterprise of reconstruction. Memory now came to their aid, as did, unwittingly, the Holocaust. The world of their fathers had left no history, for like any traditional society, it had seen itself as always having been what it was; and when little has changed, there is little to tell, much less to explain. Of that world, there were, now, only the memories of the uprooted and the echo of those memories among their children; and memories are pliant, for recollection comforts as much as it recounts. Memories are our teddy bears no less than our informants, treasured fragments of an idealized past that we clutch for reassurance in the face of an unfamiliar present. The strangest and most unsettling aspect of the world in which the *haredim* now found themselves was its relentless mandate for change. Memory filtered and transmuted, and the past of *haredi* recollection soon took on a striking similarity to the emerging present. Nor was there, after the Holocaust, an ambiguous reality to challenge *their* picture of *its* past. The cataclysmic events of the 1940s gave a unique intensity to the reconstruction of the *haredim*, as no one else was now left to preserve the flame; it also gave them free reign to create a familiar past, of which the present was simply a faithful extension.

Among the immigrants, especially those of the post–World War II wave, this new past was, in many ways, the creature of recollection[50] but not among their offspring. Nor could the memory of the parents now be transmitted, as in the past, by word of mouth, for the children had acquired alien ways of knowing, even in the most sacred of all activities, the study of the Torah. Halakhic literature, indeed, traditional Jewish literature generally, has no secondary sources, only primary ones. The object of study from childhood to old age was the classic texts—the *Humash* (Pentateuch), the Mishnah and the *Gemara* (Talmud). For well over a millennium all literary activity had centered on commenting and applying those texts,[51] and every several centuries or so, a code would be composed that stated the upshot of these ongoing commentarial discussions. Self-contained presentations of a topic, works that would introduce the reader to a subject and then explain it in full in the language of laymen did not exist. There were few, if any, serious works that could be read independently, without reference to another text which it glossed.[52] Indeed, the use of such a work would have been deeply suspect, for its reader would be making claim to knowledge which he had not elicited from the primary texts themselves. Knowledge was seen as an attainment, something that had been wrested personally from the sources. Information, on the other hand, was something merely obtained, passed, like a commodity, from hand to hand, usually in response to a question.

Study of primary sources is a slow and inefficient way to acquire information, but in traditional Jewish society the purpose of study (*lernen*) was not information, nor even knowledge, but a lifelong exposure to the sacred texts and an ongoing dialogue with them.[53] *Lernen* was seen both as an intellectual endeavor and as an act of devotion; its process *was* its purpose. The new generation, however, obtained its knowledge in business and daily affairs, in all its walks of life, from books, and these books imparted their information in a self-contained, straightforward and accessible format. They saw no reason why knowledge of the Torah should not equally be available to them in so ready and serviceable a fashion, not as substitutes, God forbid, for the study of primary sources, but rather as augmentation.[54] Learning groups (*havrutot*) and classes in Talmud were now flourishing in the "new country" as never before, and the resurgence of these traditional modes of study could only gain by such a natural supplement. In response to this widespread feeling, the past twenty years have produced a rapidly growing, secondary halakhic literature, not only guides and handbooks but rich, extensive, topical presentations, many of high scholarly caliber.[55]

In Israel these books are in modern Hebrew; in America and England they are in English. And this constitutes yet a greater break with the past. Since the late Middle Ages, Ashkenazic Jewish society was "diglossic," that is to say, it employed both a "higher" and "lower" language. Yiddish was used for common speech and all oral instruction; Hebrew for prayer and all learned writing, whether halakhic, ethical, or kabbalistic.[56] The only halakhic works published in Yiddish were religious primers, basic guides written, ostensibly, for women—in reality, also for the semiliterate but viewed by all as "woman's fare."[57] Even Hasidic tales and aphorisms, concerned as the writers were to preserve every nuance of the holy man's Yiddish words, were nevertheless always transcribed in Hebrew.[58] Things have changed dramatically over the past twenty-five years. Admittedly, the revival of the Hebrew language in Israel and its attendant secularization have diminished some of Hebrew's aura as "the sacred tongue"; nevertheless, the emergence of a rich and sophisticated halakhic literature in English stems less from the fact that Hebrew has been desacralized than because English is now the mother tongue of the Anglo-Saxon *haredi* society, as is modern Hebrew to their Israeli counterpart.[59] The contemporary Jewish community is linguistically acculturated, unlike the communities of Eastern Europe, 80 percent of whom, in Poland, for example, still gave, as late as 1931, Yiddish rather than Polish as their first language.[60] The flood of works on halakhic prerequisites and the dramatic appreciation of the level of religious observance are proud marks of the *haredi* resurgence. This flow and swift absorption are possible, however, only because that community has unwittingly adopted the alien ways of knowing of the society in which it is enmeshed and whose language it now intuitively speaks.

With this acculturation came also the discovery of "the historicity of things." The secular education of many of the *haredim* was rudimentary, but it was enough for them to know that the record of the past is found in books. Any doubt of this was put to rest by experience. In life, one had to anticipate the future, in some way, so as better to get a handle on it. The only way to do that was by knowing the past—one's medical past, the past performance of a stock, of a business, or of a politician. There could be little memory of such pasts, but there was information, written records, and from these documents, a "history" could be reconstructed. If all else had a history, they too had one. To be sure, theirs was not "History," in the upper case, the sacred, archetypical record of the Bible and Midrash, with its "eternal contemporaneity,"[61] but the more mundane sort, "history" in the lower case, replete with random figures and chance happenings. Hardly paradigmatic for posterity, still it was sufficiently significant to its immediate successors to merit their pondering its lessons. So alongside the new genre of secondary works in Halakhah, there has appeared, in the past generation, a second genre, equally unfamiliar to their fathers—that of "history," written accounts of bygone events and biographies of great Torah scholars of the recent past, images of a nation's heritage that once would have been impaired by the vibrant voices of home and street but now must be conveyed, like so much else in the "new world," by means of book and formal instruction.[62]

These works wear the guise of history, replete with names and dates and footnotes, but their purpose is that of memory, namely, to sustain and nurture, to inform in such a way as to ease the task of coping. As rupture is unsettling, especially to the traditional, these writings celebrate identity rather than difference. Postulating a national essence which is seen as immutable, this historiography weaves features and values of the present with real and supposed events of the past. It is also hagiographic, as sacred history often is. Doubly so now, as it must also provide the new text culture with its heroes and its educators with their exemplars of conduct.

Didactic and ideological, this "history" filters untoward facts and glosses over the darker aspects of the past. Indeed, it often portrays events as they did not happen.[63] So does memory; memory, however, transmutes unconsciously, whereas the writing of history is a conscious act. But this intentional disregard of fact in ideological history is no different from what takes place generally in moral education, as most such instruction seems to entail a misrepresentation of a harsh reality. We teach a child, for example, that crime does not pay. Were this in fact so, theodicy would be no problem. Yet we do not feel that we are lying, for when values are being inculcated, the facts of experience—empirical truth—appear, somehow, to cease to be "true."

If a value is to win widespread acceptance, to evoke an answering echo of assent in the minds of many, it must be experienced by them not simply as a higher calling, but as a demand that emerges from the nature of things.[64] When we state that honesty is "good," what we are saying is that, ultimately, this is what is best for man—what we call, at times, "true felicity," to distingush it from mere "happiness." We believe that were we to know all there is to know of the inner life of a Mafia don and that of an honest cobbler, we would see that honesty is, indeed, the best policy. The moral life makes claim to be the wise life, and the moral call, to most, is a summons to realism, to live one's life in accord with the deeper reality.[65] A statement of value is, in this way, a statement of fact, a pronouncement about the true nature of things.

When we say that crime doesn't pay, we are not lying; we are teaching the child the underlying reality that we believe in or intuit, rather than the distorted one of our fragmentary experience. Just as moral instruction imparts the lessons of a reality deeper than the one actually perceived, so too must sacred history reflect, to the believer, the underlying realities of the past, rather than the distortions arising from the contingencies of experience coupled with the haphazardness of documentation.

And the underlying reality of Jewish history to the *haredim* has been the Covenant that they had sealed with the Lord long ago at Sinai and which alone explains their miraculous continuance. There had been backsliding enough in their long and stiff-necked history, for which the foretold price had been exacted with fearful regularity. But when they had lived rightly, they had done so by compliance with that pact, living, as it were, "by the book"—abiding fully in their "portable homeland" and living only by the lights of His sacred texts. How else *could* the People of the Book have lived?

So alongside its chiaroscuro portrait of the past—the unremitting struggle between the sons of Light and Darkness—common to all sacred history, comes the distinctive *haredi* depiction of the society of yesteryear, the world of their fathers, as a model of text-based religiosity, of which their own is only a faithful extension. The past is cast in the mold of the present, and the current text-society emerges not as a product of the twin ruptures of migration and acculturation but as simply an ongoing reflection of the unchanging essence of Jewish history.

And before we reject out of hand this conception of the past, we would do well to remember, even if it be only for a moment, that at the bar of Jewish belief and perhaps even over the longer arc of Jewish history, it is the mimetic society "moving easy in harness" that must one day render up an account of itself.

Though born of migration and acculturation and further fueled, as we shall see, by the loss of a religious cosmology, the current grounding of religion in written norms is well suited to, indeed, in a sense is even sustained by the society in which Orthodox Jews now find themselves. Religion is a move against the grain of the tangible, but only for the very few can it be entirely that. As deeply as any ideology may stand apart from, even in stark opposition to, its contemporary environment, if this outlook is to be shared beyond the confines of a small band of elite souls, who need no supportive experience to confirm them in their convictions, its beliefs must in some way correspond to, or at the very least somehow be consonant with, the world of people and things that is daily experienced.

The old religiosity of prescriptive custom fitted in well with, indeed could be seen as a natural extension of, the Eastern European pattern of authority, of compliance with accustomed ways and submission to long-standing prerogative. Authority came with age in the old country. The present received its empowerment from the past, so it seemed only right and natural to do things the way they always had been done.

The world now experienced by religious Jews—indeed by all—is rule-oriented and, in the broadest sense of the term, rational. Modern society is governed by regulations, mostly written, and interpreted by experts accounting for their decisions in an ostensibly reasoned fashion. The sacred world of the Orthodox and the secular one that envelops them function similarly. While sharing, of course, no common source, they do share a similar manner of operation. As men, moreover, now submit to rule rather than to custom, the Orthodox and the modern man also share a common mode of legitimacy; that is, they have a like perception of what makes a just and compelling claim to men's allegiance, a corresponding belief in the kind of yoke people should and, in fact, do willingly bear. Religion can endure under almost all circumstances, even grow under most, but it flourishes more easily when the inner and outer worlds, the world as believed and the world as experienced, reflect and reinforce one another, as did a mimetic religiosity in a traditional society and as does now, to a lesser but still very real extent, a text-based religiosity in a modern, bureaucratic society.[66]

The shift of authority to texts and their enshrinement at the sole source of authenticity have had far-reaching effects. Not only has this shift contributed, as we have seen, to the policy of religious stringency and altered the nature of religious performance, but it has also transformed the character and purpose of religious education, redistributed political power in non-Hasidic circles, and defined anew the scope of the religious in the political arena.

A religiosity rooted in texts is a religiosity transmitted in schools, which was hardly the case in the old and deeply settled communities of the past. There the school had been second by far to the home in the inculcation of values. Basic schooling (*heder*) had provided its students with the rudimentary knowledge and skills necessary to participate in the Jewish way of life, while reinforcing and occasionally refining the norms instilled in the family circle. The advanced instruction (yeshivah) given a small elite was predominantly academic, cultivating, intellectual virtuosity and providing its students with the expertise necessary for running a society governed by Halakhah. Admittedly, underlying all study was the distinctive Jewish conviction that knowledge gave values greater resonance and that in the all-consuming intellectual passion that was called love of "learning," as in mundane love to which it was compared, the self was submerged, and one fused with that toward which one strained: understanding, the truth—the Torah.[67] And indeed, more was demanded of those who knew more. Useful as this cultural expectation may have been in tempering both behavior and character and in moderating, perhaps, the prerogative of a clergy, it only intensified the emphasis on study in traditional education. The affective powers of knowledge were held to be so great that the need of schooling to concentrate on its acquisition seemed ever more essential.

Now, however, the school bears most of the burden of imprinting Jewish identity; for the shift from culture to enclave that occurred in the wake of migration means precisely the shinkage of the religious agency of home and street and the sharp contraction of their role in cultural transmission. This contraction has become ever more drastic in recent decades. Indeed, it verged on elimination, as a result of developments in the larger community, where, with the full advent of modernity, the sense of right and wrong was no longer being instilled at the hearth. The family in America, indeed, in the West generally, almost ceased to serve as the inculcator of values, and the home lost much of its standing as moral educator. While the religious home was generally stronger than the one of the host society, nevertheless, it too suffered from the general depreciation of parental authority and from their rapidly diminishing role both as exemplars of conduct and as guides to the true and the proper. As the neighborhood will not and the family now cannot adequately instill fealty to a way of life different from the one that envelopes them, formal education has now become indispensable for imbuing a religious outlook and habituating religious observance. The time spent by all in school has also been immeasurably lengthened, for convictions must be ingrained and made intimate, proprieties of behavior need to be imprinted by the deliberate enterprise of teaching, and for the impress to be durable, the individual must be kept in the mold during his formative years. So youth and early manhood too are now spent within the "walls of the yeshivah," for the current purpose of that institution is not simply higher education but also, indeed, predominantly an apprenticeship in the Jewish way of life.[68]

Having stepped into the breach left by the collapse of the traditional agencies of Jewish upbringing, the yeshivah has become a mass rather than elite establishment, more a religious institution than a academic one. To be sure, contemporary yeshivot seek to produce great scholars now no less than in the past and often successfully so, but currently their major function is molding the cadres of the Orthodox enclave, people whose religious character and countenance are a product not of home breeding but of institutional minting. Sensing this shift in the educational imprimatur, intuiting that the new source of religious identity entails changes in the old religious model, the enclave has already coined a distinctive term for the new, emergent exemplar, namely, the *ben Torah*, the young adult who will bear the yeshivah ethos throughout his life, despite continuous exposure to the invasive culture of the surroundings.[69]

So great is this transformation in the traditional role of education that, at the outset, very few perceived it. Nor, for that matter, was it immediately felt. It is remarkable just how scant a number of educational institutions were erected by the immigrants or by their children, and not for lack of energy or dearth of organizational impulse. No sooner were the new arrivals off the boat, than they created free-loan societies, burial societies, immigrant aid associations, and *landsmannschaften*. Synagogues, lodges, and ladies auxiliaries were formed, hospitals established, networks of social services instituted, and charities for every sort erected for local needs, for overseas kin, and for the nascent settlements in Palestine. Temples, communtity centers, and YMHAs soon dotted the residential landscape.[70] Jewish schools, however, were scarcely to be found. True, Hebrew schools were established in abundance, but attendance there ended with the onset of adolescence, and the education received was, at best, rudimentary. These were Americanized versions of the *hedarim* that the immigrants had known in the old country, imparting the basic skills of reading and writing Hebrew, only here they bore the additional burden of preparing boys for their Bar Mitzvah.

Nor did Orthodoxy present a much different picture. At the end of World War II, only thirty day schools of any sort existed in the entire United States, with a total student population of some 5,800.[71] Yeshivot were far, far fewer, and the population of these institutions was minuscule.[72] Seminaries for the training of rabbis had, of course, been swiftly erected by each and every religious stream—Orthodox,

Conservative, and Reform.[73] The need for rabbis was perceived by all, and all equally realized that rabbis were made rather than born. Jews, however, were seen as simply being born—for Jewishness was something almost innate, and no school was needed to inculcate it. And if there chanced to be some Jews who thought they had eradicated their Jewishness, one could always rely on the *goyyim* (gentiles) to remind them that they hadn't. To be sure, the ideology of the "melting pot" played a very significant role in this educational passivity, as did equally the natural aspiration of immigrants that their children receive native certification and imprimatur. Yet it would be a mistake to view this inaction solely as surrender or default. It stemmed also from the conviction that their children's *yidishkeyt* (Jewishness), like their own, was something deep in their bone, and that schools need not—in all probability, could not—instill it. Certainly, there was nothing in their own experience nor in the rich educational past of their Eastern European forefathers that could, in any way, have led them to think otherwise. Until midcentury, the children of the immigrants on the right imbibed their religiosity primarily from home and ethnic neighborhood, much as the children of their far more numerous brethren on the left and center imbibed their Jewishness from much the same sources.

And for a while, this sufficed. So palpable the heritage of the past, so primary and nonnegotiable in this period was the sense of Jewish otherness that intermarriage was a rarity; and so self evident was then Jewish identity that it was seen as concordant with the widest variety of views. Indeed, this identity dwelled in vigorous harmony with what, at least in retrospect, seem to be the most incompatible ideologies. Jewish intellectuals and activists passionately advocated Jewish communism, Jewish socialism, and even "secular Judaism," though the same people, one suspects, would have been the first to smile at a similar claim of "Protestant communism" or secular Catholicism." These ideologies may well have been confined to a small and articulate minority, but large segments of the population shared their underlying assumptions—that the essence of Judaism lay not in law or ritual, but in a social vision (*yoysher*) and a moral standard of conduct (*mentshlikhkeyt*), that Jews, almost innately, shared this vision,[74] and that in the still moment of truth these values would rise to reclaim all allegiances.[75] To the immigrants and to those raised in immigrant homes, identity was fixed; it was ideology that was variable. The next generation, the first one to be raised in American homes, found identity to be anything but a given and ideological identification a necessity. The mimetic religiosity came to an end soon after the twentieth century rounded the halfway mark, at approximately the same time as "secular Judaism" was fading from the horizon, as were the low intermarriage rates.[76] Their common disappearance marked the end of the Eastern European heritage of self-evident Jewishness, the close of an age in which religious and irreligious alike, each in their own way, were Jewish by virtue of what they thought, were, in other words, still Jews by upbringing rather than by education.

Then—around midcentury—the hour of education arrived. Within the last fifty years, the number of day schools has leapt from 30 to 570; its population skyrocketed from under 6,000 to well over 160,000, while the count of advanced yeshivah students has increased more than fifteenfold.[77] The religiosity of the culture gave way to that of the enclave, and the mimesis of home and street was replaced by the instruction and apprecticeship of the school. Just how essential this instruction and apprenticeship are, even in the *haredi* world—indeed, even for its most insulated sector—may be seen in the numerous Hasidic yeshivot now in existence and almost all of recent origin. For close to two hundred years, Hasidism had looked askance at the institution of yeshivot, viewing them not only as competing sources of authority to that of the Hasidic rabbi (*rebbe*) but also as simply far less effective in inculcating religiosity than the Hasidic home and the local Hasidic synagogue (*shtibel*), not to speak of the court of the *rebbe* himself. To be sure, several dynasties with a more intellectual bent had founded their own yeshivot.[78] These, however, were the exception and not the rule. Moreover, these institutions addressed a tiny, elite body only, and their role in the religious life of the community was peripheral. Within the past thirty years, Hasidic yeshivot have become a commonplace, and attendance is widespread, as Hasidim have decisively realized that, in the world in which they must currently live, even the court of the holy man may well fail without the sustained religious apprenticeship of the school.

This apprenticeship is long and uncompromising, but it has proven surprisingly attractive. The prevalance of higher education in modern society makes the time now spent in the yeshivah quite acceptable, but it does not, in itself, make yeshivah attendance alluring. The draft exemption in Israel does, indeed, provide strong inducement; but this leaves unexplained the same resurgence of yeshivah in the United States and England. Unquestionably, the new affluence of the religious plays a major role in maintaining the new and growing network of schools. Wealth, however, enables many things, and massive support of higher non-career-oriented education need not necessarily be one of them.[79] The yeshivah has won its widespread support, and young men now flock to its gates, not only because it has become the necessary avenue to the religious perspective and behavior but also because it holds forth a religious life lived without the neglects and abridgements of the mundane environment. Resolutely set off from society, yet living in closest proximity to the ideals to which the larger community aspires, the yeshivah has, to some, all the incandescence of an essentialized world. Institutions of realization, such as monasteries, kibbutzim, or yeshivot, where the values of society are most uncompromisingly translated into daily life, often prove to be attended to youth's recurrent quest for the authentic. When the tides of the time do flow in their direction, their insulation from life appears less a mark of artificiality than a foretaste of the millennium, when life will finally be lived free from the pressures of a wholly contingent reality. Needless to say, such institutions have generally exercised an influence on society wholly disproportionate to their numbers.

What animates the yeshivah in so intensive a form also works its effect on the daily life of the enclave. One of the most striking phenomena of the religious resurgence is the new ubiquity of Torah study and the zeal with which it is pursued, something which had not characterized the previous generation, even in *haredi* circles. Classes in Talmud and Halakhah, at all hours of the day, have sprung up, numerous small study groups (*havrutot*) dot the religious community as never before, scholarly secondary works on halakhic topics are snapped up and read, and the institution of *daf yomi* (literally, "daily page") has become widespread. And the latter is emblematic of the wider developments. In 1923, an educational curriculum, as it were, of talamudic study for those outside yeshivot established a uniform "page a day" of the Talmud to be studied by Jews the world over. Its pace was rapid, and if scarcely conducive to profundity, nevertheless, it enabled the Talmud to be studied from beginning to end within seven years. For close to half a century, the institution languished, as both the pace and quantity were far too much for most. The past twenty years has witnessed its dramatic resurgence. The twenty thousand people who thronged Madison Square Garden in spring 1990 for the festive conclusion of the seven year cycle,[80] were, even after all allowances are made for the inevitable sightseers, still only a portion of those actually engaged in this enterprise. To meet the growing demand for Torah study and to further ease access to it, modern technology has been mobilized. Tapes of classes of Halakhah and of Talmud are widely distributed. These are played at leisure moments and when traveling to and from work. In the United States, there are toll-free lines, where a record of that day's lesson is available for those either too busy to attend *daf yomi* classes or who occasionally missed them. The traffic is so great, at times, that some communities have several lines operating simultaneously. Nor is this service restricted to the *daf yomi*. In major cities, there is now dial-a-*mishnah*, dial-a-halakhah, dial-a-*mussar* (ethics) and more.[81] To be sure, the level of instruction often leaves something to be desired, as might be expected of any mass enterprise; however, the broad-based aspiration and widespread effort are new and noteworthy.

To the religious, this is only proof again of their supernatural continuance and of the Divine assurance that regardless into what new and alien world the Torah may be cast, Jews will always return to it as their predestined home. The will to survival of any group, its determination to maintain its singularity and transmit it undiminished to the next generation, eludes, indeed, full explanation. However, the different guises that this will assumes and the reason one form is more effective at certain times than another do lend themselves to analysis.

For at least two millennia, Torah study (*talmud Torah*) had been axial to Jewish experience. Indeed, it was believed by Jews the world over to be necessary for their very existence as a people. As central as *talmud Torah* my have been to national identity, it had not been essential for the Jewish identity of the individual. That had come automatically with birth. Imbibed from infancy—first in the family circle, then from street and school—cultural identity is primordial. Coeval with conscious life, it is inseparable from it. In contemporary society, however, Jewish identity is not inevitable. It is not a matter of course but of choice; a conscious preference of the enclave over the host society. For such a choice to be made, a sense of particularity and belonging must be instilled by the intentional enterprise of instruction. Without education there is now no identity, for identity in a multiculture is ideological. Once formed, this identity required viligant maintenance, for its perimeter is continually eroded by the relentless, lapping waves of the surrounding culture. Assaulted daily by contrary messages from the street and workplace, enclave identity needs ongoing reinforcement: its consciousness of proud difference must be steadily replenished and heightened. Identity maintenance and consciousness raising are ideological exigencies, needs that can be met only by education. Not surprisingly, then, does the still mysterious impulse for Jewish survival—for the preservation of Jewish distinctiveness—currently translate itself into a desire for Jewish instruction, into an avidity for Torah study in all its varied forms. The necessity of *talmud Torah* to Jewish existence, which in the traditional society of the old country had been only a metaphysical proposition,[82] at most a religious belief, has become, in the enclaves of the new world, a simple, sociological fact.

If religion is now transmitted to the next generation by institutional education, small wonder that the influence of the educators has increased dramatically, especially the sway of the scholar, the one most deeply versed in the sacred texts. For the text is now the guarantor of instruction, as the written word is both the source and the touchstone of religious authenticity. This, in turn, has entailed a shift in political power in non-Hasidic circles.[83] Authority long associated in Eastern Europe with the city rabbi, who functioned as a quasi-religious mayor, has now passed, and dramatically so, to talmudic sages, generally the heads of talmudic academies—*roshei yeshivah*.[84] Admittedly, the traditional European rabbinate, urban, compact, and centralized, had no chance of surviving in America or Israel. It was ill-suited to the United States with its sprawling suburbs and grassroots, federal structure of authority. It was no less redundant in Israel, where the state now provides all the vital religious and social services previously supplied by the community (*kahal*), of which the rabbi was the head. However, the power lost by the rabbinate did not have to accrue necessarily to the *roshei yeshivah*. It is their standing as the masters of the book par excellence that has given them their newly found authority. In Eastern Europe of the last century,[85] the *rosh yeshivah* was the equivalent of a head of an advanced institute, distinguished and respected but without significant communal influence. He was appointed because of his mastery of the book, and to the book and school he was then confined. This mastery now bestows upon him the mantle of leadership.

And that mantle has become immeasurably enlarged, as the void created by the loss of a way of life (the *orah hayyim*), the shrinkage of a culture, manifests itself. Social and political issues of the first rank are now regularly determined by the decisions of Torah sages. Lest I be thought exaggerating, the formation of the 1990 coalition government in Israel hinged on the *haredi* parties. For months, Shamir and Peres openly courted various talmudic scholars and vied publicly for their blessings. Indeed, the decision to enter the Likud coalition lay in the hands of a ninety-five-year-old sage, and when he made public his views, his speech was nationally televised—understandably, as it was of national consequence.

Admittedly this need for direction and imprimatur is partly the product of the melding of Hasidic and *misnaggdic* ways of life, as the two joined forces against modernity. The Hasidim have adopted the mode of talmudic study and some of the ideology of *misnaggdim*. In turn, the *misnaggdim* have adopted some of the dress of the Hasidim and something of the authority figure who provides guidance in the tangled problems of life. This blending of religious styles is, to be sure, part of the story, but the crisis of confidence in religious circles is no less a part.

This new deference is surprising, as political issues generally lie beyond the realm of law, certainly of Jewish law (Halakhah), which is almost exclusively private law. When political issues do fall within its sphere, many of the determinative elements—attainability of goals, competing priorities, trade-offs, costs—are not easily reducible to legal categories. Yet the political sphere has now come, and dramatically so, within the religious orbit.

Political reactions are not innate. Opinions on public issues are formed by values and ways of looking at things. In other words, they are cultural. What had been lost, however, in migration was precisely a "culture." A way of life is not simply a habitual manner of conduct but also, indeed above all, a coherent one. It encompasses the web of perceptions and values that determines the way the world is assessed and the posture one assumes toward it. Feeling now bereft, however, of its traditional culture, intuiting something akin to assimilation in a deep, if not obvious way, the acculturated religious community has lost confidence in its own reflexes and reactions. Sensing some shift in its operative values, the enclave is no longer sure that its intuitions and judgments are what it has aptly termed—"Torah-true."[86] It turns, then, to the only sources of authenticity, the masters of the book, and relies on *their* instincts and *their* assessments for guidance. Revealingly, it calls these assessments *da'as Torah*—the "Torah-view" or the "Torah-opinion."[87]

To be sure, shifts in power are rarely without struggle, and authority that appears, from without, as total and monolithic is only too often partial and embattled when seen from within. And *da'as Torah* is no exception. Much of the current politics in some religious organizations in America[88] and certainly the rivalry between certain *haredi* parties in Israel (Agudat Yisrael and Degel Ha-Torah) reflect the clash between the old order and the new power of the *roshei yeshivah*. This, however, is never stated publicly—indeed, *can* never be stated publicly—for in the religious atmosphere that now prevails, especially among the younger generations, the primacy of *da'as Torah* is almost axiomatic.

One could hardly overemphasize the extent of the transformation. The lay communal leadership had always reserved political and social areas for itself. Even in the periods of maximum rabbinic influence, as in sixteenth century Poland, political leadership was firmly in the hands of laymen.[89] Indeed, as there is no sacerdotal power in Post-Exilic Judaism, the structure of authority in the Jewish community is such that the rabbinate has social prerogative and deference but little actual power, unless the lay leadership allows them to partake in it. Lacking the confidence to decide, that leadership now shares its power with rabbinic authority to an extent that would have astonished preceding generations.[90]

Losing confidence in one's own authenticity means losing confidence in one's entitlement to power—that is, delegitmation—and a monopoly on authority swiftly becomes a monopoly on governance. It is the contraction of a once widely diffused legitimacy into a single sphere, and the change in the nature of authority that this shrinkage entails is the political tale told by the shift from culture to enclave.

Authority was broadly distributed in traditional Jewish society, for the Torah, the source of meaning and order, manifested itself in numerous forms and spoke through various figures. It was expressed, for example, in the home, where domestic religion was imparted; in the *shul* (synagogue), where one learned the intricacies of the daily Divine service and was schooled in the venerated local traditions; and in the local *beys medrash* (study hall), where the widest variety of "learning" groups met under different local mentors to engage in various ways in the study of the Torah (*lernen*). These and other institutions were linked but separate domains. Each had its own keepers and custodians who, in authoritative accents, informed men and women what their duties were and how they should go about meeting them.

The move from a corporate state to a democratic one and from a deeply ethnic to an open society meant a shift from a self-contained world to one where significant ways of thinking and acting received some of their impress from the mold of the environment. This acculturaton diluted the religious message of home and synagogue, compromised their authenticity, and finally, delegitimated them. Only the texts remained untainted, and to them alone was submission owed. As few texts are self-explanatory, submission meant obedience to their interpreters. The compartmentalization of religion, typical of modern society, shrinks dramatically religion's former scope and often weakens its fiber. But where belief still runs strong, this constriction of religion means its increasing concentration in a single realm and a dramatic enhancement of the authority of the guardian of that realm. The broad sway of their current prerogative stems from the shrinkage of the other agencies of religion, and it is the deterioration of these long-standing counterweights that gives this newly found authority its overbearing potential.

Thus, modernity has, in its own way, done to the non-Hasidic world what the Hasidic ideal of religious ecstasy had done to large tracts of traditional Jewish society in the eighteenth century.[91] This consuming aspiration marginalized synagogue, school, and family alike, for they could, at most, instill this pious ambition but scarcely show the path to its achievement. This, only the holy man, the *zaddik* could do. It also delegitmated the rabbi and the traditional communal structure whose authority and purposes were unlinked to this aspiration. Then, in the eighteenth century, the intensification of one institution depreciated the authority of the others; now, the devaluation of other institutions has appreciated the power of the remaining one. The end result is the same: a dramatic centralization of a previously diffused authority. This centralization is now all the more effective because modern communications—telephone, newspaper, and cassette—enables the center to have ongoing contact with its periphery as never before.[92]

This concentration of authority has also altered its nature. Some nimbus attends all figures of authority, for if one did not feel they represented some higher order, why else submit? Yet when authority is broadly distributed among father and mother, elders and teachers, deference to them is part of the soft submission to daily circumstance. There are, moreover, as many parents as there are families, and every village and hamlet has its own mentors. Their numbers are too large and the figures far too familiar for them to be numinous.

Concentration of authority in the hands of the master Talmudists shrinks the numbers drastically and creates distance. Such men are few and solitary. Moreover, they now increasingly validate the religious life of the many, as acculturation undermines not only authority but also identity. Even partial acculturation is a frightening prospect for a chosen people, especially for one that was bidden "never to walk in the ways of the Gentiles" and, faithful to that mandate, had long "dwelt alone." Threatened with a loss of meaningful existence, the enclave's deepest need is for authentication. Those who answer that need, who can provide the people with the necessary imprimatur, are empowered as never before. True, a divinity had always hedged great scholars in the Jewish past. Now, however, they validate religious life rather than simply embody it, and their existence is a necessity, not simply a blessing. To a community of progressively derivative identity, these guarantors of meaning appear unique and wholly other, as if some chaste and potent spirit "inhabited them like a tabernacle." Though grounded in verifiable, intellectual excellence, their authority has become ever more charismatic. Proof of that spiritual singularity, of their religious election, is now provided by the growing accounts of their supernatural power. The non-Hasidic culture, in which the mockery of the miraculous doings of holy men had been, in the past, a comic leitmotif,[93] has currently begun to weave its own web of wonder stories around the figure of the talmudic sage.[94]

The increasing fusion of the roles of *rosh-yeshivah* and Hasidic rabbi is, then, not simply a blending of religious styles, as noted before, but flows also from a growing identity in the nature of their authority. For religious Jews sense that in the modern world, which they must now inhabit, unblemished knowledge of the Divine mandate is vouchsafed to few, and that religious authenticity is now as rare and as peremptory as was once the gift for Divine communion in the old, enclosed world in which they had long lived.

I have discussed the disappearance of a way of life and the mimetic tradition. I believe, however, the transformations in the religious enclave, including the *haredi* sector, go much deeper and affect fundamental beliefs. Assessments of other peoples' inner convictions are always conjectural and perhaps should be attempted only in a language in which the subjunctive mood is still in vigorous use. I can best convey my impression—and I emphasize that it is no more than an impression—by sharing a personal experience.

In 1959, I went to Israel before the High Holidays. Having grown up in Boston and never having had an opportunity to pray in a *haredi* yeshivah, I spent the entire High Holiday period—from Rosh Hashanah to Yom Kippur—at a famous yeshiva in Bnei Brak. The prayer there was long, intense, and uplifting, certainly far more powerful than anything I had previously experienced. And yet there was something missing, something that I has experienced before, something, perhaps, I had taken for granted. Upon reflection, I realized that there was introspection, self-ascent, even moments of self-transcendence, but there was no fear in the thronged student body, most of whom were Irsaeli-born.[95] Nor was that experience a solitary one. Over the subsequent thirty-five years, I have passed the High Holidays generally in the United States or Israel and occasionally in England, attending services in *haredi* and non-*haredi* communities alike. I have yet to find that fear present, to any significant degree, among the native-born in either circle. The ten-day period between Rosh Hashanah and Yom Kippur are now Holy Days, but they are not *Yamim Noraim*—Days of Awe or, more accurately, Days of Dread—as they have been traditonally called.

I grew up in a Jewishly non-observant community and prayed in a synagogue where most of the older congregants neither observed the Sabbath nor even ate kosher. They all hailed from Eastern Europe, largely from shtetlach, like Shepetovka and Shnipishok. Most of their religious observance, however, had been washed away in the sea-change, and the little left had further eroded in the "new country." Indeed, the only time the synagogue was ever full was during the High Holidays. Even then the service was hardly edifying. Most didn't know what they were saying, and bored, wandered in and out. Yet, at the closing service of Yom Kippur, the *Ne'ilah*, the synagogue filled, and a hush set in upon the crowd. The tension was palpable, and tears were shed.

What had been instilled in these people in their earliest childhood and what they never quite shook off was that every person was judged on Yom Kippur, and as the sun was setting, the final decision was being rendered (in the words of the famous prayer) "who for life, who for death, / who for tranquility, who for unrest."[96] These people did not cry from religiosity but from self-interest, from an instinctive fear for their lives.[97] Their tears were courtroom tears, with whatever degree of sincerity such tears have. What was absent among the thronged students in Bnei Brak and in other contemporary services—and lest I be thought to be exempting myself from this assessment, absent in my own religious life too—was that primal fear of Divine judgment, simple and direct.[98]

To what extent God was palpably present on Yom Kippur among the different generation of congregants in Boston and Bnei Brak is a matter of personal impression, and moreover, it is one about which opinions might readily and vigorously differ. The pivotal question, however, is not God's sensed presence on Yom Kippur or on the *Yamim Noraim*, the ten holiest days of the year, but on the 355 other—commonplace—days of the year: To what extent is there an ongoing experience of His natural involvement in the mundane round of everyday affairs? Put differently, the issue is not the accuracy of my youthful assessment, but whether the cosmology of Bnei Brak and Borough Park differs from that of the shtetl, and if so, whether such a shift has engendered a change in the sensed intimacy with God and the felt immediacy of His presence? Allow me to explain.

We regularly see events that have no visible cause: we breathe, we sneeze, stones fall downward, and fire rises upward. Around the age of two or three, the child realizes that these events do not happen of themselves but are made to happen; they are, to use adult terms, "caused." He also realizes that often the forces that make things happen cannot be seen but that older people, with more experience of the world, know what they are. So begins the incessant questioning: "Why does . . . ?" The child may be told that the invisible forces behind breathing, sickness, and falling are "reflex actions," "germs," and "gravitation." Or he may be told that they are the workings of the "soul," of "God's wrath," and of "the attractions of like to like" (which is why earthly things, such as stones, fall downward, while heavenly things, such as fire, rise upward). These causal notions imbibed from the home are then reinforced by the street and refined by school. That these forces are real, the child, by now an adult, has no doubt, for he incessantly experiences their potent effects. That these unseen forces are indeed the true cause of events, seems equally certain, for all authorities—indeed, all people—are in agreement on the matter.

When a medieval man said that his sickness was the result of the wish of God, he was no more affirming a religious posture than is a modern man adopting a scientific one when he says that he has a virus. Each is simply repeating—if you wish, subscribing to—the explanatory system instilled in him in earliest childhood, which alone makes sense of the world as he knows it. Though we have never actually seen a germ or a gravitational field, it is true only in a limited sense to say that we "believe" in them. Their existence to us is simply a given, and we would think it folly to attempt to go against them. Similarly, one doesn't "believe" in God, in the other explanatory system, one simply takes His direct involvement in human affairs for granted.[99] One may, of course, superimpose a belief in God, ever a passionate and all-consuming one, upon another casual framework, such as gravity or DNA. However, a God "believed" over and above an explanatory system, functioning *through* it as indirect cause, in brief, a God in a natural cosmology, is a God "believed" in a different sense than the way we now "believe" in gravitation or the way people once "believed" in God in a religious cosmology, a God whose wrath and favor were the explantory system itself.

God's palpable presence and direct, natural involvement in daily life (and I emphasize both "direct" and "daily"), His immediate responsibility for everyday events, *was* a fact of life in the Eastern European shtetl as late as several generations ago. Let us remember Tevye's conversations with God portrayed by Sholom Aleichem. There is, of course, humor in the colloquial intimacy and in the precise way the most minute annoyances of daily life are laid, package-like, at God's doorstep. The humor, however, is that of parody, the exaggeration of the commonly known. The author's assumption is that his readers themselves share, after some fashion, Tevye's sense of God's responsibilty for man's quotidan fate. If they didn't, Tevye would not be humorous; he would be crazy.

Tevye's outlook was not unique to the shtetl or to Jews in Eastern Europe; it was simply one variation of an age-old cosmology that dominated Europe for millennia, which saw the universe as directly governed by a Divine Sovereign.[100] If regularity exists in the world, it is simply because the Sovereign's will is constant, as one expects the will of a great sovereign to be. He could, of course, at any moment change His mind, and things contrary to our expectations would then occur—what we call "miracles." However, the recurrent and the "miraculous" alike are, to the same degree, the direct and unmediated consequence of His wish. The difference between them is not of kind but rather of frequency. Frequency, of course, is a very great practical difference, and it well merits, indeed demands of daily language, a difference in terms. However, this verbal distinction never obscures for a moment their underlying identity.

As all that occurs is an immediate consequence of His will, events have a purpose and occur because of that purpose. Rationality, or as they would have it, wisdom, does not consist in detecting unvarying sequences in ever more accurately observed events and seeing in the first occurrence the "cause" of the second. Wisdom, rather, consists in discovering His intent in these happenings, for that intent is their cause, and only by grasping their cause could events be anticipated and controlled. The universe is a moral order reflecting God's purposes and physically responsive to any breaches in His norms. In the workings of such a world, God is not an ultimate cause; He is a direct, natural force, and safety lies in contact with that force. Prayer has then a physical efficacy, and sin is "a fearful imprudence." Not that one thinks much about sin in the bustle of daily life, but when a day of reckoning does come around, only the foolhardy are without fear.

Such a Divine force can be distant and inscrutable, as in some strains of Protestantism, or it can be intimate and familial, as in certain forms of Catholicism. In Eastern Europe it tended toward intimacy, whether in the strong Marian strain of Polish Catholicism or in the much supplicated household icon, the center of family piety in the Greek Orthodox devotion. And much of the traditional literature of the Jews, especially as it filtered into common consciousness through the Commentaries of Rashi and the *Tzenah Re'enah*,[101] contained a humanization of the deity that invited intimacy. God visits Abraham on his sickbed; He consoles Isaac upon the death of his father. He is swayed by the arguments of Elijah or the matriarchs, indeed by any heartfelt prayer; and decisions on the destiny of nations and the fate of individuals, the length of the day and the size of the moon, are made and unmade by apt supplications at the opportune moment. The humor of Sholom Aleichem lay not in the dialogues with God but in having a "dairyman" rather than the Baal Shem Tov conduct them.[102] The parody lay not in the remonstrances but in their subject matter.

The world to which the uprooted came and in which their children were raised, was that of modern science, which had reduced nature to "an irreversible series of equations," to an immutable nexus of cause and effect, which suffices on its own to explain the workings of the world. Not that most, or even any, had so much as a glimmer of these equations but the formulas of the "new country" had created a technology which they saw, with their own eyes, transforming their lives beyond all dreams. And it is hard to deny the reality of the hand that brings new gifts with startling regularity.

There are, understandably, few Tevyes today, even in *haredi* circles. To be sure, there are seasons of the year, moments of crest in the religious cycle, when God's guiding hand may be tangibly felt by some and invoked by many, and there are certainly occasions in the lives of most when the reversals are so sudden, or the stakes so high and the contingencies so many, that the unbeliever prays for luck, and the believer, more readily and more often, calls for His help. Such moments are only too real, but they are not the stuff of daily life. And while there are always those whose spirituality is one apart from that of their time, nevetheless I think it safe to say that the perception of God as a *daily, natural* force is no longer present to a significant degree in any sector of modern Jewry, even the most religious. Indeed, I would go so far as to suggest that individual Divine Providence, though passionately believed as a theological principle—and I do not for a moment question the depth of that conviction—is no longer experienced as a simple reality.[103] With the shrinkage of God's palpable hand in human affairs has come a marked loss of His immediate presence, with its primal fear and nurturing comfort. With this distancing, the religious world has been irrevocably separated from the spirituality of its fathers, indeed, from the religious mood of intimate anthropomorphism that had cut across all the religious divides of the Old World.

It is this rupture in the traditional religious sensibilities that underlies much of the transformation of contemporary Orthodoxy. Zealous to continue traditional Judaism unimpaired, religious Jews seek to ground their new, emerging spirituality less on a now unattainable intimacy with Him than on an intimacy with His Will, avidly eliciting Its intricate demands and saturating their daily lives with Its exactions. Having lost the touch of His presence, they seek now solace in the pressure of His yoke.

## Notes

Several points very much need underscoring at the outset. First, the Orthodox community described here is of European origin. This essay does not discuss religious Jewry issuing from Muslim countries, commonly called *Sefaredim*, primarily because, unlike their Western brethren, their encounter with modernity is very recent. Second, it deals with *misnaggdic* and not Hasidic society, though I do believe that many of my observations apply to those Hasidic groups with which I am most familar, as Ger (Gora Kalwaria), for example. Nevertheless, Hasidic sects are so varied and my acquaintance with the full spectrum of them so spotty, that, despite their occasional mention, it seems wiser not to include them in the analysis. Third, the essay focuses on the *contemporary* communities of Israel, England, and America, each, alike, the product of migration. Contrast is made with the tradtional community of Eastern Europe of the past century. Migration is a sharp and dramatic rupture with the present, as well as with the past. People, however, can undergo change on their native soil, as did the Jews of Eastern Europe, in the waning years of the nineteenth century and early decades of the twentieth, as their long and deeply settled communities encountered the emergent movements of modernity. Not surprisingly, a number of the traits and some of the outlook described here first made their appearance, albeit in an inflected form, among the religious elite of these communities. This process intensified in the interwar period, in the wake of the successive dislocations of World War I and the Russian Revolution. No transformation is without roots and antecedents, and the current text culture is no exception. However, a nuanced filiation of each characteristic of contemporary Orthodox society lies beyond the scope of this study. Fourth, the transformations that were then set in train by the advent of modernity were first sensed by the Hafetz Hayyim. Indeed, in one sense, much of this essay is simply an elaboration of an insight he expressed in his ruling on women's education (see below n. 6).

As the transformations studied here generally occur first in the *haredi* world and only later spread to the modern Orthodox one, often a phenomenon discussed is currently to be found with point and clarity in the first community, but only incipiently in the second; in other cases, it is already found to an equal degree in both. Not surprisingly, my analysis shuttles to and from these two worlds. If some readers find this constant shifting and tacking disconcerting, I can only ask their forbearance. I am equally aware that some readers will occasionally feel that the developments that I describe as characteristic of the *haredim* typify already the world of modern Orthodoxy and, conversely, that some of the traits ascribed to the broader religious community are still only the hallmarks of the ultra-Orthodox. The transformations discussed in this essay are in the process of evolving, and where on the religious spectrum any given development stands at a given moment often depends on the location of the observer and the contingencies of his or her personal experience. I hope that these occasional and inevitable differences of perspective between author and reader will not detract from the overall suasion of the analysis.

Anyone who distinguishes between a traditional society and an orthodox one is drawing on the categories of Jacob Katz, set forth in print, somewhat belatedly, in 1986 (see below n. 16), but adumbrated over the past several decades in talks and colloquia. In general, the debt owed to Katz by all discussion of tradition and modernity in Jewish history exceeds what can be registered by bibliographical notation.

Two subjects are notably missing from the current presentation, ideology and women's education. The essay treats the factors contributing to the new power of the *roshei yeshiva*; it does not address, at least not adequately, the ideological climate that legitimated this shift in authority. While the religious practice of both men and women had in the past been mimetic, their educational paths had diverged: male instruction had been predominantly textual, female instruction predominantly mimetic. The disappearance of the traditional society and the full-scale emergence of the text culture could not fail then to impact on women's education. I hope to address both subjects in the future.

The ideas advanced here were first presented in a lecture at the Gruss Center of Yeshiva University in Jerusalem in March 1984, and then again, at a conference of the Kotler Center for the Study of Contemporary Judaism of Bar-Ilan University in the summer of 1985. I do not believe that I would have dared venture into an area well over 500 years removed from that of my expertise had I not known that the leading authority on *haredi* society, Menahem Friedman, agreed with my basic ideas. Friedman's article "Life Tradition and Book Tradition in the Development of Ultraorthodox Judaism" appeared in Harvey E. Goldberg, ed., *Judaism from Within and from Without: Anthropological Studies* (Albany: State University of New York Press, 1987), pp. 235–55.

This essay appeared in a somewhat altered form and with far fewer footnotes in Martin E. Marty and R. Scott Appleby, eds., *Accounting for Fundamentalism* (Chicago: Chicago University Press, 1994).

Hebrew and Yiddish, though sharing a common alphabet, have different rules of transliteration. The different spellings employed for identical letters, even identical words, depend on whether a Yiddish or Hebrew word is being transcribed.

Working far from my habitat, I was very fortunate in my friends and critics. Arnold Band, Yisrael Bartal, Menahem Ben-Sasson, David Berger, Saul Berman, Louis Bernstein, Marion Bodian, Mordecai Breuer, Richard Cohen, David Ebner, Yaakov Elman, Emanuel Etkes, David Fishman, Rivka (Dida) Frankel, Avraham Gan-Zvi, Zvi Gitelman, David Goldenberg, Judah Goldin, Jeffrey Gurock, Lillian and Oscar Handlin, Samuel Heilman, Jacob Katz, Steven Katz, Benjamin Kedar, Norman Lamm, Leo Levin, Charles Liebman, Mosheh Meiselman, Jacob Rabinowitz, Aviezer Ravitzky, Sara Reguer, David Roskies, Tamar and Yaakov Ross, Sol Roth, Anita Shapira, David Shatz, Margalit and Shmuel Shilo, Michael Silber, Emmanuel Sivan, Chana and Daniel Sperber, Prudence Steiner, Aviva and Shlomo Sternberg, Yaakov Sussman, Chaim I. Waxman, Leon Wieseltier, Maurice Wohlgelernter, and Avivah Zornberg all read and commented on various drafts. Todd Endelman and Zvi Gitelman provided me with bibliographic guidance in the respective fields of acculturation and Eastern European nationalism. I am especially grateful to the Jerusalem-Constance Center for Literary Studies and its directors, Sanford Budick and Wolfgang Iser, who enabled me to present this study for discussion at their conference in Jerusalem in the late summer of 1991. Wolfgang Iser was kind enough to further spend a Friday afternoon with me discussing some assumptions of the essay. Had I followed all the wise counsel I received from my numerous readers, the final product would have been far better.

A final debt must be gratefully acknowledged. Without the unfailing assistance of the staffs of both the Gottesman and Pollack libraries of the Yeshiva University, especially Rabbi Dov Mandelbaum, Zvi Ehrenyi, Hayyah Gordon, and John Moryl, much of the research for this essay would scarcely have been accomplished.

1. The term *haredi* has gained recent acceptance among scholars because of its relative neutrality. Designations such as "ultra-Orthodox" or the "Right" are value-laden. They assume that the speaker knows what "Orthodoxy," pure and simple, is or where the "center" of Orthodoxy is located.
2. Eating fish on Sabbath is mentioned in *Bereshit Rabbah* and was already noted by Persius, a Roman satirist of the first century. See Menahem Stern, ed., *Greek and Latin Authors on Jews and Judaism* (Jerusalem: Israeli Academy of Sciences and

Humanities, 1976), pp. 436–37. For the rich lore on fish and its consumption on Sabbath, see Stern's notes to the above-cited passage, to which should be added Ya'akov Nacht, "Dagim" *Sinai* 8 (1939): 326–33; idem, "Akhilat Daggim be-Shabbat," *Sinai* 11 (1942–43): 139–55; Moshe Halamish, "Akhilat Dagim be-Shabbat—Ta'amim u-Fishrehem," in Moshe Halamish, ed., *Alei Shefer: Mehkarim be-Sifrut he-Haggut ha-Yehudit Mukkdashim li-Khevod ha-Rav Dr. Alexander Safran* (Bar-Ilan University Press: Ramat Gan, 1990), pp. 67–87. (Popular lore has it that gefilte fish was introduced into the Sabbath menu to avoid the very problem of *borer*. Be the accuracy of this popular explanation as it may, gefilte fish is an East European dish, and Jews had been eating fish on Sabbath for some fifteen centuries before this culinary creation. Even in Eastern Europe, I know of no instance of someone being labeled a *mechallel Shabbas* and run out of town for eating "non-gefilte" fish. Indeed, in the famous communal ordinances against laxity in Sabbath observance, there is no mention of fish eating whatsoever. See H. H. Ben Sasson, "Takkanot Issurei Shabbat u-Mashme'utan ha-Hevratit ve-ha-Kalkalit," *Zion* 21 [1957]: 183–206.)

3. *Mishnah Berurah* 319:4. For critique, see A. Y. Karelitz, *Hazon Ish, Orah Hayyim* (Bnei Brak: n.p., 1973), 53:4. (For contemporary comments see Isaac Maltzan, *Shevitat ha-Shabbat* (reprint: Jerusalem, 1976) *Melekhet Borer*, fol. 10b–11b). This case has been used for simplicity's sake only. This mode of reasoning is atypical of its author, as we so emphasize in the text. Any of the rulings of the *Arukh ha-Shulhan* cited in n. 7 would have been far more typical. However, their presentation in the text would have been more complicated. The instance of *Orah Hayyim* 345:7, for example, would have entailed explaining details of the laws of *hotza'ah* and *'eruv*. The example of fish, once chosen, does, however, have its virtues. It illustrates at the same time (as does the ultimate *conclusion* of 345:7) that the emerging text culture of the *Mishnah Berurah* had its clear bounds. There were, then, limits to the critique of common practice, and the plausibility that widespread practice could be egregiously in error, while conceivable (see n. 7 end), was not fully entertained even by the Hafetz Hayyim. See also the article of Menachem Friedman, "The Lost Kiddish Cup," cited below n. 11.
4. R. Yehiel Michel Epstein, *Arukh ha-Shulhan*, first printed late in the author's life and parts even posthumously, in the years 1903–1909. See n. 6.
5. Haym Soloveitchik "Religious Law and Change: The Medieval Ashkenazic Example," *AJS Review* 12 (1987): 205–13. This phenomenon finds its most evident expression in the *Tosafot* on *Avodah Zarah*. Full documentation will be found in my forthcoming book on *yeyn nesekh*.
6. Israel Meir ha-Kohen, *Mishnah Berurah*. This six-volume work, which has been photo-offset innumerable times, was initally published over the span of eleven years, 1896–1907 and appears contemporaneous with the *Arukh ha-Shulhan*. Bibliographically, this is correct; culturally, nothing could be farther from the truth. Though born only nine years apart, their temperaments and life experiences were such that they belong to different ages. The *Arukh ha-Shulhan* stands firmly in a traditional society, unassaulted and undisturbed by secular movements, in which rabbinic Judaism still "moved easy in harness," R. Israel Meir Ha-Kohen, better known as the Hafetz Hayyim, stood, throughout his long life (1838–1933), in the forefront of the battle against Enlightenment and the growing forces of Socialism and Zionism in Eastern Europe. His response to the growing impact of modernity was not only general and attitudinal, as

noted here and below (n. 20 sec. c), but also specific and substantive. When asked to rule on the permissibility of Torah instruction for women, he replied that, in the past, the traditional home had provided women with the requisite religious background; now, however, the home had lost its capacity for effective transmission, and text instruction was not only permissible but necessary. What is remarkable is not that he perceived the erosion of mimetic society, most observers by that time (1917–18) did, but rather that he sensed at this early a date, the neccessity of a textual susbtitute. (*Likkutei Halakholt, Sotah* 21a [Pieterkow, 1918].) The remarks of the Hafetz Hayyim should be contrasted with the traditional stand both taken and described by the *Arukh ha-Shulhan, Yorch De'ah* 246:19. One might take this as further evidence of the difference between these two halakhists set forth in the text and documented in n. 7. One should note, however, that this passage was written at a much later date than the *Mishnah Berurah* at the close of World War I, when traditional Jewish society was clearly undergoing massive shock. (For simplicity's sake, I described the *Mishnah Berurah* in the text as a "code," as in effect, it is. Strictly speaking, it is, of course, a commentary to a code.)

7. Contrast the differing treatments of the *Arukh ha-Shulhan* and the *Mishnah Berurah* at *Orah Hayyim* 345:7, 539:15 (in the *Arukh ha-Shulhan*) 539:5 (in the *Mishnah Berurah*), 668:1, 560:1, 321:9 (*Arukh ha-Shulhan*) 321:12 (*Mishnah Berurah*). See also the revelatory remarks of the *Arukh ha-Shukhan* at 552:11. For an example of differing arguments, even when in basic agreement as to the final position, compare 202:15 (*Arukh ha-Shulhan*) with 272:6 (*Mishnah Berurah*). This generalization, like all others, will serve only to distort if pushed too far. The *Mishnah Berurah*, on occasion, attempts to justify common practice rather unpersuasively, as in the instance of eating fish on Sabbath, (319:4), cited above n. 3, and de facto, ratifies the contemporary *eruv* (345:7). Nor did the *Arukh ha-Shulhan* defend every common practice; see, for example, *Orah Hayyim* 551:23. (S. Z. Leiman has pointed out to me the distinction between the *Arukh ha-Shulhan* and the *Mishnah Berurah* is well mirrored in their respective positions as to the need for requisite *shiurim* in the standard *tallit katan*, noted by Rabbi E. Y. Waldenburg in the recently published twentieth volume of his *Tzitz Eliezer* [Jerusalem, 1994], no. 8, a responsum that itself epitomizes the tension between the mimetic culture and the emerging textual one.)
8. To give a simple example: blessings over food (*birkhot ha-nehenin*) is a classic area of the mimetic tradition. The five basic *berakhot* are taught to children as soon as they begin to speak, and, by the age of four or five, their recitation is already reflexive. Grade school adds a few refinements and pointers about compounds, such as, sandwiches, or hot dogs, and there things more or less stand for the rest of one's life. Or at least, so it stood in the past. This is no longer so. In 1989 *The Hakachos of Berachos* by Yisroel P. Bodner appeared in both hardcover and paperback form and has been reprinted three times in as many years. Nevertheless, it did not slake the current thirst, for 1990 saw the appearance in the Art Scroll Series of *The Law of Berachos* by Binyamin Furst, a large and full tome of some 420 pages (Bodner's work was only 289 pages), and which, within a year, was already into its third printing! (The Bodner volume was printed in Lakewood, New Jersey, and copyrighted by the author; the Art Scroll book was printed by Mesorah Publications, New York.) (A comparison becomes all the more telling if one considers that attempts at translation and mass diffusion, analogous—in a sense—to Art Scroll, were made of both these books. The

*Seder Birkhot ha-Nehnin* of the *Shulhan Arukh of the Rav* was translated into Yiddish [Wilno, 1851] as was the *Hayyei Adam* [Wilno, 1884]. The popular handbooks of or those that included *birkhot ha-nehenin*, such as the *Kehillat Shelomoh* of Shelomoh Zalman London or the *Birkhot Menahem* of Gershon Menahem Mendel Shapira, are skeletal. [In the attempt at popularization, the translators of the *Hayyei Adam* felt they needed, in addition to the discussions of the original, a straightforward product guide and incorporated that of the *Birkhot Menahem.* Even this combined text has nothing of the scope of the above cited English works.]) The Israeli counterpart is well exemplified by the two volumes, comprising some 630 pages, on the laws and customs of *'omer* and *sefirat ha'omer*, published recently in Bnei Brak, a subject that had rarely, if ever, rated more than a hundred lines in the traditional literature. (Tzvi Cohen, *Sefirat ha-Omer* [Bnei Brak: n.p., 1985], idem, *Bein Pesach le-Shevu'ot* [Bnei Brak: n.p., 1986.])

9. See, for example, Carol Silver Bunim, *Religious and Secular Factors of Role Strain in Orthodox Jewish Mothers* (Ph.D. diss. Wurzweiler School of Social Work, Yeshiva University, 1986), pp. 161–76.
10. The essay is now readily available in *Hazon Ish, Orah Hayyim, Mo'ed* (Bnei Brak: n.p., 1957), sec. 39 (*Kuntras ha-Shi'urim*). I have presented the famous upshot of his argument, germane to our discussion rather than the formal argument itself.
11. Menachem Friedman, "Life Tradition and Book Tradition in the Development of Ultraorthodox Judaism" in Harvey E. Goldberg, ed., *Judaism Viewed from Within and from Without* (Albany: State University of New York Press, 1987), pp. 235–38; idem, "The Lost *Kiddush* Cup: Changes in the Ashkenazi Haredi Culture: A Lost Religious Tradition," in Jack Wertheimer, ed., *The Uses of Tradition: Jewish Continuity in the Modern Era* (New York: Jewish Theological Seminary, 1992), pp. 175–86. (See also David Singer, "Thumbs and Eggs," *Moment* 3 [Sept. 1978]: 36–37.)
12. *Tzion le-Nefesh Hayyah (Tzlah)* (Prague, 1782), to *Pesahim*, fol. 116b; the opinion of the GRA is reported in the *Ma'aseh Rav* (Zolkiew, 1808).
13. This point needs underscoring. The scholarly elite lived their lives, no less than did the common folk, according to the mimetic tradition. They may well have tried to observe more scrupulously certain aspects of that tradition and to fine-tune some of its details, but the fabric of Jewish life was the same for scholar and layman alike. The distinction in traditional Jewish society was not between popular and elite religion but between religion as received and practiced and as found (or implied) in the theoretical literature. This is what distinguishes the mimetic tradition from the "Little Tradition" formulated by Redfield. See Robert Redfield, *The Little Community and Peasant Society and Culture* (Chicago: University of Chicago Press, 1960.)
14. Two points bear stating. First, because I am presenting the traditional society solely as a foil for my analysis of the contemporary condition, I present only those facts necessary for my argument. No world is homogeneous when seen from within; it admits of such a description only when viewed comparatively, as here. Second, Orthodox society is composed of Jews of Russian, Lithuanian, Polish, Galician, and Hungarian origin. In their contemporary form, these Jews have, I believe, common characteristics. When, however, one traces their past in a single paragraph, telescoping is inevitable. The dates given in the text are those that roughly approximate the Eastern European process. The Central European (i.e., Hungarian) encounter with modernity has its own time frame. Experiencing modernity without migration, Hungarian Orthodoxy

displayed, often in an inflected form, several of the characteristics of current *haredi* society. The tendency to stringency appeared there early, though one feels it was more a response to the allowances of the Reform than to the processes described here. Similarly, the return to texts expressed itself not in a reconstruction of religious practice, as the received ones remained much entrenched, as in a total submission to the text of the *Shulhan Arukh*, a work which hitherto had been of great, but not binding, authority. On Hungary, see Michael Silber, "The Historical Experience of German Jewry and Its Impact on the Haskalah and Reform in Hungary," in Jacob Katz, ed., *Towards Modernity: The European Model* (New Brunswick, N.J.: Transaction Books, 1987), pp. 107–59; and the latter's outstanding essay, "The Emergence of Ultra-Orthodoxy: The Invention of a Tradition" in Jack Wertheimer, ed., *The Use of Tradition: Jewish Continuity in the Modern Era* (above n. 11), pp. 43–85, and Jacob Katz's forthcoming work on Orthodoxy and Reform in Hungary, to be published by Mercaz Shazar, Jerusalem. The shtetl remained culturally isolated and wholly cut off from the surrounding gentile society to the end; see Ben Cion Pinchuk, *Shtetl Jews under Soviet Rule: Eastern Poland on the Eve of the Holocaust* (Oxford: Blackwell, 1990), pp. 12–20; Celia Heller, *On the Edge of Destruction: The Jews in Poland between the Two World Wars* (New York: Columbia University Press, 1977), pp. 7–20.

15. In these two sentences, I borrow and rearrange phrases from Oscar Handlin, *The Uprooted*, 2nd ed. (Boston: Little, Brown, 1973), pp. 5–6.
16. Jacob Katz, "Orthodoxy in Historical Perspective," in P. Y. Medding, ed., *Studies in Contemporary Jewry* (Bloomington: Indiana University Press, 1986), 2:3–17, and idem, "Traditional Society and Modern Society," in Shlomoh Deshen and W. P. Zenner, eds., *Jewish Societies in the Middle East* (Washington, D.C., 1982), pp. 33–47.
17. For a survey of the legal status of custom, see M. Elon, ed., *The Principles of Jewish Law* (Jerusalem: Keter Publishing House, 1975) s.v. *Minhag*. For overriding written law (*minhag mevattel halakhah*), see columns 97–99, and see "Laws of the Day of Atonement," in *Code of Maimonides, Book of Seasons* (New Haven: Yale University Press, 1961), 3:3; *Peri Hadash, Orah Hayyim* 496:2: 10; *Sedei Hemed, Ma'arekhet Mem, Kelal,* 39. (As consent is the controlling factor in most areas of civil law, common usage is usually taken as a self-understood, mutually agreed upon condition.)
18. The traditional kitchen provides the best example of the neutralizing effect of tradition, especially since the mimetic tradition continued there long after it was lost in most other areas of Jewish life. Were the average housewife (*bale-boste*) informed that her manner of running the kitchen was contrary to the *Shulhan Arukh*, her reaction would have been a dismissive "Nonsense!" She would have been confronted with the alternative, either that she, her mother, and grandmother had, for decades, been feeding their families nonkosher food (*treifes*) or that the *Code* was wrong or, put more delicately, someone's understanding of that text was wrong. As the former was inconceivable, the latter was clearly the case. This, of course, might pose problems for scholars; however, that was their problem not hers. Neither could she be prevailed on to alter her ways, nor would an experienced rabbi even try. There is an old saying among scholars, "A *yidishe bale-boste* takes instruction from her mother only."
19. Chaim I. Waxman, "Towards a Sociology of Pesak" *Tradition* 25 (1991): 15–19. As n. 40 points out, a dramatic swing toward *humra* occurred in the Ashkenazic community during the waning of the Middle Ages. However, as further noted there, what is comparable is not necessarily similar and the parameters of this essay are the last three

hundred years of Eastern Europe Jewish history. There was something akin to a movement toward *humra* in Ashkenazic society with the advent of Lurianic kabbalah. That movement is so complex that any comparison to contemporary developments is beside the point. Suffice it to point out that what fueled much of that impetus was the perceived theurgic nature of religious performances, which led equally to the creation of new religious rites. See Gerson Scholem, "Tradition and New Creation in the Ritual of the Kibbalists," in Scholem, *On the Kabbalah and Its Symbolism* (New York: Schocken Books, 1971), pp. 118–57. One of the salient characteristics of contemporary religious society is the disappearance among them of the animistic and symbolic universe that had nurtured this ritual impetus. Indeed, their intensification of ritual is partly a counterbalance to the defoliation of theurgic ritual that occurred in the wake of the acceptance by religious Jews, including the *haredi* sector, of the mechanistic cosmos of modern technology. See text below.

I find it difficult to view the *ba'al teshuvah* (new religious) movement as instrumental in the recent empowerment of texts, though the construction of religious life on the basis of texts is most noticeable with them, as they have no home tradition whatsoever. First, the process begins in *haredi* circles well before any such movement came into existence. Second, the impact of *ba'alei teshuvah* on such *haredi* bastions as Bnei Brak, Borough Park, and Stamford Hill, not to speak of such elitist institutions as the yeshivah, is less than negligible. It would be a mistake to equate their occasional prominence in the modern orthodox world, especially in outlying communities, with the deferential and wholly backseat role they play in the *haredi* order. Finally, the *ba'al teshuvah* movement is phenomenologically significant, not demographically.

20. (a) These tendencies have gained further impetus from the publication developments and the photo-offset revolution. The past thirty years have seen the publication of manuscripts of innumerable medieval commentators (*rishonim*), and photo-offset has further made them widely available. The number of different opinions currently available on any given issue far exceeds that of the past. One who has abandoned the past as a reliable guide for conduct in the present must now contend with a hitherto unheard of variety of views.

(b) Hasidim, arriving in groups, rather than as individuals, and clustering centripetally around the court of the *rebbe*, generally maintained the mimetic observance a generation or so longer than their non-Hasidic counterparts. However, the past fifteen to twenty years has witnessed the inital absorption of the younger male generation of some Hasidic groups, such as Ger, for example, into the dominant text culture. Similarly, many married women of Ger have begun to attend classes on practical religious observance, as ongoing supplements to their education. As Hasidic women have been, traditionally, among the most ignorant segments of the religious population, the proliferation of such classes is a major development. The current need for some manner of education for women is clear, though its practical implications are viewed as undesirable, and attempts made to neutralize them. Hasidic women are taught that, when in conflict, book knowledge always yields to home practice. See Tamar El-Or, *Educated and Ignorant* (Boulder and London: Lynne Rienner, 1994), pp. 89–135, esp. pp. 111–26.

(c) The contemporary shift to text authority explains the current prevalence in yeshivah circles of the rulings of the GRA. The GRA, while far from the first to subject the corpus of Jewish practice to textual scrutiny, did it on an unprecendented scale and with unprecedented rigor. No one before him (and quite possibly, no one since) has so often and relentlessly drawn the conclusion of jettisoning practices that did not square with the canonized texts. Great as was the GRA's influence upon the *mode* of talmudic *study* and awesome as was his reputation generally, nevertheless, very few of his radical rulings were accepted in nineteenth-century Lithuania, even in the yeshivah world. (To give a simple example: the practice in the Yeshivah of Volozhin was to stand during the *havdaleh* service as was customary, rather than to sit as the GRA had insisted.) See also Aryeh Leib Fromkin, *Sefeer Toldot Eliyahu* (Wilno, 1990), pp. 70–71. Seeking there to demonstrate, to an elite Lithuanian audience at the close of the nineteenth century, the uniqueness of his distinguished father and uncle, Fromkin points out that they were numbered among the very few who followed the rulings of the GRA. Most towns in Eastern Europe had traditions going back many centuries, and even the mightiest names could alter a practice here and there but could effect no wholesale revision of common usage. Indeed, the GRA's writ rarely ran even in Vilna (Wilno), outside of his own *kloyz* (the small synagogue where he had prayed). (I have heard this point made by former residents of Vilna. See also *Mishnah Berurah, Biur Halakhah*, 551:1, and note how rare such a comment is in that work.) Mark should be made of the striking absence of the GRA from the *Arukh ha-Shulhan, Orah Hayyim*, written by one who was a distinguished product of the Yeshivah of Volozhin and rabbi of that bastion of Lithuanian talmudism, Navahrdok (Novogrudok). Indeed, the first major work known to me that *systematically* reckons with the *Biur ha-Gra* is the *Mishnah Berurah* and understandably so, as that work is one of the first to reflect the erosion of the traditional society (see, above, text and n. 6). With the further disappearance of the traditional *orah hayyim* in the twentieth century, the ritual of daily life had to be constructed anew from the texts; the GRA's work exemplified this process in its most intense and uncompromising form and with the most comprehensive mastery of those texts. It is this consonance with the contemporary religious agenda and mode of decision making (*pesak*) that has led to the widespread influence of the GRA today in the yeshivah and *haredi* world. (See below n. 68.) (S. Z. Leiman pointed out to me that S. Z. Havlin arrived at similar conclusions as to the delayed influence of the GRA on *pesak* and further corroborated them by a computer check of the Responsa Project of Bar-Ilan University. He presented his findings, in a still unpublished paper, at the Harvard Conference on Jewish Thought in the Eighteenth Century, April 1992.) (1) I emphasize that my remarks are restricted to *pesak* and do *not* refer to modes of study. In the latter field, the GRA's impact was both swift and massive. (2) In light of my remarks above, I should take care to add that though the GRA is noticeably absent as an *authority* in the *Arukh ha-Shulhan*, that work is written in the spirit of the GRA, whereas the *Mishnah Berurah*, for all its deference to the GRA, is penned in a spirit antithetical to the one of the Gaon. The crux of the Gaon's approach both to Torah study and *pesak* was its independence of precedent. A problem was to be approached in terms of the text of the Talmud as mediated by the *rishonim* (and in the Gaon's case even that mediation was occasionally dispensed with). What subsequent commentators had to say about the issue was, with few exceptions (e.g., Magen Avraham, Shakh), irrelevant. This approach is writ large on every page of the *Biur ha-Gra*, further embodied in the *Hayyei Adam* and the *Arukh ha-Shulhan*, and has continued on to our day in the works of such Lithuanian *posekim* as the

Hazon Ish and R. Mosheh Feinstein. The *Mishnah Berurah* rejects de facto this approach and returns to the world of precedent and string citation. Decisions are arrived at only after elaborate calibration of and negotiation with multiple "aharonic" positions.

21. See also Michael Oakeshot, *Rationalism in Politics and Other Essays* (Indianapolis: Liberty Press, 1991), p. 474. The entire essay "The Tower of Babel" is relevant to our larger theme, as is the one announced in the title.
22. The impetus to *humra* is so strong and widespread that the principle of *le-hotzi la'az 'al rishonim* has, for all practical purposes, fallen into desuetude. (*Le-hotzi la'az* states that any new stringency implicity casts aspersion on the conduct of past generations and, hence, is to be frowned upon.)
23. I am addressing the intensification of ritual, not the nature of ritual in a highly performative religion, such as Judaism.
24. I make this observation on the basis of personal experience and conversations with members of the *haredi* community. The note of newness is noticeable in the 1954 statement of Moshe Scheinfeld, quoted in Menachem Friedman, "Haredim Confront the Modern City," in Medding, *Studies in Contemporary Jewry* (above n. 16), 2:81–82. On the exact text of that citation, see Chaim I. Waxman, "Towards a Sociology of *Pesak*," in Moshe Z. Socol, ed., *Rabbinic Authority and Personal Autonomy* (Northvale, N.J.: Jason Aronson, 1992), p. 225, n. 17. In Israel the trend had crystallized by 1963, but it was still viewed then, even by a perceptive observer, as a local phenomenon, characteristic of Bnei Brak and its satellite communities; see the citation of Elberg in Friedman's article (above n. 11), p. 235.
25. *Haredim* in America are at most third-generation, as there was no *haredi* presence or group formation in the period 1880–1920. See also Egon Mayer, *From Suburb to Shtetl: The Jews of Boro Park* (Philadelphia: Temple University Press, 1989), pp. 47–51, and Samuel C. Heilman and Steven M. Cohen, *Cosmopolitans and Parochials* (Chicago: University of Chicago Press, 1989), pp. 191–92. Orthodoxy in America is, indeed, older; however, the text culture emerges from the *haredi* community. Its aptness is sensed by the younger orthodox generation, the first generation that was not raised in a Yiddish-speaking home, and has been swiftly appropriated by them.
26. I owe this observation to Samuel Heilman.
27. Mayer, *From Surburb to Shtetl*, p. 55. Eastern European Jewry encountered modernity with migration; Hungarian Jewry first encountered modernity in the nineteenth century and migration only in the mid-twentieth. As mentioned in n. 14, Central Europe had its own time frame. In this essay I deal primarily with the Eastern European experience while attempting to make some references to and allowances for the Hungarian one.
28. Certain Hasidic groups, segments of the *yishuv ha-yashan*, and those in *kolelim*. "Yeshivah towns," settlements built around a famous yeshivah or clusters of *kolelim* tend to have a far more modest lifestyle. This is a function in part of lower income, in part of ideology—not surprisingly, as people of university towns tend generally to live more simply than their urban brethren. The test of nonacculturation to the consumer culture comes when young couples leave the *kolel* environment for the city enclaves and move up the economic ladder.
29. Mayer, *From Suburb to Shtetl*, ch. 4, and his remarks at pp. 138–39. In this section I discuss the factors operative in the American *haredi* community (not to speak of the

one of modern Orthodoxy). The same forces are at work, in my opinion, in the Israeli community. However, because Israeli society first began to experience affluence only in the 1970s and because religious Jews there, especially *haredim*, constitute a far larger percentage of the general population than they do in America, the Israeli acculturation is less advanced, and forces exist that still resist the consumer culture. But acculturation there is, as any acquaintance with *haredim* will evince and as Menachem Friedman and Samuel C. Heilman document in their article "Religious Fundamentalism and Religious Jews: The Case of the Haredim," in Martin E. Marty and R. Scott Appleby, eds., *Fundamentalism Observed* (Chicago: Chicago University Press, 1991), pp. 197–264. Its presentation, however, would have entailed breaking both the format and the space limitations of the essay. For the portrayal would have to describe, for example, the pull of the *yishuv* and *kelitah*, which was similar to but far from identical with that of the melting pot. The loss of social and cultural control by the men of *aliyah bet* and the decline of the Socialist and Zionist ideologies after the establishment of the State of Israel would have to be placed alongside and compared with the loss of the authority by the WASP establishment in the 1960s. Nor could any analysis of the orthodox resurgence in Israel avoid making some correlation with the contemporary Sefaredic reassertion, much as the American Orthodox resurgence is linked, as we shall soon note in the text, with the civil rights movement of the 1960s.

30. The first record of the *neo-nigunim* was made by Sholomo Carlebach, *Haneshamah Loch*, cut in 1959. His compositions, thought innovative, were not rock. His numerous successors adopted wholeheartedly the contemporary beat. By the 1970s this music had reached floodtide and has continued unabated. See Mordechai Schiller, "Chassidus in Song—Not for the Record," *Jewish Observer*, March 1975, p. 21. Bodily response to syncopation seems a natural reaction. We do not syncopate, however, to Indian or Japanese music. Syncopation, which is experienced as a primal, almost involuntary response to a felt correspondence between an outside beat and the natural rhythm of the body is in reality culturally acquired. Precisely because it seems elemental, is it so significant an indicia of acculturation. Undeniably, the high sales and diffusion of the "neo-niggunim" also reflect the growing ubiquity, even need, of music by the populace, engendered by the high-fi revolution and that of the Walkman. This, however, would only underscore the extent to which all wings of the religious community partake in this transformation of taste of the host culture. The recently instituted *hakkafot sheniyyot* amply make this point. See "Music to Tame the Heart or to Incite the Beast," *Jewish Observer,* January 1988, pp. 39–41. (Note also the arguments made by the critic in Mordechai Schiller, "Postscript #2: Jewish Music for the Record," *Jewish Observer*, December, 1975, pp. 25–26.)

31. See the newspaper articles quoted in Mayer, *From Suburb to Shtetl*, p. 171 n. 30; and see Chaim I. Waxman, *American Jews in Transition* (Philadelphia: Temple University Press, 1983), pp. 164–65; and Samuel C. Heilman, *Defenders of the Faith* (New York: Schocken Books, 1992), p. 123.

32. To give the reader some idea of the order of magnitude involved, I would simply note that the Union of Orthodox Congregations alone currently has some sixty to eighty thousand (!) products under its supervision. (So I have been informed by sources both in that organization and in the Rabbinical Council of America.) All figures are fluid, as much depends on how one should count, for example, the 57 varieties of Heinz's soup; by company, by item, or by number of separate ingredients

requiring rabbinic supervision? Even by a very restrictive count, the number would seem to be around 16,000, see 'Food, Food: A Matter of Taste," *Jewish Observer*, April 1987, pp. 37–39. In my readings, I came across this passage and jotted it down: "The proliferation of Continental or Oriental eateries, Caribbean cruises, and Passover vacation packages, all under the strictest rabbinic supervision, serve witness to the fact that an upwardly mobile (conspicuous) consumer need not compromise his religious principles." Although somewhat exaggerated, the point is well taken. Unfortunately, I forgot to note the source. The parallel between the *embourgeoisement* of the lifestyle of contemporary Orthodoxy and that of the nineteenth-century German one is striking; see Mordecai Breuer, *Modernity within Tradition: The Social History of Orthodox Jewry in Imperial Germany* (New York: Columbia University Press, 1992), pp. 225–36.

33. See, for example, Sylvia-Ann Goldberg, *Les deux rives du Yabbok: la maladie et la mort dans le dans le judaïsme ashkénaze: Prague XVI^c^–XIX^c^ siècle* (Paris: Cerf, 1989). During most of this period the practices of Central and Eastern Europe were much the same. See, for example, the matter of *wachmacht*, in the next note.

34. On *wachmacht*, See Herman Pollack, *Jewish Folkways in German Lands* (Cambridge, Mass.: M.I.T. Press, 1971), pp. 19–20; and Elliot Hurwitz, "The Eve of Circumcision: A Chapter in the History of Jewish Nightlife," *Journal of Social History* 23 (1989): 46–69, esp. n. 9. The practice was scarcely restricted to Central Europe, as the Weinreich's and Herzog's studies show. Uriel Weinreich, "Mapping a Culture," *Columbia University Forum* 6 no. 3 (1963): 19, map 3; Marvin Herzog, *Yiddish Language in Northern Poland: Its Geography and History* (Bloomington: Indiana University Press, 1965), pp. 28–29. Any study of the primary sources cited by Pollack or by Joshua Trachtenberg, *Jewish Magic and Superstition: A Study of Folk Religion* (reprint: New York: Atheneum, 1970) shows to what extent Polish Jewry shared common folkways with their brethern in German-speaking lands.

Mention of demons evokes nowadays unease in most religious circles, including *haredi* ones. For the contemporary Ashkenazi community is acculturated, and one of its hallmarks, as will be noted subsequently in the text (and below n. 103), is its basic acceptance of the mechanistic universe of modern science with its disallowance of ghosts and demons. The simple fact, however, is that demons are part of both the talmudic and kabbalistic cosmology and equally, if not more so, of the traditional, Eastern European one. Only one major halakhic figure, Maimonides, influenced by the no less mechanistic universe of Aristotle, denied their existence. For this he was roundly castigated by the GRA, who equally pinpointed the source of Maimonides' skepticism on the matter *Bi'ur ha-Gra, Yoreh De'ah*, 179:13). Despite the enormous influence of the GRA today (see above n. 20), his words on this issue have fallen on deaf ears, or rather, consigned to oblivion.

Significantly, demons and ghosts are still part of the popular Israeli Sefaredi cosmology, and this is reflected in the preachings available on cassettes in Israel. This difference should be corollated with the divergence that exists on the issue of "hell-fire." Direct appeals to the horrors that await sinners are strikingly absent from contemporary Ashkenazic writings and equally from the burgeoning cassette literature. It is found abundantly, however, on the cassettes by Sefaredic preachers (e.g., R, Nissim Yagen in the series *Ner Le-Me'ah*: no. 41, *Neshamot*, no. 86, *Ha-Parpar ha-Kahol*, part 1, no. 140, *Ha-Shoshanah she-Navlah*; in the series *Hasdei Naomi*: no. 3, *Omek ha-Din*). This suggests that in the Ashkenazic community, after some five or six generations of exposure to modernity, thoughts of the afterlife have lost much of their vivacity. The Jews from Muslim countries arrived in Israel soon after its founding in 1948. For those who came from rural areas this was their first encounter with the modern world; the same was true even for some coming from more urbanized settlements. Only a generation removed from their former culture, their vivid sense of the afterlife has not been dulled by modernity. See below n. 103. (Terror of the afterworld, one should add, has little to do with religious observance, for such fears continue as "popular beliefs," long after religious observance and even belief have been discarded.) The difficulty in proving such an assertion lies in the fact that in the written Ashkenazic literature of previous centuries, to the best of my very limited knowledge, there is equally little hellfire. Judaism did not have its Jonathan Edwards; and hellfire, even when preached, was not committed to writing. For example, the most famous hellfire preacher of nineteenth-century Lithuania was R. Mosheh Yitzhak, the *maggid* (preacher) of Kelm (d. 1900). Yet his published sermons, *Tokhahas Hayyim* (Wilno, 1896), reflect little of this. Unless my cursory reading of contemporary Sefaredic works misleads me, there is equally little in Sefaredic writings that compares, either in extent or intensity, with their cassette literature. These issues are vital in understanding contemporary Jewish religiosity, and they well merit study by more knowledgeable people than myself, employing methods more sophisticated than the ones at my disposal. (For a similar transformation in spirituality, see our discussion of Divine Providence in the close of the essay.)

([1] There is little on contemporary Sefaredic religiosity, for the moment, see H. E. Goldberg, "Religious Response among North African Jews in the Nineteenth and Twentieth Centuries," in Jack Wertheimer, ed., *The Uses of Tradition: Jewish Continuity in the Modern Era* [New York: Jewish Theological Seminary, 1992], pp. 119–44, and the essay by Shelomoh Deshen "Ha-Datiyyut shel ha-Mizrahim: ha-Tzibbur, ha-Rabbanim ve-ha-Emunah," in the fall 1994 issue of *Alpayyim*. [2] A society without movies, television or radio, where the written word may inform but not titillate, will turn to preaching for both edification and entertainment. The growing popularity, indeed ubiquity, of cassette literature in *haredi* society is not then surprising. Its diffusion is further facilitated by free lending libraries run by both *haredi* institutions and public-spirited individuals. Thus, cassette tapes, the spoken word itself and not some written transcription thereof, constitute a major source for the study of contemporary spirituality. Yet to the best of my knowledge, this repository has remained virtually untapped by scholars. The only works known to me that have employed cassettes are the recently published study of Menahem Blondheim and Kim Caplan, "On Communication and Audio-Cassettes in the Haredi World," *Kesher* 14 (1993): 51–63, and an essay bt the same Kim Caplan, "Al Derashot Mukklatot be-Hevrah ha-Haredit," in *Yahadut Zemaneinu*, summer 1996. Indeed, with the notable exception of the Harvard College Library, whose Judaica librarian, Charles Berlin, has repeatedly shown himself to be some ten years ahead of scholars in recognizing what is essential material in their own disciplines, no library even collects these tapes systematically.)

35. See Heilman, *Defenders of the Faith*, pp. 98–100, 248–52; and Tamar El-Or, *Educated and Ignorant: Ultraorthodox Jewish Women and Their World* (above n. 20), pp. 189–200. I am unacquainted with a single religious leader who has not bemoaned the growing *embourgeoisement* of the Orthodox community.

36. I say "something about which to be genuinely different," for much that goes under the name "new ethnicity" appears, to my untutored eye, to have been aptly characterized by Gans as "symbolic ethnicity." See Herbert Gans, "Symbolic Ethnicity: The Future of Ethnic Groups and Culture in America," *Ethnic and Racial Studies* 2 (January 1979): 1–20. Characterize it as you will, Jewish religious distinctness is far more substantive than that of most ethnic groups in the United States and has a far more assured future.
37. This holds true, mutatus mutandis, of Israel; see above n. 29.
38. On the background of this "swing to the right" in the general Jewish community, see Heilman and Cohen, *Cosmopolitans and Parochials*, pp. 183–93. For the broader American scene, see, for example, Charles Y. Glock and Robert N. Bellah, *The New Religious Consciousness* (Berkeley: University of California Press, 1976).
39. To give a small but characteristic example: The previous generation has accepted as a matter of course the use, in documents, publications, even letterheads, of English name forms, as Moses, Nathan, Jacob, and the like. The members of the current generation decline to allow a hegemonic majority to first appropriate their own names and then return it to them in an altered state. They sign Moshe, Nosson, or Yakov.
40. *Berakhot* 8a. Some of the phenomena outlined here have parallels in previous periods of Jewish history, such as the retreat to "the four cubits of the Halakhah" mentioned here, the shift away from orality that attended the writing down of the Mishnah, the wholesale audit of contemporary practice in light of newly explicated texts that came in the wake of the intellectual revolution of the eleventh and twelfth centuries, and the dramatic swing to stringency during the waning years of the Middle Ages. Nor should the developments in post-Expulsion Sefaredic communities be forgotten. What is parallel, however, is not necessarily comparable. Each occurred in a different historical setting, and its significance varied considerably from context to context. Be that as it may, the point of the essay is that this development is new in the sweep of Eastern European Jewish history of the last 350 years. See also above, n. 19.)
41. Nathan Glazer, *American Judaism*, rev. ed. (Chicago: Chicago University Press, 1972), pp. 171–72. Among other things, he writes, "Indeed, when *Commentary* addressed a series of questions on Jewish belief to a large group of young Jewish religious thinkers and writers in 1966, the Holocaust did not figure among the questions, nor, it must be said, did it figure much among the answers."
42. O. U. Schmelz and Segio DellaPergola, "The Demographic Consequences of U.S. Jewish Population Trends," *American Jewish Yearbook* 92 (1992): 124–28. The precise numbers are subject to some controversy, as is often the case with such statistics. There is, however, little question as to the overall magnitudes.
43. "Incognito ergo sum" is not a phrase of my own minting but one I once heard in my college days.
44. I have used the term "close to a millennium" because there is considerable controversy as to the nature—indeed, the very existence—of asceticism in rabbinic Judaism. The various positions are discussed in Steven D. Fraade, "Ascetic Aspects of Ancient Judaism" in Arthur Green, ed., *Jewish Spirituality: From the Bible through the Middle Ages* (New York: Crossroads Publishing, 1987), pp. 253–88.
45. Unfortunately, no single work on medieval Jewish asceticism exists. Linked as it is with the purpose of human existence, its ubiquity is not surprising in a world steeped in Neoplatonic thought and which had its eye fixed steadily on the afterlife. The reli-

gious impulse continued long after the original philosophical component had disappeared. The ascetic ideal begins with what is perhaps the most influential ethical work in Jewish thought, Bahya Ibn Paquda's *Hovot ha-Levavot*. The ideal wends its way through such influential works as *Sefer Hassidim, Sha'arei Teshuvah, SeferHaredim, Reshit Hokhmah, Shevet Mussar, Mesillat Yesharim*, down to the writings of R. Israel Salanter and his school in the late nineteenth century. (On *Hovot ha-Levavot*, see Alan Lazaroff, "Bahya's Asceticism against Its Rabbinic and Islamic Background," *Journal of Jewish Studies* 9 (1970): 11–38, with bibliography, and more recently, Hayyim Kreisel, "Asceticism in the Thought of R. Bahya ibn Pakuda and Maimonides," *Da'at* 21 (1998): 5–22. Much material on the later Middle Ages, often slighted in general surveys, can be found in Yaakov Elbaum, *Teshivah be-Lev ve-Kabbalat Yissurim* (Jerusalem: Magnes Press, 1993). The waning of the ascetic and pessimistic dualism is already noticeable among some of R. Israel's successors, if I read them correctly. See Tamar Ross, *Ha-Mahshavah ha-Iyyunit be-Khitvei Mamshikhav shel R. Israel Salanter* (Ph.D. diss., Hebrew University, 1986).

46. See, for example, the formulations of the *Shulhan Arukh* on conjugal relations, in *Orah Hayyim*, 240:8–9. Maimonides' position, expressed in the *Moreh Nevukhim* (2:36) that sexual activity was shameful, indeed, bestial, was rejected in view of the religious imperative of marriage and procreation. However, sexual relations beyond the minimum required by the Law or with any intent other than that of fulfilling the Law, or of a theurgic nature, were decried by *most* writers, such as Rabad of Posquieres in his influential *Ba'alei ha-Nefesh, Sha'ar ha-Kedushah*; Nahmanides, in his *Perush al ha-Torah* (to Lev. 18:6, 19:2); and the influential *Iggeret ha-Kodesh*. To what extent the ascetic ideal could and did compromise the most basic family obligations, including the most elementary conjugal ones, even among the most religiously scrupulous, as late as the nineteenth century, see Emmanuel Etkes, "Marriage and Torah Study among *Lomdim* in Lithuania in the Nineteenth Century," in David C. Kraemer, ed., *The Jewish Family: Metaphor and Memory* (New York: Oxford University Press, 1989), pp. 153–78, esp. pp. 170–73 and the citations of and about the GRA at pp. 154–55. (The GRA was probably conforming to R. Bahya's admonition in the *Sha'ar ha-Bittahon* against allowing a concern for wife and children to deflect attention from one's proper spiritual endeavors.) (There is, unfortunately, no serious study in either English or Hebrew of the traditional Jewish perception, or perceptions, of marital relations. A brief but convenient survey, indeed the only one on this subject, is George Vajda's "Continence, mariage et vie mystique selon le doctrine du judaïsme," now available in his *Sages et penseurs sépharades de Bagdad á Cordoue* [Paris: Cerf, 1989], pp. 45–56. The introduction and notes of Charles Mopsic's translation of *Iggeret ha-Kodesh*, namely *Lettre sur la saintété* [Paris: Verdier, 1986], contain much useful and some out of the way material. See also J. Katz, *Tradition and Crisis*, translated and with an Afterward by Bernard Dov Cooperman [New York: Schoken Press, 1993], p. 212. I should, perhaps, emphasize that the subject of the *Iggeret ha-Kodesh* is sexual relations, not pleasure. One might, at most, infer from a doctrine that it *logically* entails a legitimation of pleasure. Entailment, however, is not existence. For the latter, evidence must be brought that the thinker actually drew such a conclusion. I know of no medieval writer who legitimized pleasure or even entertained such a notion. Cf. Moshe Z. Socol, "Attitudes towards Pleasure in Jewish Thought: A Typological Proposal," in Jacob J. Schacter, ed., *Reverence, Righteousness, and Rahmanut;*

*Essays in Memory of Rabbi Dr. Leo Jung* [Northvale, N.J.: Jason Aronson Inc., 1992], pp. 293–314).

47. This conclusion is tentative, as I have made no thorough study of contemporary ethical literature. I can state that asceticism is noticeably absent from the writings of two of the most influential figures of our times, R. Eliyahu Dessler and the Hazon Ish. Nor have I found it, except in the most attenuated form, in a random sample of thirty-odd works of contemporary *mussar*, whether in English or Hebrew, by writers both famous and little known. The contrast between these writers, many of whom are the spiritual heirs of the *mussar* movement, and the writings of that movement itself is striking. See R. Eliyahu Dessler, *Mikhtav me-Eliyahu* 4 vols. (reprint; Jerusalem: n.p., 1987) (the passage in vol. 3, pp. 152–53 is the exception that proves the rule); Hazon Ish, *Sefer ha-Emunah ve-ha-Bittahon* (Jerusalem: n.p., 1954); idem, *Kovetz Iggrot*, 3 vols. (Bnei Brak: n.p., 1990). Further indications may be found in the absence of any accounts of ascetic practices in the biographies, possibly hagiographies, that are published now. Whether the various talmudic greats of recent memory practiced asceticism awaits determination. Clearly, however, tales of such practices either are not current or they would not be well received by the contemporary audience. For sample biographies, see the volumes mentioned in n. 62, as well as Aaron Sorasky, *Reb Elchonon: The Life and Ideals of Rabbi Elchonon Bunim Wasserman of Baranovich* (New York: Mesorah Publications, 1982); Shimon Finkelman, *Reb Chaim Ozer: The Life and Ideals of Rabbi Chaim Ozer Grodzenski of Vilna* (New York: Mesorah Publications, 1987).
48. To be sure, there still are some groups among Hasidim that practice some forms of asceticism. For example, Ger (or elite groups in Ger) looks askance at sexual foreplay and seeks to restrict sexual relations to the reproductive act itself. Slonim discourages eating precisely those foods for which one has a strong preference. Significantly, however, these aspirations and directives are kept secret, and great pains are taken to insure that they are not made known to the larger public, who being totally unattuned to the ascetic impulse, indeed, unable even to comprehend it, would immediately stamp these Hasidic groups as strange and extremist. The pamphlet of Ger on sexual relations is literally unobtainable to outsiders and is known beyond the circle of Ger only by word of mouth, though it has generated a counterliterature, e.g., *Mishkan Yisrael* 3rd ed. (Jerusalem: n.p., 1991). Any comparison of this work, which has the approbation of such distinguished Talmudists as Rabbis Y. S. Elyashiv, N. Karelitz, and S. Volbeh, with the classic works cited above (n. 46) will evidence just how far contemporary Orthodoxy, including its *haredi* sector, has moved from the asceticism of the past. (I am indebted to Rabbi Mosheh Meiselman both for the information about Slonim and for the reference of *Mishkan Yisrael*.)
49. Not that the ascetic impulse has now wholly disappeared from the surrounding society. There seems to be a fixed quantity of pain that people, in all periods, which to inflict upon themselves for the sake of some distant, possibly unattainable *summum bonum*. The rigors of monastic asceticism or of the flagellants find their equivalent in our ceaseless exercise and unremitting self-starvation undertaken for the sake of Beauty or in the name of something called Fitness. Now, as then, it is those free from the immediate burdens of subsistence who most hear the call of that higher good and voluntarily undertake to wear the hair shirt. This impulse is often linked to an attempt to move backward in time. We strive, no less than medieval men, to move backward

in time, we to Youth, they to Eden. To them the body was born with the taint of original concupiscence; to us it acquires too swiftly the odor of Age. They mortified the flesh to enable the soul to escape the confines of the body, we to enable the body to escape the ravages of time—each of the two equally impossible, by all rules of common sense, yet each pursued with equal vigor. To be sure the overwhelming majority of people eschewed the rigors of asceticism but probably never denied the rightness of the enterprise. Man, perhaps, even made some half-hearted attempts to engage in it themselves, much as exercise bikes and running shoes gathering dust in countless homes stand as witnesses to an aspiration rather than to any actual endeavor. (My remarks refer to American society generally, rather than to the religious Jewish community, who participate tepidly, at best, in this form of asceticism. In this regard, at least, contemporary Orthodoxy is still unacculturated. Nevertheless, as this community is the subject of this essay, I felt it more appropriate to use "original concupiscence" rather than "Original Sin." The latter is alien to Jewish thought; the former is not. On man's fall and his diminished, concupiscent state, see, for example, Bezalel Safran, "Rabbi Azriel and Nahmanides: Two Views of the Fall of Man," in Isadore Twersky, ed., *Rabbi Moses Nahmanides: Explorations in His Religious Virtuosity* [Cambridge, Mass.: Harvard University Press, 1983], pp. 75–106.)

50. My remarks are based on personal acquaintance. I am unaware of any study of the recollections of the "old country" in the religious or *haredi* community in the decades following the Holocaust.
51. Creativity took the form of exegesis for the reasons spelled out by Gershom Scholem, in "Revelation and Tradition as Religious Categories in Judaism," in his *The Messianic Idea in Judaism* (New York: Schoken Books, 1972), pp. 289–90.
52. The *Sefer ha-Hinukh* comes to mind, as does the *Tzedah le-Derekh*. The former, however, is a primer, and the latter a handbook. I should underscore that I am referring to scholarly, secondary sources and not to codes, though there was no lack of opposition to codes, not only because of their tone of finality but also on account of their detachment from the life-giving, primary texts. On the opposition to codes, see Menahem Elon, *Ha-Mishpat ha-Ivri* (Jerusalem: Magnes Press, 1973), vol. 3, pp. 1005–18, 1140–41, 1145–72.
53. On the dialogic aspects of *lernen*, see the remarks of Benjamin Harshav, *The Meaning of Yiddish* (Berkeley: University of California Press, 1990), pp. 16–24, esp. pp. 18–20.
54. The current popularity of the *Beit ha-Behirah* of R, Menahem ha-Meiri reflects this change in modes of learning. Meiri is the only medieval Talmudist *(rishon)* whose works can be read almost independently of the talmudic text upon which it ostensibly comments. The *Beit ha-Behirah* is not a running commentary on the Talmud. Meiri, in quasi-Maimonidean fashion, intentionally omits the give and take of the *sugya*; he focuses, rather, on the final upshot of the discussion and presents the differing views of that upshot and conclusion. Also, he alone, and again intentionally, provides the reader with background information. His writings are the closest thing to a secondary source in the library of *rishonim*. This trait coupled with the remarkably modern syntax of Meiri's Hebrew prose have won for his works their current widespread use. It is not, as commonly thought, because the *Beit ha-Behirah* has been recently discovered. True, the massive Parma manuscript has been in employ only for some seventy years. However, even a glance at any Hebrew bibliography will show that much of the *Beit ha-Behirah* on *seder mo'ed*, for example, had been published long before Avraham

Sofer began his transcriptions of the Parma manuscript in the 1920s. (E.g. *Megillah*—Amsterdam, 1759; *Sukkah*—Berlin, 1859; *Shabbat*—Vienna, 1864.) Rather, Meiri's works had previously fallen stillborn from the press. Sensing their alien character, most scholars simply ignored them, and judging by the infrequent reprintings, if any, they also appear not to have found a popular audience. They have come into their own only in the past half-century. (On Meiri's quasi-Maimonidean intentions, see *Beit ha-Behirah, Berakhot*, ed. Y. Dickman [Jerusalem, 1965], introduction, pp. 25–32. Meiri consciously follows Maimonides in addressing the halakhic dicta rather than the talmudic discussion, in gathering scattered halakhic dicta under one roof, and in writing in neo-Mishnaic rather than rabbinic Hebrew. He parts company with Maimonides and follows R. Judah ha-Nassi in writing not topically but tractatewise and in registering multiple views. Indeed, no one writing after the dialectical revolution of the Tosafists could entertain again the Maimonidean notion of halakhic univocality.)

55. E.g. David I. Sheinkopf, *Issues in Jewish Dietary Laws: Gelatin, Kitniniyyot and Their Derivatives* (Hoboken, N.J.: Ktav, 1988); Chaim B. Goldberg, *Mourning in Halachah* (New York: Mesorah Publications, 1991); not to speak of J. David Bleich's series *Contemporary Halakhic Problems* (New York and Hoboken: Ktav/Yeshiva University Press, 1977, 1981). The first large-scale, serious halakhic presentation in English was, to the best of my knowledge, that of Shimon D. Eider, 1970), which went through five printings in as many years. This, however, might yet be understood as an attempt to grapple with halakhic status and permissibility on Sabbath of the hundreds of new products of the modern consumer market, parallel to the groundbreaking work of Y. Y. Neuwirth, *Shemirat Shabbat ke-Hilkhatah*, which had appeared in Jerusalem some five years earlier. Whatever its nature at the time of publication, in retrospect it was clearly a harbinger. (The first scholarly, secondary text in Halakhah known to be was Y. Y. Greenwald, *Ah le-Tzarah* [New York, 1939]. It was well received, for it dealt with the laws of mourning, an area of religious observance that second-generation American Jews by and large still kept. Its success was due to its utility as a rabbinical handbook, rather than to any cultural receptivity to secondary texts, as nothing similar appeared for the next quarter of a century. *Ah le-Tzarah* has been republished recently under the title *Kol Bo 'al Aveilut* [New York: Feldheim, 1973].)

56. Max Weinreich, *History of the Yiddish Language* (Chicago: Chicago University Press, 1980), pp. 247–57. There is, strictly speaking, no proper term for the phenomenon described. "Diglossia" is the use of an upper and lower dialect of the same language, as classical and colloquial Arabic. However, I find this term preferable to "internal bilingualism" and other such locutions used to distinguish the case of Yiddish and Hebrew in the Ashkenazic world from ordinary "bilingualism." Bilingualism, generally, denotes the use of two languages, such as English and French, reflective of two distinct cultures, rather than, as here, the use of two separate languages, both of which are the exclusive products of a single culture.) Whether the cleavage fell along the lines of oral and written discourse, rather than learned and popular or sacred and secular, is irrelevant to our presentation.

57. Khone Shmeruk, *Sifrut Yiddish be-Polin* (Jerusalem: Magnes, 1981), pp. 52–56; idem, *Sifrut Yiddish, Perakim le-Toldotehah* (Tel Aviv: Mif'alim Universita 'iyyim le-Hotza'ah le-Or, 1978), pp. 9–24, 37. See also *Teshuvot Maharil he-Hadashot* (Jerusalem: Machon Yerushalayim, 1977), no. 93.

58. Shmeruk, *Sifrut Yiddish, Perakim le-Toldotehah*, pp. 20–21 and n. 16. So deep ran the perceived necessity of Hebrew that works originally composed in Yiddish would be translated and printed in Hebrew. The printed Hebrew text would then be translated back into Yiddish, and this translation, rather than the original Yiddish text, would be published. A book that was published in Yiddish was not perceived as really "existing"; Hebrew books alone existed, and, translations could only be made of "existing" works. See Sara Zfatman, *Nissuei Adam ve-Shedah* (Jerusalem: Akademon, 1988), pp. 21–24. The "non-existence" of Yiddish works expressed itself also in their frequent destruction. Unlike books printed in Hebrew, no aura of sanctity attended them, and no effort was made to preserve them. See Shmeruk, *Sifrut Yiddish be-Polin*, p. 23.
59. Despite almost uniform *haredi* insistence, in the United States, England, and Israel, on the use of Yiddish, both in the yeshivah and at all official functions, nevertheless, there is little tape literature in Yiddish. The preachers are only too well aware that to reach people they had best speak in the mother tongue of the community. (The flat statement in the text of linguistic acculturation is somewhat less true of the more separatist and better segregated sectors of the Hasidic community, which, unlike the yeshivah world, make specific efforts to speak Yiddish also in the house—and with some degree of success. Yet the evidence of the tapes, together with the nigh total absence of any Yiddish works in the current explosion of religious publications, would seem to indicate the ultimate failure of their valiant efforts.)
60. Ezra Mendelsohn, *The Jews of Central Europe between the World Wars* (Bloomington: Indiana University Press, 1983), pp. 29–32. For Lithuania, see pp. 233–35, 227; Latvia, pp. 250–52; Rumania, pp. 180–83.
61. See Yosef Hayim Yerushalmi, *Zakhor: Jewish History and Jewish Memory* (Seattle and London: University of Washington Press, 1982), pp. 5–52.
62. E.g., the biographies cited above in n. 47 and the works cited below in n. 94 (most of which were initially published in Hebrew); to which one could add Nisson Wolpin, ed., *The Torah Profile: A Treasury of Biographical Sketches. Collected from the Pages of The Jewish Observer* (New York: Mesorah Publications, 1988); Jacob H. Sinason, *The Gaon of Posen: A Portrait of Rabbi Akiva Guens-Eger* (London: J. Lehman, 1989); Yaakov M. Rapoport, *The Light from Dvinsk: Rav Meir Simcha, The Ohr Sameyach* (Southfield, Mich.: Targum Press, 1990). To be sure, biographical notes and reminiscences appeared in the previous century soon after the death of numerous famous Talmudists. These, however, were more in the nature of eulogies and necrologies than of biographies. More significantly, these were read by few, if at all. The popular image was a product of collective memory, scarcely of these ephemera.
63. To be sure, the line between the writing of history as it must have happened and the rewriting of history as it should have happened is fine indeed, as is often the line between believer and committed partisan. It is, however, no less real for the fact. A good example of ideological history in English (without any stand taken on which side of that thin line it falls) is Berel Wein, *Triumph of Survival: The Story of the Jewish People in the Modern Period* (Monsey: Sha'ar Press, 1990); see Monty N. Penkower's review in *Ten Daat* 6 (1992): 45–46. Another instance is the recent and much publicized withdrawal from print, by a famous yeshivah, of a translation of a well-known early-twentieth-century autobiography *(Mekor Barukh)*, because its accounts do not square with the current image of the past. See Jacob J. Schacter, "Haskalah, Secular Studies and the Close of the Yeshiva in Volozhin in 1892," *The Torah U-Madda*

*Journal* 2 (1990): 76–133. (See, further, nn. 1 and 5 for examples of intentional censuring by the translator himself.) A good Hebrew example of this genre is Yehudah Salomon, *Yerushalayyim shel Ma'alah* (Jerusalem: Carmel, 1992).

64. These remarks are psychological rather than philosophic: not what makes the moral act, obedience or insight, but how is the sense of the dictate's rightness instilled? What evokes the answering echo of assent to its mandate?
65. More broadly, see Clifford Geertz, *The Interpretation of Cultures* (New York: Basic Books, 1973), pp. 126–41, and idem, *Islam Observed* (Chicago: Chicago University Press, 1968), pp. 35–55.
66. Ibid.
67. I am indebted to Robert Redfield's essay "The Genius of the University" for the analogy and, for all purposes, also for the very phrasing. The passage is found in Redfield, *The Social Uses of Social Science: The Papers of Robert Redfield* (Chicago: Chicago University Press, 1963), vol. 2, pp. 244–45. (I altered the verbs, as I felt that "submerged" was more apt than "lost.")
68. Argument might be made, and indeed it has, that the widespread attendance of yeshivot is a major cause of the emergence of the text culture. No doubt there is currently some mutual reinforcement; however, to my mind, such a contention confuses cause with effect. The text culture arose as the mimetic society faded, and that *same* disappearance created the new role of the yeshivot. As long as the mimetic society was vibrantly alive, as it was during the lifetime of the Yeshivah of Volozhin, practice was governed by tradition rather than by text, even in the archetypical yeshivah bastion of the GRA. See above n. 20. Indeed, to the best of my limited personal knowledge, religious practice in the yeshivot of both Mir and Telz (Telsiai) in the interwar years, was still governed by tradition. The text culture, as we know it today, was not then present in those institutions. The current practice of *shiurim*, for example, was restricted to isolated individuals, usually one who had some family tradition on the matter.
69. Thus, the plaint voiced in some quarters, that in Europe, unlike contemporary America or Israel, only a handful of students, and an elite group at that, studied in yeshivot or *kolelim*, while today it has become mass education, even for the untalented, is historically correct but sociologically beside the point. The role of yeshivot and *kolelim* has changed dramatically, and the new demographics—the mass attendance—simply mirror this fact.
70. See Oscar and Mary F. Handlin, "A Century of Jewish Migration to the United States," *American Jewish Year Book* (1948–49): 30–42, 45–64. The full list may be found in *The Jewish Communal Registrar of New York, 1917–1918* (New York: Kehillah [Jewish Community], 1918). (I would like to thank Jeffrey Gurock for providing me with the last reference.)
71. The figures given are for the year 1942, which was investigated by Dr. Don Well in a study based on demographic data collected by the Board of Jewish Education of New York. I would like to thank him for sharing with me his findings. (The term "day schools" includes both day schools and what are called "yeshivah high schools," i.e., the number cited is for institutions both of the "right" and of the "center.")
72. The term *yeshivot* is here used to denote post–high school education. Exact figures are hard to come by but not the order of magnitude. It would be surprising if the number of yeshivah students exceeded 750 at the close of World War II.

73. Charles Liebman, "The Training of American Rabbis," *American Jewish Year Book* 69 (1968): 3–112 (reprinted in idem, *Aspects of the Religious Behavior of American Jews* (New York, 1974), pp. 1–110.
74. For a convenient collection in English by one of the secularists, see Saul L. Goodman, ed., *The Faith of Secular Jews* (New York: Ktav, 1976). See also Ruth Wisse, "The Politics of Yiddish," *Commentary* 80 (July 1985): 29–35. (I would like to thank David Fishman for drawing my attention to Goodman's book.)
75. Such a moment, to some, was *Slihos* time, early September of 1910, when labor and management reached agreement on the famous "Protocol" that resolved the Cloakmakers' Strike.
76. The social ideologies disappeared as the Jews moved out of the proletariat. "Secular Judaism," however, was rooted in cultural rather than class assumptions, and the reasons for its demise lie outside the economic sphere. Ethnic neighborhoods disappeared at the same time and for the same reason. As long as Jews felt themselves, however resentfully and unwillingly, as essentially different, in some sense, from the rest of the populace, living alongside Gentiles, not to speak of close friendships with them, was not realistic. With the sharp shrinkage of the sense of social alienation from both within and without, that is, with the disappearance of the felt sense of otherness by third-generation Jews, on the one hand, and the concomitant or parallel lessening of social anti-Semitism, on the other, Jewish residential patterns changed. Jews moved into neighborhoods that were partially or even predominantly Jewish, but these were a far cry from the tightly meshed, almost hermetically sealed, ethnic neighborhoods of the first half of the century, in which one could walk for blocks without ever seeing a Gentile face.
77. Study of Dr. Don Well cited above, n. 71. (The numbers given in the study are 5,800 and 168,300.)
78. Notably the dynasties of Fer, Sochaczew, and Alexandròw. Lubavitch established a yeshivah toward the end of the nineteenth century. (Not that *talmud torah* was peripheral to these dynasties, rather its institutional expression in the form of yeshivah was.) I am unaware of any study of Hasidic *yeshivot*. Some basic data may be obtained from Samuel K. Mirsky, ed., *Mosdot Torah be-Iropa be-Binyanam u-be-Hurbanam* (New York: Ogen, 1956). There is much information on the rise in the axiological standing of Torah study *talmud Torah* in Polish Hasidism of the late nineteenth and early twentieth century in Mendel Piekarz, *Hassidut Polin: Megamot Ra'ayoniyyot Bein Shetei ha-Milhamot u-be-Gezeirot Tash-Tashah* (Jerusalem: Mosad Bialik, 1990), pp. 50–81. He sees this rise as a response to the growing inroads of secularization, which would, mutatus mutandis, dovetail with our basic thesis, as would equally—what others have told me—that the yeshivah played a progressively more central role in Ger during the interwar period. Eastern European *haredi* communities were severely affected by the dislocations wrought by World War I and the Russian Revolution. Indeed, the more one studies the interwar period, the more one senses that a number of the traits of the text culture outlined in this chapter began first to then take shape.
79. To explain the *haredi* resurgence by its newly acquired affluence leaves unexplained why in the 1930s and 1940s every step up the economic ladder meant a step away from Orthodoxy and why that same upward mobility now makes simply for an affluent Orthodox Jew. As large a role as money may play in human aspirations, nevertheless, a bank account in itself neither reduces nor induces religiosity.

80. *New York Times*, April 26, 1990, section B. pg. 1; *The Jewish Observer*, May 1990, pp. 4–14.
81. Eliezer Bruchstein, "The Impact of Automation on the Torah World," *Jewish Observer*, September 1987, pp. 47–51. TCN (Torah Communications Network) has twenty-six centers in major cities of the United States and Canada.
82. Most explicitly by R. Hayyim of Volozhin, *Nefesh ha-Hayyim* (reprint: New York, 1972), *Sha'ar ha-Revi'i*. See Norman Lamm, *Torah Lishmah: Torah for Torah's Sake in the Works of Rabbi Hayyim of Volozhin and His Contemporaries* (Hoboken, N.J.: Ktav, 1989).
83. The political and religious power of the *rebbe* remains intact, though unless I am very much mistaken, the growth of Hasidic yeshivot will ultimately take its political toll, not in the delegitimation of the *rebbe*'s political power but in the marked restriction of his competency in halakhic matters, with all its far-reaching implications.
84. I say "generally," for power could equally shift to the other master of the book, the *posek* (religious decisor), who rules on the unending stream of questions that members of a text society inevitably pose. Indeed, in Israel it would appear that the successors to the current embodiment of *da'as Torah* will be prominent *dayyanim* (judges) and *posekim*, such as Rabbis N. Karelitz and S. Z. Auerbach. (I am indebted to Rabbi Mosheh Meiselman for this point.)
85. (a) I emphasize "in the last century," for the nineteenth century is the proper foil for the twentieth-century developments being described here. In prior centuries, yeshivot had been municipal institutions. The standard rabbinical contract gave the rabbi the right to maintain a yeshivah of a specific size, to be supported by the local community. The founding of the Yeshivah of Volozhin in 1803 established the yeshivah as a regional institution. It proved archetypical of most major yeshivot founded subsequently. See Shaul Stampfer, *Shalosh Yeshivot Lita'iyyot be-Me'ah ha-Tesha-Esreh* (Ph.D. diss., Hebrew University, 1981), pp. 1–8, and more generally, Jacob Katz, "Jewish Civilization as Reflected in the Yeshivot," *Journal of World History* 10 (1966–67): 674–704. I have found little evidence that the traditional authority of the rabbinate was eroded over the course of the nineteenth century (cf. Emmanuel Etkes, "Talmudic Scholarship and the Rabbinate in Lithuanian Jewry," in Leo Landman, ed., *Scholars and Scholarship: The Interaction between Judaism and Other Cultures* [New York: Yeshiva University Press, 1990], pp. 127–29). Until the death of R. Hayyim Ozer Grodzienski in 1940, political leadership was firmly in the hands of the rabbinate. Prestigious rabbinic posts were seen as the true reward of scholarship, and the attainment of such posts as Kovna (Kaunas), Vilna, and Dvinsk (Daugavpils) was the widespread aspiration of talmudic scholars the world over. (The Hungarian pattern was somewhat different; however, as stated in n. 14, our discussion follows the lines of development in Eastern rather than Central Europe.) (b) One should add that while it is correct that R. Hayyim of Volozhin and his son R. Yitzhak did exercise political power and were viewed, on occasion, as the representatives of the Jewish community of Russia, this was due more to R. Hayyim's stature as the leading pupil of the GRA and the mystique that attended his personal relationship with that almost legendary figure (a mystique that carried over to his son), not to their standing as *roshei yeshivah* of Volozhin. Significantly, their successor, R. Naftali Tzvi Yehudah Berlin, commonly known as the Netziv, had no similar status during his long and distinguished tenure as *rosh yeshivah*. Indeed, he was not even first among rabbinic equals.

That sobriquet, in the latter half of the nineteenth century, would have been bestowed on his contemporary, R. Isaac Elchanan Spector of Kovna.

86. This was a creative mistranslation of the German *Thoratreu* (faithful to the Torah), used by the neo-Orthodoxy of Germany. It was first used by modern Orthodoxy but subsequently attained far greater currency among what is called right-wing (though not *haredi*) Orthodoxy. See Jenna W. Joselit, *New York's Jewish Jews: The Orthodox Community in the Interwar Years* (Bloomington: Indiana University Press, 1990), p. 4.

87. *Da'as Torah* first made its appearance, in the modern sense of the word, in Hasidic writings of the late nineteenth century and was amplified in the interwar period by the Agudat Yisrael in Poland to advance claims of empowerment of a scholarly body *(Mo'etzes Gedolei ha-Torah)* that remained, nevertheless, largely powerless. It comes into its own as a political and ideological force only in the postwar period. On Hasidic Poland, see Mendel Piekarz, *Hassidut Polin: Megamot Ra'ayoniyyot Bein Shetei ha-Milhamot u-be-Gezeirot Tash-Tashah*, pp. 86–96. On Agudat Yisrael, see Gerson Bacon, "Da'at Torah ve-Hevlei Mashiah," *Tarbiz* 52 (1983): 497–508. See Lawrence Kaplan, "Daas Torah: A Modern Conception of Rabbinic Authority" in Moshe Z. Socol, ed., *Rabbinic Authority and Personal Autonomy* (Northvale, N.J.: Jason Aronson, 1992), pp. 1–60, esp. n. 84. Jacob Katz, in the introductory essay of his *Ha-Halakhah be-Metzar* (Jerusalem: Magnes Press, 1992), pp. 19–21, sees the origin of the current *da'as Torah* in the religious struggles with the Reform movement in Central Europe. This etiology may well be correct and does not conflict in any way with our interpretation. Nevertheless, I think that, if left unqualified, it may obscure more than enlighten. The struggle with Reform was a religious struggle and fought on religious issues. It is one thing for the laity to believe that decisions on ritual, even those that were halakhically neutral, should be in the hands of the rabbinate and that their decisions on such matters should be binding, even if no halakhic chapter and verse could be cited for such rulings. It is a wholly different thing to defer to rabbinic authority on social and political issues that are only tangentially religious, if at all. It is the latter, the new political empowerment, that is the subject of both Bacon's study and this essay. I should add as a caveat that I have made no personal study of the *term* (as opposed to the reality of) *da'as Torah* but have relied here on the studies of others. (See also the understandable *haredi* reaction to the suggestion that *da'as Torah* is a modern phenomenon, in Yaakov Feitman, "Daas Torah—an Analysis," *Jewish Observer*, May 1992, pp. 12–27. Talmudic authorities did indeed take stands on political issues in the past. What is new in the contemporary scene is the unprecedented frequency and scope of these stands and the authority currently ceded to them.)

88. I am indebted to Rabbi Mosheh Meiselman for this point. (The term "old order" merits comment. The "old order" in the Eastern European past was predominantly a lay one, composed of powerful *ba'alei battim*, and in this sense has this term, or its equivalent, been used throughout the essay. The "old order" of contemporary Orthodoxy, the subject of this paragraph, is the alliance of members of the traditional establishment—influential laymen, Hasidic rabbis, and elements of the old rabbinate—currently arrayed against the masters of the book.

89. Edward A. Fram, *Jewish Law and Social and Economic Realities in Sixteenth and Seventeenth Century Poland* (Ph.D. diss., Columbia University, 1991).

90. *Da'as Torah* may not be wholly as strange as it first appears to an American outsider.

The United States similarly believes that issues as broad as racial integration and as intimate as birth control can best be decided by nine sages steeped in the normative texts of the society and rendering their opinions in its legal idiom. And a Jewish historian might note that America, equally, has no mimetic tradition, either of peasantry or aristocracy—nor of clergy, for that matter. Perhaps a nation that saw its birth in one text and was bonded by another, and had throughout its history amalgamated its ceaseless flow of immigrants by fealty, yet again, to a text, has something in common with contemporary Orthodox society.

91. See Katz, *Tradition and Crisis* (above, n. 46), pp. 197–213. I have used ecstatic religiosity for expositional purposes only. I take no stand on what unique aspect of the Hasidic *zaddik* delegitimized the traditional religious structure: his virtuosity in religious ecstasy or his standing as the *axis mundi*, the channel through which the Divine force nurtures the world. See Arthur Green, "Typologies of Leadership and the Hasidic Zaddiq," in Green, ed., *Jewish Spirituality: From the Sixteenth Century to the Present* (London: Routledge and Kegan Paul, 1987), pp. 127–56, and notes throughout. (For a full bibliography on this issue, see Rachel Elior, "Temurot be-Makshevah ha-Datit be-Hassidut Polin: Bein Yir'ah ve-Ahavah le-Omek ve-Gavvan," *Tarbiz* 62 [1994]: 387 n. 9.)
92. I am indebted to Michael Silber for this point.
93. A. A. Droyanov, *Otzar ha-Bedihah ve-ha-Hiddud* (Tel Aviv: Devir, 1939), vol. 1, chap. 6. This collection is of the gentler humor. The more mordant jokes still await compilation. (I am not referring to literary satire, of which there was no lack, but to popular humor, which is probative of our point.)
94. For examples in English, see Shimon Finkelman, *The Chazon Ish: The Life and Ideals of Rabbi Avraham Yeshayah Karelitz* (New York: Mesorah Publications, 1984), pp. 203–12; idem, *Reb Moshe: The Life and Ideals of Hagaon Rabbi Moshe Feinstein* (New York: Mesorah Publications, 1986), pp. 237–49. (a) It is true that for several decades in the late eighteenth and early nineteenth centuries, some wonder stories circulated about the GRA. This arose both as a counter to Hasidic *rebbeim* and as a consequence of the singular charisma of the GRA. Here, as occasionally elsewhere [see n. 85], this charisma spilt over to his prime pupil, R, Hayyim of Volozhin, and in the general atmosphere of the time, some stories told of any subsequent *misnaggdic* rabbi, including R. Hayyim's son, R, Isaac of Volozhin. On wonder tales of the GRA and R, Hayyim, see Emmanuel Etkes, "Darko u-Fo'alo shel R, Hayyim mi-Volozhin," *Proceedings of the American Academy for Social Research* 38–39 [1972]" 44 n. 128. (b) The loss of antipathy to miracles, albeit still told about Hasidic rabbis, may well have begun earlier. Note the surprising signatories of the letters of approbations *[haskamot]* of Gerson E, Stashevski's *Sefer Gedulat Mordecai u-Gedulat ha-Tzaddikim* [Warsaw, 1934]. David Tamar once pointed out this text to me in a different context.) (The growing iconic role of the Torah sage also reflects, to an extent, the sensed uniqueness of his religious authenticity and the comfort that his visual presence provides for an increasingly acculturated community. See Richard I. Cohen's recent essay on the role of pictures of *gedolei Torah*, "Ve-Yihiyu Enekha Ro'ot et Morekha: ha-Rav ke-Ikunin," *Zion* 58 [1993]: 407–52.)
95. Needless to say, some of the older congregants, including, of course, the *roshei yeshivah*, were Eastern European-born, and the fear that had been instilled in them in their youth was palpable.

96. I have borrowed the vivid lines of the *u-netaneh tokef* prayer only to convey the atmosphere of *Ne'ilah*. The prayer itself is, of course, recited in *musaf*. (I should add that the borrowing is apt, for the only other time the synagogue filled up was at the recitation of the starkly personal and anthropomorphic *u-netaneh tokef*.)

97. For an *analogous* instance of the persistence in Eastern European immigrants of early notions of causation and punishment, see Barbara Meyerhoff's account of the efficacy of curses in *Number Our Days* (New York: Dutton, 1979), esp. pp. 164, 183.

98. I shared this impression with my father in 1969 and discovered that he was of a similar mind, at least about the American community with which he was familiar. Indeed, he had given expression to something much akin to this in a speech a few years before; see J. B. Soloveitchik, *Al ha-Teshuvah* (Jerusalem: Histadrut ha-Tziyyonit ha-Olamit, 1975), p. 199.

99. See, for example, Lucien Fevre, *The Problem of Unbelief in the Sixteenth Century* (Cambridge, Mass.: Harvard University Press, 1982). It is worth adding that a religious cosmology, or what is sometimes mistakenly called an "Age of Faith," does not necessarily entail greater religious observance, though this is sometimes assumed. There is no necessary relation between the two. The difference between a religious cosmology and a natural one lies in the way the notion of God is entertained: as a belief or as an invisible reality. The question of religious observance lies in the strange disjunction that exists in human beings between knowledge and action. One can take the reality of God as a physical given and still be casual about *kashrut* or eating meat on Friday, just as one can smoke and lead the life of a couch potato without for a moment doubting the reality of cancer cells or cholesterol.

100. See, for example, Keith Thomas, *Religion and the Decline of Magic* (London: Weidenfeld and Nicolson, 1971); David D. Hall, *Worlds of Wonder, Days of Judgment* (Cambridge, Mass.: Harvard University Press, 1989); W. I. Thomas and Florian Znaniecki, *The Polish Peasant in Europe and America* (Boston: Badger, 1918), vol. 1, pp. 205–306.

101. The *Tzenah Re'enah*, of R, Jacob of Janow, is far more than simply an amplified translation of the Torah, it is rather a vade mecum to the entire Midrashic world. Between 1622 and 1900 it was reprinted no less than 173 times (Shmeruk, *Sifrut Yiddish: Perakim le-Tolodotehah* [above, n. 57], p. 115), and its cumulative impact on the religious outlook and spirituality of Eastern European Jewry was incalculable.

102. Much source material on this theme can now be conveniently found in Anson Laytner, *Arguing with God: A Jewish Tradition* (Northvale, N.J.: Jason Aronson, 1990).

103. The striking, palpable silence of the Ashkenazic *haredi* community in the Peretz affair is, to my mind, indicative of this loss. Rabbi Isaac Peretz, a Sefaredi *haredi* and Israeli minister of interior, stated that the seventeen children and five adults killed when a train ran over their school bus died because of the recent public desecration of Sabbath in Petah Tikvah. These remarks caused a furor in the general community. Yet, other than a statement of support by Rabbi Shakh immediately after the storm broke (*Ha-Modi'a*, June 28, 1986, pp. 1, 3), the Ashkenazi *haredi* press made no further mention of the matter despite the furor of the next two months. Not for lack of opportunity, however, as those months witnessed continuous demonstrations against the theaters in Petah Tikvah, all of which was covered in the *haredi* press, both in *Ha-Modi'a* and the newly formed *Yated Ne'eman*. Rabbi Peretz's remarks simply expressed the classic religious explanation of linking misfortune with guilt *(pishpush*

*be-ma'asim)*, which would have been uttered by a preacher of the past millennium. Indeed, R. Nissim Yagen, the Sefaredi preacher, brought further proof of the causal link, as would have preachers of the past, by pointing out a number of correlations: first, that the number of the dead totaled twenty-two, which was also the date of the public opening of the movie theaters in Petah Tikvah (22 Sivan); second, the sum total of the dead and wounded amounted to thirty-nine, which corresponds to the number of types of work forbidden on the Sabbath *(lamed-tet avot melakhot)*. As noted above (nn. 34, 19), the Sefaredic world has encountered modernity only recently, and in many ways, as in the palpable sense of the rewards and terrors of the afterlife and of God's immediate involvement in human affairs, remains far closer to the religious sensibilities of their fathers than does the more unconsciously acculturated members of the Ashkenazic community. This distance is true even of one of the least acculturated elements of the Ashkenazic *haredi* world, Hasidic women; see Tamar El-Or, *Educated and Ignorant* (above, n. 20), p. 154. (R. Peretz's remarks were first reported in the Jerusalem weekly, *Kol Ha-Ir* of June 21, 1985. [I am indebted to Chaim I. Waxman for this reference.] Rabbi Yagen's remarks are on the tape series, *Ner le-Me'ah*: no. 41, *Neshamot*.)

# 17 Jack Wertheimer

# Religious Movements in Collision

## A Jewish Culture War?

An analysis of shifts in the policies and practices of each Jewish denomination provides a necessary context in which to assess why relations between the religious groups have deteriorated in recent years. All of the movements have responded to a series of new challenges faced by the American Jewish community: the rising rate of intermarriage and the resulting question of how to integrate the children of such marriages into the Jewish community; the feminist revolution and the demands of Jewish women for equality in religious life; and the declining levels of synagogue affiliation and involvement of third- and fourth-generation American Jews, which has forced all Jewish institutions to compete for members. The policies of Jewish denominations have been shaped as well by the aggressive tenor of religious disputation that characterizes relations between segments of American Christianity—and indeed religious antagonists throughout the world.

### Heightened Religious Tensions

Each Jewish movement has responded differently to the new challenges and has embraced policies unilaterally, with little or no consultation with its counterparts in American Judaism. The resulting policies are shaped by profoundly different conceptions of Jewish identity, religious reform, and the future of American Judaism. The Reform and Reconstructionist position on patrilineality is incompatible with Conservative and Orthodox definitions of who is a Jew. The ordination of women as rabbis is viewed by some as a logical extension of Jewish ethical values and by others as an unacceptable deviation from Judaism's differentiation between gender roles. And the self-segregation of Orthodox Jews, many of whose leaders refuse to participate in communal organizations that include non-Orthodox rabbis lest such participation confer legitimacy on inauthentic leaders, raises the question of whether Jews can act in concert. As Irving Greenberg has suggested, both extremes on the religious spectrum seem to have written each other off; both extremes assume that other Jews can be ignored because those others will become increasingly irrelevant to the Jewish future. Specifically, the majority of Orthodox rabbis act as if they expect the non-Orthodox world to assimilate; and the unilateralism of Reform and Reconstruction on the issue of patrilineality suggests a belief that adherents of halakhah are a dying or fossilized breed. Only those on the Conservative right and the Orthodox left seem overly concerned about religious polarization, perhaps because they have ties to all segments of the Jewish community.[1]

Although much of this disagreement has been confined to the journals of various rabbinic organizations, a few widely reported incidents have focused public attention on the heightened religious divisiveness. One episode that came to symbolize the possibilities as well as lost opportunities for greater religious unity has become known as the Denver experiment.[2] Beginning in 1978, Reform, Conservative, and Traditional[3] rabbis formed a joint *Beit Din* (rabbinic court) to oversee conversions. (Orthodox rabbis refused to participate, and there was no Reconstructionist rabbi in Denver at the time.) The purpose of this program was to avoid a situation in which rabbis in Denver did not recognize each other's converts to Judaism. Under the Denver program, each rabbi still retained autonomy to perform his own conversions, but a very significant number—approximately 750 individuals—underwent conversion in Denver through the communal rabbinic court.

In order to function in concert, all participating rabbis compromised some of their views: the Traditional rabbis "were prepared to say that even though we knew that all of the students coming out of the general conversion process would not be authentic Orthodox Jews, we were prepared to say as long as they were beginning an effort to learn Judaism and aspire to be committed Jews, we were prepared to offer our signatures." Or as another Traditional rabbi put it: "Our compromise was simply that we did not make the thorough investigation that we might have made of our own converts—whether the person, in practice, was prepared to embrace a larger measure of traditional Judaism." The Reform rabbis, in turn, compromised by agreeing to teach about traditional observances, such as Jewish dietary laws and special Passover regulations. In addition, the Reform rabbis compromised by acceding to the Traditional and Conservative rabbis' insistence that converts must go to a ritual bath *(mikveh)* and undergo a symbolic circumcision *(hatafat dam brit)*.[4] Not coincidentally, the lone Conservative rabbi in Denver, whose conception of conversion represented a centrist position, served as the chairman of the board for most of its history. But the actual conversion ceremony was supervised by three Traditional rabbis.

In 1983, after six years of relatively smooth functioning, the Denver *Beit Din* was dissolved. The move was precipitated by the resolution on patrilineality adopted that year by the Central Conference of American Rabbis. This decision to redefine Jewish identity, as well as the designation of Denver as a pilot community for a new Reform outreach effort to recruit converts, convinced the Traditional and Conservative rabbis that they could no longer participate in the joint board. Although the Reform rabbis of Denver held varying views on the question of patrilineality, the national decision of the Reform rabbinate placed the Traditional and Conservative rabbis in an untenable position. They could not cooperate in a conversion program with rabbis who held so different a conception of Jewish identity. And furthermore, they could not supervise conversions that would occur with increasing frequency due to a Reform outreach effort that was inconsistent with their own understanding of how to relate to potential proselytes. Thus, the Denver program, a model for other local Jewish communities, foundered because of decisions taken far away from that community at the national convention of Reform rabbis.

The possibility of future cross-denominational cooperation in other Jewish communities was further undermined by the response of Orthodox groups to the Denver program. When the existence of that program became public knowledge (ironically, through the announcement of its demise), Orthodox groups raised a hue and cry over the folly of Traditional rabbis for even participating in a joint conversion effort. As the *Jewish Observer*, an English-language periodical of the Orthodox right, crowed:

> While compromise for the sake of unity can often make good sense, when dealing with basic principles of faith, "compromise" is actually a sell-out. . . . It is time that all Orthodox rabbis recognized that Reform and Conservative Judaism are far, far removed from Torah, and that *Klal Yisroel* [the totality of the Jewish people] is betrayed—not served—when Orthodoxy enters in religious association with them.

In the judgment of the *Jewish Observer*, "the Traditional rabbis of Denver have been party to an outrageous fraud." And lest anyone fail to grasp the implications of this fraud, the periodical's editor went on to warn "other communities contemplating this type of denominational cooperation . . . [to] take note of the awesome pitfalls involved and step back from the abyss."[5]

Since the collapse of the Denver program, denominational relations have continued to deteriorate. Among the key flash points have been the veto exercised by Orthodox rabbis of the Rabbinical Council of America to prevent the newly independent Reconstructionist movement from joining the Synagogue Council of America, an umbrella agency linking the rabbinic and congregational bodies of all the other Jewish religious movements;[6] the reconstitution of the Jewish Welfare Bureau's Chaplaincy Board, which provided chaplains and other support to Jews in the military since World War I, in response to the application of a woman rabbi seeking to serve as a Jewish military chaplain;[7] and the placement of advertisements by rabbinic groups of the Orthodox right urging Jews to stay home on the

High Holidays rather than worship in a non-Orthodox synagogue.[8] When the *New York Times* published a front-page article with the headline, "Split Widens on a Basic Issue: What Is a Jew?" the divisions among rabbis began to attract wider attention in the Jewish community.[9] One organization in particular, the National Jewish Center for Learning and Leadership (CLAL), headed by Rabbi Irving Greenberg, sought to focus communal attention on the growing rift by inviting the leaders of all four Jewish religious movements to a conference that posed the provocative question, "Will There Be One Jewish People by the Year 2000?"[10]

The wider Jewish community was most actively drawn into the fray during the "who is a Jew" controversy in late 1988. An international debate erupted when it appeared that the Israeli government would grant the Orthodox rabbinate the exclusive right to determine the Jewish status of converts, thereby guaranteeing the delegitimation of all conversions not performed under Orthodox auspices.

Long after Israeli leaders had finished with the matter, the bitterness engendered by the controversy continued to fester within the American Jewish community. Opponents of the amendment faulted Orthodox leaders in the United States, particularly the Lubavitcher Rebbe, who resides in Brooklyn, New York, for pressuring Israeli groups to pass the amendment. Orthodox groups were castigated as divisive and mean-spirited. It was frequently argued that Orthodox Jews in America were taking their battle against other Jewish denominations to Israel because as a small minority they could not win such a struggle in the United States. Moreover, non-Orthodox spokespeople claimed that *their* identity as Jews was under attack. Shoshana Cardin, then the chairperson of the Council of Jewish Federations' Committee on Religious Pluralism put it as follows: "What we're dealing with here is perceived disenfranchisement of millions of Jews. And in this case, perception is reality."[11]

Orthodox groups counterattacked. Though some Orthodox organizations supported the campaign to remove the issue of "who is a Jew" from the Israeli political agenda (principally, the Rabbinical Council of America), other Orthodox groups banded together to blame Reform Judaism for causing a religious schism. In an "Open Letter to American Jews" signed by several Orthodox organizations, the halakhic definition of Jewish identity was described as "universally accepted among all Jews for thousands of years. Reform, however, has done away with *Halacha*; and the Conservative movement is forever tampering with it."[12] In a similar vein, Rabbi Marc Angel, one of the most moderate members of the centrist Orthodox rabbinate, lashed out at those who criticized Orthodoxy for its stand on "who is a Jew": "Those leaders who speak so passionately for Jewish unity ought to have launched a major attack on the decision of Reform Judaism to consider 'patrilineal Jews' as Jews. There has probably been nothing more divisive in modern Jewish history than this decision to unilaterally change the definition of Jewishness to include the child of a Jewish father."[13] The recrimination and bitterness over this issue brought religious hostility between Orthodox and non-Orthodox groups to a fever pitch.

## The Great Rift

The "who is a Jew" controversy set into sharp relief the central features of recent religious warfare between Jews. First, it demonstrated the inextricable connection between Israeli religious and political developments and religious divisions that characterize American Jewry. Remarkably, actions taken by rabbis in Israel who have virtually no constituency other than Orthodox Jews can spark religious conflict in the United States, where the non-Orthodox groups represent the vast majority of Jews. The hostility of Jewish religious leaders in Israel toward non-Orthodox Jews strengthens the hands of militant Orthodox groups in the United States and antagonizes non-Orthodox groups. It is disturbing enough to some that the chief rabbis of Israel do not set foot in non-Orthodox synagogues when they visit the United States. But when leading Orthodox rabbinic decisors of *both* the right-wing *Haredi* sector and the more moderate faction rule that "in principle it is forbidden to save the life of a Reform or Conservative Jew on Shabbat on the same basis that one is not allowed to desecrate the Sabbath to save a gentile's life,"[14] there is a serious likelihood that the religious mind-set developing within the official Israeli rabbinate will further poison relations between Orthodox and non-Orthodox Jews in the United States. In turn, the attitudes of the latter toward Israel have been affected adversely because of the perceived link between the Israeli government and the Orthodox religious establishment. According to a recent survey, the attitudes of Reform Jews toward Israel are strongly correlated with the extent to which they link Israel with its Orthodox rabbinate; the greater the perceived link, the more alienated from Israel Reform Jews felt.[15]

Second, the intensity of the recriminations indicates that issues of personal status are now at the heart of the struggle between religious factions. The explosion, after all, came over the question of "who is a Jew." Religious polarization became more intense when Jews could no longer agree on questions of boundaries: Who is part of the group and who is outside? Whom may their children marry? Will their grandchildren be considered Jewish and permitted to celebrate a Bar or Bat Mitzvah if those grandchildren have a Christian mother and a Jewish father? If their rabbi was born to a Jewish father and Christian mother, is that ordained rabbi considered to be a Jew? In the past, Jewish religious movements held diverse theological views and observed religious rituals differently; but the observances of one group of Jews had only a limited impact on those of another group; they could be ignored if deemed offensive. Issues of personal status, by contrast, have far wider repercussions: at stake is the community's recognition or rejection of an individual as a Jew. Soaring rates of intermarriage coupled with disputes over patrilineal descent will only worsen the situation: Rabbi Irving Greenberg has warned that by the end of the century, there will be perhaps as many as half a million children, born to mothers converted by Reform rabbis or accepted as Jewish under the patrilineal definition, whose Jewishness will not be accepted by other Jews.[16] Thus, regardless of whether the matter is ever raised again in the State of Israel, American Jews do not agree on the question of "who is a Jew."

Third, there is even no agreement as to the number of American Jews who care about these matters. One survey found that on the issue of patrilineality, the vast majority of Orthodox Jews would be "upset" if their children married someone of patrilineal descent, but only one-third of Conservative Jews and one-tenth of Reform Jews would be "upset." Thus, perhaps no more than one-quarter of American Jewry rejects the new definition of Jewish identity put forward by Reform and Reconstuctionism.[17] This has led to speculation that the rejection of patrilineality by Orthodoxy and by segments of the Conservative movement will give way in time to sociological realities, namely, mass support for patrilineality by American Jewry. Other observers are not so certain, especially as evidence mounts about the minimal Jewish identity of children raised in mixed-married homes and as fears of intermarriage intensify. Orthodox Jews are not about to alter their opposition, and Conservative rabbis who overwhelmingly voted to expel from their association any colleague who accepted patrilineality may yet convince their congregants to reject patrilineality.

Finally, and most important, the "who is a Jew" controversy made it evident that the critical fault line running through the Jewish community separates Orthodox from non-Orthodox Jews. Reform and Reconstructonist Jews explicitly reject Halakhah (rabbinic law) as normative; accordingly, they do not define Jewish identity on the basis of those laws. By contrast, the Conservative movement does regard rabbinic law as normative and agrees with some Orthodox positions on questions of personal status. But in the debate over "who is a Jew" and other controversies in Israel, the Conservative movement has linked arms with the Reform and Reconstructionist movements, thereby blurring its own more nuanced stance: it agrees with Orthodoxy that Jewish identity must conform to rabbinic law, but it sides with Reform on the need to break the Orthodox monopoly on interpreting Jewish law. In order to wage that political battle, Conservative Judaism has allied itself with nonhalakhic movements. The critical divide thus runs between non-Orthodox movements on one side and the Orthodox on the other.

Since the "who is a Jew" controversy, relations between these camps have continued to worsen.

*Item*: Rabbi Aaron Soloveitchik, the heir apparent to his brother Joseph as the spiritual leader of centrist Orthodoxy, declared that any unified effort to resolve the chaotic issues of personal status through a Jewish court that included a non-Orthodox Jew would be invalid. Moreover, he likened the very act of cooperation with non-Orthodox groups to the biblical sin of the golden calf because it would "mislead ignorant Jewish masses to worship the idol of Reform and Reconstructionist Judaism."[18]

*Item*: Rabbi J. D. Bleich, his colleague at Yeshiva University, the preeminent institution of centrist Orthodoxy, "proposed to resolve the problem of 'who is a Jew?' by recognizing Reform converts in Israel the same way the law recognizes Moslem and Christian converts, that is, as members of a separate religion."[19]

*Item*: A planned meeting between American rabbis and Pope John Paul II was almost torpedoed by denominational bickering. The Synagogue Council of America, an umbrella agency that coordinates the national policies of Jewish rabbinical and congregational organizations, was paralyzed by the insistence of the Union of Orthodox Jewish Congregations on its right to veto the composition of the delegation. The matter became moot after the pope postponed his visit to the United States. But it is unlikely that the umbrella organization will be able to avert conflict in the future. The head of the Orthodox rabbinic group insisted on the right to veto the appointment of a homosexual or patrilinear rabbi to a position of leadership on the Synagogue Council of America.[20]

*Item*: The Conservative movement has embarked on a program to free itself from reliance on Orthodox functionaries. Since the late 1980s the Jewish Theological Seminary of American has sponsored programs to train Jewish physicians to perform ritual circumcision *(brit milah)* and has taught rabbis how to supervise *kashrut* (Jewish dietary requirements) in their communities.[21] Conservative institutions are also building their own ritual baths as a response to Orthodox efforts to obstruct the performance of Conservative conversion ceremonies at communal *mikvaot*.[22]

Not surprisingly, these policy decisions are accompanied by increasingly uncivil outbursts by leaders of the various factions. Name-calling and invective are now routinely injected into Jewish public discourse. In an address to the Reform rabbinate, Rabbi Alexander Schindler of the Union of American Hebrew Congregations opined: "Where Orthodoxy alone prevails—stale repression, fossilized tradition, and ethical corruption hold sway."[23] Orthodox writers, in turn, label Reform Judaism a "sect" or an expression of "deviance."[24] The upcoming generation of rabbis is likely to be even more polarized. According to a recent study, large majorities of rabbinical students at the Conservative, Reform, and Reconstructionist seminaries viewed Orthodoxy as intolerant, lacking in compassion, and dominated by their isolationist wing. Almost all Orthodox rabbinical students surveyed and two-thirds of Conservative rabbinical students regarded Reform Judaism as "assimilationist."[25]

Although some observers dismiss these rifts as minor rabbinic squabbling over turf, fragmentary evidence is surfacing of a more widespread social consequence to the religious polarization. There is some evidence of a withdrawal on the part of broader segments of the Orthodox community away from social interaction, let alone friendship, with non-Orthodox Jews.[26] Though it is not widely publicized, the implicit, if not explicit, stance of the more right-wing Orthodox groups is to avoid such social contacts.[27] One writer who examined audio tapes prepared for Orthodox children found "a universe of discourse . . . [that] is exclusively Orthodox. . . . Jews who are other than Orthodox rarely appear, and then only . . . as negative foils," as Jews who are not very smart or as potential converts.[28] Moreover, as the overwhelming majority of Orthodox youngsters now attend their own denomination's day schools, summer camps, and youth programs through their high school years, they increasingly inhabit an exclusive social world that does not even allow for contact with non-Orthodox peers. These moves toward separatism, in turn, have antagonized non-Orthodox Jews: a survey of American Jews conducted in the late 1980s found that the majority claimed to be "very offended" "by Orthodox Jews who show no respect for the way you choose to be Jewish."[29] Social barriers between the Orthodox and non-Orthodox worlds are growing higher as the religious conflict intensifies.

Recognizing the dangers to Jewish unity inherent in religious polarization, some groups have tried to bridge the divide. This is a central item on the agenda of CLAL, the national Jewish Center for Learning and Leadership, which has a specific department called Am Echad—One People. The American Jewish Committee has also acted through its Department of Communal Affairs to bring leaders of opposing groups together.[30] In local communities rabbis from across the spectrum have initiated programs to keep the lines of communication open and to cooperate on issues of pan-Jewish concern.[31] Even some of the antagonists are edging away from conflict: the increasingly right-wing Young Israel movement within the Orthodox camp saw fit at the time of the "who is a Jew" controversy to publish an advertisement in the Jewish press to express its understanding "of the pain of those who mistakenly believe that Orthodoxy has denied their authenticity as Jews." "A Jew is a Jew," the ad declared, "regardless of his affiliation—Orthodox, Conservative, Reform, or non-believer—all are, and ever will remain Jews, to be loved and cherished."[32] Rabbis across the spectrum overwhelmingly assert that Jewish leaders should display unity in public and not delegitimize other Jews. It is those very same rabbis who carry on the disputes, however.[33]

Nevertheless, despite the many laudable efforts to bridge divisions, disputes over Jewish personal status remain unresolved; profound disagreements over religious definition, legitimacy, and change fester; social interactions between different types of Jews continue to be strained or nonexistent. And in the background, Israeli political groups, which do not concern themselves with questions of religious diversity, periodically hurl incendiary challenges into the volatile brew that is American Judaism.

## A Jewish Culture War?

The informed observer of Jewish religious conflict cannot fail to note the significant parallels between developments within American Judaism and the religious upheaval within Christian denominations. "On all sides," writes Robert Wuthnow about the general pattern, "American religion seems to be embroiled in controversy. . . . Scarcely a statement is uttered by one religious group on the issues without another faction of the religious community taking umbrage. The issues themselves shift almost continuously, but the underlying sense of polarization and acrimony continues."[34] Certainly, the tone of discussion and the polarized mood within American Judaism parallel those in American Christianity. But what about the substance of the dispute? To what extent does the great rift between non-Orthodox and Orthodox Jews mirror the great divide in American Protestantism between conservatives and liberals? How apt are comparisons between Protestant fundamentalists and Orthodox Jews? And is the religious struggle gripping the Jewish community the same as the culture war waged in some sectors of American society at large?

The broad brush strokes show many similarities in both the causes and the consequences of religious conflict in American Judaism and in American Christianity. To begin with, the antagonists—religious conservatives and liberals—share a common worldview with their counterparts in other religions. As defined by James Davison Hunter, the worldview of orthodoxy in its various permutations "is the commitment on the part of adherents to an external, definable, and transcendent authority," whereas progressivists[35] share in common "the tendency to resymbolize historical faiths according to the prevailing assumptions of contemporary life."[36] This distinction applies to Jewish religious movements, which are separated by their willingness to accept a normative religious structure that is commanded by divine (transcendent) authority: Orthodoxy in all its shadings affirms such a structure; the Conservative movement officially offers a nuanced acceptance of such religious norms; and the Reform and Reconstructionist movements explicitly advocate the need to resymbolize Judaism according to contemporary assumptions and to reject a binding religious structure. Clearly, the acceptance or rejection of a normative, divinely mandated Judaism with a legal structure based on commandments is central to Jewish religious division.

Moreover, as Hunter notes, those worldviews then shape social assumptions, especially regarding matters of public policy. Until the 1960s, conservative groups believed that their views of marriage and sexual morality were widely shared. But since the revolutions of the 1960s those comfortable assumptions have been shattered by new social patterns—increasing rates of divorce, permissive sexual mores, divergent lifestyles, changing gender roles, the perceived collapse of the family, more openly expressed homosexuality, and the availability of abortion on demand.[37] Some segments of the Orthodox Jewish community have sympathized with like-minded Christians over these symptoms of declining "family values." For their part, conservative activists have worked to build alliances with Orthodox Jews, as is attested by Jerry Falwell's (founder of the moral majority) proud declarations of his kinship with Orthodox Jews and the publication of approving reports about the warm family life of Lubavitch Hasidim by a conservative "think tank."[38]

In truth, however, only a small segment of the Jewish population is comfortable with these alliances. To some extent, Jews are held back by political considerations: there is an ingrained fear of right-wing groups, because they have traditionally harbored anti-Semites and advocated the Christianization of America. Furthermore, most Jews, including many in the Orthodox camp, cannot subscribe to the total conservative social agenda. To take the most controversial issue, most Jews of all shades support present public policy on abortion; and even the most right-wing Orthodox Jews, who reject abortion on demand, cannot support a ban on abortion, because under certain circumstances they too rule that abortion is permissible. Even Agudath Israel, an ultra-Orthodox, explicitly pro-life organization, which opposes *Roe v. Wade*, stops short of supporting a ban on public funding and facilities for abortions.[39] Similarly, all religious groupings in Judaism maintain that divorce is a legitimate option. Thus, while religious liberals, the vast majority of American Jewry, actively support liberal social policies and sometimes take a high-profile stance at pro-choice rallies,[40] more religiously conservative Jews are not generally active in the American culture war over social policies—even when they sympathize with part of the conservative agenda.

This is true even of those Orthodox Jews conventionally lumped together with fundamentalists, the right-wing Orthodox, or *Haredim*, as they are now more commonly known in Jewish circles. To understand why, we first need to clarify where these Orthodox Jews converge with Christian fundamentalists. If we ignore the original defining feature of fundamentalism, the belief in biblical inerrancy,[41] it is possible to discern some important areas of convergence between the most ultra-Orthodox Jews and the right wing of evangelical Protestantism and Catholicism. Both ultra-Orthodoxy and fundamentalism are responses to the challenges posed by modernity to traditional religion, and therefore both are most likely to exist "where tradition is meeting modernity rather than where modernity is most remote." Both also engage in a struggle with their own coreligionists who are perceived as "agents of assault on all that is held dear."[42]

*Haredim* conform to many of the characteristics listed in a recent attempt by Martin Marty and R. Scott Appleby to classify the commonalities shared by all fundamentalists.[43]

1. They are militant. "Fundamentalists begin as traditionalists who perceive some challenge or threat to their core identity, both social and personal. . . . They react, they fight back with great innovative power."
2. They share a "certain understanding of gender, sex roles, the nurturing and education of children."
3. They fight with a chosen repertoire of resources, including "real or presumed pasts, to actual or imagined ideal original conditions and concepts, and select what they regard as fundamental."
4. They "fight under God."
5. "They will fight for a changed civil polity."

With the exception of the last point, all of these traits characterize the outlook of ultra-Orthodox Jews in the United States

This is not to suggest, however, that ultra-Orthodoxy derives its strategies and programs from American fundamentalism. Ultra-Orthodoxy was born in Europe, and its most important techniques were imported to America at the time of the Holocaust. These include a reliance on separatism in Jewish communal matters—secession from official communal functions and refusal to recognize the legitimacy of non-Orthodox rabbis, even non-ultra-Orthodox rabbis; and the elevation of the Jewish school over the synagogue as the central institution of Jewish life, thereby granting most power to rabbinic authorities in the yeshiva world, rather than to pulpit rabbis. The recent resurgence of ultra-Orthodoxy has been reinforced by the successful application of these transplanted approaches rather than by the model of American fundamentalism.

In matters of American politics, as well, ultra-Orthodox Jews pursue an approach that differs from that of Christian fundamentalists. Undoubtedly, some Orthodox Jews support conservative policy stances; indeed, certain segments of Orthodox Jews tend to vote for political conservatives.[44] But ultimately, these Jews invest little energy and money in conservative social causes—however much they may sympathize. The critical battles for Orthodox Jews are with non-Orthodox Jews and revolve around entirely different matters.

To take up the first distinction, Orthodox Jews for the most part are not invested in the struggle over public policy, the key battleground in the American religious and culture wars.[45] To be sure, Orthodox Jews sometimes become activists on behalf of specific candidates, but they are drawn into politics in order to protect their communal interests, to get their fair share of government funding and protection—not in order to change American society. The conventional right-wing Orthodox perspective was colorfully expressed by Rabbi Yehuda Levin: "I had very little contact with the Gentile world. I was living in a ghetto without walls. . . . It is inbred in our community that what goes on in the outside world is *meshugah* (crazy). . . . So if it is *meshugah*, why should we bother with it."[46] Levin nevertheless became a militant antiabortion and anti–gay rights activist, but he is the exception that proves the rule. Most Orthodox Jews do not see American public policy as their domain. They fight for their narrow political interests, not to remake American society.[47]

The only society ultra-Orthodox Jews wish to remake is Israel—for both ideological and pragmatic reasons. Orthodox groups in the United States and Israel have invested in the issue of "who is a Jew" and other questions of Israeli public policy because it offends them that Israel is not governed by traditional Jewish law. They have no such expectations of American society. Moreover, ultra-Orthodox Jews, the so-called *Haredim*, have a powerful vested interest in Israeli political life since they are supported by massive government subsidies. As Samuel Heilman and Menachem Friedman put it: "The [international Jewish] fundamentalism train is pulled by the Israeli *[Haredi]* locomotive; that locomotive is traveling very fast on rails maintained" by the Israeli government.[48]

By contrast, the Orthodox/non-Orthodox rift in the United States focuses not on governmental policy but on communal conflict, particularly regarding the definition of Jewish personal status. True, the various Jewish religious movements differ in their evaluations of modern culture and American mores; and they also assess gender and sexual matters differently. But the critical divide between Jewish religious groups concerns questions of personal status—marriageability and Jewish identity—which have no counterpart in Christian religious disputes. Put differently, the culture war engulfing some sectors of Christianity concerns the proper ordering of American society; at stake in Judaism are issues of group survival and cohesion. As Christians clash over theology and public policy, religious Jews battle over the boundaries of their own society—indeed, they cannot even agree on whether some of their co-religionists are actually Jewish.

## Notes

1. On Irving Greenberg's views, see Gary Rosenblatt, "Judaism's Civil War: How Deep Is the Rift?" *Baltimore Jewish Times*, January 29, 1988, pp. 56–59; Greenberg, "Will There Be One Jewish People in the Year 2000?" *Moment*, June 1985; and idem, "The One in 2000 Controversy" *Moment*, March 1987.
2. The most complete account of this experiment, which includes interviews with all of the participating rabbis, appeared in a special section entitled "Conversion and Patrilineality," *Intermountain Jewish News*, December 2, 1983.
3. Traditional synagogues and rabbis are largely a midwestern phenomenon; Traditional congregations permit men and women to sit together and utilize a microphone during religious services; their rabbis, mainly graduates of the Hebrew Theological Seminary in Skokie, identify with Modern Orthodoxy.
4. For a history of the board written by the leading Reform rabbi in Denver, see Steven E. Foster, "The Community Rabbbinic Conversion Board: The Denver Model," *Journal of Reform Judaism*, summer 1984, esp. pp. 27–28.
5. Nisson Wolpin, "Compromise on the Great Divide: Questionable Conversions in Denver," *Jewish Observer*, January 1984, pp. 32–34.
6. Editorial, "The Synagogue Council of America," *Reconstructionist*, July–August 1986, p. 6.
7. When the CCAR placed a female candidate in the chaplaincy program, the commission was reconstituted as the Jewish Chaplains Council in 1986. See *JTA Bulletin*, August 29, 1985, p. 3; and *American Jewish Yearbook* 86 (1986), p. 399; and *American Jewish Yearbook* 87 (1987), p. 400, on the name change.
8. *New York Times*, February 28, 1986, p. A1.
9. Ibid.
10. For information on this conference, see *Materials from the Critical Issues Conference*, which includes press clippings from Jewish newspapers compiled by CLAL to publicize the discussions held in mid-March 1986.
11. Cardin is quoted in Arthur J. Magida, "'Who Is a Jew' Dominates Assembly," *Jewish News* (Detroit), November 25, 1988, p. 1. See also "'Who Is a Jew' Issue Threatens

Funding," and "Leaders Protest 'Who Is,'" *Atlanta Jewish Times*, December 2, 1988, pp. 12, 13, as well as "'Who Is a Jew' Furor Erupts," *Atlanta Jewish Times*, November 8, 1988, p. 16A.

12. The open letter appeared in the *New York Times*, December 19, 1988, p. B9. On Orthodox divisions over the issue, see Alan Richter and Walter Ruby, "Rift Develops among Orthodox over Law of Return," *LI Jewish World*, December 2–8, 1988, p. 3.
13. Marc D. Angel, "Leaders of U.S. Jewry Have Fear of Losing Power," *Jewish Week*, December 16, 1988, p. 26.
14. This is the summary offered by Irving Greenberg, "Will There Be One Jewish People by the Year 2000?—Further Reflections," in *Conflict of Cooperation: Papers on Jewish Unity* (New York: American Jewish Committee, 1989), pp. 9–10.
15. Steven M. Cohen, "Are Reform Jews Abandoning Israel?" *Reform Judaism*, spring 1988, pp. 4–5.
16. See the exchange between Greenberg and Steven M. Cohen in Greenberg, "The One in 2000 Controversy."
17. Steven M. Cohen, *Unity and Polarization in Judaism Today: The Attitudes of American and Israeli Jews* (New York: American Jewish Committee, 1988), p. 5.
18. Lawrence Grossman, "Jewish Communal Affairs," *American Jewish Yearbook* 91 (1991), p. 200.
19. Greenberg, "Will There Be One . . . Further Reflections," p. 10.
20. Ira Rifkin, "Intra-Jewish Tension Delays Papal Meeting," *Baltimore Jewish Times*, November 2, 1990, pp. 43–44.
21. Rahel Musleah, "Surgically Simple, Ritually Complex," *LI Jewish World*, January 19, 1990, p. 3; Debra Nussbaum Cohen, "Conservative Rabbis Get Training in Kashrut Supervision," *JTA Report*, July 23, 1992.
22. Lawrence Troster, "Conversion and *Mikveh*," *RA Newsletter*, summer 1989, p. 4.
23. Alexander Schindler, "Remarks by the President of the UAHC," *CCAR Yearbook* 92 (1982), p. 63.
24. Alan J. Yuter, "Is Reform Judaism a Movement, a Sect, or a Heresy," *Tradition*, spring 1989, p. 94; N. Wolpin, "One Straw, How Many Camels?" *Jewish Observer*, September 1986, p. 16.
25. Samuel Heilman, *Jewish Unity and Diversity: A Survey of American Rabbis and Rabbinical Students* (New York: American Jewish Committee, 1991), pp. 27–35.
26. Samuel Heilman and Steve M. Cohen, *Cosmopolitans and Parochials: Modern Orthodox Jews in America* (Chicago: University of Chicago Press, 1989), pp. 122–23.
27. Hints of this social stance appear occasionally. It is the subject of an editorial column written by Gary Rosenblatt, a journalist who identifies with Orthodoxy but has many contacts with the rest of the community. Rosenblatt claims that "Orthodox rabbis . . . tell their congregants not to associate with non-Jews, or even non-Orthodox families," and as a result these congregants "feel they have hardly any common points of reference or connection with their so-called brethren." Rosenblatt, "'Frum' Here to Modernity," *Baltimore Jewish Times*, September 25, 1992, p. 10.
28. Ira Robinson, "The Marvelous Midos Machine: Audio Tapes as an Orthodox Educational Medium," in *Essays in the Social Scientific Study of Judaism and Jewish Society*, vol. 2, ed. Simcha Fishbane and Stuart Schoenfeld (Hoboken, N.J.: Ktav, 1992), p. 165.
29. Steven M. Cohen, *Content or Continuity? Alternative Bases for Commitment* (New York: American Jewish Committee, 1990), p. 71.

Few spokespersons for Orthodoxy will go on record with their views, but it is no secret that many regard non-Orthodox versions of Judaism as another religion. One right-wing activist has spoken as follows: "If we give them a test, use any standard recognized by the most uneducated, uninitated Gentile as to what would constitute Jewish affiliation—Sabbath observance, eating kosher, frowning on adultery, the Ten Commandments—these people would not match up in any way. So therefore I say that they are practicing a religion which is not Judaism." Quoted by James Davison Hunter, *Culture Wars: The Struggle to Define America* (New York: Basic Books, 1991), p. 15.

30. See the joint publication of CLAL and the AIC, *Conflict or Cooperation: Papers on Jewish Unity.*
31. See, for example, "A Message from Our Rabbis," *Community Review*, December 15, 1988, p. 1, which issues an appeal for unity in the name of all the rabbis in Harrisburg, Pa.
32. "An Open Letter to Our Brethren," *Jewish Week*, December 30, 1988, p. 19.
33. Heilman, *Jewish Unity and Diversity*, pp. 16–17.
34. Robert Wuthnow, *The Restructuring of American Religion* (Princeton, N.J.: Princeton University Press, 1988), p. 6.
35. Hunter prefers the terms *orthodox* and *progressivist* for what others call religious conservatives and religious liberals.
36. Hunter, *Culture Wars*, pp. 44–45.
37. Wade Clark Roof and William McKinney, *American Mainline Religion: Its Changing Shape and Future* (New Brunswick, N.J.: Rutgers University Press, 1987), p. 37.
38. Jerry Falwell, "An Agenda for the 1980s," in *Piety and Politics: Evangelicals and Fundamentalists Confront the World*, ed. Richard J. Neuhaus and Michael Cromartie (Lanham, Md.: University Press of America, 1987), pp. 113–14; Edward Hoffman, "Thriving Families in Urban America: The Lubavitcher Hasidim," *Family in America* (The Rockford Institute Center on the Family in America) 4 (October 1990), pp. 1ff.
39. See Grossman, "Jewish Communal Affairs," pp. 191–92, for a discussion of Jewish organizational responses when the U.S. Supreme Court took up a Missouri law denying public funding and facilities for abortion.
40. Sarah Gold, "Where Do Jews Stand in the Debate over Abortion," *LI Jewish World*, October 23–29, 1992, p. 3.
41. The claim of biblical inerrancy fundamentally asserts the literal truth of the Bible; such literalism was rejected by rabbinic Judaism, and even the most Orthodox of Jews believes in the necessity for rabbinic interpretations, which sometimes flatly contradict the literal words of the text. For a brief analysis of the theological meaning of inerrancy, see James D. Hunter, *Evangelicalism: The Coming Generation* (Chicago: University of Chicago Press, 1987), pp. 20–25.
42. Nancy Ammerman, *Bible Believers: Fundamentalism in the Modern World* (New Brunswick, N.J.: Rutgers University Press, 1987), p. 8. For a trenchant analysis of the early history of Jewish ultra-Orthodoxy in Europe, see Michael K. Silber, "The Emergence of Ultra-Orthodoxy: The Invention of a Tradition," in *The Uses of Tradition: Jewish Continuity in the Modern Era*, ed. Jack Wertheimer (New York and Cambridge, Mass.: Jewish Theological Seminary of America and Harvard University Press, 1993), pp. 23–84.

43. Martin E. Marty and R. Scott Appelby, eds., *Fundamentalisms Observed* (Chicago: University of Chicago Press, 1991), pp. ix–x.
44. Heilman and Cohen, *Cosmopolitans and Parochials*, pp. 160–73.
45. For the two most important works on the transformation of American religious life under the impact of these political/cultural battles, see Wuthnow, *The Restructuring of American Religion*; and Hunter, *Culture Wars*.
46. Hunter, *Culture Wars*, p. 13.
47. One area of public policy that has attracted Orthodox attention is the question of church/state separation, specifically regarding government support for parochial schools and the public display of religious symbols, such as the Hanukkah menorah. But here too they have pursued the matter out of narrow interest, rather than on broad principle. On other issues such as abortion rights, there is little unity, given the openness of traditional Judaism to abortion under certain circumstances. On separation issues, see Naomi W. Cohen, *Jews in Christian America: The Pursuit of Religious Equality* (New York: Oxford University Press, 1992), pp. 240–41; on abortion rights issues, see Grossman, "Jewish Communal Affairs," pp. 191–92; and Gold, "Where Do Jews Stand in the Debate over Abortion?" p. 3.
48. Samuel Heilman and Menachem Friedman, "Religious Fundamentalism and Religious Jews: The Case of Haredim," in Marty and Appelby, *Fundamentalisms Observed*, p. 258.

# Part VI

## Conclusion

# 18 Roberta Rosenberg Farber and Chaim I. Waxman

# Postmodernity and the Jews

## Identity, Identification, and Community

Social transformations are consequences of social, political, and economic changes. The most recent paradigmatic change occurring in America and throughout the world pivots on the change from a materialist to a postmaterialist society. Like other religious cultures, Judaism filters the process and nature of change experienced by American Jews, so in many cases distinctive characteristics remain even as transformation occurs. In this essay we discuss the way in which changes in American society may affect the American Jewish population in the twenty-first century.

The journey from Eastern European shtetl life to the segmented world of postmodern America spans the major social transformations that started with the Industrial Revolution in the 1700s. These changes, which typically center on the means of production, radically transformed the structure of ordinary life. The shift from a preindustrial to an industrial society necessitated the relocation of populations from rural, agricultural communities to urban, industrially centered economies. It greatly altered the bonds that brought and held people together and dramatically altered, as well, relationships between the social, political, and economic sectors of society. The change from a preindustrial to an industrial society shifted the center of the economy from agriculture to the production of goods. In a postindustrial society the center again changed, this time to the provision of services and, importantly, the production and application of knowledge (Bell 1973).

Most recently, the term *postmodern* (Inglehart 1990, 1997) has been used to describe a new paradigm, distinct from the preindustrial-to-postindustrial path of development observed in advanced industrial societies. During the first half of the century, persons were concerned with meeting the basic needs of food, shelter, and safety. But with the harnessing of the earth's resources, these daily concerns, in addition to the ever-present fear of extinction due to famine, flood, and/or war, became unnecessary. As a result, individuals were more likely to experience economic security during their formative years of growth than the economic scarcity that had been the more common experience. According to Inglehart (1990) this experience of economic security leads to the culture shift from materialist to postmaterialist values in a postmodern society.

The central idea of the culture shift is that since survival concerns are no longer a relevant motive for action, energy can be and is devoted to higher-level, nonsurvival concerns. This is consistent with Maslow's need hierarchy, in which he notes that the need for food, shelter, and sex are on the lowest rung and must be satisfied before a person can move up the pyramid to its apex, self-actualization. It is not that higher needs cannot be sought before moving up the pyramid; it is just that the lower, more fundamental ones keep getting in the way of achieving them. Materialists are those for whom economic scarcity remains a psychological and/or material reality; postmaterialists are those for whom scarcity is no longer an issue. It is interesting to note that, even though economic prosperity brings about this culture shift, when it does occur, the change in values leads to an economic decline. This is because postmaterialists give priority to environmental and quality-of-life issues over and above industrial growth and economic development. Although Inglehart (1990) uses terms like *materialist* and *postmaterialist*, which imply a polarity, change actually occurs along a continuum with numerous intermediate stages (75). As expected, postmaterialist values are expressed in far greater numbers by younger generations than older ones.

Three value changes are central to the culture shift, as confirmed in survey research throughout the world (Inglehart 1990). The first is a more permissive attitude expressed toward divorce by younger generations, as indicated in the increasing divorce rate. The second is the fact that younger groups place far less emphasis on having children than do older ones, an attitude expressed in lower fertility rates. The third is the far greater tolerance afforded to homosexuality by youth than by older persons, which is expressed in attitude surveys and legislation intended to protect homosexual rights. Some of these changes, such as lower fertility rates, have occurred simultaneously with processes of industrialization. However, when viewed in conjunction with the other value shifts, such as the more permissive attitude toward divorce and the greater tolerance for homosexuality, the changes suggest a greatly lessened concern with the future of the species. Specifically, it suggests a radically different view of the family and procreation, both of which had always functioned implicitly, if not explicitly, to protect humankind against extinction.

Within the American Jewish population, especially the baby boomer population, behavioral patterns strongly suggest the presence of postmaterialist values. Divorce rates are much higher, approximating the national level. Fertility rates are significantly lower than in earlier generations and even lower than the national level. The fact that the American Jewish population has had a low fertility rate for many years (Rebhun, DellaPergola, and Tolts, this volume) suggests that the early economic success of the second generation and the subsequent economic security they provided for *their* children during their formative years of growth led to easy acceptance of the values characteristic to a postmaterialistic, postmodern society. Attitudes toward homosexuality among Jewish persons are also more tolerant than those found in the national population (Liebman & Cohen, this volume). In addition, concern with environmental and quality-of-life issues are consistent with the liberal orientation prevalent within the American Jewish baby boomer population.

Because the three central values so clearly pertain to the traditionally defined moral realm, their presence creates conflict within American society (Hunter 1991, Wuthnow 1989) and within the Jewish population as well. Wertheimer (1993) identifies three factors that account for the divisiveness found in all denominations of Christianity and Judaism: (1) the interrelated sexual and feminist revolution, (2) a spirit of religious individualism, and (3) a quest for community and personal meaning. The first factor, the interrelated sexual and feminist revolutions, is conceptually and practically related to the three value shifts mentioned by Inglehart (1990): the permissive attitude towards divorce, lessened emphasis on having children, and a greater tolerance toward homosexuals. The spirit of religious individualism signals a general decline in survival concerns and the perceived need to ban together for protection. The third factor, the quest for community and meaning in life are also concerns characteristic to a postmodern society. This analysis strongly suggests that for the majority of the Jewish population the culture shift has already occurred.

American Jews have always had a high level of literacy and education, and thus they have had no difficulty adjusting to the requirements of a postindustrial economy. The challenge presented by a postmodern society, however, is not found in the accomplishments it requires but rather in its value structure. One specific challenge of postmodernity for the American Jewish population is in its lack of concern with the "package" of survival behaviors, including procreation, in-marriage, and the condemnation of homosexual relationships.

According to Inglehart (1990; 1997), adoption of postmaterialist values is a response to the experience of economic security during the formative years of growth and the more generalized economic security experienced by the society. Since Jewish populations have always been beset by survivalist concerns, we might expect this aspect of the culture shift to affect them somewhat differently. Survival concerns among Jewish populations, however, are not necessarily rooted in the forms and variegations of production but rather in a fear of anti-Semitism. From a historical perspective this fear is certainly a legitimate and reasonable one, but for a person with scant, if any, knowledge of Jewish history, such fear makes little sense, especially for someone living within a pluralistic, democratic society like the United States. Thus, the majority of American Jews are unlikely to experience either a sense of economic insecurity or the fear of anti-Semitism.

Nevertheless, contemporary survival concerns within the American Jewish population do reflect the threat of postmaterialist values that can be said to be expressed in the high intermarriage rate, which reached 52 percent for first marriages since 1985 (Kosmin et al. 1991). This rate suggests a lack of concern with the future of the Jewish people in that groups with the higher rates of intermarriage are also those with the lowest rates of Jewish involvement and affiliation. The high intermarriage rate also reflects higher rates of assimilation and thus persons more apt to express postmaterialist values.

From a cultural perspective, intermarriage is consistent with American values, and it is difficult to see how or why it should be otherwise. Tolerance and diversity are American values and as such have been largely accepted by the American Jewish population. America's greatness has always been in the multiplicity of religious, ethnic, and racial groups that claim adherence to the same national identity. The price of this pluralistic diversity, combined with a lack of persecution, is a fluidity of personal commitment and a subsequent weakened and or symbolic sense of minority group identity. For the more assimilated American Jew this weakness is not problematic even if, or when, it includes intermarriage. The rise in Jewish intermarriage is, after all, consistent with the national trend to intermarry among all racial, religious, and ethnic groups (Alba 1990; Spickard 1989). For others however, this figure brings forth the fear of extinction, not because of an outside force but because of decisions made by Jews who, by their actions, seem to express a lack of concern with or commitment to traditional Jewish ideals.

To the extent that intermarriage expresses the wholehearted acceptance of American pluralism, it also reflects changes in the perception of religion in America. In the 1950s, Herberg (1960) noted that all Americans were expected to have a religion, but which one a person chose didn't really matter. All that mattered was that a person have a religion. This equality between religions implied that they were interchangeable, which, in turn, implied that intermarriage would not result in the loss of a distinctive religious tradition. The understanding of religion as an individual belief system was generally accepted by 1960s and 1970s. It implied that intermarriage would not impose on a person's "private" religiosity. A person could retain his or her own religiosity irrespective of the spouse's religious behavior or affiliation. Amid a declining level of Jewish observance and knowledge, the traditional rationale to in-marry, that is, to continue the Jewish People, sounded old-fashioned at best and, at worst, suggested that being Jewish was at odds with being an American. For Jews, especially those with little or no Jewish background, being American was the more prominent and more important identity.

Dissonance between American and Jewish values is perhaps most apparent in an examination of the source of the authority that governs individual and social action. From its inception, American life has always been primarily concerned with individual freedom and expression over and above the interests of the community. Self-autonomy, in other words, is primary. For more assimilated Jews, with little or no Jewish background, self-autonomy is likewise a central principle in determining appropriate action. It expresses the independence and self-reliance of an individual as well as his or her right to decide which action to take. Nevertheless, some criteria or measure is still needed to determine the appropriate action. Since all lifestyle choices are valued equally in America, there are no objective measures to use in this determination. Therefore, the primary criterion is that of personal feeling. The concept of authenticity is invoked as a way to determine whether or not the feeling is real. Self-autonomy thus intertwines with that of authenticity in its use as an authoritative principle or guide to action. Practically, this means that action must *feel* right before a person will accept it as authentically his or her own and therefore be willing to do it. According to Taylor (1991), this measure is an honest attempt to fill the void created by a largely secular society that has rejected science as an all-encompassing authority and eschews religious values.

Reliance on authenticity as a guide to action means that there are neither principles nor laws that can be shared in common. The absence of shared behavior guidelines makes it nearly impossible for religion to be the center of one's life and or community. Since religious behavior in America is regarded as within the realm of individual free choice, neither standards nor guidelines compel a person to act in a particular way. Everything must first be subjected to an individual determination of whether or not an action or idea is authentic to his or her self. And even if it were possible to reach general agreement on specific goals or ideals, no one need feel obligated to follow them.

This is obviously problematic, especially since the search for community among all Americans, including Jews, suggests a desire for values and ideals shared in common. The situation is less problematic for traditional Jews who are observant of Jewish law (Halakhah) because Jewish religious law determines ideal, if not always actual, behavior. Since Jewish religious law governs the most minute to the grandest aspects of a person's life, even when differences do exist, a fundamental life structure is still shared. Everyone may not do all that Halakhah obligates them to do, but nevertheless, they share an ideal as well as general expectations of behavior.

The principle of self-autonomy is also invoked as the source of authority for the interpretation of Jewish texts from a modern or postmodern perspective. This means that everyone has a right to his or her own opinion, irrespective of authoritative sources. As a result, there can be no shared-in-common meanings: the process of text interpretation is completely open. Consequently, neither can the practical implications of text interpretation be shared, in the sense that they might function as an agreed upon basis for Jewish life.

The situation is very different from a traditional perspective, in which text interpretation is understood to require extensive scholarship and a deep and abiding faith that is thought to be expressed in the writings of great rabbis. Therefore, their interpretations are always taken into consideration. This does not mean that creativity is inhibited, but it does restrict creative or novel interpretations by requiring that they share an underlying logic and consistency with more traditional sources of interpretation. This is similar to the requirements of secular scholarship. These two approaches have vastly different implications for behavior, in that disagreement regarding interpretation translates directly into disagreement about what being a Jew means and how it is related to the structure and content of Judaism. Since learning about Judaism is understood to provide the foundation on which a Jewish identity must be constructed, in reality, then, the struggle between and within the American Jewish denominations pivots on the right to interpret Judaism and thereby to define what being Jewish means.

The problem is that, without the knowledge base that traditional Judaism provides, Jewish identity can be defined only from the perspective of one's culture, that is, from an American political, ethical, and religious framework. More assimilated Jews, who are most numerous within the Reform and Conservative denominations, inevitably define what being Jewish means from a primarily postmaterialist or postmodern American value perspective. When applied to religious behavior, a postmodern American perspective supports the conceptual framework for an individualistic interpretation and expression of religious belief and action. A basic example of this is evident in the radically changed perception of and concern with the connection between a personal decision regarding marriage and family and the implications of this decision for the future of the Jewish People. Concern with the communal consequences of such a clearly personal decision regarding marriage and family is antithetical to the individualistic pursuit of personal happiness and satisfaction typical to a postmodern consciousness. Within traditional Judaism, however, recognizing and responding to the connection between personal action and communal well-being are accepted as fundamental necessities to ensure the continuity of the Jewish people and therefore are incumbent upon all Jews.

Different approaches to the observance of Jewish rituals and ceremonies (Liebman, this volume) also reflect the two conceptions of authority. According to a traditional framework, commitment to and consistency of observance is the basis of ritual observance, whereas within the modern framework, commitment is seldom made to something other than personal self-development. Thus, rituals and ceremonies are chosen and used in accordance with one's own needs and feelings. This latter approach, referred to as "salad bar" or "smorgasbord" Judaism, is completely at odds with traditional Judaism, in which the commandments that constitute the foundation of all ritual and ceremonial actions are exactly that—commandments—not options one chooses whether or not to perform.

This does not mean that all persons who adhere to traditional Judaism do everything they are obligated to do. Rather, it means that this idea constitutes the ideal one strives to achieve. Since the ideal is objectively stated, it can be known and shared in common and can thereby provide the basis for community. Even though change has clearly occurred within traditional religious Jewish communities, Jewish law has remained the primary source of personal and communal values and behavior. Change, in other words, has not impinged on the unifying and stabilizing force of Jewish law. The very openness of American society, however, has reduced the effectiveness of Jewish law in regulating behavior, in part because the informal censure created by autonomous community life no longer exists. The multiplicity of options available to Americans are equally available to religiously Orthodox Jews. Even within Orthodox communities there is the sense that one can do anything he or she chooses. The traditional censure of communal life is greatly reduced; thus, all persons who remain within the realm of religious orthodox observance can be said to have chosen their way of life.

The linking of an individual to a community requires the perception of connection. This perception can be imposed from without or emerge from within or be some combination of the two. In part the transformation of the American Jewish community can be seen as a cultural shift in the loci of this definition, moving from an externally imposed perception to a voluntary internal one. From another perspective the transformation of the American Jewish community can be seen as the movement from life lived as a nondiscursive integrated web of meaning and behavior (Zborowski and Herzog 1952) to a discursively comprehended world in which the content of each realm is interchangeable. Whereas Jewish life in Europe consisted of shared meanings that bound one to the other, life in America is constructed individually, with an emphasis on shared feelings that in no way obligate a person. Each person is regarded as fully responsible for his or her life and destiny and for what he or she chooses to believe. The personal and voluntary nature of religious life in America (Bellah et al. 1985) de-emphasizes the act of commitment and so undermines the very basis of traditional Jewish life, which holds that each Jew is responsible for every other Jew. This obligation has always provided the foundation for group support and coordinated group action, and its absence has already spawned behavior that places political power and self-interest above the broader needs of Jewish life and unity (Wertheimer 1997).

Still another critical disjunction between being Jewish in America and in the Eastern European ghetto is the process by which knowledge of one's Jewish identity is acquired and transmitted. What had been thought of as intuitive turns out to have been the behavioral consequence of a holistically integrated, religiously based culture that was formally and informally transmitted, supported, and enforced by the closed nature of Eastern European ghetto life and frequent bouts of anti-Semitism. The result was a strong intuitive perception of being Jewish that led Jews to take their identity for granted. Thus, immigrants of the Great Migration of 1880–1924 made relatively little effort to transmit specific Jewish values, ideals, and practices to their children. Behavior that was transmitted often lacked a coherent rationale to make it meaningful in a land that prized material comfort, personal freedom, and the exercise of choice above all other values. Today it is recognized that great and coordinated effort must be extended to instill a strong Jewish identity in children. Techniques to achieve this include, but are not limited to, formal Jewish education, summer camp, and trips to Israel and Holocaust centers in Europe. All of these, however, must be reinforced by a clear, unambiguous

(Medding et al., this volume) Jewish identity expressed in the home. This is most easily and fruitfully achieved by the observance of home-based religious rituals combined with synagogue or temple attendance.

A large part of the assimilation to American life has been separating the previously intertwining roles of religion and ethnicity in Jewish life and then choosing which elements to keep. This sense of creating or, as Conzen et al. (1991) phrase it, inventing ethnicity, occurs for all immigrant groups. It reflects the simultaneously held desires to retain or acknowledge the past even while fully participating in the present and anticipating a future quite different from the past. For the Jewish community, the separation of the religious and ethnic dimensions of Jewish life proved especially problematic, as the particularity of Jewish religious ritual and the necessary institutional forms are intricately connected to the persistence and purpose of the Jewish People. Sharot (1997) notes: "From a materialist perspective, religious institutions are the objective conditions which make possible the persistence of a relatively strongly-held ethnicity" (40).

Two cultural paradigms are thus present within advanced industrial societies that yield radically different and often conflicting goals and values, not unlike the culture wars phenomenon noted by Hunter (1990). The rising intermarriage rate is but one instance of dissonance between American and traditional Jewish values. The decline in moral standards noted by traditionalists and others would seem to be part of a much larger cultural change, embedded and dependent on economic development and prosperity that affects not only America but all advanced industrial societies. Assuming the absence of a major economic disaster, this perspective suggests that the background culture in twenty-first-century America will be primarily postmaterialist in its value orientation and that the future of American Jewry in the twenty-first century depends on its response to the values and ideals of a postmaterialist culture.

In traditional societies the source of religious authority is, typically expressed, within a Judaic framework through the writings and legal decisions of learned rabbis and scholars. Modernity, on the other hand, extols the individual human capacity to reason. Thus, each person is believed to have the capacity as well as the right to decide what is true, of value, and meaningful and to take action based on these determinations. The shift from reliance on religious authority to personal authority means that individuals are no longer dependent on the writings or pronouncements of a religious hierarchy, either for their spiritual interpretation of Scripture or for guidance as to the right way to live. The resulting individualistic approach to religious practice and belief makes it that much more difficult to achieve and sustain a shared understanding of what being Jewish is all about. Since greater reliance on personal authority is prevalent throughout American society—not only among Jewish Americans—it also makes being Jewish less of a distinctive identity and therefore harder to differentiate from the dominant religious and civic culture. Such cultural distinctiveness of a minority group within a dominant cultural community is always a difficult perception to sustain, but it is especially so when members of the subgroup participate in the dominant culture as fully as do American Jews. The movement away from large centers of Jewish population to less dense areas in the United States both reflects and reinforces this lack of distinctiveness (Goldstein & Goldstein 1996, Hammond and Warner 1993, Kosmin and Lachman 1993).

As the level of Jewish literacy among American Jews declined, American culture and values, more than traditional Jewish ones, assumed the status of "the way things should be" and functioned as a measure against which Jewish life and thought were evaluated. This is seen in the acceptance of American-based notions like pluralism, diversity, and equality as values to emulate in the practice of Jewish life. Acceptance and integration of American cultural values is most fully articulated within the Reform and Conservative denominations, although they are present within Orthodoxy as well. The former denominations place greater value on the incorporation of American values into Jewish life than do the latter, who look to past Jewish communities for guidance. The former also lack a clearly defined model of an alternative community as is found in the religiously based culture of an Orthodox Jewish community. For these reasons, among more modernized American Jews, it is American society that functions as the dominant cultural model in defining the nature of relationships between individuals and society as well as in the construction of "strategies of action" (Swidler 1986) to achieve various goals.

Religion in contemporary America is conceptualized as expressive behavior that can meet personal needs for meaning and for spiritual growth and development, as well as the desire for belonging. This reflects two seemingly antithetical qualities: an individualistic pursuit of personal meaning and spirituality and the quest for community and sense of belonging. Wuthnow (1994) explores how these needs merge in Christian and other groups throughout America; Davidman (1994) explores this theme within a Jewish feminist group. Within traditional Jewish life these needs are structurally intertwined, but the segmented quality of American life and the vast array of available choices necessitates their integration be a personal rather than communal enterprise. From an American perspective one religion is equally as valid as another, irrespective of consequences, so intermarriage is not regarded as a problem. Rather it is seen as a benefit, legitimately enabling families to choose from a more plentiful assortment of religious rituals and ceremonies. Greater value, in other words, is given to the act of choice than to its substance (Taylor 1991), so for most American Jews, as for most Americans, religious identification is but one aspect of a larger personal identity. In this respect, religious choice intertwines with the psychological processes of self-development and actualization. This emphasis on individual choice yields a balance between individual and communal needs that is radically different from a traditional orientation, in which community needs are always a consideration.

## The Twenty-first Century

The remaking of Judaism and thereby of Jewish life in accordance with values taken from the larger host culture has occurred continuously throughout the thousands of years of the Diaspora. Nevertheless, as made clear at the beginning of this essay, postmodern values, especially when combined with the extensive assimilation that has occurred and the relatively low level of Jewish knowledge among America Jews, pose a critical threat to Jewish life and therefore to the Jewish population in twenty-first-century America. On the basis of these trends, three analytically distinct responses can be seen within the American Jewish population as it enters the twenty-first century

From a traditional Jewish perspective, the most distressing path is that of complete assimilation, intermarriage and/or conversion. This path is not necessarily an intentional one, as would be the case in an act of conversion. Rather, it is a natural movement for primarily secular or religiously neutral Jews whose behavior is characterized by a lack of Jewish observance, observance of "national" Christian holidays like Christmas, and the absence of a sustained, conscious effort to retain and transfer the Jewish heritage to their children. These Jews are part of a largely non-Jewish culture, whether they adopt Christianity, choose an alternative religious system, or create their own individualized spiritual system. That this often occurs within the context or communities in which intermarriage is acceptable and even prevalent makes the assimilation that much easier.

The second response within the American Jewish population is that taken primarily by Reform Jews. They will continue the ongoing redefinition of what being Jewish means that was begun in Germany by the Reform movement. Essentially, this movement retains the title of Judaism even as it alters everything that had for centuries been understood to define Judaism. In terms of the quest for unity of the Jewish population, the radical changes in the fundamental definitions of traditional Judaism, such as adoption of patrilineal descent, has created unbridgeable divisions with the more traditionally oriented Jews of all denominations.

Ironically, the arena for this struggle to define who is a Jew and the nature of Judaism is the State of Israel, which, since its creation in 1949, had been a strong unifying force for American Jews. That the conflict between the denominations is expressed and played out in the Jewish homeland suggests that Israel is still a center of Jewish life in the sense that its legal rulings on Judaism matter to Diaspora Jews. On the other hand, the fact that the struggle has become overtly political, including threats to withhold funds for organizations that serve the entire Israeli population, suggests that the state is no longer regarded as central to American Jewish life. That threats are made even when research finds that Israelis do not share the same ideal of religious pluralism, as interpreted by Reform and Conservative American denominations, supports the latter interpretation (Sorkin 1997).

A third direction, the formation of enclave Judaism, consists of Jews moving closer to traditional Judaism through increased ritual observance and greater religious education for both children and adults. Formation of largely homogeneous communities provides a supportive cultural milieu for religious observance and social life. These communities provide an interlocking fabric of relationships that in turn provide a bulwark against unwanted inroads of influence from the majority culture (Kranzler 1995). The enclave culture makes sense for groups who choose to belong to and raise their children in an American subculture. Since the acquisition of wealth and the provision of economic security for one's family have always been valued within a traditional Jewish culture, in itself the experience of economic security during one's formative years will not lead to the adoption of postmaterialist values that result in lessened religious observance. Rather, increased economic resources will be spent on ritual observance and the necessary provision of an extended Jewish education for all members of the family. Whereas previous generations, for example, had to choose between education for a son or a daughter, today all children are expected to receive long years of Jewish schooling. In any case, the high birthrate in many religious communities suggests that a high level of economic security will remain a fairly elusive goal. Thus, postmaterialist values, though they clearly encroach on the values of traditionally observant communities, are not likely to erode them.

Studies find that American Jews who identify their Jewishness by religion are far more likely to engage in other Jewish behaviors and are far less likely to intermarry, and that religiously observant Jews have the lowest rate of intermarriage. The American Judaism adopted largely by Reform Jews, on the other hand, with its changed definitions of the transmission and definition of a Jewish identity and of what this identity means is statistically along the path to further assimilation and intermarriage. We can expect the religiously affiliated, especially the Orthodox, to endure, but whether the former type of Judaism will constitute an identity distinct enough to endure as more than a political group and whether it will be transferred from generation to generation are questions to be answered in the twenty-first century.

## References

Alba, Richard D. 1990. *Ethnic Identity: The Transformation of White America.* New Haven: Yale University Press.

Bell, Daniel. 1973. *The Coming of Post-Industrial Society: A Venture in Social Forecasting.* New York: Basic Books.

Bellah, Robert, Richard Madsen, William M. Sullivan, Ann Swidler, and Steven M. Tipton. 1985. *Habits of the Heart: Individualism and Commitment in American Life.* New York: Harper & Row.

Conzen, Neils Kathleen, David A. Gerber, Ewa Morawska, George E. Pozzetta, and Rudolph J. Vecoli. 1991. "The Invention of Ethnicity: A Perspective from the U.S.A." *Journal of American Ethnic History* (1), pp. 3–41.

Davidman, Lynn. 1994. 'I Come Away Stronger': The Religious Impact of a Loosely Structured Jewish Feminist Group. In Wuthnow, Robert, ed., *"I Come Away Stronger" How Small Groups Are Shaping American Religion*. Grand Rapids, Mich.: William B. Eerdmans Publishing Co., pp. 322–43.

Goldstein, Sidney, and Alice Goldstein. 1996. *Jews on the Move: Implications for Jewish Identity*. Albany: State University of New York Press.

Hammond, Phillip E., and Kee Warner. 1993. "Religion and Ethnicity in Late-Twentieth-Century America." *Annals of the American Academy of Political and Social Science* 527 (May), pp. 55–66.

Herberg, Will. 1960. *Protestant–Catholic–Jew: An Essay in American Religious Sociology*, rev. ed. New York: Anchor Books.

Hunter, James Davison. 1991. *Culture Wars: The Struggle to Define America*. New York: Basic Books.

Inglehart, Ronald. 1990. *Culture Shift in Advanced Industrial Society*. Princeton, N.J.: Princeton University Press.

Kosmin, Barry A., Sidney Goldstein, Joseph Waksberg, Nava Lerer, Ariella Keysar, and Jeffrey Scheckner. 1991. *Highlights of the CJF 1990 National Jewish Population Survey*. New York: Council of Jewish Federations.

———. 1977. *Modernization and Postmodernization: Cultural, Economic, and Political Change in 43 Societies*. Princeton, N.J.: Princeton University Press.

Kosmin, Barry A., and Seymour P. Lachman. 1993. *One Nation under God: Religion in Contemporary American Society*. New York Harmony Books.

Kranzler, George. 1995. *Hasidic Williamsburg: A Contemporary American Hasidic Community*. Northvale, N.J., and London: Jason Aronson.

Maslow, Abraham. 1954. *Motivation and Personality*. New York: Harper and Brothers.

Sharot, Stephen. 1997. "A Critical Comment on Gans' 'Symbolic Ethnicity' and 'Symbolic Religiosity' and Other Formulations of Ethnicity and Religion." *Contemporary Jewry* 18:25–43.

Sorkin, J. S. 1997. "Religious Pluralism in Israel." *Midstream*, August/September, pp. 15–18.

Spickard, Paul A. 1989. *Mixed Blood: Intermarriage and Ethnic Identity in Twentieth Century America*. Madison: The University of Wisconsin Press.

Swidler, Ann. 1986. "Culture in Action: Symbols and Strategies." *American Sociological Review* 51:273–86.

Taylor, Charles. 1991. *The Ethics of Authenticity*. Cambridge and London: Harvard University Press.

Waxman, Chaim I., 1983. *America's Jews in Transition*. Philadelphia: Temple University Press.

Wertheimer, Jack. 1993. *A People Divided: Judaism in Contemporary America*. New York: Basic Books.

Wertheimer, Jack. 1997. "Politics and Jewish Giving." *Commentary* 104 (December), pp. 32–36.

Woocher, Jonathan S. 1985. "Sacred Survival: American Jewry's Civil Religion." *Judaism*, spring, pp. 151–62.

Wuthnow, Robert. 1989. *The Struggle for America's Soul: Evangelicals, Liberals, and Secularism*. Grand Rapids, Mich.: William B. Eerdmans Publishing Co.

———. 1994. *Sharing the Journey: Support Groups and America's New Quest for Community*. New York: The Free Press.

Zborowski, Mark, and Elizabeth Herzog. 1952. *Life Is with People: The Culture of the Shtetl*. New York: Schocken.

## Contributors

**Steven Bayme** is national director of the Jewish Communal Affairs Department, American Jewish Committee, and an adjunct professor at the Wurzweiler School of Social Work, Yeshiva University.

**Jerome A. Chanes** is associate executive director of the National Foundation for Jewish Culture, senior research fellow at the Center for Jewish Studies of the CUNY Graduate Center, and adjunct professor at Yeshiva University's graduate division. He is the editor of *Antisemitism in America Today: Exploding the Myths*, co-editor of *A Portrait of the American Jewish Community*, and author of the forthcoming *From Anti-Judaism to Antisemitism: A History of Antisemitism.*

**Carmel U. Chiswick** is professor of economics at the University of Illinois at Chicago. Her current research addresses the economic aspects of work, family life, and religious observance in the United States, focusing on the experience of American Jews.

**Steven M. Cohen** teaches at the Melton Centre for Jewish Education of The Hebrew University. He is currently working on a book with Arnold Eisen on the Jewish identity of moderately affiliated American Jews.

**Sergio DellaPergola** is a professor of demography and former chairperson of The A. Harman Institute of Contemporary Jewry, The Hebrew University of Jerusalem.

**Daniel J. Elazar** is Senator N. M. Patterson Professor of Political Studies at Bar-Ilan University, director of the Center for the Study of Federalism at Temple University, and director of the Jerusalem Center for Public Affairs. He is the founder and editor of the *Jewish Political Studies Review*.

**Roberta Rosenberg Farber** is adjunct associate professor of sociology at Stern College for Women, Yeshiva University.

**Sylvia Barack Fishman** is the author of three books: *American Jewish Lives in Cultural Context; A Breath of Life: Feminism in the American Jewish Community*; and *Follow My Footprints: Changing Images of Women in American Jewish Fiction*. She is assistant professor of contemporary Jewish life in the Near Eastern and Judaic Studies Department at Brandeis University and is co-director of the International Research Institute on Jewish Women, established by Hadassah at Brandeis University.

**Jerome S. Legge, Jr.,** is professor of political science at the University of Georgia. His current work is concerned with anti-foreign sentiment and antisemitism in Germany.

**Charles S. Liebman** is a professor of political science at Bar-Ilan University in Israel and has written many books and articles on Jews in Israel and in the United States.

**Peter Y. Medding** is the Dr. Israel Goldstein Professor of the History of Zionism and the State of Israel in the Department of Political Science and the Institute of Contemporary Jewry at the Hebrew University of Jerusalem.

**Uzi Rebhun** is a research fellow at The A. Harman Institute of Contemporary Jewry, The Hebrew University of Jerusalem.

**Mordechai Rimor** is an Experimental Psychologist and is Senior Lecturer at the Department of Behavioral Sciences, College of Management, Tel Aviv.

**Haym Soloveitchik** is professor of Jewish history and literature at Yeshiva University, Bernard Revel Graduate School.

**Gary A. Tobin** is director of the Maurice and Marilyn Cohen Center for Modern Jewish Studies at Brandeis University, and the author of several books, including *Jewish Perceptions of Antisemitism* and *Church and Synagogue Affiliation*.

**Mark Tolts** is a senior researcher at The A. Harman Institute of Contemporary Jewry, The Hebrew University of Jerusalem.

**Chaim I. Waxman** is a professor of sociology at Rutgers University and has written widely on America's Jews.

**Jack Wertheimer** is provost and professor of American Jewish history at the Jewish Theological Seminary of America.

**University Press of New England** publishes books under its own imprint and is the publisher for Brandeis University Press, Dartmouth College, Middlebury College Press, University of New Hampshire, Tufts University, and Wesleyan University Press.

**Library of Congress Cataloging-in-Publication Data**
Jews in America : a contemporary reader / [edited by] Roberta Rosenberg Farber and Chaim I. Waxman.
p. cm. — (Brandeis series in American Jewish history, culture, and life)
Includes bibliographical references.
ISBN 0–87451–899–7
(pbk. : alk. paper)
1. Jews—United States—Social conditions. 2. Judaism—United States. 3. Judaism—20th century. 4. Jews—United States—Identity. I. Farber, Roberta Rosenberg, 1944– . II. Waxman, Chaim Isaac. III. Series.
E184.36.S65J49 1999
305.892'4073—dc21 98-47529